Lecture Notes in Computer Science 2642

Edited by G. Goos, J. Hartmanis, and J. van Leeuwen

Springer

Berlin
Heidelberg
New York
Barcelona
Hong Kong
London
Milan
Paris
Tokyo

Xiaofang Zhou   Yanchun Zhang
Maria E. Orlowska (Eds.)

Web Technologies and Applications

5th Asia-Pacific Web Conference, APWeb 2003
Xian, China, April 23-25, 2003
Proceedings

 Springer

Series Editors

Gerhard Goos, Karlsruhe University, Germany
Juris Hartmanis, Cornell University, NY, USA
Jan van Leeuwen, Utrecht University, The Netherlands

Volume Editors

Xiaofang Zhou
Maria E. Orlowska
The University of Queensland
School of Information Technology and Electrical Engineering
Brisbane QLD 4072, Australia
E-mail: {zxf, maria}@itee.uq.edu.au

Yanchun Zhang
University of Southern Queensland
Department of Mathematics and Computing
Toowoomba, QLD 4350, Australia
E-mail: zhang@usq.edu.au

Cataloging-in-Publication Data applied for

A catalog record for this book is available from the Library of Congress

Bibliographic information published by Die Deutsche Bibliothek
Die Deutsche Bibliothek lists this publication in the Deutsche Nationalbibliographie;
detailed bibliographic data is available in the Internet at <http://dnb.ddb.de>.

CR Subject Classification (1998): H.3, H.4, H.5, C.2, K.4

ISSN 0302-9743
ISBN 3-540-02354-2 Springer-Verlag Berlin Heidelberg New York

Springer-Verlag Berlin Heidelberg New York
a member of BertelsmannSpringer Science+Business Media GmbH

http://www.springer.de

© Springer-Verlag Berlin Heidelberg 2003
Printed in Germany

Typesetting: Camera-ready by author, data conversion by PTP-Berlin GmbH
Printed on acid-free paper   SPIN: 10926383   06/3142   5 4 3 2 1 0

Preface

The papers in this volume were presented at the 5th Asia Pacific Web Conference (APWeb 2003), which was held in Xi'an, China during 23–25 April 2003.

The World Wide Web has dramatically changed our ways of working, learning, entertaining and doing business in the last 10 years. The Asia Pacific region has emerged in recent years as the fastest growing region in the world in the use of Web technologies as well as in making significant contributions to WWW research and development. APWeb this year received 136 submissions from 21 countries and regions, including Australia, Belgium, Brazil, Canada, China, Finland, France, Germany, Greece, Hong Kong, Italy, Japan, Korea, Kuwait, New Zealand, Singapore, Switzerland, Taiwan, Turkey, UK, and USA. Each submission was carefully reviewed by three members of the Program Committee. Only 39 regular papers and 16 short papers were accepted. While XML-related technologies continued to dominate at this year's APWeb conference, this volume reveals some emerging trends, such as the formal foundations of Web data management, architectures and methodologies in Web information systems engineering, Web-based workflow management systems, and the applications of data mining and distributed data management techniques in the new context of the Web. Also included in this volume are two high-quality papers from leading research groups on the topic of web mining (organized by Wen-Ying Ma of Microsoft Research Asia). One highlight of APWeb 2003 was its high-profile keynote speakers, Marek Rusinkiewicz (Telcordia Technologies, USA), Minoru Etoh (NTT DoCoMo USA Labs) and Beng Chin Ooi (National University of Singapore). Two keynote papers are included here.

The conference received financial support from Microsoft, Netec and a number of Xi'an software industry and government agencies. We also received help and logistical support from the University of Queensland, the City University of Hong Kong, the Web Information Systems Engineering (WISE) Society, and Xi'an Jiaotong University. We are grateful to Jian Chen, Xiaohua Jia, Markus Kirchberg, Miranda Lee, Qing Li, Xuemin Lin, Wei Liu, Kevin Xu and Jeffrey Yu for their great effort in supporting the conference organization. Finally, we would like to take this opportunity to thank all Program Committee members and external reviewers for their expertise and help in evaluating papers.

February 2003

Xiaofang Zhou
Yanchun Zhang
Maria Orlowska

Conference Organization

General Chair: Maria Orlowska, University of Queensland, Australia
Tutorials Chair: Jeffrey X. Yu, Chinese University of Hong Kong, China
Publication Chair: Yanchun Zhang, Univ. of Southern Queensland, Australia
Publicity Chair: Xuemin Lin, University of New South Wales, Australia
Industry and Demo Chair: Jian Chen, Netec Co. Ltd., China

Program Committee Chair

Xiaofang Zhou, University of Queensland, Australia

Program Committee Members

Wojciech Cellary, Poznan University of Economics, Poland
Shama Chakravarthy, University of Texas, Arlington, USA
Guihai Chen, Nanjing University, China
Hanxiong Chen, Tsukuba University, Japan
Phoebe Chen, Queensland University of Technology, Australia
Ping Chen, Xidian University, China
Gillian Dobbie, University of Auckland, New Zealand
Guozhu Dong, Wright University, USA
Jin Song Dong, National University of Singapore, Singapore
Xiaoyong Du, Renmin University of China, China
Wendy Feng, University of Sydney, Australia
Le Gruenwald, University of Oklahoma, USA
KeunHo Ryu, Chungbuk National University, Korea
Joshua Z. Huang, University of Hong Kong, China
Zhiyong Huang, National University of Singapore, Singapore
Xiaohua Jia, City University of Hong Kong, China
Markus Kirchberg, Massey University, New Zealand
Masaru Kitsuregawa, University of Tokyo, Japan
Ee Peng Lim, Nanyang Technological University, Singapore
Mingshu Li, Institute of Software, Chinese Academy of Sciences, China
Qing Li, City University of Hong Kong, China
Xue Li, University of Queensland, Australia
Tao Lin, SAP, USA
Chengfei Liu, South Australia University, Australia
Sanjay Madria, University of Missouri, Rolla, USA
Xiaofeng Meng, Renmin University of China, China
Mukesh Mohania, IBM India Research Lab, India
Jan Newmarch, Monash University, Australia
Wee Keong Ng, Nanyang Tech. University, Singapore
Beng Chin Ooi, National University of Singapore, Singapore
Zhiyong Peng, Wuhan University, China

Pearl Pu, EPFL, Switzerland
Xiaolin Qin, Nanjing University of Aeronautics and Astronautics, China
Shazia Sadiq, University of Queensland, Australia
Wasim Sadiq, SAP Research, Australia
Junyi Shen, Xi'an Jiaotong University, China
Timothy K. Shih, Tamkang University, Taiwan
Kian Lee Tan, National University of Singapore, Singapore
Katsumi Tanaka, Kyoto University, Japan
Li Xie, Nanjing University, China
Cheng-Zhong Xu, Wayne State University, USA
Hongji Yang, De Montfort University, UK
Qiang Yang, Hong Kong University of Science and Technology, China
Yun Yang, Swinburne University of Technology, Australia
HongJiang Zhang, Microsoft Research, China
Aoying Zhou, Fudan University, China
Wanlei Zhou, Deakin University, Australia

External Reviewers

Manish Bhide	Sebastian Link	Takayuki Tamura
Zheng Chen	Jixue Liu	Masashi Toyoda
Rui Ding	Qincai Liu	Alexei Tretiakov
Marlon Dumas	Daofeng Luo	Jing Wang
Chris A. Freyberg	Qiang Ma	Yitong Wang
Song Fu	Wei-Ying Ma	Krzysztof Walczak
Jiangfeng Gao	Yufei Ma	Jirong Wen
Sven Hartmann	Natwar Modani	Khin Myo Win
Dongdong Hu	Anirban Mondal	Yew Kwong Woon
Xiaodi Huang	Satoshi Oyama	Lei Yi
Mukul Joshi	Iko Pramudiono	Jianming Yong
Wayne A. Kelly	Jarogniew Rykowski	Donggang Yu
Raymond Lau	Klaus-Dieter Schewe	Juntao Yu
Rynson Lau	Jun Shen	Koji Zettsu
Hongchen Li	Takahiko Shintani	Bin Zhao
Mingjing Li	Kazutoshi Sumiya	
Zhao Li	Dawei Sun	
Zichen Li	Katsumi Takahashi	

Table of Contents

Session 4: Web Mining

Session 5: Web Clustering, Ranking and Profiling

Session 6: Payment and Security

Session 7: Web Application Architectures

Session 8: Advanced Applications

Session 9: Web and Multimedia

Session 10: Network Protocols

Session 11: Workflow Management Systems

Session 12: Advanced Search

Session 13: Data Allocation and Replication

Trends in Mobile Multimedia and Networks

Minoru Etoh

DoCoMo Communications Laboratories USA, Inc.
181 Metro Drive, Suite 300, San Jose, CA 95110 USA
etoh@ieee.org
http://www.docomolabs-usa.com

Abstract. NTT DoCoMo is the company to "DO COmmunications over the MObile Network". It reached 43 million subscribers in Japan, early 2003. This presentation covers the multimedia services over mobile networks and give a glimpse of future directions of mobile multimedia networks and applications. DoCoMo's 2G and 3G mobile networks currently offer mobile visual phones, multimedia mails, and video clip download as well as enhanced "i-mode" services. After introducing the mobile multimedia applications and related technologies, future challenges and directions beyond the current networks are discussed, taking three keywords: hyper operator network, mobile content, and seamless service.

1 Introduction

During the recent four years, the total cellular customer based in Japan achieved a net growth of 10 million each year. As of January 2003, the mobile phone subscription in Japan was 74 million[1]. The expansion of mobile communications so far has been led by the growth of voice usage. However, voice usage will certainly saturate in the near future, simply because the population will not increase any more, and people's active hours in a day are limited. As for Internet, the number of "wired" Internet users in Japan is about 20 million , while the mobile users were 60 million , of which 36 million are i-mode[2] subscribers in early 2003. According to the forecast by Japanese government, the number of Internet users in Japan is expected to reach 77 million by 2005, pushed by the increase in the number of mobile users accessing the Internet from a mobile device. Owing to the internet access initiated by i-mode, the three major telecommunication operators in Japan (i.e, DoCoMo, KDDI, and J-phone) have maintained the revenue form the data traffic. Fig.1 shows such a revenue analysis. This means we need to generate new demands for mobile communications to further expand the market. Fortunately, the use of Internet is increasing rapidly. Therefore, we should take the challenge to combine mobile communications with the Internet, and develop it into a mobile multimedia service, which can handle not only voice and data but also image communications. Let us call it "Mobile Multimedia Frontier" as depicted in Fig.2. The figure shows an optimistic but vital view.

---

[1] For the current numbers, see http://www.tca.or.jp/index-e.html

[2] i-mode is NTT DoCoMo's mobile internet access system, and is also a trademark and/or service mark owned by NTT DoCoMo.

X. Zhou, Y. Zhang, and M.E. Orlowska (Eds.): APWeb 2003, LNCS 2642, pp. 1–9, 2003.

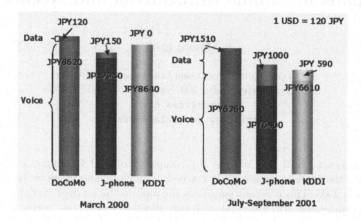

Fig. 1. Average Revenue Per User in Japan's Mobile Communication.

2   Mobile Multimedia Today

In view of Mobile Multimedia Frontier, we launched W-CDMA network(i.e., IMT-2000 network) in 2001. That network allows 384Kbps packet switch connection for down link and 64Kbps circuit connection that is N-ISDN compatible. Thus DoCoMo now operates dual generation mobile networks in which 2G network provides 28.8 Kbps packet switch connection.

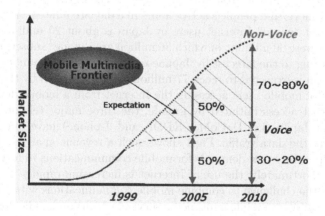

Fig. 2. Mobile Multimedia Frontier.

Fig. 3 summarizes the current and anticipated mobile multimedia services over 2G and 3G networks.

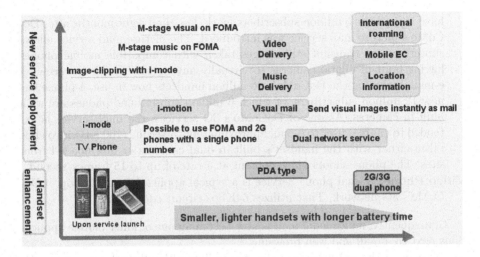

Fig. 3. Evolution Path of Mobile Multimedia Services.

e-mail: This is one of killer applications regardless of mobile network generations. You can send e-mail to other mobile phones and to anyone who has an Internet e-mail address, and recive e-mail vice versa. The two major points should be noticed here. It costs less than 1 cent and interoperability to Internet mail is guaranteed.

Web Browsing: The legacy 2G network has allowed mainly text-based HTML browsing with some small graphics. In enhanced 2G and 3G networks, JPEG was adopted and is commonly used in mobile web browsing. Now we are using a 2-inch or similar size display with a limited resolution though, the resolution will be eventually extended to VGA in the near future.

Java Application: In early 2001, DoCoMo launched Java application download service. Users now can download and store a variety of dynamic applications via the 2G and 3G networks. All new i-mode phones are now equipped with the Java capability and Secure Sockets Layer (SSL) Protocol, which provides cryptography for the safe transmission of personal information (e.g., credit card numbers). It is expected that the Java new phones will be used for financial service and other e-commerce businesses in addition to video games.

Videoclip Download: The 3G service, dubbed "i-motion" will enable users to obtain video content at speeds of up to 384 kbps (64 kbps uplinks) from sites accessed via DoCoMo's official portal with new DoCoMo's 3G handsets. Movie trailers, news highlights and music files will be among the many types of increasingly rich content to be offered. Data will be provided in three formats: video with sound for promotional videos, news, etc. still frames with sound for famous movie scenes etc., and sound-only music files.

Multimedia Mail: Mobile picture mail services have proved a major hit with the Japanese market. In early 2003, penetration of camera phone handsets have topped the 5 million subscribers mark, less than eight months after Do-CoMo's picture mail service was introduced. The picture mail service allows subscribers to transmit still images taken with compatible mobile phones having built-in digital cameras to virtually any device capable of receiving e-mail, including the DoCoMo's 36 million handsets now in use. J-phone has now 12 million subscribers, of which 6 million subscribers' phones are with built-in cameras. As one of DoCoMo's 3G services, the mail service is extended to enables user to e-mail approximately 15-second/100 KB video clips taken either with the handset's built-in dual cameras or downloaded from sites. The phone shoots video content at a rate of up to 15 frames/second.

Video Phone: Visual phone Service is a typical application on the top of Do-CoMo's 3G network. That utilizes 64Kbps circuit connection.

Consequently, multimedia mail is now becoming one of killer mobile applications next to e-mail and web browsing.

Concerning the web browsing, due to the limited bandwidth and screen display size on the phone, Internet standards for web service could not be directly applied to mobile internet service. Thus, a new standard needed to be introduced. In Japan, two standards were introduced. First is the i-mode HTML, which is the standard, created by NTT DoCoMo, based on Internet protocol. The other standard is WAP, (Wireless Access Protocol), specified by the WAP Forum, an industry forum comprised of wireless operators and manufacturers worldwide. The standard established is a public/open standard integrated with cellular protocol. Fig. 4 summarizes two streams of mobile markup language formats. At this point, we have a very optimistic view to such an "estranged" situation. One reason is that the current mobile web browsing is mainly for database access such

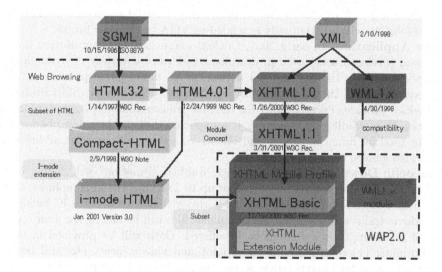

Fig. 4. Compact HTML and WAP.

as inquiring train time table, weather forecast,and mobile news, in which web contents are automatically generated by a front-end system which knows "user agent" information from each cell phone. The majority of mobile web content with valued information is dynamically and automatically created. The other reason is that we will eventually have convergence into an Internet dominant content format, which is supposed to be (X)HTML or its derivatives. Since the cell phone's capability and bandwidth environment are now growing to follow the wired environments, i.e., legacy Internet, then we will have to consider the interoperability between mobile content and legacy content more than ever.

3   Technology Research Trends

Breathtaking advances in LSI technologies, expanding network bandwidth, advanced coding technology and heterogeneous access networks will change the way we use mobile networks forever. Future users will interact with the network using any device, in any location and demand consistent, familiar service. They will expect completely reliable delivery of virtually any type of content or service including real time high quality video audio, games, text and video conferencing. The ultimate goal of mobile multimedia technology development is to make any type of multimedia content and services be available anywhere and anytime. Here let me focus on three research topics: Hyper Operator Network, Mobile Content, Seamless and Ubiquitous Service technologies.

3.1   Hyper Operator Network as Overlay Network

Fig. 5 illustrates an ideal mobile future network including a forth generation(4G) radio access network. As we can see in the figure, heterogeneous, rather than homogeneous, user terminals, wireless access networks, backbone networks, and even service operators/contents providers gradually become a reality. The heterogeneity will bring much more choices to customers to meet their preferred requirements individually. On the other hand, however, a conventional operator may face a difficulty to provide all satisfied services required by users with its own resources. The concept of hyper operator comes to absorb this heterogeneity by using the resources from both itself and other parties. The word "Hyper" is to signify a coherent set of characterizing concepts: seamlessness in mobile subscriber and third party service provider experience; heterogeneity in wireless access networks, backbone networks, mobile terminals, as well as applications; openness in terms of allowing and supporting third party service providers to deploy and compose any kind of application services such as web services, and mobile users to engage in all kind of Internet transactions and services with appropriate trust and security relationship management support and open interfaces support. Different from the conventional concept, not only mobile subscribers including human beings, pets and machines but also service providers probably providing radio access, Internet access/backbone, and contents or application services will become customers of a hyper operator. Then, a hyper operator

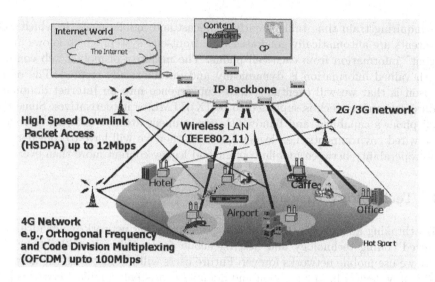

Fig. 5. Heterogeneous Network as Future Mobile Network.

will market comprehensive wireless Internet services to consumers, manage mobile subscribers, and offer them seamless services across heterogeneous wireless systems, networks, applications, terminals, and service providers at anytime in anywhere by anyway with minimum investment on infrastructure by using all possible resources.

A hyper operator will have different configurations. In a horizontal business model of wireless Internet services, possible service providers would be applied to radio access network (RSP), Internet access/core network (ISP), application (ASP). A hyper operator may be established based on any combination of these service providers. That is, it might be an RSP, an RSP+ISP, an RSP+ISP+ASP, etc. Nevertheless, a hyper operator must have a hyper operator overlay architecture/platform/network to provide seamless services.

Besides the services provided by existing operators, such as connectivity services by network service providers, applications and contents services by ASPs, the hyper operator overlay network is constructed to provide value added services including AAA (authentication, authorization, and account) services, service portal services for seamless applications, hyper handover support, and so on. As for AAA services, we know that different access networks have different level of security, in terms of authentication/ authorization/identification management. It is necessary to provide a uniform security level in heterogeneous access networks. Integrated AAA and composed AAA services will be considered. To provide third parties' applications seamlessly to mobile subscribers in terms of user's preference/profiles and device's diversities, a hyper operator service portal is needed for service selection, device adaptation, service decomposition, and service integration. Handover in the heterogeneous network environment is different from that in the same wireless access system (e.g., from one base station to another). While the handover within the same system is defined as horizontal handover, the handover between different administrative domains, different access technologies, user terminals, or applications is defined as hyper handover. Hyper operator overlay network will support the hyper handover. A plausible objective is thus to develop an overlay network on which a hyper operator can construct an application platform to provide new value added service and provide cross-provider/-layer coordination to absorb the heterogeneity. Mobility management and AAA are identified as key technologies here.

3.2   Mobile Multimedia Content and Seamless/Ubiquitous Service

Here let us take a question. What factors differentiate mobile multimedia content from conventional one? There are many futures including:

- Relatively Limited Bandwidth
- Error Prone Environment
- Terminal Capabilities such as Speakers, Displays and Limited Power Consumption Batteries, and
- Mobile Specific Emerging Applications (e.g., multimedia mail)

Although our next generation radio access technology is expected to provide higher bandwidth to users, compression still remains essential one due to the limited radio resources. This is especially true in image coding and hyper media that has more dimensions and requires the certain amount of data. Providing the best coding efficiency still remains essential technologies.

Speech is and will continue to be the traditional medium for communication, whether wired or wireless. Improved speech coding therefore remains a significant objective. Fundamental research work is delivering real advances both in coding efficiency and subjective performance. On the other hand, from the viewpoint of practical preparation toward the next decade, a speech CODEC suitable for Voice over mobile IP Network shold be also considered. Imaging and video are emerging media in wireless communications as we discussed. Further advances in coding efficiency and subjective performance will in the future enhance the user experience by providing sharper images with higher resolution and higher frame rate.

The research in this area is not limited to the compression. In the upcoming generation networks, devices, communication, available resources, and services are expected to become ever more diversified. Against this background, end users and service providers want both a "seamless" experience and ease of use without being confused by the multitude of available alternatives. Out of the many issues involved, the following topics are essential for mobile applications:

- Management, adaptation, and use of the diversity in user devices
- Management, adaptation, and use of the diversity in available networks and changes in operating conditions
- Discovery, adaptation, and use of various resources and services

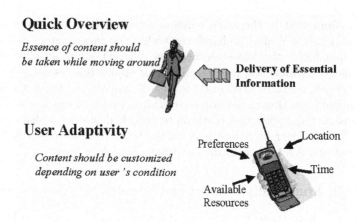

Fig. 6. Mobile Content Delivery Environment.

Here let us point out characteristics of a content delivery for mobile users as follows:

- Mobile content consists of spatially and temporally localized information in addition to that of non-mobile content(e.g., TV programs). "Spatially localized" means for example that the information within a mile radius from the user is useful for shopping or finding a fancy restaurant. "Temporally localized" means also for example that the present information, say 30 minutes before or later is useful for the abovementioned localized purpose
- Viewing time of mobile content is very limited by its nature. Mobile users are usually moving around, thus they do not have enough time to enjoy 2-hour movies

Mobile terminal are now highly personalized. Many personal data including user's preference on content viewing, terminal capability, or geometrical location will be stored or signaled by a mobile terminal. Mobile content should be customized so that its essential information can be presented properly depending on user's environment. Fig. 6 summarizes the mobile specific environments for the content delivery.

Here let us point out again the importance of metadata for seamless service customization since it provides hint information on how to customize the target content. In the context of content delivery, description of "user", "system (terminal and network)", and "mobile content" should be considered so that a content delivery system can respond the dynamic change of the content delivery environment (Fig. 7). Content description data represents semantic structure of the content to be delivered, which is required to identify what part of video data has to be delivered. For example, RDF framework has been specified to annotate semantics of the web content. Second one is the delivery environment description consisting of terminal description and network resource description. CC/PP defines the framework for specifying metadata dictionary for this type of information. Thirdly, user description addresses user's personal data or content viewing conditions, which can be dynamically changed. Thus representation of the environments (i.e., delivery context), and the adaptation mechanism based on the representation are essential.

New media processing, handling, and coding technologies together with networking technologies will inevitably revolutionize the way users interact with the mobile and fixed networks.

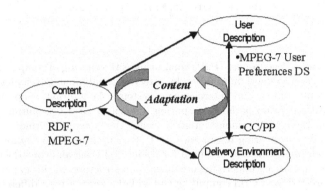

Fig. 7. Environment Description for Content Adaptation.

4   Conclusion

We have introduced the current mobile multimedia applications first. There would be two principles for creating killer applications. One is to follow what successfully happened in the legacy Internet. E-mail and web browsing are typical examples. The other one is to recognize what value 'mobile' adds. Multimedia mail is becoming a killer application and is particular to mobile environments, in which cell phones eventually will be equipped with 1M pixel CCD built-in cameras and VGA full color displays. Future generations of wireless networks will provide virtually unlimited opportunities to the global, connected community. Innovations in network technology will provide an environment in which virtually anything is available, anywhere, at any time, via any connected device. In that context, we have discussed future directions with three key words: hyper operator network, mobile content, and seamless service, in which mobility support, AAA, environment/delivery context representation and adaptation mechanism are identified as key technologies. We anticipate that the new technologies will be realized soon.

DB-Enabled Peers for Managing Distributed Data

Beng Chin Ooi, Yanfeng Shu, and Kian Lee Tan

Department of Computer Science
National University of Singapore
3 Science Drive 2, Singapore 117543
{ooibc,shuyanfe,tankl}@comp.nus.edu.sg

Abstract. Peer-to-peer (P2P) computing is the sharing of computer resources, services and information by direct negotiation and exchange between autonomous and heterogeneous systems. An alternative approach to distributed and parallel computing, known as Grid Computing, has also emerged, with a similar intent of scaling the system performance and availability by sharing resources. Like P2P computing, Grid Computing has been popularized by the need for resource sharing and consequently, it rides on existing underlying organizational structure. In this paper, we compare P2P and Grid computing to highlight some of their differences. We then examine the issues of P2P distributed data sharing systems, and how database applications can ride on P2P technology. We use our Best-Peer project, which is an on-going peer-based data management system, as an example to illustrate what P2P computing can do for database management.

1 Introduction

Peer-to-peer (P2P) technology, also called peer computing, is an emerging paradigm that is now viewed as a potential technology that could re-architect distributed architectures (e.g., the Internet). In a P2P distributed system, a large number of nodes on the edge (e.g., PCs connected to the Internet) can potentially be pooled together to share their resources, information and services. These nodes, which can both consume as well as provide data and/or services, may join and leave the P2P network at any time, resulting in a truly dynamic and ad-hoc environment. The distributed nature of such a design provides exciting opportunities for new killer applications to be developed.

The concept of P2P is not new. The pervasiveness of the Internet and the publicity gained as a result of music-sharing have caused researchers and application developers to realize the untapped resources, both in terms of computer technology and information. Edge devices such as personal computers are connecting to each other directly, forming special interest groups and collaborating to become a large search engine over information maintained locally, virtual clusters and file systems. Indeed, over the last few years, we have seen many systems

X. Zhou, Y. Zhang, and M.E. Orlowska (Eds.): APWeb 2003, LNCS 2642, pp. 10–21, 2003.

being developed and deployed; e.g., Freenet [5], Gnutella [6], Napster [15], ICQ [10], Seti@home [20] and LOCKSS [14].

The initial thrusts on the use of P2P platform were mainly social. Applications such as ICQ [10] and Napster [15], enable their users to create online communities that are self-organizing, dynamic and yet collaborative. The empowerment of users, freedom of choice and ease of migration, form the main driving force for the initial wide acceptance of P2P computing. To deploy P2P in a business organization, the accesses and dynamism can be constrained as data and resource sharing may be compartmentalized and restricted based on the roles users play. While most researchers and businessmen realize the potential of P2P, it remains a difficult task to find a business model for exploiting P2P fully. Consequently, various forms of P2P architectures have emerged and will evolve and adapt over time to find a natural fit for different application domains. One such success story is the deployment of the paradigm of edge-services in content search, where it has been exploited in pushing data closer to the users for faster delivery and solving the network and server bottle-neck problems.

From database perspective, most of these P2P systems are limited in several ways. First, they provide only file level sharing (i.e., sharing of the entirety of a file) and lack object/data management capabilities and support for content-based search. Second, they are limited in extensibility and flexibility. As such, there is no easy and rapid ways to extend their applications quickly to fulfill new users needs. Third, a node's peers are typically statically defined, without taking system and network traffic into consideration. The limitations are due to the lack of database's richness in semantics and relationships, and adaptability based on data size and access patterns.

Fueled by the need for sharing remote resources and datasets, and pooling computing resources for large-scale resource intensive data analysis, Grid Computing [3,4] has concurrently emerged as an alternative approach to distributed and parallel computing. Like P2P computing, Grid technology exploits shared resources and rides on existing underlying organizational structure. While they are similar in philosophy, they differ in several ways. In the next section, we provide some comparison between P2P and Grid computing, and argue that while Grid computing will continue to play an important role in specialized applications, the P2P technology has its own merits and offers more research challenges in view of the scale and unstability of the network. In the Section 3, we examine the issues of P2P distributed data sharing systems, and how database applications can ride on P2P technology. In Section 4, we present our BestPeer [16] project and its features, which is an on-going peer-based data management system, as an illustration of what P2P computing can do for database management. We conclude in Section 5.

2   P2P vs. Grid Computing

An alternative approach known as Grid Computing to distributed and parallel computing has also emerged, with a similar intent of scaling the system performance and availability by sharing resources. Like P2P computing, Grid Computing has been popularized by the need for resource sharing and consequently, it rides on existing underlying organizational structure. However, there are differences that distinguish the two as of today.

First, the grid network involves higher-end resources as compared to edge level devices in the P2P network. While the former requires large amount of money to be pumped in, the latter can tap into existing resources that are idling and hence require less upfront cost commitment.

Second, the participants in the Grid network are organizations which agree in good faith to share resources with a good degree of trust, accountability and common understanding; membership can be rather exclusive and hence the number of participants is usually not large. The common platform for sharing is usually clusters that have been demonstrated to be cost effective to super-computing, and together they provide an enormous amount of aggregated computing resources. In contrast, the participants of the P2P network are mainly end-users and the platform of sharing is mainly individual Personal Computer (PC). However, due to the mass appeal, the network grows in a much faster rate and may scale up to thousands of nodes. Because of the loose integration, it is more difficult and critical to manage trust, accountability and security.

Third, the Grid network is very much well structured and stable. As a result, resource discovery is less of an issue. On the contrary, P2P network is very unstable - nodes can join and leave the network anytime. This complicates the design of resource discovery mechanisms. Nodes that leave the network may mean some directories may be temporarily "unavailable".

Fourth, Grid computing can exploit traditional distributed query processing techniques and ensure that answers are complete. In contrast, nodes in the P2P network containing data may not be connected at the time of query, answers are likely to be incomplete.

Finally, computational grids are largely set up in anticipation of resource intensive applications, e.g. BioGrid for bioinformatics. However, to date, there has been no reported successful story. On the other hand, "killer" applications have surfaced in P2P naturally. For example, the Napster [15] MP3 music file sharing applications served over 20 million users by mid-2000 before it was finally shut down. As another example, the SETIhome [20] program has accumulated over 500,000 years of CPU time through more than 2 million users!

In summary, we believe Grid computing will continue to play an important role in specialized applications, although architecturely, Grid computing could be considered a special case of P2P computing, where each participating node has a larger capacity and collaboration is more constrained and organized. Notwithstanding, we believe P2P technology is more "user friendly" in the sense that it allows users (particularly those at the edges) to share their resources and information easily and freely. P2P also offers more research challenges in view of the scale and unstability of the network.

3   How Has P2P Been Used for Databases?

While database technologies are mature, P2P promises the power of autonomous and distributed resource sharing. Though these two have their different research focus, researchers are now trying to seek out possible ways to integrate the two to leverage on their respective strengths. We shall review some of these efforts here.

[7] is the first paper that discusses data management issues in P2P environment from a database research perspective. Its focus, however, is largely on *what database technologies can do for P2P applications*. Though a preliminary architecture for peer data management (Piazza) is described in [7], little is discussed about how peers cooperate. Different from [7], PeerOLAP [11] sought to address the problem in a different way - it looks at *what P2P technologies can do for database applications*. Essentially, PeerOLAP is still a client/server system, however, the cooperation among clients (peers) is explored: all data within clients is shared together.

In a P2P system, each peer maintains its data independently. In order to support semantically meaningful search, some kind of understanding among peers is required. In PeerDB[18,17], we adopted IR-based approach to mediate peer schemas with the help of a global thesaurus. In [19], a data model(LRM) is designed for P2P systems with domain relations and coordination formulas to describe relationships between two peer databases. Data Mapping [13] is a simplified implementation of this model.

Due to the autonomy of the peer nodes and the databases each maintains, data integration naturally becomes an important research area. However, unlike traditional data integration systems, where a global schema is assumed with a few data sources, a P2P system cannot simply assume a global schema, due to its high dynamicity and large number of data sources. Nevertheless, it may be possible to compose mediators, having some mediators defined in terms of other mediators and data sources, thus achieving system extensibility. This is the main thrust of [8] and [12]. While [8] focuses on how queries are reformulated with views, [12] focuses on selective view expansion as opposed to full view expansion which may be prohibitively expensive.

4   Peer-Based Data Management in the BestPeer Project

The BestPeer project started in 1999, and an extensible P2P platform, the Best-Peer platform, was developed fully in Java [16]. We have built several applications on top of the BestPeer platform, including BuddyWeb, PeerOLAP, PeerIS, PeerCQ and PeerDB. We shall focus here on the PeerDB system that is a prototype P2P application that provides database capabilities. This system has been developed at the National University of Singapore in collaboration with Fudan University, and is being enhanced with more features and applications.

PeerDB [17] is an instance of DBMS application over the BestPeer platform. The concept behind PeerDB is similar to the analogy of publishing personal web sites, except that it is now applied to personal databases. Unlike personal web sites which are usually hosted together in a central web server, personal databases are stored in the person's own PC. In addition, it is increasingly common for people to keep their data in common personal DBMS like MySql, and MSAccess. Therefore, a PeerDB node allows an user to index and publish his/her personal database for other peers to query.

4.1   The PeerDB Network

In the PeerDB network, there are two types of entities: a large number of nodes (PeerDB nodes), and a relatively fewer number of location independent global names lookup (LIGLO) servers. Each participating node runs the PeerDB (Java-based) software that enables it to communicate or share resources with any other nodes in the PeerDB network, thus realizing a P2P distributed data management and sharing environment. Each node is essentially a data management system and retains its autonomy: it determines its degree of participation - which relations to share with other nodes, amount of resources to share, and access control.

A LIGLO server is a "super" peer with fixed IP address, and is used to uniquely recognize nodes whose IP addresses may change frequently. Thus, a node's peer whose IP address may be different at different time remain uniquely recognizable. To avoid the server from being a bottleneck, we adopted a distributed approach where several LIGLO servers exist in the PeerDB network to cater to the nodes.

Like existing P2P systems, each PeerDB node maintains addresses of a set of nodes that it can directly reached. We shall refer to these nodes as *neighbors* or *directly connected peers* of the node. Each PeerDB node also maintains metadata of objects/services provided by its neighbors. If a request can be satisfied locally at a node, it is done; if it can be satisfied by some of its neighbors, it is routed to them; otherwise, the request is routed to all neighbors, which in turn may route it to their neighbors, and so on. Answers, however, are returned directly to the node that initiates the query without passing through the search path.

PeerDB exploits BestPeer's ability to reconfigure the network to keep promising peers in close proximity based on some criterion. Currently, PeerDB supports the following reconfiguration policies, the last strategy is newly designed:

1. **MaxCount**. MaxCount maximizes the number of objects a node can obtain from its directly connected peers. It works in two steps. First, the node sorts the peers based on the number of answers (or bytes) they returned. Those that return more answers are ranked higher, and ties are arbitrarily broken. The assumption here is that a peer that returns more answer is likely to be useful for future queries. Second, the k peers with the highest values are retained as the k directly connected peers, where k is a system parameter that can be set by a participating node.
2. **MinHops**. MinHops, implicitly exploits collaboration with peers by minimizing the number of Hops. It requires that peers piggyback with their

answers the value of Hops. This will indicate how far the peers are from the initiator of the request. More importantly, this information provides an indication on what one can access from one's indirect peers. The rationale is as follows: If one can get the answers through one's not-too-distant peers (with small Hops value), then it may not be necessary to keep those nodes (that provide the answer) as one's immediate peers; it is better to keep nodes that are further away so that all answer can be obtained with the minimal number of Hops. Thus, this policy simply orders peers based on the number of Hops, and picks those with the larger Hops values as the immediate peers. In the event of ties, the one with the larger number of answer is preferred.

3. **TempLoc.** TempLoc is a temporal locality based strategy that favors nodes that have most recently provided answers. It uses the notion of stack distance to measure the temporal locality. The idea works as follow. Consider a stack that stores all the peers that return results. For each peer that returns answers, move the peer to the top of the stack, and push the existing peers down. The temporal locality of a peer is thus determined by its depth in the stack. The top k peers in the stack are retained as the k directly connected peers, where k is a system parameter that can be set by the node.

4.2 Architecture of PeerDB

Figure 1 illustrates the internals of a PeerDB node. There are essentially four components that are loosely integrated. The first component is a data management system that facilitates storage, manipulation and retrieval of the data at the node. We note that the interface of the data management system is essentially an SQL query facility. Thus, the system can be used on its own as a stand alone DBMS outside of PeerDB.

For each relation that is created (through the PeerDB interface), the associated meta-data (schema, keywords, etc) are stored in a **Local Dictionary**. There is also an **Export Dictionary** that reflects the meta-data of objects that are sharable to other nodes. Thus, only objects that are exported can be accessed by other nodes in the network. We note that the meta-data associated with the Export Dictionary is a subset of those found in the Local Dictionary, and the distinction here is a logical one.

The second component is a database agent system called DBAgent. DBAgent provides the environment for mobile agents to operate on. Each PeerDB node has a *master agent* that manages the query of the user. In particular, it will clone and dispatch *worker agents* to neighboring nodes, receive answers and present them to the user. It also monitors the statistics and manages the network reconfiguration policies.

The third component is a cache manager. We are dealing with caching remote meta-data and data in secondary storage, and the cache manager determines the caching and replacement policies.

The last component is the user interface. This provides a user-friendly environment for user to submit their queries, to maintain their sharable objects,

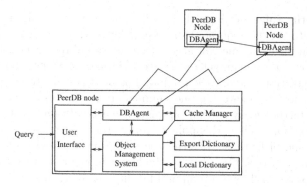

Fig. 1. PeerDB node architecture

and to insert/delete objects. In particular, users search for data using SQL-like queries.

4.3   Key Features of PeerDB

PeerDB has two main distinguishing features. First, it allows users to query data in a SQL-like interface without knowing the schema of data in other nodes. To address this issue, we adopt an Information Retrieval (IR) based approach. For each relation that is created by the user, meta-data are maintained for each relation name and attributes. These are essentially keywords/descriptions provided by the users upon creation of the table, and serve as a kind of synonymous names. DBAgents are sent out to the peers to find out potential matches and bring the corresponding meta-data back. By matching keywords from the meta-data of the relations, PeerDB is able to locate relations that are potentially similar to the query relations.

Second, in PeerDB, we adopt a two-phase agent-assisted query processing strategy. In the first phase, the relation matching strategy (as described in the first feature) is applied to locate potential relations. These relations (meta-data, database name, and location) are then returned to the query node for two purposes. One, it allows user to select the more relevant relations. This is to minimize information overload when data may be syntactically the same (having the same keywords) but semantically different. That is, different schemas are mediated. Moreover, this can minimize transmitting data that are not useful to the user, and hence better utilizes the network bandwidth. Two, it allows the node to update its statistics to facilitate future search process. Phase two begins after the user has selected the desired relations. In phase two, the queries will be directed to the nodes containing the selected relations, and the answers are finally returned (and cached). The two phases are completely assisted by agents. In fact, it is the agents that are sent out to the peers, and it is the agent that interacts with the DBMS. Moreover, a query may be rewritten into another form by the DBAgent (e.g., a query on a single relation may be rewritten into a join query involving multiple relations).

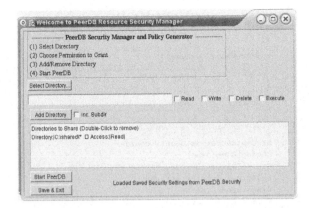

Fig. 2. Interface for specifying security policy

4.4 Security in PeerDB

Due to the security risks posed by such a potentially powerful platform, PeerDB has also been enhanced to provide a secure access to a node's computing resources and databases. Recall that each node comprises two types of data, private data and sharable data. Nodes can only access data that are sharable. This is enforced by a security policy that restricts applications to user-specified locations established during platform initialization. Figure 2 shows the interface to realize this. Communications between nodes have also been provided with 128 bit encryption to protect the sensitive data from being eavesdropped and viewed as they travel through the BestPeer network.

4.5 Implementation of PeerDB

PeerDB is fully implemented in Java. In our current implementation, we use MySQL as the underlying database management systems. Users need to enter keywords/descriptions and the columns of the table when they want to share the table to others. An example is shown in in Figure 3. In the figure, the table **studentcourses** has keywords **student** and **course**. Similarly, the attribute **CourseID** has keywords **course code** and **course number**.

The metadata is very useful as the incoming agent would determine whether the table is relevant to the query according to it. Our agent could also carry the relevant metadata from the query originating host to destination host to compare the similarity of the two metadata, and bring the set of possible relevant results back. Once the results arrive at the query originating host, the user would need to select the one he/she believe is relevant to his query, and perform the query.

Users will also need to maintain the relationship among those shared tables. i.e, they need to specify which tables can be joined and on what attributes. This is to facilitate better accuracy and more results. When an agent reaches the host, it not only searches for single tables, but also checks whether those "joinable" tables could be relevant to the query.

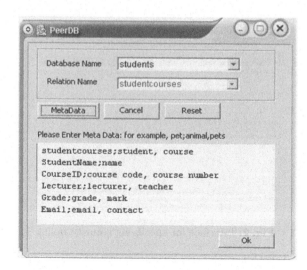

Fig. 3. A sample metadata for a PeerDB relation

When a user submits a query to our system, we will first check whether there is any cached information about the relevant tables. If yes, we will query those tables first. Our system will dispatch the agent to find more tables if the user is not satisfied with the number of results.

PeerDB maintains two thresholds input by the users, threshold1 and threshold2, to help find relevant tables. Our agent will carry the two thresholds with it; and when it arrives at a particular node, it will ask for the metadata of all the shared tables. For each shared table, it will then compute the similarity, sim1, between the two tables using the two set of metadata. If the sim1 is larger than threshold1, it will indicate the table as potentially relevant. It also computes the similarity, sim2, between the original metadata and the metadata of the "joinable table". If sim2 is larger than threshold2 and the sum of sim1 and sim2 is larger than threshold1, it will also indicate the joined table as potentially relevant. Note that in searching for relevant "joinable tables", threshold1 is for improving accuracy and threshold2 is for improving efficiency. The keywords for table name is assigned a higher weight.

After the computation, it will bring the metadata of those potential relevant tables to the query originating host. When the result is returned back, the user would need to indicate which table is relevant to his query and perform the query. The system automatically constructs a new query and directly sends the query to the destination node without dispatching the agent. We note that the reconstructed query may replace the names of the attributes and/or drop some attributes that are not relevant to the original query. PeerDB currently supports queries that join relations from multiple nodes. The user could also choose to save the metadata of the relevant tables (in the form of view), so that a subsequent search on the same tables do not require any agents to be dispatched. The view can then be propagated to other peers and maintained based on the statistics on how often it is being used.

Figure 4 shows the PeerDB query interfaces - the first figure shows the query interface; the second figure shows a sample where the user specifies that Table Students and Table Courses (both tables are results from the relation matching strategies) should be joined on the field Students.courseID and Courses.courseID; and the last figure displays the answer tuples from a selected relation.

4.6 Joining Tuples Based on 'Contents'

Query-by-keywords is the standard information retrieval mechanism to search for text documents. Recently, keyword search has also been proposed for searching centralized relational databases(eg. DBXplore [1], Discover[9] and BANKS[2]). In general, it is technically very challenging to query a database using keywords due to the semantics of keywords. In PeerDB, an on-going work is to provide keyword search in a peer-based data management system setting. Unlike centralized systems, the key challenges are the autonomy of peers, the lack of a global schema and the dynamics of the peer connectivity. To this end, we introduce the notion of peer-to-peer join that combines tuples from relations that contain certain keywords in the query. Compared to SQL queries, which can be only posed according to peers' local schema, keyword-based queries efface differences among peers to some extent, providing an integrated interface for the users. In addition, it is worthwhile to note that keyword-based queries in our system are answered in a semantically meaningful way, which is quite different from IR experiences.

Each peer maintains its data in a relational database. When a query is processed, the peer will search its database and return tuples that may include all or subsets of keywords in the query. Our focus is not on how keywords are searched in local relational databases, but on how partial and incomplete information from different peers can be combined and integrated. Within each peer, local keyword searching is an indispensable and important component.

Peer-to-Peer Join is a join operation that combines two (or more) relations from two (or more) peers based on the semantics of keywords and syntax of join operation of relational database systems. Each relation either contains at least one unique keyword in the query or acts as a connector that is necessary for joining other relations, but includes no query keywords by itself. To facilitate efficient peer-to-peer join processing, various network reconfiguration and query processing strategies are designed. Hueristics are formulated to select peers to improve the 'completeness' of the answer while returning the answer as quickly as possible to the user.

5   Conclusion

In this paper, we have relooked at P2P technology, and compare it against grid computing. We believe that P2P technology offers interesting research problems.

(a) Query submission.

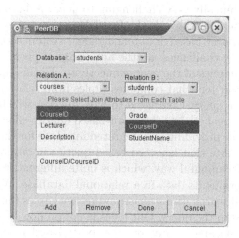

(b) Specifying joins.

(c) Answer tuples.

Fig. 4. Query interface.

We also presented how P2P technology has been applied to support data management, and described our current on-going work on building a peer-based data management system.

References

1. S. Agrawal, S. Chaudhuri, and G. Das. Dbxplorer: A system for keyword-based search over relational databases. In *Proceedings of the 18th International Conference on Data Engineering*, San Jose, CA, April 2002.
2. G. Bhalotia, C. Nakhe, A. Hulgeri, S. Chakrabarti, and S. Sudarshan. Keyword searching and browsing in databases using banks. In *Proceedings of the 18th International Conference on Data Engineering*, San Jose, CA, April 2002.
3. I. Foster. The grid: A new infrastructure for 21st century science. In *Physics Today*, 2002.
4. I. Foster and C. Kesselman, editors. *The Grid: Blueprint for a New Computing Infrastructure*. Morgan Kaufmann, 1999.
5. Freenet Home Page. *http://freenet.sourceforge.com/*.
6. Gnutella Development Home Page. *http://gnutella.wego.com/*.
7. S. Gribble, A. Halevy, Z. Ives, M. Rodrig, and D. Suciu. What can databases do for peer-to-peer. In *WebDB*, 2001.
8. A. Y. Halevy, Z. G. Ives, and D. Suciu. Schema mediation in peer data management systems. In *Proceedings of the 19th International Conference on Data Engineering*, 2003.
9. V. Hristidis and Y. Papakonstantinou. Discover: Keyword search in relational databases. In *VLDB'2002*, 2002.
10. ICQ Home Page. *http://www.icq.com/*.
11. P. Kalnis, W.S. Ng, B.C. Ooi, D. Papadias, and K.L. Tan. An adaptive peer-to-peer network for distributed caching of olap results. In *ACM SIGMOD 2002*, 2002.
12. T. Katchaounov. Query processing in self-profiling composable peer-to-peer mediator databases. In *Proc. EDBT Ph.D. Workshop 2002*, 2002.
13. A. Kementsietsidis, M. Arenas, and R. Miller. Data mapping in peer-to-peer systems. In *Proceedings of the 19th International Conference on Data Engineering*, 2003 (Poster Paper).
14. LOCKSS Home Page. *http://lockss.stanford.edu/*.
15. Napster Home Page. *http://www.napster.com/*.
16. W. S. Ng, B. C. Ooi, and K. L. Tan. BestPeer: A self-configurable peer-to-peer system. In *Proceedings of the 18th International Conference on Data Engineering*, San Jose, CA, April 2002 (Poster Paper).
17. W. S. Ng, B. C. Ooi, K. L. Tan, and A. Zhou. PeerDB: A p2p-based system for distributed data sharing. In *Proceedings of the 19th International Conference on Data Engineering*, Bangalore, India, March 2003.
18. B.C. Ooi, K.L. Tan, A.Y. Zhou, C.H. Goh, Y.G. Li, C.Y. Liau, B. Ling, W.S. Ng, Y. Shu, X.Y. Wang, and M. Zhang. PeerDB: Peering into personal databases. In *Proceedings of ACM SIGMOD Intl. Conf. on Management of Data*, San Diego, June 2003.
19. A. B. Philip, G. Fausto, K. Anastasios, M. John, S. Luciano, and Z. Ilya. Data management for peer-to-peer computing: A vision. In *WebDB Workshop*, 2002.
20. SETI@home Home Page. *http://setiathome.ssl.berkely.edu/*.

Functional Dependencies for XML

Millist W. Vincent and Jixue Liu

School of Computer and Information Science
University of South Australia
{millist.vincent, jixue.liu }@unisa.edu.au

Abstract. In this paper we address the problem of how to extend the definition of functional dependencies (FDs) in incomplete relations to XML documents. An incomplete relation is said to strongly satisfy a FD if every completion of the relation, obtained by replacing all null values by data values, satisfies the FD in the ordinary sense. We propose a syntactic definition of strong FD satisfaction in a XML document (called a XFD) and then justify it by proving that for a very general class of mappings of a relation into a XML document, a relation strongly satisfies a unary FD if and only if the XML document also strongly satisfies the equivalent XFD.

1 Introduction

XML has recently emerged as a standard for data representation and interchange on the Internet [13,1]. While providing syntactic flexibility, XML provides little semantic content and as a result several papers have addressed the topic of how to improve the semantic expressiveness of XML. Among the most important of these approaches has been that of defining integrity constraints in XML [5]. Several different classes of integrity constraints for XML have been defined including key constraints [5,6], path constraints [7], and inclusion constraints [9] and properties such as axiomatization and satisfiability have been investigated for these constraints. However, one topic that has been identified as an open problem in XML research [13] and which has been little investigated is how to extended the oldest and most well studied integrity constraint in relational databases, namely *functional dependencies* (FDs), to XML and then how to develop a normalization theory for XML. The only paper that has specifically addressed this problem is the recent paper [3]. Before presenting the contribution of [3] and comparing it with our paper, we briefly outline the approaches to defining FD satisfaction in incomplete relational databases.

There are two approaches, the first called the *weak satisfaction* approach and the other called the *strong satisfaction* approach [4]. In the weak satisfaction approach, a relation is defined to weakly satisfy a FD if there exists *at least one* completion of the relation, obtained by replacing all occurrences of nulls by data values, which satisfies the FD. A relation is said to strongly satisfy a FD if *every* completion of the relation satisfies the FD. Both approaches have their advantages and disadvantages (a more complete discussions of this issue can

X. Zhou, Y. Zhang, and M.E. Orlowska (Eds.): APWeb 2003, LNCS 2642, pp. 22–34, 2003.
© Springer-Verlag Berlin Heidelberg 2003

be found in the full version of our paper [12]). The weak satisfaction approach has the advantage of allowing a high degree of uncertainty to be represented in a database but at the expense of making maintenance of integrity constraints much more difficult. In contrast, the strong satisfaction approach restricts the amount of uncertainty that can be represented in a database but makes the maintenance of integrity constraints much easier. However, as argued in more detail in [12], both approaches have their place in real world applications and should be viewed as complementary rather than competing approaches. Also, it is possible to combine the two approaches by having some FDs in a relation strongly satisfied and others weakly satisfied [10].

The contribution of [3] was, for the first time, to define FDs in XML (what we call XFDs) and then to define a normal form for a XML document based on the definition of a XFD. However, there are some difficulties with the definition of a XFD given in [3]. The first is that although it is explicitly recognized in the definitions that XML documents have missing information, the definitions in [3], while having some elements of the weak instance approach, are not a strict extension of this approach since there are XFDs that are violated according to the definition in [3] yet there are completions of the tree that satisfy the XFDs (see the full version of our paper [12] for an example). The second difficulty is that the definition of an XFD in [3] assumes the existence of a DTD. One problem with this assumption is that a XML document does not require the existence of a DTD and so XFDs cannnot be defined in such documents. The other problem with this assumption is that it raises the issue of possible interaction of FDs with the DTD. It is well known that for a variety of integrity constraints in XML, such as keys and foreign keys, the integrity constraints and the DTD interact in the sense that there are integrity constraints implied by the combination of the set of integrity constraints and the DTD that are not implied by either the set of integrity constraints or the DTD alone [2,6,8]. It was shown in [12] that the same situation occurs with XFDs. However the effects of the possible interaction between XFDs and DTDs were not investigated in [3].

The main contributions of our paper are as follows. The first is that we give a precise syntactic definition of the strong satisfaction of a XFD in a XML document which overcomes the difficulties just mentioned with the approach of [3]. Our approach is simpler and more direct than the one used in [3] and has the additional flexibility of not requiring the existence of a DTD for the definition. The second contribution of our paper is to provide formal justification for our syntactic definition of a XFD by proving that for a very general class of mappings of a relation into a XML document, a relation strongly satisfies a unary FD if and only if the XML document also strongly satisfies the equivalent XFD. We note also that in the full length version of our paper [12] another justification for our definition of a XFD is provided. There we prove that a XML document strongly satisfies a XFD if and only if every completion of the XML document also satisfies the XFD. This is the XML equivalent of Lemma 6.1 in [4] which proves the equivalence between a syntactic definition of strong satisfaction of FDs in incomplete relations and the semantic definition (the one previously given).

2 Preliminary Definitions

In this section we present some preliminary definitions that we need before defining XFDs. We model a XML document as a tree as follows.

Definition 1. *Assume a countably infinite set* $\mathbf{E}$ *of element labels (tags), a countable infinite set* $\mathbf{A}$ *of attribute names and a symbol* S *indicating text. An XML tree is defined to be* $T = (V, lab, ele, att, val, v_r)$ *where* V *is a* finite *set of nodes in* T*; lab is a function from* V *to* $\mathbf{E} \cup \mathbf{A} \cup \{S\}$*; ele is a partial function from* V *to a sequence of* V *nodes such that for any* $v \in V$*, if* $ele(v)$ *is defined then* $lab(v) \in \mathbf{E}$*; att is a partial function from* $V \times \mathbf{A}$ *to* V *such that for any* $v \in V$ *and* $l \in \mathbf{A}$*, if* $att(v,l) = v_1$ *then* $lab(v) \in \mathbf{E}$ *and* $lab(v_1) = l$*; val is a function such that for any node in* $v \in V, val(v) = v$ *if* $lab(v) \in \mathbf{E}$ *and* $val(v)$ *is a string if either* $lab(v) = S$ *or* $lab(v) \in \mathbf{A}$*;* v_r *is a distinguished node in* V *called the root of* T *and we define* $lab(v_r) = root$*. Since node identifiers are unique, a consequence of the definition of val is that if* $v_1 \in \mathbf{E}$ *and* $v_2 \in \mathbf{E}$ *and* $v_1 \neq v_2$ *then* $val(v_1) \neq val(v_2)$*. We also extend the definition of val to sets of nodes and if* $V_1 \subseteq V$*, then* $val(V_1)$ *is the set defined by* $val(V_1) = \{val(v) | v \in V_1\}$*.*

For any $v \in V$*, if* $ele(v)$ *is defined then the nodes in* $ele(v)$ *are called* subelements *of* v*. For any* $l \in \mathbf{A}$*, if* $att(v,l) = v_1$ *then* v_1 *is called an* attribute *of* v*. Note that a XML tree* T *must be a tree. Since* T *is a tree the set of ancestors of a node* v*, is denoted by* $Ancestor(v)$*. The children of a node* v *are also defined as in Definition 1 and we denote the parent of a node* v *by* $Parent(v)$*.*

We note that our definition of *val* differs slightly from that in [5] since we have extended the definition of the *val* function so that it is also defined on element nodes. The reason for this is that we want to include in our definition paths that do not end at leaf nodes, and when we do this we want to compare element nodes by node identity, i.e. node equality, but when we compare attribute or text nodes we want to compare them by their contents, i.e. value equality. This point will become clearer in the examples and definitions that follow.

We now give some preliminary definitions related to paths.

Definition 2. *A* path *is an expression of the form* $l_1.\cdots.l_n$*,* $n \geq 1$*, where* $l_i \in \mathbf{E} \cup \mathbf{A} \cup \{S\}$ *for all* $i, 1 \leq i \leq n$ *and* $l_1 = root$*. If* p *is the path* $l_1.\cdots.l_n$ *then* $Last(p)$ *is* l_n*.*

For instance, in Figure 1, `root` and `root.Division` are paths.

Definition 3. *Let* p *denote the path* $l_1.\cdots.l_n$*. The function* $Parnt(p)$ *is the path* $l_1.\cdots.l_{n-1}$*. Let* p *denote the path* $l_1.\cdots.l_n$ *and let* q *denote the path* $q_1.\cdots.q_m$*. The path* p *is said to be a* prefix *of the path* q *if* $n \leq m$ *and* $l_1 = q_1, \ldots, l_n = q_n$*. Two paths* p *and* q *are* equal*, denoted by* $p = q$*, if* p *is a prefix of* q *and* q *is a prefix of* p*. The path* p *is said to be a* strict prefix *of* q *if* p *is a prefix of* q *and* $p \neq q$*. We also define the intersection of two paths* p_1 *and* p_2*, denoted but* $p_1 \cap p_2$*, to be the maximal common prefix of both paths. It is clear that the intersection of two paths is also a path.*

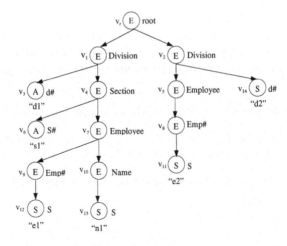

Fig. 1. A XML tree

For example, in Figure 1, `root.Division` is a strict prefix of
`root.Division.Section` and
`root.Division.d#` ∩ `root.Division.Employee.Emp#.S` = `root.Division`.

Definition 4. *A path instance in an XML tree T is a sequence $\bar{v}_1.\cdots.\bar{v}_n$ such that $\bar{v}_1 = v_r$ and for all $\bar{v}_i, 1 < i \leq n, v_i \in V$ and $\bar{v}_i$ is a child of $\bar{v}_{i-1}$. A path instance $\bar{v}_1.\cdots.\bar{v}_n$ is said to be* defined over the path $l_1.\cdots.l_n$ *if for all $\bar{v}_i, 1 \leq i \leq n$, $lab(\bar{v}_i) = l_i$. Two path instances $\bar{v}_1.\cdots.\bar{v}_n$ and $\bar{v}'_1.\cdots.\bar{v}'_n$ are said to be* distinct *if $v_i \neq v'_i$ for some i, $1 \leq i \leq n$. The set of path instances over a path p in a tree T is denoted by $Paths(p)$*

Definition 5. *An* extended XML tree *is a tree $(V \cup N, lab, ele, att, val, v_r)$ where N is a set of marked nulls that is disjoint from V and if $v \in N$ and $v \notin E$ then $val(v)$ is undefined.*

Definition 6. *Let T be a XML tree and let P be a set of paths. Then (T, P) is* consistent *if:*
   (i) For any two paths $l_1.\cdots.l_n$ and $l'_1.\cdots.l'_m$ in P such that $l'_m = l_i$ for some i, $1 \leq i \leq n$ then $l_1.\cdots.l_i = l'_1.\cdots.l'_m$;
   (ii) If v_1 and v_2 are two nodes in T such that v_1 is the parent of v_2, then there exists a path $l_1.\cdots.l_n$ in P such that there exists i and j, where $1 \leq i \leq n$ and $1 \leq j \leq n$ and $i < j$ and $label(v_1) = l_i$ and $label(v_2) = l_j$.

Definition 7. *Let T be a XML tree and let P be a set of paths such that (T, P) is consistent. Then a minimal extension of T, denoted by T_P, is an extended XML tree constructed as follows. Initially let T_P be T. Process each path p in P in*

*an arbitrary order as follows. For every node in v in T such that lab(v) appears
in p and there does not exist a path instance containing v which is defined over
p, construct a path instance over p by adding nodes from* **N** *as ancestors and
descendants of v. Also, assign to any null node in T_P the corresponding label in
p.*

The next lemma follows easily from the construction procedure.

Lemma 1. *Let T be a XML tree and let P be a set of paths such that (T, P) is
consistent. Then T_P is unique up to the labelling of the null nodes.*

For instance, the minimal extension of the tree in Figure 1 is shown in Figure 2.

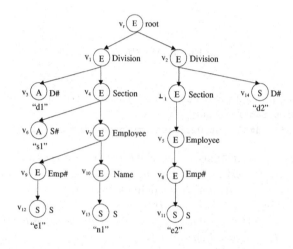

Fig. 2. The minimal extension of an XML tree.

Definition 8. *A path instance $\bar{v}_1.\cdots.\bar{v}_n$ in T_P is defined to be complete if
$\bar{v}_i \notin$ **N** for all i, $1 \leq i \leq n$. Also we often do not need to distinguish between
nulls and so the statement $v =\perp$ is shorthand for $\exists j(v =\perp_j)$ and $v \neq\perp$ is
shorthand for $\not\exists j(v =\perp_j)$.*

The next function returns all the final nodes of the path instances of a path
p.

Definition 9. *Let T_P be the minimal extension of T. The function $N(p)$, where
p is the path $l_1.\cdots.l_n$, is defined to be the set $\{\bar{v}|\bar{v}_1.\cdots.\bar{v}_n \in Paths(p) \wedge \bar{v} = \bar{v}_n\}$.*

For example, in Figure 2, $N(\text{root.Division.Section.Employee}) = \{v_7, v_5\}$
and $N(\text{root.Division.Section }) = \{v_4, \perp_1\}$.

We now need to define a function that is related to ancestor.

Definition 10. *Let T_P be the minimal extension of T. The function $AAncestor(v, p)$ where $v \in V \cup N$, p is a path and $v \in N(p)$, is defined by $AAncestor(v, p) = \{v'|v' \in \{\bar{v}'_1, \cdots, \bar{v}'_n\} \wedge v = \bar{v}'_n \wedge \bar{v}'_1. \cdots .\bar{v}'_n \in Paths(p)\}$.*

For example, in Figure 2, $AAncestor(v_5, \texttt{root.Division.Section.Employee})$ $= \{v_r, v_2, \perp_1, v_5\}$. The next function returns all nodes that are the final nodes of path instances of p and are descendants of v.

Definition 11. *Let T_P be the minimal extension of T. The function $Nodes(v, p)$, where $v \in V \cup N$ and p is a path, is the set defined by $Nodes(v, p) = \{x|x \in N(p) \wedge v \in AAncestor(x, p)\}$. Note that $Nodes(v, p)$ may be empty.*

For example, in Figure 2, $Nodes(v_r, \texttt{root.Division.Section.Employee}) = \{v_5, v_7\}$, $Nodes(v_1, \texttt{root.Division.Section.Employee}) = \{v_7\}$, $Nodes(v_7, \texttt{root.Division}) = \emptyset$.

Lastly we extend the definition of the *val* function so that $val(\perp_j) = \perp_j$. Note that different unmarked nulls are not considered to be equal and so $val(\perp_i) \neq val(\perp_j)$ if $i \neq j$.

3 Strong Functional Dependencies in XML

This leads us to the main definition of our paper.

Definition 12. *Let T be a XML tree and let P be a set of paths such that (T, P) is consistent. A XML functional dependency (XFD) is a statement of the form: $p_1, \cdots, p_k \rightarrow q$ where $p_1, \cdots, p_k$ and q are paths in P. T strongly satisfies the XFD if $p_i = q$ for some $i, 1 \leq i \leq k$ or for any two distinct path instances $\bar{v}_1. \cdots .\bar{v}_n$ and $\bar{v}'_1. \cdots .\bar{v}'_n$ in $Paths(q)$ in T_P, $((\bar{v}_n = \perp \wedge \bar{v}'_n = \perp) \vee (\bar{v}_n \neq \perp \wedge \bar{v}'_n = \perp) \vee (\bar{v}_n = \perp \wedge \bar{v}'_n \neq \perp) \vee (\bar{v}_n \neq \perp \wedge \bar{v}'_n \neq \perp \wedge val(\bar{v}_n) \neq val(\bar{v}'_n)) \Rightarrow \exists i, 1 \leq i \leq k$, such that $x_i \neq y_i$ if $Last(p_i) \in E$ else $\perp \notin Nodes(x_i, p_i)$ and $\perp \notin Nodes(y_i, p_i)$ and $val(Nodes(x_i, p_i)) \cap val(Nodes(y_i, p_i)) = \emptyset$, where $x_i = \{v|v \in \{\bar{v}_1, \cdots, \bar{v}_n\} \wedge v \in N(p_i \cap q)\}$ and $y_i = \{v|v \in \{\bar{v}'_1, \cdots, \bar{v}'_n\} \wedge v \in N(p_i \cap q)\}$.*

We note that since the path $p_i \cap q$ is a prefix of q, there exists only one node in $\bar{v}_1. \cdots .\bar{v}_n$ that is also in $N(p_i \cap q)$ and so x_i is always defined and unique. Similarly for y_i.

We now outline the thinking behind the above definition firstly for the simplest case where on the l.h.s. of the XFD contains a single path. In the relational model, if we are given a relation r and a FD $A \rightarrow B$, then to see if $A \rightarrow B$ is satisfied we have to check the B values and their corresponding A values. In the relational model the correspondence between B values and A values is obvious - the A value corresponding to a B value is the A value in the same tuple as the B value. However, in XML there is no concept of a tuple so it is not immediately clear how to generalize the definition of an FD to XML. Our solution is based on the following observation. In a relation r with tuple t, the value $t[A]$ can be seen as the 'closest' A value to the B value $t[B]$. In Definition 12 we generalize this observation and given a path instance $\bar{v}_1. \cdots .\bar{v}_n$ in $Paths(q)$, we first compute the 'closest' ancestor of $\bar{v}_n$ that is also an ancestor of a node in $N(p)$ (x_1 in the above definition) and then compute the 'closest p-nodes' to be the set of nodes which terminate a path instance of p and are descendants of x_1. We then proceed in a similar fashion for the other path $\bar{v}'_1 \cdots \cdot \bar{v}'_n$ and compute the 'p-nodes' which are closest to $\bar{v}'_n$. We note that in this definition, as opposed to the relational case, there will be in general more than one 'closest p - node' and so $Nodes(x_1, p)$ and $Nodes(y_1, p)$ will in general contain more than one node. Having computed the 'closest p-nodes' to $\bar{v}_n$ and $\bar{v}'_n$, if $val(\bar{v}_n) \neq val(\bar{v}'_n)$ we then require, generalizing on the relational case, that the $val's$ of the sets of corresponding 'closest p-nodes' be disjoint.

The rationale for the case where there is more than one path on the l.h.s. is similar. Given a XFD $p_1, \cdots, p_k \rightarrow q$ and two paths $\bar{v}_1 \cdots \cdot \bar{v}_n$ and $\bar{v}'_1 \cdots \cdot \bar{v}'_n$ in $Paths(q)$ which end in nodes with different val, we firstly compute, for each p_i, the set of 'closest p_i nodes' to $\bar{v}_n$ in the same fashion as just outlined. Then extending the relational approach to FD satisfaction, we require that in order for $p_1, \cdots, p_k \rightarrow q$ to be satisfied there is at least one p_i for which the $val's$ of the set of 'closest p_i nodes' to $\bar{v}_n$ is disjoint from the $val's$ of the set of 'closest p_i nodes' to $\bar{v}'_n$. We now illustrate the definition by some examples.

Example 1. Consider the XML tree shown in Figure 3 and the XFD
root.Department.Lecturer.Lname $\rightarrow$
root.Department.Lecturer.Subject.SubjName.S. Then $v_r.v_1.v_5.v_{13}.v_{17}.$ v_{22} and $v_r.v_2.v_9.v_{15}.v_{21}.v_{24}$ are two distinct path instances in
$Paths($root.Department.Lecturer.Subject.SubjName.S$)$ and $val(v_{22}) =$ "n1" and $val(v_{24}) = $ "n2". So $N($root.Department.Lecturer.Lname$\cap$
root.Department.Lecturer.Subject.SubjName.S$)$ $= \{v_5, v_6, v_9\}$ and so $x_1 = v_5$ and $y_1 = v_9$. Thus $val(Nodes(x_1, $root.Department.Lecturer.Lname$))$ $= \{$"11"$\}$ and $val(Nodes(y_1, $root.Department.Lecturer.Lname$))$ $=$ $\{$"11"$\}$ and so the XFD is violated. We note that if we change val of node v_{10} in Figure 3 to "13" then the XFD is satisfied.

Consider next the XFD root.Department.Head $\rightarrow$ root.Department. Then $v_r.v_1$ and $v_r.v_2$ are two distinct paths instances in $Paths($root.Department$)$ and $val(v_1) = v_1$ and $val(v_2) = v_2$. Also
$N($root.Department.Head $\cap$ root.Department$) = \{v_1, v_2\}$ and so $x_1 = v_1$ and $y_1 = v_2$. Thus $val(Nodes(x_1, $root.Department.Head$)) = \{$"h1"$\}$ and $Val(Nodes(y_1, $root.Department.Head$)) = \{$"h2"$\}$ and so the XFD is satisfied. We note that if we change val of node v_8 in Figure 3 to "h1" then the XFD is violated.

Consider next the XFD root.Department.Lecturer.Lname,
root.Department.Dname $\rightarrow$
root.Department.Lecturer.Subject.Subject#. Then $v_r.v_1.v_5.v_{13}.v_{16}$ and $v_r.v_2.v_9.v_{15}. \perp_1$ are two distinct path instances in
$Paths($root.Department.Lecturer.Subject.Subject#$)$ and $val(v_{16}) =$ "s1" and the final node in $v_r.v_2.v_9.v_{15}. \perp_1$ is null.

Then $N(\text{root}.\text{Department}.\text{Lecturer}.\text{Lname} \cap$

root.Department.Lecturer.Subject.Subject#) $= \{v_5, v_6, v_9\}$ and so $x_1 = v_5$ and $y_1 = v_9$ and so

$val(Nodes(x_1, \text{root}.\text{Department}.\text{Lecturer}.\text{Lname})) = $ "11" and

$val(Nodes(y_1, \text{root}.\text{Department}.\text{Lecturer}.\text{Lname})) = $ "11". We then compute $N(\text{root}.\text{Department}.\text{Dname} \cap$

root.Department.Lecturer.Subject.Subject#) $= \{v_1, v_2\}$ and so $x_2 = v_1$ and $y_2 = v_2$ and so $val(Nodes(x_2, \text{root}.\text{Department}.\text{Dname})) = $ "d1" and

$val(Nodes(y_2, \text{root}.\text{Department}.\text{Dname})) = $ "d2". Similarly, for the paths $v_r.v_2.v_9.v_{15}.\perp_1$ and $v_r.v_1.v_6.v_{14}.v_{18}$, we derive that $x_1 = v_6$ and $y_1 = v_9$ and so

$val(Nodes(x_1, \text{root}.\text{Department}.\text{Lecturer}.\text{Lname})) = $ "12" and

$val(Nodes(y_1, \text{root}.\text{Department}.\text{Lecturer}.\text{Lname})) = $ "11" and so the XFD is satisfied.

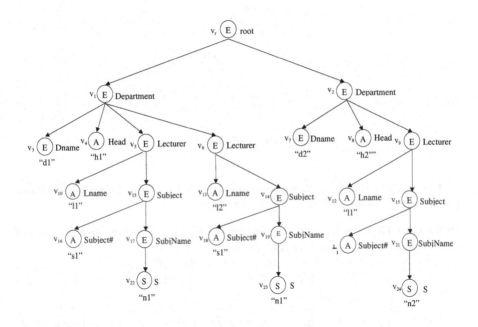

Fig. 3. A XML tree illustrating the definition of a XFD

4   XFDs in XML Trees and FDs in Relations

In this section we provide a formal justification for the definition of a XFD given in the previous section. We prove that for a very general class of mappings of a relation into a XML document, a relation strongly satisfies a unary FD if and only if the XML document also strongly satisfies the equivalent XFD. As our technique for mapping relations to XML Trees is done via nested relations, we firstly present the definitions for nested relations.

Let U be a fixed countable set of atomic attribute names. Associated with each attribute name $A \in U$ is a countably infinite set of values denoted by $DOM(A)$ and the set **DOM** is defined by **DOM** $= \cup DOM(A_i)$ for all $A_i \in U$. We assume that $DOM(A_i) \cap DOM(A_j) = \emptyset$ if $i \neq j$. A *scheme tree* is a tree containing at least one node and whose nodes are labelled with nonempty sets of attributes that form a partition of a finite subset of U. If n denotes a node in a scheme tree S then:

- $ATT(n)$ is the set of attributes associated with n;
- $A(n)$ is the union of $ATT(n_1)$ for all $n_1 \in Ancestor(n)$.

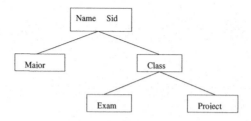

Fig. 4. A scheme tree

Figure 4 illustrates an example scheme tree defined over the set of attributes {Name, Sid, Major, Class, Exam, Project}.

Definition 13. *A* nested relation scheme *(NRS) for a scheme tree S, denoted by $N(S)$, is the set defined recursively by:*

(i) If S consists of a single node n then $N(S) = ATT(n)$;

(ii) If $A = ATT(ROOT(S))$ and $S_1, \cdots, S_k, k \geq 1$, are the principal subtrees of S then $N(S) = A \cup \{N(S_1)\} \cdots \{N(S_k)\}$.

For example, for the scheme tree S shown in Figure 4, $N(S) = \{$Name, Sid, {Major}, {Class, {Exam}, {Project}}$\}$. We now recursively define the domain of a scheme tree S, denoted by $DOM(N(S))$.

Definition 14. *(i) If S consists of a single node n with $ATT(n) = \{A_1, \cdots, A_n\}$ then $DOM(N(S)) = DOM(A_1) \times \cdots \times DOM(A_n)$;*

(ii) If $A = ATT(ROOT(S))$ and $S_1, \cdots, S_k$ are the principal subtrees of S, then $DOM(N(S)) = DOM(A) \times P(DOM(N(S_1))) \times \cdots \times P(DOM(N(S_k)))$ where $P(Y)$ denotes the set of all nonempty, finite subsets of a set Y.

The set of *atomic attributes* in $N(S)$, denoted by $Z(N(S))$, is defined by $Z(N(S)) = N(S) \cap U$. The set of higher order attributes in $N(S)$, denoted by $H(N(S))$, is defined by $H(N(S)) = N(S) - Z(N(S))$. For instance, for the example shown in Figure 4, $Z(N(S)) = \{$Name, Sid$\}$ and $H(N(S)) =$ $\{\{$Major$\}, \{$Class, $\{$Exam$\}, \{$Project$\}\}\}$.

Finally we define a nested relation over a nested relation scheme $N(S)$, denoted by $r^*(N(S))$, or often simply by r^* when $N(S)$ is understood, to be a finite nonempty set of elements from $DOM(N(S))$. If t is a tuple in r^* and Y is a nonempty subset of $N(S)$, then $t[Y]$ denotes the restriction of t to Y and the restriction of r^* to Y is then the nested relation defined by $r^*[Y] = \{t[Y]|t \in r\}$. An example of a nested relation over the scheme tree of Figure 4 is shown in Figure 5.

A tuple t_1 is said to be a *subtuple* of a tuple t in r^* if there exists $Y \in H(N(S))$ such that $t_1 \in t[Y]$ or there exists a tuple t_2, defined over some NRS N_1, such that t_2 is a subtuple of t and there exists $Y_1 \in H(N_1)$ such that $t_1 \in t_2[Y_1]$. For example in the relation shown in Figure 5 the tuples

$<$ CS100, $\{$mid-year, final$\}, \{$Project A, Project B, Project C$\}$ $>$ and $<$ Project A $>$ are both subtuples of

$<$ Anna, Sid1, $\{$Maths, Computing$\}, \{$CS100, $\{$mid-year, final$\}$, $\{$Project A, Project B,Project C$\}\}$ $>$.

Name	Sid	{Major}	{Class	{Exam}	{Project}}
Anna	Sid1	Maths	CS100	Mid-year	Project A
		Computing		Final	Project B
					Project C
Bill	Sid2	Physics	P100	Final	Prac 1
					Prac 2
		Chemistry	CH200	Test A	Experiment 1
				Test B	Experiment 2 1

Fig. 5. A nested relation.

We now introduce the nest and unnest operators for nested relations as defined in [11].

Definition 15. *Let Y be a nonempty proper subset of $N(S)$. Then the operation of nesting a relation r^* on Y, denoted by $\nu_Y(r^*)$, is defined to be a nested relation over the scheme $(N(S) - Y) \cup \{Y\}$ and a tuple $t \in \nu_Y(r^*)$ iff:*
(i) there exists $t_1 \in r^*$ such that $t[N(S) - Y] = t_1[N(S) - Y]$ and
(ii) $t[\{Y\}] = \{t_2[Y]|t_2 \in r^* \text{ and } t_2[N(S) - Y] = t[N(S) - Y]\}$.

Definition 16. *Let $r^*(N(S))$ be a relation and $\{Y\}$ an element of $H(N(S))$. Then the unnesting of r^* on $\{Y\}$, denoted by $\mu_{\{Y\}}(r^*)$, is a relation over the nested scheme $(N(S) - \{Y\}) \cup Y$ and a tuple $t \in \mu_{\{Y\}}(r^*)$ iff there exists $t_1 \in r^*$ such that $t_1[N(S) - \{Y\}] = t[N(S) - \{Y\}]$ and $t[Y] \in t_1[\{Y\}]$.*

More generally, one can define the *total unnest* of a nested relation r^*, denoted by $\mu^*(r^*)$, as the flat relation defined as follows.

Definition 17. *(i) if r^* is a flat relation then $\mu^*(r^*) = r^*$;*

(ii) otherwise $\mu^*(r^*) = \mu^*((\mu_{\{Y\}}(r^*)))$ where $\{Y\}$ is a higher order attribute in the NRS for r^*.

It can be shown [11] that the order of unnesting is immaterial and so $\mu^*(r)$ is uniquely defined. Also, we need the following result from [11]. Let us denote the NRS of nested relation r^* by $N(r^*)$.

Lemma 2. *For any nested relation r^* and any $Y \subseteq N(r^*)$, $\mu_{\{Y\}}(\nu_Y(r^*)) = r^*$.*

We note the well known result [11] that the converse of the above lemma does not hold, i.e. there are nested relations such that $\nu_Y(\mu_{\{Y\}}(r^*)) \neq r^*$.

Mapping from relations to XML. The translation of a relation into a XML tree consists of two phases. In the first we map the relation to a nested relation whose nesting structure is arbitrary and then we map the nested relation to a XML tree.

In the first step we let the nested relation r^* be defined by $r_i = \nu_{Y_{i-1}}(r_{i-1}), r_0 = r, r^* = r_n, 1 \leq i \leq n$ where r represents the initial (flat) relation and r^* represents the final nested relation. The Y_i are allowed to be arbitrary apart from the obvious restriction that Y_i is an element of the NRS for r_i.

The nest operator as defined above only works for complete relations so we have to indicate how we handle nulls. Our approach is in the first step to consider the nulls to be marked, and hence distinguishable, and to treat these unmarked nulls as though they are data values. Thus the definition of the nest operator and r^* remain unchanged.

In the second step of the mapping procedure we take the nested relation and convert it to a XML tree as follows. We start with an initially empty tree. For each tuple t in r^* we first create an element node of type Id and then for each $A \in Z(N(r^*))$ we insert a single attribute node with a value $t[A]$. We then repeat recursively the procedure for each subtuple of t. The final step in the procedure is to compress the tree by removing all the nodes containing nulls from the tree. We now illustrate these steps by an example.

Example 2. Consider the flat relation shown in Figure 6.

If we then transform the relation r in Figure 6 by the sequence of nestings $r_1 = \nu_{PROJECT}(r)$, $r_2 = \nu_{EXAM}(r_1)$, $r_3 = \nu_{CLASS,\{EXAM\},\{PROJECT\}}(r_2)$, $r^* = \nu_{MAJOR}(r_3)$ then the relation r^* is shown in Figure 7. We then transform the nested relation in Figure 7 to the XML tree shown in Figure 8

This now leads to the main result of this section which establishes the correspondence between satisfaction of FDs in relations and satisfaction of XFDs in XML. We denote by T_{r^*} the XML tree derived from r^*.

Theorem 1. *Let r be a flat relation and let $A \rightarrow B$ be a FD defined over r. Then r strongly satisfies $A \rightarrow B$ iff T_{r^*} strongly satisfies $p.A \rightarrow q.B$ where $p.A$ denotes the path in T_{r^*} to reach A and $q.B$ denotes the path to reach B.*

Name	Sid	Major	Class	Exam	Project
Anna	Sid1	Maths	CS100	Mid-year	Project A
Anna	Sid1	Maths	CS100	Mid-year	$\perp_1$
Anna	Sid1	Maths	CS100	Final	Project A
Anna	Sid1	Maths	CS100	Final	$\perp_1$
Anna	Sid1	$\perp_2$	CS100	Mid-year	Project A
Anna	Sid1	$\perp_2$	CS100	Mid-year	$\perp_1$
Anna	Sid1	$\perp_2$	CS100	Final	Project A
Anna	Sid1	$\perp_2$	CS100	Final	$\perp_1$
$\perp_4$	Sid2	Chemistry	CH200	Test A	Prac 1
$\perp_4$	Sid2	Chemistry	CH200	$\perp_3$	Prac 1
$\perp_4$	Sid2	Chemistry	CH200	Test A	Prac 2
$\perp_4$	Sid2	Chemistry	CH200	$\perp_3$	Prac 2

Fig. 6. A flat relation.

Name	Sid	{Major}	{Class	{Exam}	{Project}}
Anna	Sid1	Maths	CS100	Mid-year	Project A
		$\perp_2$		Final	$\perp_1$
$\perp_4$	Sid2	Chemistry	CH200	Test A	Prac 1
				$\perp_3$	Prac 2

Fig. 7. A nested relation derived from a flat relation.

Proof. See full length version of the paper [12].

To illustrate the above result, consider the relation given in Figure 6. This relation satisfies the FDs Major → Sid and violates the FDs Class → Exam and Exam → Project. One can see that the XML tree in Figure 8 satisfies the XFDs root.Id.Id.Major → root.E.Sid and violates the XFDs root.Id.Id.Subject → root.Id.Id.Exam and root.Id.id.Id.Exam → root.Id.Id.Id.Project.

5 Conclusions

In this paper we have investigated the issue of defining XFDs in XML documents. We have defined a strong XFD in XML and justified it by proving that for a very general class of mappings of a relation into a XML document, a relation strongly satisfies a unary FD if and only if the XML document also strongly satisfies the equivalent XFD.

There are several other topics related to the ones investigated in this paper that warrant further investigation. Firstly, the approach used in this paper can also be extended to defining weak XFDs in XML. Also, how to extend the approach to defining multi-valued dependencies in XML is an important problem.

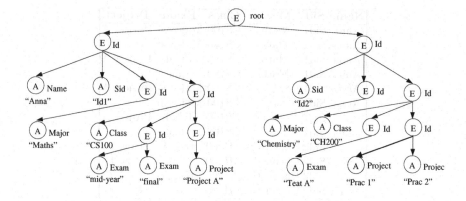

Fig. 8. A XML tree derived from a nested relation

References

1. S. Abiteboul, P. Buneman, and D. Suciu. *Data on the Web*. Morgan Kauffman, 2000.
2. M. Arenas, W. Fan, and L. Libkin. On verifying consistency of xml specifications. In *Proc. ACM PODS Conference*, pages 259–270, 2002.
3. M. Arenas and L. Libkin. A normal form for xml documents. In *Proc. ACM PODS Conference*, pages 85–96, 2002.
4. P. Atzeni and V. DeAntonellis. *Foundations of databases*. Benjamin Cummings, 1993.
5. P. Buneman, S. Davidson, W. Fan, and C. Hara. Reasoning about keys for xml. In *International Workshop on Database Programming Languages*, 2001.
6. P. Buneman, S. Davidson, W. Fan, C. Hara, and W. Tan. Keys for xml. *Computer Networks*, 39(5):473–487, 2002.
7. P. Buneman, W. Fan, and S. Weinstein. Interaction between type and path constraints. In *Proc. ACM PODS Conference*, pages 129–138, 1999.
8. W. Fan and L. Libkin. On xml integrity constraints in the presence of dtds. *Journal of the ACM*, 49(3):368–406, 2002.
9. W. Fan and J. Simeon. Integrity constraints for xml. In *Proc. ACM PODS Conference*, pages 23–34, 2000.
10. M. Levene and G. Loizu. Axiomatization of functional dependencies in incomplete relations. *Theoretical Computer Science*, 206:283–300, 1998.
11. S.J. Thomas and P.C. Fischer. Nested relational structures. In P. Kanellakis, editor, *The theory of databases*, pages 269–307. JAI Press, 1986.
12. M.W. Vincent and J. Liu. Strong functional dependencies and a redundancy free normal form for xml. Submitted for publication, 2002.
13. J. Widom. Data management for xml - research directions. *IEEE data Engineering Bulletin*, 22(3):44–52, 1999.

On Transformation to Redundancy Free XML Schema from Relational Database Schema

Chengfei Liu[1], Jixue Liu[1], and Minyi Guo[2]

[1] Advanced Computing Research Centre, School of Computer and Information
Science, University of South Australia, SA 5095, Australia
{chengfei.liu, jixue.liu}@unisa.edu.au
[2] Department of Computer Software, The University of Aizu, Aizu-Wakamatsu City,
Fukushima, 965-8580, Japan
minyi@u-aizu.ac.jp

Abstract. While XML is emerging as the universal format for publishing and exchanging data on the Web, most business data is still stored and maintained in relational database management systems. As a result, there is an increasing need to efficiently publish relational data as XML documents for Internet-based applications. One way to publish relational data is to provide virtual XML documents for relational data via an XML schema which is transformed from the underlying relational database schema, then users can access the relational database through the XML schema. In this paper, we discuss issues in transforming a relational database schema into corresponding schema in XML Schema. We aim to achieve high level of nesting while introducing no data redundancy for the transformed XML schema. In the paper, we first propose a basic transformation algorithm which introduces no data redundancy, then we improve the algorithm by exploring further nesting of the transformed XML schema.

1 Introduction

While XML [4,1] is emerging as the universal format for publishing and exchanging data on the Web, most business data is still stored and maintained in relational database systems. As a result, there is an increasing need to efficiently publish relational data as XML documents for Internet-based applications. One approach to publish relational data is to create XML views of the underlying relational data. Through the XML views, users may access the relational databases as though they were accessing XML documents. Once XML views are created over a relational database, queries in an XML query language like XML-QL [6] or XQuery [3] can be issued against these XML views for the purpose of accessing relational databases. SilkRoute [8] is one of the systems taking this approach. In SilkRoute, XML views of a relational database are defined using a relational to XML transformation language called RXL, and then XML-QL queries are issued against these views. The queries and views are combined together by a query composer and the combined RXL queries are then translated into the

X. Zhou, Y. Zhang, and M.E. Orlowska (Eds.): APWeb 2003, LNCS 2642, pp. 35–46, 2003.

corresponding SQL queries. XPERANTO [12,5,11] takes a similar approach but uses XQuery [3] for user queries.

Another approach [10] to publish relational data is to provide virtual XML documents for relational data via an XML schema which is transformed from the underlying relational database schema, then users can access the relational database through the XML schema. In this approach, there is a need to transform a relational database schema to the corresponding XML schema.

Currently, there are two options for defining an XML schema. One is the Data Type Definition (DTD) and the other is the XML Schema [7]. We choose XML Schema because Data Type Definition (DTD) has a number of limitations.

XML Schema offers great flexibility in modeling documents. Therefore, there exist many ways to map a relational database schema into a schema in XML Schema. For examples, XViews [2] constructs graph based on primary key/foreign key relationship and generate candidate views by choosing node with either maximum in-degree or zero in-degree as root element. The candidate XML views generated achieve a high level of nesting but suffer considerable level of data redundancy. NeT [9] derives nested structures from flat relations by repeatedly applying the *nest* operator on tuples of each relation. The resulting nested structures may be useless because the derivation is not at the type level.

In this paper, we discuss issues in transforming a relational database schema into the corresponding schema in XML Schema. We aim at achieving a high level of nesting while introducing no data redundancy for the transformed XML schema. In the paper, we first propose a basic transformation algorithm which is redundancy free, then we improve the algorithm by exploring further nested structures.

The rest of the paper is organized as follows. In Section 2, we give a brief introduction of the XML Schema, especially the features which will be used in the schema transformation. In Section 3, we present the mapping rules of a basic transformation algorithm which converts a relational schema to the corresponding schema in XML Schema. The improvement of the basic algorithm is discussed in Section 4 with more nested structure explored. Section 5 concludes the paper.

2   XML Schema

XML Schema [7] is the W3C XML language for describing and constraining the content of XML documents. It is replacing the Data Type Definition (DTD) because DTD has a number of limitations, e.g., it is written in a non-XML syntax; it has no support of namespaces; it only offers extremely limited data typing. XML Schema is a more comprehensive and rigorous method for defining content model of an XML document. The schema itself is an XML document, and so can be processed by the same tools that read the XML documents it describes. XML Schema supports rich built-in types and allows complex types built based on built-in types. It also supports key constraint and unique constraint which are important to map relational database schema to XML schema. XML Schema supports two mechanisms to represent identity and reference: one is ID/IDREF which is also supported in DTD, the other is KEY/KEYREF which is not supported by DTD. ID and IDREF only apply to a single element/attribute while KEY and KEYREF can apply to multiple elements/attributes.

Shown below is a schema *Company_XML* in XML Schema for a company.

```
<xs:element name="Company_XML">
 <xs:complexType>
  <xs:sequence>
   <xs:element name="Employee" minOccurs="0" maxOccurs="unbounded">
    <xs:complexType>
     <xs:sequence>
      <xs:element name="name" type="xs:string"/>
      <xs:element name="city" type="xs:string"/>
      <xs:element name="salary" type="xs:int"/>
     </xs:sequence>
     <xs:attribute name="eno" type="xs:ID"/>
     <xs:attribute name="dno" type="xs:IDREF"/>
    </xs:complexType>
   </xs:element>
   <xs:element name="Dept" minOccurs="0" maxOccurs="unbounded">
    <xs:complexType>
     <xs:sequence>
      <xs:element name="dname" type="xs:string"/>
      <xs:element name="city" type="xs:string"/>
      <xs:element name="DeptLoc" minOccurs="0" maxOccurs="unbounded">
       <xs:complexType>
        <xs:attribute name="dno" type="xs:IDREF"/>
        <xs:attribute name="city" type="xs:string"/>
       </xs:complexType>
       <xs:key name="PK_DeptLoc"/>
        <xs:selector xpath="Dept/DeptLoc/"/>
        <xs:field xpath="@dno"/>
        <xs:field xpath="@city"/>
       </xs: key>
      </xs:element>
     </xs:sequence>
     <xs:attribute name="dno" type="xs:ID"/>
     <xs:attribute name="mgrEno" type="xs:IDREF"/>
    </xs:complexType>
   </xs:element>
   <xs:element name="Project" minOccurs="0" maxOccurs="unbounded">
    <xs:complexType>
     <xs:sequence>
      <xs:element name="pname" type="xs:string"/>
      <xs:element name="city" type="xs:string"/>
     </xs:sequence>
     <xs:attribute name="pno" type="xs:ID"/>
     <xs:attribute name="dno" type="xs:IDREF"/>
    </xs:complexType>
```

```
    </xs:element>
    <xs:element name="WorksOn" minOccurs="0" maxOccurs="unbounded">
     <xs:complexType>
      <xs:element name="hours" type="xs:int"/>
      <xs:attribute name="eno" type="xs:IDREF"/>
      <xs:attribute name="pno" type="xs:IDREF"/>
      <xs:key name="PK_WorksOn"/>
       <xs:selector xpath="WorksOn/"/>
       <xs:field xpath="@eno"/>
       <xs:field xpath="@pno"/>
      </xs: key>
     </xs:complexType>
    </xs:element>
   </xs:sequence>
  </xs:complexType>
</xs:element>
```

Under the root element *Company_XML*, there are four set elements: *Employee, Dept, Project* and *WorksOn*. Each of these four elements is used to hold a set of instances conformed to the complexType defined within the element. In element *Employee*, there are three elements *name, city* and *salary*, and two attributes *eno* and *dno*. *eno* serves as the identity of the instances of *Employee*, *dno* intends to reference an instance of element *Dept*. In *Dept*, there are three elements *dname, city* and *DeptLoc*, and two attributes *dno* and *mgrEno*. *dno* serves as the identity of the instances of *Dept* while *mgrEno* intends to reference an instance of *Employee*. *DeptLoc* itself is also a set element which has two attributes *dno* and *city*, these two attributes together serve as the identity of the instances of *DeptLoc* using KEY element definition rather than ID type. In *Project*, there are two elements *pname, city*, and two attributes *pno* and *dno*. *pno* serves as the identity of the instances of *Project* while *dno* intends to reference an instance of *Dept*. In *WorksOn*, there are one element *hours*, and two attributes *eno* and *pno*. *eno* and *pno* together serve as the identity of the instances of *WorksOn* using KEY element definition. Individually, *eno* and *pno* intend to reference an instance of *Employee* and *Project* respectively.

3   Schema Transformation

The schema transformation from a relational database schema into the corresponding XML schema must take into account the integrity constraints associated with a relational schema, e.g., primary keys (PKs), foreign keys (FKs), null/not-null, unique, etc. The null/non-null constraint can be easily represented by properly setting *minOccurs* of the transformed XML element for the relation attribute. The unique constraint can also be represented by the unique mechanism in XML Schema straigtforwardly. In this paper, we focus on the mapping of PK/FK constraints. In the target XML schema, we aim to generate possible nested XML structure, however, we also aim to avoid introducing redundancy.

As introduced in the previous section, both ID/IDREF and KEY/KEYREF are supported by XML Schema. KEY/KEYREF can be used to represent keys with multiple attributes but ID/IDREF cannot. However, ID/IDREF supports the dereference function in path expressions in most XML query languages. Therefore, we will differentiate the single attribute primary/foreign keys from multi-attribute primary/foreign keys while transforming the relational database schema to XML schema and try to use ID/IDREF where possible because of dereference function support. We also classify a relation into the four categories based on different types of primary keys.

Definition 31 *regular relation*
A regular relation is a relation where the primary key contains no foreign keys.

Definition 32 *component relation*
A component relation is a relation where the primary key contains one foreign key which references its parent relation. The other part of the primary key serves as a local identifier under the parent relation.

The component relation is used to represent a component or a multi-valued attribute of its parent relation.

Definition 33 *supplementary relation*
A supplementary relation is a relation where the primary key as a whole is also a foreign key which references another relation.

The supplementary relation is used to supplement another relation or to represent a subclass for transforming a generalization hierarchy from a conceptual schema.

Definition 34 *association relation*
An association relation is a relation where the primary key contains more than one foreign keys, each of which references a participant relation of the association.

Based on above discussion and definitions, we give the set of mapping rules.

3.1   The Basic Algorithm

Input: A relational database schema *Sch* with primary key and foreign key definitions.
Output: A corresponding XML schema *Sch_XML* which is redundancy free.

Rule 1 *For a relational database schema* Sch, *a root element named* Sch_XML *is created in the corresponding XML schema as follows.*

```
<xs: element name = "Sch_XML">
  <xs: complexType>
    <xs: sequence>
      <!-- transformed relation schema of Sch -->
    </xs: sequence>
  </xs: complexType>
</xs: element>
```

Rule 2 *For each regular or association relation R, the following element with the same name as the relation schema is created and then put under the root element.*

```
<xs: element name = "R" minOccurs = "0" maxOccurs = "unbounded">
  <xs: complexType>
    <xs: sequence>
      <!-- the attributes of R -->
    </xs: sequence>
  </xs: complexType>
</xs: element>
```

Rule 3 *For each component relation R_1, let its parent relation be R_2, then an element similar to Rule 2 and with the same name as the component relation is created and then placed as a child element of R_2.*

Rule 4 *For each supplementary relation R_1, let the relation which R_1 references be R_2, then the following element with the same name as the supplementary relation schema is created and then placed as a child element of R_2. Notice, there is a difference between the transformed element of a component relation and the transformed element of a supplementary relation on* maxOccurs.

```
<xs: element name = "R1" minOccurs = "0" maxOccurs = "1">
  <xs: complexType>
    <xs: sequence>
      <!-- the attributes of R1 -->
    </xs: sequence>
  </xs: complexType>
</xs: element>
```

Rule 5 *For each single attribute primary key with the name PKA of regular relation R, an attribute of the element for R is created with ID data type as follows.*

```
<xs: element name = "R" minOccurs = "0" maxOccurs = "unbounded">
  <xs: complexType>
    <xs: attribute name = "PKA" type = "xs:ID"/>
  </xs: complexType>
</xs: element>
```

Rule 6 *For each multiple attribute primary key PK of a regular, a component or an association relation R, suppose the key attributes are $PKA_1, \cdots, PKA_n$, an attribute of the element for R is created for each $PKA_i (1 \leq i \leq n)$ with the corresponding data type. If R is a component relation and PKA_i is a single attribute foreign key contained in the primary key, then the data type of the created attribute is IDREF. After that a key element is defined with a selector to select the element for R and several fields to identify $PKA_1, \cdots, PKA_n$. The key element can be defined inside or outside the element for R. The name of the element PK should be unique within the namespace.*

```
<xs: element name = "R" minOccurs = "0" maxOccurs = "unbounded">
  <xs: complexType>
    <xs: attribute name = "PKA1" type = "xs:PKA1_type"/>
    ... ...
    <xs: attribute name = "PKAn" type = "xs:PKAn_type"/>
  </xs: complexType>
  <xs: key name = "PK"/>
    <xs: selector xpath = "R/"/>
    <xs: field xpath = "@PKA1"/>
    ... ...
    <xs: field xpath = "@PKAn"/>
  </xs: key>
</xs: element>
```

Rule 7 *Ignore the mapping for primary key of each supplementary relation.*

Rule 8 *For each single attribute foreign key FKA of a relation R except one which is contained in the primary key of a component or supplementary relation, an attribute of the element for R is created with IDREF data type.*

```
<xs: element name = "R" minOccurs = "0" maxOccurs = "unbounded">
  <xs: complexType>
    <xs: attribute name = "FKA" type = "xs:IDREF"/>
  </xs: complexType>
</xs: element>
```

Rule 9 *For each multiple attribute foreign key FK of a relation R except one which is contained in the primary key of a component or supplementary relation, suppose FK references PK of the referenced relation, and the foreign key attributes are $FKA_1, \cdots, FKA_n$, an attribute of the element for R is created for each $FKA_i (1 \leq i \leq n)$ with corresponding data type. Then a keyref element is defined with a selector to select the element for R and several fields to identify $FKA_1, \cdots, FKA_n$. The keyref element can be defined either inside or outside the element. The name of the element FK should be unique within the namespace and refer of the element is the name of the key element of the primary key which it references.*

```
<xs: element name = "R" minOccurs = "0" maxOccurs = "unbounded">
  <xs: complexType>
    <xs: attribute name = "FKA1" type = "xs:FKA1_type"/>
    ... ...
    <xs: attribute name = "FKAn" type = "xs:FKAn_type"/>
  </xs: complexType>
  <xs: keyref name = "FK" refer = "PK"/>
    <xs: selector xpath = "R/"/>
    <xs: field xpath = "@FKA1"/>
    ... ...
    <xs: field xpath = "@FKAn"/>
  </xs: keyref>
</xs: element>
```

Rule 10 *For each non-key attribute of a relation R, an element is created as a child element of R. The name of the element is the same as the attribute name.*

3.2   Example and Discussion

Let us have a look of a relational database schema *Company* for a company. Primary keys are underlined while foreign keys are in *italic* font.

Employee(eno, name, city, salary, *dno*)

Dept(dno, dname, *mgrEno*)

DeptLoc(*dno*, city)

Project(pno, pname, city, *dno*)

WorksOn(*eno*, *pno*, hours)

If the above schema is given as an input to the basic schema transformation algorithm, the schema in XML Schema *Company_XML* shown in Section 2 will be generated.

As XML allows nested structure, redundancy may be brought in when transforming flat relation structure to nested XML structure. For example, if we put element Dept under element Project, same department will be repeated in all projects in the department. However, if we put elements Dept and Project at the same level or put element Project under element Dept, there is no data redundancy introduced.

From the algorithm and the transformation example, we can see that the mapping rules bring no data redundancy provided the underlying relational schema is redundancy free. So we have the following.

Theorem 31 *If the relational database schema Sch is redundancy free, the XML schema Sch_XML generated by the basic transformation algorithm is also redundancy free.*

This theorem is easy to prove. For a regular or an association relation R, an element with the same name R is created under the root element, so the relation R in Sch is isomorphically transformed to an element in Sch_XML. For a component relation R, a sub-element with the same name R is created under its parent R_p. Because of the foreign key constraint, we have the functional dependency $PK_R \to PK_{R_p}$, i.e., there is a many to one relationship from R to R_p, therefore it is impossible that a tuple of R is placed more than one time under different element of R_p. Similar to a component relation, there is no redundancy introduced for a supplementary relation.

4   Exploring Nested Structures

As we can see, the basic transformation algorithm introduced above fails to explore all possible nested structures. For example, the *Project* element can be moved to under the *Dept* element if every project belongs to a department. Nesting is important in XML schema because it allows navigation of path expressions to be processed efficiently. If we use IDREF instead, we may use system supported dereference function to get the referenced elements. In XML, the dereference function is expensive because ID and IDREF types are value based. If we use KEYREF, we have to put an explicit *join* condition in an XML query to get the referenced elements. Therefore, we need to explore all possible nested structure by investigating the referential integrity constraints in the relational schema. For this purpose, we introduce a reference graph as follows:

Definition 41 : *Given a relational database schema $Sch = \{R_1, \cdots, R_n\}$, a reference graph of the schema Sch is defined as a labeled directed graph $RG = (V, E, L)$ where V is a finite set of vertices representing relation schema $R_1, \cdots, R_n$ in Sch; E is a finite set of arcs, if there is a foreign key defined in R_i which references R_j, an arc $e = < R_i, R_j > \in E$; L is a set of labels for edges by applying a labeling function from E to the set of foreign keys.*

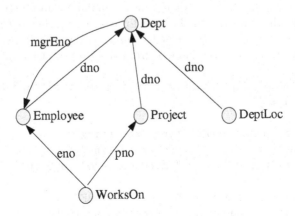

Fig. 1. A Reference Graph

The reference graph of the relational schema *Company* is shown as in Figure 1. In the graph, we can see that the element of node *DeptLoc* has been put under the element of node *Dept* by the basic algorithm. The element of node *Project* could be put under the element of node *Dept* if the foreign key *dno* is defined to NOT-NULL. This is because that node *Project* only references node *Dept* and a many to one relationship from *Project* to *Dept* can be derived from the foreign key constraint. In addition, the NOT-NULL foreign key means every project has to belong one department. As a result, one project can be put under one department and cannot be put twice under different departments in the XML document. In the graph, we also see a loop between *Employee* and *Dept*, what we can get from this is a many to many relationship between *Employee* and *Dept*. In fact, the foreign key *mgrEno* of Dept reflects a one to one relationship from *Dept* to *Employee*. Unfortunately, this semantic got lost when we map the conceptual model (e.g., E-R or UML) to the logical model. With the guide of a designer, the element of the node *Employee* can also put under the element of the node *Dept* if the foreign key *dno* is defined to NOT-NULL. The node *WorksOn* references two nodes *Employee* and *Project*. The element of *WorksOn* can be put under either *Employee* and *Project* if the corresponding foreign key is NOT-NULL. However, which node to choose to put under all depends on which path will be used often in queries. We will also leave this decision to be chosen by a designer.

Based on the above discussion, we can at least improve the basic algorithm by the following.

Theorem 41 *If a relation R_1 has only one foreign key FK which references to another relation R_2 and FK is defined as NOT-NULL, then we can move the element for R_1 to under the element for R_2 without introducing data redundancy.*

The proof of this theorem has already explained by the relationship between *Project* and *Dept* in Figure 1. The NOT-NULL FK suggests a many to exact one relationship from R_1 to R_2. Therefore, for each instance of R_1, it is put only once under exactly one instance of R_2, no redundancy will be introduced.

If we apply this theorem to the transformed XML schema *Company_XML*, the element for *Project* will be moved to under *Dept* as follows, the attribute *dno* with IDREF type can be removed from the *Project* element.

```
<xs:element name="Dept" minOccurs="0" maxOccurs="unbounded">
 <xs:complexType>
  <xs:sequence>
   <xs:element name="dname" type="xs:string"/>
   <xs:element name="city" type="xs:string"/>
   <xs:element name="DeptLoc" minOccurs="0" maxOccurs="unbounded">
    <xs:complexType>
     <xs:attribute name="dno" type="xs:IDREF"/>
     <xs:attribute name="city" type="xs:string"/>
    </xs:complexType>
```

```
<xs:key name="PK_DeptLoc"/>
  <xs:selector xpath="Dept/DeptLoc/"/>
  <xs:field xpath="@dno"/>
  <xs:field xpath="@city"/>
  </xs: key>
</xs:element>
<xs:element name="Project" minOccurs="0" maxOccurs="unbounded">
 <xs:complexType>
  <xs:sequence>
    <xs:element name="pname" type="xs:string"/>
    <xs:element name="city" type="xs:string"/>
  </xs:sequence>
  <xs:attribute name="pno" type="xs:ID"/>
 </xs:complexType>
 </xs:element>
</xs:sequence>
<xs:attribute name="dno" type="xs:ID"/>
<xs:attribute name="mgrEno" type="xs:IDREF"/>
</xs:complexType>
</xs:element>
```

5   Conclusion and Future Work

This paper addressed the issues in mapping relational database schema to XML schema. To generate high quality XML schema from relational schema, a schema transformation algorithm should have two features: exploring all possible nested structures and preserving data redundancy free property of a relational schema. The work in XViews and NeT satisfy the former only. The algorithm presented in this paper satisfies both features. It brings no data redundancy while achieving high level of nesting.

We believe that the proposed algorithm is effective and practical. In the future, we will investigate schema transformation from non-normalized relational database schema to redundancy free XML schema.

Acknowledgements. This work was supported in part by the visiting research program award R-5-2 from the University of Aizu, Japan.

References

1. S. Abiteboul, P. Buneman, and D. Suciu. *Data on the Web: From Relations to Semistructured Data and XML*. Morgan Kaufmann Publishers, 2000.
2. C. Baru. Xviews: Xml views of relational schemas. In *Proceedings of DEXA Workshop*, pages 700–705, 1999.
3. S. Boag, D. Chamberlin amd M. Fernandez, D. Florescu, J. Robie, J. Simeon, and M. Stefanescu. *XQuery 1.0: An XML Query Language*, April 2002. W3C Working Draft, http://www.w3.org/TR/2002/WD-xquery-20020430/.

4. T. Bray, J. Paoli, C. Sperberg-McQueen, and E. Maler. *Extensible Markup Language (XML) 1.0 (Second Edition)*, October 2000. W3C Recommendation, http://www.w3.org/TR/REC-xml.

5. M. Carey, J. Kiernan, J. Shanmugasundaram, E. Shekita, and S. Subramanian. Xperanto: Middleware for publishing object-relational data as xml documents. In *Proceedings of VLDB*, pages 646–648, 2000.

6. A. Deutsch, M. Fernandez, D. Florescu, A. Levy, and D. Suciu. *XML-QL: A Query Language for XML*, August 1998. Submission to W3C, http://www.w3.org/TR/NOTE-xml-ql/.

7. D. Fallside. *XML Schema Part 0: Primer*, May 2001. W3C Recommendation, http://www.w3.org/TR/xmlschema-0/.

8. M. Fernandez, W. Tan, and D. Suciu. Silkroute: Trading between relations and xml. In *Proceedings of WWW*, pages 723–725, 2000.

9. D. Lee, M. Mani, F. Chiu, and W. Chu. Nesting-based relational-to-xml schema translation. In *Proceedings of the WebDB*, pages 61–66, 2001.

10. C. Liu, M. Guo, and J. Liu. Accessing relational databases via xml schema. Technical report, School of Computer and Information Science, University of South Australia, December 2002.

11. J. Shanmugasundaram, J. Kiernan, E. Shekita, C. Fan, and J. Funderburk. Querying xml views of relational data. In *Proceedings of VLDB*, pages 261–270, 2001.

12. J. Shanmugasundaram, E. Shekita, R. Barr, M. Carey, B. Lindsay, H. Pirahesh, and B. Reinwald. Efficiently publishing relational data as xml documents. In *Proceedings of VLDB*, pages 65–76, 2000.

Constraint Preserving XML Updating*

Kun Yue, Zhengchuan Xu, Zhimao Guo, and Aoying Zhou

Department of Computer Science & Engineering, Fudan University
200433 Shanghai, China
{kuny, zcxu, zmguo, ayzhou}@fudan.edu.cn

Abstract. With the rapid development of Internet, XML becomes the standard for data representation, integration and exchange on the web. In order to fully evolve XML into a universal data representation and sharing format, it is necessary to update XML documents efficiently while preserving constraints. We consider an important class of constraints, XML keys. In this paper, based on XML keys and the constraint-preserving normalized storage of XML over relational databases, we present a novel method for updating XML data. Our method first propagates the update on XML into the relational database. Then taking the updated relational data and the original document as input, the resulting XML document updated can be produced through locating the positions of updates in the original one by annotation technology. Preliminary performance studies have shown that our method is very effective and efficient.

1 Introduction

XML has been adopted as the mark-up language for preserving semantics of on-line document. It has been extensively studied in many aspects, such as query processing, indexing, storage and so on. There has been a growing interest in mapping XML data into relational databases [1,2,3,4,5,6,7]. Considering the capability of supporting updates in database management systems, it is indispensable to specify updates to XML document and evaluate them efficiently.

It is known that current XML query processors cannot support updates on XML. In the past few years, such query languages as Xpath [8], Xquery [9], etc., have been developed as the standard query languages for XML, but none of them has considered the update on XML. To the change detecting for XML view, *diff*-algorithm [10] detects the unchanged subtrees between the old version and the new one of XML document to match as many nodes as possible. *Archiving* technology [11] implements the version control of XML and archives the multi-versioned data in unified format by annotation technology. Work on XML query processing based on relational databases never concerns XML updating, e.g., XPERANTO [12] and Clock [13]. Tatarinov et al. presented the update language for XML by extending XQuery, and implemented

---

* This work is supported by the "973" National Foundational Research Program of China (G1998030404) and National Natural Science Foundation of China (No. 60003016).

X. Zhou, Y. Zhang, and M.E. Orlowska (Eds.): APWeb 2003, LNCS 2642, pp. 47–58, 2003.

the updates over relational databases through XML views, in which the RDB was updated instead of the XML document itself [1]. Using this method, if the updated XML document is demanded, the entire document must be reconstructed by publishing all the related data from RDB. In addition, there exists high cost to process the large XML document; moreover, the key constraints cannot be preserved.

For the first time, we present a novel method for updating XML document while preserving the important class of constraints, XML keys [14]. First, the storage of XML document over RDB is normalized based on the functional dependencies, which are derived from XML keys using the *Propagating algorithm* [2]. Then the XML data is mapped into RDB of 3NF schemas. Within a specific domain of XML applications, key constraints are preserved by means of preserving the functional dependencies over RDB. In our method, the relational data is regarded as the view of XML documents. At first, updates on XML are translated into SQL statements. Then the relational data is updated according to the submitted SQL statements. Next, the updates on RDB are propagated into XML. The updated XML document can be got from the original one and the updated relational data. We focus on two core update operations: insertion and deletion. We summarize our contributions as follows:

• Key constraints can be preserved after XML data is updated based on the normalized storage over relational databases. Also we present the technique that is applied to the problem of updating XML documents through RDB view.

• A novel annotation technology is presented to locate positions of the updates on XML. It associates each tuple in RDB to the exact data block in XML document.

• With our method, XML documents can be updated efficiently by only dealing with the updated relational data and the annotation retrieved from RDB. Experimental results show that our method can be used to update XML documents more efficiently than the naive publishing one; furthermore, it is not sensitive to the size of the original XML document and the depth of the XML nodes to be updated.

The paper is organized as follows. We begin with the XML storage model over RDB based on XML keys in section 2. In section 3, we present the method for updating XML preserving key constraints. In section 4, we describe the experimental results and performance studies. Finally, we conclude and discuss the future work in section 5.

2   Background

In our method, XML keys define the semantics of XML document, and the normalized relational storage of XML is used to preserve the constraints.

2.1   Keys for XML

Buneman et al. present the definition of XML keys with path expression independent of DTD [14]. Definition 1 presents the keys for XML, which is based on the *value equality* of tree structure [14].

Definition 1. XML tree satisfies the key constraint written as $(Q, (Q', \{P_1, \cdots, P_k\}))$, iff $\forall n \in \llbracket Q \rrbracket$, $\forall n_1, n_2 \in n\llbracket Q' \rrbracket$, if for all $i \in [1, \cdots, k]$, $\exists x \in n_1\llbracket P_i \rrbracket$, $\exists y \in n_2\llbracket P_i \rrbracket$, $x =_v y$, then $n_1 = n_2$, in which $=$ denotes *node equality* (Whether two nodes are the exact same node) and $=_v$ denotes *value equality* (two nodes are *value equal* if the trees rooted at the nodes are isomorphic by an isomorphism that is an identity on string values).

Keys in the form $(Q, (Q', \{\}))$ mean that all nodes in $n\llbracket Q' \rrbracket (n \in \llbracket Q \rrbracket)$ differ from each other. For example, Fig.1 corresponding to the XML fragment specified in Xmach-1 [15] shows an XML tree. We use *doc_id, cid, sid, Ssid* to represent the *id* attribute of document, chapter, section and sub-section respectively. Keys describing the semantics can be defined as $(*.document, \{doc\_id\})$ and $(*.document, (chapter, \{cid\}))$. The key $(*.document, (author\{\}))$ means each document has only one author.

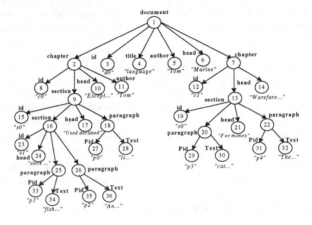

Fig. 1. An instance of XML tree

2.2 Normalized XML Storage Model over RDB

Storing XML document into relational databases is to map XML tree into relational tables. Much work is available for the relational storage of XML document recently. For example, based on DTD, Shanmugasundaram et al. presented the approach that some XML nodes are mapped as separate relations and their related child nodes are inlined as fields of these relations [3]. However, none of these methods can generate the normalized relational, so that the update on RDB may be performed incorrectly. Davidson et al. presented a transformation language that specifies transformations from XML data to relational databases. Moreover, they proposed a PTIME *propagating* algorithm for determining whether a functional dependency is propagated from XML keys through the transformations [2].

The propagating algorithm [2] can be summarized as follows. For a set Σ of XML keys and a well-formed mapping δ from XML data to RDB of schema R, an XML tree T satisfying Σ, if $\delta(T)$ satisfies a functional dependency ϕ, then it is called that Σ implies ϕ logically, or ϕ is a functional dependency propagated from Σ.

The propagating algorithm searches the tree space made up of certain mapping rules, and validates the possible FDs (functional dependencies) on the relational schema. In our method, we first map the XML data into the RDB of a universal relational schema; then on this schema, derive the canonical cover of FDs implied by XML keys using propagating algorithm; finally decompose the universal relational schema into 3NF schemas according to the canonical cover [16].

Fig. 2 illustrates the key constraints of the XML data in Fig. 1. For the universal relational schema, Fig. 3 illustrates the canonical cover of FDs derived from XML keys by propagating algorithm. Fig. 4 presents the normalized relational schemas.

```
(*.document,{doc_id});                        (*.document,(author,{}));
(*.document,(chapter,{cid}));                 (*.document,(title,{}));
(*.document.chapter, (section,{sid}));        (*.document.chapter,(Cauthor,{}));
(*.document.chapter.section,(*.section,{Ssid}));  (*.document.chapter,(Chead,{}));
(*.document.chapter.section,(paragraph,{Pid}));   (*.document.chapter.*.section,(Shead,{}));
(*.document.chapter.section.*.section,        (*.document.chapter.*.section.paragraph,
   (paragraph,{Pid}))                            (SPText,{}))
```

Fig. 2. XML keys of Fig. 1

```
doc_id  → title
doc_id  → author                              Document (doc_id, Title, Author);
(doc_id,cid) → Chead                          Chapter (doc_id, cid, Cauthor, Chead);
(doc_id,cid) → Cauthor                        Section (doc_id, cid, sid, Shead);
(doc_id,cid,sid) → Shead                      Ssection (doc_id, cid, sid, Ssid, Sshead);
(doc_id,cid,sid, Pid) → PText                 Paragraph (doc_id, cid, sid, Pid, PText);
(doc_id,cid,sid,Ssid) → Sshead                SParagraph (doc_id, cid, sid, Ssid, SPid, SPText)
(doc_id,cid,sid,Ssid, Pid) → SPText
(doc_id,chapter_id,Ssid,SPid,Sid) → SPText
```

Fig. 3. Canonical cover of FDs   **Fig. 4.** Normalized relational schemas

2.3 Assumptions

In real applications, any XML document as data source is specified within a certain domain and based on the specific applications. Most of the XML documents have hierarchical key structures [11]. Moreover, each node in an XML tree can be uniquely identified by a path from the root; thus we assume that the keys are defined level by level and cover all nodes in the XML tree. For example, all the nodes on the path */document/chapter/section/paragraph* should be constrained by the associated keys.

Further, the updates on XML document will be pointless unless it is executed within the given domain. With respect to the XML documents in various fields, most of them have a well-organized key system, e.g., scientific data [11]. Therefore, the XML data updated must satisfy the constraints pre-defined in the certain domain. Thus, we will only update the XML data in which all the nodes have keys, while any XML fragment that is to be inserted but not constrained by the given keys will be excluded.

3   Updating XML with Constraints

Tatarinov et al. proposed XUpdate [1] as an XML query language to update XML document based on XQuery. In this paper, we focus on two core operations: insertion and deletion; update commands of XML are submitted in XUpdate. The system architecture of XML updating is illustrated in Fig. 5.

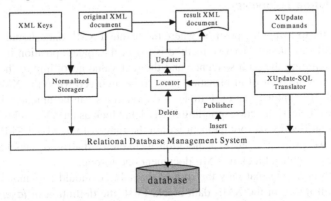

Fig. 5. System architecture of XML Updating

The update process can be described as follows. First, *Normalized storager* maps XML data into RDB while preserving XML keys, and *XUpdate-SQL Translator* rewrites update commands on XML into SQL statements. Then the *Locator* locates the position of the update. Finally, with *Updater*, the insertion is implemented by adding XML fragments to the original XML document in appropriate positions; the deletion is along the same lines except that it is free from constructing XML data. Key constraints are preserved by the mechanism of checking provided by RDBMS.

3.1   Update Operations on XML Document

XUpdate defines four primary update operations: Deletion, Renaming, Insertion and Replacement [1]. Because Renaming is the substitution for element names, and Replacement can be carried out through Deletion and Insertion, we are just to deal with Deletion and Insertion. In this paper, updates of IDREF are ignored. Now we describe the two core update operations.

(1) Deletion:
   Delete(child): where child can be any attribute or element, and it will be removed from the original XML document. The operation is specified as:

```
FOR $binding1 IN XPath-expr,   ···
    WHERE predicate1,  ···
DELETE $binding1,  ···
```

(2) Insertion:
   Insert(content): where content can be any attribute or element, and it will be inserted into the original XML document. Inserting an attribute with the same name as an existing one will fail. And the ordered insertion can be carried out by sorting tech-

nology [4]. In this paper, we ignore the order when insertion is implemented. The operation is specified as:

```
FOR $binding1 IN XPath-expr, ...
    WHERE predicate1, ...
    INSERT content1, ...
```

3.2 Annotation Technology

It is necessary to locate the position where the updated XML data should reside in the original XML document. A naive method is to get the update position in XML documents by archiving the path sequence and the text value according to the conditions. However, large amount of information need to be archived when the XML document is traversed. It is known that each tuple in the relations can be uniquely identified by its key; nevertheless, the corresponding XML data block as an XML subtree cannot be uniquely identified by its root element within the range of the whole XML document. Therefore, we propose a novel annotation technology that associates each tuple in RDB to the exact data block in XML document one-to-one.

It is worth notifying that only the root of the subtree should be annotated uniquely instead of all nodes in the XML data block. First, the definition of *layer* is given to identify and classify the nodes that should be annotated.

Definition 2. XML data in the document T can be mapped into the relational database R with the mapping δ, where $R=(R_1,\cdots, R_n)$, $\delta =(Rule(R_1), \cdots,Rule(R_n))$, R_i is the separate relation in R and $Rule(R_i)$ is the mapping rule from XML nodes to $R_i, i \in [1,\cdots,n]$. Given node set V in T, if $\forall v \in V$, $\exists R_i$ in R, such that v is mapped as R_i with $Rule(R_i)$, then *the layer of v* is denoted by $layer(v)$ and $layer(v)= R_i$, otherwise $layer(v) = \phi$. The set $LT = \{Ri \mid \exists v \in V, layer(v) = Ri\}$ is called the *layer set that T can be mapped to*. The number of layers in T is the cardinality of LT, and $|LT|=n$.

The relationship among XML nodes, corresponding relational schemas and the *layer* of XML nodes can be interpreted by the example in Fig. 6, in which both of the two chapter nodes are of the same layer — *chapter*, and there are 2 *layers* in it. Consequently, only the document and chapter nodes are to be annotated.

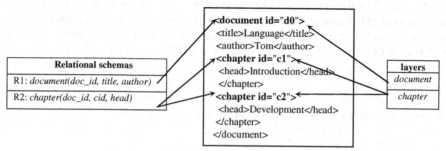

Fig. 6. Layers of XML fragment

Definition 3. Annotation on XML tree T is made up of extra annotation elements named *Tag_NodeName* (with an *id* attribute). For each node v in T, if there exist

$Ri \in LT$, such that $layer(v) = Ri$, then the *Tag_NodeName* element corresponding to R_i is added to *T* as the parent of *v*, and the value of its *id* attribute is different from the other ones of this *Tag_NodeName*. These values are called **annotation values on XML**. Thus, any nodes ($layer(v) \neq \phi$) of the same *layer* ($layer(v) = R_i \in LT$) must have the same *Tag_NodeName* but different values of *id* attributes, while the nodes of the different layers have different *Tag_NodeName*s. Correspondingly, annotation on RDB consists of new *annotation* fields for each R_i in *R*. The newly added field for each R_i is to store the id attribute values of such *Tag_NodeName* element as the annotation of node *v* that satisfies $layer(v)= R_i$. The values of these fields are called **annotation values on RDB**.

In XML documents, an extra *Tag_NodeName* element with an *id* attribute is added for each node *v* that is of the same layer and $layer(v) \neq \phi$. E.g., in Fig. 1, the corresponding nodes document, chapter, section and paragraph are annotated. Also an extra field is added to each separate relation in RDB, and its values are those of *id* attributes of *Tag_NodeName* elements in the XML document. E.g., the annotated relation of *Chapter* is *Chapter(doc_id, cid, Cauthor, Chead, **Tag_chapter**)*.

Newly added annotation elements divide the XML document into data blocks, and data in each block only comes from a certain tuple in RDB. The annotation value in each tuple will be assigned by RDBMS automatically. From this point, within the certain domain for the specific applications, the storage of an XML document can be implemented when it is inserted into an empty one. Fig. 7 shows the annotated XML fragment and the annotated *chapter* relation. To locate the chapter whose head has label "Except have million" in Fig. 7, we can get *Tag_chapter* field and its value "*1*" from RDB. Locating can be done just by hitting the element *<Tag_chapter id="1">*.

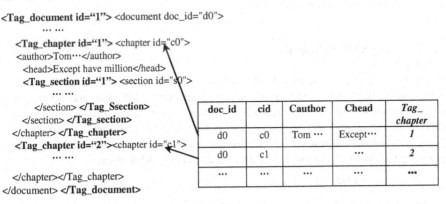

Fig. 7. Annotated XML fragment and annotated *chapter* relation

3.3 Updating Relational Storage of XML

Each update on XML may involve multiple relations in RDB. All the relational data corresponding to the update should be modified. The update is valid if the SQL can be executed correctly. In this paper, the objects of update operations consist of leaf nodes and subtrees. With respect to the RDB, leaves are mapped as separate fields in the corresponding relation while the subtrees are mapped as tuples in one or more relations. Due to the space limitation, re-writing will not be discussed here in detail.

3.3.1 Deletion of Relational Data

As for the deletion of leaf node, the operation of an update on XML is translated into a SQL statement, which sets the value of the relevant field as *null* in the tuple that satisfies the given condition. The SQL statement is expressed as:

`UPDATE relation-name SET column-name=' ' WHERE condition.`

For the deletion of subtree, the update expressed in XUpdate is translated into the SQL statement that is to remove the relational data corresponding to the root of the subtree. It is expressed as below:

`DELETE FROM relation-name WHERE condition.`

Since the subtree to be removed may be across one or more tuples in one or more relations, all the tuples *referencing* the root of the subtree will be removed thoroughly. In our method, the mechanism of cascading deletion in RDBMS is put into use.

3.3.2 Insertion of Relational Data

The insertion of the leaf node in XML document is translated into "UPDATE" SQL statement(s), which set the value of the corresponding field as new data. The leaf to be inserted must not exist in the original XML document; that is, the field must be *null*.

The insertion of subtree is similar to storing XML data into RDB, and the data is stored into RDB as a series of tuples top-down. The *referential integrity* is preserved by RDBMS. Further, in RDB, the annotation values for the newly inserted tuple (such as values of the fields *Tag_document*, *Tag_chapter* etc.) are assigned automatically layer by layer in line with definition 3.

3.4   Updating XML Efficiently

RDB must keep consistent with XML document all along, vice-versa. RDB is just a view of an XML document during the course of updating XML data, and we preserve the constraints with the normalized RDB. However, getting the XML document updated is the target, and it is unnecessary to publish all the relational data completely. Using our method, the resulting XML document can be generated efficiently by only retrieving the updated relational data, and the unchanged XML data.

3.4.1 Deletion of XML Data

As for the deletion of the leaf node in XML document, according to the conditions demanded, the value of the field corresponding to the leaf has been updated — set as *null* with the method in section3.3. The annotation value of the tuple that the field belongs to, can be obtained by querying RDB.

For the deletion of subtree, the root of it can be located with the annotation and its value got by querying RDB. For example, the `chapter` annotated by <Tag_chapter id="1"> can be removed by leaving out all the XML data of the fragment between <Tag_chapter id="1"> and the corresponding </Tag_chapter>.

3.4.2 Insertion of XML Data

The insertion of leaf node is just similar to the deletion, except that the counterpart will be inserted into the XML. According to definition 2, the subtree inserted has one layer at least and each layer corresponds to a separate relation in RDB. And the XML data related to the subtree may be across multiple tuples and relations in RDB. Thus, a naive method is to construct the fragment for each layer by retrieving the triggered data, and insert them into the original XML document separately. The subtree T will not be inserted thoroughly until such processes are done for |LT| times (|LT| is the account of layers) with a few useless intermediate ones.

Because of the deficiency above, we propose an efficient approach called bulk-insertion. The entire XML fragment to be inserted can be constructed from the related data that is obtained by triggers. Based on the method and strategy of publishing relational data [17], the construction is performed top-down. Annotation values relevant to the fragment inserted are assigned by RDBMS when the corresponding XML data is mapped into RDB. Motivated by the referential integrity among the layers in XML document, the XML data of each fragment will have to be inserted within the region of its parent. For the parent node, the annotation value on XML can be obtained by retrieving the data in the corresponding relation according to the given conditions, while the parent-child relationship among relations is inherent.

The example below shows the insertion of a 3-layer XML subtree in Fig. 8. RDB is updated by executing the SQL statements in Fig. 9. If the bulk-insertion is adopted, the annotation and its values are propagated to the XML document. The XML fragment will be constructed as Fig. 10.

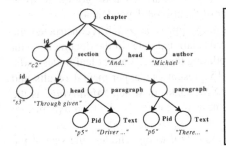

```
INSERT INTO chapter
    VALUES ('d0', 'c2', 'Michael', 'And…')
INSERT INTO section
    VALUES ('d0', 'c2', 's3', 'Through given')
INSERT INTO paragraph
    VALUES ('d0', 'c2', 's3', 'p5', 'Driver…')
INSERT INTO paragraph
    VALUES ('d0', 'c2', 's3', 'p6', 'There…')
```

Fig. 8. An XML subtree   **Fig. 9.** SQL statements for Fig.7

```
<Tag_chapter id="3"> <chapter id="c2">
    <author > Michael </author>
    <head> And … </head>
    <Tag_section id="4"> <section id="s3">
        <head> Through given </head>
        <Tag_para id = "4"> <paragraph id = "p5">Driver … </paragraph> </Tag_para>
        <Tag_para id ="5"> <paragraph id = "p6">There … </paragraph> </Tag_para>
    </section> </Tag_section >
</chapter> </Tag_chapter>
```

Fig. 10. Annotated XML fragment

The data in *Document* relation is shown as Fig. 11. Before inserting the fragment of Fig. 10 into the original XML document, the annotation of its parent — document ("d0") will be obtained by querying RDB according to the given condition. The SQL statement is expressed as below:

SELECT tag_document FROM Document WHERE doc_id='d0'.

doc_id	Title	Author	*Tag_document*
d0	Language	Tom	*1*
...	...	...	...

Fig. 11. *Document* relation with annotation

4 Experimental Results

In this section, we present the experimental results and the performance studies of our method. We deal with deletion and insertion of the XML leaf and the subtree respectively, also the update at different depth of the original XML document. Our code was written in Java, and used JDBC to communicate with Oracle9i. Our experiments were conducted on the same machine with a 500MHz PIII processor, 256M of memory, running the operating system of Windows 2000 Server.

XML documents of 478K, 1.82M, 2.29M and 6.06M were generated by the benchmark tool of Xmach-1 [15]. First, we presented key constraints of the XML document and the mapping rules from XML to the relational schemas. Then we got the RDB of 3NF schemas according to the canonical cover of functional dependencies.

We compared our method with the *Publishing* approach, which reconstructed the entire XML document by publishing the related relational data. In the documents with various sizes, we tested the performance of updating the XML data of leaf nodes and a subtree with the size of 70K. Fig. 12 - Fig.15 present our experimental results and performance of two approaches for updating XML data, in which *"Modifying"* is the method proposed in this paper. *Logarithm* scale was adopted for the time axis in Fig. 12 and Fig. 14 due to the significant difference of these two methods.

It is obvious that *Modifying* is much better than *Publishing*. The less the size of the XML data updated is, the less the cost of *Modifying* will be; however, for the *Publishing* method, the cost is very high even though the document has small size.

Fig. 12. Insertion of leaf node   **Fig. 13.** Insertion of subtree

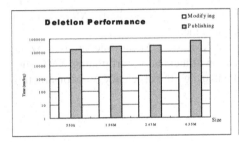
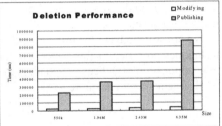

Fig. 14. Deletion of leaf node   **Fig. 15.** Deletion of subtree

Further, when the size of the original XML document increases, the performance of *Modifying* has no significant change.

To get the resulting XML document by *Modifying*, only the updated relational data is published, and the cost will be unchanged if the XML data to be inserted is fixed. The total cost of deletion is even less because it is unnecessary to reconstruct any XML fragments from RDB. It is not sensitive to the size of the original document. Thus, it is effective even for the large XML document while *Publishing* is not.

We also examined the performance of updating the same XML data at various hierarchies using *Modifying*. The experimental result is illustrated in Fig. 16. The performance will not be influenced greatly by the depth where the updated XML nodes locate. Therefore, our method is efficient even for the deeper XML nodes.

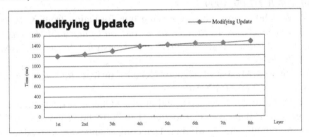

Fig. 16. Updates at different hierarchies

5 Conclusions

In order to fully evolve XML into a universal data representation and sharing format, it is necessary to update XML documents while preserving key constraints, and develop techniques to process them efficiently. In this paper, we present a novel method for updating XML based on the constraint-preserving normalized storage of XML over RDB. To our knowledge, it is the first proposal that updates XML document while preserving key constraints. Our method first propagates the updates on XML into the RDB. Then taking the updated relational data and the original document as input, the resulting XML document can be generated through locating the positions of updates by annotation technology. Preliminary performance study indicates that our method significantly speeds up the processing of updates on XML by more than an order of magnitude, and improves the performance of updating XML. Moreover, our method is not sensitive to the size of original document.

We are still studying the ordered updates on XML data. Meanwhile, aroused by the techniques proposed in this paper, optimization strategies of partitioning XML sub-tree, application of indices in updating, and enhancing the efficiency of reconstructing XML fragment are our future work.

References

1. Igor Tatarinov, Zachary G. Ives, Alon Y. Halevy, and et al.: Updating XML. In *Proc.Of ACM Int'l Conf. On Management of Data (SIGMOD)*, 2001
2. S. Davidson, W. Fan and C. Hara. Propagating XML Keys to Relations. In *Int'l Conf. On Data Engineering (ICDE)*, 2003
3. J. Shanmugasundaram, C. Zhang, and et al.: Relational Databases for Querying XML Documents: Limitations and Opportunities. In *Proc. of the 25th Int'l Conf. on Very Large Databases (VLDB)*, Edinburgh, Scotland, September 1999
4. Igor Tatarinov, Stratis D. Viglas and et al.: Storing and Querying Ordered XML Using a Relational Database System. In *Proc.Of ACM Int'l Conf. On Management of Data (SIGMOD)*, 2002
5. Alin Deutsch, Mary Fernandez, and Dan Suciu: Storing semi-structured data in relations. Workshop on Query processing for Semi-structured Data and Non-standard Data Formats. In *conjunction with ICDT'99*, 1999
6. D. Lee and W. W. Chu: Constraints-preserving transformation from XML document type definition to relational schema. In *Proc.Of Int'l Conf. on Conceptual Modeling (ER)*, 2000
7. Yi Chen, Susan B.Davidson and Yifeng Zheng. Constraint Preserving XML Storage in Relations. In *WebDB* 2002
8. J. Clark and S. Derose: XML Path Language (XPath). In *W3C Recommendation* 16 November 1999, http://www.w3.org/TG/XPath
9. D. Chamberlin, D. Florescu, J. Simeon, and et al.: XQuery: A query Language for XML. *Technical report. World Wide Web Consortium*, Feb 2001, http://www.w3.org/TR/ Xquery
10. G. Cobena, S. Abiteboul, and A. Marian: Detecting changes in XML documents. In *Int'l Conf. On Data Engineering (ICDE)*, 2002
11. Peter Buneman, Sanjeev Khanna, Keishi Tajima, and Wang-Chiew: Archiving Scientific Data. In Proc. *Of ACM Int'l Conf. On Management of Data (SIGMOD)*, 2002
12. M. J. Carey, D. Florescu, Z. G. Ives, and et al.: XPERANTO: Publishing object-relational data as XML. In *ACM SIGMOD WebDB Workshop*, 2000
13. Xin Zhang, Gail Mitchell, Wang-Chien Lee, and et al.: Clock: Synchronizing Internal Relational Storage with External XML Documents. In *Eleventh Intl. Workshop on Research Issues in Data Engineering (RIDE)*, IEEE Computer Society, April 2001
14. P. Buneman, S. Davidson, W. Fan, and et al.: Keys for XML. In *WWW10*, 2001
15. T. Bohme, E. Rahm: Xmach-1: A Benchmark for XML Data Management. In *Proc. Of German database conf. BTW2001, Oldenburg*, 7-9. March, Springer, Berlin 2001
16. ZhengChuan Xu, Xueqing Gong and et al.: Normalized storage of XML document in rela-tional database. To be published in *Mini-Micro System*
17. J.Shanmugasundaram, K. Tufte, C. Zhang and et al.: Efficiently Publishing Relational Data as XML Documents. In *Proc. of the Int'l Conf. on Very Large Databases (VLDB)*, Cairo, Egypt, September 2000
18. Hector Garcia-Molina et al.: Database System Implementation. *Prentice Hall*, 2000

ENAXS: Efficient Native XML Storage System*

Khin-Myo Win, Wee-Keong Ng, and Ee-Peng Lim

Centre for Advanced Information Systems, School of Computer Engineering, NTU
Nanyang Avenue, N4-B3C-13, Singapore 639798, SINGAPORE
khinmyo@pmail.ntu.edu.sg, wkn@acm.org, aseplim@ntu.edu.sg

Abstract. XML is a self-describing meta-language and fast emerging as a dominant standard for Web data exchange among various applications. With the tremendous growth of XML documents, an efficient storage system is required to manage them. The conventional databases, which require all data to adhere to an explicitly specified rigid schema, are unable to provide an efficient storage for tree-structured XML documents. A new data model that is specifically designed for XML documents is required. In this paper, we propose a new storage system, named *Efficient Native XML Storage System* (ENAXS), for large and complex XML documents. ENAXS stores all XML documents in its native format to overcome the deficiencies of the conventional databases, achieve optimal storage utilization and support efficient query processing. In addition, we propose a path-based indexing scheme which is embedded in ENAXS for fast data retrieval. We have implemented ENAXS and evaluated its performance with real data sets. Experimental results show the efficiency and scalability of the proposed system in utilizing storage space and executing various types of queries.

1 Introduction

Within a few decades, the Web has been growing incredibly and has become the main information interchange among various organizations. Many applications produce and consume semistructured data which contains irregularities and evolves rapidly making the use of predefined rigid schemas infeasible. XML is emerging as a dominant standard for representing and exchanging semistructured data among applications over the Web. With the tremendous growth of XML data, an efficient storage system is required to manage them.

Several XML storage solutions [1,2,4,6,9,11,12,15] proposed in recent years are based on the conventional databases, such as *relational* (RDBMS) and *object* (ODBMS). The main reason is that these databases are matured enough to handle large volume of data and provide robust data management features. But in practice, they have a lot of limitations to deal with their rigid schema and XML irregular structure. They require an additional transformation to map XML data into their formats and vice-versa. This process is complex and requires more space when the document structure is deep and nested. In addition, they have to

---

* This work is partially supported by the SingAREN21 research grant M48020004

X. Zhou, Y. Zhang, and M.E. Orlowska (Eds.): APWeb 2003, LNCS 2642, pp. 59–70, 2003.
© Springer-Verlag Berlin Heidelberg 2003

convert XML queries into appropriate patterns understood by underlying query engines. It is time-consuming and performance degradation in data retrieval.

Due to above deficiencies and limitations, a new data model which is specifically designed for XML is emerging recently. This system is able to store XML in its native hierarchical structure and eliminates transformation processes. It provides efficient query processing and document navigation. Currently proposed solutions [8,10,14,17] are designed to provide such advantages but they have not addressed how to efficiently store large collection of documents which contain data with similar hierarchical structure. They disregard the common structural properties of elements, as a result, the storage consumes additional space to maintain redundant structural information and requires more I/O accesses when all elements or contents (values) with a unique path from multiple documents are retrieved.

In this paper, we propose a new schema-conscious efficient native XML storage system, named ENAXS. It organizes a large volume of XML documents with common hierarchical structures and collectively stores elements and contents according to their paths. The new storage aims to eliminate transformation overhead produced in the conventional databases, and overcome inefficient space utilization and query processing of the existing native XML storages. We also embed a new path-based XML indexing scheme into ENAXS to speed up tree traversing and reduce I/O cost for loading and scanning data in query execution.

The rest of the paper is organized as follows. Section 2 reviews related work and Section 3 explores the proposed index structure and storage design for XML data. Section 4 contains the results of our experiments using real data sets and Section 5 concludes the paper.

2   Related Work

Some native XML storage models have been proposed in recent years. *Lore* is an object-based storage that uses *OEM* in which all elements are stored as objects and linked by the use of labels [14]. Lore provides forward traversal but an additional index is needed to traverse backward. *Natix* uses a hybrid approach in which a certain level of data is stored in its structured part and the rest in the flat object part [10]. *Natix* uses an intuitive algorithm to split input document tree into subtrees which are able to be stored in the physical records. This approach provides faster data retrieval when an entire document is needed but inefficient for the query to find all elements with a unique path in multiple documents. *Timber* organizes XML documents as the collection of ordered-labelled trees manipulated by the use of bulk algebra and maps it into *Shore* [8]. *Tamino* is built on the foundation of hierarchical *ADABAS* database [17]. It groups input documents into collections by the definition of an open content model. Each collection contains several document types and each type is assigned a common schema. These schemas are stored in the repository and used in query evaluation.

Several path indexes are also proposed to support faster query processing. *Lore* uses *DataGuides* as a structural summary for document navigation and implements a set of indexes for query execution [7,13]. *ToXin* introduces hash table based indexing scheme that allows efficient traversing along the document [16].

Index Fabric proposes a prefix encoding scheme that encodes all tags along the path and places together with value as a keyword in the Patricia tries [5]. *APEX* uses a structural summary and a hash table to navigate the document and to resolve frequently used path queries [3].

3   ENAXS

We focus to the scenario of storing nodes with a same path expressions together in a group. It may reduce storage space and provides faster data retrieval as most queries expect data with a same structural attribute from multiple documents. ENAXS deals with the approach that all root nodes, internal nodes (elements) and external nodes (contents) from multiple documents are collectively grouped according to their paths, and stored together in the repository. The overall structure of ENAXS is shown in Fig. 1.

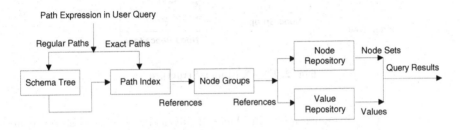

Fig. 1. The Overall Structure of ENAXS

We describe some brief definitions used in ENAXS as follows:

- *Node repository* maintains all root and internal nodes.
- *Value repository* contains binary form of all external nodes.
- *Node group* is a set of node-references grouped together according to their paths regardless of which document they belong.
- *Schema tree* is an abstract representation of the structure of XML documents.
- *Path index* maintains a set of keys which are hash values generated from the path expressions. The leaf nodes of the index tree contain references pointing to the associated node groups.

3.1   Index Structure

A path index is necessary to support queries that requires exhaustive path traversals. With its support, a query processor executes queries without traversing along the given path to fetch the required nodes. The path index in ENAXS comprises of three components: path index, node group and schema tree.

Path Index. Index is uploaded into memory and frequently accessed during query execution, so that, the size, processing efficiency and flexibility of index structure greatly effect on resource utilization and speed of query processing. ENAXS is a path-based storage in which *path index* is embedded as a crucial component by considering above issues. Instead of indexing long strings of path expressions, we generate hash values from it and employ as index keys in order to reduce the overall size of index structure and processing overhead in searching exact-matched string keys. Fig. 2 illustrates the ENAXS index structure.

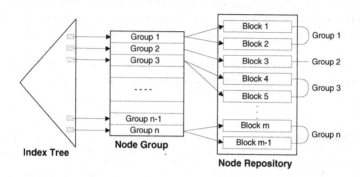

Fig. 2. ENAXS Index Structure

We collectively organize nodes in blocks of physical records and store in the node repository. Each block is addressed by a *block pointer*. We implement the path index using the B^+-tree structure, a balanced tree in which leave nodes are *group pointers* referring to the node groups. Since all index keys in the B^+-tree are numerical hash values, simple arithmetic comparison can be applied in key matching, and the number of B^+-tree levels can be significantly reduced.

Node Group. In order to perform efficient node insertion, update and deletion, we add a layer, named node group, between the index and node repository. Each group in this layer contains references pointing to blocks of nodes in the node repository as depicted in Fig. 2. Since the hash function may generate a same hash key for different paths, ENAXS organizes all path groups and forms a single large one. Fig. 3 shows the general format of a group record.

Each record is composed of *header* and *body*. *Number of groups* in the header indicates the number of node groups in a record, *pointer to group* points to the associated group of node-references and *path expression* consists of a full-path expression that represents a group. As node-references may exceed a block size, *pointer to next block* in the body is used to link an aggregated block and then *group of node-references* is used to point nodes in the node repository. Node insertion, update and deletion in ENAXS become easy because the node group can be updated directly. The following algorithm describes the node insertion procedure.

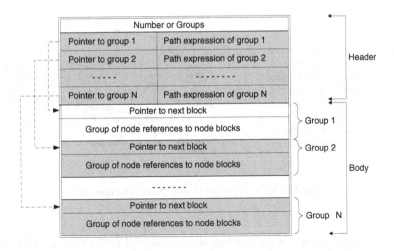

Fig. 3. The Node Group Record Format

Algorithm: Insert(node)

1 **path** ← path expression of node
2 **sig** ← hash(**path**)
3 Search for **sig** in path index
4   If not found, then
5   Store **node** to the node repository in a new block
6   Allocate a new block **new_block** in node group file
7   Create a new node group record, **new_group**, and
          add the reference to **new_block** into **new_group**
8   Insert **sig** and reference to **new_group** into path index
9   else
10   Get the pointer to existing group **old_group**
11   Store **node** into **block** pointed by the last pointer in **old_group**
12   if **block** is full
13   Create **new_block**
14   Store **node** into **new_block**
15   Append **new_block** pointer to **old_group**
16   end if
17   end if
18 end

Schema Tree. In order to deal with regular-path queries, we introduce a structure called *schema tree*, a tree representation of the common structure for a set of XML documents. It is constructed by the use of DTD and provides the parent-child relationship of a pair of nodes. Fig. 4 describes a sample DTD and a XML document and Fig. 5(a) shows its equivalent schema tree.

Each node in the schema tree is assigned a unique identifier so that two nodes from different paths with a same node name can be differentiated. ENAXS

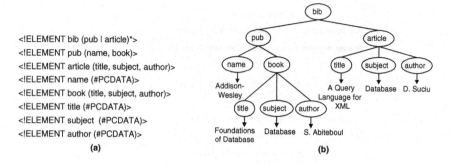

<!ELEMENT bib (pub | article)*>
<!ELEMENT pub (name, book)>
<!ELEMENT article (title, subject, author)>
<!ELEMENT name (#PCDATA)>
<!ELEMENT book (title, subject, author)>
<!ELEMENT title (#PCDATA)>
<!ELEMENT subject (#PCDATA)>
<!ELEMENT author (#PCDATA)>

Fig. 4. The Sample DTD and XML Document

traverses along the schema tree to find all possible full-paths that match a given regular path. We employ *bottom-up approach* that enables traversing from the bottom to the root of the schema tree by reducing the possibilities of paths to choose. We implement an *inverted list* illustrated in Fig. 5(b) to support that traversing.

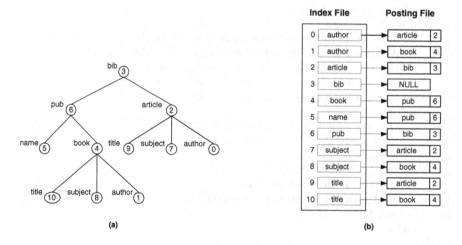

Fig. 5. The Schema Tree and Its Inverted Representation

For a given regular path, we first extract the last tag and then lookup in the index file to locate its parent node in the posting file. We use the resulting node as an index entry to go next level up. This procedure continues till the root node is reached, and all possible full-paths are obtained. Then, the query processor uses the resulting paths to resolve the query. This approach magnifies the capabilities of schema tree not only providing efficient exploring of structure but also enhancing the query processing because the query can be answered preliminarily by identifying whether a given tag exists in the schema tree, without needing to search in all documents.

3.2 Storage Structure

Typically, internal nodes (root and internal) shape the structure of document and external nodes retain scalar values that are the majority of the document. ENAXS stores structure and contents separately so that the node operations can be performed independently. A unique *document identifier* (DID) is assigned to each document and a *node identifier* (NID) to each node (except external) so that a particular node can be identified by a pair ⟨DID, NID⟩ within the storage.

Value Repository. Value repository is a collection of records that are the physical representations of all external nodes. The record format is depicted in Fig. 6(a). An external node record is composed of *DID*, its *Parent Node ID* (PID), *Parent Node Block Pointer* and *Value*. The record size varies with the value length but it is limited by block size. For a record that exceeds a block size, we employ *splitting* to make two parts; the first one is allocated in current block and the rest in a new block, so that documents with long contents such as novels can be stored and the node operations can be performed efficiently.

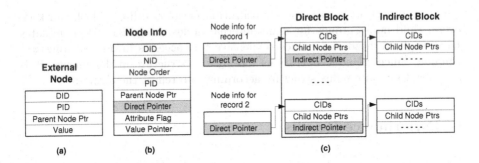

Fig. 6. The External Node and Internal Node Record Format

Insertion of a node is straightforwardly appended to the last block. The *splitting* is applied for a long record to span it over multiple blocks.

Updating of a record invokes the *reallocation* to rearrange all subsequent records by moving up or pushing down within a block. This may acquire a new block if necessary.

Deletion of a node releases space occupied and applies reallocation within the block.

Node Repository. Node repository is a collection of all internal nodes records. (The record format is shown in Fig. 6(b) and (c)). A record is composed of three main parts: node info, direct block and indirect block. A *node info* basically maintains the internal node information that can be used to identify whether it is an element or an attribute and whether it has a value or child nodes. It also maintains a reference that points to its value (value pointer) or a *direct block* (direct pointer) where information of a particular number of child nodes are stored. The additional child nodes, if any, are maintained in an *indirect block*. ENAXS uses a parameter, called the *node set threshold* denoted by α, that predefines the maximum number of child nodes which can be allocated in a direct block. If the number of child nodes is greater than α, indirect pointer is set to reference an indirect block where additional child nodes are stored, otherwise, it is always set to NULL. The value of α is set to 10 by default but it can be fine-tuned by an administrator to achieve the optimal storage utilization. Since node information is fragmented into parts, the node operations can avoid unnecessary loading of vast data.

Insertion of a new node involves creating a new node info, and capturing child nodes information in the direct and indirect blocks or value in the value repository.

Updating of a node simply modifies the node info.

Deletion of a node uses the bottom-up approach that removes value of that node from the value repository or child nodes from direct and indirect blocks. Then it deletes the node info and performs the necessary updating in its parent node.

Our approach improves storage utilization because a direct block can keep several child nodes groups for many internal nodes. It significantly eliminates the storage overhead and reduces expensive I/O accesses in data loading and scanning. Since all node operations modify the structure of documents, it is necessary to update index structure accordingly to reflect the changes.

4   Performance Results

In this section, we present the performance results measured on two aspects: space utilization and I/O cost for storing and querying XML data with ENAXS. We developed the system using Java. IBM XML 4J Parser[1] was used as a parser. The evaluations were performed on a Pentium-III 800MHz machine with 256MB RAM under Windows 2000 using 20GB disk. We use two data sets: Shakespeare's Plays[2] (D1) that contains deep and nested node hierarchy with 327K elements in 37 files (7.6MB in size) and KJV Bible[3] (D2) that is relatively flat with 32K elements in 1 file (4.9MB).

---

[1] http://www.alphaworks.ibm.com/tech/xml4j

[2] http://www.ibiblio.org/bosak/xml/eg/

[3] http://www.assortedthoughts.com

4.1   Storage Space Utilization

We evaluate the system by altering block sizes (BS) and α to determine how
the size of data files (node and value repository, node group and index) reflects
the changes. We did not keep track the size of the schema tree as it was small
and unaffected by changes in both data sets. Fig. 7(a) shows the growing trend
of data files sizes for D1 when BS=4KB and 8KB respectively with α=25, and
Fig. 7(b) depicts the situation if α=10.

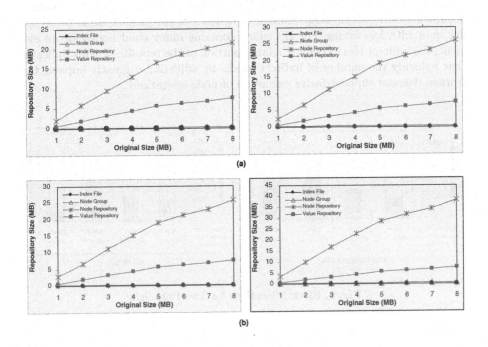

Fig. 7. Size of Data Files

Index File. The path index size is small and the curve is relatively flat no matter
how BS changes. It occupies 3 blocks (1 for root and 2 for internal nodes) for
D1 as it contains 57 distinct paths and 1 block for D2 as it has only 5.

Node Group File. We found that the size of the node group file increases
linearly with respect to data set size. From the experiment with D1, the number
of blocks occupied by 57 node groups is 59 when BS is set to 4KB and 57 when
BS=8KB. This shows that the number of blocks does not significantly decrease
when BS is expanded because each group occupies at least one block. It gives
an advantage that there are more spaces available in each block flexible enough

to add more node references when the size of data set increases and reduces I/O accesses for loading fragmented data. We got a similar result for D2.

Node Repository. Node repository is the majority of the storage and it increases linearly with the size of each data set (shown in Fig. 7(a) and (b)). Fig. 8 shows the number of blocks required to store node info, direct blocks and indirect blocks for D1 and D2 respectively. From the several experiments, we observed that ENAXS gives more efficient storage utilization with larger α (25) in both data sets. We also found that larger BS spends less storage space for complex documents that contain large number of nodes, but the smaller BS is better for flat ones with less nodes. For D2 which contains many child nodes for an element, the indirect blocks occupy a large portion of the repository. This indicates that reducing the number of indirect blocks by adjusting α greatly impacts the storage size and support faster execution of node operations.

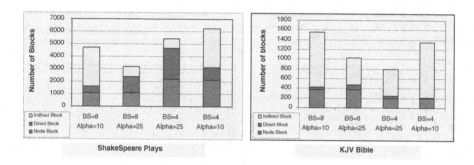

Fig. 8. Block Allocations for Two Data Sets

Value Repository. Value repository is almost the same size as the original data set because values are the majority of both sets.

4.2   Query Performance

We evaluated the performance of ENAXS by executing various queries (described in Fig. 9(a)) using XQuery[4] language on D1 and examined the number of block I/Os accessed during the execution with and without the support of index. We set BS to 8KB and α to 10 and examined the number of blocks read. The results from Fig. 9(b) show that execution of Q1 speeds up approximately 500 times with the support of the index. The execution of Q2 does not cost much than Q1, means that, navigating document with the support of the schema tree spends only a few traversal cost. Q3 and Q4 examine the performance of the value

---

[4] http://www.w3.org/TR/xquery/

repository. The results show that both queries are substantially faster with the support of the index. Q3 costs more because additional I/Os are needed to access the value repository.

	Query	Description
Q1	PLAY.ACT.SCENE.SPEECH.SPEAKER	Exact-match query to extract all *speaker* in *speech*
Q2	*.SPEAKER	Reqular path query to retrieve all *speaker* in all *play*
Q3	PLAY.ACT.SCENE.TITLE.#	Value query to extract all values of *scene/title*
Q4	PLAY.ACT.SCENE.TITLE	Query to extract all *title*

(a)

	Query	Index	Node Group	Node Repository	Value Repository	Total	No. of Nodes
With Index	Q1	1	1	183	0	185	30972
	Q2	7	6	188	0	201	31067
	Q3	1	1	5	752	759	630
	Q4	1	1	5	0	7	748
Without Index	Q1	0	0	101350	0	101350	30972
	Q2	-	-	-	-	-	-
	Q3	0	0	4658	752	5410	630
	Q4	0	0	4658	0	4658	748

(b)

Fig. 9. Queries and Block I/Os Costs in Query Executions

5   Conclusions

In this paper, we proposed a new schema-conscious native XML storage system called ENAXS to address the shortcoming of maintaining large and complex structured XML documents with similar schema in the existing systems. We take the advantage of the common schema of the XML documents and collectively organize according to their structures so that the system substantially eliminates storage and processing overheads. We also embed a path-based indexing scheme to provide direct access to the nodes. It significantly reduces the number of blocks to be scanned during query processing. With the support of the schema tree, the system can resolve complex regular path queries efficiently.

We conducted various experiments and evaluated the performance of ENAXS in terms of space utilization, I/O assess and query processing costs. The results through experiments have shown that ENAXS supports an efficient and scalable storage for the real XML documents. We will extend ENAXS by adding additional features such as concurrency control, transaction management and multiuser control in our future work.

References

1. D. Alin, F. Mary, and D. Suciu. Storing Semistructured Data with STORED. *SIGMOD Record*, pages 431–442, 1999.
2. V. Christophides, S. Abiteboul, S. Cluet, and M. Scholl. From Structured Documents to Novel Query Facilities. In *Proc. ACM SIGMOD Conf.*, Minneapolis, Minnesota, May 1994.
3. C. W. Chung, J. K. Min, and K. Shim. APEX: An Adaptive Path Index for XML Data. *ACM SIGMOD*, 4(6), June 2002.
4. T. S. Chung, S. Park, S. Y. Han, and H. J. Kim. Extracting Object-Oriented Database Schemas from XML DTDs Using Inheritance. In *Proc. 2nd Int. Conf. EC-Web*, Munich, Germany, September 2001.
5. B. F. Cooper, S. Neal, J. F. Michael, R. H. Gisli, and S. Moshe. A Fast Index for Semistructured Data. In *Proc. 27th Int. Conf. on Very Large Data Bases*, pages 341–350, Roma, Italy, 2001.
6. D. Florescu and D. Kossmann. Storing and Querying XML Data using an RDBMS. *In Bullettin of the Technical Committee on Data Engineering*, 22(3):27–34, September 1999.
7. R. Goldman and J. Widom. DataGuides: Enabling Query Formulation and Optimization in Semistructured Databases. In *Proc. 23rd Int. Conf. on Very Large Data Bases*, Athens, Greece, 1997.
8. H. V. Jagadish, Shurug AI-Khalifa, Laks V. S., Andrew Nierman, Stylianos Paparizons, Jignesh Patel, Divesh Srivastava, and Yuqing Wu. TIMBER: A Native XML Database. *VLDB Journal (To appear)*, 2002.
9. S. Jayavel, T. Kristin, H. Gang, Z. Chun, D. David, and N. Jeffrey. Relational Databases for Querying XML Documents: Limitations and Opportunities. In *Proc. 25th Int. Conf. on Very Large Data Bases*, Edinburgh, Scotland, 1999.
10. C. C. Kanne and G. Moerkotte. Efficient Storage of XML Data. In *Proc. 16th Int. Conf. on Data Engineering*, San Diego, CA, February 2000.
11. M. Klettke and H. Meyer. XML and Object Relational Database Systems Enchancing Structural Mapping Based on Statistics. In *Int. Workshop on the Web and Database (WebDB)*, Dallas, 2000.
12. K. Loney and G. Koch. *Oracle 8i : The Complete Reference*. McGrawHill, 2000.
13. J. McHugh, S. Abiteboul, R. Goldman, D. Quass, and J. Widom. Lore: A Database Management System for Semistructured Data. *SIGMOD Record*, 26(3), September 1997.
14. D. Quass, J. Widom, R. Goldman, K. Haas, Q. Luo an J. MchHugh, S. Nestorov, A. Rajaraman, H. Rivero, S. Abiteboul, J. Ullman, and J. Wiener. LORE: A Lightweight Object REpository for Semistructured Data. *ACM SIGMOD*, 25(2):549–549, June 1996.
15. M. Rays. Bringing the Internet to Your Database: Using SQL Server 2000 and XML to Bulid Loosely-Coupled Systems. In *Proc. 17th IEEE Int. Conf. on Data Engineering*, Heidelberg, Germany, April 2001.
16. F. Rizzolo and A. Mendelzon. Indexing XML Data with ToXin. In *Proc. 4th Int. Workshop on the Web and Database (in Conjunction with ACM SIGMOD)*, Santa Barbara, CA, May 2001.
17. H. Schoning. Tamino: A DBMS Designed for XML. In *Proc. 17th Int. Conf. on Data Engineering*, pages 149–154, Heidelberg, Germany, April 2001.

A Fast Index for XML Document Version Management

Nicole Lam and Raymond K. Wong

School of Computer Science and Engineering
University of New South Wales
Sydney, NSW 2052, Australia
wong@cse.unsw.edu.au

Abstract. With the increasing popularity of storing content on the WWW and intranet in XML form, there arises the need for the control and management of this data. As this data is constantly evolving, users want to be able to query and retrieve previous versions efficiently. This paper proposes an efficient index that support fast version updates and retrievals. Experimental results have shown that the system carries little overhead compared to those without version management support.

1 Introduction

With the increasing popularity of storing content on the WWW and intranet in XML form, there arises the need for the control and management of this data. As this data is constantly evolving, users want to be able to query previous versions, query changes in documents, as well as to retrieve a particular document version efficiently.

A possible solution to the version management of data would be to store each complete version of data in the system. Although this would maintain a history of the data stored on the system so far, the performance of such a system would be poor. This leads to the use of change detection mechanisms to identify the differences between data versions. The storage of these differences may provide an increased performance of the system, especially in relation to its space requirements.

Traditional change detection systems which computed the differences between two documents (such as GNU diff) were based on a line-by-line comparison. This was appropriate for flat textual files but cannot be extended to handle semistructured data, such as XML documents.

Change detection algorithms have been proposed by [5] and [9]. In each case, the algorithm utilises the concept of persistent identifiers and node signatures in order to find matchings between nodes of the 2 input documents. We adopt a similar approach. An alternative solution to the change detection problem is via object referencing as suggested by [3].

Marian et. al. [6] developed a change-centric method for version management, which is similar to our approach. In [6], the system stores the last version of a

X. Zhou, Y. Zhang, and M.E. Orlowska (Eds.): APWeb 2003, LNCS 2642, pp. 71–82, 2003.

document and the sequence of forward completed deltas. In contrast to the approach by [6], we also store intermediate complete versions of the document. A disadvantage of [6] is: if we have already stored 100 versions of a document, retrieving the 3rd version would involve applying 97 deltas to the curent version - a very inefficient process. On the other hand, by storing intermediate versions, our system is likely to result in a more efficient retrieval of the 3rd version (for example, by working forward from the initial version).

In this paper, we present an efficient content-based version management system for managing and querying changes on XML documents based on update logging. Our proposed system uses complete deltas for the logical representation of document versions. We generate deltas through the application of a change detection algorithm in the style of [9]. Our storage policy includes the conditional storage of complete document versions (depending on the proportion of the document that was changed). Furthermore, we define a mapping between forwards and backwards deltas in order to improve the performance of the system, in terms of both space and time. We also adapt a set of basic edit operations, which provide the necessary semantics to describe the changes between documents, from our previous work regarding the extensions of XQL with a useful set of update operations [10].

Finally we discuss the query mechanisms to facilitate meaningful queries to our proposed version management system, The mechanisms behind querying previous versions of data (such as a document) are greatly dependant on the logical and physical model of the version management system in question. That is, it is impossible to explore query mechanisms of a version management system without considering the context in which previous versions of data are stored in the system.

Our intended Version Management System allows for content-based change detection, which enables content-based queries in relation to changes in documents. Our system provides performance efficiency by constructing a given version from one of the intermediate complete versions rather than from the current version only, as suggested in [6]. Furthermore, we provide a mapping between backwards and forward deltas, hence reducing the space requirements for the system. The prototype of our proposed Version Management System has been integrated with a native XML database system called SODA3 and is available at [8].

2   System Model

For the purposes of this paper, we define a system model for version management. The logical model of the system consists of the representation of intermediate versions using the notion of Complete Deltas in the style of [6]. We also define an efficient storage policy for the document versions to reduce the storage requirements of the system. Finally, the system also maintains the time at which the document was loaded into the system in order to perform time related queries on this data.

2.1   Complete Deltas

Our proposed system uses the concept of Complete Deltas to store the different versions of a document in the database. That is, instead of storing the complete versions of all documents in the system, we chose to represent only the differences between versions to conserve storage space.

The Complete Deltas used here are representations of the differences between versions. They are termed 'Complete' as it is possible, given two versions, V_i and V_j and their Complete Delta $\Delta_{i,j}$ to reconstruct either document version. That is, given V_i and $\Delta_{i,j}$, we can reconstruct V_j; and given V_j and $\Delta_{i,j}$, we can reconstruct V_i.

2.2   Storage Policy

We define an efficient storage policy for our proposed system. Suppose there many differences between two versions of a document, it may be more efficient to store the complete version of the more recent document, rather than storing the large complete delta. This is the intuition behind the storage policy defined.

Depending on the relative size of a complete delta, as compared to the complete document version, we either store the complete delta or the complete version. This reduces the storage requirements of the system significantly. However, due to this unconventional storage policy, there arises the need to define new query mechanisms in order to efficiently query these document versions.

3   Diff and Edit Operations

In this section, we describe the key of a version management system, i.e., the *diff* operator, and a set of edit operations that are closely related to that *diff* operator. Firstly, we look at the complete deltas used, the xDiff algorithm, followed by the types of edit operations that the complete deltas contain. Next, several user operations for version insertion and retrieval are defined.

3.1   Complete Deltas

One of the main components of our proposed system is the use of complete deltas for change detection. Several other change detection algorithms [2,1,3,5, 9] have been proposed. However, we utilise the concept of deltas, rather than object references [4], or node annotations [1], as deltas are more intuitive.

Firstly, we define a forward (backward) **delta** to be an edit script that can be applied to a complete version of a document to obtain the next (previous) complete version of a document. Such deltas are also termed 'lossy' as, given two versions V_i and V_j such that f is the forward delta which can be applied to V_i to obtain V_j, it is not possible to obtain V_i from V_j and f. Similarly for a backward delta. Hence, such deltas contain operations that are not invertable.

Next, we define a **complete delta** to be an edit script such that there exists a 1 to 1 mapping between the forward and backward deltas between two versions.

Although a lot of redundancy is introduced to the edit operations in a complete delta, this method is preferred as we argue that complete deltas enable our system more flexibility and efficiency.

3.2 Edit Operations

In addition to the two basic operations: Insert and Delete, we define three more main operations: Update, Move and Copy. Although the Insert and Delete operations are sufficient to describe the differences between two versions, we find that the three additional operations provide a more meaningful and intuitive approach to the description of differences.

For simplicity and clarity, we assume here simple path expressions, in the style of [7], to present the edit operations of our system. In our actual prototype implementation, we use a more complicated, extended XQL expressions as described in [10].

For the insert, delete, move and copy operations, it is necessary to include the element's final index as this facilitates the inversion of the operations. The operations also contain some redundant information (for example the *oldvalue* in Update operation) so as to aid in the mapping between forward and backward deltas.

We consider the following operations:

1. **Insert:** We define three sub-operations under the Insert operation: **insertInto, insertBefore, insertAfter**.
   insertInto: `path!insertInto(`
   `insertedpath)` inserts `insertedpath` as a subtree of `path`, given that `path` has no children.
   insertBefore: `path!insertBefore(`
   `insertedpath, i)` assumes that there exists a subtree, t, rooted at `path`, such that t has nodes other than the root. This operation inserts `insertedpath` before subtree t, such that it has a final element index i.
   insertAfter: `path!insertAfter(`
   `insertedpath, i)` assumes that there exists a subtree, t, rooted at `path`, such that t has nodes other than the root. This operation inserts `insertedpath` after subtree t such that it has a final element index i.

2. **Delete:** This operation is the inverse of the Insert operations. That is, `path!delete(x, elem, isBefore)` removes the subtree x (which has nodes other than the root node) rooted at `path`. The subtree x is the raw XML that represents the subtree being deleted. Also, `elem` is the node that was adjacent to x before it was moved. `isBefore` identifies if `elem` is the left/right neighbour or neither.
   We also define `path!delete(elem, isBefore)` which assumes that `path` describes a leaf node and thus removes the leaf node.

3. **Update:** Intuitively, `path!update(newvalue, oldvalue)` updates the `oldvalue` of `path` to the `newvalue` specified. It is necessary to keep track of the `oldvalue` in order to invert the operation.

4. **Move:** We define three sub-operations under the Move operation: `moveInto`, `moveBefore`, `moveAfter`.
   a) `dstpath!moveInto(srcpath, elem, boolean)`
   b) `dstpath!moveBefore(srcpath, elem, boolean, path)`
   c) `dstpath!moveAfter(srcpath, elem, boolean, path)`
   We also include extra parameters for these operations to aid in the mapping between backward and forward deltas. For example, in `path!moveAfter(srcpath, origNeighbour, isBefore, newpath)`, newpath is the final path of `srcpath` in its new location. The parameters for the other move operations are similarly defined.

5. **Copy:** We define three sub-operations under the Copy operation: `copyInto`, `copyBefore`, `copyAfter`.
   a) `dstpath!copyInto(srcpath)`
   b) `dstpath!copyBefore(srcpath, index)`
   c) `dstpath!copyAfter(srcpath, index)`

4 Implementation

The Version Management System for Semistructured Data has been implemented as a C++ application. Built on top of SODA3 [8], a native semistructured database management system, the application provides an interactive prompt which allows the user to perform actions on the database system.

4.1 Organisation of Data

As with the current implementation of SODA3, the current version of all documents are stored under the `<data>` node of the storage structure. The corresponding schema for the current document versions are also stored under the `<schema>` node of the storage structure.

In addition to the basic node structure, we include (as another child of the `<root>` node) a `<version_root>` node. This node holds all information relating to the version management of the different document versions, and hence represents a significant portion of the Version Management System storage structure. Figure 1 shows the significant portions of the storage structure of our proposed system. Omitted node elements in the figure are those that are standard to the SODA3 storage structure (as described previously).

Each document is associated with a single `<tagIndex>` which represents the the edit operations performed on the document, sorted according to tag names. This index facilitates near constant time retrieval of operations related to a given tag. The `<version>` node immediately following the `<tagIndex>` of a document represents the initial complete version of the document (i.e. the version of the document that was first loaded into the system using the `load` function). All `<version>` nodes at this level contain complete versions of the corresponding document. The `<complete_delta>` nodes, found between `<version>` nodes, represent the difference between the complete versions that are adjacent to it. The sequence of complete deltas between complete versions are represented here as a simple complete delta in the form of the Path Index structure.

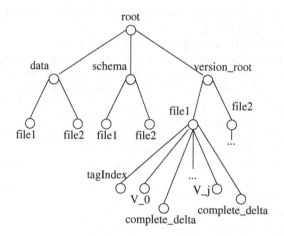

Fig. 1. Storage Structure of Version Management System

We found that by loading a non-empty document into the Version Management System, it is possible to reduce the size of the Path Index structure. In this case, each node in the document was not represented in the Path Index. Hence, each `<indexNode>` in the Path Index has to store extra information in terms of the *canonical path* that it represents, as the `indexNode`'s position in the Path Index is insufficient to determine it's *canonical path*. The Path Index structure can thus be seen as a compressed trie.

Each subtree rooted at `<complete_delta>` contains `<indexNode>`s which have a series of edit operations associated with them. With the exception of the delete operation, each edit operation is represented by the version and operation identifier, together with the tag, at the root of the subtree, affected by the operation. Each `<tag>` node optionally has an attribute-value `type="char"` if it represents character data. This is important because, in SODA3, character data nodes are represented differently from element nodes (i.e. tags), and hence affects the reconstruction of complete versions of a document. For `delete`, instead of having a tag name, the entire subtree that was deleted is copied into the `<tag>` node. This was done to facilitate the inverting of a delete operation in order to facilitate both forward and backward deltas.

Example To illustrate the structure of the Path Index, Figure 2 shows a sample XML document, sample.xml. Suppose the document (sample.xml) above is loaded into the Version Management System. Initially, only the `<data>` and `<schema>` subtrees exist in the system. That is, the `<version_root>` subtree is only created on demand - when the current document is being edited. Suppose the user executes the operations: `a/c!delete()` and `a/b!insertBefore("e")`. Assuming that the MAX_RATIO for the document is large such that a complete version of the document is not stored in the system, the subtree rooted at `<version_root>` would look like Figure 3.

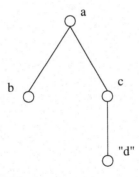

Fig. 2. Sample XML document for Example 6.2

In addition, the Version Management System also has a `<workspace>` node, which is a child of the `root` node. This node is the temporary location used for intermediate computations. For example, this location is used in version retrieval to temporarily hold the result of applying each complete delta to the closest complete version stored in the system.

4.2   Edit Operations

Insert, delete, update, move and copy operations are implemented in the application. In the design, the edit operations had additional arguments to specify the node's final index location after the operation was executed and several other redundant information. In the implementation, we found that this index information, as well as the redundant information, need not be specified by the user and can be determined by the application itself - based on the target path expression. For example, with the moveBefore operation, it is unnecessary for the user to specify the original neighbour, etc to facilitate the mapping of edit operations because the edit operation information is logged in the `<complete_delta>` subtree using the *Canonical Path* representation of the node affected. Hence, such information about the node's location is irrelevant because the delta stores the absolute location of the node. Similarly for insert, update and copy. The delete operation takes no arguments as the subtree that is being deleted can be obtained from the current data version itself. Hence, this subtree is then copied into the index to facilitate the mapping of the delete operation for version retrieval.

4.3   Functions

The application provides several functions through its interactive interface:

load(*filename*)**:** Loads *filename* into the database (under the `<data>` node of the SODA data structure), while maintaining the schema associated with the document.

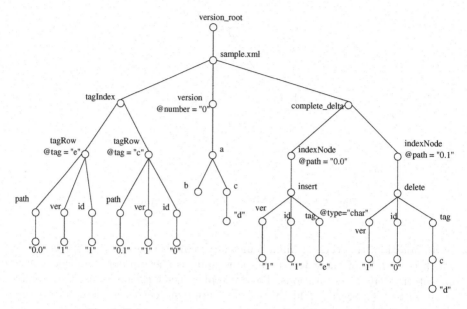

Fig. 3. Subtree rooted at `<version_root>` (Example 6.2)

begin_version(*filename, MAX_RATIO*): This function is called by the user before any transactions are performed on the current version of *filename* to enable the versioning mechanism. Note that if this function is not called before edit operations are performed on the data, the versioning facility will be unavailable. *MAX_RATIO* is specified as one of the arguments to the function to allow the user to specify the maximum number of operations that the sequence of consecutive complete deltas can contain. This value can vary between versions. This function performs most of the computation including the updating of the `<version_root>` subtree based on the specified value of *MAX_RATIO* for the previous version.

commit_version(*filename*): Signals the end of transactions for the current version of *filename*.

retrieve_version(*filename, version_number, FORWARD_CONSTANT*):
Retrieves the version of *filename* specified by *version_number*. As with `begin_version`, the constant *FORWARD_CONSTANT* is an argument to this function.

4.4   Version Insertion

Version insertion is implemented in the application via edit operations performed on the data. That is, a user begins editing the current document version by calling the `begin_version` function. All subsequent edit operations performed on that document will be logged in the `<complete_delta>` subtree. When the user is finished editing the document, `commit_version` is called.

When each operation is executed on the current data version, where versioning is enabled, the `<complete_delta>` subtree is updated. Here, each operation is represented by a 4-tuple: (*version_number, id, tag, path*). *version_number* is the version number associated with the operation being executed.

In general each node affected by an edit operation is assigned an integer value (starting from 0) for its id number. The numbering convention for the operation id is straightforward for the insert and delete operations, where a 4-tuple is used to represent each node affected by the operation. Each node inserted in the `<data>` subtree is represented by an operation, *OpRep*. Suppose the number of nodes represented by the target path of an insert operation is n and the simple path contains m elements. (m * n) node operations *OpRep* will be inserted into the `<complete_delta>` to represent the insert operation.

For update operations, it is necessary to store the old label of the target nodes in order to reverse the operation for version retrieval. There exists a one to one mapping between the node operation *OpRep* representing the current, updated node label and the node operation *OpRep* for the old label, where both *OpReps* have the same (*version_number, id*). To distinguish the two, the *OpRep* for the old label is also annotated with an attribute-value pair op="update_old".

The id numbering for copy and move operations are slightly more complex as the operations involve a source/argument path, in addition to the target path. It is necessary to log both the source and target path affected by the edit operation to facilitate version retrieval, as well as querying changes. Assuming the current unused id is x. The nodes specified by the target path will be assigned id numbers starting from x, while the nodes in the source/argument path will also be assigned id numbers starting from x. In order to differentiate between source and target node operations (as (*version_number, id*) are supposed to uniquely identify a node operation), operations representing the source nodes are annotated with a triple (start, end, size), where *start* is the first operation id of the target node operations (in this case: x), *end* is the last operation id of the target node operations and *size* is the number of nodes in the source path. This information is essential in version retrieval as these values are used to recompute the corresponding edit operations that were performed. Thus, for a copy operation, which has n destination nodes and m source nodes, m * n *OpRep* nodes will be inserted into the version indexes to represent the copyDest. On the other hand, m *OpRep* nodes will be inserted into the version indexes to represent the copySrc operation.

Note that this complexity could have been avoided, in exchange for a larger `<complete_delta>` subtree. Instead of associating a single set of source node operations with multiple target node operations, it could have been implemented such that there exists a one to one mapping between source and target sets. However, this would have increased the space requirements of the application as each set of source operations will have to be duplicated n times, where n is the number of nodes in the target path.

This approach to operation id numbering has implications on the semantics of the canonical paths associated with the edit operations. In contrast to insert, delete and update operations (where each node's canonical path is evaluated individually), copy and move operations have their target and source nodes' canonical path evaluated as a group such that the canonical paths are valid before the operation is executed and not after. This is best explained with an example.

Example Given the XML document in Fig. 2, suppose a user performs the edit operation: `a/b!moveBefore(a/c)`. The target canonical path is `0.0`, while the source canonical path is `0.1`. Note that after the move operation is executed, the canonical path `0.0` does not define the correct target node anymore.

4.5   Version Retrieval

To retrieve a version of a document, the `retrieve_version` function is called. This function obtains the necessary edit operations from the corresponding `complete_delta` subtree and applies the operations to the current working complete version, which is temporarily stored at the `<workspace>` node. In the pseudo-code below, the current working complete version is represented as `cur_ver`.

```
retrieve_version(v):
1     ver = closest complete version (to v) satisfying Eq 3.2 stored in system
2     cur_ver = copy(ver)
3     for i from ver to v:
4         e = get_edit_operations(i)
5         if ver > v:
6             cur_ver = apply_delta_reverse(cur_ver, e)
7         else:
8             cur_ver = apply_delta(cur_ver, e)
9     return cur_ver
```

`get_edit_operations(i)` retrieves all edit operations in the complete_delta associated with version i of the document. Each edit operations is represented by a target path, argument and edit operation type. Where appropriate, paths are in their canonical form to improve the efficiency of applying these edit operations.

The operation id numbering conventions impose implicit constraints on the way the operations are handled. Instead of handling each operation individually, we introduce the notion of sets of operations that are executed at a given instant. The system treats insert, delete and update operations as singleton sets of operations, while copy and move operations are grouped into sets of operations where each set of operations contains operations that were the result of a single user edit operation.

Example 6.4: Referring to Figure 4 and the edit operations e1 and e2 performed by the user on the data. e1 results in 3 `<insert>` nodes to be added to `<complete_delta>` and e2 results in 4 `<copyDest>` nodes and 2 `<copySrc>` nodes to be added. e1 results in 3 sets of operations, where each set contains a single insert operation. e2 results in one set of operations because the 6 *copy* nodes in the `<complete_delta>` are the result of the single user edit operation, e2.

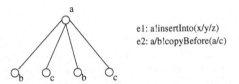

e1: a!insertInto(x/y/z)
e2: a/b!copyBefore(a/c)

Fig. 4. Sample XML document and user operations(Example 6.4)

Hence, each set of operations is applied individually on the current working complete version in order to retrieve the appropriate version correctly.

The target path of each edit operation specifies the final location of the affected node. Hence, the problem of identifying which type of edit operation (i.e. *op*Into, *op*Before or *op*After) to execute, reduces to the problem of identifying whether the path specifies a node in the current working complete version (*op*Before will be used) or the path represents a non-existant node (*op*Into will be used). This technique is used for applying insert, delete and update operations to the current working complete version in `apply_delta`. The alogithm handles copy and move operations differently as the source/argument canonical paths represented in each edit operation determine the location of the required nodes before any operation is executed. Thus, `apply_delta` first evaluates the source nodes of the copy or move operation, this is followed by iteratively applying the copy or move operation to each target node. Due to the semantics of the move operation, applying the move operation to the current working complete version is equivalent to performing a copy operation, followed by deleting the source node set.

This technique is used similarly in `apply_delta_reverse()`, together with the mapping of edit operations to their inverse. Note that applying the inverse of a move operation to a complete version involves deleting all destination nodes except the last destination node, which is moved back to the original (or source) location. The implementation for the other edit operations are similar.

4.6   Querying Versions

In the current implementation of the system, we provide query facilities via XQL. Due to our approach of logging user edit operations, the `<complete_delta>` subtrees are expressive enough for the user to query directly using xql. For example, the user can query the content of a subtree that was deleted because the deleted subtree is explicitly described in the edit operation node stored in the `complete_delta`.

Example. From Fig. 2 and 3, a user can issue a query to retrieve the version where the character data "d" was deleted. This is accomplished via the XQL statment: `retrieve_version("sample.xml", root/version_root/ sample.xml/ complete_delta// indexNode/ delete[tag//"d"] /ver/*, 1)`.

5 Conclusions

This paper presented an efficient content-based version management system that allows authors to manage and query different versions of their documents. The storage policy and logical representation of changes (in terms of complete deltas and edit operations) of the system result in its high performance.

By storing intermediate versions of the document as complete deltas, users are able to efficiently query these data versions without having to reconstruct each version. Efficient version retrieval is also possible due to the system's storage policy of storing intermediate complete version of the document within the storage structure. Performance testing of our prototyped system revealed a highly efficient, scalable version management system that was able to handle large sizes of documents, as well as a large number of edit operations and version insertions. Due to space limitations, detailed performance measurement can be found from http://dba.cse.unsw.edu.au

References

1. S. Chawathe, S. Abiteboul, and J. Widom. Representing and querying changes in semistructured data. In *Proceedings of the International Conference on Data Engineering*, February 1998.
2. S. Chawathe and H. Garcia-Molina. Meaningful change detection in structured data. In *Proceedings of the ACM SIGMOD International Conference on Management of Data*, pages 26–37, May 1997.
3. S-Y. Chien, V. Tsotras, and C. Zaniolo. Copy-based versus edit-based version management schemes for structured documents. In *RIDE-DM*, pages 95–102, 2001.
4. S-Y. Chien, V.J. Tsotras, and C. Zaniolo. Efficient management of multiversion documents by object referencing. In *Proceedings of VLDB*, September 2001.
5. G. Cobena, S. Abiteboul, and A. Marian. Detecting changes in xml documents. In *ICDE (San Jose)*, 2002.
6. A. Marian, S. Abiteboul, G. Cobéna, and L. Mignet. Change-centric management of versions in an xml warehouse. In *Proceedings of VLDB*, September 2001.
7. W3C Recommendation. Xml path language (xpath) version 1.0. *http://www.w3.org/TR/xpath*, November 1999.
8. Soda Technologies. Soda3 xml database management system version 3.0. *URL: http://www.sodatech.com*.
9. Y. Wang, D. J. DeWitt, and J-Y. Cai. X-diff: An effective change detection algorithm for xml documents. Technical report, University of Wisconsin, 2001.
10. R.K. Wong. The extended xql for querying and updating large xml databases. In *Proceedings of the ACM International Symposium on on Document Engineering (DocEng)*, November 2001.

A Commit Scheduler for XML Databases

Stijn Dekeyser and Jan Hidders

University of Antwerp

Abstract. The hierarchical and semistructured nature of XML data may cause complicated update-behavior. Updates should not be limited to entire document trees, but should ideally involve subtrees and even individual elements. Providing a suitable scheduling algorithm for semistructured data can significantly improve collaboration systems that store their data — e.g. word processing documents or vector graphics — as XML documents. In this paper we improve upon earlier work (see [5]) which presented two equivalent concurrency control mechanisms based on Path Locks. In contrast to the earlier work, we now provide details regarding the workings of a commit scheduler for XML databases which uses the path lock conflict rules. We also give a comprehensive proof of serializability which enhances and clarifies the ideas in our previous work.

1 Introduction

Semistructured data [1] is an important topic in Information Systems research that has been studied extensively — especially regarding query languages — in the past and which has regained importance due to the popularity of XML. Even though XML is not meant to replace traditional database systems, lately an interest in native XML databases has surfaced. Consequently, all features present in relational and object-oriented databases will be revisited in the context of semistructured data. One such feature is the necessity of a concurrency control mechanism in any type of database.

Concurrency control [8] has been extensively studied in the context of traditional database management systems [2,6,7]. It is possible to re-use these results for providing concurrency control in semistructured databases. However, as we have shown in earlier work [5], the traditional solutions we mentioned — while guaranteeing serializability — do not allow a sufficient degree of concurrency; i.e., they are too restrictive.

As a consequence, the problem statement is "what kind of conflict rules and scheduling algorithm for semistructured databases can guarantee both serializability and a high degree of concurrency?"

In previous work, we have investigated the use of path locks to solve the research problem mentioned in the introduction. We introduced two equivalent locking protocols: path locks satisfiability and path locks propagation. For both systems, we introduced conflict rules and analyzed their complexity. We showed that the conflict rules were sufficient to ensure two actions from different transactions can be swapped if no conflict occurs.

X. Zhou, Y. Zhang, and M.E. Orlowska (Eds.): APWeb 2003, LNCS 2642, pp. 83–88, 2003.

In this paper, however, we introduce the scheduler that makes use of the path locks and the conflict rules. The second contribution of this paper is the inclusion of a comprehensive proof of serializability, which was lacking in earlier work. The proof also enhances and clarifies the ideas presented earlier.

2   Data Model and DML

The data model we assume for XML documents is a simplification of the standard XPath data model [3] and essentially node-labeled trees. However, for the purpose of locking we allow also acyclic graphs. We label nodes with a set of transaction identifiers to indicate that the node has been deleted by these transactions.

Definition 1 (Instance graph, actual instance). *The instance graph (N, B, r, ν, δ) is a rooted acyclic graph with vertices N, edges $B \subseteq N \times N$, the root r, nodes labeled with element names by $\nu : N \to E$ and with sets of transaction identifiers by $\delta : N \to 2^T$. The subgraph defined exactly by the nodes that are labeled by δ with the empty set is called the* actual instance *and is presumed to be always a tree with root r.*

The query language is based on a subset of XPath expressions as defined by the following grammar.

$$\mathcal{P} ::= \mathcal{F} \mid \mathcal{P}/\mathcal{F} \mid \mathcal{P}//\mathcal{F}$$
$$\mathcal{F} ::= E \mid *$$

where E is the universal set of strings representing the names of elements.

The following definition enumerates the operations offered by the data manipulation language that can be used to alter a document.

Definition 2 (Operations on the instance graph). *The following four operations are defined on an instance graph.*

A(n, a). *This update operation adds a new edge starting from n and ending in a new node with label a. The new node is returned as the result of the operation. If in the new instance graph the actual instance is not a tree with root r then the operation fails[1].*

D(n). *This update operation adds the transaction identifier of the transaction that requests the operation to $\delta(n)$. This operation returns no result. If in the new instance graph the actual instance is not a tree with root r then the operation fails.*

---

[1] Failure means here that the scheduler does not execute the operation and reports this to the transaction that requested it.

Q(n, p). *This query operation returns as its result all nodes in the instance graph such that there is in the* actual *instance a path from n to this node that satisfies the path p.*

C$()$. *This update operation removes all nodes n from the instance graph with $\delta(n)$ containing the identifier of the executing transaction. The operation returns no result. The operation fails if in the resulting instance graph the actual instance is not a tree[1] with root r.*

Now that we have defined the operations of the data manipulation language, we turn to some traditional definitions from transaction management theory.

Definition 3 (Action, Transaction, and Schedule). *An action is a pair (t, o) where t is a transaction identifier and o is one of the operations given in Def. 2. A transaction is a finite list of actions having the same transaction identifier and in which there is exactly one commit operation (the last pair). A schedule is an interleaving of several transactions. A schedule is said to be node-correct if for every operation that uses a certain node there is an earlier action (containing an addition or a query) of the same transaction that had this node in its result.*

Following tradition, two schedules are equivalent if (1) one is a permutation of the other, (2) the resulting instance graph is in both cases the same, and (3) all the queries in one schedule return the same result as the corresponding queries in the other schedule. A schedule is said to be serializable if it is equivalent with a serial schedule.

3   Path Locks

We now turn to the locking scheme that is used by the scheduler to ensure serializability.

We start with the definition of the read locks. A *read lock* is defined as a tuple $\mathrm{rl}(t, n, p)$ where t is a transaction identifier, n is the node identifier in the instance graph for which the lock holds and p is a path expression in $\mathcal{P}$. The informal meaning of such a lock is that the transaction has issued a query p starting from node n.

The *initial read lock* that must be obtained for a given query operation **Q**(n, p) that is issued by transaction t is simply $\mathrm{rl}(t, n, p)$. From the initial read lock we derive other read locks that must also be obtained by a process called *read-lock propagation*. The process of read-lock propagation causes read locks on a node to be propagated to nodes just below this node in the instance graph. This is done with the rules shown in the next table. The process of read-lock propagation is applied until no more new read locks are added. For more information on the Path Lock Propagation mechanism, we refer the reader to [5].

1. $rl(t, n, a/p) \rightarrow rl(t, n', p)$ if $(n, n') \in B$ and $\mathbf{name}(n') = a$.
2. $rl(t, n, */p) \rightarrow rl(t, n', p)$ if $(n, n') \in B$.
3. $rl(t, n, a//p) \rightarrow rl(t, n', p)$ if $(n, n') \in B$ and $\mathbf{name}(n') = a$.
4. $rl(t, n, a//p) \rightarrow rl(t, n', *//p)$ if $(n, n') \in B$ and $\mathbf{name}(n') = a$.
5. $rl(t, n, *//p) \rightarrow rl(t, n', p)$ if $(n, n') \in B$.
6. $rl(t, n, *//p) \rightarrow rl(t, n', *//p)$ if $(n, n') \in B$.

Fig. 1. Read lock propagation rules.

We proceed with the definition of the write locks. A *write lock* is defined as a tuple $wl(t, n, f)$ where t is a transaction identifier, n is the node identifier for which the lock holds and f is an expression over $\mathcal{F}$.

The following defines which write locks must be obtained for which update operator:

$A(n, a)$: A write lock $wl(t, n, a)$ on node n for transaction t.

$D(n)$: Write locks $wl(t, n, *)$ and $wl(t, n', a)$ where n' is the parent of n in the instance graph and a is the label of n. If n or n' does not exist, then the corresponding write lock does not need to be obtained.

To end this section, we need to define when locks conflict. A read lock $rl(t, n, a)$ or $rl(t, n, *)$ conflicts with a write lock $wl(t', n, a)$ and a write lock $wl(t', n, *)$ if $t \neq t'$. All other locks do not conflict. Two write locks do not conflict due to the node-correctness property of transactions. This property implies that consecutive additions and deletions always commute.

4   The Commit Scheduler

In this section we detail the working of the commit scheduler. The term is based on the theoretical notion of *commit serializability* [8]. Thus, a commit scheduler guarantees that the schedules it accepts are serializable.

Definition 4 (Commit Scheduler). *The commit scheduler is the automaton whose state consists of a schedule S of actions that it has previously accepted and processed, a set of locks L and an instance graph I. Its transition function γ maps S, I and a newly requested action $a(o, t)$ to a schedule S', a set of locks L' and an instance graph I' as follows:*

1. *The new instance graph I' is obtained by applying operation o to instance graph I. If the operation fails, then γ is not defined[2].*

---

[2] If γ is undefined, the sending process is notified that its action is not accepted, and the scheduler waits for a new action. Thus deadlocks cannot occur.

2. *For update and query operations, the set of locks L' is obtained by adding to L the locks required by the operation o. For the commit operation, L' is obtained by removing all locks from L which are owned by the transaction that commits, plus those locks on the nodes that are now deleted from the instance graph.*
   If L' contains conflicting locks, then γ is not defined[2].
3. *The schedule S' is S augmented with $a(o,t)$ provided that γ did not become undefined due to the previous points.*
4. *The sending process receives the result of o, if any.*

The execution of the commit scheduler on a given instance graph I starts with the empty schedule S, the empty set of locks L, and the instance graph I. It receives the actions of S sequentially, and its result is either (1) the output schedule S, the set of locks L, and the instance graph I transformed according to each iteration of the commit scheduler, or (2) undefined.

5 Serializability

In this section, we give a sketch of the serializability proof. The full proof can be found in the Technical Report [4]. We will first give some preliminary definitions.

Definition 5 (Legal and Fail-free Schedules). *A schedule is said to be fail-free if all its operations can be executed without any of them failing. A schedule is said to be a legal schedule if (1) it is node correct, (2) fail-free and (3) all sets of locks in the scheduler's state contain only compatible locks.*

It is easy to see that the output schedule of the scheduler is always a legal schedule.

Theorem 1. *Every legal schedule is serializable.*

Sketch of the proof. We presume some ordering on the transaction identifiers used in S such that $t_i < t_j$ if the commit of t_i preceeds the commit of t_j in S or there is a commit of t_i but not a commit of t_j in S. We serialize the schedule by repeatedly swapping two consecutive actions (t_i, o_i) and (t_{i+1}, o_{i+1}) if $t_i \neq t_j$ and $t_j < t_i$. It is easy to see that if there are no more such pairs then the schedule is serialized. It can also be shown that after a swap of such a pair the result will be an equivalent legal schedule if the schedule before the swap is a legal schedule. Assume that S is a legal schedule and we swap two consecutive actions (t_i, o_i) and (t_{i+1}, o_{i+1}) in S and $t_i \neq t_j$ and o_i is not a commit, then we prove that the following holds: (1) the two swapped operations will not fail in S', (2) all locks in $L_i^{S'}$ are compatible, (3) $I_{i+1}^{S'} = I_{i+1}^{S}$, (4) if they exist the results of o_i and o_{i+1} remain the same, (5) $L_{i+1}^{S'} \subseteq L_{i+1}^{S}$, and (6) S' is node correct. It follows from these points that S' is equivalent with S, fail-free and in all sets $L_j^{S'}$ there are no incompatible locks, i.e., S' is legal.

References

1. S. Abiteboul, P. Buneman, and D. Suciu. *Data on the Web: From Relations to Semistructured Data and XML.* Morgan-Kaufmann, San Francisco, 1999.
2. P. Bernstein, V. Hadzilacos, and N. Goodman. *Concurrency Control and Recovery in Database Systems.* Addison Wesley, Reading, Mass., 1987.
3. J. Clark and S. DeRose. XML Path Language (XPath). *W3C Recommendation,* November 1999.
4. S. Dekeyser and J. Hidders. A path-lock scheduler for XML databases. Technical Report 02-13, University of Antwerp, 2002.
   ftp://win-ftp.uia.ac.be/pub/dekeyser/scheduler.ps.
5. S. Dekeyser and J. Hidders. Path locks for XML document collaboration. In *Proceedings of the Second WISE Conference,* 2002.
6. J. Gray. Notes on database operating systems. In *Operating Systems: an Advanced Course.* Springer-Verlag, New York, 1978.
7. C. Papadimitriou. *The Theory of Database Concurrency Control.* Computer Science Press, Rockville, MD, 1986.
8. G. Weikum and G. Vossen. *Transactional Information Systems.* Morgan Kaufmann, 2002. ISBN: 1-55860-508-8.

An Efficient Path Index for Querying Semi-structured Data

(Extended Abstract)

Michael Barg, Raymond K. Wong, and Franky Lam

School of Computer Science and Engineering
University of New South Wales
Sydney, NSW 2052, Australia
{mbarg,wong,flam}@cse.unsw.edu.au

Abstract. The richness of semi-structured data allows data of varied and inconsistent structures to be stored in a single database. Such data can be represented as a graph, and queries can be constructed using *path expressions*, which describe traversals through the graph.

Instead of providing optimal performance for a limited range of path expressions, we propose a mechanism which is shown to have consistent and high performance for path expressions of any complexity, including those with descendant operators (path wildcards). We further detail mechanisms which employ our index to perform more complex processing, such as evaluating both path expressions containing links and entire (sub) queries containing path based predicates. Performance is shown to be independent of the number of terms in the path expression(s), even where these expressions contain wildcards. Experiments show that our index is faster than conventional methods by up to two orders of magnitude for certain query types, is compact, and scales well.

1 Introduction

Semi-structured data allows data of varied and inconsistent structures to be stored in a single database. For example, an online catalog may integrate heterogeneous data adhering to multiple schema from multiple sites. Semi-structured data can be represented as a graph, and queries can be constructed using *path expressions* [1], which describe traversals through the graph. Path expressions may contain *descendant operators* (path wildcards) which enable queries to be posed over multiple or imperfectly understood data sources.

A large number of path indexes have been proposed for semi-structured data. Such indexes, however, typically trade off performance with the expressiveness of the path expressions they can process.

We propose a path indexing mechanism which is shown to have consistent and high performance for path expressions of any complexity, including those with descendant operators. Performance is shown to be independent of the number of query terms. Our mechanism always allows path expressions to be evaluated with a single index access.

X. Zhou, Y. Zhang, and M.E. Orlowska (Eds.): APWeb 2003, LNCS 2642, pp. 89–94, 2003.

Path expression evaluation typically occurs in the context of a more complex "branchy" query, involving path based predicates, filters etc. Evaluating path expressions individually and combining the result can lead to explosively large intermediate sets which can significantly degrade query evaluation performance [5]. Most existing path indexes focus on the relatively simple task of single path expression evaluation.

In contrast, our index supports more complex processing, such as evaluating entire (sub) queries with path-based predicates, ancestor operators and links.

Recent work on indexing semi-structured data [3,7], has proposed encoding various aspects of the data. Such methods generally have the advantage that the encoding size is insensitive to key length. We extend this notion, encoding multiple aspects of a data set in a very small space (a typical encoding is no more than 8 bytes). The encodings are stored in a data structure that enables comparison of arbitrary length paths in near constant time, using a variety of bitwise operations.

This extended abstract gives a brief summary of the main findings of our work. More detail can be found in the full version of this paper [2,4].

2   Overview

2.1   Encoding Schemes

A semi-structured schema can be thought of as a graph which captures the structural information about the full data graph [8]. A materialised path through the schema is referred to as a *Materialised Schema Path* (MSP).

Our searching mechanism requires us to represent two different aspects of the data - the MSP itself, and the location of a particular node within the graph of the data (called a *path encoding*). Each aspect is represented by a different encoding scheme, which is comprised of a series of low valued, non-negative numbers. These are implemented in the *compressed array* data structure [3], which enables compressed sequence storage and failitates comparison of entire sequences in constant time.

2.2   Index Structure

The index consists of a series of multi-phase inverted lists. MSPs are stored in inverted lists, where the head of the inverted list represents the *last* element in the MSP. Each such element then indicates a secondary list containing the individual nodes and the path encodings which represent them.

List searching is facilitated by arranging the elements in numerographic order of the encodings. Numerographic order is similar to lexicographical order, except that it only considers sequences of numbers, and comparisons are based on the value of each number, rather than the ASCII value of each digit. For example, the sequences {1-2-7, 1-3, 1-3-2-4, 1-3-2-10} appear in numerographic order. Note that if lexicographic ordering was used, the order of the last two sequences would be reversed.

Storing the encodings in numerographic order has the important property that all elements which share a common prefix are contiguous. This is especially important when we only wish to consider nodes with a particular ancestor, or a path with a fixed initial sequence of terms.

Numerographic order further enables logarithmic time access to individual elements using a modified binary search.

2.3   Path Expression Evaluation

Any search has a number of different physical execution plans. These execution plans can be optimised by selecting more than one *focus*. A focus is a query term which reduces the search space by "focusing" the search on the smaller set of nodes which are likely to be of interest. The last query term is always a focus.

We present algorithms which optimally evaluate both single and multi-focus queries. The processing is efficient for all path expressions, including those with path and label wildcards. For large amounts of irregular data, multi-focus processing is shown to reduce query evaluation time by many orders of magnitude.

2.4   Extended Query Evaluation

We present non-trivial extensions to the index and the multi-focus processing algorithm which enable our index to evaluate:

Links: Links (such as XLinks and hypertext links), are an important extension to the XML specification, and are a fundamental feature of many XML documents. For this reason, we have incorporated a "link" operator (->) into our query syntax. The link operator can appear anywhere a path separator (/) can appear.

Whilst it is always possible to "follow" links using traditional joins, such a mechanism is relatively expensive, especially when dealing with paths. By including a virtual node in the data graph to represent the link, we present a modification of our multi-focus processing algorithm which efficiently evaluates a path expression with links for only the cost of an additional focus.

Path based predicates: Path-based query predicates (or "branchy" queries) are potentially expensive for the underlying DBMS to process. Typical processing may require multiple index lookups, joins and/or pointer chasing to evaluate such queries.

Predicate query processing is possible due to the fact that we encode the physical location of each node in the graph. By comparing path encodings, we are thus able to effectively perform "graph traversal" by utilising bitwise comparisons on our indexed encodings.

3   Results

Tests were run on a computer with a Pentium III 800MHz processor, 256MB RAM, running Linux Redhat 7.0. The data was stored in the Soda2 [13] database.

We ran tests over two sets of data - one with a simple, well defined schema, and one with no pre-defined structure at all. Whilst most data will fall between these two extremes, we felt this approach gives good upper and lower bounds on the effects of data structure on index performance.

3.1   Path Expression Length

Figure 1 shows the effect of the length of the path expression on query time. Queries were generated with an equal proportion containing a) no wildcards, b) path wildcards, c) label wildcards, d) a combination of path and label wildcards. In these results, a "query term" refers to either a label or label wildcard. (i.e. /a/b/*//c has 4 query terms).

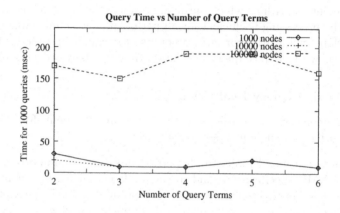

Fig. 1. Number of Query Terms vs Time

Results were obtained for various path expression selectivities. These were held relatively constant to provide a fair comparison. For 100,000 nodes, the result sets tended to be significantly larger (in number of pages) and so additional I/Os were required to load the OIDs.

These results demonstrate that path expression evaluation is independent of the number of query terms for all path expressions, including those with wildcards.

3.2   Query Cost

We compare our index with two other techniques: the basic *edge-mapping* scheme [14], and [7], which also encodes MSPs. (These are stored in a modified patricia trie and path expressions are evaluated by traversing the trie). Figure 2 shows the average number of I/Os to evaluate a single query of the specified type.

Single Path Expression without Wildcards. Query 1 represents a simple path expression with no wildcards. For both regular and random data, edge

Query	I/O - Pages Regular Data						I/O - Pages Random Data					
	Edge Map		Cooper et al		MSP Index		Edge Map		Cooper et al		MSP Index	
	value	Δ	value	Δ	value	Δ	value	Δ	value	Δ	value	Δ
1 /a/b/c	97	1.0	64	1.5	69	1.4	194	1.0	3	64.7	9	21.6
2 //a//b//c	4207	1.0	603	6.7	607	6.6	81056	1.0	9766	8.3	349	232
3 /a/b[d]/c	135	1.0	-	-	13	10.3	235	1.0	-	-	17	13.8
4 //a//b[.//d]//c	5938	1.0	-	-	16	371	135158	1.0	-	-	694	194

Fig. 2. Performance Results

mapping is significantly slower than the other two approaches, due to the number of joins required to evaluate the path expression.

For both the other approaches, the regular data required substantially more I/Os than for the random data, due to the higher number of MSPs (around 2 orders of magnitude).

Single Path Expression with Wildcards. Query **2** represents a simple path expression with path wildcards. To evaluate such a query, Cooper et al search the index using a top down traversal. The random data contained over 800,000 MSPs, spread over many pages. As such, traversing such a trie requires many I/Os. Our approach required only a single scan of the relevant MSP list, with significantly fewer I/Os.

The advantage of our approach becomes more pronounced as the structure of the data becomes less consistent. This becomes increasingly prevalent for large databases with heterogeneous data and/or very loose schema.

Branchy Queries. Query **3** represents a branchy query with no wildcards, whilst query **4** represents a branchy query with wildcards. It is not possible to compare our work with Cooper et al, as they do not support branchy query processing for arbitrary queries. Edge mapping requires a significantly greater number of I/Os, as each query term results in at least one join.

By utilising the path encodings stored with the OIDs, we alleviate the need to visit the actual data. As we only need to load the data for the (reduced) result set, we require a significantly reduced number of I/Os.

4 Related Work

The wide number of existing path indexes have tended to fall into two categories. One approach is to label nodes in the graph according to some numbering scheme based on the pre and post order traversal of the XML tree [6,11,9]. This numbering scheme is used to identify the containment relationship between nodes. Path expressions are then evaluated by performing a structural join for the set of nodes which corresponds to each path expression term.

The other main approach is to generate a structural summary of the data, and then evaluate path expressions by traversing this summary [7,8,10,12]. Most summary structures are labeled, directed graphs. Cooper et al [7] encode paths as strings and store these in a modified patricia trie.

[7] and [10] provide limited support for "branchy" query evaluation.

5   Conclusion

In this abstract we describe a method for implementing a fast, versatile path index. Our index is shown to be effective for evaluating all path expressions, including those with wildcards, as well as supporting more complex processing such as evaluating path expressions with links and evaluating entire (sub) queries with path based predicates. Performance is shown to be independent of the number of terms in the path expression(s), even where these expressions contain wildcards. Our index is shown to be faster than conventional methods by up to two orders of magnitude for certain query types, irrespective of whether the data adheres to any pre-defined schema. Experiments show our index is compact, enables efficient searching, and scales well.

References

1. S. Abiteboul. Querying semi-structured data. In *ICDT*, 1997.
2. M. Barg and R. K. Wong. Fast and versatile path index for querying semi-structured data. Full paper. Technical Report 0209, University of NSW, 2002. Available at: ftp://ftp.cse.unsw.edu.au/pub/doc/papers/UNSW/0209.ps.Z.
3. M. Barg and R.K. Wong. Structural proximity searching for large collections of semi-structured data. In *ACM CIKM*, 2001.
4. M. Barg and R.K. Wong. A fast and versatile path index for querying semi-structured data. In *8th Intl. Conf. on Database Systems for Advanced Applications (DASFAA'03)*, Kyoto, Japan, March 2003.
5. N. Bruno, N. Koudas, and D. Srivastava. Holistic twig joins: Optimal xml pattern matching. In *SIGMOD*, 2002.
6. S. Chien, V. Tsotras, C. Zaniolo, and D. Zhang. Efficient complex query support for multiversion XML documents. In *EDBT*, 2002.
7. B. Cooper, N. Sample, M. Franklin, G. Hjaltason, and M. Shadmon. A fast index for semi-structured data. In *VLDB*, 2001.
8. R. Goldman and J. Widom. Dataguides: Enabling query formulation and optimization in semistructured databases. In *VLDB*, 1997.
9. T. Grust. Accelerating xpath location steps. In *SIGMOD*, 2002.
10. R. Kaushik, P. Bohannon, J. Naughton, and H. Korth. Covering indexes for branching path queries. In *SIGMOD*, 2002.
11. Q. Li and B. Moon. Indexing and querying xml data for regular path expressions. In *VLDB*, 2001.
12. J. McHugh, S. Abiteboul, R. Goldman, D. Quass, and J. Widom. Lore: A database management system for semistructured data. In *SIGMOD*, 1997.
13. University of New South Wales. The Soda2 project. http://www.cse.unsw.edu.au/ soda/.
14. J. Shanmugasundaram, K. Tufte, C. Zhang, G. He, D. DeWitt, and J. Naughton. Relational databases for querying XML documents: Limitations and opportunities. In *VLDB*, 1999.

Integrating Path Index with Value Index for XML Data*

Jing Wang[1], Xiaofeng Meng[2], and Shan Wang[2]

[1] Institute of Computing Technology, Chinese Academy of Sciences,
100080 Beijing, China
cuckoowj@btamail.net.cn
[2] Information School, Renmin Univerisity of China,
100872 Beijing, China
{xfmeng, suang}@public.bta.net.cn

Abstract. With the advent of XML, it is becoming the de facto standard required by the Web applications. To facilitate path expression processing, we propose an index structure adopted in our native XML database system Orient-X. Our index is constructed by utilizing DTD to get paths that will appear in the XML documents. It represents structural summary of XML data collection conforming to certain DTD, so we can process any label path query without accessing original data. In addition, it is integrated with value indexes. Preliminary experiments show quite promising results.

1 Introduction

As more and more data sources on the Internet switch over and express their data content using XML [1] format, the volume of XML data is increasing rapidly. This trend calls for efficient XML data management solutions. In line with the tree centric nature of XML data, path expression plays an important role in XML query [2]. Recent proposals put their focus on efficient support for sequence of "/" steps from the document root, but is not efficient for the processing of partial path matching and "//" due to the exhaustive navigation of the indexes. In this paper, we propose SUPEX (Schema gUided Path indEx for XML data). In contrast to traditional path index, SUPEX is constructed by utilizing DTD to get paths that will appear in XML documents. With SUPEX, we can process any label path query without accessing original data. Value based conditions are crucial in querying any kind of data. In SUPEX, path index and value indexes are integrated to facilitate query evaluation.

The remainder of this paper is organized as follows. In Section2, we present some back knowledge and related works. An overview of SUPEX is given in Section 3. Section 4 describes the procedure of query processing. Section 5 contains the results of our experiments. Finally, conclusion and future work are given in Section 6.

---

* This research was partially supported by the grants from 863 High Technology Foundation of China under grant number 2002AA116030, the Natural Science Foundation of China (NSFC) under grant number 60073014 and 60273018, and the Excellent Young Teachers Program of MOE (EYTP).

X. Zhou, Y. Zhang, and M.E. Orlowska (Eds.): APWeb 2003, LNCS 2642, pp. 95–100, 2003.

2 Background and Related Work

Document Type Definition (DTD) is part of XML standard [1], and specifies the structure of an XML element by specifying the names of its sub-elements and attributes. We define an XML data set as a set of XML documents conforming to certain DTD. A key issue in XML query processing is how to efficiently determine the ancestor-descendant relationship between any two elements. We adopt the encoding scheme proposed by [5]. Every node in XML document tree is associated with an 3-tuple (DocId, Order: Size, Level). This numbering scheme is applied to our document tree and index graph.

Recent proposals on path index include DataGuides [3], 1-indexes [4], and so on. These indexes are not efficient for the processing of partial path matching due to the exhaustive navigation of the indexes. Furthermore, the construction cost is expensive. Cooper et al. [6] presented the Index Fabric which encodes each label path to each XML element with a value as a string and inserts them into an efficient index structure for string. This index loses relationships between elements, and only supports label path query from document root. XISS[5] proposed an index based path evaluating approach, and supported path query through structural join.

3 Overview of SUPEX

3.1 SUPEX: Its Structure

SUPEX consists of a structural graph (SG) and an element map (EM). SG is constructed based on DTD, and represents the structure summary of XML data. So all possible path starting from the roots of XML documents conforming to special DTD will appear in SG. EM provides fast entries to nodes in SG, and is useful in finding all elements with the same tag.

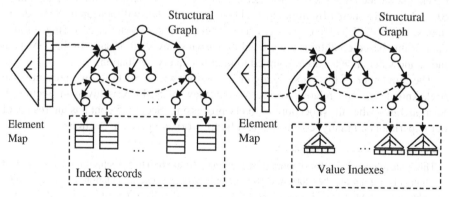

Fig. 1. SUPEX structure with value indexes

SG has one root node. Each node in SG except the root node has a label defined in DTD, called E-Label. All nodes with the same E-Label in SG are linked through a pointer named Next-Element. Each node in SG corresponds to a set of fixed-length index records which is called extent of the corresponding SG node. The extent of SG node includes index records of elements having an identical incoming label path, and these index records are sorted by DocId and Order values. Each index record includes an element descriptor and other related information. SG is tree-shaped when there is no cycle in DTD graph. When DTD graph is cyclic, SG is still tree-like except the reverse edges from descendant nodes to ancestor nodes. Element Map (EM) is implemented as a B+-tree using element name as key. Each entry in a leaf node points to the first node of a list with an identical E-Label in SG. EM allows us to quickly find all SG nodes with the same E-Label.

In traditional database systems such as relational database systems, value indexes are usually created on columns of a relation. But due to tree-shaped nature of XML data, it is difficult to define the granularity of values indexes. In SUPEX, value indexes are constructed with respect to the context of data elements. Each SG node may have one or several pointers to value indexes that are constructed on the attributes or text values of elements in its extent. These value indexes are implemented as B+-tree, and their construction and destruction are user's decisions. Fig. 1 gives the structure of SUPEX.

3.2 Construction of SUPEX

DTDs have proved important in a variety of areas: transformation between XML and databases, XML data storage, and so on. SUPEX is generated from DTD, and the main issues that must be addressed include:

1. Simplifying DTD. Practical DTD can be very complex, and most of the complicity of DTD comes from the complex specification of elements. We choose a set of transformations to eliminate constraints on occurrence time of elements, transform "|" to ",", and group sub-elements having the same name. Such simplification loses information such as relative order of the elements, but retains information about all possible sub-elements, which is enough to generate our structure graph.
2. Constructing structural graph. The simplified DTD can be represented as DTD graph. Through depth first traversal of DTD graph starting at the element nodes without incoming edge, we expand DTD graph into the structural graph. The SG nodes with an identical E-Label are linked to form a list. Element Map can be constructed on all element tags.
3. Data Loading. SUPEX can be constructed before data loading. During XML documents loading procedure, each element is encoded, and its corresponding index record is inserted into the extent of corresponding node in SG. As for value indexes, users can choose to create appropriate value indexes on attributes or text values of elements conforming to certain context.

4   Query Processing with SUPEX

SUPEX contains information of path index and value indexes. With SUPEX, we can efficiently process path expression with value based condition predicate. SUPEX supports two basic queries: (1) given a tag, all elements with this tag can be obtained by the lookup of EM. (2) Simple label paths from the root of document can be matched by traversal of SG starting from the root node. Except these two, SUPEX can be used to evaluate query in the following ways.

4.1   Path Expression

A complex path expression can be decomposed into a set of basic structural relationships between nodes. These basic structural relationships include ancestor-descendant and parent-child relationship. Path queries like "E1/E2" and "E1/*/E2" can be supported by Parent-Child (E1, E2) and Ancestor-Descendant(E1, E2) algorithms, respectively. The procedure of algorithm Ancestor-Descendant(E1,E2) is as follows. By the lookup of EM, we can get two nodes in SG that are the head nodes of lists with E-Label E1 and E2 respectively. Following the two lists, we determine the ancestor-descendant relationship between the current nodes in the two lists according to their numbers. If they are ancestor and descendant, the element records in their extent are sort-merged and appended into result. Otherwise, one pointer is moved to the next node accordingly.

```
Algorithm Ancestor-Descendant (E1,E2)
Input: Ancestor element E1,descendant element E2
Output: Pairs of matching nodes

1: Get the head node of List E1 in SG through EM;
2: Get the head node of List E2 in SG through EM;
3: For each node in List E1 do
4:    Skip over unmatchable nodes in List E2;
5:    For each matching node in List E2 do
6:        Sort-merge the extents of current nodes of
            List E1 and E2;
7:        Append the result to output;
8:    End for
9: End for
```

In addition to these basic structural relationships, our index can support partial label path matching. For label paths like "//E1/E2/.../En", we needn't traverse the whole index graph to get result. By the lookup of EM, we can obtain the head node of the list with E-Label E1. For each node in this list, the sub-tree rooted at it will be traversed to find nodes matching "E1/E2/.../En". So only a part of SG will be traversed to get the result. This will greatly reduce the cost of partial label path matching. The detailed procedure is omitted due to space limit.

4.2 Query Evaluation with Value Indexes

Value based condition predicates are important in query evaluation. In XML query, condition predicates are often on elements matching certain label path expression. In SUPEX, value indexes are created according to the requirements of users, and can be used in the evaluation of condition predicates. Through the traversal of SG, we can get SG nodes matching certain label path expressions. If there are value based conditions on these nodes and appropriate value indexes, query can be evaluated through existing indexes. When there are a large number of data nodes matching path expressions, value indexes will be a good choice with lower cost compared with executing predicates on all candidate nodes.

5 Preliminary Experiment Results

We empirically evaluated the performance of SUPEX on a variety of XML documents. We report results here for a representative dataset: the XMark benchmark [7]. The experiments were performed on Pentium IV-1.4GHz platform with MS-Windows 2000 and 256 Mbytes of main memory. The XERCES-C++ parser was used to parse and generate XML data. We implemented our index in the C++ programming language. The data sets were stored on a local disk.

To get controllable document size, we used the XML generator XMLgen developed by the XMark benchmark project. For a fixed DTD modeling an Internet auction site, XMLgen produces document instances of controllable size. Table 1 lists the characteristics of the data sets used in our experiments. The numbers in columns of the table represent the parameter of XMLgen, the size of generated document, and the number of elements in the generated documents, respectively.

Table 1. XML document size and number of elements in documents

Scaling Factor	Document Size(MB)	Element number
0.01	1.12	17132
0.05	5.6	83533
0.1	11.3	167865
0.5	56.2	832911
1.0	113	1666315

We implemented the element index and element-element join algorithm in XISS [5], and compare its performance with SUPEX. Fig. 2 and 3 report the query response time for //open_auction//description and //description/text against XMark documents of increasing size respectively. As shown in these figures, SUPEX is faster than XISS, and attains more cost reduction compared with XISS with the increasing of document size.

We have found preliminary experiment results quite motivating. Further performance evaluation will be made in the future.

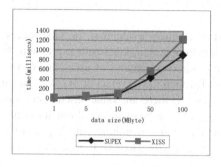

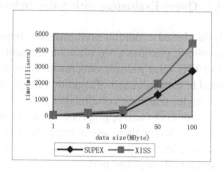

Fig. 2. Open_auction//description   **Fig. 3.** Description/text

6 Conclusion and Future Work

Our research group is working on a native XML data management system. We are implementing SUPEX as the index module of our system. In the future, we will test our method with large volume of data, and compare it with existing index schemes. Furthermore, values indexes will be added into SUPEX structure to accelerate the evaluation of predicate conditions.

References

1. T. Bray, J.Paoli, C. M. Sperberg-McQueen, and E. Maler(Eds). Extensible Markup Language (XML) 1.0 (Second Edition). W3C Recommendation 6 October 2000,
   http://www.w3.org/TR/2000/REC-xml-20001006
2. D. Chamberlin, D. Florescu, J. Robie, J. Simeon, and M. Stefanescu(Eds). Xquery: A Query Language for XML. W3C Working Draft, 15 February 2001,
   http://www.w3.org/TR/2001/WD-xquery-2001215
3. R. Goldman, J. Widom. DataGuide: Enabling Query Formulation and Optimization in Semistructured Databases. In Proceedings of the 23th International Conference on Very Large Data Bases, Athens, Greece,1997
4. T. Milo and D. Suciu. Index structures for path expression. In Proceedings of the 7th International Conference on Database Theory, pages 277–295, January 1999
5. Quanzhong Li , Bongki Moon. Indexing and Querying XML Data for Regular Path Expressions. In Proceedings of the 27th International Conference on Very Large Data Bases, Roma, Italy, 2001
6. Brian F. Cooper, Neal Sample, Michael J. Franklin, Gisli R. Hjaltason, Moshe Shadmon. A Fast Index for Semistructured Data. In Proceedings of the 27th International Conference on Very Large Data Bases, Roma, Italy, 2001
7. Albrecht R. Schmidt, Florian Waas, Martin L. Kersten, Daniela Florescu, Ioana Manolescu, Michael J. Carey, and Ralph Busse. The XML Benchmark Project. Technical Report INS-R0103, CWI, Amsterdam, The Netherlands, April 2001

Automatic Layout Generation with XML Wrapping

Istvan Beszteri and Petri Vuorimaa

Telecommunications Software and Multimedia Laboratory,
Department of Computer Science and Engineering,
Helsinki University of Technology,
P.O.Box 5400, FI-02015 HUT, Finland
{istvan.beszteri, petri.vuorimaa}@hut.fi

Abstract. Because of the increasing variety of user terminals, there is a great demand for server side content adaptation. This paper describes a method to generate different layouts of an XML document automatically on server side, according to some information about the client needs. As a result of the algorithm, an XHTML document is generated from an XML source. The layout of the resulting XHTML adapts to the client's requirements. The information about the client is sent to the server by CC/PP protocol. The generation of the layout is done dynamically on the server according to a predefined general layout template. A simple document is introduced, and tested with the most common web browsers as an example.

1 Introduction

The XML (Extensible Markup Language [1]) based content provision has become very popular in the last few years. The main reason is that, XML makes it possible to separate the document data from the visualization.

In the practice it means that the document consists of two files: an XML data file, and a separated stylesheet file. This setup has many benefits. One of them is that, one can provide several stylesheets for an XML document, describing different layouts for the same data. A useful usage of this property is to support different client terminals from a web server.

Today it seems that there will be a great demand in the near future for supporting various client terminals from web servers. Unfortunately, the most web pages are designed for large color displays with at least 640x480 resolution. The new kinds of mobile devices are different. Their screen is much smaller and in many cases only capable of displaying the content in gray scale. Making direct presentation of documents on mobile devices, which were designed for high-resolution displays, results bad looking pages, which are difficult to browse, or in the worst case totally unusable. Because of the high variety of different clients, it is not possible to redesign a web document for every target device, so it is obvious that some kind of content adaptation is needed.

X. Zhou, Y. Zhang, and M.E. Orlowska (Eds.): APWeb 2003, LNCS 2642, pp. 101–107, 2003.

2   The Adaptation Problem

Concentrating on the document layout, a typical web document is built up from some basic structures. For instance an opening page of a site, usually contains a fancy banner indicating the content, a menu that links to other pages of the site, some links to other sites with similar or relevant content and some text and image flow, containing the information that the site wants to provide.

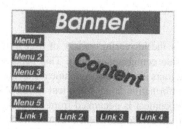

Fig. 1. A typical web page layout

Figure 1. shows such a typical layout of a web page on a desktop computer. It can be seen that a device with smaller screen size is not able to show the page as it is, because the components of the page require the whole available width and height of the actual screen. The page should be split up to several pages, the components should be resized, and these new pages should contain the same information.

The question is: what kinds of information should this new layout generation be based on? Many papers have been presented on this topic, and almost all the presented content adaptation methods are based on some semantic knowledge about the objects of the page.

Bickmore et al. [2] classifies the adaptation methods into five categories:
1. device-specific authoring
    The web page is created in as many versions as many devices are supported.
2. multiple-device authoring
    The designer of the page provides different stylesheets for every supported devices, so the presentation adapts to the specific hardware (e.g., [3]).
3. client-side navigation
    The user can interactively navigate a web page, displaying a portion of the page at any given time.
4. automatic re-authoring
    Modifies the original content and layout of the page dynamically.
5. web page filtering
    Lets the users get only those web pages they are interested in.

The presented method can be classified into the automatic re-authoring category. Good examples for the same category are the UC Berkley Pythia proxy [4] and Digestor [5]. The Pythia proxy was developed to reduce bandwith latency for such clients which suffer from low data transmission speeds. Although Pythia does not modify the layout of the document, it is a good example, because it makes some adaptation dynamically on the document, and this adaptation does not happen on the client hardware. Another project of the same research group resulted a proxy-assisted web browser for handheld devices [6]. Digestor adapts the content and the layout with heuristic methods. It analyses the document both from semantic and syntactic point of view, and chooses from predefined heuristic adaptation methods.

Heuristic adaptation methods give acceptable results for most pages, but the designer of the page has no control on the layout on every device. The pages are still supposed to be designed for a specific environment and the re-authoring transformers, try to correct the imperfection of the design for another environment.

Another limitation of most content adaptation solutions is that they are restricted to one document description language. They are browsing the document source for certain tags, and modify the source. The method described in this paper is rather wrapping the original document fragments into special XML tags, and does not care about the target language itself.

The currently used document and layout description languages are not fully designed for dynamic modifications. The following method gives a solution, which resolves the lack of information by adding extra layout information to flow based XML document description languages like XHTML (Extensible HyperText Markup Language) [7], by wrapping fragments of the document to specific space description tags. This only solves the layout problem and does not deal with the semantic adaptation, but similar wrapping tags could be designed to describe the meaning of document fragments.

3 Layout Adaptation

Chen at al. has proposed a function-based object model (FOM) for content adaptation [8]. Instead of semantic understanding of the functions of the web page objects are used for adaptation.

Similarly to FOM, in this solution, the objects of a web page are classified into two categories:

- basic objects (BO)
- compound objects (CO)

A basic object is an XML document fragment, which the designer does not want to be modified, by the adaptors. It can contain alternative versions for the same content, but the adaptor cannot modify them, only choose one of them.

A compound object is a complex object that can be built up from basic, and other compound objects. The current implementation distinguishes three kinds of compound objects:

- vertical list
- horizontal list
- page

A vertical list can be imagined as a table with one column. Every cell can contain basic or compound objects.

A horizontal list, is similar to the vertical list, but as it follows from its name, in horizontal direction. It can be imagined as a table with one row.

Since every cell in a compound object can contain other compound objects, tables and more complex structures can be described by nested compound objects. For instance a table with three rows and four columns can be described with a vertical list with three objects, where every object is a horizontal list with four objects, or vice versa.

A page is a special list (vertical or horizontal) and gets role in the optimization part of the algorithm.

To help the layout adaptation, for every object in the page, the designer should decide if that is a compound or basic object, and wrap the document fragment, representing the object into special XML tags, which provide information about the object to the optimization algorithm.

The wrapping tag has to have attributes, which describe the width and height of the object in percentage compared to the composing object. In addition the wrapping tags of the basic objects have to have attributes describing the minimum width and height of the object in pixels (display units). The algorithm does not check if the object is really can be displayed in the given minimum area. It is the designers responsibility. Wrapping tags for a basic and a compound object can be the followings:

```
<basic name="basic example" sizeX="40%" sizeY="30%" minX="50px"
minY="40px">
… here comes the wrapped document fragment …
</basic>
<vertical_list name="compound example" sizeX="20%" sizeY="80%">
… here comes the wrapped document fragment …
</vertical_list>
```

The algorithm first parses the document to a tree structure. Since every object is wrapped by a special tag, at the highest level the root element should be a page compound object, and by default it is considered as if it was a vertical list.

Before the optimization the program has to get the space information (width and height in pixels), which is available to display the page. This information is sent to the server by the CC/PP protocol [10]. Starting from the size data, with the help of the wrapping relative size attributes, the program recursively calculates the available space, for every contained object.

At the point, where the recursion reaches a basic object, the algorithm compares the calculated available space and the required minimal space in the wrapping tag of the basic object. If the calculated space is not big enough this fact propagates back to the container objects, up to highest level.

Since the page is a special list, it can be split up to two lists. After the split, both of the lists are considered as full pages, and get the full available space. For the new pages, the algorithm is run again and again, until all the pages fit to the available space.

If a page, as a result of splitting, contains only one compound object, then that is not a real list anymore. Thus the contained object will be considered as the page, and the direction of the page list is determined by the type of the contained object. This flatting is repeated iteratively, while finally the page contains multiple objects, or only one basic object.

If the page contains only one basic object, and the available space is still not enough, the page is ignored completely. To avoid this situation, the designer has the possibility to provide multiple alternative objects for a basic object. If alternatives available, the minimum required space in the wrapping tag is determined by the required space of the smallest alternative.

The following XML code shows an example for the alternatives:

```
<basic name="basic example" sizeX="40%" sizeY="30%" minX="60px"
minY="30px">
  <alternatives>
    <alternative>
      <img src="example_80x50.jpg"/>
    </alternative>
    <alternative>
      <img src="example_60x30.jpg"/>
    </alternative>
  </alternatives>
</basic>
```

The multiple alternative objects, also has another advantage. It can happen, that a compound object should be split, because the available space is not enough even for the contained smallest basic objects, but after the splitting the new lists get so much space that a bigger version of the basic objects can be displayed. So, when all the pages fit to the available area as a result of the splitting, the algorithms checks all the basic objects, and chooses the biggest possible alternatives, which still can be displayed in the calculated area of the basic object.

4   Tests and Results

The method described in the previous sections is implemented as a Java application, and generates XHTML files from an input stylesheet template. As a test, the program generates outputs for various screen sizes. Both the width and the height of the test screen sizes vary from 50 up to 1200.

The output pages in the XHTML document were modeled by tables. The content of the testing page can be seen in Figure 1. It visualizes the page that was adapted to 600x400 screen size. It is built up from the following objects:

A page object (considered as a vertical list) containing a basic object (banner image), a horizontal list which contains the menu and the content, and another horizontal list for the links.

The horizontal list of the menu and the content, contains a vertical list for the menu items, and a basic object that represents the content (content image or text).

The banner, the menu items, the content and the link items are basic objects, represented by images or texts as alternative objects.

(a)

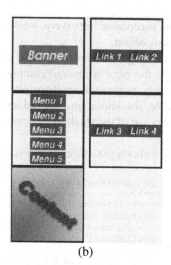
(b)

Fig. 2. Adapted pages: a) 300x200 screen size, b) adapted to 120x120 screen size

Figure 2. a). shows the layout in the case of a 300x200 screen size. Since the screen was not high enough to contain all components, the page was split up to two pages. The first page contains the basic object that represents the banner, while the second page holds the two horizontal lists of the original page. Note, that another alternative image was chosen for the banner, which fills the available place better, and the same is true for the content image.

Figure 2. b). shows a case, where the layout is adapted for 120x120 screen size. Because of the extremely small screen size, all the compound objects were placed into separate pages. The two original horizontal lists (menu-content and links) were split further because of the small width of the screen. The screen is high enough to show all the menu items within one page, but it is not wide enough to show all the link items within one page, not even in the smallest size, so the horizontal list of the links was split up to two horizontal lists. The two new lists got their own pages, and in the new situation there is enough space, to show the links even as images.

Table 1. Number of generated pages and size of the banner for different screen sizes

Screen size (pixels)	Number of pages	Banner size (pixels)
600x400	1	500x80
300x200	2	300x200
120x120	5	100x30
200x300	4	200x300

5 Conclusions

In the previous sections an effective layout adaptation method was introduced. The adaptation is based on special XML tags, which wrap the objects of the original document. Because the adaptation does not use information from the document itself, the method is usable for all well formed XML document languages.

The presented implementation adapts only document layouts, since the wrapping tags are holding size information, and does not deal with the content, but it is easy to see, that algorithm can be extended to adapt any feature of the document with other wrapping tags. The drawback of the solution that the provision of the correct size information is the designer's responsibility, and it is possibly an error prone task. To minimize the probability of wrong size attributes, the visual document editing tools could be extended so that they add the wrapping tags automatically to the document objects.

The presented implementation proved that the algorithm adapts the document layout well, and the resulting documents are acceptable on all tested screen sizes. The components of the testing application can be used to implement a servlet, which could adapt the documents online. The user could send the information about itself to the servlet with the help of the CC/PP protocol.

A future improvement of the algorithm might be to consider other kinds of wrapping tags to adapt other features of the documents. It also would be interesting to see, what kinds of strategies could be used at the list splitting part of the algorithm to improve the output layout.

References

1. Bray T, et al., Extensible Markup Language (XML) 1.0 (Second Edition), W3C Recommendation 6. October 2000., http://www.w3c.org/TR/2000/REC-xml-20001006, 2000.
2. Bickmore T., et al., Web Page Filtering and Re-Authoring for Mobile Users, Computer Journal special issue on Mobile Computing, vol. 42, no. 6, 1999, pp. 534–546.
3. Beszteri I. And Vuorimaa P. Server Side XML Formatting, The Eight International Conference on Distributed Media Systems, San Francisco, California, USA, September 2002, pp. 723–727.
4. Fox A. and Brewer E., Reducing WWW Latency and Bandwith Requirements by Real-Time Distillation, Fifth International World Wide Web Conference, Paris, May 1996.
5. Bickmore T. W. and Schillit B. N., Digestor: Device-independent Access to the World Wide Web, Sisth International World Wide Web Conference, Santa Clara, California, April 1997.
6. Brewer E., et al., Experience with Top Gun Wingman: A proxy-based graphical web browser for the 3Com PalmPilot, IFIP Int. Conf. On Distributed Systems Platforms and Open Distributed Procssing (Middleware 98'), pp. 407–424. Springer, Berlin
7. Pemberton S., et al., XHTML™ 1.0 The Extensible HyperText Markup Language (Second Edition), W3C Recommendation 26. January 2000, revised 1. August 2002, http://www.w3.org/TR/xhtml1/, 2002.
8. Chen J., et al., Function-Based Object Model Towards Website Adaptation, 10th World Wide Web Conference (Best Paper for the Content and Coding Session), Hong Kong, May 1–5, 2001.
9. Adler S., et al., Extensible Stylesheet Language (XSL) Version 1.0, W3C Recommendation 15. October 2001. http://www.w3c.org/TR/xsl/, 2001.
10. Ohto H., Hjelm J., CC/PP exchange protocol based on HTTP Extension Framework, W3C Note 24. June 1999. http://www.w3.org/TR/NOTE-CCPPexchange, 1999.

Efficient Evaluation in XML to XML Transformations*

Qing Wang[1], Junmei Zhou[2], Hongwei Wu[1], Yizhong Wu[1], Yang Yuan[1], and Aoying Zhou[1]

[1] Department of Computer Science and Engineering, Fudan University,
220 Handan Rd., Shanghai, China
{qingwang, hwwu, yzwu, yyang, ayzhou}@fudan.edu.cn
http://www.cs.fudan.edu.cn/indexen.jsp
[2] Shanghai R&D Institute of ZTE Corporation,
396 Guilin Rd., Shanghai, China
zhou.junmei@zte.com.cn
http://www.zte.com.cn/english/

Abstract. Different communities specify different standards (DTDs) and only those XML documents conforming to the given DTD can be processed inside a certain community. The goal of DTD-conforming XML to XML transformations with XML Transformation Grammars is to make exchanging XML documents between two communities whose DTDs are distinct feasible. However, in essence XTG evaluation is the process of executing a number of XML queries and thus this presents new challenges to query optimization. In this paper, we investigate each step of evaluating an XTG, and after modelling XML queries, we propose some optimization techniques to speed up XTG evaluation. Finally, the experimental results indicate that those techniques are efficient to XTG evaluation.

1 Introduction

With the rapid development of the Internet, XML [1] has been the prime standard format for data exchange on the Web. In practical applications, a community or industry always agrees on a certain DTD [1], and requests all members of the community to provide XML documents conforming to the DTD, such as E-commerce applications. If an XML document is exchanged from one site belonging to a community to another site which belongs to another community, the document may be converted into another one conforming to the DTD specified by the latter before it can be used.

Based on this motivation the paper of [2] proposes a very useful conception – *XML Transformation Grammar* XTG – for DTD-conforming XML to XML transformations. However, as it describes, to evaluate an XTG is the process of

---

* This work is supported by the National Natural Science Foundation of China under Grant No. 60228006 and the Fok Ying Tung Education Foundation under Grant No. 81062.

X. Zhou, Y. Zhang, and M.E. Orlowska (Eds.): APWeb 2003, LNCS 2642, pp. 108–119, 2003.

executing many XML queries associated with the production rules. Naive query submissions are expensive, therefore we describe some optimization techniques in response to this need in this paper.

To the best of our knowledge, the problem on query optimization is a popular issue and many systems, mechanisms and indices are proposed aiming at this problem. For example, in the Lore [3] system, designed specifically for managing semistructured data, includes a Lorel [4] query compilation layer which consists of a parser, a preprocessor, a query generator, and a query optimizer. All of them, as well as the indices [5,6], are used to optimize the query after compiling it. In the VXMLR [7] system the structural-map [8] is used for rewriting regular path expressions into simple path expressions, and so forth. Additionally, indices, such as the Index Fabric in the paper of [9], the F&B-Index in the paper of [10], the A(k)-index in the paper of [11], the APEX in the paper of [12] and the T-index in the paper of [13], etc, are also proposed to accelerate the query processing. Without considering indices, the paper of [14] proposes a novel bottom-up mechanism to process XPath in PTIME after investigating those traditional top-down approaches which are all EXPTIME. Besides only those which are used to optimize XML queries or XPath without back-end databases (e.g. RDB) can be used for evaluating an XTG, there are some other special techniques in the context of transformation.

More close to our work are those methods adopted in the XML-publishing systems (e.g. XPERANTO [15], SilkRoute [16] and PRATA [17]) for the purpose of efficient evaluation: the paper of [18] addresses the problem of efficiently constructing materialized XML views of relational databases and focuses on how to combine some SQL queries into a single query which specifies an XML view, and then execute the single query only to gain the best performance without having control over the target RDBMS; the paper of [17] presents materialization technique and partitioning technique when publishing relational data with the predefined DTD.

But because XML transformations present new challenges and thus demand new solutions, the optimization method for them is not the same as any previous work mentioned above.

In this paper, we address the problem of efficiently constructing cached XML fragments after investigating the steps of evaluating an XTG. Then we model the queries in an XTG as functions and the result of each function can be cached for reusing when the same function with the same parameters is invoked. We show the difference between the breadth first evaluation and the depth first evaluation when using this technique. Finally, inside a query we adopt path expansion to reduce unnecessary traversals on the XML tree, which is commonly used in many systems.

The remainder of the paper is organized as follows: section 2 reviews the conceptions on DTD and XTG, then introduces the query model and the caching mechanism during evaluating an XTG; section 3 and section 4 describe two optimization techniques at different levels – inter-query and inside-query; the performance study is given in section 5 and we summarize this paper in section 6.

2   Preliminaries

2.1   DTD

Definition 1. *A DTD is a tuple $D = (Ele, P, r)$, where:*

- *Ele is a finite set of element types;*
- *P is a set of production rules that define the element types in terms of regular expressions over $Ele \cup \{\texttt{PCDATA}\}$: for each τ in Ele, $P(\tau)$ is a regular expression α:*

$$\alpha ::= \texttt{PCDATA} \mid \tau' \mid \epsilon \mid \alpha + \alpha \mid \alpha, \alpha \mid \alpha *$$

where PCDATA denotes the string type, τ' is an element type in Ele, ϵ denotes the empty word (EMPTY), and "+"(to avoid confusion, "|" is not used here), ",", and "" denote union, concatenation and the Kleene closure, respectively.*

- *The unique label r ($\in Ele$) denotes the element type of the root, referred to as the root type.*

To simplify the discussion, we do not consider attributes in a DTD in the paper. An XML tree T conforming to D, iff 1) there is a unique node whose label is r, called the *root* of T; 2) each node in T is labeled either with an element type $\tau \in Ele$, called a τ element node, or with PCDATA, called a text node; 3) for each τ element node, the list of labels of its element children and text children can be accepted by the regular expression $P(\tau)$; 4) each text node carries a string value and is a leaf of the tree.

Taking advantage of the notion of *normal form DTD*, we add *Ety* which is a finite set of entities to D and redefine P on element types and entities such that for each τ in $Ele \cup Ety$, $P(\tau)$ has the form:

$$\alpha ::= \texttt{PCDATA} \mid \epsilon \mid \tau_1' + \ldots + \tau_n' \mid \tau_1', \ldots, \tau_n' \mid \tau' *,$$

where τ', τ_i' are in $Ele \cup Ety$ and $n \geq 1$. It is denoted by $\tau \to \alpha$. To distinguish with D, we use D' to denote the DTD in normal form after redefining.

As stated in [17], for any DTD D, a DTD D' in the normal form can be computed from D in linear time such that D and D' are *equivalent*. For example, Fig. 1 shows an example of a DTD D_0 and its normal form D_0', where **papers** and **urlnourl** are entities. The tree in Fig. 1 conforms to the DTD D_0'. And we can obtain an XML tree T conforming to D_0 by removing each entity node in T' and connecting its children to its parent repeatedly. In this paper we consider those DTDs in the normal form only.

2.2   XTG

Next we introduce XTG proposed in [2]. It is the backbone of the solution to the transformation problem, which is: given an XML document S and a target DTD D, how do we extract real data from S and construct another document T such that T conforms to D?

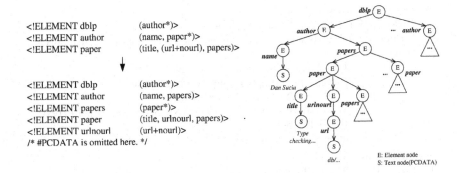

```
<!ELEMENT dblp        (author*)>
<!ELEMENT author      (name, paper*)>
<!ELEMENT paper       (title, (url+nourl), papers)>
```
                        ↓
```
<!ELEMENT dblp        (author*)>
<!ELEMENT author      (name, papers)>
<!ELEMENT papers      (paper*)>
<!ELEMENT paper       (title, urlnourl, papers)>
<!ELEMENT urlnourl    (url+nourl)>
/* #PCDATA is omitted here. */
```

Fig. 1. An example of a DTD D_0 and its normal form D_0' and an XML tree conforming to D_0'

Definition 2. *Let $D = (Ele, P, r)$ be a DTD in the normal form and S be an XML tree. An XML Transformation Grammar σ from S to D, denoted by $\sigma : S \to D$, consists of:*

- *Grammar: the DTD D.*
- *Semantic rules: if $\tau \to \alpha$ and $\tau \in Ele$, for each $\tau' \in Ele \cup \{$PCDATA$\}$ that occurs in α, there is a rule (query) that specifies how the subtree rooted at each τ' element (if $\tau' \in Ele$) or the value of each τ' (if $\tau' = $ PCDATA) is evaluated.*

To explain it clearly, we give an example first. Consider DBLP XML records as the source document and suppose that one wants to construct a target XML document T that contains all the papers coauthored by Suciu and published in 2000, along with all the papers that are cited directly or indirectly by these papers and published in or after 1995, and conforms to D_0' in Fig. 1. The XTG can be specified as follows.

dblp → author*
Q_1: $author ← LET $doc:=document("dblp.xml")
      FOR $author IN DISTINCT ($doc//author)
      WHERE CONTAINS($author, "Suciu")
      RETURN $author

author → name, papers
Q_2: $name = RETURN <name>$author/text()</name>
Q_3: $papers = <papers>
       LET $doc:=document("dblp.xml")
       FOR $inproceedings IN ($doc/inproceedings[year="2000"])
       WHERE $inproceedings/author = $author
       RETURN $inproceedings
      </papers>

papers → paper*
Q_4: $paper ← FOR $inproceedings IN ($papers/inproceedings)
      RETURN <paper>$inproceedings</paper>

paper → title, urlnourl, papers
Q_5: $title = RETURN $paper/inproceedings/title
Q_6: $urlnourl = RETURN <urlnourl>$paper/inproceedings/url</urlnourl>
Q_7: $papers =<papers>
      LET $doc:=document("dblp.xml")
      FOR $cite IN ($paper/inproceedings/cite)
      FOR $cp IN ($doc/inproceedings)
      WHERE $cp/year .>=. 1995 AND $cp/@key = $cite/text()
      RETURN $cp
     </papers>

urlnourl → url+nourl
Q_8: $url = RETURN $urlnourl/url
Q_9: $nourl = RETURN IF (NOT(EXISTS($urlnourl/url)))
      THEN <nourl>"Not available"</nourl> ELSE $urlnourl/nourl

A → PCDATA   /* A is one of name, title, url, nourl */
Q_{10}: $PCDATA = RETURN $A/text()

Observe that each query is a Quilt [19]-like query because for each query Q' from τ to τ' (we call Q' is associated with τ'), there may exist a variable $\$\tau$. Its value determined at run time is the result of the higher query, i.e. the query associated with τ.

The process of evaluating the XTG is as follows: 1) the root tagged with dblp is created first; 2) the authors are obtained by computing Q_1. Then the author elements are created in the target tree under the root dblp as its children. For each author element, it will have two children – a name element and a papers element, which are obtained by executing Q_2 and Q_3 respectively. Note that in Q_2, $author is a variable and before executing Q_2 it is given a value, which is one of subtrees rooted at author elements returned by Q_1; 3) for each papers element, it has some paper elements as its children, which are the results after executing Q_4; 4) for each paper element, the target tree continues to be expanded like this way. Observe that under each paper element, it has a papers child and under each papers, it may have some paper children, which forms a recursion. And then each papers is processed as described in 3); 5) for each urlnourl element, it may have either a url child or a nourl child but not both. The decision is made by Q_8 and Q_9: if Q_8 returns a url element, then the url element becomes the child. Otherwise, Q_9 will return a nourl element which becomes the child. To this end, it is certain that the target tree constructed in this way conforms to the DTD D_0'.

We next model each query in an XTG as a function and introduce the caching mechanism.

Definition 3. *An XML query Q is defined to be a function mapping a list of XML trees to another list of XML trees, that is, $(t_1, ..., t_n) = Q(s_1, ..., s_m)$, where $s_1, ..., s_m$ are called source trees of Q and $t_1, ..., t_n$ are called target trees of Q with the parameters $s_1, ..., s_m$.*

Note that the source forest and the target forest are order sensitive.

The query Q' associated with τ' cannot be executed directly until it is rewritten by substituting an XML tree for the variable $\$\tau$, where τ' is in $P(\tau)$. However,

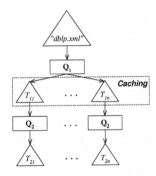

Fig. 2. An example to illustrate caching

because the XML tree is one of target trees of the higher query Q associated with τ, it is dynamically decided by Q according to source trees of Q. Hence, for Q', its source tree is unknown at compile time, referred to as *nondeterministic source tree* of Q'. On the other side, those trees which are statically embedded in the query Q' are referred to as *deterministic source trees* of Q', e.g. "dblp.xml" in Q_1. They are fixed if Q' is fixed.

For any query Q' from τ to τ' in an XTG, 1) if it is used to compute the children of the root of the target XML tree T, i.e. τ is the root type, it has no nondeterministic source tree, otherwise, it has only one nondeterministic source tree; 2) Q' outputs one target tree iff τ' is not followed by "*" in $P(\tau)$. For Q', 1) if τ is the root type, we use a triangle named as the source XML document to denote it; 2) if τ is a non-root element type and it is denoted by m $(m > 0)$ triangles named as $T_1, ..., T_m$ respectively, for each T_i, we use a rectangle named as Q' to denote the query Q' first, treat T_i as the nondeterministic source tree of Q', add the triangles of deterministic source trees of Q', and then i) if τ' is not followed by "*" in $P(\tau)$, use a triangle named as the target tree $Q'(T_i)$ to denote the element type τ', ii) or else, use a group of triangles named as the target trees $Q'(T_i)$ to denoted τ', where $Q'(T_i) = T'_1, ..., T'_n$ and $n \geq 0$. In this way, an XTG plan can be obtained.

As mentioned early, the process of evaluating an XTG is the process of executing some queries from the top down and the queries at a lower layer may use the target tree of the query at a higher layer. Therefore, the intermediate query results can be cached and reused through substituting the results for the variable in a query, which is called *caching*.

Fig. 2 depicts an example to illustrate the mechanism of caching. Q_1 is a function mapping "dblp.xml" to $T_{11}, ..., T_{1n}$, which are a bunch of authors. For each subtree T_{1i}, Q_2 is another function mapping T_{1i} to T_{2i}, where T_{2i} is the **name** subtree of T_{1i}. After the query Q_1 is executed and the **author** elements are created, the target trees $T_{11}, ..., T_{1n}$ of Q_1 are cached in the main memory. At the next stage of the evaluation, say Q_2 for creating **name** element for each author, the cached subtrees $T_{11}, ..., T_{1n}$ can be reused to get the names of those authors. As opposed to [17], to reduce the time consumption of fetching cache,

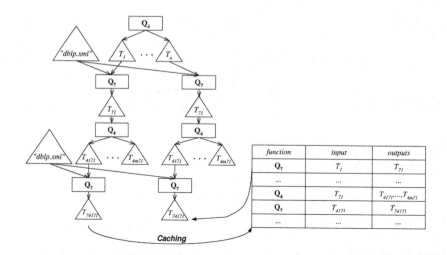

Fig. 3. An example to illustrate graph reduction

we keep the intermediate results as DOM trees in the main memory and the buffer is maintained by a swapping algorithm.

3   Graph Reduction

To reduce unnecessary repeated computations, an optimization technique *graph reduction*, which is intensively studied for functional programming, is adopted to speed up evaluating XTGs which contain recursions. The key idea is that for a function f and certain inputs $s_1, ..., s_m$, the result $f(s_1, ..., s_m)$ is cached and if f is invoked with the same parameters next time, the cached result is fetched and repeated computation is not needed.

Fig. 3 explains the theory of graph reduction. An auxiliary table which is composed of three attributes (**function**, **input** and **outputs**) is maintained in the main memory. As mentioned above, the deterministic source trees of a query are constants to the query and we maintain the nondeterministic source tree of the query only in the attribute **input**. Note that if a DOM tree needs to be cached, e.g. T_1, just the pointer pointing to the root of T_1 instead of the actual DOM tree is stored. After a query associated with an element type in a recursion is executed, its result needs to be cached. For example, if Q_7 is executed with the parameters "dblp.xml" and T_1, a record ("Q_7", "T_1", "T_{71}") is appended to the table, where T_{71} is the target tree $Q_7(T_1)$. When Q_7 will be executed again with the parameters "dblp.xml" and T_n ($= T_1$), the entry ("Q_7", "T_1") is looked up in the table first and the pointer to T_{71} is returned without any computation.

Definition 4. *Let D be the target DTD and T be the target tree conforming to D. If a tree T' is a subtree of T, denoted by $T' \subseteq T$, then T' is final.*

For example, in Fig. 1 the subtree rooted at the **author** Dan Suciu is final because it is a subtree of the target tree. The difference between a final tree and a intermediate tree (intermediate result) is that the final tree partially conforms to the target DTD and there is no query executed on it for evaluation.

Consider a query Q in an XTG plan. Q and all queries lower than Q form a sub-plan ς of the XTG plan. Give a nondeterministic source tree S_j of Q, after evaluating the sub-plan, we can obtain result trees $T_1, ..., T_n$, where T_i are all final and n is equal to the out-degree of Q. We say $T_1, ..., T_n$ are *final target trees* of the sub-plan ς with the parameter S_j. For example, the subtrees rooted at author elements under the root dblp of the target tree T (see Fig. 1) are final target trees of the sub-plan starting from Q_1 in Fig. 2 and composed of all queries Q_1–Q_{10} in the XTG.

Proposition 1. *For any query Q in an XTG plan, if two nondeterministic source trees S_j and $S_{j'}$ of Q are the same, then the final target trees of the sub-plan starting from Q with the parameter S_j are the same as those of the sub-plan with the parameter $S_{j'}$.*

As described early, the process of evaluation is a top-down approach. Hence, it is a breadth first evaluation. In this mode, for example, the target tree T can be expanded by processing Q_7 on T_i in Fig. 3 one by one: if Q_7 has not been executed on T_i before, say T_1, Q_7 must be executed and the target trees $Q_7(T_i)$ are cached, otherwise, say T_n, the pointer of the corresponding record in the auxiliary table is returned. However, for the path from T_1, Q_4 is executed on T_{71} and then the target trees $Q_4(T_{71})$ ($=T_{4171}, ..., T_{4m71}$) are cached. Later, for the path from T_n, we look up (Q_4, T_{71}) in the table and return $T_{4171}, ..., T_{4m71}$. From Proposition 1, the final target tree of the sub-plan from Q_7 with the parameter T_n is the same as that of the sub-plan with the parameter T_1. Therefore, we can evaluate the sub-plan from Q_7 with the parameter T_1 first and cache its final target tree in the table, and then fetch the cached tree directly when evaluating the same sub-plan with the parameter T_n. This depth first evaluation reduces the time consumption of frequent lookup and swapping in the memory, especially when the recursion is too deep. We adopt the depth first mode during evaluation.

Proposition 2. *For a sub-plan ς from a query Q and another sub-sub-plan ς' from a query Q' where Q' is a query in the sub-plan ς, given a nondeterministic source tree S_j of Q and a nondeterministic source tree $S_{j'}$ of Q', each final target tree $T'_{i'}$ of ς' with the parameter $S_{j'}$ is a subtree of T_i, where T_i is one of the final target trees of ς with the parameter S_j. That is, $T'_{i'} \subseteq T_i$.*

For example, in Fig. 1, given the sub-plan ς starting from Q_3 and the sub-sub-plan ς' from Q_7, the final target tree of ς' is a subtree of the final target tree of ς with the parameter S_j, where S_j is the tree rooted at the author element "Dan Suciu" after executing Q_1. It is shown in Fig. 4 (b) and (c).

According to Proposition 2, there is only one copy kept in the memory for each final target tree of a sub-plan and those of the sub-sub-plans are not maintained. The pointers are all stored in the attribute outputs of the table. Adopting the depth first evaluation, the mechanism of Fig. 3 is changed into Fig. 5.

4   Path Expansion

Quilt queries heavily use XPath expressions, which are major cost of XTG evaluation. To reduce the cost, an auxiliary structure is maintained in advance and

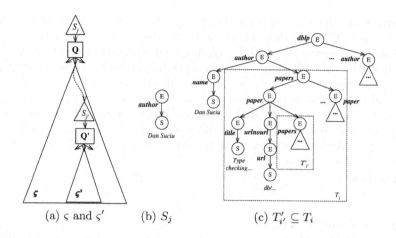

(a) ς and ς'   (b) S_j (c) $T'_{i'} \subseteq T_i$

Fig. 4. An example to illustrate Proposition 2

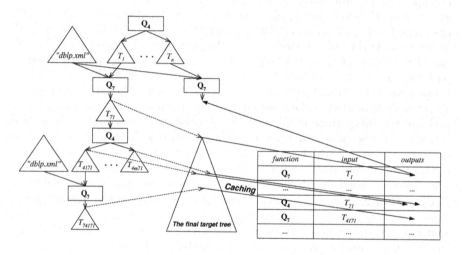

Fig. 5. Using the depth first evaluation in graph reduction

serves as an index for the queries. Given the source document S, it is parsed and concrete (simple) paths are extracted from it and stored into the auxiliary structure. After a query is submitted and before executed, the XPath expressions in it are rewritten by substituting concrete paths for expensive traversals "//" (descendant). This inside-query technique is done at compile time, referred to as *path expansion*.

When the DTD of the source document is available, the DTD can be used for certain expansions without looking into the source document. However, if the DTD contains recursion, the actual depth of the recursion is not known by parsing the DTD only and thus the source document is used.

startstep	endstep	path
dblp	author	article, inproceedings, ...
dblp	cite	article, inproceedings, ...
dblp	title	article, inproceedings, ...
...	...	...

(a) paths starting from `dblp`

startstep	endstep	path
article	author	NULL
article	cite	NULL
article	title	NULL
...	...	...

(b) paths starting from `article`

startstep	endstep	path
inproceedings	author	NULL
inproceedings	cite	NULL
inproceedings	title	NULL
...	...	...

(c) paths starting from `inproceedings`

Fig. 6. Structural maps for path expansion

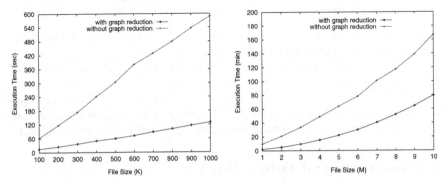

Fig. 7. Benefits of graph reduction

For example, the DTD "dblp.dtd" is parsed and some tables in Fig. 6 are created. In order to locate the right record in the table quickly, the records are classified according to the attribute startstep and each table is sorted alphabetically by the attribute endstep. Suppose Q_1 is submitted. The XPath "\$doc//author" can be rewritten into "\$doc/article/author | \$doc/inproceedings/author | ...".

5   Performance

We next present some preliminary experimental results, which demonstrate that our optimization techniques – graph reduction and path expansion – are effective.

Our experiments were conducted on a 1.8GHz Pentium 4 machine with 40G of hard disk and 512MB of main memory running Windows 2000. We adopted a variant of DBLP XML records presented earlier as source XML documents. Those XML fragments with different sizes for experiments are extracted from "dblp.xml". We used some XTGs similar to the one described in Section 2.2.

Fig. 7 depicts the impact of graph reduction as a function of the source document size. Here graph reduction is in the depth first evaluation mode. We evaluated the XTG both with and without graph reduction. The execution time measures the time from loading the XTG file until the target XML document T is generated. The experimental results indicate that graph reduction can speed

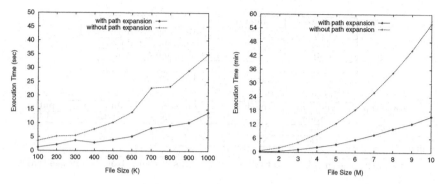

Fig. 8. Benefits of path expansion

up the evaluation by a factor of up to 9.6. The benefit of the technique is more evident when the size of the source document increases.

The next experiment demonstrates the benefit of path expansion: the XTG was evaluated both with and without path expansion. The results, shown in Fig. 8, tell us that path expansion can reduce the traversing time and improve the performance by a factor of up to 4.5. Better still, as the size of the source document increases, the benefit of path expansion becomes more significant.

6   Conclusion and Future Work

In this paper, we have addressed the problem of efficiently constructing cached XML fragments when evaluating an XTG for XML to XML transformation. Through modelling a query in the XTG, an XTG plan can be obtained from the XTG dynamically. By analyzing each step of evaluation, we can mainly propose some special optimization techniques to speed up the process. The inter-query technique graph reduction is efficient to the situation that there exist recursions in the XTG because some queries are executed many times with the same inputs. And the inside-query technique path expansion processes "//" in a query. It reduces the unnecessary traversals. Preliminary performance study shows the effect of those techniques is significant to evaluation, especially when the source XML document is large. The issue on XML to XML transformations also arouses some other interesting optimization issues, e.g., whether node IDs rather than fragments can be cached, whether indices for internal XPath are constructed, and how to compose some queries in an XTG into a single query in order to reduce traffic to the query processor, etc.

References

1. Bray, T., Paoli, J., Sperberg-McQueen, C.M.: Extensible Markup Language (XML) 1.0. W3C Recommendation (1998). http://www.w3.org/TR/REC-xml/
2. Zhou, A., Wang, Q., Guo, Z., Gong, X., Zheng, S., Wu, H., Xiao, J., Yue, K., Fan, W.: TREX: DTD-Conforming XML to XML Transformations. In: Proc. of ACM SIGMOD Conf. on Management of Data (2003). To be appeared.

3. McHugh, J., Abiteboul, S., Goldman, R., Quass, D., Widom, J.: Lore: A database management system for semistructured data. SIGMOD Record, Vol. 26 No. 3 (1997)
4. Abiteboul, S., Quass, D., McHugh, J., Widom, J., Wiener, J.L.: The Lorel query language for semistructured data. Int. J. Digit. Libr. 1 (1997) 68–88
5. McHugh, J., Widom, J., Abiteboul, S., Luo, Q., Rajaraman, A.: Indexing semistructured data. Technical report, Standford University (1997)
6. Goldman, R., Widom, J.: Dataguides: Enabling query formulation and optimization in semistructured databases. In: Proc. of Int'l Conf. on Very Large Databases (1997)
7. Zhou, A., Lu, H., Zheng, S., Liang, Y., Zhang, L., Ji, W., Tian, Z.: VXMLR: A Visual XML-Relational Database System. In: Proc. of Int'l Conf. on Very Large Databases (2001)
8. Zheng, S., Zhou, A., Yu, J.X., Zhang, L., Tao, H.: Structural-map: A new index for xml path expression query processing. In: Proc. of Int'l Conf. on Web Age Information Management (2002)
9. Cooper, B.F., Sample, N., Franklin, M.J., Hjaltason, G.R., Shadmon, M.: A fast index for semistructured data. In: Proc. of Int'l Conf. on Very Large Databases (2001)
10. Kaushik, R., Bohannon, P., Naughton, J.F., Korth, H.F.: Covering indexes for branching path queries. In: Proc. of ACM SIGMOD Conf. on Management of Data (2002)
11. Kaushik, R., Shenoy, P., Bohannon, P., Gudes, E.: Exploiting local similarity for indexing paths in graph-structured data. In: Proc. of IEEE Int'l Conf. on Data Engineering (2002)
12. Chung, C.-W., Min, J.-K., Shim, K.: Apex: An adaptive path index for xml data. In: Proc. of ACM SIGMOD Conf. on Management of Data (2002)
13. Milo, T., Suciu, D.: Index structures for path expressions. In: Proc. of Int'l Conf. on Database Theory (1999)
14. Gottlob, G., Koch, C., Pichler, R.: Efficient algorithms for processing xpath queries. In: Proc. of Int'l Conf. on Very Large Databases (2002)
15. Carey, M.J., Florescu, D., Ives, Z.G., Lu, Y., Shanmugasundaram, J., Shekita, E.J., Subramanian, S.N.: XPERANTO: Publishing object-relational data as XML. In: WebDB (2000) 105–110
16. Fernandez, M.F., Tan, W., Suciu, D.: SilkRoute: Trading between relations and XML. In: Proc. of Int'l World Wide Web Conf (2000)
17. Benedikt, M., Chan, C.Y., Fan, W., Rastogi, R., Zheng, S., Zhou, A.: DTD-directed publishing with attribute translation grammars. In: Proc. of Int'l Conf. on Very Large Databases (2002)
18. Fernandez, M.F., Morishima, A., Suciu, D.: Efficient evaluation of XML middleware queries. In: Proc. of ACM SIGMOD Conf. on Management of Data (2001) 103–114
19. Chamberlin, D., Robie, J., Florescu, D.: Quilt: An XML query language for heterogeneous data sources. In: WebDB (2000) 53–62

Formalizing Semantics of XSLT Using Object-Z

Hong Li Yang[1,3*], Jin Song Dong[2], Ke Gang Hao[1], and Jun Gang Han[3]

[1] Department of Computer Science
Northwest University, Xi'an China
yanghon1@hotmail.com
hkg@nwu.edu.cn
[2] School of Computing,
National University of Singapore,
dongjs@comp.nus.edu.sg
[3] Department of Computer Science
University of Xi'an Post & Telecomm. China
hjg@xiyou.edu.cn

Abstract. In this paper, a formal object-oriented semantic model for XSLT in Object-Z is presented. The semantic model is constructed based on XSLT's W3C Working Draft (August 2002). Formal description of XSLT language can provide deeper understanding of the language and support the standardisation effort for XSLT. All XSLT language constructs are modeled as Object-Z classes and the XSLT stylesheet itself is also specified by a formal class. This highly structured semantic model is concise, composable and extensible.

1 Introduction

Formal models of programming languages support language understanding and standardisation, program reasoning and software reliability. The Extensible Stylesheet Language Transformation (XSLT) [2] is a language for transforming XML[8] documents to other XML documents. It is one of the core technologies in XML. It is desirable to have a full complete formal semantic model for XSLT.

The semantics of XSLT has been described in natural language with examples [2]. There are some recent work in the research of the semantics of XML related technologies. For instance, Wadler [9] has presented a formal semantics of the patterns using traditional denotational semantics and a formal semantics of the path expressions using judgements and inference rules are also defined in [6]. We are interested in presenting a more complete and highly structured formal semantic model for the XSLT language based on the object-oriented views of programming language semantics [3,4].

In this paper, Object-Z[5] is used as the meta language for presenting the XSLT semantics. All XSLT language constructs such as expressions, patterns, content constructors, instructions, templates and stylesheet, are specified as

---

* This paper was written during the first author's visit to the School of Computing of National University of Singapore as part of the UNU/IIST Fellowship Programme.

X. Zhou, Y. Zhang, and M.E. Orlowska (Eds.): APWeb 2003, LNCS 2642, pp. 120–131, 2003.

Object-Z classes. This highly structured semantic model is concise, composable and reusable.

The remainder of this paper is organized as follows: Section 2 presents the data model of XML document. Section 3 presents the semantics of expressions. Section 4 presents the semantics of instructions. Section 5 presents the semantics of templates and stylesheets. Section 6 concludes the paper.

2   Data Model of XML Document

The data model used by XSLT is the same as that used by XPath [1].

Firstly, the character sets are defined as a Z free type definition

$$Char ::= \text{`a'} \mid \text{`b'} \mid \cdots \mid \text{`A'} \mid \text{`B'} \mid \cdots \mid \text{`1'} \mid \text{`2'} \mid \cdots \mid \text{`\_'} \mid \text{`:'} \mid \text{`-'} \mid \text{`.'} \mid \cdots$$

The *String* type is defined as a sequence of characters:

$$String == \text{seq } Char$$

An empty string is defined as a constant *empty*.

$$\begin{array}{|l}
empty : String \\
\hline
empty = \langle\,\rangle
\end{array}$$

An XML name is a special kind of string: it must be non-empty, its first character must be a letter, an underscore or a colon, and the remaining characters can be letters, digits, a hyphen, an underscore, a colon or a period. Here we define the *QName* as a subset of *String* which subjects to those constraints.

$$QName == \{s : String \mid \#s > 0 \wedge \text{head } s \in \{\text{`a'}, \text{`b'}, \cdots, \text{`A'}, \text{`B'}, \cdots, \text{`\_'}, \text{`:'}\} \wedge$$
$$\text{ran } s \subseteq \{\text{`a'}, \text{`b'}, \cdots, \text{`A'}, \text{`B'}, \cdots, \text{`1'}, \text{`2'}, \cdots, \text{`\_'}, \text{`:'}, \text{`-'}, \text{`.'}\}\}$$

The basic datatype is *Node*. Each node is one of seven kinds: document, element, attribute, text, comment, processing instruction, namespace. The node type is defined as Z free type definition.

$$\begin{aligned}
nodeType ::=\ & docType \mid elemType \mid attrType \\
& \mid textType \mid commType \mid piType \mid nmType
\end{aligned}$$

A *Node* object contains a node type, *type*, a node name, *name*, a node value, *value*, a node parent, *parent*, a sequence of children nodes, *children*, a sequence of attribute nodes, *attribute*, a sequence of namespace nodes, *namespace*. In addition, the secondary attribute *doc* is a document node. *descend* is a sequence of descendant nodes. *ancestor* is a sequence of ancestor nodes. There are several laws related with these attributes which has been captured by the class invariants. For example, the names of root node, text node and comment node are empty string. Only a document or element node can have children. Each child is either an element node, text node, comment node or processing instruction node. Only element nodes may have related attribute nodes and namespace nodes.

```
┌─ Node ─────────────────────────────────────────────────────┐
│  ┌──────────────────────────────────────────────────────┐  │
│  │ type : nodeType                                       │  │
│  │ name : QName                                          │  │
│  │ value : String                                        │  │
│  │ parent : Node                                         │  │
│  │ children, attribute, namespace : seq Node             │  │
│  │ Δ                                                     │  │
│  │ doc : Node                                            │  │
│  │ descend, ancestor : seq Node                          │  │
│  ├──────────────────────────────────────────────────────┤  │
│  │ ∀ x, y : Node •                                       │  │
│  │   x.type ∈ {docType, textType, commType} ⟹ x.name = empty │
│  │   y ∈ ran x.children ⟹ y.type ∈ {elemType, textType, commType, piType} │
│  │   y = x.parent ⟹ y.type ∈ {elemType, docType}        │  │
│  │   y ∈ ran x.attribute ⟹ y.type = attrType ∧ x.type = elemType │
│  │   y ∈ ran x.namespace ⟹ y.type = nmType ∧ x.type = elemType │
│  │   y = x.doc ⟹ y.type = docType                        │  │
│  │   y ∈ ran x.descend ⟹ y ∈ ran x.children ∨           │  │
│  │       ∃ z : Node • z ∈ ran x.descend ∧ y ∈ ran z.descend │
│  │   y ∈ ran x.ancestor ⟹ y = x.parent ∨                │  │
│  │       ∃ z : Node • z ∈ ran x.ancestor ∧ y ∈ ran z.ancestor │
│  └──────────────────────────────────────────────────────┘  │
└────────────────────────────────────────────────────────────┘
```

3 Semantics of Expressions

An expression is either a number-expression, a string-expression, a bool-expression, a path-expression or a variable reference.

The type of expressions are defined as scalar types $ScalType$

$$ScalType ::= numType \mid strType \mid boolType \mid nodesType$$

The value of an expression can be either real, string, boolean or sequence of nodes. The set of scalar values is defined using the free-value construct.

$$ScalVal ::= numval\langle\!\langle \mathbb{R} \rangle\!\rangle \mid strval\langle\!\langle String \rangle\!\rangle \mid boolval\langle\!\langle \mathbb{B} \rangle\!\rangle \mid nodesval\langle\!\langle seq\ Node \rangle\!\rangle$$

The function $type\_of$ returns the type of an expression value.

```
┌──────────────────────────────────────────────────────────────┐
│ type_of : ScalVal → ScalType                                 │
├──────────────────────────────────────────────────────────────┤
│ ∀ n : ℝ; st : String; b : 𝔹; ns : seq Node •                 │
│   type_of(numval(n)) = numType ∧ type_of(strval(st)) = strType │
│   type_of(boolval(b)) = boolType ∧ type_of(nodesval(ns)) = nodesType │
```

The class *Exp* is defined as class union.

$$Exp \;\hat{=}\; numExp \cup strExp \cup boolExp \cup pathExp \cup Varef$$

The common properties of all expressions are specified as class *baseExp*.

```
┌─ baseExp ──────────────────────────────────────────────────────────────
│   ┌──────────────────────────────┐   ┌─ outVal ──────────────────┐
│   │  type : ScalType             │   │  val! : ScalVal           │
│   │  Δ                           │   ├───────────────────────────┤
│   │  context : Node              │   │  val! = val               │
│   │  val : ScalVal               │   └───────────────────────────┘
│   ├──────────────────────────────┤
│   │  type_of(val) = type         │
│   └──────────────────────────────┘
└────────────────────────────────────────────────────────────────────────
```

The path expression class *Path* requires the definition of the class *Step*, which represents step expressions.

Firstly, the type *Axis* is defined as a free type definition

$$Axis \;::=\; child \mid desc \mid attr \mid self \mid desOrself \mid followSib \mid$$
$$follow \mid nmsp \mid parent \mid ance \mid preSib \mid preced \mid ancOrself$$

The type *Test* is defined as a free type definition

$$Test \;::=\; text \mid comm \mid pi \mid nd \mid qnm\langle\!\langle QName \rangle\!\rangle$$

The type *Pred* is simply defined as *Exp* type.

$$Pred == Exp$$

A step expression consists of an axis to express the relationship between the context node and the nodes to be selected, a node test, to actually specifies what is to be selected, and optionally, predicates, which filters the nodes selected by the node test. A step expression is defined as an object of class *Step*. A path expression contains a sequence of step expressions. It is defined as an object of class *Path*.

The function *evalStep* is defined to evaluate a step expression. Function *evalPath* is defined to evaluate a path expression.

```
│  evalStep : Node × Axis × Test × Pred → seq Node
│  evalPath : Node × seq Step → seq Node
```

```
┌─ Step ────────────────────────────┐   ┌─ Path ───────────────────────────┐
│  baseExp                          │   │  baseExp                         │
│  ─────────────────────────────    │   │  ──────────────────────────      │
│  axis : Axis                      │   │  steps : seq Step                │
│  test : Test                      │   │  ──────────────────────────      │
│  pred : Pred                      │   │  type = nodesType                │
│  ─────────────────────────────    │   │  val = evalPath(context, steps)  │
│  type = nodesType                 │   └──────────────────────────────────┘
│  val = evalStep(context, axis, test, pred) │
└───────────────────────────────────┘
```

A pattern is a specific path expression. Each step in a pattern is constrained to use only the *child* or *attr* axis. The class *Patt* is defined by inheriting class *Path*.

$$\begin{array}{|l}
\underline{\;Patt\;} \rule{4cm}{0pt} \\
\hline
Path \\
\hline
\forall\, sp : Step \bullet sp \in \text{ran } steps \Rightarrow \\
\quad sp.axis = child \vee sp.axis = attr \\
\hline
\end{array}$$

$$\begin{array}{|l}
\underline{\;base\,VarLoc\;} \rule{3cm}{0pt} \\
\hline
type : ScalType \\
cont : ScalVal \\
\hline
type\_of(cont) = type \\
\hline
\end{array}$$

There are two elements in XSLT that can be used to bind variables: variable and parameter. The variable reference class *Varef* requires the definition of the class *VarLoc*, which represents variable locations. A variable was given initial value by two ways: evaluating result of an expression or a content constructor. The *VarLoc* is defined as class union. The common attributes of *VarLoc* are defined as class *baseValLoc*.

$$VarLoc \,\hat{=}\, selVarLoc \cup conVarLoc$$

The class *selVarLoc* specifies the initial value of a variable as the evaluating result of contained expression. The class *conVarLoc* specifies the initial value of a variable as the evaluating result of contained constructor. Where *Cons* class is defined in section 4.

$$\begin{array}{|l}
\underline{\;selVarLoc\;} \rule{3cm}{0pt} \\
\hline
baseVarLoc \\
\hline
sel : Exp \\
\hline
\underline{\;\text{INIT}\;} \\
type = sel.type \\
cont = sel.val \\
\hline
\end{array}$$

$$\begin{array}{|l}
\underline{\;conVarLoc\;} \rule{3cm}{0pt} \\
\hline
baseVarLoc \\
\hline
content : Cons \\
\hline
\underline{\;\text{INIT}\;} \\
type = nodesType \\
cont = content.val \\
\hline
\end{array}$$

A variable reference object contains an identified name(nm) and a reference(vl) to a *VarLoc* object. The class *Varef* is specified by inheriting class *baseExp*. There is no assignment operation to class *Varef*. Once a variable has been given a value, the value cannot subsequently be changed. The parameter reference class *Paref* extends the definition of class *Varef* to have additional operations *OutLoc* and *ReLoc* to facilitate the specification of reference parameter substitutions in a calling template instruction which is defined in section 4.

$$
\begin{array}{|l}
\hline \; Varef \underline{\hspace{4cm}} \\
\hline \begin{array}{|l} \hline BaseExp \\ \hline nm : QName \\ vl : VarLoc \\ \hline type = vl.type \\ val = vl.cont \\ \hline \end{array} \\
\hline
\end{array}
$$

$$
\begin{array}{|l}
\hline \; Paref \underline{\hspace{4cm}} \\
\hline Varef \\
\begin{array}{|l} \hline ReLoc \underline{\hspace{1cm}} \\ \hline \Delta(vl) \\ vl? : VarLoc \\ \hline vl' = vl? \\ \hline \end{array}
\begin{array}{|l} \hline outLoc \underline{\hspace{1cm}} \\ \hline vl! : VarLoc \\ \hline vl! = vl \\ \hline \end{array} \\
\hline
\end{array}
$$

4   The Semantics of Instructions

The instructions in XSLT can be classified as either constructor instructions or other instructions such as value_of instruction, copy_of instruction, choose instruction, applying template instruction and calling template instruction. The instruction class *Ins* is specified as class union.

$$Ins \;\widehat{=}\; ContIns \cup ValueofIns \cup CopyofIns \cup ChooseIns \cup AppIns \cup CallIns$$

The common properties of all instructions can be modelled as class *baseIns*.

$$
\begin{array}{|l}
\hline \; baseIns \underline{\hspace{6cm}} \\
\hline \begin{array}{l} context : Node \\ \Delta \\ val : seq\ Node \end{array} \\
\hline
\end{array}
$$

A content constructor instruction is either a creating instruction, shallow copy instruction, repeating instruction or conditional instruction. The class *ContIns* is specified as class union.

$$
\begin{aligned}
ContIns \;\widehat{=}\; & CreAttrIns \cup CreCommIns \cup CreElemIns \cup CreTextIns\cup \\
& CreNmsIns \cup CrePiIns \cup CopyIns \cup RepIns \cup IfIns
\end{aligned}
$$

The *ContIns* class requires the definition of the class *Cons* and the class *Module*. The class *Cons* represents content constructors. It consists of a sequence of instructions, which are evaluated to produce a sequence of nodes. The function *evalIns* is defined to evaluate a sequence of instructions.

$$
\begin{array}{|l}
\hline \; Cons \underline{\hspace{4cm}} \\
\hline \begin{array}{l} ins : seq\ Ins \\ \Delta \\ context : Node \\ val : seq\ Node \\ \hline \forall\, x : Ins \bullet x \in ran\ ins \Rightarrow \\ \quad x.context = context \\ val = evalIns(ins) \end{array} \\
\hline
\end{array}
$$

$$
\begin{array}{|l}
\hline \; baseContIns \underline{\hspace{3cm}} \\
\hline Module \\
\begin{array}{l} cont : Cons \\ parent : Template \cup StySheet \\ \Delta \\ val : seq\ Node \\ \hline cont.context = context \\ vscope = parent.vscope \oplus vdecs \end{array} \\
\hline
\end{array}
$$

The class *Module* consists of variable declarations *vdecs*, a list of local variable references *lvars*, and additionally, secondary attributes *vscope* and *context*.

___ *Module* _____

$vdecs : QName \rightarrowtail VarLoc_{\circledcirc}$
$lvars : \text{seq } Varef_{\circledS}$
Δ
$vscope : QName \rightarrowtail VarLoc$
$context : Node$

$\#\{v : (Varef \cap scontain) \bullet v.nm\} = \#(Varef \cap scontain)$
$\hfill$ [pred1]
$\{vr : (Varef \cap scontain) \bullet vr.nm \mapsto vr.vl\} \subseteq vscope$ $\hfill$ [pred2]

Where the notation '$_\circledcirc$' is used to specify the local scope of each variable. The notation '$_\circledS$' is a syntactic simplification identifying the directly contained but sharable objects.

The attribute *vdecs* is one-one mappings from identified name to variable locations. The whole scope of a module is specified by the value of the secondary variables, *vscope*. The precise meaning of this variable depends on whether the module is inherited as either an instruction, a template or a stylesheet; therefore only the signature of the *vscope* appears in the class *Module*.

The class invariant *pred1* specifies that there are no two distinct variables having the same name in a module. The predicate *pred2* specifies that applied occurrences of the variables are bounded in the scope.

The common properties of all content constructor instructions are specified as class *baseContIns*, which is defined by inheriting class *Module*. In addition, it consists of a content constructor, *cont*, a parent template or stylesheet, *parent*, and a secondary attribute, *val*. The invariant specifies that the whole access scope of an instruction is the scope of parent template or stylesheet overridden by the local variable declarations.

An instruction which creates either a text node, a comment node, an attribute node, a processing instruction node or a namespace node, returns a newly created node. The common properties of these instructions are modelled as class *baseCreIns*. Where *catVal* function is specified to concatenate the string value of sequence of text nodes, to form a single string.

$\mid$ $catVal : \text{seq } Node \rightarrow String$

___ *baseCreIns* _____
baseContIns

$\#val = 1$
$cont.val = \langle \, \rangle \Rightarrow val(1).value = empty$
$cont.val \neq \langle \, \rangle \Rightarrow val(1).value = catVal(cont.val)$

The creating element instruction class *CreElemIns* is defined by inheriting the class *baseContIns*. In addition, it contains a name property, *nm*, which is the name of created element node. The *create* function is defined to create a new element node.

$$create : QName \times \text{seq } Node \rightarrow Node$$

─── *CreElemIns* ─────────────
baseContIns
─────────────────────
nm : QName
─────────────────────
#val = 1
val(1).type = elemType
val(1) = create(nm, cont.val)

─── *ValueofIns* ─────────────
baseIns
─────────────────────
sel : Exp
─────────────────────
#val = 1 \land sel.type = strType
val(1).type = textType
val(1).value = sel.val

A *value_of* instruction is evaluated to construct a new text node. The value of new node is the evaluating result of contained expression. The class *ValueofIns* is defined by inheriting class *baseIns*.

The copy instruction provides an easy way of copying the context item. The function *shwCopy* is defined to shallow copy a node.

$$shwCopy : Node \times Cons \rightarrow \text{seq } Node$$

Function *copy* is defined to deeply copy a node.

$$copy : Node \rightarrow \text{seq } Node$$

Function *deepCopy* is defined to deeply copy a sequence of nodes.

$$deepCopy : \text{seq } Node \rightarrow \text{seq } Node$$

A *copy* instruction is modelled as an object of the class *CopyIns*, which inherits the class *baseContIns*. A *copy_of* instruction object contains a path expression, *sel*, which is evaluated to produce a sequence of nodes to be copied. The class *CopyofIns* is defined by inheriting the class *baseIns*.

─── *CopyIns* ─────────────
baseContIns
─────────────────────
val = shwCopy(context, cont)

─── *CopyofIns* ─────────────
baseIns
─────────────────────
sel : Path
─────────────────────
val = deepCopy(sel.val)

There are two kinds of instructions in XSLT that support conditional processing in a template. An *if* instruction provides simple if-then conditionality.

```
┌─ IfIns ──────────────────────────────────────────────
│ baseContIns
│ ┌───────────────────────────────────────────────────
│ │ test : Exp
│ │ ─────────────────────────────────────────────────
│ │ test.type = boolType
│ │ boolval(test.val) ⇒ val = cont.val
│ │ ¬ boolval(test.val) ⇒ val = ⟨ ⟩
└─┴───────────────────────────────────────────────────
```

A *choose* instruction contains a sequence of *if* instructions, *wh*, and a content constructor, *th*. The class *ChooseIns* is defined by inheriting the class *baseIns*.

```
┌─ ChooseIns ──────────────────────────────────────────
│ baseIns
│ ┌───────────────────────────────────────────────────
│ │ wh : seq IfIns
│ │ th : Cons
│ │ ─────────────────────────────────────────────────
│ │ th.context = context
│ │ (∃ i : 1 .. #wh • boolval(wh(i).te.val)) ⇒ val = wh(i).cont.val
│ │ (∄ i : 1 .. #wh • boolval(wh(i).te.val)) ⇒ val = th.val
└─┴───────────────────────────────────────────────────
```

A *repeat* instruction contains a path expression, *sel*, and a content constructor, *cont*. The function *rep* is defined to evaluate a content constructor for each node in a sequence.

$$rep : seq\, Node \times Cons \to seq\, Node$$

An *apply_templates* instruction contains a path expression, *sel*, which is evaluated to produce a sequence of nodes. The *app* function is defined to find a matched template for each node in the sequence, then evaluate the chosen template rules and return a resulting sequence of nodes.

$$app : seq\, Node \to seq\, Node$$

```
┌─ RepIns ─────────────────────────┐   ┌─ AppIns ─────────────────────────┐
│ baseContIns                      │   │ baseIns                          │
│ ┌───────────────────────────────┐│   │ ┌───────────────────────────────┐│
│ │ sel : Path                    ││   │ │ sel : Path                    ││
│ │ ──────────────────────────────││   │ │ ──────────────────────────────││
│ │ val = repeat(sel.val, cont)   ││   │ │ val = app(sel.val)            ││
└─┴───────────────────────────────┘┘   └─┴───────────────────────────────┘┘
```

A *CallIns* instruction object contains a template reference, tr, and an actual reference parameter list, $arpl$. A template reference object contains a name, nm and a template, tem.

Teref _____

> $nm : QName$
> $tem : Template$

CallIns _____

> *baseIns*
> _____
>
> $tr : Teref_{\circledS}$
> $arpl : \text{seq } Paref_{\circledS}$
> _____
>
> $\#arpl = \#tr.tem.frpl$ [pred1]
> $\forall j : \text{dom } arpl \bullet arpl(j).type = tr.tem.frpl(j).type$ [pred2]
> $tr.context = context$
> $val = tr.tem.val$
> _____
>
> $RefSubs \mathrel{\widehat{=}} \wedge\ i : \text{dom } arpl \bullet arpl(i).outLoc \parallel tr.tem.frpl(i).ReLoc$

The invariant $pred1$ specifies that the length of the actual parameter list from a call instruction is equal to length of the formal parameter list of the called template. The predicate $pred2$ specifies that the type of an actual parameter matches to the type of the corresponding formal parameter. The result value of the instruction is the value of referenced template. The operation *RefSubs* represents the relocation of the parameter location(vl) of the reference parameters.

5   Semantics of Templates and Stylesheets

The template class *Template* is defined by inheriting class *Module*, and therefore contains all the information which is specified in the class *Module*. In addition, a *Template* object consists of a pattern pat, a content constructor, $cont$, a stylesheet parent, $parent$, a formal reference parameter list, $frpl$, and a secondary attribute val. The function *match* is defined to check if a node matches a pattern.

> $match : Node \times Pattern \to \mathbb{B}$

```
┌─ Template ──────────────────────────────────────────────────
│ Module
│ ┌──────────────────────────────────────────────────────────
│ │ frpl : seq Paref_⑤
│ │ pat : Patt
│ │ cont : Cons
│ │ parent : StySheet
│ │ Δ
│ │ val : seq Node
│ ├──────────────────────────────────────────────────────────
│ │ val = cont.val
│ │ match(context, pat)                                  [pred1]
│ │ vscope = parent.vscope ⊕ (vdecs ∪ {vr : ran frpl • vr.nm ↦ vr.vl})
│ │                                                       [pred2]
│ │ #{vr : ran(lvars ∪ frpl) • vr.nm} = #lvars + #frpl    [pred3]
│ └──────────────────────────────────────────────────────────
└──────────────────────────────────────────────────────────────
```

The state invariant $pred1$ specifies that the context node of a template matches the pattern of the template. Predicate $pred2$ specifies that the whole access scope of a template is the scope of the parent stylesheet overridden by the local variable and parameter declarations. Predicate $pred3$ specifies that any two different local parameters or variables have different identified names.

```
┌─ StySheet ──────────────────────────────────────────────────
│ Module
│ ┌──────────────────────────────┐ ┌─ modify ──────────────────
│ │ ts : seq Template            │ │ Δ(result)
│ │ source : Node                │ │
│ │ Δ                            │ │ result'.children = find(context).val
│ │ result : Node                │ │ result'.type = docType
│ ├──────────────────────────────┘ └───────────────────────────
│ │ vscope = vdecs
│ │ source.type = docType ∧ context = source
│ │ result.type = docType ∧ result.children = ⟨ ⟩
│ └──────────────────────────────
└──────────────────────────────────────────────────────────────
```

The stylesheet class $StySheet$ is defined by inheriting class $Module$. In addition, it contains a template list, ts, a source document node $source$, and a secondary attribute $result$, which is a result document node. The $find$ function is defined to return the matched template of a node.

$$| \quad find : Node \rightarrow Template$$

The whole access scope of a stylesheet is the scope of the global variable declarations. For simplicities, we only consider a simple transformation of a single stylesheet document. It is convenient to set both the initial input sequence and the initial context node to the document node of the source document to be transformed. The operation *modify* is defined to modify the implicitly created result document node with new evaluated children.

6   Conclusion

In this paper, the formal semantics of XSLT has been specified by using the Object-Z notation. A uniform semantic view, the Object-Z class view, has been taken to model all XSLT language constructs, i.e., patterns, content constructors, templates and stylesheet. This highly structured semantic model is concise, composable and reusable. The semantic model has also used Object-Z inheritance to present an incremental formal description. One interesting aspect is that Object-Z itself has an XML environment [7] which supports automatic expansion of Object-Z inheritance and generation of UML diagrams. With this tool, the formal semantic model for XSLT can be studied and understood more readily and visually.

One research direction will be to model common semantic constructs of all XML related languages as a semantic library, and then to reuse this library to specify the semantics of all those XML related languages. One interesting aspect is that Object-Z itself has an XML environment [7] which support automatic expansion of Object-Z inheritance.

Acknowledgements. We would like to thank Adnan Sherif, Neil Loughran and and anonymous referees for many helpful comments. This work is supported by the UNU/IIST fellowship programme.

References

1. Scott Boag etc. Anders Berglund. *XML Path Language (XPath) 2.0*, 2002. http://www.w3.org/TR/xpath20/.
2. James Clark. *XSL Transformations (XSLT) Version 2.0*, 2002. http://www.w3.org/TR/xslt20/.
3. J. S. Dong. *Formal Object Modelling Techniques and Denotational Semantics Studies*. PhD thesis, University of Queensland, 1995.
4. J. S. Dong, R. Duke, and G. Rose. An object-oriented approach to the semantics of programming languages. *Australian Computer Science Communications*, 16, 1994.
5. R. Duke and G. Rose. *Formal Object Oriented Specification Using Object-Z*. Macmillan, 2000.
6. Denise Draper etc. *XQuery 1.0 and XPath 2.0 Formal Semantics*, 2002. http://www.w3.org/TR/query-semantics/.
7. J. Sun, J. S. Dong, J. Liu, and H. Wang. Object-Z Web Environment and Projections to UML. In *WWW-10: 10th International World Wide Web Conference, refereed papers track*, pages 725–734. ACM Press, May 2001.
8. C. M. Sperberg-McQueen Tim Bray, Jean Paoli. *Extensible Markup Language (XML) 1.0 (Second Edition)*, 2000. http://www.w3.org/TR/REC-xml/.
9. P. Wadler. *A formal semantics of patterns in XSLT, Markup Languages, MIT Press*, June 2001.

An XML-Based Context-Aware Transformation Framework for Mobile Execution Environments

Tzu-Han Kao[1], Sheng-Po Shen[1], Shyan-Ming Yuan[1], and Po-Wen Cheng[2]

[1] Department of Computer and Information Science, National Chiao Tung University,
1001 Ta Hsueh Rd., Hsinchu 300, Taiwan.
{gis89539, gis91513, smyuan}@cis.nctu.edu.tw

[2] Internet System Technology Department, Computer & Communications Research
Laboratories, Industrial Technology Research Institute,
195, sec. 4, Chung Hsing Rd. Chutung, Hsinchu 310, Taiwan.
sting@itri.org.tw

Abstract. We propose an XML-based Context-Aware transformation Framework (X-CAF). In X-CAF, we design three main techniques - (1) an XML-based programming model to program applications, (2) a user interface adaptation mechanism to adjust UIs of applications, and (3) a transformation scheme to transform programs adapt to various MExE environments. Moreover, we design two methods, Static-time Component Generation and Runtime XUL Transformation for transforming efficiently and flexibility. Through applying these techniques, this framework may make applications device-independent.

1 Introduction

With the development of these mobile devices technologies, there are various mobile applications which can be designed, downloaded and installed to execute on Mobile Execution Environment (MExE)[8] devices. In the research of device independence, context definition and context protocols, the Device Independence Working Group (DI WG)[5][6][7], a Working Group as defined by the W3C process, study issues related to authoring, adaptation and presentation of Web content and applications that can be delivered effectively through different access mechanisms. And the Composite Capabilities/Preferences Profile Working Group[13][14][15] is defining a general framework for representing capabilities and preferences.

Some research investigate a concept of context awareness[1][2][11] including context awareness application and context aware mobile portal. These applications or systems will sense the changes of users' preferences or users' device capabilities[9][10][13][14][15][16] to provide suitable service.

The development of mobile applications on client devices, however, is very difficult for programmers to write mobile programs. In the execution environments of client devices, 3GPP Mobile Execution Environment (MExE) service TS[8] defines the stage one description of the MExE. Because there are a great many of different

X. Zhou, Y. Zhang, and M.E. Orlowska (Eds.): APWeb 2003, LNCS 2642, pp. 132–143, 2003.

devices with the various MExE classmarks such as WAP[16], Personal JAVA[18], J2ME[18] and Microsoft CLI, and with diverse capabilities including screen size, color number, graphic or text representation, and so on.

In order to approach the following- (1) mobile programs can be written regardless of the kind of their devices; (2) these programs can be adjust automatically to adapt to the various MExE environments and device capabilities when downloading them from a MExE server or gateway, we propose a XML-based Context-Aware transformation Framework(X-CAF). In X-CAF, we design three key techniques in this paper. (1) An XML-based programming model to program applications, we applied an XML-based user interface description language- XUL[3] and an XML-based description language of event-handling logic- LGML proposed in this paper. This separates a mobile program into two parts inclusive of XUL and LGML to program rapidly, concern-separately and device-independence. (2) A user interface adaptation mechanism to adjust UIs of applications. For this purpose, we design context-awareness profiles by using two kinds of context information- User Device Profile, and User Preference Profile to adjust them to adapt to devices. (3) Finally, this paper proposes an transformation by applying XSLT/XPath[4] to achieve cross-platform. Moreover, we design two methods, Static-time Component Generation and Runtime XUL Transformation, to transform efficiently and flexibility. This transforming scheme dynamically and automatically accommodates UIs of downloading programs to the MExE environments. Through applying these techniques, this framework may make applications device-independent.

2 XML-Based Context-Aware Framework

Device Tier: The first layer is all kinds of devices used by the clients such as Java phones, smart phones, and PDAs. Furthermore, there are four different MExE Environments established on these devices.

Bearer Tier: The second is network infrastructure. This layer is the wireless and mobile access technologies by which the different mobile devices communicate with each other ubiquitously. A Java phone, for instance, can enjoy telecom service and contents in the internet via 2.5G or 3G network. However wireless LAN, IEEE 802.11 b/a provides higher bandwidth than that of these telecom network. All of them provide the capability of mobile and wireless access.

Portal tier: The third one, portal tier of X-CAF, consists mainly of a web server called MExE server shown in figure 1 providing mobile clients can communicate with the server by HTTP Request/Reply, CC/PP exchange protocol and CC/PP content negotiation.

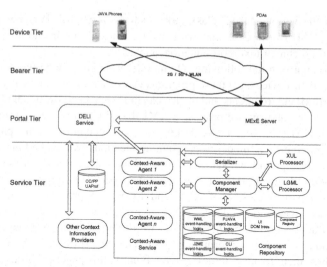

Fig. 1. The overview of our system framework inclusive of four layers: *Device Tier, Bearer Tier, Portal Tier*, and *Service Tier*.

In context awareness, we designed a DELI[9][10] service in this framework by applying DELI, a Java servlet[17] version with JENA[9][10] API developed by HP Lab, can handle clients' requests via the UAProf[16] W-HTTP Protocol and Profile Resolution. Furthermore, this service possesses the context processing functions e.g. content selection, generation, and transformation. In this framework, it plays the role to resolve clients' requests and to process the context profiles including these requests, like the CC/PP and UAProf profiles. In addition, it provides the context processing interface which can be invoked to obtain the context information for the user interface adaptation mechanism mentioned in section 4.2.

Service tier: The forth layer is the kernel we can explain it by dividing it into three parts. The first part is the storage modules storing the CC/PP and UAProf[16] profiles, and the compiled files of event-handling logics in the four MExE languages in the component repository as well as other context information providers. Event-handling logics were written as LGML at the beginning. Then each of them can be parsed and transformed into the four MExE languages, e.g. Java *class* file.

The second part has two modules. The first module includes two processor, XUL processor and LGML processor. The former can validate and parse an XUL file and then can transform the result tree generated from parsing. However, the latter processes LGML files. The second module is the serializer which can generate files in the four MExE languages from the adjusted tree produced in the adaptation mentioned in section 4.2.

The third part has modules consisting of Context-Aware Service (CAS) and Component Manager operating to serve clients. We explain exhaustively as follows:

- *CC/PP, UAProf*: It is context information database storing the CC/PP and UAProf[16] profiles. In addition, other context information providers are profile sources which can be connected to obtain profiles by using URLs. If so, the overhead need to transmit profiles can be reduced, since clients issue part of an UAProf profile instead of whole of it to the MExE server.

- *Component Repository*: The program of an application, in fact, is an execution unit conceptually, like Microsoft Outlook. Our framework divides it into two parts- user interface- XUL and event-handling logic- LGML. The repository stores the compiled files of event handling logics and UI DOM trees. Before inserting the logic files, the files were transformed to one of MExE language after adjustment and then compiled by the corresponding compilers. As to UI DOM trees, these trees were generated from parsing its XUL files, and then were stored to wait for clients' requests. These details will be discussed in chapter 4. In order to maintain the stored files and UI DOM trees and to retrieve them efficiently while clients issue request message, we design the component repository which records three fundamental tables including: (1) application table recording applications' IDs as their primary keys and names, (2) application component table recording the MExE classmarks and the locations of their event-handling logic files associate with, and (3) application UI table recording the locations of their UI DOM trees.

- *XUL Processor*: This processor can parse a XUL file and then produce a result tree. After completing this validating and parsing, the result would be inserted into the component repository and be registered in the component registry through component manager.

- *LGML processor*: Its function is similar to the function of the XUL processor. However, the difference is that it parses LGML files, event-handling logics of programs.

- *Serializer*: This module would serialize the result trees generated from parsing XUL files to the MExE languages. For example, the serialized format could be a Java *class* file if the value of the classmark_no is set two or three. It means that the MExE classmark two is Personal Java and the MExE classmark three is J2ME.

- *Component Manager*: It manages the complied files of event-handling logics of applications and their UI DOM trees. Moreover, these files and trees were collected in a DBMS like Microsoft SQL Server actually. If the component manager need to access these data, it might invoke the database accessing interface e.g. JDBC.

- *Context-Aware Service (CAS)*: the CAS contain several Context Aware Agents (CAAs). Each of them is like a thread, an execution unit sharing the CPU time. Once a CAS receives a client request, it would select a CAA from its agent pool to serve the client. This design is to efficiently perform clients' requests, because that creating and initiating a CAA to serve a client when receiving the client's request is very time-consuming.

3 XML-Based Programming Model

3.1 LoGic ML (LGML)

In order to accomplish the objectives that programs can be written regardless of the kind of devices and that they can be adjusted automatically to adapt to various MExE execution environments and device capabilities. In the other words, applications are device-independent and they could execute on various execution platforms e.g. Java, Microsoft CLI and etc. However, achieving this goal is difficult greatly, because transforming languages such as Java, c++, or c from one of them to another is very complex to design. To solving this problem, instead of transforming two different kinds of MExE languages, we applied the XSLT\XPath transforming technology. In addition, we design an XML-based language to describe the event-handling logic of an application. This method is similar to the XUL describing the user interface of an application. A Programmer can write the code handling the events triggered by the corresponding items of an application UI. For example, he could write the method, testBut-ton.onClick(); in a XUL file. And then he writes the corresponding LGML of the following code to implement the method.

```
onClick(){
  if (y==0) { result = x;  find = true; }
  }
```

The corresponding LGML is showed as bellow:

```
<lg:if>
<lg:test>
 <lg:equal>
 <lg:operand select="y" />
 <lg:operand type="int" value="0" />
 </lg:eqaul>
</lg:test>

<lg:action>
 <lg:assign arg1="result" arg2="x" />
 <lg:assign arg="find">
   <lg:operand type="boolean" value="true" />
 </lg:assign>
</lg:action>
</lg:if>
```

The above LGML can define the event-handling logic. If so, there are several advantages listed as follows:
- The transforming is very ease to design due to validation and well-form of XML.
- It benefits cross-platform and device-independence, because that XML, essentially a universal representation technology, is used in companies collaborating and documents exchanging.
- It also never to concern what are MExE environments programs execute in.

3.2 The Programming Model

The programming model of X-CAF is illustrated as shown in figure 2. The concept of this model is that a program of an application can be divided into two parts consisting of a XUL file and a LGML file. This division has two advantages. One is that writing the program could be separate-of-concern. A programmer write the part of the UI without considering the implementation of the event-handling logic, and oppositely a programmer write the logic without understanding the layout of the UI. The other purpose is to efficiently and flexibly determine a MExE environment of an application while a CAA is receiving a client request. Let's take flexibility and efficiency into consideration:

- *The flexibility aspect*: a program of an application UI is transformed and compiled in runtime. It means that representation style of the UI is adjusted dependent upon the context information of a client device when receiving a client request. Completing the adjustment, the adjusted UI DOM tree would be transformed to execution code conforming to a MExE environment of the device.
- *The efficiency aspect*: the part of event-handling logic of an application can be transformed and complied beforehand. In other words, its execution code for the four MExE environments was generated and stored in the component repository. Once receiving a client's request, a UI DOM tree of the desired application would be processed. Then the processing result and the complied file obtained from the repository would be packed and sent to the client device.

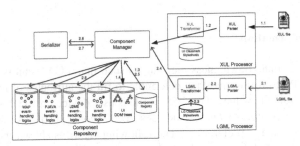

Fig. 2. The programming model and its sequence flow

3.3 Static-Time Component Generation

- *XUL processing*:

1. (1.1): an XUL file is sent to the XUL processor.
2. (1.2): after parsing the XUL, a result tree would be produced and then sent to the component manger.
3. (1.3): when the component manager receives the tree, the manager would query to check whether it duplicates or not.

4. (1.4): if there are no duplicate names or identifiers, it would be inserted into the component repository and registered in the component registry. There are many policies can be designed. For example, the old record in the repository can be replaced with the new one when inserting.

● *LGML processing*:

1. (2.1): a LGML file is delivered to the LGML processor.
2. (2.2): after the LGML processor parses the received LGML file, a result tree will be generated and be passed to the LGML transformer.
3. (2.3): the LGML transformer transforms the tree to the four MExE languages separately according to their corresponding MExE classmark stylesheets (XSLT files).
4. (2.4): it compiled these files or not dependent upon its configuration. Assume the `complied_by_itself` is set `false`, it sent the transformed result tree to the component manager
5. (2.5), (2.6): when the component manager receives the trees, it will pass them to the serializer. Then, the trees would be serialized to files in the four MExE languages. These files would be complied and then returned to the component manager.
6. (2.7), (2.8): they would be inserted into the component repository and registered in the component registry by the component manager.

4 Context-Awareness

4.1 Context Information

We designed the context-awareness mechanism such that a CAA can be aware of the CC/PP and UAProf profiles and then determine to fill the attributes of nodes of an UI DOM tree with suitable values. The first profile is user device profile describing capabilities and configuration of clients' devices. The second profile is user preference profile describes clients' preferences. The following figure is shown the part of user preference profile and the part of user device profile:

Fig. 3. On the left a RDF[12] graph of the user device profile, on the right the RDF graph of the user preference profile

4.2 User Interface Adaptation Mechanism

User interface adaptation is an adjustment procedure based on the context information, CC/PP and UAProf profiles. We can clearly explain when and how to adapt UIs by this scenario that a CAA received a client's request is illustrated as follows: (you can refer to the figure 4 showed above)

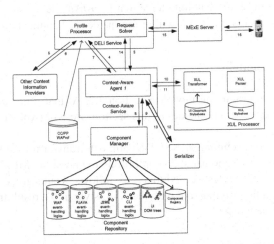

Fig. 4. The sequence diagram of the user interface adaptation mechanism. It is described as follows:

1. (1): the client issues the request message with a URI of a profile and profile-diff to the MExE server.
2. (2): when the MExE server receives the request message, it will deliver the request to the DELI service. The DELI service, a Java servlet, has a request solver and a profile processor which can parse the request message containing profile information.
3. (3): after the DELI receiving, the request solver parses the request and afterwards passes it with the related context information to the CAS.
4. (4), (5), (6), (7): once receiving the request, the CAS would select a CAA, a Java thread[18] in essence, from its agent pool to perform the client's request. Each of clients' requests can be handled by a CAA. For example, CAA *1* as shown in figure 4, is allocated to serve this client. It will invoke a method of the profile processor interface to obtain the related profile information. As to how to obtain the information, the URI and the profile-diff of the profile can be used when processing the profile. A *vector* object, a Java abstract collection object[18], consists of the information of the profiles. In addition, it is returned to the CAA after invoking the method of the profile processor interface.
5. (8), (9): after that, the CAA will retrieve the designated event-handling logic from the component repository according to the client's request and the classmark information of the profile. As well as its corresponding UI DOM tree will be retrieved.

The attributes of the tree's nodes are filled with the appropriate values guided by the *vector*. This mechanism to adjust the tree on the basis of user preference profiles and device capability profiles will be explained in the next section.

6. (10), (11): the XUL transformer in the server side would transform the tree into the designated MExE language.
7. (12), (13): the CAA would serialize the tree to files, and then integrate these files with the files of the event-handling logic to a Java *JAR* file.
8. (14), (15), (16): finally, the CAA will return the desired application to client.

4.3 Code Transformation

We introduce the programming model in section 3.2. At that time, we mentioned the runtime XUL transformation scheme. In this section, we will explain how the scheme operates in detail.

The transformation technology, XSLT\XPath, can transform a DOM tree with the XUL or LGML style into another style conforming to one of the MExE languages. For example, the following stylesheet exhibited as follows would guide the XUL transformer to transform the original tree with the XUL style into a result tree whose nodes expanded in J2ME language.

```
<?xml version="1.0"?>
<xsl:stylesheet version="1.0"
xmlns:xsl="http://www.w3.org/1999/XSL/Transform" >
 <xsl:output method="text"/>
  <xsl:template match="/">
  import javax.microedition.lcdui.*;
  import javax.microedition.midlet.*;
  class <xsl:value-of select="//window/@title"/> extends Form
    implements CommandListener{
      <xsl:for-each select="//window/button"> Command
      <xsl:value-of select="@label"/>Cmd = new
         Command("<xsl:value-of select="@label"/>", Command.OK, 1);
      </xsl:for-each>
   ...
   }
  </xsl:template>
 ...
</xsl:stylesheet>
```

Assume the following XUL file:

```
<window  xmlns:html="http://www.w3.org/1999/xhtml"
         xmlns:rdf="http://www.w3.org/1999/02/22-rdf-syntax-ns#"
         title="example">
           <button label="play"/>
           <button label="stop"/>
         </window>
```

After transforming it, to serialize the content of this tree would be:

```
import javax.microedition.lcdui.*;
import javax.microedition.midlet.*;
```

```
class example extends Form implements CommandListener{
  Command playCmd = new Command("play", Command.OK, 1);
  Command stopCmd = new Command("stop", Command.OK, 1);
  ...
}
```

Runtime XUL transformation: By applying this transforming scheme, we might design the transformation stylesheets of the MExE languages to guide the transformer. In order to improve the performance, we separate the scheme into two procedures, and each of them runs in different moments. It is presented as follows:

1. A XUL file would be validated after a programmer wrote it and then it would be parsed after passing it into the XUL parser. The result tree will be delivered to the component manager, and it is inserted into the component repository afterwards. Figure 2 shows the sequence.
2. After client issue a request message to the MExE server, an allocated CAA would obtain the designated UI DOM tree. The attributes of its nodes are filled with the appropriate values guided by the user preference profile and the device capability. This mechanism adapts the tree according to these profiles. That is shown as in figure 4.

LGML transformation: processing files of the event-handling logic of an application is not necessary to break into two procedures performed in two different occasions individually. Its transformation is easier than that of XUL transformation. During the static-time component generation, the LGML processor would transform a LGML DOM tree into four result trees with the style adapt to the four MExE languages dependent upon the LG classmark stylesheets as shown in figure 2.

Notice that there are two modules, a serializer and a XUL transformer, dedicated to the CAS. Programmers also have these modules in their computers. The next section will explain why we design that.

4.4 Application Aggregation and Serialization

The last section mentioned how and when the transformation performs. In the section, we describe how a CAA integrates two partitions, the event-handling logic and the UI of an application, into a whole when a client issues a request message. Then, the CAA returns the program to him. Taking J2ME into example, we illustrate a downloading scenario listed as follows:

1. An application manger on a client device issues a request message.
2. When receiving the request, the MExE server delivery it to the DELI and then the CAS. In addition, the CAS will allocate a CAA to serve this client. The agent would retrieve the requested files of the event-handling logic and the corresponding

UI DOM tree from the component repository. This sequence is shown in figure 4 clearly.

3. The CAA will execute the user interface adaptation described in section 4.2, and then filling the attributes of the result tree's nodes with appropriated values.

4. The CAA would deliver the adjusted tree to the XUL transformer. Then, the transformer will insert the following lines during expanding the nodes of the tree. Similarly, the files of the event-handling logic have had the same lines, but the insertion occurred when transforming the LGML files.

```
package org.xcaf.application_name;
...
import org.xcaf.application_name.Event_handling_logic_interface;
...
```

5. The CAA compiles the UI of the requested program and integrates it and the files of the event-handling logic into a Java *jar* file. And then, this file, *application_name.jar*, will be send to the client device.

Though applying Static-time Component Generation and Runtime XUL Transformation, the cost of time can be reduced. Because that the LGML files of a program is not necessary to be transformed while receiving a client request except the XUL.

5 Conclusions and Future Work

In order to approach the device-independence that automatically adapting to various MExE environments and device capabilities when downloading, we design the X-CAF. It includes three fundamental techniques. The XML-based programming model divides programs of an application into two partitions. The objective of the division is to program rapidly, concern-separately and device-independence. In addition, we applied XSLT\XPath to transform a DOM tree to conform to one of the MExE languages. According the transformation scheme, we design Static-time Component Generation and Runtime XUL Transformation to transform files efficiently and flexibility. Furthermore, this framework provides user interface adaptation mechanism on the basis of user device profile and user preference profile. To implement it, we use some technologies such as Web server, Java servlet, Java RMI, and an agent pool to enhance the usability and efficiency.

In the future works, we will focus on self-adaptation. The self-adaptation means that the content of an application UI can be adjusted automatically and intelligently. For examples, an UI can be shown clearly on the screen of a PC but it shown worse on that of a PDA. In this manner, self-adaptation could examine this circumstance, and then tailoring the UI. It might be one main frame to be tailored into two sub-frames. To consider this instance, a picture with high quality is shown well on a PC, it can be resized, transcoded to a low quality or translated to text which can be displayed better on a handheld device. Eventually, we can integrate our solution and content adaptation to develop more automatic and intelligent system.

References

1. Ricky Robinson. *Context Management in Mobile Environments.* World Wide Web, http://www.itee.uq.edu.au/~ricky/thesis.doc, October 2000.
2. Knut Ola Topand. *Mobile learning technological challenges on multi-channel e-learning services.* World Wide Web, http://siving.hia.no/ikt02/ikt6400/g05/Rapport_files/Diplom%20Knut%20Ola.pdf, spring 2002.
3. Neil Deakin. *XUL Tutorial.* World Wide Web, http://www.xulplanet.com/tutorials/xultu/, July 2002
4. Hiroshi Maruyama, Kent Tamura, Naohiko Uramoto, Makoto Murata, Andy Clark, et al. *XML and Java Second Edition: Developing Web Applications.* Addison-Wesley, 2002.
5. Mark H. Bulter. *Current Technologies for Device Independencel.* World Wide Web, http://www-uk.hpl.hp.com/people/marbut/currTechDevInd.htm, March 2001.
6. Mark Bulter, Fabio giannetti, roger gimson, and Tony wiley. Device Independence and the Web. *IEEE internet computing,* October 2002.
7. W3C, *Device independence working group charter.* World Wide Web, http://www.w3.org/2002/06 /w3c-di-wg-charter-20020612.html .
8. 3GPP TS 22.057 V5.4.0. *3rd Generation Partnership Project; Technical Specification Group Services and System Aspects; Mobile Execution Environment (MExE); Service description, Stage 1 (Release 5).* World Wide Web, http://www.3gpp.org, 2002.
9. Mark H. Butler. *DELI: A Delivery context LIbrary for CC/PP and UAProf. External Technical Report HPL-2001-260,* HP Labs. World Wide Web, http://delicon.sourceforge.net /.02/08/2002 , 2002.
10. Mark H. Butler. *Implementing Content Negotiation using CC/PP and WAP UAProf. External Technical Report HPL-2001-190,* World Wide Web, http://www.hpl.hp.com /techreports/2001/HPL-2001-190.html, 2001.
11. Kovacs, E., Rohrle, K., Schiemann, B. Adaptive mobile access to context-aware services. *Agent Systems and Applications 1999 and Third International Symposium on Mobile Agents. Proceedings. First International Symposium,*1999.
12. Dan Brickley, R.V. Guha. *RDF Vocabulary Description Language 1.0: RDF Schema.* W3C Working Draft. World Wide web, http://www.w3.org/TR/rdf-schema/, November 2002.
13. Franklin Reynolds, Johan Hjelm, Spencer Dawkins, and Sandeep Singhal. *Composite Capability/Preference Profiles(CC/PP): A user side framework for content negotiation.* W3C Note. World Wide Web, http://www.w3.org/TR/NOTE-CCPP/ , July 1999.
14. Johan Hjelm, Lalitha Suryanarayana. *CC/PP Implementors Guide: Harmonization with Existing Vocabularies and Content Transformation Heuristics.* W3C Note. World Wide Web, http://www.w3.org/TR/CCPP-COORDINATION/, December 2001.
15. Hidetaka Ohto, Johan Hjelm. *CC/PP exchange protocol based on HTTP Extension Framework.* W3C Note, World Wide Web, http://www.w3.org/TR/NOTE-CCPPexchange, June 1999.
16. WAP Forum. *User Agent Profiling Specification.* World Wide Web, http://www1. wapforum.org/tech/terms.asp?doc=WAP-248-UAProf-20011020-a.pdf, October 2001.
17. Sun Microsystems. *Java Servlet technology.* World Wide Web, http://java.sun.com /products/servlet/ .
18. Sun Microsystems. *Tutorials & Short Courses.* World Wide Web, http://developer. java.sun.com/developer/onlineTraining/ .

FIXT: A Flexible Index for XML Transformation[1]

Jianchang Xiao, Qing Wang, Min Li, and Aoying Zhou

Department of Computer Science and Engineering, Fudan University,
220 Handan Rd, Shanghai, China
{jcxiao, qingwang, leemin, ayzhou}@fudan.edu.cn
http://www.cs.fudan.edu.cn/indexen.jsp

Abstract. XML is emerging as the main standard of presentation and exchange on the Internet. This highlights the important question of XML to XML transformation. In this paper, a flexible index structure, FIXT, is presented for efficient XML transformation. It is easy to extract and reconstruct subparts of FIXT index to build indexes for intermediate results. Thus, it can improve the performance of XML to XML transformation.

1 Introduction

With the rapidly increasing popularity of XML for data representation, it is more and more common to find data in XML format in the World Wide Web. This highlights an important question that how to extract data from various data sources and construct another document that conforms to a fixed DTD. Usually it is referred to as XML to XML transformation.

A number of XML query languages [1, 2, 3, 4, 6] are currently being used to transform XML data. During the execution of queries, some intermediate results would be generated and be queried later, which are usually the combo of subparts of the source documents. Indexing them would be helpful and a convenient way to do this is to extract and reconstruct the corresponding subparts of the source index. Therefore, XML transformation requires the index structure to be flexible.

To achieve this goal, we have developed FIXT, which is easy to extract and reconstruct subparts. In summary, this paper makes the following contributions:

- This paper illustrates building index for intermediate results from the source indexes in XML transformation.
- We design a flexible index structure, FIXT, which is suitable for XML transformation. The index structure is efficient in not only query evaluation but also index reconstruction.

The remainder of this paper is organized as follows: Section 2 reviews the related work. We will discuss our index structure in section 3 and experiments in section 4. In section 5 we conclude with a summary.

---

[1] This work is supported by the National Natural Science Foundation under grant No: 60228006 and Fok Ying Tung Education Foundation.

X. Zhou, Y. Zhang, and M.E. Orlowska (Eds.): APWeb 2003, LNCS 2642, pp. 144–149, 2003.

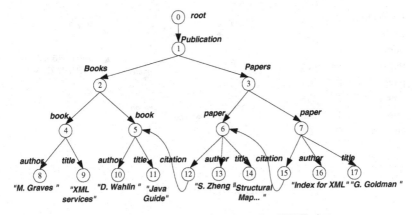

Fig. 1. The graph structure of an example of XML data

2 Background

In this section, we review some basic concepts and definitions that will be useful throughout the paper.

structural graph: An structural graph for an XML data graph G is a graph $I(G)$ where an extent is associated with each node in it. If A is a node in the structural graph $I(G)$, then *extI (A)*, the extent of A, is the union of target sets of all label paths that can come to node A from the root.

k-bisimilarity: [5] explores the problem of building index graphs that takes advantage of local similarity and brings out the k-bisimilarity, $\approx^k$:

- For any two nodes, u and v, $u \approx^0 v$ iff u and v have the same label,
- Node $u \approx^k v$ iff $u \approx^0 v$ and for every parent u' of u, there is a parent v' of v such that $u' \approx^{k-1} v'$ and vice versa.

XTG: XTG [6] presents a novel approach to handle DTD-conforming XML transformation. It extends a DTD by incorporating semantic rules defined with XML queries and allows users to specify how to extract relevant data from source XML documents via the queries, and to construct a target XML document directed by the embedded DTD. Hence, the queries can cite the result of each other and indexes of intermediate results can be built.

3 FIXT: A Flexible Index for XML Transformation

As we saw above, XML to XML transformation needs an index that not only can accelerate query evaluation but also can extract subparts from source indexes easily. Our index definition schema is towards this.

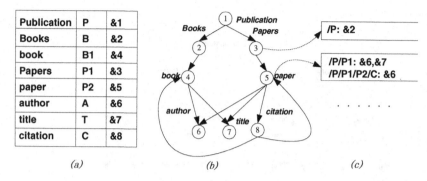

Publication	P	&1
Books	B	&2
book	B1	&4
Papers	P1	&3
paper	P2	&5
author	A	&6
title	T	&7
citation	C	&8

/P: &2

/P/P1: &6,&7
/P/P1/P2/C: &6

(a)   (b)   (c)

Fig. 2. Overview of FIXT

3.1 Overview of FIXT

A FIXT index structure consists of three parts: a hash table (H), a structural graph (G) and an extent (Ext).

Structural Graph: We apply k-bisimilarity to the structural graph and will see that, when k is zero, the structural summary will have much fewer nodes, just as many as types of elements that appear in the source documents. As shown in Fig. 2 (b), each type of element has just one corresponding node in the structural graph. We can now easily extract the sub index without thinking of comparing and combining sub trees.

Extent: After zero-bisimilarity is used in the structural summary, another problem comes forth: how can we tell the incoming path of nodes in the extents? Zero-bisimilarity merges different nodes of same element type in the structural graph, but it also merges the target sets of them. All extents of the nodes in the structural summary are now "maybe-sets". If we use the method of validating nodes against the original document like [5], that means we must look up the source XML document frequently. It would be very inefficient.

To solve this problem, we use encoded paths to group the extents. We assigned a designator to each element type. A designator is a unique character or character strings. For each target set, we use the designators to encode the incoming path into character string, and use these character strings to group different target sets in the extents. When queried with a path expression l, the index encodes l into character string and constructs a DFA to match the string with the group names in the corresponding extent. If a group name reaches an accept state, this group should be returned.

Hash Table: Since each element type has just one node in the structural graph, we will reach the same node for querying the same element type even though following different incoming paths. For fast access to the target node, we add a hash table to the index and store a pointer for each node in the structural graph. The hash table is also a good place to store the designators. So each entry of the hash table has three fields: element label, pointer and designator.

Fig. 2 depicts the corresponding FIXT index for Fig. 1. The hash table H (a) includes all the element types that appear in the source XML document. Each entry in H contains an element name, a designator, and a pointer. The pointer points to a node in G (b) so that one can access the relevant graph node fast. The structural graph G acts as the structural summary and each node in it has an extent. The extent (c) comprises all the nodes in the XML document that have the same name as in the hash table entry, and the nodes in it are grouped by encoded incoming paths.

3.2 Query Evaluation

Next, we demonstrate how to evaluate queries with FIXT. At first, we introduce some operations as follows:

- *Locate(l)*: find all the node in G reached by a regular path l, and there may be multi nodes returned;
- *Matching(l)*: encode and match the group names in the extent of a node with regular path l, and return the matching target sets;
- *Select(E; Exp)*: select the elements from E satisfying the expression *Exp*;
- *UNION*: union the nodes of multi target sets;
- *JOIN*: join the multi target sets.

Operations 1 to operation 4 act as their names imply. We just explain operation 5 here. The *JOIN* operation is used to intersect two sets according to a common ancestor. The common ancestor, like key and foreign key in relation database, is called anchor here. If two data nodes have the same anchor node, they should be picked out. It is usually used in the evaluation of branching path expressions.

A query can be evaluated by the above operations easily. Note that any complex query can be decomposed into three path components: path expression l, a predicate $E[Exp]$, and a combination of two sets. Each path expression can be evaluated by a *Locate* and a *Matching* operation. A predicate can be evaluated by *Selection* operation. Finally, the results of each component can be combined by *UNION* operation or *JOIN* operation to produce the total result for the whole query.

3.3 Rebuilding the Sub Index

Because most sub indexes are parts of the source index, we depict how to extract subpart form the source first. Extracting subparts includes two sides: One is to build the sub graph; the other is to pick out correct target sets for each node. Rooting from target nodes of a path expression, the rebuilding process browses the structural graph in depth first fashion and picks out all the descendant nodes to form the sub graph. And for each node in the sub graph, only the nodes that are descendants of the query result should be selected into the target sets. The algorithm is given in Fig. 3 (a).

Besides extracting nodes from source data, the query may add some nodes or combine graphs from different documents. Thus we need to define some operations to accomplish them.

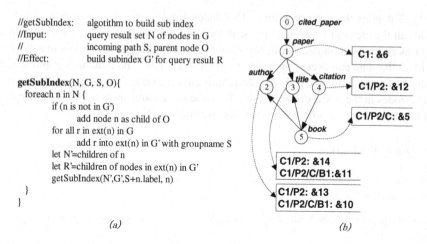

```
//getSubIndex:    algotithm to build sub index
//Input:          query result set N of nodes in G
//                incoming path S, parent node O
//Effect:         build subindex G' for query result R

getSubIndex(N, G, S, O){
    foreach n in N {
        if (n is not in G')
            add node n as child of O
        for all r in ext(n) in G
            add r into ext(n) in G' with groupname S
        let N'=children of n
        let R'=children of nodes in ext(n) in G'
        getSubIndex(N',G',S+n.label, n)
    }
}
```

(a)   (b)

Fig. 3. Algorithm to build sub index (a) and an example of sub index (b)

- *NewNode(label)*: new a node with given label;
- *Combine(G1, G2)*: combine two graphs;
- *Concatenate(node1, node2)*: link *node2* as a child of *node1*.

To illustrate this, let us use Q as example.

> **Q:**   FOR $X IN //paper [author="G. Goldman"]/citation/paper
>   RETURN <cited_paper>$X</cited_paper>

Building index for Q can be done by a sequence of operations as follows: *NewNode*(cited paper), *getSubIndex()*, then *Concatenate* the node cited paper and root node of *getSubIndex()*. The final index for Q is shown in Fig. 3 (b). Note that node 1 in Fig. 3 (b) has no extent. It means the node is constructed by the query and does not exist in any document. The hash table is the same as the one in Fig. 2 except adding entry cited paper encoded as *C1*, so it is ignored here.

4   Experiments

We conducted experiments to explore the performance of the FIXT index structure. All the experiments are over XMark XML benchmark and DBLP. We specify five XTGs for each data set. These XTGs cover a wide range of processing features of XML transformation. The experiments were performed on a machine with 1.4G PIV CPU and 256M RAM. All the results of FIXT will be compared against the ones of using DataGuide as structural graph.

We can see in Fig. 4 that for some XTG FIXT performances better than DataGuide and some does not. The reasons could be found by analyzing the feathers of XTGs. For XTG2 and XTG8, it is because FIXT built indexes for intermediate result to avoid looking up the source document again and again. For XTG1, XTG3, XTG4 and XTG5, query combination made them have no need to build intermediate index. But because the path expressions in them are regular path expressions and FIXT overcomes DataGuide in regular expression evaluation, FIXT performs still better than DataGuide here. For the other XTGs, they needn't built intermediate index, and the path expressions are simple ones. These made DataGuide come out a little faster.

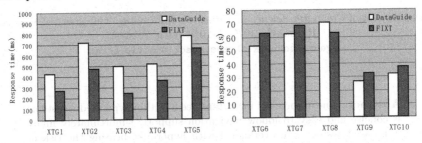

Fig. 4. XTG Evaluation Performances

From above we can see that intermediate index and regular path evaluation are the two reasons that make FIXT performance better.

5   Conclusion

In this paper, we have presented FIXT, a new index structure for XML to XML transformation. We examine the transformation process and find that index for intermediate results will help to improve performances. So we adopt zero-bisimilarity in the structural graph and assign names to each group in extents to avoid the "maybe-set" problem. Preliminary performance study shows that FIXT is efficient in XML transformation.

References

1. P. Buneman, S. B. Davidson, G. G. Hillebrand, and D. Suciu. A query language and optimization techniques for unstructured data. In ACM SIGMOD International Conference on Management of Data, pages 505–516, 1996.
2. D. Chamberlin et al. XQuery 1.0: An XML Query Language. W3C Working Draft, June 2001. http://www.w3.org/TR/xquery.
3. J. Clark. XSL Transformations (XSLT). W3C Recommendation, Nov. 1999. http://www.w3.org/TR/xslt.
4. J. Clark and S. DeRose. XML Path Language (XPath). W3C Working Draft, Nov. 1999. http://www.w3.org/TR/xpath.
5. R. Kaushik, P. Shenoy, P. Bohannon, and E. Gudes. Exploiting local similarity for indexing paths in graph-structured data. ICDE, 2002.
6. A. Zhou, Q. Wang, Z. Guo, X. Gong, S. Zheng, H. Wu, J. Xiao, K. Yue, and W. Fan. TREX: DTD-Conforming XML to XML Transformations. SIGMOD accepted, Fudan University and Bell laboratories, 2003.

Formal Foundation of Web Navigation Stereotypes and Their Transformation into XML

Georg Sonneck and Thomas Mueck

Department of Computer Science and Business Informatics, University of Vienna
Rathaustr. 19/9, A-1010 Wien, Austria
{georg.sonneck,thomas.mueck}@univie.ac.at

Abstract. One of the most important needs within hypermedia systems is concise and easy to follow navigation support. Unfortunately many web-based systems are overloaded with hyperlinks bearing the risk of "getting lost" within the site, which leads subsequently to frustrated end users and less frequency of the site. To solve this problem web navigation patterns which represent well-established navigation paths within hypermedia systems have been proposed in the literature and have consequently been integrated into web design languages.

Feeling the need for a formal foundation we propose a labeled graph which describes the overall navigational structure of web-based systems. This graph constitutes a basis for the formal definition of web navigation patterns which are in turn the base for high-level UML stereotypes. These UML stereotypes are transformed into XML structures and finally into HTML. This approach to support navigation design of web-based systems is exemplified using the case of the filtered index navigation pattern.

1 Introduction

Nowadays the importance of the world wide web increases more and more, not only by providing a pool of information, but also by becoming a platform for intranet, internet and extranet applications. All systems, web-based systems and also web applications, use hyperlinks to connect related information. This ability to provide fast access to interrelated information can be a benefit on the one hand. On the other hand, it incorporates the risk of creating systems which are overloaded with navigation paths, making it hard for end users to find their way within the system.

Because of that, web navigation patterns have been integrated into web design languages like Araneus [5], OOHDM [6] or WebML [2], describing well-established and broadly accepted navigational structures. In this way the same navigation patterns appear within several design languages and publications such as [4] with slightly different semantics. To overcome this deficiency we propose a formal foundation of web navigation stereotypes by introducing the *navigation graph*. Starting from this foundation we show the formal definition of one selected navigation pattern.

X. Zhou, Y. Zhang, and M.E. Orlowska (Eds.): APWeb 2003, LNCS 2642, pp. 150–155, 2003.
© Springer-Verlag Berlin Heidelberg 2003

Based on this formal definition of the pattern, we introduce a high-level UML stereotype (as in [8]) which represents the navigational structure of the pattern.

Subsequently we show how an automatic transformation of the high-level model into XML structures can be done. These XML skeletons are exclusively based on the XLink [11], XForms [10] and XMLQuery [12] specifications of the W3C to guarantee extensibility. XML has been chosen as result of the transformation because it encodes navigation information in a device independent way. In conducting a further transformation several output formats (e.g. HTML) can be created. Currently, the last transformation from XML to a final output format has to be done manually.

Some web design languages provide extensions to support the implementation phase as well: OOHDM-Web [6], for example, provides a library of functions in the CGI scripting environment CGI-LUA. In this way navigation and interface constructs can be mapped to functions in this library. WebML [2] is fully implemented in a Web design tool suite called ToriiSoft. To support the implementation, the ToriiSoft tool suite maps abstract references to content elements into data retrieval instructions in some server-side scripting language. Web design languages based on UML like W2000 [1] do not specify, to the best of the authors knowledge, how the implementation phase can be supported.

The paper is structured as follows: This section gives an introduction and presents related work, leading to section 2 where the navigation graph is formally defined and described. Based on this definition, one navigation pattern, namely the filtered index navigation, is formally defined in section 3. Afterwards a high-level UML stereotype representing the navigation pattern and the subsequent transformation into corresponding XML structures is described. Finally, in section 4, we come to the conclusions and issues for further research.

2 The Navigation Graph

In this section we introduce a formal foundation for the definition of web navigation patterns. See definition 1 for the formal definition of the *navigation graph* which will be the basis for all formal definitions of web navigation patterns.

Definition 1 (navigation graph) *A navigation graph is a labeled graph (over two fixed alphabets Ω_V and Ω_E for node and edge labels) which is a tuple $G = \langle G_V, G_E, G_F, s^G, t^G, lv^G, le^G \rangle$, where G_V is a set of nodes, G_E is a set of edges, $s^G, t^G : G_E \to G_V$ are the source and target functions, and $lv^G : G_V \to \Omega_V$ and $le^G : G_E \to \Omega_E$ are the node and the edge labeling functions, respectively. G_F incorporates the node where the graph starts with $G_F \subseteq G_V$ and $|G_F| = 1$.*

Within this publication the node and edge labels are: $\Omega_V = \{INF\}$ and $\Omega_E = \{1, ..., n\}$. The node label INF corresponds to a node with type informational which means that it exclusively presents information to end users (see [9] for other node types in the field of web applications). Edges are drawn as arrows from source to the target and the label of each node or edge is written after its identity, separated by a colon. Web navigation patterns (e.g. index navigation, filtered index navigation or guided tour) can be described as navigation graphs with specific properties that must be fulfilled.

3   Filtered Index Navigation Pattern

To exemplify the steps starting from the formal foundation
of a pattern up to a corresponding HTML representation,
we take the filtered index navigation pattern: The web
navigation pattern starts at node $P1$ (see figure 1) from
which a navigation to related target nodes which fulfill
specific filter criteria is possible. If a related target node
does not fulfill all filter criteria (see for example node $P4$
of figure 1), the navigation paths between this node and
$P1$ are no longer allowed. For each valid target node an
uplink back to $P1$ must exist and no direct links between
target nodes are allowed in this pattern.

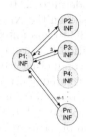

Fig. 1.   Navigation graph

3.1   Formal Definition

Figure 1 depicts the navigation graph of the filtered index navigation pattern.
The pattern can be formally described by extending the definition of the navigation graph with several constraints that have to be satisfied. See definition 2
for a formal definition of the filtered index navigation pattern.

Definition 2 (navigation graph of the filtered index navigation) *The
graph of the filtered index navigation is an extended navigation graph and can
be described as a tupel* $FING = \langle G_V, G_E, G_F, G_Z, P, s^G, t^G, lv^G, le^G \rangle$ *where* G_F
represents the node where the pattern starts and G_Z *is the set of target nodes
with* $G_F \subset G_V$, $G_Z \subset G_V$, $G_V = G_F \bigcup G_Z$ *and* $|G_F| = 1$. *The set* P *includes
predicates with* $P : G_Z \to \{true, false\}$. *The following conditions have to be
met:*

- $\forall x \in G_Z, y \in G_F : (\exists p \in P : p(x) = false) \Rightarrow (\neg \exists k_1 \in G_E : (s(k_1) = x) \wedge (t(k_1) = y)) \wedge (\neg \exists k_2 \in G_E : (s(k_2) = y) \wedge (t(k_2) = x))$.
- $\forall x \in G_Z, y \in G_F : (\forall p \in P : p(x) = true) \Rightarrow (\exists k_1 \in G_E : (s(k_1) = x) \wedge (t(k_1) = y)) \wedge (\exists k_2 \in G_E : (s(k_2) = y) \wedge (t(k_2) = x))$.
- $\forall x, y \in G_Z : (\neg \exists k \in G_E : (s(k) = x) \wedge (t(k) = y))$.

3.2   UML Notation

Figure 2 shows the filtered index navigation pattern modeled as a new UML
stereotype (as in [8]). This high-level model shows the relation between the two
pages by introducing the stereotype <<index navigation>> for the unidirectional
association representing the relationship between one instance of class A and 1
to n associated instances of class B. Additionally the filter criteria $co_1, ..., co_n$
are specified below the association enlarging the functionality of the index navigation. In this way the navigation paths are restricted allowing exclusively a
navigation from one instance of class A to related instances of class B which
fulfill these criteria. The up link from one instance of class B to its associated
instance of class A is modelled using the stereotype <<link>> (see [3]).

To be able to generate the corresponding XML structure, the attributes *id*, *name*, *file_name* and *tag_name* are mandatory. The attribute *id* is an identifier for each instance, whereas attribute *name* includes a human readable description for the instance. The attributes *file_name* and *tag_name* have class scope. Additionally, attributes $att_1, ..., att_n$ can be present.

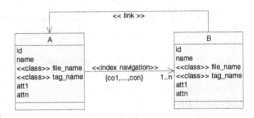

Fig. 2. Filtered Index Navigation in UML

3.3   Abstract Construction of XML Structures

After navigation from the starting page has begun, the user has to specify filter criteria constraining the set of appropriate target pages. The specified filter criteria will consequently result in a dynamically generated link list incorporating target pages which satisfy the provided filters. This link list can be used to navigate to a specific target page.

Figure 3 depicts the required steps between the user and involved system components: The filtered index navigation starts when a user requests a starting resource (element with name *A*) of A.xml (steps 1, 2). Within this resource a XForms is integrated which exclusively enables a navigation to the servercomponent *generate_search_page* (step 3). This servercomponent creates a XHTML file including another XForms which can be used to insert filter criteria (in step 4 this file is submitted to the user).

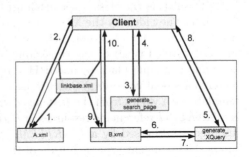

Fig. 3. Filtered Index Navigation in XML

The inserted filter criteria are submitted to the servercomponent *generate_XQuery* in step 5. This servercomponent integrates the filter criteria into a XQuery-template, submits the completed XQuery (step 6) and retrieves a link list as result (step 7). This link list is forwarded to the user (step 8) who can finally navigate to a specific target page (steps 9, 10).

The complete listings for all these steps can be found in [7]. As example we show here the generation of the XQuery-template and the structure of the resulting link list which is returned to the user.

Servercomponent *generate_XQuery* completes the XQuery-template with the *instance data* representing the filter criteria of the user. The pseudo-code is executed only once to generate the XQuery-template.

```
A a; B b; int several_filters = 0;
namespace my_app="http://www.example.com/Mapping"
<LINKLIST xmlns:xlink="http://www.w3.org/1999/xlink">
 {
  for $x in document("b.file_name")//my_app:b.tag_name where
 foreach c in all_constraints {
  if(several_filters) { and }
  several_filters = 1;
  if(c.d_type == "string") { $x/my_app:c.n[contains(string(.), [PH c.n]]
  } else { $x/my_app:c.n = [PH c.n] }
 }
     and $x/my_app:EntrypageLink[@xlink:href = "a.file_name#
        xpointer(//*[local-name()='a.tag_name'
                    and @id='" + [PH submitid] + "'])"]
   return
    <LINKITEM xlink:type="simple"
       xlink:title="{ $x/my_app:name/text() }"
       xlink:href="b.file_name#xpointer(//*[local-name()=
                   'b.tag_name' and @id='{ string($x/@id) }'])">
     { $b/my_app:name/text() }
    </LINKITEM>
 }
</LINKLIST>
```

In this listing the class scope attributes *file_name* and *tag_name* are used the first time. They identify the XML structure (e.g. *file_name* and *tag_name* of class A are "A.xml" and "A"). For each constraint a selection predicate according to the *data_type* (d_type) of the constraint is inserted into the XQuery-template, including a unique place holder [**PH c.n**] for the constraint. At runtime, the servercomponent *generate_XQuery* replaces the place holders within the XQuery-template with values from the *instance data* and submits the XQuery. The result is a *LINKLIST* referencing resources in *B.xml* which fulfill the filter criteria. Each resource is addressed by a *LINKITEM* via a *simple link*. The following listing shows the document type definition of the link list.

```
<?xml version="1.0" encoding="UTF-8"?>
<!ELEMENT LINKLIST (LINKITEM)*>
<!ATTLIST LINKLIST xmlns:xlink CDATA #FIXED "http://www.w3.org/1999/xlink">
<!ELEMENT LINKITEM (#PCDATA)>
<!ATTLIST LINKITEM xlink:type (simple) #FIXED "simple"
  xlink:title CDATA #IMPLIED xlink:href CDATA #REQUIRED>
```

4   Conclusions and Further Work

In this publication we are supporting navigation design in web-based systems on several levels: We introduce the *navigation graph* as a formal foundation for the definition of web navigation patterns. On the level of abstract navigation design, UML web navigation stereotypes are introduced representing the navigational semantics of the patterns. On this level several web design languages exist which try to express the same semantics with different models. To support the implementation phase, we describe an automatic transformation which starts at the high-level UML model and leads to implementation near XML structures which encode the navigation capabilites of the patterns in a device independent manner. These XML structures use exclusively W3C specifications to guarantee openness and extensibility of the solution.

Further research will deal with the semi-automated generation of web-pages and hence address the transformation between XML and other representation formats.

References

1. L. Baresi, F. Garzotta, and P. Paolini. Extending UML for Modeling Web Applications. In *Proc. HICSS 2001*, page 3055, Maui, Hawaii, USA, 2001.
2. S. Ceri, P. Fraternali, and A. Bongio. Web Modeling Language (WebML): a modeling language for designing Web sites. *WWW9 / Computer Networks*, 33(1-6):137–157, May 2000.
3. J. Conallen. *Building Web Applications with UML*. Addison Wesley Longman, Massachusetts, 2000.
4. F. Garzotto, P. Baolini, D. Bolchini, and S. Valenti. Modeling-by-Patterns of Web Applications. In *Proc. ER Workshops 1999*, volume 1727 of *Lecture Notes in Computer Science*, pages 293–306, Paris, France, 1999. Springer.
5. T. Isakowitz, E.A. Stohr, and P. Balasubramanian. RMM: A Methodology for structured Hypermedia Design. *Communications of the ACM (CACM)*, 38(8):34–44, August 1995.
6. D. Schwabe, R. Almeida, P. Moura, and I. Moura. OOHDM-Web: An Environment for Implementation of Hypermedia Applications in the WWW. *SigWEB Newsletter*, 8(2):207–225, June 1999.
7. G. Sonneck. Formal Foundation of Web Navigation Stereotypes and Their Transformation into XML. Technical report, Department of Computer Science and Business Informatics, University of Vienna, December 2002.
8. G. Sonneck, R. Motschnig, and T. Mueck. Mapping UML Web Navigation Stereotypes to XML Data Skeletons. In *Proc. EC-Web 2002*, volume 2455 of *Lecture Notes in Computer Science*, pages 294–303, Aix-en-Provence, France, September 2002. Springer.
9. G. Sonneck and T. Mueck. Optimized One-to-One Personalization of Web Applications using a Graph Based Model. In *Proc. IPDPS 2003 (ICEC Workshop)*, Nice, France, April 2003. IEEE Computer Society.
10. XForms. XForms 1.0 from the World Wide Web Consortium (W3C). http://www.w3c.org/MarkUp/Forms/, June 2002.
11. XLink. XLink (XML Linking Language) from the World Wide Web Consortium (W3C). http://www.w3.org/TR/xlink/, January 2002.
12. XMLQuery. XML Query from the World Wide Web Consortium (W3C). http://www.w3c.org/XML/Query, June 2002.

Mining "Hidden Phrase" Definitions from the Web

Hung. V. Nguyen[1], P. Velamuru[1], D. Kolippakkam[1], H. Davulcu[1], H. Liu[1], and M. Ates[2]

[1]Department of Computer Science and Engineering
Arizona State University,
Tempe, AZ, 85287, USA
{hung, prasanna.velamuru, n.kolippakkam, hdavulcu,
hliu}@asu.edu
[2]Cash-Us.com
21 Helen Way, Berkeley Heights, NJ, 07922, USA
mates@cash-us.com

Abstract. Keyword searching is the most common form of document search on the Web. Many Web publishers manually annotate the META tags and titles of their pages with frequently queried phrases in order to improve their placement and ranking. A "hidden phrase" is defined as a phrase that occurs in the META tag of a Web page but not in its body. In this paper we present an algorithm that mines the definitions of hidden phrases from the Web documents. Phrase definitions allow (i) publishers to find relevant phrases with high query frequency, and, (ii) search engines to test if the content of the body of a document matches the phrases. We use co-occurrence clustering and association rule mining algorithms to learn phrase definitions from high-dimensional data sets. We also provide experimental results.

1 Introduction

Keyword searching is the most common form of document search on the Web. Most search engines do their text query and retrieval using keywords. Search engines pull out and index words and phrases that are deemed significant. Phrases and words that are mentioned in the URL, TITLE or META tags of the document as well as those that are repeated many times in the body are more likely to be deemed important. The average keyword query length is under three words (2.2 words [3], 2.8 words [5]). Nowadays, many Web publishers frequently use phrase frequency databases, like Overture [12] and Word Tracker [13], to identify phrases that are queried with high frequency and attach them to their document titles or META tags in order to improve their placement and ranking. If a phrase occurs in the META tag of a Web page but not in its body then we call it a "hidden phrase".

Mining the definitions of "hidden phrases" or phrases in general, would allow (i) publishers to easily find relevant phrases with high query frequency, and, (ii) search engines to test if the content of the body of a document matches the phrases in its TITLE and META tags. As an example, if a catalog publisher knows that a "leather jacket" is a "motorcycle jacket" then, the publisher can use the second phrase as a META tag or to enrich the product descriptions. Similarly, if a Web page contains the META tag "luxury bedding" and the search engine knows that only "silk, satin or

X. Zhou, Y. Zhang, and M.E. Orlowska (Eds.): APWeb 2003, LNCS 2642, pp. 156–165, 2003.

designer beddings" are considered to be "luxury" then it can determine the relevance of a page that has the "luxury bedding" as a hidden phrase.

In this paper we present an algorithm that mines the definitions of hidden phrases from the Web documents. We introduce a novel framework based on (i) sampling highly ranked documents that matches a hidden phrase by using a keyword search engine, (ii) extracting frequent sets of highly co-occurring phrases from the pages using co-occurrence clustering and (iii) use association rule mining for learning the phrase definitions.

The first step of the algorithm yields high dimensional data, such as ~1000 co-occurring phrases per hidden phrase. The second step of our algorithm provides preprocessing steps for reducing the dimensionality of the phrase sets using co-occurrence clustering during the phrase definition mining using association rules. In the experimental results, we demonstrate that these techniques are effective for mining the definitions of hidden phrases.

The rest of the paper is organized as follows. Section 2 is related work. Section 3 presents our phrase definition-mining algorithm. Experimental results and analysis are discussed in Section 4. Section 5 concludes the paper and discusses future work.

2 Related Work

In [8] linguistic analysis is employed to mine the description of phrases/queries. Specifically, that work is based on patterns such as *is a, or, such as, especially, including, or other, and other, etc.*, in order to recognize the meaning of a phrase/query. This approach, however cannot work well with domains where the target phrase does not associate within the context of the above patterns. Another related work is described in [7]. In this work, the trends in text document are discovered based on sequential pattern mining in order to trace phrases. Then, each phrase is assigned an ID number and history of each phrase is tracked by partitioning documents into time intervals. From this, the trends of phrases are identified using trend queries. The output, however, is not the definition but trends of the usage of the phrases through a period. In [1], techniques called *generalized episodes* and *episodes rules* are used for Descriptive Phrase Extraction. *Episodes rules* are the modification of association rules and *episode* is the modification of frequent set. These concepts are used associated with some weighting measures in order to determine the (episode) rules that define a phrase. Because *episode* as described in [1] is a collection of features vectors with a partial order for that collection, authors claimed that their approach is useful in phrase mining in Finnish, a language that has the relaxed order of words in a sentence.

3 Algorithm

The algorithm essentially consists of three components. A Web wrapper collects all relevant Web pages by posing a query, a hidden phrase, to a search engine. We used Google [9] search engine in our experiments. The wrapper extracts co-occurring phrase sets using specialized algorithms from resulting pages. The second component, called preprocessor, builds a phrase-document matrix and pre-processes the data before feeding it to an association rule miner. The third component is an association rule miner [11] that produces the phrase definition rules, with predetermined *Support* and *Confidence* values. Figure 1 is the outline of the algorithm. In Figure 2, the architecture of the mining system is shown.

Subsequent sections discuss in detail the components of the mining algorithm.

```
Begin

  1. Retrieve a set of documents (Web pages) by querying a search
     engine with the target phrase and extract relevant phrases from
     the documents

  2. Construct the phrase-document matrix M. Cell (i,j) has the
     value as TF (term frequency) value of phrase i in document j.

  3. Construct the correlation matrix C of phrases C = M x Mᵀ.

  4. Partition the collection of phrases into co-occurrence clusters
     by utilizing the correlation matrix C

       -  Initially, each phrase forms a cluster

       -  Repeatedly merge two nearest clusters until the size of
          the cluster exceeds a threshold t. (The notion of
          distance between two clusters is discussed in Section
          3.2)

  5. Select relevant documents and reconstruct the phrase-document
     matrix for each cluster and run the association rule miner to
     extract the description rules.

End.
```

Fig. 1. Outline of Definition Mining Algorithm

3.1 Extraction of Related Phrases

Finding sets of co-occurring phrases that are pertinent to a hidden phrase is a very important issue. We first need to identify a good keyword-based search engine that could serve as a trusted entry point to automatically retrieve the Web documents that contain information relevant to the hidden phrase. Google [9] was specifically chosen as the keyword-based search engine of choice due to its superior PageRank algorithm for ranking Web pages. After a thorough analysis of the source code structure of a set of typical and atypical Web pages authored in HTML for different hidden phrases, such as *Sexy Shoes* and *Baby Gifts*, the following three locations were identified as the best sources to gather relevant phrases in order to mine definitions of the hidden target phrase:

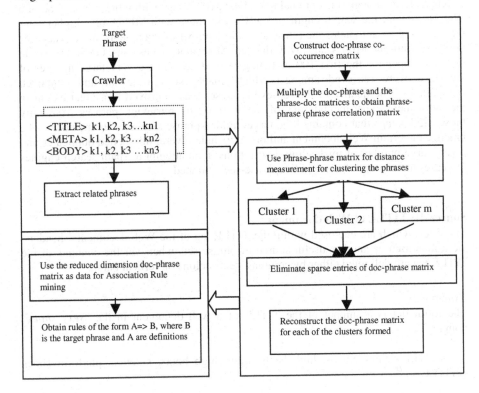

Fig. 2. Architecture of the Phrase Definition Mining System

Source – I: Phrases in the Keyword and Description META tags

Phrases included within the keyword and description META tags are valuable precursors to the contents of the document. Usually, the page author manually fills-up the phrases in these tags. Whenever the hidden phrase is mentioned in these META tags, our algorithm extracts the corresponding set of phrases as a relevant set of terms.

Example 1:
The following is a snippet of the source code of a web document retrieved using *Sexy Shoes* as the hidden phrase:

<META name="keywords" content="sexy high heeled shoes, platform shoes, high heeled boots, platform heeled boots, woman's sexy shoes, thigh high boots, exotic high heeled pumps, stiletto shoes boots, high heeled sandals, big sizes shoes, closed toed shoes, pumps really high heels, sandals, sexy boots, **sexy shoes**, shoe fashions, ... , women's stiletto shoes in large sizes, black satin high heeled shoes, stiletto shoes">

It can be observed that the set of keywords are usually related to one another and thus help us in understanding the latent semantic meaning of any one of them in terms of others. Even though it is optional to include META tags within the source code of a Web document, the search engine usually ranks those with META tags higher. Our Google wrapper automates the retrieval of any number of documents and extracts the phrases within the META tags, with the help of regular expressions. On an initial run of the wrapper for the first 100 matching Web documents, a very large number of keywords were retrieved amongst which, many were irrelevant and contained misspellings. The quality of the retrieved phrases was improved to a great extent in the subsequent experimental runs of the wrapper by retrieving phrases from only those META tags that contained the target hidden phrase as one of its members. The practice of certain Web document authors to include several misspelled duplicates and a very large number of misleading descriptions in an attempt to spam search engines increases the amount of noise in the phrase-sets obtained.

Source-II: TITLE of Web documents

The titles, which are enclosed within the TITLE tag of the Web documents' headers, were identified as another useful source of phrase sets whenever the contents of the TITLE tag are delimited either by commas, semi-colons or vertical bars.

Example 2:
The following is a snippet of the TITLE of a web document in the *"sexy shoes"* domain:

<TITLE> Sexy Shoes, high heels, thigh high boots, stilettos, platform shoes </TITLE>

Each phrase separated by a delimiter within the TITLE tag is considered as a potential phrase that could be used to define the target phrase. The set of irrelevant phrases in this case too was high when we considered all the titles retrieved by the crawler. Hence the same methodology adopted as in the case of META tags was used in this case too i.e., to consider only those titles that contain the target phrase within its contents.

Source –III: From the BODY tag of a Web document

Though the information within the BODY tag is not hidden, we consider it as a valid data source, because we hope to get rules of higher support. A Document Object Model (DOM) based HTML parser was used to parse the contents enclosed within the BODY of the Web document. The parse tree is also used as a source to retrieve collections of related phrases for the hidden phrase. First, we matched the leaf nodes that contain the hidden phrase. Then, the root to leaf path was computed and applied within the page to collect phrases that appeared at similar "positions" in the DOM tree.

Example 3:

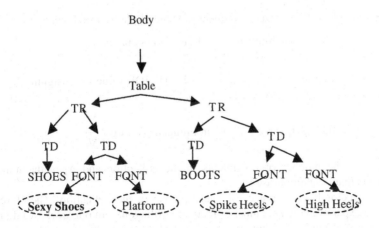

In the above example the HTML tag path to phrase "Sexy Shoes" is "Body \Table \TR \TD \FONT". When we match this path in the DOM tree we obtain the set of phrases {**Sexy Shoes**, Platform, Spike Heels, Knee High, High Heels} that co-occur at similar positions as our target phrase and are hence extracted as a co-occurrence set.

DOM tree analysis is extremely useful in case of mining definitions of target phrases that do not occur frequently in the TITLE and META tags of relevant documents. In such circumstances, the BODY may serve as an important source of co-occurrence sets.

The above three sources provide the raw collections of co-occurring phrases. The most relevant sets of correlated phrases and co-occurrence sets are systematically determined using data mining algorithms described below.

3.2 Dimensionality Reduction of the Phrase-Document Matrix

In data mining algorithms, the data preprocessing and data cleaning steps are very important. Preprocessing data affects the quality and the efficiency of the data mining algorithms. In our case, we obtained an average of around 1000 phrases for every 100 pages we crawled for a hidden phrase. We would like to reduce the dimension of the phrase-document matrices to an, empirically determined, N dimensions. We constructs such sets of phrases by first computing strongly correlated phrase sets. We compute such sets by co-occurrence clustering.

Our preprocessor first constructs the correlation matrix C, between phrases by using the original phrase-document matrix, M, that contains the TF (term frequency) values of all phrases in all documents. The number of rows of the matrix M corresponds to the number of documents in the collection and the number of columns corresponds to the number of distinct phrase that occur in all documents. Hence, for a given document d_j:

$Vector(d_j) = (ph_{1j}, ph_{2j}, ..., ph_{mj})$
$ph_{ij} > 0$ whenever phrase $ph_i \in d_j$.
The value ph_{ij} is the TF (term frequency) value of phrase i in document j.

$$TF\ (i,j) = \text{frequency of phrase } i \text{ in document } j. \tag{1}$$

Other weighting methods normally use the TF*IDF value for assigning the weight in vectors.

$$IDF(i)\ (\text{Inverse Document Frequency}) = Log \frac{N}{N_i} \tag{2}$$

Where N is the number of documents in the collection and N_i is the number of documents that contain phrase i.

Each vector holds a place for every phrase in the collection. Therefore, most vectors are sparse and hence, most of them are orthogonal. In our work, we do not use IDF factor as it tends to reduce the weight of phrases that occur in many documents and in most cases, these phrases are important in terms of descriptiveness of the hidden phrase.

In Equation 3, we define a matrix S is a phrase-phrase or Correlation matrix among phrases in the collection.

$$S = M \times M^T \tag{3}$$

$$C_{u,v} = \frac{S_{u,v}}{S_{u,u} + S_{v,v} - S_{u,v}} \tag{4}$$

Matrix C (in Equation 4) is the "*normalized matrix*" of matrix S. That means each cell in C has the value less than or equal 1.0 and every cell in diagonal has the value 1.0 (e.g. phrase i is 100% correlated with itself). C contains the normalized correlation values between phrases in the collection. Two phrases are correlated if they have high co-occurrence in the documents. The size of the matrix C is $m \times m$, where m is the number of phrases in the collection. As a consequence, the dimensionality of the matrix C is still very large. It is necessary to reduce the dimension for two main reasons. First, there is lot of noise in the data i.e. there are a lot of phrases that occurs rarely and do not contribute to the meaning of the hidden phrase. Second, the large dimension of the matrix makes the association rule miner run very inefficiently. In order to reduce the dimensions, we partition the collection of phrases into clusters. Co-occurrence clustering helps reduce the dimensionality of phrases and also increases the correlation degrees within the clusters of phrases that will be used as phrase sets for association rule mining. More specifically, we employ the idea of Hierarchical Agglomerative Clustering (HAC) [4] technique to do the co-occurrence clustering of phrases. The basic idea of HAC is as follows. At the beginning, each single phrase forms a cluster. Subsequently, we try to merge two *closest* clusters. The clustering process stops when the cardinality of merged cluster exceeds a threshold t. There are several ways to measure the distance between clusters [10]. In this work we followed the UPGMA scheme as described in [4, 6]. The correlation (distance) between two clusters is computed as in Equation 5. Specifically, suppose we have two clusters of phrases named c_1 and c_2, then

$$\text{Correlation}(c_1, c_2) = \frac{\sum_{i \in c1, j \in c2} Correlation(i, j)}{size(c1) \times size(c2)} \tag{5}$$

Where the correlation value between two phrases i and j is Correlation (i,j) = C(i,j).

Example 4:

For *"sexy shoes"* domain, some of the clusters we obtained with the above co-occurrence clustering algorithm are as follows:
{*sexy boots, sandals, stiletto*}, {*high heel, cat suit, boots*}, {*platform shoes, thigh high boots, pumps, high heels*}.
Each cluster contains phrases that have high co-occurrence correlation values amongst each other and their combinations are likely to yield good definitions for the hidden phase, *sexy shoes*.
During the experimental phase, we set t to 15. The experimental results and the performance of the algorithm are detailed in the next section.

4 Experimental Results and Evaluation

After the phrase clusters have been created, it is necessary to determine the relationships between the phrases that define the target phrase. Once the document-term matrices were created for each cluster as discussed in the previous section, the association rule miner can determine the possible relationships, which define the target phrase.

Association rules [2] are of the form A=>B, where A is the precedent and B is the antecedent. Here, A corresponds to the phrases that define the target hidden phrase B. If there are k attributes (phrases) including target phrase, then there are potentially 2^k possible association rules. Association rules can be evaluated by two measures: *Support* and *Confidence*. The generality of a rule defines *Support*, and the precision of the rule defines *Confidence*. Association rules that have both high Support and Confidence are general enough, yet precise. We used WEKA [11], a machine learning workbench to perform Association rule mining experiments.

For every cluster of each problem domain considered, we generated the association rules. Then we filtered out the rules that did not have the class label (target phrase) as its antecedent. Finally, those rules that had the best support values were chosen as candidates. This was performed for every cluster of each hidden phrase.

We performed experiments on three selected hidden phrases, namely: *sexy shoes*, *baby gifts* and *luxury beddings*. The following are the rules that were obtained for *sexy shoes* and *baby gift*. A domain expert judged the results to be *acceptable* for *"sexy shoes"* and *"baby gifts"* and as *poor* for *"luxury bedding"* since it missed some relevant phrases such as "silk", "satin", "designer", etc.

Table 1. Definition Rules for Hidden Phrase *Sexy Shoes*

Source		Rules for target phrase = sexy shoes	Support
Hidden	TITLE	Boots ➔ sexy shoes	9%
	META Tag	High heel, boots ➔ sexy shoes	15%
		Sandals, stiletto ➔ sexy shoes	12.5%
		Platform shoes ➔ sexy shoes	68%
Non-hidden	BODY	Knee high boots ➔ sexy shoes	5.2%
		Platform boots ➔ sexy shoes	5.2%
		Thigh high boots ➔ sexy shoes	5.2%

Table 2. Definition Rules for Hidden Phrase *Baby Gift*

Source		Rules for target phrase = baby gifts	Support
Hidden	TITLE	Toy ➔ baby gifts	4.8%
	META Tag	Baby clothes ➔ baby gifts	5.2%
		Infant toy ➔ baby gifts	5.2%
		Blankets, stuffed animals ➔ baby gifts	5.2%
		Teddy bears ➔ baby gifts	10.5%
		Growth charts, piggybanks ➔ baby gifts	8.7%
Non-hidden	BODY	Baby gift baskets ➔baby gifts	3.8%

As can be seen from the results, the phrases that are obtained from the hidden parts (META tag, TITLE) of pages produce rules with higher Support than those that are obtained from the non-hidden parts (BODY). This is an intersting find, as our goal in thie paper for mining hidden phrases is justified.

5 Conclusions and Future Work

The performance of our algorithm can be improved by extracting more relevant phrases and co-occurrence sets from the web document bodies. For example, the missing phrases "silk bedding", "satin bedding" and "designer bedding" for *"luxury bedding"* can be obtained by better analyzing the document contents. Sometimes, there are semantic hierarchies within web pages, such as; the "silk bedding" phrase is visually located under the "luxury bedding" in product taxonomy. Then, since root to leaf paths are different for different levels of the taxonomy we cannot extract such co-occurrences. The rules obtained from the hidden phrases can be used to better describe the content of the web page by web publishers. We propose to work on better algorithms for the extraction of relevant phrases from document contents. Also, we would like to mine "semantic" sets of phrases, such as, a set of vendor names, a set of colors, and a set of types so that we can extract phrase definitions that are cross products of these distinct attributes. For sexy shoe, such sets could enable us to mine a parametric rule that says: red, high-heel, Etienne Aigner ➔ sexy shoes.

References

1. H. Aholen, O. Heinonen, M. Klemettinen, and A. I. Verkamo.: Applying Data Mining Techniques for Descriptive Phrase Extraction in Digital Collections. Proceedings of ADL'98, Santa Barbara, USA (4, 1998)
2. R. Agrawal and R. Srikant.: Fast Algorithms for mining association rules. In Proc. 20th Int. Conf. VLDB (1994) 487–499
3. Cutting and R. Douglas.: Real life information retrieval: Commercial search engines. Part of a panel discussion at SIGIR 1997: Proc. of the 20th Annual ACM SIGIR Conference on Research and Development on Information Retrieval (1997)
4. R. C. Dubes and A. K. Jam.: Algorithms for Clustering Data, Prentice Hall, (1988)
5. J. Karlgren.: Non-topical factors in information access. Invited talk at WebNet '99, Honolulu, Hawaii, USA, (10,1999)
6. L. Kaufman and P. J. Rousseeeuw.: Finding Groups in Data: an Introduction to Cluster Analysis, John Wiley and Sons, (1990).
7. B. Len, R.Agrawal, and R. Srikant.: Discovering trends in text databases. In D. Heckerman, H. Mannila,D. Pregibon, and R. Uthrysamy, editors, Proceedings of the Third International Conference on Knowledge Discovery and Data Mining (KDD'97), Newport Beach, California, USA (8,1997). AAAI Press 227–230
8. Y. K. Liu.: Finding Description of Definitions of Words on the WWW. Master thesis, University of Sheffield, England, 2000. Available at : http://dis.shef.ac.uk/mark/cv/publications/dissertations/Liu2000.pdf
9. L. Page and S. Brin: The anatomy of a large-scale hyper-textual Web search engine. Proceedings of the Seventh International Web Conference WWW 1998
10. M. Steinbach, G. Karypis, and V. Kumar.: A Comparison of Document Clustering Techniques. Technical Report #00-034, Department of Computer Science and Engineering, University of Minnesota, USA.
11. I. Witten and E. Frank: Data Mining: Practical Machine Learning tools and techniques with Java Implementations. Morgan Kaufman 2000
12. www.overture.com
13. www.wordtracker.com

Extending a Web Browser with Client-Side Mining

Hongjun Lu, Qiong Luo, and Yeuk Kiu Shun

Hong Kong University of Science and Technology
Department of Computer Science
Clear Water Bay, Kowloon
Hong Kong, China
{luhj, luo, rayshun}@cs.ust.hk

Abstract. We present WBext (Web Browser extended), a web browser extended with client-side mining capabilities. WBext learns sophisticated user interests and browsing habits by tailoring and integrating data mining techniques including association rules mining, clustering, and text mining, to suit the web browser environment. Upon activation, it automatically expands user searches, re-ranks and returns expanded search results in a separate window, in addition to returning the original search results in the main window. When a user is viewing a page containing a large number of links, WBext is able to recommend a few links from those that are highly relevant to the user, considering both the user's interests and browsing habits. Our initial results show that WBext performs as fast as a common browser and that it greatly improves individual users' search and browsing experience.

1 Introduction

Both individual web sites and common search engines have made significant efforts in organizing their contents and improving search quality in order to ease users' browsing and searching activities. Nevertheless, it is difficult and costly for these sites to tailor their content and service for every single one of the vast web population. Moreover, the interests and browsing habits of individual users are changing over time. Finally, even though some server-side personalization features are available, users usually hesitate to adopt them due to privacy concerns.

Motivated by these problems in server-side personalization, we developed a novel personalized web browser, WBext (Web Browser extended), based on client-side mining. Without the extensions activated, it is just an ordinary web browser (currently using Microsoft Internet Explorer). With the extensions activated, WBext learns user interests and habits from the browser side and provides assistance for the user to locate the desired information at any web sites or search engines.

A screen shot of WBext in use is shown in Figure 1. Click on the menu bars titled "Activity", "Search", "Recommendation", "Setting", and "Log" below the main browser window, the corresponding results from the extensions will be shown in the window at the bottom.

X. Zhou, Y. Zhang, and M.E. Orlowska (Eds.): APWeb 2003, LNCS 2642, pp. 166–177, 2003.
© Springer-Verlag Berlin Heidelberg 2003

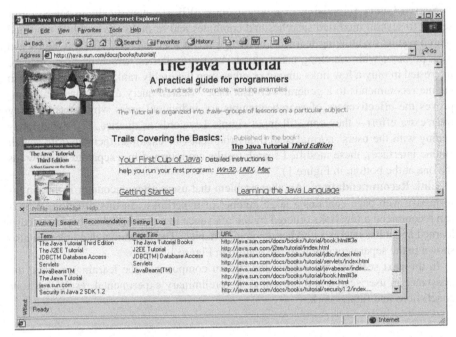

Fig. 1. WBext with Internet Explorer

The system has the following novel features:

Automatic, privacy-preserving personalization. WBext uses unsupervised learning; therefore, it does not need the users to predefine their interests or to manage their preferences as previous work based on pre-defined user profiles [5, 13]. Rather, the system continuously monitors user activities, learns user interests and habits, and adapts itself to current user interests. Because it accumulates and updates its knowledge base along with the user's browsing activities, it is able to assist users more effectively over time. In addition, the knowledge discovered is owned by the users for improving their browsing experience, not shared with any web sites for any privacy-violating actions.

Efficient and effective client-side mining. Compared with existing client-side agents supporting personalization, such as the Personal WebWatcher and others [10, 14], WBext tailors and integrates various data mining techniques, including clustering, association mining, and text mining, to discover and to maintain sophisticated user interests in the browser environment. While interests are mainly content-related, WBext further mines user browsing habits, which make link recommendations more focused and truly personalized. Compared with server side usage mining [1, 11, 12], WBext captures user activities more accurately and identifies user interests better. With detailed user activity logs, the system is able to efficiently and reliably resolve sessions and transaction entities, to evaluate importance of different textual contents, as well as to understand users' frequent navigational patterns. This ensures the high quality and completeness of knowledge discovered.

Search Query Expansion. Upon activation, WBext automatically expands a user search to several modified searches and combines and re-ranks the multiple modified search results by utilizing learned knowledge about user interests. This is motivated by a problem with searching using simple keyword queries, which is, users may be interested in only a few links among or other than the highly-ranked ones that a search engine recommends to a general web user base. Search query expansion greatly improves the effectiveness of search attempts for individual users while not requiring their extra effort – they can still input simple keywords as queries. To avoid intervening with the users' normal search environment (for example, their favorite search engine interface), these modified search results are returned in a separate window (as the one at the bottom in Figure 1).

Link Recommendation. Another problem that users often encounter is that an informative web page contains a large number of hyperlinks. In this situation, WBext can recommend a few links ordered by the relevance to a user based on the knowledge learned about her interests and her navigation habits. The recommended links are also shown in the separate window at the bottom in Figure 1.

In the next sections, we present the system components, the learning process, the assistance in user search and browsing, the preliminary experimental results, and our conclusions and future work.

2   WBext: The System

2.1   System Components

Figure 2 shows the system architecture of WBext. It consists of the following sets of main components: WBext Interface, Activity Log, Knowledge Base, WBext Miner, and WBext Agents.

The **WBext Interface** is embedded in the browser and serves as an interface layer between the web browser and other components of the system. It has two major functions: capturing activities that a user performs at the browser, and passing the results of WBext agents to the web browser.

The **Activity Log** stores user activities captured by the WBext Interface. Each entry in the Activity Log is an activity carried out by the user at the web browser. Seven kinds of activities are captured: page visit, search initiation, link following, bookmarking, text selection, page focusing, and new window spawning.

The **Knowledge Base** of WBext has two components, user interests and habits. User interests are frequently searched topics of the user, learned from the user activities. User habits refer to the navigational patterns presented in browsing activities of the user. Both types of knowledge are discovered from the Activity Log.

The **WBext Miner** consists of four modules, Log Processor, Habit Miner, Feature Extractor, and Interest Miner. The Log Processor prepares the activity log for mining. The Feature Extractor and Interest Miner discover knowledge relevant to user inter-

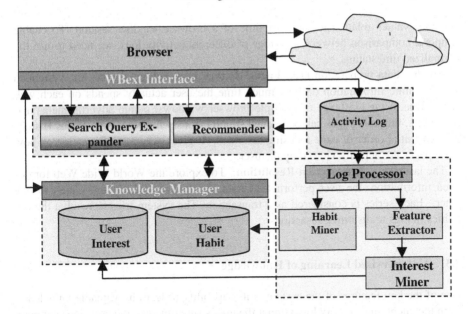

Fig. 2. WBext: The System Architecture.

ests, and the Habit Miner mines the habit of the user. The resulting knowledge is sent to the Knowledge Base.

Two types of **WBext Agents**, a Search Query Expander and a Recommender, have been implemented in the system to make use of the mined knowledge. The search query expander expands a keyword-based search query into a number of queries that better reflect the user's requirements. The Recommender provides the user with a selected list of hyperlinks appeared in the Web page that the user is browsing in the order of relevancy based on both user interests and habits.

WBext works as follows. When a user uses the browser to surf the Web, her activities are captured. The two types of knowledge are mined and accumulated in the knowledge base. After the system accumulates sufficient knowledge, the search query expander will be active when the system detects that the user is issuing a keyword search to search engines, and the recommender will be active when the user browses a Web page. All the functions can be turned off so that WBext will work just as a plain browser.

2.2 Data Preparation

The WBext interface produces an activity log for the activities carried out in each browser window. To prepare the activity logs into data that are digestible by data mining algorithms, three data preparation tasks are performed by the Log Processor: Timestamp Normalization, Focus History Generation, and Transaction Resolution.

Timestamp Normalization is to normalize the timestamps of all user activities to an absolute time value. This is because activities in different browser window sessions can be interrelated while the timestamps of activities stored in activity logs are temporal values relative to the start time of a browser window session. To enable temporal comparison between activities of different activity logs, we need to use the normalized timestamps.

Another data preparation task, **Focus History Generation**, enables the system to have accurate information on how much time the user actually spends on each web page. Due to the existence of multiple browser windows, popup advertisements and frame sets, multiple pages can be opened simultaneously for browsing. Focus History is a sequential order of page focusing activities. It gives accurate information on how these pages are actually viewed by the user.

The last task is **Transaction Resolution**. To explore the World Wide Web for desired information, the user performs a series of activities, which are related to one other. Each series is considered as a transaction. The system tries to resolve the activities in logs to disjoint transactions.

2.3   Unsupervised Learning of Knowledge

One of the key features of the system is its capability of learning valuable knowledge from the client-side activity log without the user's supervision – the user does not need to assist the system in analyzing the activity data. Two types of knowledge, User Interest and User Habit, are learned by the system, using data mining algorithms.

2.3.1   Mining of User Interest

A user has a number of interest areas, which are reflected in the activities carried out in the transactions. To capture the characteristics of user interests, similar transactions are grouped together to form clusters. Each cluster represents one interest area of the user. The vector-based model is used for this clustering analysis process. Whenever a new transaction is performed by the user and its activities is captured by the system, important features are extracted from the transaction to produce a feature vector. A cluster in the user interest base is composed of transactions whose feature vectors are similar to each other.

2.3.2   Mining of User Habit

When browsing the web, users usually have some habits that are reflected in the associations among activities. For instance, while visiting news websites, the user tends to look at the technology and sports section. Such user browsing habits are represented by association rules of form A→B, where A and B are sets of user activities. Such a rule indicates that, if the user's current activities are A, the next activity is most likely B. We developed a modified version of the Apriori Algorithm, which we call the Partial Apriori Algorithm. It can mine adaptable and generic rules from the activity data.

2.4 Application of Knowledge

When a user uses WBext for a period of time, the knowledge base grows in depth and breadth. With a proper scale of knowledge, the system can aid the user by expanding search queries and offering link recommendations.

2.4.1 Search Query Expansion

Common users use only a few keywords in their search queries, which often fail to precisely describe to the search engines what the users really want. As a result, most search attempts produce a large number of "matched" URLs. The user needs to decide the relevance manually by browsing through the result list, or to navigate deeper following the links in the result list.

When the user submits a simple keyword query to a search engine through WBext, the system will try to identify the user's current interest against the interest areas in the User Interest Base. If the activities in the current session are similar enough to one of the interest clusters, the system expands the original search query to multiple extended queries, each of which is produced by adding extra query terms to the original query. Such terms are extracted from the feature vectors in the identified interest cluster.

The results from the extended search queries are merged together and re-ranked to produce a list of extended search results. This list has improved precision as more specific keywords are added; therefore, the search attempt becomes more focused on the user's interest. Furthermore, the recall of a search attempt is also improved as a wider variety of vocabulary is introduced. Finally, since the ranking of the list is also based on the user's interest, the user will find the ranking of expanded query results closer to their preference.

2.4.2 Link Recommendation

When the user is viewing a web page with a large number of hyperlinks, the system will recommend a few links that are expected to be more relevant to the user. Each link is given a ranking score, and the links whose scores are above a threshold form the list of recommendation.

The ranking is divided into habit-based ranking and interest-based ranking. To enable habit-based ranking, the system keeps comparing the activities with the rules in the user habit base during the course of web browsing. Links that match the rules in the user habit base are given high scores. For interest-based ranking, terms in the links are compared to the terms and weights in the feature vectors within the identified cluster. Scores are then given to links according to their corresponding weights. The system combines habit-based ranking and interest-based ranking for recommending primary links.

3 Experimental Results

We have conducted preliminary experiments to evaluate the system. The browser extensions are implemented in Visual C++ as a Browser Helper Object (BHO) of the

Microsoft Internet Explorer. The experiments were done on an Intel Pentium III 800Mhz machine with 512 MB memory. The operating system was Microsoft Windows 2000 Professional. In all of the experiments, the browsing speed of WBext was comparable to that of a plain browser (the difference was hardly noticeable). In this section, we show results concerning the effectiveness of knowledge discovery, search query expansion, and link recommendations.

3.1   On Knowledge Discovery Algorithms

To show the effectiveness of knowledge discovery capability of our system, we performed an experiment during which the user browsed a number of pages related to the interests of "Java", "News" and "Data Mining" in an interleaved fashion (Table 1).

Table 1. The user browsing sessions for mining

Session	Interest	Description
01	Java	Java certification information
02	News	News, mainly technology, little sports
03	Java	Java servlets
04	News	News, sports, science and technology
05	Java	Java certification mock papers
06	Java	Java tutorials in J2EE and JDBC
07	News	News of major IT firms
08	News	Sports news
09	News	News on IT, NBA
10	News	Sports news, NBA
11	Java	Preparation of certification exams, mainly Java
12	Java	Java online tutorials
13	Data Mining	General data mining research topics
14	Data Mining	General knowledge discovery research topics
15	News	General sports news
16	Java	Java server side programming
17	News	General news browsing
18	News	News from portal sites, from different content providers
19	News	News from portal sites, from different content providers
20	Data Mining	Clustering analysis algorithms
21	Data Mining	SIGKDD conferences and papers
22	Data Mining	Theories in data mining in large databases
23	News	Cable news
24	Data Mining	Web mining
25	Java	Java sample code
26	Data Mining	Association rule mining
27	Java	Java Server Pages (JSP)
28	Data Mining	Client side web mining
29	Java	Comparison of J2EE and .Net
30	Java	JDBC and JDO

The system captured the browsing activities and identified a number of transactions. The interest miner grouped the transactions into clusters, as shown in Figure 3. It can be clearly seen that most transactions are correctly grouped into the clusters representing the interests. Nevertheless, there are a few transactions scattered around the main clusters due to the large variance in the features of the transactions. This is most prominent in the transactions of the News interest.

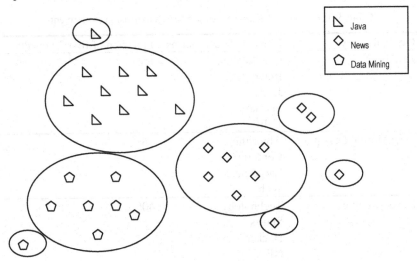

Fig. 3. Clustering user sessions

3.2   On Search Query Expansion

We then performed search query expansion experiments based on the knowledge discovered from the previous experiment. The user submitted a simple search keyword query for each topic, and the system used the user interest knowledge to perform search query expansion. The precision of a search query is defined as the percentage of the results that match the user's interest. The effectiveness of search query expansion is measured by the ratio of the precision of the first 20 expanded search results to that of the first 20 original search results. The experiments show (Tables 2 and 3) that search query expansion is capable of improving precision of a search attempt by a ratio of 2 to 3.4.

For example, an original search query was "Java Book" and the precision of the first 20 matches returned from a search engine (Google) was 25%. WBext expanded the query into five queries and sent them to the same search engine, each with one of the following terms identified from the user interest knowledge base: "Certification", "Enterprise", "J2EE", "Servlet", and "JDBC". The precision of the first 20 matches of the combined and re-ranked expanded query results was 85%, which led to a precision ratio 3.40.

Table 2. The original search queries in search expansion experiments

Search query	Interest	Precision of the first 20 results
Java Book	Java	25%
Data Mining example	Data Mining	35%
News Archive	News	20%

Table 3. The expanded search queries in search expansion experiments

Original query	Expanded query terms	Precision of first 20 results
Java Book	Certification	85%
	Enterprise	
	J2EE	
	Servlet	
	JDBC	
Data Mining example	Algorithm	75%
	Conference	
	Large-Scale	
	Web	
News Archive	Technology	40%
	Sports	
	Hacker	
	NBA	
	Entertainment	

3.3   On Link Recommendation

The last set of experiments assessed the effectiveness of link recommendation by measuring the precision and recall of the recommendation lists. The precision was defined as the percentage of recommended links that match the interests of the user. The recall was defined as the percentage of interesting recommended links to the interesting links in the web page.

We performed four web browsing sessions A, B, C, and D (Table 4). In each session, the user first conducted a number of initial browsing activities and then started to get recommendations of links from the system when encountering web pages with a large number of hyperlinks in them. We evaluated the effectiveness of three recommendations for each session.

Session A was random browsing with no interest areas; therefore, only habit-based recommendation was performed. Sessions B, C, and D focused on Java programming readings, news headlines of the day, and Data Mining reading materials, respectively. Both user interests and habits were used for recommendation in sessions B, C, and D.

As shown in Figures 4 and 5, the precision of the link recommendations was high (80-100%) and the recall varied from 20% to 94%. The random session A had a high precision value (88-100%) due to the reliability of user habits, while it suffered from a lowest recall value (20%) in the first recommendation. The effectiveness of session C was lower than that of sessions B and D, due to the diversity of terms used in news headlines. The effectiveness of sessions B was especially encouraging because the topics had distinctive terms such as "JDBC", "Servlet", and others.

Table 4. The web browsing sessions in link recommendation experiments

Session	Interest	Description of initial activities
A	None	Browsing through various interest areas
B	Java	Reading pages about Java programming
C	News	Looking for the news headlines of the day
D	Data Mining	Reading pages about data mining techniques

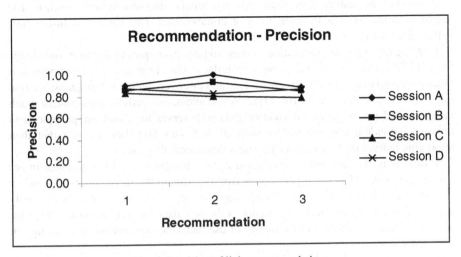

Fig. 4. Precision of link recommendations

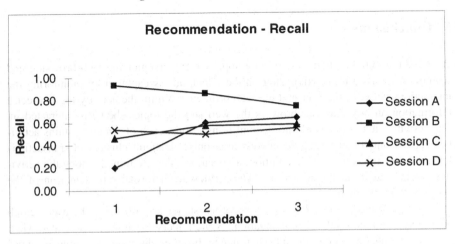

Fig. 5. Recall of link recommendations

4 Related Work

Work related to ours comes from three areas: collaborative filtering, web log mining, and intelligent agents.

Collaborative filtering, or collaborative personalization, is a technique to tailor content for specific users based on some collaborative measures that requires participation of the users. The web content provider use this means of personalization extensively. Examples include portal sites [15], online radio [5], news [8], and online learning [4]. Such systems keep user profiles and perform recommendations in the form of a personalized starting point, which straightly directs the user to the location of proper contents. In addition to recommendations, the profiles are also used for purposes such as pushing appropriate advertisements. In these systems, each profile has to be constructed with some form of collaboration with the user. In contrast, WBext does not require any collaborative efforts from the user.

Web log mining is an application of data mining techniques to discover knowledge from HTTP access logs of web servers. Similar to our client side mining approach, it requires pre-processing [3] steps on the logs and discovers patterns through association rules mining and clustering ([16], [7]). Nevertheless, our activity logs contain much more detailed and accurate information than web server logs, and our purpose is to improve individual user experience with all web sites that they access rather than improving individual web sites for the users that access those sites.

WBext is in the category of intelligent agents that provide users assistance in accessing the Web. Most intelligent agents ([6], [9]) run on the server side or depend on a server side component [2], which may cause privacy concerns. Moreover, they only track link following and web page visits as the raw data for learning tasks. In comparison, WBext monitors a wider variety of user activities and enhances the quality of knowledge discovered.

5 Conclusions

We have presented a client side mining approach to personalizing web browsing and search. A detailed user activity log on the client side is captured by monitoring the interactions between the user and the web browser. Within the activity log is precise information on how the user browses the web and the topics she/he is interested in. The activities log is resolved into disjoint transactions, each of which contains activities carried out for one specific interest area only. Disjoint clusters of transactions form the user interest base. In addition, association rules are mined among the activities carried out in each transaction. These rules are a formal representation of the user's web browsing habits.

Using the mined knowledge, two types of assistance are offered to the user: search query expansion and link recommendation. Search query expansion is activated when the user initiates a search attempt when he/she browses the web. A simple keyword query specified by the user is expanded to multiple extended queries, which are compositions of the original query terms and additional terms extracted from the cluster that represents the current interest of the web browsing session. Link recommendation is provided whenever the user visits a web page. Both the user interest and user habit knowledge can be utilized for this purpose.

We have evaluated the effectiveness of our approach on WBext, our prototype system. The initial results of the experiments are encouraging. Future work on the client side activity log mining approach includes finer distinction of topics within the same interest area hierarchically and generation of association rules that applies to particular interest areas.

References

1. A. G. Buchner, M. Baumgarten, S. S. Anand, M. D. Mulvenna, and J. G. Hughes: User-Driven Navigation Pattern Discovery from Internet Data. WebKDD, 1999.
2. L. Chen and K. Sycara: WebMate: Personal Agent for Browsing and Searching. In Proc. 2nd Int'l Conf on Autonomous Agents, pp. 132–139. 1998.
3. R. Cooley, B. Mobasher, and J. Srivastava: Data Preparation for Mining World Wide Web Browsing Patterns. Journal of Knowledge and Information Systems, 1(1), 1999.
4. C. Groeneboer, D. Stockley, and T. Calvert: Virtual-U: A collaborative model for online learning environments. In Proc. Second International Conference on Computer Support for Collaborative Learning, Toronto, Ontario, December 1997.
5. D. B. Hauver and J. C. French: Flycasting: Using Collaborative Filtering to Generate a Playlist for Online Radio. International Conference on Web Delivering of Music, 2001.
6. T. Joachims, D. Freitag, and T. Mitchell: WebWatcher: A tour guide for the World Wide Web. In Proc. IJCAI-97, Nagoya, Japan.
7. A. Joshi and R. Krishnapuram: On Mining web Access Logs. In Proc. 2000 ACM SIGMOD Workshop on Research Issues in Data Mining and Knowledge Discovery 2000, pp. 63–69, 2000.
8. K. Lang: NewsWeeder: Learning to Filter Netnews. In Proc. 12th International Conference on Machine Learning, pp. 331–339, 1995.
9. J.P. McGowan, N. Kushmerick, and B. Smyth: Who do you want to be today? Web Personae for personalized information access. International Conference on Adaptive Hypermedia and Adaptive web-Based Systems (AH2002), Malaga, Spain.
10. D. Mladenic: Personal WebWatcher: Implementation and Design. Technical Report, IJS-DP-7472, Dept. of Intelligent Systems, J. Stefan Institute, Slovenia, 1996.
11. B. Mobasher, H.Dai,T.Luo,M.Nakagawa,Y.Sun, and J.Wiltshire: Discovery of Aggregate Usage Profiles for Web Personalization, WebKDD 2000.
12. M.D. Mulvenna, S.S. Anand, and A.G. Buchner: Personalization on the Net Using Web Mining. CACM, Vol. 43(8):pp. 123–125, August 2000.
13. R. Rafter, B. Smyth: A domain analysis methodology for collaborative filtering. 23rd BCS European Annual Colloquium on Information Retrieval Research, Darmstadt, Germany, April 2001.
14. C. Shahabi: Knowledge Discovery from users web-page navigation. ICDE-RIDE 1997.
15. Yahoo! Inc.: Welcome to My Yahoo! http://my.yahoo.com
16. O. R. Zaïane, Man Xin, Jiawei Han: Discovering Web Access Patterns and Trends by Applying OLAP and Data Mining Technology on Web Logs. ADL 1998: 19–29.

Real-Time Segmenting Time Series Data

Aiguo Li, Shengping He, and Zheng Qin

Department of Computer Science, Xi'an Jiaotong University, 710049, Xi'an, Shaanxi, China
liag@xust.edu.cn, zhqin@xjtu.edu.cn

Abstract. There has been increased interest in time series data mining recently. In some cases, approaches of real-time segmenting time series are necessary in time series similarity search and data mining, and this is the focus of this paper. A real-time iterative algorithm that is based on time series prediction is proposed in this paper. Proposed algorithm consists of three modular steps. (1) Modeling: the step identifies an autoregressive moving average (ARMA) model of dynamic processes from a time series data; (2) prediction: this step makes k steps ahead prediction based on the ARMA model of the process at a crisp time point. (3) Change-points detection: the step is what fits a piecewise segmented polynomial regressive model to the time series data to determine whether it contains a new change-point. Finally, high performance of the proposed algorithm is demonstrated by comparing with Guralnik-Srivastava algorithm.

1 Introduction

There has been increased interest in time series data mining and similarity search recently [1-4,7-10]. The application background of segmenting time series methods includes using data-mining techniques to extract interesting patterns from time series data generated by sensors. Some batch or incremental algorithms have been proposed for segmenting time series [5,6]. However, in some real-time application situations, it is necessary for real-time detection of events from time series data. We will consider a real-valued time series denoted by x_t, $t = 1, 2, \dots$, where t is a time varying parameter. When a crisp observed value x_t is obtained at time point t, we need an algorithm to determine whether the time point t is a new change-point or not before next time point $t + 1$. The problem is the focus of this paper.

We propose two iterative real-time segmenting time series algorithms based on time series prediction. Proposed algorithms consist of three modular steps: Modeling, Prediction, and Change-point detection. (1) Modeling: the step identifies the ARMA (Autoregressive Moving Average) model of a dynamic process from time series data; (2) Prediction: this step predictions that future k time points states based on the ARMA model of the process. The k steps Kalman predictor of ARMA model is employed in this paper; (3) Change-points detection: the step is that fits a piecewise poly

X. Zhou, Y. Zhang, and M.E. Orlowska (Eds.): APWeb 2003, LNCS 2642, pp. 178–186, 2003.

nomial regressive model to a time segment, and maximum likelihood principles is applied to determine whether it contains a new change-point or not.

The remainder of the paper is organized as follows: section 2 describes the segmenting time series problem briefly. Section 3 presents the real-time segmenting time series algorithms. Section 4 describes experiments involved in comparing our algorithms with the batch algorithm proposed by Guralnik and Srivastava [6]. Finally, section 5 concludes the paper.

2   Real-Time Segmenting Time Series

It is supposed that a real valued time series x_t, $t = 1,2,...,$ N can be modeled mathematically, where each model is characterized by a set of parameters, the segmenting time series problem becomes the change-point detection problem [6], so we don't discriminate segmenting time series from change-point detection in this paper.

2.1   Segmenting Time Series

Consider a real-valued time series denoted by

$$x_t, t = 1,2,..., N .$$ (1)

Where t is a time varies. We can find a piecewise segmented model M, given by

$$X = \begin{cases} f_1(t,w_1) + e_1(t), (0 < t \le \alpha_1) \\ f_2(t,w_2) + e_2(t), (\alpha_1 < t \le \alpha_2) \\ ...... \\ f_k(t,w_k) + e_k(t), (\alpha_{k-1} < t \le \alpha_k = N) \end{cases} .$$ (2)

Where $f_i(t,w_i), 1 \le i \le k$ is a basis class function (with its vector of parameters w_i) that is fit in segment i; the vector $\mathbf{\alpha} = (\alpha_1, \alpha_2,..., \alpha_k)$ is the change points set of time series x_t, $t = 1,2,..., N$; and $e_i(t), i = 1,2,..., k$ is error term in ith segment.

Likelihood L is defined as below:

$$L = \sum_{i=1}^{k} l_i = \sum_{i=1}^{k} s_i .$$ (3)

Where k is the number of change-points; l_i is the likelihood of ith segment; and s_i is the residual sum of squares for the model of ith segment. Here s_i is defined as below

$$s_i = \sum_{j=0}^{m_i} (x_{\alpha_{i-1}+j} - f_i(\alpha_{i-1} + j, w_i))^2 . \qquad (4)$$

Where $m_i = \alpha_i - \alpha_{i-1}$ is the number of time points in ith segment.

The maximum likelihood estimate (MLE) of change points set $\boldsymbol{\alpha} = (\alpha_1, \alpha_2, ..., \alpha_k)$ and parameters vector w_i of $f_i(t, w_i), i = 1, 2, ..., k$ can be found by means of minimizing the likelihood L.

2.2 Real-Time Segmenting Time Series

Consider a time series defined in Eq. (1), we suppose that actual sample value $x_1, x_2, ..., x_{i-1}$ and $\boldsymbol{\alpha} = (\alpha_1, \alpha_2, ..., \alpha_k)$ have been known. When a crisp sample value x_i is obtained at sample time instant i, it is necessary to determine whether time instant i is a new change point or only a candidate by means of minimizing the likelihood L.

3 Proposed Algorithms

The real-time algorithms we have proposed consist of three modular steps: modeling, prediction, and change-point detection. The step of modeling identifies the ARMA model of a dynamic process from time series data. The ARMA model of the time series can be identified either in a priori or in iterative processes of the algorithms. The step of prediction is to predict future k time point states based on the ARMA model. Many approaches of modeling and prediction have been proposed [11]. In our experiments of the paper, the k steps Kalman predictor of ARMA model is employed (see section 4). The step of change-points detection is that fits a piecewise regressive model to a time segment, and maximum likelihood principles is applied to determine whether it contains an new change-point or not.

The basis idea of the real-time algorithms is that the k steps prediction are made which are denoted by $x_i(1), x_i(2), ..., x_i(k)$ at every crisp sample i, then i is examined to see whether it is an new change point or a candidate, according to x_i and $x_i(1), x_i(2), ..., x_i(k)$. The algorithms work under the assumption that a dynamic process can be described by an ARMA(n ,m) model:

$$\varphi(q^{-1})x_t = \theta(q^{-1})a_t \; . \tag{5}$$

Where

$$\varphi(q^{-1}) = 1 + \varphi_1 q^{-1} + \varphi_2 q^{-2} + \dots + \varphi_n q^{-n} \; . \tag{6}$$

$$\theta(q^{-1}) = 1 + \theta_1 q^{-1} + \theta_2 q^{-2} + \dots + \theta_m q^{-m} \; . \tag{7}$$

The parameters vector of the ARMA model is

$$\Phi = (\varphi_1, , \varphi_2, \dots, \varphi_n; \theta_1, \theta_2, \dots, \theta_n) \; . \tag{8}$$

3.1 The Algorithm A

Many approaches to identify the ARMA model of dynamic processes from time series data have been proposed [11]. If there are enough time series data, the ARMA model of the time series could be identified a priori. When the ARMA model of the time series is known a priori, the framework of the real-time segmenting algorithm is described as follows:

1) Given a time series Eq.(1); regressive model Eq(2), and model set Mset
   of $f_i(t, w_i), i = 1, 2, \dots, k$; ARMA model

2) Initialize $x_0, x_{-1}, \dots, x_{-n-m}$; $\mathbf{\alpha} = \{ \alpha_1 = 0 \}$, L=0;

   maximum prediction steps K; new change point ncp= 0.

3) for t= 2:1:N

   a). k steps prediction: $x_t(1), x_t(2), \dots, x_t(k)$

   Where $k <= K$;

   b). for i= ncp:1:t % change point detection

   Compute likelihood: $l1 = l(ncp, t+k)$; and $l2 = l(ncp, i) + l(i, t+k)$;

   if $((l1 - l2)/l1) > \mu$

   $ncp = I$; $l1 = l2$; $l3 = l(ncp, i)$;

   end if

   end for

   $\alpha = \alpha \cup ncp$; $L = L + l3$;

   end for

4) Output α, L.

5) End.

3.2 The Algorithm B

If the ARMA model of a dynamic process is unknown, we have to on-line identify the ARMA model of the dynamic process. Many iterative algorithms of identifying the ARMA model have been proposed. An assumption is what the orders of the ARMA model are known a priori. In this case, the framework of the real-time segmenting algorithm is described as follows:

1) Given a time series Eq.(1); regressive model Eq(2), and model set Mset
   of $f_i(t, w_i), i = 1, 2, ..., k$; the orders of ARMA model n and m

2) Initialize $x_0, x_{-1}, ..., x_{-n-m}$; $\alpha = \{ \alpha_1 = 0 \}$, $L=0$;

   maximum prediction steps K, new change point: $ncp= 0$.
3) for $t= n:1:N$
   a) Identifying ARMA model parameters Φ_t

   b) k steps prediction: $x_t(1), x_t(2), ..., x_t(k)$
      Where $k<=K$
   c) for $i= ncp:1:t$ % change point detection
      Compute likelihood: $l1= l(ncp, t+k)$; and $l2= l(ncp, i)+ l(i, t+k)$;
      if $(l1- l2)/ l1> \mu$

            $ncp=I$; $l1= l2$; $l3= l(ncp, i)$;
      end if
   end for
   $\alpha = \alpha \cup ncp$; $L= L+ l3$;

   end for
4) Output α, L;
5) End.

4 Experimental Results

The data used in our experiments is taken from a vibration experiment of a bus. In the raw data set D, the sample period is 5 milliseconds, and the data length is 512. At each sample instant, the amplitude of the bus vibration is recorded, and the unit of the amplitude is millimetre. The raw data set D is divided into two data subsets D1, and D2. D1 contains 400 data that come from the front elements of set D, and D2 contains 112 data that come from the rest data of set D. Set D, D1, and D2 are denoted respectively by D= { $d_1, d_2, ..., d_{512}$ } ; D1= { $d_1, d_2, ..., d_{400}$ }; D2= { $d_{401}, d_{402}, ..., d_{512}$ }. The raw data is shown in Figure 1.
Data set D1 is used to off-line identify the ARMA model of the time series for real-time segmenting algorithm A described in section 3.1. However, set D2 is used to examine the real-time algorithms described in above.

We are interested in how our real-time segmenting algorithms performed compared to the batch algorithm proposed by Guralnik and Srivastava [6].

For experimental purposes, the regressive model set Mset of $f_i(t, w_i)$, $i = 1,2,...,k$ in Eq. (2) is a group of polynomials as below:

$$f_i(t, w_i) = 1 + w_{i,1}t + w_{i,2}t^2 + ... + w_{i,p}t^p \tag{9}$$

$$i = 1,2,...,k$$

In our experiments, p_{max}=3.

The k steps ahead prediction algorithm used in our experiments is a Kalman prediction algorithm. Supposed the ARMA(n, m) model is described by Eq. (5), (6), and $n=m$. The k steps ahead Kalman prediction algorithm is described as below:

$$\theta(q^{-1})x_t(k) = G_k(q^{-1})x_t \tag{10}$$

Where the coefficient vector of $G_k(q^{-1})$ is

$$\mathbf{g}_k = (g_{k1}, g_{k2}, ..., g_{kn})^T = A^{k-1}K_P \tag{11}$$

$$A = \begin{bmatrix} -\varphi_1 & \\ -\varphi_2 & I_{n-1} \\ ... & \\ -\varphi_n & 0 \ ... \ 0 \end{bmatrix} \tag{12}$$

$$K_P = (\theta_1 - \varphi_1, \theta_2 - \varphi_2, ..., \theta_n - \varphi_n)^T \tag{13}$$

Obviously, only would Eq. (13) be changed slightly, when $n \neq m$.

The experimental results are shown in Figure 2, 3, and 4, and Table 1, 2. Figure 2 shows the results of Guralnik-Srivastava (GS) batch algorithm; Figure 3 and Figure 4 show the results of our algorithms described respectively in section 3.

The orders of ARMA model the process used in our algorithms are n= 6 and m= 5. Box-Jenkins method is used to off-line identify the ARMA model of the process in the real-time segmenting algorithm A. However, iterative least square method is used to on-line identify the ARMA model of the process in the algorithm B.

According to the results in Table 1, the likelihood value L of GS batch algorithm is nearly 3 times than that of proposed algorithm A and B, the likelihood value L of the algorithm B is slightly larger than that of the algorithm A, so the segmenting result of algorithm A is best, and that of the GS batch algorithm is worst. The compute speeds of our algorithm A and B are great faster than that of GS batch algorithm. In fact, the memory demand of the algorithm A and B are less than that of batch algorithm too.

Fig. 5 shows daily closing price data of IBM stock from Jan. 1, 1980 to Oct. 8, 1992 (http://www-personal.buseco.monash.edu.au/~hyndman/TSDL/korsan/dailyibm.dat),

totally 3333 points. The 1000 points of the front of the raw dataset were used for estimating prediction model, and the remaining 2333 points for evaluating the proposed
algorithms. ARMA(5, 4) models were used in algorithm A and B. The basis class
functions were polynomial functions, and pmax=3. Because computing efficiency of
batch GS algorithm is low in large dataset, incremental GS algorithm [6] is used for
comprising with algorithm A and B. The experimental results are shown in Table 3.
In Table 3, the likelihood value of algorithm A and B are very small, so the evaluating
results of algorithm A and B are better than that of GS algorithm.

5   Conclusions

In this paper, we presented two real-time segmenting time series algorithms that based
on time series prediction. We have analyzed how ARMA model of a process could be
used in segmenting time series. The experiments show that proposed algorithms are
superior to Guralnik-Srivastava batch algorithm.

Table 1. Comparison of likelihood estimation and run time of the three algorithms

Algorithm	μ	L	CPU Time (sec)
GS Algorithm	0.02	4747.4	41.08
Algorithm A	0.9	1052.9	2.03
Algorithm B	0.9	1190.4	3.51

Table 2. The results of segmenting the bus vibration data by the three algorithms respectively

Algorithm	Chang Point Set
GS Algorithm	0, 13, 21, 29, 37, 44, 57, 66, 74, 84, 97, 105, 112
Algorithm A	0, 7, 14, 21, 28, 35, 43, 50, 57, 73, 80, 87, 94, 101, 108
Algorithm B	0, 7, 15, 25, 32, 44, 51, 58, 65, 72, 79, 86, 93, 100, 108

Table 3. The results of segmenting daily closing price of IBM stock with GS algorithm and
proposed algorithms respectively

Algorithm	μ	L	CPU Time (sec)	Number of change points
GS Algorithm	0.02	155080	14572	10
Algorithm A	0.2	1497.9	14.44	328
Algorithm B	0.9	1437.6	38.05	334

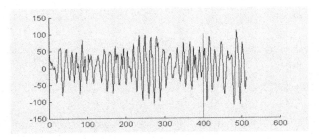

Fig. 1. Bus vibration time series data

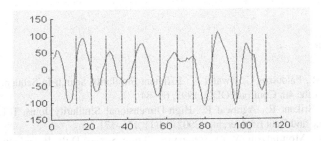

Fig. 2. Result of segmenting bus vibration time series using GS batch algorithm

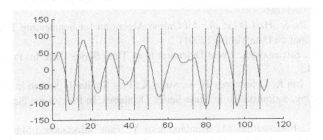

Fig. 3. Result of segmenting bus vibration time series using the algorithm A

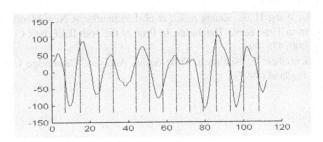

Fig. 4. Result of segmenting bus vibration time series using the algorithm B

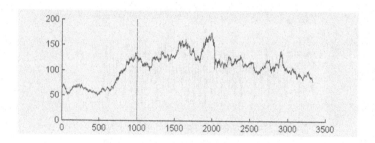

Fig. 5. Daily closing price time series data of IBM stock

References

1. Agrawal R., Faloutsos C., Swami A.: Efficient Similarity Search In Sequence Databases. In: Proc of the 4th Conf on FODO, 1993, 69–84
2. Shim K., Srikant R., Agrawal R.: High-Dimensional Similarity Joins. IEEE Trans. on Knowledge and Data Engineering (2002) 14(1): 156–171
3. Rafiai D., Mondelzon A. O.: Querying Time Series Data Based on Similarity. IEEE Trans on Knowledge and Data Engineering (2000) 12(5): 675–693
4. Keogh E., Chakrabarti K., Pazzani M., Mehrotra S.: Dimensionality Reduction for Fast Similarity Search in Large Time Series Databases. Knowledge and Information Systems (2001) 3(3): 263–286
5. Keogh E., Chu S., Hart D., et al.: An Online Algorithm for Segmenting Time Series. In: IEEE Int'l Conf on Data Mining (2001)
6. Guralnik V., Srivastava J.: Event Detection from Time Series Data. In: Proc of SIGKDD (1999) 33–42
7. Agrawal R., Lin K. I., Sawhney H. S., Shim K.: Fast Similarity Search in the Presence of Noise, Scaling, andranslation in Time-Series Databases. In Proc of the 2lst VLDB (1995) 490–50
8. Faloutsos C., Ranganathan M., Manolopoulos Y.: Fast Subsequence Matching in Time-Series Databases. In Proc. of the ACM SIGMOD Conf. on Management of Data (1994) 419–429
9. Chan K. P., Fu A. W.: Efficient Time Series Matching by Wavelets. In Proc of the 15th ICDE (1999)
10. Perng C. S., Wang H. X., Zhang S. R., et al: Landmarks: A New Model for Similarity-Based Pattern in Time Series Databases. In Proc of the 16th IEEE Int'l Conf on Data Engineering (2000) 475–693
11. Kantz H., Schreiber T.: Nonlinear Time Series Analysis, Cambridge University Press, Cambridge, England (1997)

An Efficient Data Mining Algorithm for Discovering Web Access Patterns

Show-Jane Yen[1] and Yue-Shi Lee[2]

[1] Department of Computer Science & Information Management, Fu Jen Catholic University,
510 Chung Cheng Rd., Hsinchuan, Taipei 242, Taiwan, R.O.C.
sjyen@csie.fju.edu.tw
[2] Department of Information Management, Ming Chuan University,
5 The-Ming Rd., Gwei Shan District, Taoyuan County 333, Taiwan, R.O.C.
leeys@mcu.edu.tw

Abstract. In this paper, we propose a data mining technology to find *non-simple frequent traversal patterns* in a web environment where users can travel from one object to another through the corresponding hyperlinks. We keep track and remain the original user traversal paths in a web log, and apply the proposed data mining techniques to discover the complete traversal path which is traversed by a sufficient number of users, that is, non-simple frequent traversal patterns, from web logs. The non-simple frequent traversal patterns include forward and backward references, which are used to suggest potentially interesting traversal path to the users. The experimental results show that the discovered patterns can present the complete browsing paths traversed by most of the users and our algorithm outperforms other algorithms in discovered information and execution times.

1 Introduction

The definitions about mining non-simple frequent traversal patterns are presented as follows: A *page* is corresponding to a web page or object in the web. A *traversal sequence* is a set of pages ordered by increasing traversal-time, which is represented as $<s_1, s_2, \ldots, s_n>$ and s_i is a page. For two traversal sequences $<a_1, a_2, \ldots, a_n>$ and $<b_1, b_2, \ldots, b_m>$, if there exists an ordered integers $i_1 < i_2 < \ldots < i_n$, $1 \leq i_k \leq m$, such that $a_1 \subseteq bi_1, \ldots, a_n \subseteq bi_n$, then $<a_1, a_2, \ldots, a_n>$ is contained in $<b_1, b_2, \ldots, b_m>$. A traversal sequence is *maximal* if this sequence is not contained in any other sequence.

A *user sequence* is a complete traversal sequence for a user from entering to existing the web system. A *user sequence database* contains a set of user sequences traversed by all users in the system, which includes user identifiers, traversal pages and traversal-time. A user sequence c *supports* a traversal sequence s if s is contained in c. The *support* for a traversal sequence s is the number of user sequences that supports s. If the support for a traversal sequence s satisfies the user-specified *minimum support* threshold, then s is called *frequent traversal sequence*. The *length* of a traversal se

X. Zhou, Y. Zhang, and M.E. Orlowska (Eds.): APWeb 2003, LNCS 2642, pp. 187–192, 2003.
© Springer-Verlag Berlin Heidelberg 2003

quence s is the number of pages in the sequence. A traversal sequence of length k is called a *k-traversal sequence*, and a frequent traversal sequence of length k a *frequent k-traversal sequence*. If a frequent traversal sequence is maximal among all the other frequent traversal sequences, then the frequent traversal sequence is a *frequent traversal pattern*. If there are repeated pages in a traversal sequence, then this sequence is called *non-simple traversal sequence*. Otherwise, the traversal sequence is called *simple traversal sequence*.

In this paper, we propose an efficient algorithm to discover all the non-simple frequent traversal patterns from a user sequence database in a web environment. For the convenience, the non-simple frequent traversal sequence is also called *frequent traversal sequence*. Before generating the frequent traversal sequences, we need to generate the *candidate traversal sequences*, and scan the database to count the support for each candidate traversal sequence to decide if it is a frequent traversal sequence. A candidate traversal sequence of length k is called a *candidate k-traversal sequence*.

Mining path traversal patterns is to discover web access patterns in a distributed information-providing environment. M.S. Chen and et al. [2] proposed a method for mining path traversal patterns. They first devised an algorithm, called MF algorithm, to convert the original log sequence into a set of maximal forward references which will loss the information about backward references. Second, they devised two algorithms full-scan (FS) and selective-scan (SS) for finding frequent traversal sequences from the maximal forward references, which utilize some techniques on hashing to prune the candidates and trim the database for each database scan. However, since the information about backward references has been removed by applying MF algorithm, the discovered frequent traversal sequences are also lost some information. Besides, if the minimum support threshold decreases, that is, the number of frequent traversal sequences increases, then the 2-candidate sequences which can be pruned by the hash method are very few and the size of the database almost cannot be trimmed. Hence, the performance of FS (SS) with MF algorithm can be degraded.

2   Mining Non-simple Frequent Traversal Sequences

Owing to the web structure is designed by experts, there must be the relationships between every two pages which are linked together. We want to analyze the traversal paths traversed by all the users in the web structure to understand the users' interests.

Some algorithms for mining sequential patterns [1, 3, 4] are for different applications, such as improving the designs of web sites. Our research focuses on the application for understanding user behaviors and suggesting potentially interesting traversal paths to the users. We want to discover the frequent traversal sequences that allow the same page appearing in a sequence more than once, that is, non-simple frequent traversal sequences. We propose an efficient algorithm to find all the non-simple frequent traversal sequences in a web-training environment, which can provide users with connecting to the next desired page rapidly and obtaining the needed information immediately, such that the search time and the waiting time can be reduced.

2.1 The Algorithm for Mining Non-simple Frequent Traversal Sequences

We propose an efficient algorithm MFTP (Mining Frequent Traversal Patterns) to mining the non-simple frequent traversal sequences in which each page has a directed link to the next page from a web environment. This algorithm considers the structure of the web site.The method to generate candidate (k+1)-traversal sequences (k ≥ 1) is as follows: for every two frequent k-traversal sequences $<r, S_1, S_2, ..., S_{k-1}>$ and $< S_1, S_2, ..., S_{k-1}, t>$, the candidate (k+1)-traversal sequence $< r, S_1, S_2, ..., S_{k-1}, t>$ can be generated. In order to clearly explain our algorithm MFTP, we give the following example:

Example 1: The web structure is shown in Fig. 1 and the user sequence database is shown in Table 1. Suppose the minimum support threshold is set to 40%. We shall find all the non-simple frequent traversal sequences in which each page has a directed link to the next page from the user sequence database.

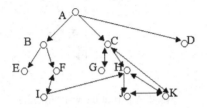

Fig. 1. A web structure

Table 1. User sequence database

User ID	User sequences
User 001	ABEBFIH
User 002	ABFIHKCHKCHK
User 003	ACGCGCKJKC
User 004	ACHKJKC
User 005	BFIFH

First, the database is scanned to count the support for each page. After generating all the candidate 2-traversal sequences, the candidate 2-traversal sequence can be pruned if there is no directed link from the first page to the next page in the candidate 2-traversal sequence. From this method, the number of candidate 2-traversal sequences can be reduced. For the second database scan, we count the support for each candidate 2-traversal sequence.

2.2 A Special Database Scanning Method

After finding the frequent 2-traversal sequences, we can generate the candidate 3-traversal sequences ABF, ACH, BFI, CHK, FIH, HKC, HKJ, IHK, JKC, JKJ, KCH, and KJK. In the following, we propose a *special database scanning method* to generate all the frequent k-traversal (k ≥ 3) sequence. We use another example to explain this method: Suppose there is a user sequence {ABCDEFDGHIGJDK}, and a part of the web structure is shown in Fig. 2.

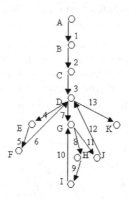

Fig. 2. A part of the web structure

After generating all the candidate 3-traversal sequences, we need to scan each user sequence in the database to count the support for each candidate 3-traversal sequence. The key point is how to generate all the combinations of the traversal sequences of length 3, in which each page has a directed link to the next page in the web structure, for counting the supports of the candidate 3-traversal sequences. We use the *directed linked traversal sequence table* (DLTS) to explain the special database scanning method, which is shown in Table 3, and the traversal order for the user sequence is shown in Table 2.

In Table 3, when the third page C is scanned, the 3-traversal sequence {ABC} can be sequentially generated to check if this sequence exists in the set of the candidate 3-traversal sequences. If the sequence has ever been generated from the same user sequence, then this sequence is ignored. Similarly, when the forth page D is scanned, the 3-traversal sequence {BCD} can be sequentially generated. When the seventh page D is scanned, because page D has appeared in the forth page and its previous page, that is, the third page is C, a ready sequence {CD} is generated. When the eighth page G is scanned, except that the 3-traversal sequence {FDG} is sequentially generated, the 3-traversal sequence {CDG} is also generated by combining the ready sequence {CD} and the page G. For the generated traversal sequence {CDG}, there are directed link from each page to the next page in the web structure in Fig. 2, but we cannot generate this sequence if we just sequentially generate the traversal sequences from this user sequence.

Similarly, when the eleventh and the thirteenth pages G and D are scanned, the ready sequences are also generated for generating the traversal sequences in which each page has a directed link to the next page from the user sequence when the next pages J and K are scanned, respectively. After scanning all the user sequences in the database, the support for each candidate 3-traversal sequence can be counted and the frequent 3-traversal sequences can be obtained.

Table 2. The traversal order for the user sequence {ABCDEFDGHIGJDK}

Pages	A	B	C	D	E	F	D	G	H	I	G	J	D	K
Order	1	2	3	4	5	6	7	8	9	10	11	12	13	14

Table 3. The user sequence scan for generating all the frequent 3-traversal sequences

Scanning order	Pages	Ready sequence	Generated traversal sequence	Scanning order	Pages	Ready sequence	Generated traversal sequence
1	A			9	H		DGH
2	B			10	I		GHI
3	C		ABC	11	G	DG	HIG
4	D		BCD	12	J		IGJ
5	E		CDE				DGJ
6	F		DEF	13	D	CD, FD	GJD
7	D	CD	EFD	14	K		JDK
8	G		FDG				CDK
			CDG				FDK

3 Experimental Results

We first construct a web structure, and refer to [2] to generate the synthetic user sequences. Since backward reference is an important browsing behavior, most of the users may often perform the backward references when they are traveling the web structure. We change the parameter R, which is the probability of backward references in a user sequence, to generate 4 synthetic user sequence databases P500-D100-I15-**R10**, P500-D100-I15-**R20**, P500-D100-I15-**R30**, P500-D100-I15-**R40**, and the parameter R's are set to 10%, 20%, 30% and 40%, respectively.

The relative execution times for algorithms FS with MF [2] and MFTP are shown in Table 4 and the maximum length of the frequent traversal sequences discovered by the two algorithms for each database are shown in Table 5.

Table 4. Relative execution times

Databases	MFTP	FS with MF
P500-D100-I15-**R10**	1	1.04
P500-D100-I15-**R20**	1	1.07
P500-D100-I15-**R30**	1	1.03
P500-D100-I15-**R40**	1	0.98

Table 5. The maximum length of the frequent traversal sequences generated by the two algorithms

Databases	MFTP	FS with MF
P500-D100-I15-**R10**	7	7
P500-D100-I15-**R20**	7	6
P500-D100-I15-**R30**	8	6
P500-D100-I15-**R40**	8	5

For FS with MF algorithm, a user sequence is converted into a set of maximal forward references, such that some information, such as backward references, is lost. MFTP algorithm remains the original user sequences without any information loss. Hence, the information discovered by MFTP is more than that of FS with MF algorithm. In Table 5, the maximum length of the frequent traversal sequences discovered by FS with MF is smaller than that of MFTP, especially, when the parameter R is increased to 30% and 40%. For Table 4, in some cases, The performance of FS with MF is slightly worst than MFTP, because there are more frequent traversal sequences generated when the number of the pages is reduced, such that FS with MF cannot reduce the number of the candidate 2-traversal sequences and the size of the database effectively. However, MFTP can reduce the number of candidate 2-traversal sequences significantly according to the web structure. In the case of the parameter R being set to 40%, because the maximum length of the frequent traversal sequences generated by FS with MF is only 5 (Table 5), that is, it needs only 5 database scans, but MFTP needs 8 database scans. Hence, the performance of FS with MF is slightly better than MFTP.

Achknowledgement. Research on this paper was partially supported by National Science Council grant NSC91-2213-E130-010 and NSC91-2213-E030-012.

References

1. Agrawal, R. and *et al.*: Mining Sequential Patterns. Proceedings of the International Conference on Data Engineering (ICDE), (1995) 3–14
2. Chen M.S., Park, J.S. and Yu, P.S.: Efficient Data Mining for Path Traversal Patterns. IEEE Transactions on Knowledge and Data Engineering (TKDE), (1998) 209–220
3. Pei, J., Han, J., Mortazavi-asi, B. and Zhu, H.: Mining Access Patterns Efficiently from Web Logs. Proceedings of the Pacific-Asia Conference on Knowledge Discovery and Data Mining (PAKDD), (2000) 396–407
4. Yen, S.J. and Lee, Y.S.: An Efficient Data Mining Technique for Discovering Interesting Sequential Patterns. Proceedings of the International Conference on Data Mining (ICDM), (2001) 663–664

Applying Data Mining Techniques to Analyze Alert Data[*]

Moonsun Shin[1], Hosung Moon[1], Keunho Ryu[1], KiYoung Kim[2], and JinOh Kim[2]

[1]Database Laboratory, Chungbuk National University,
48, Gaesin-dong,Cheongju, Chungbuk, Korea
{ msshin, hsmoon, khryu}@dblab.chungbuk.ac.kr

[2]Network Security Department,
Electronics and Telecommunications Research Institute, Korea
{kykim,zyno21}@etri.re.kr

Abstract. Architecture of the policy-based network management has a hierarchical structure that consists of management layer and enforcement layer. A security policy server in the management layer should be able to generate new policy, delete, update the existing policy and decide the policy when security policy is requested. Therefore the security policy server must analyze and manage alert messages received from policy enforcement system. In this paper, we propose an alert analyzer with data mining engine. It is a helpful system to manage the fault users or hosts. The implemented mining system supports the alert analyzer and the high level analyzer efficiently for the security policy management.

1 Introduction

A policy-based network management is a mechanism that provides the management for centralization of the global network with providing the update policy easily to request for the manager. And it also provides the process of the consistent policy and makes appropriately the policy for the global network[4]. With the boom in e-commerce and the increasing global interconnectedness of computer systems, infra structure protection has quickly become hot issue. Intrusion detection systems collect information from various vantage points within network, and analyze that information. However, the unknown attacks are hardly found. Therefore, many researches have been performed to apply data mining techniques to intrusion detection systems. Data mining techniques are to discover useful information from huge databases. So it is used to analyze a large audit data efficiently in intrusion detection system and select features for constructing intrusion detection models.

This paper provides an introduction to apply data mining techniques for an alert analyzer. We first outline related work. Section 2 and 3 describe the framework for policy-based network security management and data mining for IDS. In section 4 we

---

[*] This work was supported by University IT Research Center Project, KOSEF RRC Project (Cheongju Univ. ICRC) and ETRI in Korea

X. Zhou, Y. Zhang, and M.E. Orlowska (Eds.): APWeb 2003, LNCS 2642, pp. 193–200, 2003.

design a module that analyzes alert data. Section 5 and 6 presents implementation of alert data mining system and experiments of our system. We conclude by summarizing the contribution of this paper and giving directions for future work.

2 Policy-Based Network Security Management

A Policy-based network management is a network management based on policy. A policy is defined as an aggregation of policy rules. Each policy rule consists of a set of conditions and a corresponding set of actions. The condition defines when the policy rule is applicable. If policy rules activated, one or more actions contained by that policy rule may be executed. So, we can use policy for modification of system behavior. Policy-based network management for network security is the concept and technology that uses policy-based network management for network security. A framework of policy-based network management for network security consists of following components. The PMT (Policy Management Tool) generates and manages the security policy. The PDP (Policy Decision Point) makes a decision for security behavior that depends on the security rule. The PR (Policy Repository) stores the security rule and PEP (Policy Enforcement Point) enforces security behavior. There are network protocols that communicate between the PDP and PEP[5, 6].

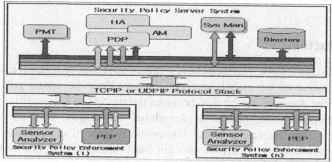

Fig. 1. Framework of Policy-based Network Management for network security

Architecture of the policy-based network management for network security is composed of a management layer and an enforcement layer. The management layer is a security policy server system. The enforcement layer is a security policy enforcement system that detects intrusions. Figure 1 shows the relationships between the components for the policy-based network management of network security in detail.

In this paper, we propose an alert analyzer including mining engine. We design and implement the alert analyzer that is a part of the policy-based network security management framework. Also we implement mining system that analyzes alert data efficiently and supports high-level analyzer for the security policy server.

3 Data Mining for Intrusion Detection System

There are many penetration points for intrusions to take place in network system. Because of large traffic volume, IDS often needs to be extended and be updated frequently and timely. Currently building effective IDS is an enormous knowledge engineering task. Some of the recent researches have started to apply data mining techniques to the IDSs. Because of the sheer volume of audit data, efficient and intelligent data analysis tools are required to discover the behavior of system activities. Data mining generally refers to the process of extracting useful information from large stores of data. Our research aim is to develop mining system for the analysis of alert data. The recent rapid development in data mining has made available a wide variety of algorithms, drawn from the fields of statistics, pattern recognition, machine learning and databases. Some algorithms are particularly useful for mining audit data. In the other cases of alert data, these algorithms are also useful. Follows are the several data mining areas that support IDS:

- **Classification**: maps data item into one of several predefined categories. An ideal application in intrusion detection will be to gather sufficient "normal" and "abnormal" audit data for a user or a program.
- **Association rules**: determines relationships between fields in the database records.
- **Frequent episodes**: models sequential patterns. These algorithms can discover what time-based sequence of audit events and frequent episodes.
- **Clustering**: gathers similar patterns to the same group and measures similarity of sequence. We design and implement the alert data mining system that consists of three components in this paper. The association rule miner performs link analysis of alert data and the frequent episodes miner can discover time based sequence of alert events. The cluster miner can measure similarity of alert sequence. In each miner, security manager can choose the attributes of interest, and then mining is performed on those interesting attributes.

4 Alert Analyzer

The security policy server system uses relational DBMS for storing alert data that were sent by security policy enforcement system. The PEP detects intrusions and sends information about intrusions to the security policy server system. These data were stored in databases by Alert Manager, and analyzed by Alert Analyzer and Black List Watcher. The High-Level Analyzer, Alert Manager and Blacklist Watcher systematically co-work together using the alert data in database. Table 1 shows the schema of alert data to be stored.

Table 1. Data Schema of Alert

Attribute name									
ALID	SID	ATID	ATTYPE	DDATE	SADDR	DADDR	SPORT	DPORT	PROTO

It is an important faculty of the security policy server that analyzes alert data that were sent by security policy enforcement system and responses against those. Recent attacks of network are hard to predict and detect. For analyzing and detecting various intrusions, we need the modules that analyze the correlation between alert data. The correlation analysis of alert data extracts the relationships between alert data, and covers analysis of behavior as well as similarity. A behavior analysis analyzes a correlated behavior between alert data[1, 2, 3]. A similarity analysis analyzes repetition of similar alerts. Details are as follows: repetitive analysis, similarity analysis, potentiality analysis, behavior analysis. For more efficient analysis of alerts, it is necessary to monitor malicious users and vulnerable hosts using alert data. So we design a Black List Watcher.

The Black List Watcher provides the systematic management of attacked hosts and intrusive users in the domain of security policy server. It extracts information about malicious users and attacked hosts from alert data and constructs black list of fault users and host by security policy rules. The Black List Watcher is composed of two functions, Black List Manager and Fault User/Host Detector. It is helpful to detect intrusion in advance and to response immediately against the attacks by malicious users and to vulnerable hosts. Consequently, the security policy server manages and controls the network security efficiently.

5 Alert Data Mining System

In order to support the security policy server we propose an alert data mining system that consists of three modules such as association rule miner, frequent episode miner and clustering miner. Association rule miner can find correlation among attributes in record, although frequent episode miner searches event patterns in records.

In addition, clustering miner discovers similar attack patterns by grouping alert data with similarity among alert data. We improved the basic mining algorithms to create candidate item sets that included only interesting attributes. The existing association rule mining algorithms search for interesting relationships in transaction database. However, we expanded Apriori algorithm without grouping items by T_id because of the characteristics of the alert data. So rules can be generated only with attributes of interest. The process of the expanded algorithm is composed of three steps. The steps of the process of the association rule miner are as follows.

1) Find all frequent item sets composed of interesting attributes
2) Generating strong association rules from the frequent item sets
3) Generating final rules:

An episode is defined by a sequence of specific events that occurs frequently. Using episodes, an infiltration detection system can detect frequently repeated patterns, and apply them to the rule or use them as guidelines for service refusal attacks. Frequent episode mining is carried out through the following 3 steps.

1) Generating candidate episodes: The tuples composed of attributes of interest are arranged by given time window units. Time within a window must be included in the time span of the window.
2) Generating frequent episodes: A set of frequent episodes, which satisfy the minimum frequency, are extracted from the set of candidate episode.
3) Generating final episodes.

In the case of cluster miner, we implemented the modified CURE algorithm, which can cluster datasets with multi-dimensional attributes because of the characteristics of alert data. Such a clustering analysis technique improves the efficiency of the analysis of alert data, and abstracts high-level meanings through grouping data. The implemented clustering miner has four steps of process: data preprocessing, clustering alert data, analyzing the result of clusters, classify new alert data. The architecture of a clustering miner system is shown in Figure 2 (a). And Figure 2 (b) shows alert cluster algorithm.

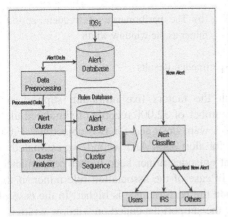

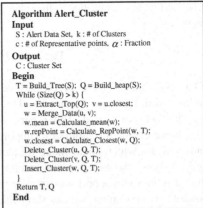

(a) Architecture   (b) Algorithm

Fig. 2. Alert Data Clustering System

6 Experiments and Evaluation

The implemented mining system using virtual alert data. Table 2 presented an example of the final rules after mining task. Here we found out correlations among alert data inter-records or intra-records. For example, the first rule meant that there was close correlation between "attack id" 50 and "destination port" 21.That also implied the strong relation between attributes "attack id" and "destination port". We were able to find sequential pattern of events as results. In the example, we might guess a fact that attack 5001 brings about attack 5007.

Table 2. Example of Final Rules

Association Rule	Meaning
50<=>21 (supp:49, conf:100%,)	Attribute 50(Atid) correlated with attribute 21(dsc_port)
21<=>tcp (supp:49, conf:100%,)	Attribute 21(dsc_port) correlated with attribute tcp(protocol)
Frequent Episode Rule	Meaning
5001:210.155.167.10:21:tcp => 5007:210.155.167.10.21 :tcp (fre:10, conf:100%, time:10sec)	If 5001(Ftp Buffer Ovrflow) occur, then 5007(Anonymous FTP) occur together.

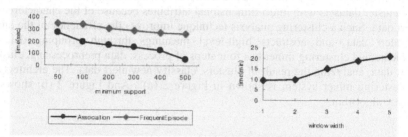

(a) The performance evaluation as the value of minimum support

(b) The performance of frequent episodes miner as the window width

Fig. 3. The Experimental Results

Our experiments were performed with the factors like minimum support and window width of frequent episodes. The number of 32,000 records of simulated alert data have been evaluated. The experiments were designed for two objectives. First, how can we decide the minimum support for alert data. And second, we estimated of window width which could make frequent episodes miner keep higher performance. Figure 3 shows the experimental results. In case of the association rule miner, if the value of minimum support was smaller then the performance is higher. In the case of frequent episodes miner, we can show that the support depended on window width.

Table 3. Results of clustering analysis

Cluster ID	PRECluster1	PRECluster2	PRECluster3	PRECluster4	PRECluster5
Cluster1	54.85 %	0.23 %	1.54%	10.45%	32.34%
Cluster2	10.4%	7.46%	1.39 %	71.23%	9.21%
Cluster3	29.09%	3.10%	32.67%	12.72%	11.88%
Cluster4	0.93%	2.49%	20.10%	67.86%	10.23%
Cluster5	2.43%	5.45%	10.44%	1.93%	76.06%

For the clustering miner, two experiments were carried out. The first experiment was to test the performance of clustering. This experiment evaluated the accuracy of each cluster generated by the clustering miner. We use the KDDCup 1999 dataset[15]. The test data were assigned to clusters with relatively high accuracy for attack types such as DOS and Probing, which were distributed in a relatively large amount in the training dataset. However, the attack types such as R2L and U2R, which were rarely distributed in the training dataset, were clustered less accurately. The second experiment was defining the previous cluster of each generated cluster, and determining if the sequence of clusters could be generated based on the defined previous clusters. The distribution of previous alert data for each cluster generated is as in Table 3.

Figure 4 showed the sequences generated from the results shown in Table 3. This experiment generated sequences of clusters by analyzing the distribution of previous alerts, which were the cause of the generation of the resulting sequences, and showed that it was possible to provide a method of forecasting the future type of alerts occurring by abstracting the sequences of clusters through integrating each sequences of clusters generated.

Fig. 4. Generated cluster sequence base on table 3

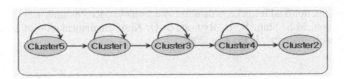

7 Conclusion

We proposed the alert analyzer with mining engine. It provides more efficient and active analysis of alert data than the analysis of alert data based on quantitative critical values, and will support to build active security policies. The major contributions of this paper are to apply data mining techniques to alert analysis for supporting security policy server in policy based network security management. Currently, we are going to apply our mining engine to real security system.

References

1. D. Schnackenberg, K. Djahandari, and D. Sterne, "Infrastructure for Intrusion Detection and Response", Proceedings of the DARPA Information Survivability Conference, Jan. 2000
2. D. Schnackenberg, H. Holliday, R. Smith, K. Djahandari, and D. Sterne, "Cooperative Intrusion Traceback and Response Architecture (CITRA) ", DISCEX'01, Anaheim, California, June. 2001.
3. S. M. Lewandowski, D. J. Van Hook, G. C. O'Leary, J. W. Haines, and L. M. Rossey, "SARA: Survivable Autonomic Response Architecture", DISCEX'01, Anaheim, California, June. 2001.
4. IPHIGHWAY, Inc., "Introduction to Policy-based network and quality of service", http://www.iphighway.com, 2002.
5. E. Lupu and M. Sloman, "Conflicts in Policy-based Distributed Systems Management", IEEE Transactions on Software Engineering", Vol. 25, No. 6, Nov. 1999.
6. Sudipto Guha, Rajeev Rastogi, and Kyuseok Shim, "CURE: An Efficient Clustering Algorithm for Large Databases", In Proceedings of SIGMOD, Vol. 27(2), pages 73–84, Jun. 1998.
7. B. Moore, E. Ellesson, J. Strassner, and A. Westerinen, "Policy Core Information Model – Ver. 1 Spec.", IETF RFC3060, Feb. 2001.
8. W. Lee, S. J. Stolfo, K. W. Mok "A Data Mining Framework for Building Intrusion Detection Models*", Computer Science Department, Columbia University
9. Valdes and K. Skinner, "Probabilistic alert correlation", In Proceedings of the 4th International Symposium on Recent Advances in Intrusion Detection (RAID 2001), pages 54–68, 2001.
10. H. Mannila, H. Toivonen and A. I. Verkamo, "Discovery of frequent episodes in event sequences", Data Mining and Knowledge Discovery, 1(3), Nov. 1997.

11. O. Dain and R.K. Cunningham, "Fusing a heterogeneous alert stream into scenarios", In Proceedings of the 2001 ACM Workshop on Data Mining for Security Applications, pages 1–13, Nov. 2001.
12. Lincoln Lab MIT. DARPA 2000 intrusion detection evaluation datasets.
13. http://ideval.ll.mit.edu/
14. KDD99Cup, ttp://kdd.ics.uci.edu/databases/kddcup99/kddcup99.html, 1999
15. H. S. Moon, M.S. Shin, K. H. Ryu and J. O. Kim "Implementation of security policy server's alert analyzer", ICIS, Aug. 2002

Web Page Clustering: A Hyperlink-Based Similarity and Matrix-Based Hierarchical Algorithms

Jingyu Hou[1], Yanchun Zhang[2], and Jinli Cao[3]

[1] School of Information Technology, Deakin University
Melbourne, Vic 3125, Australia
jingyu@deakin.edu.au

[2] Department of Mathematics and Computing, University of Southern Queensland
Toowoomba, Qld 4350, Australia
zhang@usq.edu.au

[3] Department of Computer Science and Computer Engineering, La Trobe University
Melbourne, Vic 3086, Australia
jinli@cs.latrobe.edu.au

Abstract. This paper proposes a hyperlink-based web page similarity measurement and two matrix-based hierarchical web page clustering algorithms. The web page similarity measurement incorporates hyperlink transitivity and page importance within the concerned web page space. One clustering algorithm takes cluster overlapping into account, another one does not. These algorithms do not require predefined similarity thresholds for clustering, and are independent of the page order. The primary evaluations show the effectiveness of the proposed algorithms in clustering improvement.

1 Introduction

The information explosion on the World Wide Web makes it hard for users to obtain required information from the web-searched results. One way to solve this problem is to cluster web pages, for instance the work in [28] [29] [31] and [24]. Web page clustering makes it possible to establish index on the web pages, and implement efficient information classification, navigation, storage, retrieval and integration.

To implement effective web page clustering, it is necessary to find intrinsic relationships, especially similarities, among the pages. For this purpose, web page content, hyperlinks and usage data could be utilized. In this work, we use hyperlink information because hyperlinks usually convey human judgement of whether the linked pages are semantically related [19]. The hyperlink analysis has proven success in many web-related areas, such as page ranking in the search engine *Google* [7] [8], web page community construction [19] [2] [10] [14] and relevant page finding [19] [12] [16].

When hyperlink analysis is applied to web page clustering, most of the work only considered the direct hyperlink between pages, such as the work in [23] [24] [11] and [27]. However, the hyperlinks, as well as the semantics the hyperlinks convey, usually are transitive. Some hyperlink-based work, such as the work in [28] [20], was aware

X. Zhou, Y. Zhang, and M.E. Orlowska (Eds.): APWeb 2003, LNCS 2642, pp. 201–212, 2003.

of hyperlink transitivity, but the web page similarity derived directly from hyperlink transitivity analysis was over-simplified or only out-links of the pages were considered.

Even though the hyperlink transitivity is considered, the role each page plays in the page similarity measurement is different. Up to now, there is no such web page similarity measurement that incorporates page importance and hyperlink transitivity simultaneously.

For web page clustering, some of the previous work adapted K-mean and agglomerative hierarchical clustering algorithms in information retrieval; some work used page merging methods or improved the K-mean algorithm. For example, the work in [24] [28] [31] [27] and [29] fall into these categories. However, if the initial values or predefined thresholds for these algorithms are not chosen properly, the final clustering results might be unsatisfactory.

This paper proposes a new metric from hyperlinks to measure the similarity between pages within the concerned web page space. This similarity metric incorporates hyperlink transitivity and page importance. Based on it, two matrix-based hierarchical web page clustering algorithms are proposed. The clustering algorithms do not require predefined similarity thresholds for clustering, and are independent of the page order.

In section 2, we propose the new web page similarity measurement. Section 3 gives matrix-based hierarchical clustering algorithms. Some primary evaluations of the proposed algorithms are presented in section 4. Finally, we give some conclusions and future work in section 5.

2 Web Page Similarity Measurement

Web page similarity is usually considered within a page space. Since we are concerned about clustering web search pages, we focus on the page space (source) that is related to the user's query topics.

2.1 Page Source Construction

For the users, they are usually concerned about a portion of searched pages, say the first r highest-ranked pages. Accordingly, the page source S is constructed as follow:

Step 1: Select r highest-ranked pages to form a root page set R.

Step 2: For each page p in R, select up to B pages, which point to p and whose domain names, i.e. the first levels of the URL strings, are different from that of p, and add them to the back vicinity set BV of R.

Step 3: For each page p in R, select up to F pages, which are pointed to by p and whose domain names are different from that of p, and add them to the forward vicinity set FV of R.

Step 4: Page source S is constructed by uniting sets R, BV, FV and adding original links between pages in S.

Parameters B and F are used to guarantee the page source S is of a reasonable size.

2.2 Page Weight Definition

Web page weight is defined to measure the importance of each page *within the concerned page source*. For each page P_i in the page source S, we associate a non-negative *in-weight* $P_{i,in}$ and a non-negative *out-weight* $P_{i,out}$ with it. The *in-weight* and *out-weight* of the page P_i in S are iteratively calculated as follow [19]:

$$P_{i,in} = \sum_{P_j \in S, P_j \to P_i} P_{j,out}, \quad P_{i,out} = \sum_{P_j \in S, P_i \to P_j} P_{j,in}.$$

In-weight and out-weight vectors are normalized after each iteration.

We denote the average in-weight of S as μ, and the average out-weight of S as λ,

$$\mu = \sum_{P_i \in S} P_{i,in} / size(S), \quad \lambda = \sum_{P_i \in S} P_{i,out} / size(S),$$

where $size(S)$ is the number of pages in S. Then the page weight for P_i is defined as

$$w_i = 1 + \max((P_{i,in} - \mu)/(M_{in} - m_{in}), (P_{i,out} - \lambda)/(M_{out} - m_{out})) \qquad (1)$$

where M_{in}, m_{in}, M_{out} and m_{out} are defined as follow:

$$M_{in} = \max_{P_j \in S}(P_{j,in}), \quad m_{in} = \min_{P_j \in S}(P_{j,in}), \quad M_{out} = \max_{P_j \in S}(P_{j,out}), \quad m_{out} = \min_{P_j \in S}(P_{j,out}).$$

2.3 Page Correlation Matrix

To measure the page correlation, we firstly give the following definitions.

Definition 1. If page A has a direct link to page B, then the *length of path* from page A to B is 1, denoted as $l(A,B) = 1$. If page A has a link to page B via n other pages, then $l(A,B) = n+1$. The *distance* from page A to page B is defined as $sl(A,B) = min(l(A,B))$. $l(A,A) = 0$. If there are no links from page A to page B, then $l(A,B) = \infty$.

Definition 2. The *correlation weight* between two pages i and j ($i \neq j$) is defined as $w_{i,j} = max(w_i, w_j)$ where w_i and w_j are the page weights for pages i and j respectively. If $i = j$, $w_{i,j}$ is defined as 1.

Definition 3. *Correlation factor*, denoted as F, $0 < F < 1$, is a constant that measures the correlation rate between two page with direct link, i.e. if page A has a direct link to page B, the correlation rate from page A to page B is F.

Similar to [28], the value of F is chosen as 1/2 in this paper. With the above definitions, a correlation degree between any two pages is defined as follow.

Definition 4. The *correlation degree* from page i to page j, denoted as c_{ij}, is defined as

$$c_{ij} = w_{i,k1} w_{k1,k2} \cdots w_{kn,j} F^{sl(i,j)}, \qquad (2)$$

where F is the correlation factor, $sl(i,j)$ is the distance from page i to page j, and $w_{i,k1}$, $w_{k1,k2}$, ..., $w_{kn,j}$ are correlation weights of the pages i, $k1$, $k2$, ..., kn, j that form the distance $sl(i,j)$, i.e. $i \to k1 \to k2 \to ... \to kn \to j$. If $i = j$, then c_{ij} is defined as 1.

For the page source S, we suppose the size of the root set R is m, the size of the vicinity set $V = BV \cup FV$ is n. Then the correlation degrees of all the pages in S can be expressed in a $(m+n) \times (m+n)$ matrix $C = (c_{ij})_{(m+n) \times (m+n)}$, called *correlation matrix*.

2.4 Page Similarity

In this work, we concentrate on clustering web-searched pages in the root set R. Without losing generality, we divide the correlation matrix C as follow:

$$C = (c_{ij})_{(m+n) \times (m+n)} = \begin{array}{c} R \\ V \end{array} \left[\begin{array}{c|c} \textcircled{1} & \textcircled{2} \\ \hline \textcircled{3} & \textcircled{4} \end{array} \right]_{(m+n) \times (m+n)}$$

Accordingly, the row vector that corresponds to each page i in R is in the form of $row_i = (c_{i,1}, c_{i,2}, ..., c_{i,m+n})$, $i = 1, 2, ..., m$. It represents out-$link$ relationship of page i in R with all the pages in S. Similarly, the column vector that is in the form of $col_i = (c_{1,i}, c_{2,i}, ..., c_{m+n,i})$, $i = 1, 2, ..., m$, represents in-$link$ relationship of page i in R with all the pages in S.

For any two pages i and j in R, their out-$link$ $similarity$ is defined as

$$sim_{i,j}^{out} = \frac{(row_i, row_j)}{\| row_i \| \cdot \| row_j \|},$$

where

$$(row_i, row_j) = \sum_{k=1}^{m+n} c_{i,k} c_{j,k}, \qquad \| row_i \| = (\sum_{k=1}^{m+n} c_{i,k}^2)^{1/2}.$$

Similarly, their in-$link$ $similarity$ is defined as

$$sim_{i,j}^{in} = \frac{(col_i, col_j)}{\| col_i \| \cdot \| col_j \|}.$$

Then the similarity between any two pages i and j in R is defined as

$$sim(i, j) = \alpha_{ij} \cdot sim_{i,j}^{out} + \beta_{ij} \cdot sim_{i,j}^{in}, \tag{3}$$

where the similarity weights α_{ij} and β_{ij} are determined dynamically as:

$$\alpha_{ij} = \frac{\| row_i \| + \| row_j \|}{MOD_{ij}}, \qquad \beta_{ij} = \frac{\| col_i \| + \| col_j \|}{MOD_{ij}},$$

$$MOD_{ij} = \| row_i \| + \| row_j \| + \| col_i \| + \| col_j \|.$$

With the page similarity measurement (3), an $m \times m$ $similarity$ $matrix$ SM for R is constructed as $SM = (sm_{i,j})_{m \times m}$, where

$$sm_{i,j} = \begin{cases} sim(i, j) & \text{if } i \neq j, \\ 1 & \text{if } i = j. \end{cases}$$

3 Matrix-Based Clustering Algorithms

The matrix-based web page clustering is implemented by partitioning the page similarity matrix, and the pages are accordingly clustered into clusters. Before partitioning, it is needed to conduct similarity matrix permutation.

3.1 Similarity Matrix Permutation

The similarity matrix permutation is to put those closely related pages together in the similarity matrix *SM*. For measuring how close two pages are related, we define the

affinity of two pages i and $j \in R$ as: $AF(i, j) = \sum_{k=1}^{m} sm_{i,k} \times sm_{j,k}$. The corresponding

affinity matrix is denoted as *AF*. For globally optimizing the page position, we define the *global affinity* of matrix *SM* as

$$GA(SM) = \sum_{i=1}^{m} \sum_{j=1}^{m} AF(i, j)[AF(i, j-1) + AF(i, j+1)], \qquad (4)$$

where $AF(i,0) = AF(i, m+1) = 0$. The higher the $GA(SM)$, the more likely the closely related pages are put together as neighboring pages. The purpose of the similarity matrix permutation is to get the highest $GA(SM)$.

The highest $GA(SM)$ can be obtained by swapping the positions of every pair of columns (accordingly rows) in matrix *AF* similar to the work in [22]. When the highest $GA(SM)$ is achieved, the page positions in *SM* are permuted accordingly. For simplicity, we still denote this permuted similarity matrix as *SM* hereafter.

3.2 Clustering Algorithm Based on Matrix Partition

The matrix-based page clustering is implemented by partitioning the permuted matrix *SM* into four sub-matrices along its main diagonal, i.e.

$$SM = (sm_{i,j})_{m \times m} = \begin{bmatrix} SM_{1,1} & SM_{1,2} \\ \cdots D \cdots \\ SM_{2,1} & SM_{2,2} \end{bmatrix}_{m \times m}$$

The pages corresponding to the sub-matrices $SM_{1,1}$ and $SM_{2,2}$ form two clusters.

To find the dividing point D along the main diagonal of *SM*, we define a measurement for the sub-matrix $SM_{p,q}$ $(1 \le p, q \le 2)$ as

$$M(SM_{p,q}) = \sum_{i=(p-1)*d+1}^{d+(m-d)*(p-1)} \sum_{j=(q-1)*d+1}^{d+(m-d)*(q-1)} sm_{i,j}, \qquad 1 \le p, q \le 2,$$

where d stands for the row (and column) number of D. The dividing point D is selected such that the following function is maximized

$$F_D = M(SM_{1,1}) * M(SM_{2,2}) - M(SM_{1,2}) * M(SM_{2,1}). \qquad (5)$$

This matrix partition could be recursively applied to the matrices $SM_{1,1}$ and $SM_{2,2}$ until the number of pages in every new produced cluster is less than or equal to a preferred number pn (e.g. 20). All clusters produced during this procedure hierarchically cluster the web pages. The clustering procedure is depicted as the Algorithm1, *Clustering1*, where $|SM|$ stands for the number of rows in the square matrix SM.

[**Algorithm1**] *Clustering1* (SM, pn)
[**Input**] SM: similarity matrix; pn: preferred page number in each cluster;
[**Output**] $CL = \{CL_i\}$: a set of hierarchical clusters;
Begin
>   Set $CL = \varnothing$;   Permute SM such that (4) is maximized;
>   Partition SM such that (5) is maximized;
>   **If** $|SM_{1,1}| \le pn$, **then** do
>>   converting $SM_{1,1}$ into the next CL_i; $CL = CL \cup \{CL_i\}$;
>
>   **else** do
>>   converting $SM_{1,1}$ into the next CL_i; $CL = CL \cup \{CL_i\}$;
>>   *Clustering1* ($SM_{1,1}$, pn);
>
>   **If** $|SM_{2,2}| \le pn$, **then** do
>>   converting $SM_{2,2}$ into the next CL_i; $CL = CL \cup \{CL_i\}$;
>
>   **else** do
>>   converting $SM_{2,2}$ into the next CL_i; $CL = CL \cup \{CL_i\}$;
>>   *Clustering1* ($SM_{2,2}$, pn);
>
>   Return CL;
End

3.3 Cluster-Overlapping Algorithm

For the algorithm *Clustering1*, there exists no overlapping among the clusters that are produced at the same level. In practice, however, it is reasonable that a page might belong to several same level clusters. On the other hand, the non-zero element values in $SM_{1,2}$ or $SM_{2,1}$ represent the similarity between two pages, named *cross-related pages*, that belong to two different clusters.

To determine whether a cross-related page in one cluster could be added to another cluster, we define a *centroid* of the cluster $SM_{p,p}$ ($1 \le p \le 2$) as $CE(SM_{p,p}) = \{CE^{row}(SM_{p,p}), CE^{col}(SM_{p,p})\}$, where

$$CE^{row}(SM_{p,p}) = \frac{1}{|SM_{p,p}|} \sum_{j \in SM_{p,p}} row_j, \quad CE^{col}(SM_{p,p}) = \frac{1}{|SM_{p,p}|} \sum_{j \in SM_{p,p}} col_j. \quad (6)$$

The Algorithm2 *Extending* depicts this overlapping procedure.

[**Algorithm2**] *Extending* (SM)
[**Input**] SM: similarity matrix with sub-matrices $SM_{1,1}$, $SM_{2,2}$, $SM_{1,2}$ and $SM_{2,1}$;
[**Output**] $SM'_{1,1}$, $SM'_{2,2}$: new sub-matrices with added cross-related pages;
Begin
>   Compute the centroids $CE(SM_{1,1})$ and $CE(SM_{2,2})$ according to (6);
>   Compute the threshold t, which is the average non-zero similarities in $SM_{1,2}$;

Set $N1 = [\ |\ SM_{1,1}\ |\ * 0.15\ ]$; $N2 = [\ |\ SM_{2,2}\ |\ * 0.15\ ]$; $N = \min(N1, N2)$;

Construct page set $P = \{p\ |$ at least one $sm_{p,j} \neq 0,\ 1 \le p \le d,\ d+1 \le j \le m\}$;

Construct page set $Q = \{q\ |$ at least one $sm_{i,q} \neq 0,\ 1 \le i \le d,\ d+1 \le q \le m\}$;

Compute $P\_SM22 = \{sim(p, CE(SM_{2,2}))\ |\ p \in P,\ sim(p, CE(SM_{2,2})) \ge t\}$;

Compute $Q\_SM11 = \{sim(q, CE(SM_{1,1}))\ |\ q \in Q,\ sim(q, CE(SM_{1,1})) \ge t\}$;

Add up to N pages in $SM_{2,2}$ that correspond to the N highest values in Q_SM11 into $SM_{1,1}$ to form a new sub-matrix $SM'_{1,1}$;

Add up to N pages in $SM_{1,1}$ that correspond to the N highest values in P_SM22 into $SM_{2,2}$ to form a new sub-matrix $SM'_{2,2}$;

Return $SM'_{1,1}$ and $SM'_{2,2}$;

End

The parameter d is the row number of the dividing point D in SM. The parameter N is used to restrict the number of pages to be added to $SM_{1,1}$ and $SM_{2,2}$, which guarantees the added pages could not change the main property of the original clusters.

Based on the algorithm *Extending*, the matrix-based hierarchical clustering algorithm with cluster overlapping is depicted as the Algorithm3 *Clustering2*.

[**Algorithm3**] *Clustering2 (SM, pn)*

[**Input**] SM: similarity matrix; pn: preferred page number in each cluster;

[**Output**] $CL = \{CL_i\}$: a set of hierarchical clusters;

Begin

Set $CL = \varnothing$;   Permute SM such that (4) is maximized;

Partition SM such that (5) is maximized;

$\{SM'_{1,1}, SM'_{2,2}\} = Extending (SM)$;

If $|\ SM'_{1,1}\ | \le pn$, **then** do

converting $SM'_{1,1}$ into the next CL_i; $CL = CL \cup \{CL_i\}$;

else do

converting $SM'_{1,1}$ into the next CL_i; $CL = CL \cup \{CL_i\}$;

Clustering2 $(SM'_{1,1}, pn)$;

If $|\ SM'_{2,2}\ | \le pn$, **then** do

converting $SM'_{2,2}$ into the next CL_i; $CL = CL \cup \{CL_i\}$;

else do

converting $SM'_{2,2}$ into the next CL_i; $CL = CL \cup \{CL_i\}$;

Clustering2 $(SM'_{2,2}, pn)$;

Return CL;

End

It is not difficult to prove that the complexity of the above two clustering algorithms is $O(m^2)$, where m is the number of pages to be clustered.

4 Evaluations

We chose "*Jaguar*" as the search topic for primary evaluation. The number of source pages is 3,540 and the number of hyperlinks is 17,793. The number of pages to be clustered is 472. All the clustering algorithms used for evaluation are listed in Table 1.

Table 1. The algorithms for evaluation

Algo.	Meaning
CA2(D)	Algorithm *Clustering2* with **dynamic** similarity weights (α_{ij}, β_{ij}) in (3).
CA2(S)	Algorithm *Clustering2* with **static** similarity weights (α_{ij}, β_{ij}) = (1/2, 1/2) in (3).
CA1(D)	Algorithm *Clustering1* with **dynamic** similarity weights (α_{ij}, β_{ij}) in (3).
CA1(S)	Algorithm *Clustering1* with **static** similarity weights (α_{ij}, β_{ij}) = (1/2, 1/2) in (3).
PCA2(D)	Algorithm *Clustering2* with **dynamic** similarity weights (α_{ij}, β_{ij}) in (3), not consider hyperlink transitivity and page importance.
PCA2(S)	Algorithm *Clustering2* with **static** similarity weights (α_{ij}, β_{ij}) = (1/2, 1/2) in (3), not consider hyperlink transitivity and page importance.
PCA1(D)	Algorithm *Clustering1* with **dynamic** similarity weights (α_{ij}, β_{ij}) in (3), not consider hyperlink transitivity and page importance.
PCA1(S)	Algorithm *Clustering1* with **static** similarity weights (α_{ij}, β_{ij}) = (1/2, 1/2) in (3), not consider hyperlink transitivity and page importance.
WK01A	Extended hierarchical clustering algorithm of [27], *K*-mean style, not consider hyperlink transitivity and page importance.

We adapt the precision concept in information retrieval [3] and define the following clustering accuracy. Given a page source, we denote its real clusters as the set $\{RC_i\}$ and its experimental clusters as the set $\{EC_j\}$. For a cluster EC_j, its accuracy is defined as

$$Accuracy\ (EC_j) = \frac{\max_i (|\ EC_j \cap RC_i\ |)}{|\ EC_j\ |},$$

where $|EC_j|$ is the number of pages in the cluster EC_j. For a single-page cluster, its accuracy is defined as 0.

We firstly evaluated the algorithms proposed in this work. The average accuracies of the leaf clusters produced by these algorithms are shown in Fig. 1. It is indicated that the algorithms incorporating hyperlink transitivity and page importance (*CA2(D)*, *CA2(S)*, *CA1(D)* and *CA1(S)*) have higher clustering accuracy than other algorithms. It is also shown that the algorithms considering cluster-overlapping perform better than those without considering it, such as *CA2(D)* and *CA1(D)*. For the same kind of algorithms, the algorithm with dynamic similarity weights produces better results.

The comparison of algorithms *CA2(D)*, *CA1(D)* and *WK01A* on the average leaf cluster accuracy are shown in Fig. 2. For the *WK01A*, we chose the predefined clustering similarity thresholds from 0.05 to 0.30 with the step of 0.05, and the corresponding algorithms are marked as W0.05, ..., W0.30. The merging threshold is 0.75. Single-page clusters are not considered. The average leaf cluster accuracy for all these thresholds is marked WK01A. These results show that the algorithms (e.g. *CA2(D)*, *CA1(D)*) considering hyperlink transitivity and page importance (whether considering cluster-overlapping or not) produce better clusters than the algorithm (e.g. *WK01A*) without considering hyperlink transitivity and page importance. Furthermore, the algorithm *WK01A* is sensitive to the predefined clustering thresholds, while *CA2(D)* and *CA1(D)* are independent of predefined clustering thresholds.

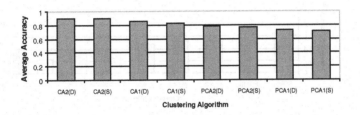

Fig. 1. The average leaf cluster accuracies of the eight clustering algorithms

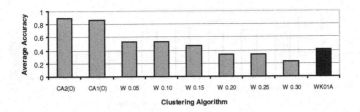

Fig. 2. The average leaf cluster accuracies of *CA2(D)*, *CA1(D)* and *WK01A*

In Fig. 3, the comparison among the average *leaf cluster accuracies* of the *CA2(D)* and *CA1(D)* and the average *base cluster accuracies* of the *WK01A* are presented. The base clusters of the *WK01A* are the first level clusters produced by the *WK01A*. The average base cluster accuracy, marked WK01A, is lower than the average leaf cluster accuracies of *CA2(D)* and *CA1(D)*.

For the matrix-based clustering algorithms *PCA2(D)* and *PCA1(D)* that do not incorporate hyperlink transitivity and page importance, the comparison of their leaf cluster accuracies with the leaf cluster accuracy and base cluster accuracy of the algorithm *WK01A* are presented in Fig. 4 and 5 separately. These results indicate that the matrix-based algorithms produce better clusters than the *K*-mean style algorithm *WK01A*.

The above evaluations demonstrate that the algorithms in this work effectively improve the clustering results. Finally, we give concrete examples of some major clusters produced by the *CA2(D)* in Table 2. The results are satisfactory as the main web pages sharing the same topic are really clustered into one cluster.

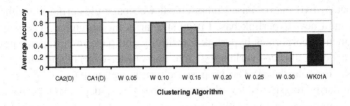

Fig. 3. The leaf cluster accuracies of *CA2(D)*, *CA1(D)* and the base cluster accuracies of *WK01A*

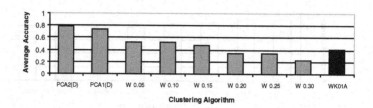

Fig. 4. The average leaf cluster accuracies of *PCA2(D)*, *PCA1(D)* and *WK01A*

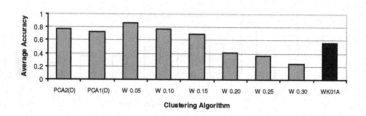

Fig. 5. The leaf cluster accuracies of *PCA2(D)*, *PCA1(D)* and the base cluster accuracies of *WK01A*

Table 2. Examples of some major clusters

Topic: **Jaguar Car**	Topic: **Jaguar Car Club**
www.jaguar.com	www.jec.org.uk
www.classicjaguar.com	www.seattlejagclub.org
www.jagweb.com	www.jag-lovers.org
Topic: **Jaguar Big Cat**	Topic: **Jaguar Reef Touring**
dspace.dial.pipex.com/agarman/jaguar.htm	www.jaguarreef.com
www.animalsoftherainforest.com/jaguar.htm	www.divejaguarreef.com
www.bluelion.org/jaguar.htm	www.belizenet.com/jagreef.html

5   Conclusions and Future Work

In this paper, two matrix-based hierarchical web page clustering algorithms are proposed from a new hyperlink-based page similarity measurement. The page similarity measurement incorporates hyperlink transitivity and page importance simultaneously. Two situations, cluster-overlapping and non-cluster-overlapping, in the clustering procedure are considered. The proposed clustering algorithms do not require predefined similarity thresholds for clustering. They are independent of page order and effectively improve web page clustering.

However, the hyperlinks only partially reveal the semantics among web pages. A proper combination of effective page hyperlink similarities and page content similarities might be another approach to increase the clustering effectiveness. The ideas in this work could also be applied to other similar areas, such as XML document clustering.

References

1. Bharat, K., Broder, A., Henzinger, M., Kumar, P., Venkatasubramanian, S.: The Connectivity Server: Fast Access to Linkage Information on the Web, *Proceedings of the 7th International World Wide Web Conference* (1998) 469–477
2. Bharat, K., Henzinger, M.: Improved Algorithms for Topic Distillation in a Hyperlinked Environment, *Proceedings of ACM 21st International SIGIR'98* (1998) 104–111
3. Baeza-Yates, R., Ribeiro-Neto, B.: *Modern Information Retrieval*, Addison Wesley, ACM Press (1999)
4. Botafogo, R. A.: Cluster Analysis for Hypertext Systems, *Proceedings of ACM 16th Annual International SIGIR'93* (1993)
5. Botafogo, R. A., Rivlin, E., Shneiderman, B.: Structural Analysis of Hypertexts: Indentifing Hierarchies and Useful Metrics, *ACM Transactions on Information Systems*, Vol 10, No 2 (1992)142–180
6. Botafogo, R. A., Shneiderman, B.: Identifying Aggregates in Hypertext Structures, *Proceedings of Hypertext'91*(1991) 63–74
7. Brin, S., Page, L.: The Anatomy of a Large-Scale Hypertextual Web Search Engine, *Proceedings of the 7th International World Wide Web Conference* (1998)
8. Brin, S., Page, L.: The PageRank Citation Ranking: Bringing Order to the Web, January 1998, *http://www-db.stanford.edu/~backrub/pageranksub.ps.*
9. Carriere, J., Kazman, R.: WebQuery: Searching and Visualizing the Web through Connectivity, *Proceedings of the 6th International world Wide Web Conference* (1997)
10. Chakrabarti, S., Dom, B., Gibson, D., Kleinberg, J., Raghavan, P., Rajagopalan, S.: Automatic Resource Compilation by Analyzing Hyperlink Structure and Associated Text, *Proc. the 7th International World Wide Web Conference* (1998) 65–74
11. Chakrabarti, S., Dom, B., Indyk, P.: Enhanced Hypertext Categorization Using Hyperlinks, *Proceedings of SIGMOD1998,* 307–318
12. Dean, J., Henzinger, M.: Finding Related Pages in the World Wide Web, *Proc. the 8th International World Wide Web Conference* (1999) 389–401
13. Dubes, R. J., Jain, A. K.: *Algorithms for Clustering Data*, Prentice Hall (1988)
14. Hou, J., Zhang, Y.: Constructing Good Quality Web Page Communities, *Proceedings of the 13th Australasian Database Conferences (ADC 2002)* 65–74
15. Hou, J., Zhang, Y.: A Matrix Approach for Hierarchical Web Page Clustering Based on Hyperlinks, *Proceedings of the 3rd International Conference on Web Information Systems Engineering, Workshop: Mining Enhanced Web Search* (2002) 207–216
16. Hou, J., Zhang, Y.: Effectively Finding Relevant Web Pages from Linkage Information, *IEEE Transactions on Knowledge & Data Engineering* (to appear)
17. Hou, J., Zhang, Y.: Utilizing Hyperlink Transitivity to Improve Web Page Clustering, *Proceedings of the 14th Australasian Database Conference (ADC2003)*
18. Jiang, H., Lou, W., Wang, W.,: Three-tier Clustering: an Online Citation Clustering System, *Proceedings of the Second international Conference on Web-Age Information Management (WAIM2001)* 237–248

19. Kleinberg, J.: Authoritative Sources in a Hyperlinked Environment, *Proceedings of the 9th ACM-SIAM Symposium on Discrete Algorithms (SODA, 1998)*

20. Marchiori, M.: The Quest for Correct Information on the Web: Hyper Search Engines, *Proceedings of the 6th International Word Wide Web Conference* (1997)

21. McCormick, W. T., Schweitzer, P. J., White, T. W.: Problem Decomposition and Data Reorganization by a Clustering Technique, *Oper. Res.* (1972), 20(5) 993–1009

22. Özsu, M. T., Valduriez, P.: *Principle of Distributed Database Systems*, Prentice-Hall, Inc., Englewood Cliffs, New Jersey, USA (1991)

23. Pirolli, P., Pitkow, J., Rao, R.: Silk from a Sow's Ear: Extracting Usable Structures from the Web, *Proceedings of ACM SIGCHI Conference on Human Factors in Computing* (1996)

24. Pitkow, J., Pirolli, P.: Life, Death, and Lawfulness on the Electronic Frontier, *Proceedings of ACM CHI'97* (1997) 383–390

25. Terveen, L., Hill, W.: Finding and Visualizing Inter-site Clan Graphs, *Proceedings of CHI-98* (1998) 448–455

26. Wang, L.: On Competitive Learning, *IEEE Transaction on Neural Networks*, Vol.8, No.5 (1997) 1214–1217

27. Wang, Y., Kitsuregawa, M.: Use Link-based Clustering to Improve Web Search Results, *Proceedings of the Second International Conference on Web Information Systems Engineering (WISE 2001)* 119–128

28. Weiss, R., Vélez, B., Sheldon, M. A., Namprempre, C., Szilagyi, P., Duda, A., Gifford, D. K.: HyPursuit: A Hierarchical Network Search Engine that Exploits Content-Link Hypertext Clustering, *Proceedings of the Seventh ACM Conference on Hypertext* (1996) 180–193

29. Wen, C.W., Liu, H., Wen, W. X., Zheng, J.: A Distributed Hierarchical Clustering System for Web Mining, *Proceedings of the Second international Conference on Web-Age Information Management (WAIM2001)* 103–113

30. Xiao, J., Zhang, Y., Jia, X., Li, T.: Measuring Similarity of Interests for Clustering Web-Users, *Proceedings of the 12th Australasian Database Conference (ADC2001)* 107–114

31. Zamir, O., Etzioni, O.: Web Document Clustering: A Feasibility Demonstration, *Proceedings of ACM SIGIR'98* (1998) 46–54

A Framework for Decentralized Ranking in Web Information Retrieval

Karl Aberer and Jie Wu

School of Computer and Communication Sciences
Swiss Federal Institute of Technology (EPF), Lausanne
1015 Lausanne, Switzerland
{karl.aberer, jie.wu}@epfl.ch

Abstract. Search engines are among the most important applications or services on the web. Most existing successful search engines use global ranking algorithms to generate the ranking of documents crawled in their databases. However, global ranking of documents has two potential problems: high computation cost and potentially poor rankings. Both of the problems are related to the centralized computation paradigm. We propose to decentralize the task of ranking. This requires two things: a decentralized architecture and a logical framework for ranking computation. In the paper we introduce a ranking algebra providing such a formal framework. Through partitioning and combining rankings, we manage to compute document rankings of large-scale web data sets in a localized fashion. We provide initial results, demonstrating that the use of such an approach can ameliorate the above-mentioned problems. The approach presents a step towards P2P Web search engines.[1]

Keywords: search engines, information retrieval, P2P systems, link analysis

1 Introduction

A number of papers in recent years have studied the approach of hyperlink structure analysis to determine the hub and authority values or reputation of web documents. One algorithm proposed, PageRank [2], is the kernel of the very successful search engine Google [1]. The main problem of this sort of solutions is that they still are based on a centralized framework. The computation cost is thus prohibitively high since they have to deal with the complete document collection of the whole web. Even worse, the computation result can never reflect precisely the *real*[2] ranking relationship since the snapshot in search engines' databases can never be complete.

---

[1] The work presented in this paper was supported (in part) by the National Competence Center in Research on Mobile Information and Communication Systems (NCCR-MICS), a center supported by the Swiss National Science Foundation under grant number 5005-67322.

[2] That is, the ideal ranking of all existing web documents on the Internet.

X. Zhou, Y. Zhang, and M.E. Orlowska (Eds.): APWeb 2003, LNCS 2642, pp. 213–226, 2003.

We give a more detailed analysis that strongly suggests that increased use of local rankings should be made as compared to global rankings. Computing local rankings not only allows to partition the problem of determining a global ranking and to derive this ranking from fresher information, but also allows to peruse information that is only locally available for the ranking computation. Examples of such information are the hidden Web and usage profiles. In this paper, we also take up the idea of sharing resources at the level of both computing and knowledge in P2P systems, and explore the possibility to determine document rankings for the use in Web search.

We first point out some of the potential that such an approach bears, such as better scalable architectures and improved usage of distributed knowledge. The key in making such an approach work lies in the ability to compose global rankings from local rankings. We develop an *algebra* to concisely specify ranking composition processes. An important contribution of the paper is the identification of the essential operators for ranking compositions that we have derived from experiences gained by composing rankings in an ad-hoc manner in our experimental environment. We then present some initial results on ranking compositions, that demonstrate their potential use: on the one hand in decomposing global ranking computation and still being able to retain the original ranking characteristics, on the other hand in composing new types of rankings depending on the desired ranking context.

The paper lays ground for many possible future developments. Most notably, these concern system architectures that allow to implement ranking composition processes efficiently and the use of the algebraic framework for potential optimizations of ranking compositions by algebraic rewriting.

2   Limitations of the Global Ranking Approach

In this section we give an overview of a number of inherent limitations of the global ranking approach, as for example used by Google. Some of those are more or less well-known facts, whereas others will be more surprising. The limitations fall into three categories:

1. Practical problems related to scalability
2. Semantic problems related to the exclusive use of global context
3. Semantic problems related to the instability of ranking algorithms

We will illustrate the problems at the example of Google, in particular the use of the PageRank algorithm, but similar problems can be expected for other ranking approaches. PageRank uses iterations of matrix multiplication on the global web adjacency matrix to compute a global ranking of the whole web graph, and returns the search results in an order that is decided by a combined factor of PageRank and the ranking of the traditional keyword-based search.

2.1 Practical Problems of Global Algorithms

We call the algorithms based-on global information "global algorithms". The practical problems of global ranking schemes are mainly related to scalability.

Dynamicity of Web content: According to the recent research result, the Web consists of approximately 2.5 billion documents in 2000, with a rate of growth of 7.3 million pages per day [7]. This web growth rate continuously imposes high pressure on existing search engines. Repetitive computation is required even if only a small part of the global web is changed. The reason is that, the global link adjacency matrix is required to compute the final PageRank.

Latency: Most search engines update on a roughly monthly basis [4]. Since the time needed to retrieve all the existing and newer Web increases, it also takes longer time to integrate it into the database, thus longer for a page to be exposed on search engines. A simpler way to demonstrate the impossibility of catching up with the growing speed of the Web for the current centralized search systems is that, in December 2001, Google announced that it was spidering 3 million pages each day where freshness had been determined to be crucial [10]. So the Web pages emerging per day are crawled by Google in about 2.5 days. As a consequence also the Web graph structure that is obtained will be always incomplete, and the global ranking computation thus less accurate.

High Computation Cost: The computation of PageRank is over the whole Web that has been grabbed into Google's servers. Therefore, the algorithm has to deal with the problem of multiplication of a huge matrices. Early in June 1 of year 2000, Google indexes 300 million pages in total, and Google's process entails 500 million variables and 2 million terms to index every month, resulting in about 1 terabyte of data to index. According to Sergey Brin, hypertext analysis of Google is computationally expensive [6]. A single matrix multiplication with 75 million URLs takes 5 hours. At that time, Google already used 4,000 PCs running Linux to provide its service.

2.2 Importance of Context for Ranking

Link-based ranking methods, such as Google's PageRank algorithm [2] and the hub and authority method by Kleinberg [3], have proven as a valuable approach in uncovering hidden, distributed knowledge in the Web. They are based on the implicit assumption that the existence of a link from a Web document to another document expresses that the referenced document bears some importance to the content of the referencing document and that frequently referenced documents are of a more general importance.

The rankings derived based on that observation are usually established in the context of a specific query, either in combination with other global ranking schemes as in Google or by post-processing query results as in Kleinberg's proposal. However, other forms of context may be considered, in particular the aspect of locality.

The first observation we make is that there exists a certain likelihood that a local link, i.e. a link that references a document within the same local domain, typically a Web site, is likely to be semantically more "precise" since the author of the link is likely to be better informed about the semantics and particular importance of the local documents than an external author.

The second observation we make is that documents that are globally considered as important, also locally will have greater importance. This second observation suggests that it might be plausible to identify documents of global importance based on there local rankings only.

The third observation we make is that each Website establishes a specific semantic context. Depending now on the context we might specifically take advantage of the semantics implicit in certain Websites in order to obtain rankings that are tuned towards certain interest profiles.

All of these three observations lead us to the conclusion that it might be worthwhile to consider from a semantic perspective instead of a single global ranking various combinations of local rankings for the following three different but not mutually exclusive purposes:

1. Obtaining more precise rankings by exploiting local knowledge;
2. Reconstructing global rankings from local rankings in order to distribute the ranking effort;
3. Using selected local rankings in order to tune the resulting ranking towards specific interest profiles.

2.3   Instability of Ranking Schemes

Little attention is generally paid to the question to which extent link-based ranking methods are sensitive to changes in context. We performed a number of experiments indicating that link-based ranking such as PageRank might have in fact some undesirable properties with respect to stability. We classified them into two problems.

Effects of Agglomerate Documents

Previous studies on the HITS algorithm [9] revealed that HITS is prone to the problem of mutual reinforcement: the hub-authority relationships between pages are mutually reinforced because people put some one-to-many or many-to-one links in web sites. This problem can be solved in a heuristic way by dividing the hub or authority weights in the computation by the in-degree or out-degree number. It seems that it has not been noticed in the literature that the same phenomenon also occurs for the PageRank algorithm. The heuristic solution used by HITS to circumvent the problem cannot be applied to PageRank, since the division by the out-degree number is already used in the PageRank algorithm.

We illustrate this phenomenon by a simple experiment. We applied the PageRank algorithm to the set of documents that can be found at the ETH Zuerich website (about 430.000 pages). Interestingly, among the top 20 documents of PageRank one finds a substantial number of pages from the Java documentation (13 out of 20), which surely are not the most relevant documents to characterize ETH Zuerich. The reason for those documents to being ranked that high is found in the strong cross-referencing the Java documentation exhibits.

Stability of Local Ranking

Computation of global rankings merges information that is drawn both from local links and remote links. An interesting question is on the influence local versus remote links can have on the outcome of the ranking computation.

We illustrate this point by another experiment we did with pages collected from the EPF Lausanne websites (domain ".epfl.ch"). We chose two subsets of pages from them, related to two different organizational units and included all pages referenced from these web sites which brought the total number of documents to 1075. We computed now local rankings for documents for both websites (*dscwww* and *icawww*) in two ways.

1. Computing a global ranking including all 1075 documents and then project- ing the resulting global ranking to the pages from one website;
2. Computing a local ranking from the documents found on each respective web site only.

The result is somewhat surprising. For the smaller (*dscwww*) of the two web- sites, both the projected global and the local ranking coincide almost completely. For the larger (*icawww*) of the two the projected global and the local ranking are substantially different. Analysis shows that by relying solely on global rankings different aspects of ranking semantics, namely the local ranking (self-assessment) and the projected global ranking (assessments by others) are merged in a some- what arbitrary manner. Therefore a separation of these concerns seems to be a promising approach in order to reveal more precise information from the avail- able link structure.

3   The Ranking Algebra

In the previous section we have argued that different rankings established in different contexts can be of interest. Thus we see rankings as first-class objects, that can be produced, exchanged and manipulated as any other data object. We introduce now a framework that defines what the type of rankings is, and how rankings are manipulated. We will use an algebraic framework for rankings, a ranking algebra, similarly as it is done for other types of data objects (such as using relational algebra for relations). The ranking algebra will allow to formally specify different methods of combining rankings, in particular, for aggregating global rankings from local rankings originating from different semantic contexts.

3.1   Definitions

First we have to define the domain of objects that are to be ranked. Since rankings can occur at different levels of granularity there will not be rankings of documents only, but more generally, rankings over subsets of documents. This leads to the following definition.

Definition 1: A partition of a document set D is a set P of disjoint, non-emtpy subsets of D where $P = \{p_1, \cdots, p_k\}$, $D = \bigcup_{i=1}^{k} p_i$. We denote $\mathcal{P}(D)$ or briefly $\mathcal{P}$ as the set of all possible partitions over the document set D. We call each of the disjoint subsets a zone.

We use $\mathbf{P_0}$ to denote the finest partition where each zone in it is a single web document. So rankings at the document levels are also expressed over elements of $\mathcal{P}$ which makes our ranking framework uniform independent of the granularity of ranking. We also use $\mathbf{P_S}$ to denote the partition according to web sites, assuming that there exists a unique way to partition the Web into sites (e.g. via DNS). Then each zone corresponds to the set of web documents belonging to an individual site.

In order to be able to compare and relate rankings at different levels of granularity we introduce now a partial order on partitions.

Definition 2: Given $\mathcal{P}(D)$, the relation *cover* over $\mathcal{P}(D)$ for $P_1, P_2 \in \mathcal{P}(D)$ is denoted as $P_1 \ll P_2$ and holds iff. $\forall p_1 \in P_1, \exists p_2 \in P_2, p_1 \subseteq p_2$.

We also say that P_1 is covered by P_2 or P_2 covers P_1. The relation $P_2 \gg P_1$ is defined analogously.

We will also need a possibility to directly relate the elements of two partitions to each other (and not only the whole partitions as with cover). Therefore we introduce the following operator.

Definition 3: For $P_1, P_2 \in \mathcal{P}, P_1 \gg P_2$ the mapping $\rho_{P_1 \gg P_2} : P_1 \to 2^{P_2}$ is defined for $p \in P_1$ and $q \in P_2$ as $q \in \rho_{P_1 \gg P_2}(p)$ iff. $q \subseteq p$.

This operator selects those elements of the finer partition that are covered by the selected element p of the coarser partition. For example, for $\mathbf{P_S} \gg \mathbf{P_0}$, given a web site $S \in \mathbf{P_S}$, the operator maps it to its set of web documents contained in this site: $\rho(S) \subseteq \mathbf{P_0}$.

The basis for computing rankings are links among documents or among sets of documents. Therefore we introduce next the notion of link matrix. Link matrices are always defined over partitions, even if we consider document links. Also we define link matrices only for sub-portions of the Web, and therefore introduce them as partial mappings. Note that it makes a difference whether a link between two entities is undefined or non-existent.

Definition 4: Given $P \in \mathcal{P}$ a link matrix $M_P \in \mathcal{M}_P$ is partial mapping $M_P : P \times P \to \{0,1\}$. In particular if M_P is defined only for values in $P_1 \subset P$ then we write $M_P(P_1)$. We say then $M_P(P_1)$ is a link matrix over P_1.

A number of operations are required to manipulate link matrices before they are used for ranking computations. We introduce here only those mappings that we have identified as being relevant for our purposes. The list of operations can be clearly extended by other graph manipulation operators.

The most important operation is the projection of a link matrix to a subset of the zones that are to be ranked.

Definition 5: For $P \in \mathcal{P}(D)$, $P_1 \subseteq P$ and $M_P \in \mathcal{M}_P$, the node projection $\Pi_{P_1} : \mathcal{M}_P \to \mathcal{M}_P(P_1)$ satisfies $\Pi_{P_1}(M_P)(p,q), p,q \in P$ defined iff. $p,q \in P_1$ and M_P is defined for p,q.

We also need the ability to change the granularity at which a link matrix is specified. This is supported by the contraction operator.

Definition 6: For $P_1, P_2 \in \mathcal{P}(D)$ with $P_1 \gg P_2$ and link matrices $M_{P_1} \in \mathcal{M}_{P_1}$ and $M_{P_2} \in \mathcal{M}_{P_2}$ the contraction $\Delta^{P_1 \gg P_2} : \mathcal{M}_{P_2} \to \mathcal{M}_{P_1}$ is the mapping that maps M_{P_2} to M_{P_1} such that for $p', q' \in P_1$, $M_{P_2}(p', q')$ defined iff. $M_{P_2}(p, q)$ defined for all $p, q \in P_2$ with $p \subseteq p', q \subseteq q'$ and $M_{P_1}(p', q') = 1$ iff. $M_{P_1}(p', q')$ defined and exists $p, q \in P_2$ with $p \subseteq p', q \subseteq q', M_{P_2}(p, q) = 1$.

for $p, q \in P_2$ $M_{P_2}(p, q) = 1$ and defined iff. for $p', q' \in P_1$ with $p \subseteq p', q \subseteq q'$ $M_{P_1}(p', q') = 1$ and defined.

In certain cases it is necessary to directly manipulate the link graph in order to change the ranking context. This is supported by a link projection.

Definition 7: For $P \in \mathcal{P}(D)$, $P_1 \subseteq P$ and $M_P \in \mathcal{M}_P$ the link projection $\Lambda_{P_1} : \mathcal{M}_P \to \mathcal{M}_P$ satisfies for $p \in P - P_1, q \in P - P_1$ $\Lambda_{P_1}(M_P)(p, q) = 0$ iff. $M_P(p, q)$ defined and $\Lambda_{P_1}(M_P)(p, q) = M_P(p, q)$ for all other p, q.

Based on link matrices rankings are computed. The domain of rankings will again be partitions of the document set.

Definition 8: For $P \in \mathcal{P}(D)$ a ranking $R_P \in \mathcal{R}_P$ is a partial mapping $R_P : P \to [0, 1]$. When the ranking is defined for $P_1 \subseteq P$ only we also denote the ranking as $R_P(P_1)$.

Normally rankings will be normalized. This leads to the following definition:

Definition 9: A normalized ranking R_P satisfies $\sum_{p \in P} R_P(p) = 1$. Given a general ranking $R_P \in \mathcal{R}_P$ the operator $\mu : \mathcal{R}_P \to \mathcal{R}_P$ derives a normalized ranking by $\mu(R_P(p)) = \frac{R_P(p)}{\sum_{p \in P} R_P(p)}$.

The connection between rankings and link matrices is established by ranking algorithms. As these algorithms are specific, we do not define their precise workings.

Definition 10: A ranking algorithm is a mapping $R_P^{alg} : \mathcal{M}_P(P_1) \to \mathcal{R}_P(P_1)$

We will distinguish different ranking algorithms through different superscripts. In particular, we will use $R^{PageRank}$, the Page rank algorithm, and R^{Count}, the incoming links counting algorithm, in our later examples.

As for link matrices we also need to be able to project rankings to selected subsets of the Web.

Definition 11: For $P \in \mathcal{P}(D)$ and $R_P \in \mathcal{R}_P$ the projection $\Pi_{P_1} : \mathcal{R}_P \to \mathcal{R}_P(P_1)$ is given as $\Pi_{P_1}(R_P) = \mu(R_P^*)$ iff. $R_P^*(p) = R_P(p)$ with $p \in P_1$ and $R_P(p)$ defined.

In many cases different rankings will be combined in an ad-hoc manner driven by application requirements. We introduce weighted addition for that purpose.

Definition 12: Given rankings $R_P^i \in \mathcal{R}_P, i = 1, \ldots, n$ and a weight vector $w \in [0, 1]^n$ then the weighted addition $\Sigma_n : \mathcal{R}_P^n \times [0, 1]^n \to \mathcal{R}_P$ is given as $\Sigma_n(R_P^1, \ldots, R_P^n, w_1, \ldots, w_n) = \mu(R_P^*)$ iff. $R_P^*(p) = \sum_{i=1}^n w_i R_P^i(p)$ and $R_P^i(p)$ defined for $i = 1, \ldots, n$.

We will in particular look into methods for systematic composition of rankings. These are obtained by combining rankings that have been obtained at different levels of granularity. To that end we introduce the following concepts.

Definition 13: A covering vector of rankings for $\mathcal{R}_Q$ over $\mathcal{R}_P$ with $Q \gg P$ is a partial mapping $R_P^Q \in \mathcal{R}_P^Q$ with signature $R_P^Q : Q \to \mathcal{R}_P$.

This definition says that for each ranking value of a ranking at higher granularity there exists a ranking at the finer granularity. Next we introduce an operation for the systematic composition of rankings using covering vectors.

Definition 14: Given a covering vector $\mathcal{R}_P^Q$ with $Q \gg P$ the folding is the mapping $\mathcal{F}^{Q \gg P} : \mathcal{R}_P^Q \times \mathcal{R}_Q \to \mathcal{R}_P$ such that for $R_P^Q \in \mathcal{R}_P^Q, R_Q \in \mathcal{R}_Q$, $\mathcal{F}^{Q \gg P}(R_P^Q, R_Q) = \mu(R_P^*)$ iff. for $p \in P$,

$$R_P^*(p) = \sum_{q \in Q \text{ st. } R_P^Q(q) \text{ and } R_Q(q) \text{ defined}} (R_Q(q) * R_P^Q(q)(p)).$$

3.2 Computing Rankings from Different Contexts

In this section we give an illustration of how to apply the ranking algebra in order to produce different types of rankings by using different ranking contexts.

Suppose $P_S = \{s_1, \ldots, s_k\} \subset \mathbf{P_S}$ is a subset of all Web sites. If we determine $D_i = \rho_{\mathbf{P_S} \gg \mathbf{P_0}}(s_i)$ we see that $D_i \subset \mathbf{P_0}$ corresponds to the set of documents of the Web site s_i. We denote with $D_S = \cup_{i=1}^k D_i$ the set of all documents occuring in one of the selected Web sites. For ranking documents from the subset P_S of selected Web sites we propose now different schemes.

Global site ranking: The global site ranking is used to rank the selected Web sites using the complete Web graph. Since only inter-site links are used the number of links considered for computing the ranking is substantially reduced as compared to the global Web graph. In addition such rankings should only be recomputed at irregular intervals. The ranking algorithm to be used is PageRank. Global site rankings for subsets of Web sites could be provided by specialized ranking providers or Web aggregators. Formally we can specify this ranking as follows. Given the Web link matrix $M \in \mathcal{M}_{\mathbf{P_0}}$ and a selected subset of Web sites $P_S \subset \mathbf{P_S}$ the global site ranking of these Web sites is given as

$$R_{P_S}^{GS} = \Pi_{P_S}(R^{PageRank}(\Delta^{\mathbf{Ps} \gg \mathbf{P_0}}(M))) \in \mathcal{R}_{\mathbf{P_S}}(P_S)$$

Local site ranking: In contrast to the global site ranking we use here as context only the subgraph of the Web graph that concerns the selected Web sites. In this case we prefer to use the ranking algorithm R^{Count} since the number of inter Web site links may be more limited for this smaller link graph. Formally we can specify this ranking as follows. Given the Web link matrix $M \in \mathcal{M}_{\mathbf{P_0}}$ and a selected subset of websites $P_S \subset \mathbf{P_S}$ the local site ranking of these websites is

$$R_{P_S}^{LS} = R^{Count}(\Pi_{P_S}(\Delta^{\mathbf{Ps} \gg \mathbf{P_0}}(M))) \in \mathcal{R}_{\mathbf{P_S}}(P_S)$$

Note that we assume that R^{count} ranks only documents for which the link matrix is defined and thus we don't have to project the resulting ranking to the subset of Web sites taken into account.

Global ranking of documents of a Web site: This ranking is the projection of the global PageRank to the documents from a selected site. Formally we can specify this ranking as follows. Given the Web link matrix $M \in \mathcal{M}_{\mathbf{P_0}}$

and the Web site $s_i \in P_S$ with $D_i = \rho_{\mathbf{P_S} \gg \mathbf{P_0}}(s_i)$. Then the global ranking of documents of a Web site is

$$R_{D_i}^{global} = \Pi_{D_i}(R^{PageRank}(M))) = \Pi_{D_i}(R_{D_S}^{global}) \in \mathcal{R}_{\mathbf{P_0}}(D_i)$$

A more restricted form of global ranking is when we only include the documents from the set $D_S = \cup_{i=1}^{k} D_i$. This gives

$$R_{D_i}^{intermediate} = \Pi_{D_i}(R^{PageRank}(\Pi_{D_S}(M)))) \in \mathcal{R}_{\mathbf{P_0}}(D_i)$$

The global or intermediate ranking of documents of a set $D' = D_{i_1} \cup \cdots \cup D_{i_m}$ of more than one web sites can be obtained similarly by simply replacing D_i with D' in the projection operators.

Local internal ranking for documents: This corresponds to a ranking of the documents by the document owners, taking into account their local link structure only. The algorithm used is PageRank applied to the local link graph. Formally we can specify this ranking as follows. Given the Web link matrix $M \in \mathcal{M}_{\mathbf{P_0}}$ and the Web site $s_i \in P_S$ with $D_i = \rho_{\mathbf{P_S} \gg \mathbf{P_0}}(s_i)$, the local internal ranking is

$$R_{D_i}^{LI} = R^{PageRank}(\Pi_{D_i}(M)) \in \mathcal{R}_{\mathbf{P_0}}(D_i)$$

Note that we assume here that the PageRank algorithm does not rank documents for which the link matrix is undefined, and therefore the resulting ranking is only defined for the local web site documents.

Local external ranking for documents: This corresponds to a ranking of the documents by others. Here for each document we count the number of incoming links from one of the other Web sites from the set P_S. The local links are ignored. This results in one ranking per other Web site for each Web site. Formally we can specify this ranking as follows. Given the Web link matrix $M \in \mathcal{M}_{\mathbf{P_0}}$ the Web site $s_i \in P_S$ with $D_i = \rho_{\mathbf{P_S} \gg \mathbf{P_0}}(s_i)$ to be ranked and the external Web site $s_j \in P_S$ with $D_j = \rho_{\mathbf{P_S} \gg \mathbf{P_0}}(s_j)$ used as ranking context. We include the case where $i = j$. Then

$$R_{D_{ij}}^{LE} = \Pi_{D_i}(R^{Count}(\Lambda_{D_j}(\Pi_{D_i \cup D_j}(M)))) \in \mathcal{R}_{\mathbf{P_0}}(D_i)$$

3.3   Ranking Aggregation

We illustrate here by using ranking algebra again how the rankings described above can be combined to produce further aggregate rankings. Thus we address several issues discussed in previous sections and demonstrate two points:

1. We show that global document rankings can be determined in a distributed fashion, and thus better scalability can be achieved. Hence ranking documents based on global information not necessarily implies a centralized architecture.
2. We show how local rankings from different sources can be integrated, such that rankings can be made precise and can take advantage of globally unavailable information (e.g. the hidden web) or different ranking contents. Thus a richer set of possible rankings can be made available.

Our goal is to produce a composite ranking for the documents in one of the selected subset of Web sites in P_S from the different rankings that have been described before. The specific way of composition has been chosen with two issues in mind: first, we want to illustrate different possibilities of computing aggregate rankings using the ranking algebra, and second, the resulting composite ranking should exhibit a good ranking quality, which we will evaluate in the experimental section, by comparing to various rankings described in Section 3.2.

The aggregate ranking for a Web site $s_i \in P_S$ with $D_i = \rho_{\mathbf{P_S} \gg \mathbf{P_0}}(s_i)$ is obtained in 3 major steps. First we aggregate the local external rankings by weighting them using the global site ranking. Since for each D_i we can compute a local external ranking $R_{D_{ij}}^{LE}$ relative to D_j, we can obtain a covering vector $RLE_{\mathbf{P_0}}^{\mathbf{P_S}}(D_i)$ over P_S by defining $RLE_{\mathbf{P_0}}^{\mathbf{P_S}}(D_i)(s_j) = R_{D_{ij}}^{LE}$. Using the global site ranking we compose an aggregate local document ranking by using a folding operation

$$R_{D_i}^{LE} = \mathcal{F}^{\mathbf{P_S} \gg \mathbf{P_0}}(RLE_{\mathbf{P_0}}^{\mathbf{P_S}}(D_i), R_{P_S}^{GS})$$

Then we combine this ranking of documents in D_i with the local internal ranking in an ad-hoc fashion, using w_E and w_I as the weights that we give to the external and internal rankings.

$$R_{D_i}^{WA} = \Sigma_2(R_{D_i}^{LE}, R_{D_i}^{LI}, w_E, w_I)$$

In this manner we have now obtained a local ranking for each D_i. We can again use these local rankings to construct a covering vector $RCL_{\mathbf{P_0}}^{\mathbf{P_S}}$ over P_S by

$$RCL_{\mathbf{P_0}}^{\mathbf{P_S}} = R_{D_i}^{WA}$$

Using this covering vector we can obtain a global ranking by applying a folding operation. This time we use the local site ranking to perform the ranking

$$R_{D_S}^{comp} = \mathcal{F}^{\mathbf{P_S} \gg \mathbf{P_0}}(RCL_{\mathbf{P_0}}^{\mathbf{P_S}}, R_{P_S}^{LS})$$

Finally we project the ranking obtained to a Web site

$$R_{D_i}^{comp} = \Pi_{D_i}(R_{D_S}^{comp})$$

This composite ranking we will compare experimentally with some of the basic rankings introduced earlier.

4   Application and Evaluation

4.1   Experimental Setting

In this section we give an illustration of how to apply the ranking algebra in a concrete problem setting. We performed an evaluation of the aggregation approach described above within the EPFL domain which contains about 600 independent Web sites ($\mathbf{P_S}$) identified by their hostnames or IP addresses. We crawled about 270.000 documents found in this domain. Using this document collection we performed the evaluations using the following approach: we chose two selected Web sites s_1 and s_2, with substantially different characteristics, in particular of substantially different sizes. For those domains we computed the local internal and external rankings. We also put the EPFL portal web server s_h (hostname www.epfl.ch) in the collection, since this is a point where most of the other subdomains are connected to. We consider this subset of documents an excellent knowledge source for information of web site importance. So we have $P_S = \{s_1, s_2, s_h\}$ here. We denote the corresponding document ses D_1, D_2, D_h as in section 3.3.

Then we applied the algebraic aggregation of the rankings obtained in that way, in order to generate a global ranking for the joint domains s_1 and s_2. For local aggregation we chose the values $(w_E, w_I) = (0.8, 0.2)$. This reflects a higher valuation of external links than internal links. One motivation for this choice is the relatively low number of links across subdomains as compared to the number of links within the same subdomain. The resulting aggregate ranking $R_{D_1 \cup D_2}^{comp}$ for the joint domains s_1 and s_2 is then compared to the ranking obtained by extracting from the global ranking $R_{D_1 \cup D_2}^{global}$ computed for the complete EPFL domain (all 270.000 documents) for the joint domains s_1 and s_2. The comparison is performed both qualitatively and quantitatively.

4.2   Qualitative Results

We report on one specific experiment performed in the way described above. The subdomains used are sicwww.epfl.ch, the home of the computing center (280 documents) and sunwww.epfl.ch, the support site for SUN machines (21685 documents). Figure 1 compares the top 25 documents resulting from the two ranking methods. We can observe some substantial differences. In the top 25 list of the aggregate ranking result, the top 4 are obviously more important than the top listed ones from the global PageRank. The 2 obviously important pages "http://sunwww.epfl.ch/" and "http://sicwww.epfl.ch/informatique/" are ranked much lower than some of the software documentation pages. We can assume that this is an effect due to the agglomorate structure of these document collections. These play obviously a much less important role in the composite ranking due to the way of how the ranking is composed from local rankings. It shows that the global page ranking is not necessarily the best possible ranking method. We obtained similar qualitative improvements in the ranking results of other domains.

4.3   Quantitative Comparison

For quantitative comparison of rankings we adopt the Spearman's Footrule. [8]:

$$F(R_0, R_1) = \sum_{i=1}^{n} |R_0(i) - R_1(i)| \tag{1}$$

In the formula, $R_j, j = 0, 1$ are the two ranking vectors to be compared. $R_j(i)$ is the rank of document i.

Doc_ID	Rank_Value	URL	Doc_ID	Rank_Value	URL
4194	0.027078119	http://sunwww.epfl.ch/	1500	0.000121	http://sicwww.epfl.ch/SIC/
82	0.005867276	http://sicwww.epfl.ch/informatique/	10714	6.00E-05	http://sunwww.epfl.ch/Admin/todorov.html
1500	0.002242407	http://sicwww.epfl.ch/SIC/	66021	4.10E-05	http://sunwww.epfl.ch/Java/jdk1.4/docs/api/overview-summary.html
10714	0.001030088	http://sunwww.epfl.ch/Admin/todorov.html	66020	3.40E-05	http://sunwww.epfl.ch/Java/jdk1.4/docs/api/index.html
66021	0.000710622	http://sunwww.epfl.ch/Java/jdk1.4/docs/api/overview-summary.html	168390	3.10E-05	http://sunwww.epfl.ch/Java/jdk1.4/docs/api/allclasses-noframe.html
66020	0.000598713	http://sunwww.epfl.ch/Java/jdk1.4/docs/api/index.html	168389	3.10E-05	http://sunwww.epfl.ch/Java/jdk1.4/docs/api/help-doc.html
168387	0.000539437	http://sunwww.epfl.ch/Java/jdk1.4/docs/api/deprecated-list.html	168388	3.10E-05	http://sunwww.epfl.ch/Java/jdk1.4/docs/api/index-files/index-1.html
168388	0.000539437	http://sunwww.epfl.ch/Java/jdk1.4/docs/api/index-files/index-1.html	168387	3.10E-05	http://sunwww.epfl.ch/Java/jdk1.4/docs/api/deprecated-list.html
168389	0.000539437	http://sunwww.epfl.ch/Java/jdk1.4/docs/api/help-doc.html	66435	3.00E-05	http://sunwww.epfl.ch/Java/jdk1.2/docs/api/overview-summary.html
168390	0.000539437	http://sunwww.epfl.ch/Java/jdk1.4/docs/api/allclasses-noframe.html	65975	2.90E-05	http://sunwww.epfl.ch/Java/jdk1.3/docs/api/overview-summary.html
66435	0.000519678	http://sunwww.epfl.ch/Java/jdk1.3/docs/api/overview-summary.html	405856	2.70E-05	http://sunwww.epfl.ch/Java/jdk1.4/docs/relnotes/devdocs-vs-specs.html
65975	0.000500968	http://sunwww.epfl.ch/Java/jdk1.3/docs/api/overview-summary.html	4194	2.40E-05	http://sunwww.epfl.ch/
405856	0.000480859	http://sunwww.epfl.ch/Java/jdk1.4/docs/relnotes/devdocs-vs-specs.html	66434	2.30E-05	http://sunwww.epfl.ch/Java/jdk1.2/docs/api/index.html
66434	0.000404271	http://sunwww.epfl.ch/Java/jdk1.3/docs/api/index.html	3709	2.30E-05	http://sicwww.epfl.ch/SIC/SIC-welcome.html
169526	0.000404097	http://sunwww.epfl.ch/Java/jdk1.3/docs/api/deprecated-list.html	169528	2.30E-05	http://sunwww.epfl.ch/Java/jdk1.2/docs/api/help-doc.html
169527	0.000404097	http://sunwww.epfl.ch/Java/jdk1.3/docs/api/index-files/index-1.html	169527	2.30E-05	http://sunwww.epfl.ch/Java/jdk1.2/docs/api/index-files/index-1.html
169528	0.000404097	http://sunwww.epfl.ch/Java/jdk1.3/docs/api/help-doc.html	169526	2.30E-05	http://sunwww.epfl.ch/Java/jdk1.2/docs/api/deprecated-list.html
65974	0.000389758	http://sunwww.epfl.ch/Java/jdk1.3/docs/api/index.html	65974	2.20E-05	http://sunwww.epfl.ch/Java/jdk1.3/docs/api/index.html
167601	0.000389583	http://sunwww.epfl.ch/Java/jdk1.3/docs/api/deprecated-list.html	167603	2.20E-05	http://sunwww.epfl.ch/Java/jdk1.3/docs/api/help-doc.html
167603	0.000389583	http://sunwww.epfl.ch/Java/jdk1.3/docs/api/help-doc.html	167602	2.20E-05	http://sunwww.epfl.ch/Java/jdk1.3/docs/api/index-files/index-1.html
167602	0.000389409	http://sunwww.epfl.ch/Java/jdk1.3/docs/api/index-files/index-1.html	167601	2.20E-05	http://sunwww.epfl.ch/Java/jdk1.3/docs/api/deprecated-list.html
406487	0.000349716	http://sunwww.epfl.ch/Java/jdk1.2/docs/api/java/lang/Object.html	406487	2.10E-05	http://sunwww.epfl.ch/Java/jdk1.4/docs/api/java/lang/Object.html
409918	0.000267882	http://sunwww.epfl.ch/Java/jdk1.2/docs/api/java/lang/Object.html	26506	2.00E-05	http://sicwww.epfl.ch/SIC/SIC-SII.html
399292	0.000255817	http://sunwww.epfl.ch/Java/jdk1.4/docs/api/java/lang/Object.html	82	1.50E-05	http://sicwww.epfl.ch/informatique/
168214	0.000235534	http://sunwww.epfl.ch/Java/jdk1.4/docs/api/java/lang/String.html	409918	1.50E-05	http://sunwww.epfl.ch/Java/jdk1.2/docs/api/java/lang/Object.html

Fig. 1. URLs ranked 1 to 25 in the composite and global ranking

Since search engines return documents in ranking order, top level documents receive generally much higher attention than documents listed later. To take this into account we customize Spearman's Footrule by a weighting scheme

$$F(R_0, R_1) = \sum_{i=1}^{n} w_0(i) w_1(i) |R_0(i) - R_1(i)| \qquad (2)$$

Since users mostly care about top listed documents we assign 90% of the weight to the T top-listed documents for $T < n$, i.e. $w_j(i) = \frac{0.9}{T}$ for $1 \leq i \leq T$ and $w_j(i) = \frac{0.1}{n-T}$ for $t+1 \leq i \leq n$. When $T = n$, $w_j(i) = \frac{1}{n}$ for $1 \leq i \leq n$.

We give now the results of the quantitative comparison for our experiment on the 2 subdomains in Figure 2. The figure shows the ranking distance computed using the adapted Spearman's rule of different rankings with respect to the global ranking $R_{D_1 \cup D_2}^{global}$ for varying values of T. Besides of the aggregate ranking we include for comparison purposes other rankings that are computed for different contexts. The "subset" ranking is the ranking obtained by selecting exactly all documents that are involved in the computation of the aggregate ranking and applying the PageRank algorithm, i.e. $R_{D_1 \cup D_2}^{intermediate}$. This ranking thus uses exactly the same information that is available to the computation of the aggregate ranking, i.e., the documents in the set P_S. The "tinyset" ranking is the ranking obtained by selecting exactly all documents that are ranked by the aggregate ranking and applying PageRank to them, which is exactly $R_{D_1 \cup D_2}^{LI}$. In addition, we included for calibration a randomly generated ranking. The results are shown in Figure 2.

One can observe that, interestingly, the result of the "composite" ranking appears to be much "worse" for low values of T than the global ranking. However, considering the qualitative analysis, the result rather indicates that the global ranking seems to be poor, whereas the aggregate ranking is to be considered as the "good" ranking to be approximated. For larger values of T the aggregate ranking approximates then the rankings computed on the selected subsets. Also

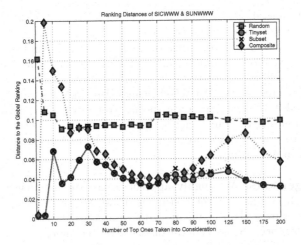

Fig. 2. Ranking Distances of SICWWW & SUNWWW

this is an interesting result, since the aggregate ranking is performed in a distributed manner, computing separate rankings for each of the three subdomains involved, whereas the "subset" and "tinyset" rankings can be considered as corresponding to a global ranking based on the union of the selected subdomains. This shows that by aggregation one can obtain at least as good results in a distributed manner as with global ranking using the same information.

Due to limit of space, we only show the main results here. More results can be found in a longer version of this paper at http://lsirwww.epfl.ch/.

4.4 Summary

From the comparison and analysis, we find that with our ranking algebra, the ranking result has been improved in two important aspects: firstly, default important pages (for example the department home) are levered to the rank that they deserve; secondly, the reinforcing effect of some agglomerate pages is defeated to a satisfactory degree.

In short, our results making use only of local information approximate the result of PageRank based on global information very well and in some cases appear to be even better with respect to importance of documents. We see this work as a first step towards a completely decentralized P2P-based search engine that offers meaningful and efficient rankings.

5   Future Work

By introducing a ranking algebra we made a first step towards an operational framework for manipulating and composing rankings. An obvious development is to determine and exploit algebraic equivalences in order to find alternative plans for computing rankings in a distributed environment most efficiently.

Having the possibility to consider different contexts for rankings, an interesting approach is to use information obtained from user interactions in order to obtain information on the relevance of documents. This kind of local feedback could greatly enhance the quality of local rankings that could be used in the framework that allows to integrate different local rankings.

Another specific context of which composite rankings can take advantage of are so-called hub sites. These are special Web sites that provide a directory function by pointing to many relevant (authority) sites. They would be particularly useful to provide Web site rankings used to fold multiple local rankings, as illustrated in our examples.

Acknowledgements. We highly appreciate the discussions with Prof. Ling Liu, Prof. Calton Pu, and their student Todd Miller from Georgia Institute of Technology during their academic sojourn at LSIR (Distributed Information Systems Laboratory), Swiss Federal Institute of Technology, Lausanne.

References

1. Sergey Brin, Lawrence Page, "The Anatomy of a Large-Scale Hypertextual Web Search Engine", 2000.
2. Larry Page, Sergey Brin, R. Motwani, T. Winograd, "The PageRank Citation Ranking: Bringing Order to the Web", 1998.
3. Jon Kleinberg, "Authoritative Sources in a Hyperlinked Environment", 1998.
4. Danny Sullivan, "New AllTheWeb.com Goes Live",
   http://searchenginewatch.com/sereport/01/08-alltheweb.html, 2001.
5. Chris Sherman, "It's Fresher at FAST",
   http://www.searchenginewatch.com/searchday/01/sd0725-fast.html, 2001.
6. Mitch Wagner, "Google Bets The Farm On Linux",
   http://www.internetwk.com/lead/lead060100.htm, 2000.
7. UC Berkeley SIMS, "How Much Information – Internet Summary",
   http://www.sims.berkeley.edu/research/projects/how-much-info/internet.html, 2000.
8. Keith A. Baggerly, "Visual Estimation of Structure in Ranked Data", PhD thesis, Rice University, 1995.
9. K. Bharat, M. R. Henzinger, "Improved algorithms for topic distillation in a hyperlinked environment", in *Proceedings of the ACM International Conference on Research and Development in Information Retrieval (SIGIR)*, pages 104–111, Melbourne, Australia, August 1998. ACM Press, New York.
10. Danny Sullivan, "Google Adds More "Fresh" Pages, Changes Robots.txt & 403 Errors, Gains iWon", http://searchenginewatch.com/sereport/02/08-google.html, Aug. 5, 2002.

A Web User Profiling Approach

Younes Hafri[1,2], Chabane Djeraba[2], Peter Stanchev[3], and Bruno Bachimont[1]

[1] Institut National de l'Audiovisuel, 4 avenue de l'Europe
94366 Bry-sur-Marne Cedex, France
{yhafri,bbachimont}@ina.fr
[2] Institut de Recherche en Informatique de Nantes, 2 rue de la Houssiniere
43322 Nantes Cedex, France
djeraba@irin.univ-nantes.fr
[3] Kettering University, USA
pstanchev@kettering.edu
3, Kettering University, Flint, MI 48504, USA

Abstract. People display regularities in almost everything they do. This
paper proposes characteristics of an idealized algorithm that would allow an automatic extraction of web user profil based on user navigation
paths. We describe a simple predictive approach with these characteristics and show its predictive accuracy on a large dataset from KDD-
Cup web logs (a commercial web site), while using fewer computational
and memory resources. To achieve this objective, our approach is articulated around three notions: (1) Applying probabilistic exploration
using Markov models. (2) Avoiding the problem of Markov model high-
dimensionality and sparsity by clustering web documents, based on their
content, before applying the Markov analysis. (3) Clustering Markov
models, and extraction of their gravity centers. On the basis of these
three notions, the approach makes possible the prediction of future states
to be visited in k steps and navigation sessions monitoring, based on both
content and traversed paths.

1 Introduction

On the web today, sites are still unable to market each individual user in a way,
which truly matches their interests and needs. Sites make broad generalizations
based on huge volumes of sales data that don't accurate an individual person.
Amazon.com tracks relationships in the buying trends of its users, and makes
recommendations based upon that data. While viewing a DVD by Dupont Du-
rand, the site recommends three other Dupont Durant DVDs that are often
bought by people who buy first DVD. The agreement calls for the participating web documents to track their users so the advertisements can be precisely
aimed at the most likely prospects for web documents. For example, a user who
looks up tourist document about Paris might be fed ads for web documents of
hotels in Paris. What would be far more useful would be if web sites were able
to understand specific user's interests and provide them with the content that
was relevant to them. Instead of requiring users to provide their interests, a website could learn the type of content that interests the users and automatically

X. Zhou, Y. Zhang, and M.E. Orlowska (Eds.): APWeb 2003, LNCS 2642, pp. 227–238, 2003.

place that information in more prominent locations on the page. Taking a film example, if a web site knew where you lived, it could provide you with information when an actor is touring in the user area. From an advertising standpoint, this technology could be used for better targeting of advertisements to make them more relevant to each user. It is evident that there are strong dependencies between web exploration and different domains and usages. The fundamental requirements that ensure the usability of such systems are: (1) obtaining compressed and exhaustive web representations, and (2) providing different exploration strategies adapted to user requirements. The scope of the paper deals with the second requirement by investigating an exploration based on historical exploration of web and user profiles. This new form of exploration induces the answer to difficult problems. An exploration system should maintain over time the inference schema for user profiling and user-adapted web retrieval. There are two reasons for this. Firstly, the information itself may change. Secondly, the user group is largely unknown from the start, and may change during the usage of exploration processes. To address these problems, the approach, presented in this paper, models profile structures extracted and represented automatically in Markov models in order to consider the dynamic aspect of user behaviors. The main technical contribution of the paper is the notion of probabilistic prediction, path analysis using Markov models, clustering Markov models and dealing with the high dimension matrix of Markov models in clustering algorithm. The paper provides a solution, which efficiently accomplishes such profiling. This solution should enhance the day-to-day web exploration in terms of information filtering and searching.

The paper contains the following sections. Section 2 situates our contribution among state of art approaches. Section 3 describes user-profiling based web exploration. Section 4 highlights the general framework of the system and presented some implementation results. Finally, section 5 concludes the paper.

2   Related Works and Contribution

The analysis of sequential data is without doubts an interesting application area since many real processes show a dynamic behavior. Several examples can be reported, one for all is the analysis of DNA strings for classification of genes, protein family modeling, and sequence alignment. In this paper, the problem of unsupervised classification of temporal data is tackled by using a technique based on Markov Models. MMs can be viewed as stochastic generalizations of finite-state automata, when both transitions between states and generation of output symbols are governed by probability distributions [1]. The basic theory of MMs was developed in the late 1960s, but only in the last decade it has been extensively applied in a large number of problems, as speech recognition [6], handwritten character recognition [2], DNA and protein modeling [3], gesture recognition [4], behavior analysis and synthesis [5], and, more in general, to computer vision problems. Related to sequence clustering, MMs has not been extensively used, and a few papers are present in the literature. Early works were proposed in [6,7], all related to speech recognition. The first interesting approach not directly linked to speech issues was presented by Smyth [8], in which clustering was faced by devising a "distance" measure between sequences using HMMs. Assuming each model structure known, the algorithm trains an HMM for each sequence so that the log-likelihood (LL) of each model, given each sequence, can be computed. This information is used to build a LL distance matrix to be used to cluster the sequences in K groups, using a hierarchical algorithm. Subsequent work, by Li and Biswas [10,11], address the clustering problem focusing on the model selection issue, i.e. the search of the HMM topology best representing data, and the clustering structure issue, i.e. finding the most likely number of clusters. In [10], the former issue is addressed using standard approach, like Bayesian Information Criterion [12], and extending to the continuous case the Bayesian Model Merging approach [13]. Regarding the latter issue, the sequence-to-HMM likelihood measure is used to enforce the within-group similarity criterion. The optimal number of clusters is then determined maximizing the Partition Mutual Information (PMI), which is a measure of the inter-cluster distances. In [11], the same problems are addressed in terms of Bayesian model selection, using the Bayesian Information Criterion (BIC) [12], and the Cheesman-Stutz (CS) approximation [14]. Although not well justified, much heuristics are introduced to alleviate the computational burden, making the problem tractable, despite remaining of elevate complexity. Finally, a model-based clustering method is also proposed in [15], where HMMs are used as cluster prototypes, and Rival Penalized Competitive Learning (RPCL), with state merging is then adopted to find the most likely HMMs modeling data. These approaches are interesting from the theoretical point of view, but they are not tested on real data. Moreover, some of them are very computationally expensive.

Each visitor of a web site leaves a trace in a log file of the pages that he or she visited. Analysis of these click patterns can provide the maintainer of the site with information on how to streamline the site or how to personalize it with respect to a particular visitor type. However, due to the massive amount of data that is generated on large and frequently visited web sites, clickstream analysis is hard to perform 'by hand'. Several attempts have been made to learn the click behaviour of a web surfer, most notably by probabilistic clustering of individuals with mixtures of Markov chains [16,9,17]. Here, the availability of a prior categorization of web pages was assumed; clickstreams are modelled by a transition matrix between page categories. However, manual categorization can be cumbersome for large web sites. Moreover, a crisp assignment of each page to one particular category may not always be feasible. In the following section we introduce the problem and then describe the model for clustering of web surfers. We give the update equations for our algorithm and describe how to incorporate prior knowledge and additional user information. Then we apply the method to logs from a large commercial web site KDDCup (http://www.ecn.purdue.edu/KDDCUP/), discuss both method and results and draw conclusions.

3   User Profiling and Web Exploration

3.1   Mathematical Modeling

Given the main problem "profiling of web exploration", the next step is the selection of an appropriate mathematical model. Numerous time-series prediction problems, such as in [18], supported successfully probabilistic models. In particular, Markov models and Hidden Markov Models have been enormously successful in sequence generation. In this paper, we present the utility of applying such techniques for prediction of web explorations.

A Markov model has many interesting properties. Any real world implementation may statistically estimate it easily. Since the Markov model is also generative, its implementation may derive automatically the exploration predictions. The Markov model can also be adapted on the fly with additional user exploration features . When used in conjunction with a web server, this later may use the model to predict the probability of seeing a scene in the future given a history of accessed scenes. The Markov state-transition matrix represents, basically, "user profile" of the web scene space. In addition, the generation of predicted sequences of states necessitates vector decomposition techniques. The figure 1 shows the graph representing a simple Markov chain of five nodes and their corresponding transitions probabilities. The analogy between the transition probability matrix and the graph is obvious. Each state of the matrix corresponds to a node in the graph and similarly each probability transition in the matrix corresponds to and edge in the graph. A set of three elements defines a discrete Markov model: $< \alpha, \beta, \lambda >$ where α corresponds to the state space. β is a matrix representing transition probabilities from one state to another. λ is the initial probability distribution of the states in α. Each transition contains the

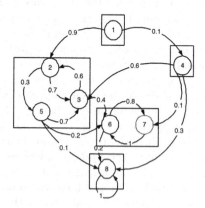

Fig. 1. Transition graph

identification of the session, the source scene, the target scene, and the dates of accesses.

The fundamental property of Markov model is the dependencies of the previous states. If the vector $\alpha(t)$ denotes the probability vector for all the states at time 't', then:

$$\alpha(t) = \alpha(t-1) \times \beta \qquad (1)$$

If there are N states in the Markov model, then the matrix of transition probabilities β is of size N x N. Scene sequence modeling supports the Markov model. In this formulation, a Markov state corresponds to a scene presentation, after a query or a browsing. Many methods estimate the matrix β. Without loss of generality, the maximum likelihood principle is applied in this paper to estimate β and λ. The estimation of each element of the matrix $\beta[v, v']$ respect the following formula:

$$\beta[v, v'] = \phi(v, v')/\phi(v) \qquad (2)$$

where $\phi(v, v')$ is the count of the number of times v' follows v in the training data. We utilize the transition matrix to estimate short-term exploration predictions. An element of the matrix state, say $\beta[v, v']$ can be interpreted as the probability of transitioning from state v to v' in one step. The Markovian assumption varies in different ways. In our problem of exploration prediction, we have the user's history available. Answering to which of the previous explorations are *good predictors* for the next exploration creates the probability distribution. Therefore, we propose variants of the Markov process to accommodate weighting of more than one history state. So, each of the previous explorations are used to predict the future explorations, combined in different ways. It is worth noting that rather than compute β and higher powers of the transition matrix, these may be directly estimated using the training data. In practice, the state probability vector $\alpha(t)$ can be normalized and threshold in order to select a list of *probable states* that the user will choose.

3.2 Predictive Analysis

The implementation of Markov models into a web server makes possible four operations directly linked to predictive analysis. In the first one, the server supports Markov models in a predictive mode. Therefore, when the user sends an exploration request to the web server, this later predicts the probabilities of the next exploration requests of the user. This prediction depends of the history of the user requests. The server can also support Markov models in an adaptive mode. Therefore, it updates the transition matrix using the sequence of requests that arrive at the web server. In the second one, prediction relationship, aided by Markov models and statistics of previous visits, suggests to the user a list of possible scenes, of the same or different web bases, that would be of interest to him, and then the user can go to next. The prediction probability influences the order of scenes. In the current framework, the predicted relationship does not strictly have to be a scene present in the current web base. This is because the predicted relationships represent user traversal scenes that could include explicit user jumps between disjointing web bases. In the third one, there is generation of a sequence of states (scenes) using Markov models that predict the sequence of states to visit next. The result returned and displayed to the user consists of a sequence of states. The sequence of states starts at the current scene the user is browsing. We consider default cases, such as, if the sequence of states contains cyclic state, they are marked as "explored" or "unexplored". If multiple states have the same transition probability, a suitable technique chooses the next state. This technique considers the scene with the shortest duration. Finally, when the transition probabilities of all states from the current state are too weak, then the server suggests to the user, the go back to the first state. In the fourth one, we refer to web bases that are often good starting points to find documents, and we refer to web bases that contain many useful documents on a particular topic. The notion of profiled information focuses on specific categories of users, web bases and scenes. The web server iteratively estimate the weights of profiled information based on the Markovian transition matrix.

3.3   Path Analysis and Clustering

To reduce the dimensionality of the Markov transition matrix β, a clustering approach is used. It reduces considerably the number of states by clustering similar states into *similar groups*. The reduction obtained is about log N, where N is the number of scenes before clustering. The clustering algorithm is a variant of k-medoids, inspired of [19]. The particularity of the algorithm (algorithm 1) is the replacement of sampling by heuristics. Sampling consists of finding better clustering by changing one medoid. However, finding the best pair (medoid, item) to swap is very costly ($O(k(nk)2)$). That is why, heuristics have been introduced in [19] to improve the confidence of swap (medoid, data item). To speed up the choice of a pair (medoid, data item), the algorithm sets a maximum number of pairs to test (num_pairs), then choose randomly a pair and compare the dissimilarity. To find the k medoids, our algorithm begins with an arbitrary selection of k objects. Then in each step, a swap between a selected object O_i and a non-selected object O_h is made, as long as such a swap would result in an improvement of the quality of the clustering. In particular, to calculate the effect of such a swap between O_i and O_h , the algorithm computes the cost C_{jih} for all non-selected objects O_j. Combining all possible cases, the total cost of replacing O_i with O_h is given by: $T_{cih} = \sum C_{jih}$. The algorithm 1 is given bellow.

```
Clustering()
  {
    Initialize num_tries and num_pairs;
    min_cost = infinitive;
    for k = 1 to num_tries do
        current=k; randomly selected items in the entire data set.
        L=1;
        repeat
                xi = a; randomly selected item in current
                xh = a; randomly selected item in {entire data set current}.
                if TCih  < 0 then
                    current = currentxi+xh;
```

```
        else
            j = j+1;
        end if
    until (j <= num_pairs)
    if min_cost < cost(current) then
        best = current;
    end if
  end for
  return   best;
}
```

Algorithm 1. Clustering function

The algorithm go on choosing pairs until the number of pair chosen reach the maximum fixed. The medoids found are very dependant of the k first medoids selected. So the approach selects k others items and restarts num_tries times (num_tries is fixed by user). The best clustering is kept after the num_tries tries.

4   Approach Implementation

We have implemented the approach, and particularly the clustering method of navigation sessions. Our objective through this implementation is articulated around two points. The first one concerns the study of the different problems that held when we deal with a great number of sessions represented by Markov models. The second one concerns the extraction of the most representative behaviors of the web site. A representative behavior is represented by a Markov model (pages, transitions between pages and the average time in each page) for which the access frequencies to their pages are homogeneous. It means that, the ideal representative user behaviors have not pages accessed frequently and pages rarely accessed, such as presented in the figure presented bellow. Figure 2 represents page frequencies calculated on the basis of the exploration session database, extracted from KDD Cup logs of a commercial web site that will be detailed bellow. In the figure, a curve in two-dimension space is shown In ab-

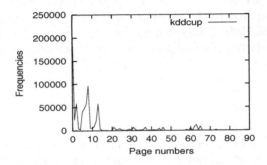

Fig. 2. Classical curve form

scise, we have the web page numbers. In the ordinate, we have the frequencies, which measure the number of access to the concerned page. The highest number in abscise represents the page numbers of the target web site. In this example, we have 90 pages. The frequency of the page number 0 is between 200000 and 250000. It means that the page number 0 has been accessed more than 200000 times and less than 250000 times. It is the highest frequency in the curve. We can deduce that the page number 0 corresponds to the root page or the main page of the web site. The frequency of the page number 80 is equal to 0. It means that no user accessed to this page. We note that the most frequently accessed pages are between 0 and 15; the less frequently accessed pages are between 15 and 46, and between 60 and 70. The pages between 48 and 58 and between 75 and 90 have never been accessed. Globally, the figure represents a typical state of web site access, where some pages are frequently accessed (ex. page number 0), others are rarely accessed (ex page number 30), and others are not accessed at all (ex. page number 90). In this typical state of web site pages, the cardinality of pages that are frequently accessed is generally less than the cardinality of pages that are rarely or never been accessed. Again, in the ideal result of our approach, we should obtain Markov models composed of a sub set of the target web site pages, and the curve of page frequencies should be homogeneous. It means that the curve should be stable, like in the figure 3. In the figure 3 the

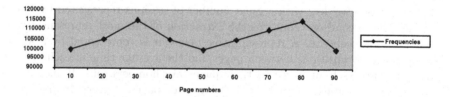

Fig. 3. Ideal curve form

page frequencies are between 100000 and 120000 access. So there is a stability of the curve compared to the classical curve form where the page frequencies are between 0 and 250000. This figure is just an example of an ideal curve form where the best behaviors contain pages that have homogeneous page frequencies.

4.1   Data Set

The used data set is provided by KDDCup (www.ecn.purdue.edu/KDDCUP/) which is a yearly competition in data mining that started in 1997. It's objective is to provide data sets in order to test and compare technologies (prediction algorithms, clustering approaches, etc.) for e-commerce, considered as a "killer domain" for data mining because it contains all the ingredients necessary for successful data mining. The ingredients of our data set include many attributes (200 attributes), and many records (232000). Each record corresponds to a session.

4.2 Results

The tests were carried out on a PC Pentium III with 500 MHz and 256 MB of RAM on the Data set of sessions composed of 90785 sessions (individual Markov models). In our tests, we considered different number of classes, iterations and maximum number of neighbors to compute run time and clustering distortion. We will focus our results on run time and distortion obtained when varying the maximum number of neighbors. So we fixed the number of classes and iterations to respectively 4 and 5. For different numbers of classes and iteration, we obtain similar results.

We tested the approach is the data set composed of 90785 markov models, and we supposed that there are 4 typical user behaviors (number of classes equal to 4) and five iteration of the clustering algorithm (number of iteration equal to 5). Previous experiments [19] proved that the distortion is conversely proportional to the number of iterations. That is why we concentrate our experiments on Run time and distortion values on the basis of respectively numbers of classes (clusters) and iterations. On the basis of the figure curve, we can highlight the

Table 1. Run Time (minutes) proposional to the number of neighbors

Run time	Classes	Iterations	Max Neighbors	Medoids	Distortion
15mn	4	5	10	123023, 294044, 328940, 343287	139004.3
15mn	4	5	10	13137, 145762, 387937, 21549	133472.47
15 mn	4	5	10	15368, 59465, 235239, 101451	136211.69
35 mn	4	5	50	101467, 233739, 145567, 5565	130836.16
35 mn	4	5	50	352195, 185969, 246696, 3782	131280.61

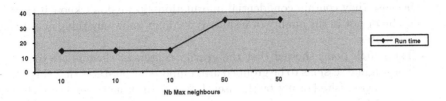

following conclusions. The run time execution is proportional to the maximum number of neighbors. For 10 neighbors, we have 15 minutes run time. For 50 neighbors, we have 35 minutes of execution. We think that the run time will be very high when the number of iteration and classes are high. However the

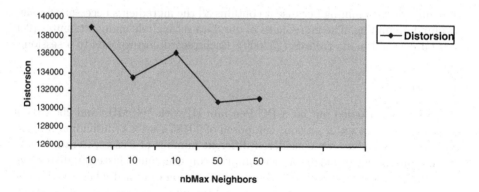

Fig. 4. Distortion conversely proportional to the number of the maximum neighbors

run time is less increasing than the maximum number of neighbors (figure 1). Another remark concerns the distortion (figure 4). The good quality of distortion is proportional to the maximum number of the neighbors. More generally, the results of tests showed some interesting points.

- The first point sub-lined the necessity to clean carefully the data set and to select the useful attribute before any application of the approach. In the data collections, we have a relation table with 200 attributes, and few of them are really useful to achieve our objective. We use only 19 attributes that specify the identification of the web pages, the identifier of the user session, the link relations between web pages and the time spent by the user in each web page.
- The second point sub-lined the necessity to create a new data set suitable for our approach. The original data set contain 230000 sessions, and only 90785 sessions are useful for our approach.
- The third point notes that the features of some attributes have been deleted, because they contain confidential information. So we don't know if they are useful or not in the quality of results as we don't know any thing about these attributes.
- The fourth point showed that the gravity centers of clusters are too small. The original sessions to be grouped are composed of 90 states that correspond to 90 pages visited or not by the user. However the gravity centers of clusters, obtained by our approach, are sessions composed of few pages, in several cases we obtain in our experiments gravity centers with less than 5 pages. We may explain this by the fact that the gravity center of a cluster represents the most typical session. And the most typical session is shared by the whole sessions in the cluster. And the shared point is necessary small when we consider a big number of sessions. The different tests showed that higher is the cardinality of the cluster, lesser is the volume of the gravity center. We think that this property is interesting to make accurate decision because the

site administrator obtains simple and easy to interpret gravity centers, as they are composed of few states and transitions.

- The fifth point concerns the sparse property of the Markov models of sessions. The original Markov models are high dimensional and too sparse. Each session is represented by a high number of states (90 states) and transitions, however not all state are used. This is the result of the fact that the data set corresponds to a web site composed of many pages, and few number of these pages are used in a session. Our approach is addressed to such voluminous sites. The problem of the high dimension and sparse Markov model matrix is that it needs important resources: too large central memory, powerful processor and a clustering algorithm adapted to this high dimensionality. In our experiment, we considered 90 pages, however many commercial web sites consider hundred pages.

- The sixth point concerns how web site administrators may use the results of our experiments. That is good to obtain the most representative behaviors, but how the representative behaviors (gravity centers of behavior clusters) may be exploited in the real e-commerce environment.

5 Conclusion

In this paper, we have presented a method to cluster and predict web surfer actions, based on their surfing patterns using Makov Models. These models, very suitable in modeling sequential data, are used to characterize the similarity between web sequences. To make this prediction possible, three concepts have been highlighted. The first one represents user exploration sessions by Markov models. The second one avoids the problem of Markov model high-dimensionality and sparsely by clustering web documents, based on their content, before applying Markov analysis. The third one extracts the most representative user behaviors (represented by Markov models) by considering a clustering method. Results shown that the proposed method is able to infer the natural clusters with patterns characterizing a complex and noisy data like the KDDCup ones.

References

1. Rabiner, L.R.: A tutorial on Hidden Markov Models and Selected Applications in Speech Recognition. Proc. of IEEE 77(2) (1989) 257–286
2. Hu, J., Brown, M.K., Turin, W.: HMM based on-line handwriting recognition. IEEE Trans. Pattern Analysis and Machine Intelligence, 18(10) (1996) 1039–1045
3. Hughey, R., Krogh, A.: Hidden Markov Model for sequence analysis: extension and analysis of the basic method. Comp. Appl. in the Biosciences 12 (1996) 95–107
4. Eickeler, S., Kosmala, A., Rigoll, G.: Hidden Markov Model based online gesture recognition. Proc. Int. Conf. on Pattern Recognition (ICPR) (1998) 1755–1757
5. Jebara, T., Pentland, A.: Action Reaction Learning: Automatic Visual Analysis and Synthesis of interactive behavior. In 1st Intl. Conf. on Computer Vision Systems (ICVS'99) (1999)

6. Rabiner, L. R., Lee, C.H., Juang, B. H., Wilpon, J. G.: HMM Clustering for Connected Word Recognition. Proceedings of IEEE ICASSP (1989) 405–408
7. Lee, K. F.: Context-Dependent Phonetic Hidden Markov Models for Speaker Independent Continuous Speech Recognition. IEEE Transactions on Acoustics, Speech and Signal Processing 38(4) (1990) 599–609
8. Smyth, P.: Clustering sequences with HMM, in Advances in Neural Information Processing (M. Mozer, M. Jordan, and T. Petsche, eds.) MIT Press 9 (1997)
9. Smyth, P.: Clustering sequences with hidden markov models. In M.C. Mozer, M.I. Jordan, and T. Petsche, editors, Advances in NIPS 9, (1997)
10. Li, C., Biswas, G.: Clustering Sequence Data using Hidden Markov Model Representation, SPIE'99 Conference on Data Mining and Knowledge Discovery: Theory, Tools, and Technology, (1999) 14–21
11. Li, C., Biswas, G.: A Bayesian Approach to Temporal Data Clustering using Hidden Markov Models. Intl. Conference on Machine Learning (2000) 543–550
12. Schwarz, G.: Estimating the dimension of a model. The Annals of Statistics, 6(2) (1978) 461–464
13. Stolcke, A., Omohundro, S.: Hidden Markov Model Induction by Bayesian Model Merging. Hanson, S.J., Cowan, J.D., Giles, C.L. eds. Advances in Neural Information Processing Systems 5 (1993) 11–18
14. Cheeseman, P., Stutz, J.: Bayesian Classification (autoclass): Theory and Results. Advances in Knowledge discovery and data mining, (1996) 153–180
15. Law, M.H., Kwok, J.T.: Rival penalized competitive learning for model-based sequence Proceedings Intl Conf. on Pattern Recognition (ICPR) 2, (2000) 195–198
16. Cadez, I., Ganey, S. and Smyth, P.: A general probabilistic framework for clustering individuals. Technical report, Univ. Calif., Irvine, March (2000)
17. Smyth, P.: Probabilistic model-based clustering of multivariate and sequential data. In Proc. of 7th Int. Workshop AI and Statistics, (1999) 299–304
18. Ni, Z.: Normal orthant probabilities in the equicorrelated case. Jour. Math. Analysis and Applications, n° 246, (2000) 280–295
19. Ng, R.T. and Han, J.: CLARANS: A Method for Clustering Objects for Spatial Data Mining. TJDE 14(5), (2002) 1003–1016

A New Algorithm for Performing Ratings-Based Collaborative Filtering

Fengzhao Yang, Yangyong Zhu, and Bole Shi

Department of Computing and Information Technology, Fudan University,
200433 Shanghai, China
yangfz@citiz.net, zhuyangyong@datamining.com.cn

Abstract. Collaborative filtering is the most successful recommender system technology to date. It has been shown to produce high quality recommendations, but the performance degrades with the number of customers and products. In this paper, according to the feature of the rating data, we present a new similarity function Hsim(), and a signature table-based Algorithm for performing collaborative filtering. This method partitions the original data into sets of signature, then establishes a signature table to avoid a sequential scan. Our preliminary experiments based on a number of real data sets show that the new method can both improve the scalability and quality of collaborative filtering. Because the new method applies data clustering algorithms to rating data, predictions can be computed independently within one or a few partitions. Ideally, partition will improve the quality of collaborative filtering predictions. We'll continue to study how to further improve the quality of predictions in the future research.

1 Introduction

The explosive growth of the world-wide-web and the emergence of e-commerce has led to the development of recommender systems. Recommender systems is a personalized information filtering technology, used to either predict whether a particular user will like a particular item(prediction problem), or to identify a set of N items that will be of interest to a certain user(top-N recommendation problem)[1]. In recent years, recommender systems have been used in a number of different applications, such as recommending products a customer will most likely buy, identifying web-pages that will be of interest.

One of the earliest and most successful recommender technologies is collaborative filtering(CF)[2,3]. CF systems recommend products to a target customer based on the opinions of other customers. These systems first find a set of customers known as neighbors, that have a history of agreeing with the target user, then use several algorithms to produce recommendations.

Although CF has been very successful in both research and practice, there remain important research questions in overcoming two fundamental challenges[4]. The first challenge is to improve the scalability of the collaborative filtering algorithms. The computational complexity of these methods grows linearly with the number of customers that in typical commercial applications can grow to be several millions. The second challenge is to improve the quality of the recommendations for the

X. Zhou, Y. Zhang, and M.E. Orlowska (Eds.): APWeb 2003, LNCS 2642, pp. 239–250, 2003.
© Springer-Verlag Berlin Heidelberg 2003

consumers. Recommender systems, like other search systems, have two types of characteristic errors: false negatives, which are products that are not recommended, though the consumer would like them, and false positive, which are products that are recommended, though the consumer does not like them. In many recommender systems, the amount of historical information for each user and for each item is often quite limited. As a result, CF-based recommender systems cannot accurately compute the neighborhood and predict how well a user will like an item.

1.1 Contributions

In this paper, we present a new recommendation algorithm which is based signature table to improve both scalability and quality of recommender systems. This paper has three primary research contribution:
1. According to the feature of quantitative transaction data, we present a new similarity function Hsim( ).
2. The signature table is extend from binary transaction data into quantitative transaction data.
3. A new algorithm for performing ratings-based collaborative filtering is discussed.

1.2 Organization

The rest of the paper is organized as follows. The next section provides a brief overview of some related research work. Section 3 descript our signature table-based algorithm for performing rating-based collaborative filtering. Section 4 provides the experimental evaluation of the proposed algorithms. Finally, Section 5 provide some conclusion and the future research.

2 Related Work

The concept of collaborative filtering descends from work in the area of information filtering[10]. The term collaborative filtering was coined by Goldberg et al.[12], who were the first to publish an account of using collaborative filtering techniques in the filtering of information.

GroupLens[2,3]first introduced an automated collaborative filtering system using a neighborhood-based algorithm. GroupLens provided personalized predictions for Usenet news articles. The original GroupLens system used Pearson correlations to weight user similarity, used all available correlated neighbors, and computed a final prediction by performing a weighted average of deviations from the neighbor's mean.

Breese et al.[11] performed an empirical analysis of several variants of neighborhood-based collaborative filtering algorithms. For similarity weighting, Pearson correlation and cosine vector similarity were used, with correlation being found to perform better.

To address the scalability concerns of user-based recommendation algorithm, item-based recommendation techniques have been developed[11,13,14,15]. These approaches analyze the user-item matrix to identify relations between the different items, and then use these relations to compute recommendations. Since they use the pre-computed model, these approaches can quickly recommend a set of items, and have been shown to produce recommendation results that in some cases are comparable to traditional, neighborhood-based CF recommender systems. But they are not better suited to provide truly personalized information.

Sparsity problem in recommender system has been addressed in [16,17]. The problems associated with high dimensionality in recommender systems have been discussed in[13], and application of dimensionality reduction techniques to address these issues has been investigated in [18].

A method for indexing market basket data efficiently for similarity search was discussed in [5]. The method shows very good pruning and accuracy performance and scales well with database size and memory availability. But the method is only adapted for binary transaction data.

3   Signature Table-Based Recommendation Algorithm

3.1   Proximity Measure

The problem of collaborative filtering is to predict how well a user will like an item that he has not rated given a set historical preference judgments for a community of users. Preference judgments can be explicit statements recorded from user or implicit measures that are inferred from available data on user activity. In a typical CF-based recommender system, the input data is usually represented as an $m{\times}n$ customer-product matrix, R, such that $r_{i,j}$ is customer i's rating on product j (Table1). In practice, many commercial recommender system are used to evaluate large product sets. In these systems, even active customers may have rated well under 1% of the products. Accordingly the matrix R is often very sparse. Obviously the total dimensionality of rating data is very high which is clearly out of the available indexing technique for continues valued attributes. Furthermore, the products which a customer rated are closely correlated. We call this kind of data quantitative transaction data. We defined the quantitative transaction data formally as follow:

Table 1. Example of the customer-product matrix

	Film1	Film2	Film3	Film4	Film5	Film6	......
User1	2	5	1		4	1	
User2				4		2	
User3	3	4		4	3		
User4			1	5		1	
......							

Let $I=\{i_1,i_2,...,i_n\}$ be a set of items. D_p is the domain of i_p, and $1\leq p\leq n$. An itemset $Z=\{i_{j_1},i_{j_2},\cdots,i_{j_m}\}$ is a non-empty subset of I. An itemset with m items is called an m-itemset. A valueset $Q=\{q_{j_1},q_{j_2},\cdots,q_{j_m}\}$ is a subset of $D_{j_1}\times D_{j_2}\times\cdots\times D_{j_m}$. Duple <tid, Z,Q> is called a quantitative transaction if tid is a transaction identifier, Z is an itemset and Q is a valueset. A quantitative transaction database $QTDB$ is a set of quantitative transactions.

In high dimensional space, the ratio of the relative distances of the different points to a given target converges to one[19]. For distance functions such as L_p-norm, this result in very poor measurement of similarity. The proximity between two customers is usually measured using either the correlation or the cosine measure. In this paper, in order to establish the efficient indexing structure, we adopt a new similarity fuction $Hsim(\ )$.

Let $X=\{tid_x, Z_x, Q_x\}$ and $Y=\{tid_y, Z_y, Q_y\}$ are two quantitative transactions. m is number of items which are in both, that is $m=|Z_x \cap Z_y|$. h is hamming distance, that is $h=|Z_x - Z_y| + |Z_y - Z_x|$.

Let the common items between X and Y be $\{i_{s_1}, \cdots, i_{s_m}\}$, the corresponding values of X and Y are $\{x_{s_1}, \cdots, x_{s_m}\}$ and $\{y_{s_1}, \cdots, y_{s_m}\}$ respectively. Then, the similarity function $Hsim(X,Y)$ between X and Y is given by:

$$Hsim\ (X,Y) = \frac{\left(\sum_{i=1}^{m} \frac{1}{1 + |x_{s_i} - y_{s_i}|^p} \right)^{1/p}}{h + m} \tag{1}$$

Note that the value of the above expression will vary between 0 and 1, higher number imply greater similarity. In our experiment, the value of p equals 1.

The analysis indicates that this definition of similarity continues to retain its meaningfulness for higher dimensionalities in terms of the relative contrasts in distances to a given target[20]. The quality of the nearest neighbor returned by such a technique is better than that provide by L_p-norm. At the same time it is possible to design index structures which are able to prune away a large part of the data while searching for closest neighbors to target.

3.2 Neighborhood Formation

The most important step in CF-based recommender systems is that of computing the similarity between customers as it is used to form a proximity-based neighborhood between a target customer and a number of like-minded customers. The main goal of neighborhood formation is to find, for each customer u, an ordered list of customers $N=\{N_1, N_2, \ldots, N_k\}$ such that $u \notin N$ and $sim(u, N_1)$ is maximum, $sim(u, N_2)$ is next maximum and so on. For a target transaction, we wish to find the k transactions which are most similar to it. The straightforward solution of using a sequential scan may require considerable I/O for very large data collections.

3.2.1 Indexing Structure

We will introduce a data structure called the Signature Table[5]. A signature is a set of items. The items in the original data are partitioned into sets of signatures. A transaction T is said to activate a signature A at level r if and only if $|A \cap T| \geq r$. This level r is referred to as the activation threshold.

For example, Consider the items in the original data are $\{a,b,c,d,e,f,g\}$. Then one possible partition of these items into signatures could be $P=\{a,e\}$, $Q=\{c,d\}$, and $R=\{b,f,g\}$. consider the transaction $T=\{a,b,c,e\}$. Then, the transaction T will activate the signatures P, Q, and R at level $r=1$, and will activate only the signature P at level $r=2$.

The set of items are partitioned into K sets of signatures. We shall refer to this value of K as the signature cardinality. The supercoordinate of a transaction exists in

K-dimensional space such that each dimension of the supercoordinate has a unique correspondence with a particular signature and vice-versa. Each dimension in this K-dimensional supercoordinate is a 0-1 value which indicates whether or not the corresponding signature is activated by that transaction. Thus, if the items are partitioned into K signatures $\{S_1,...,S_K\}$, then there are 2^K possible supercoordinates.

The signature table consists of a set of 2^K entries. One entry in the signature table corresponds to each possible supercoordinate. Thus, the entries in the signature table create a partition of the data. This partition will be used for the purpose of similarity search. The signature table is stored in main memory, whereas the actual transactions which are indexed by each entry of the signature table are stored on disk. Each entry in the signature table points to a list of pages which contain the transactions indexed by that supercoordinate.

3.2.2 Signature Table Construction

The effective construction of the signature table requires us to partition the universal set of items I into subsets of items which form the signatures. We would like the set of items in each signature to be closely correlated. If the items in each signature are closely correlated, then a transaction is likely to activate a small number of signatures. The signature table is constructed in two steps. During the first step, a weighted hypergraph H is constructed to represent the relations among different items, and during the second step, a hypergraph partitioning algorithm is used to find K partitions such that the items in each partition are highly related. In our current implementation, we use frequent item sets found by the association rule algorithm as hyperedge.

Association rules capture the relationship of items that are present in transaction[6][7]. For quantitative transaction data, let I be the universal set of items, $T=<tid,Z,Q>$ be a quantitative transaction. An itemset X is contained in transaction T if $X \subseteq Z$. Given a Quantitative transaction database $QTDB$, the support of an itemset X, denoted as $sup(X)$, is the number of transactions in $QTDB$ which contain X. An association rule $R: X=>Y$ is an implication between two itemsets X and Y is an implication between two itemsets X and Y where $X,Y \subset I$ and $X \cap Y = \varnothing$. The support of the rule, denoted as $sup(X=>Y)$, is defined as $sup(X \cup Y)$. The confidence of the rule, denoted as $conf(X=>Y)$, is defined as $sup(X \cup Y)/sup(X)$.

A number of algorithms have been developed for discovering frequent item-sets. Apriori algorithm presented in [7] is one of the most efficient algorithms available.

Once we obtain association rules implied in the $QTDB$, we can construct the hypergraph. A hypergraph $H=(V,E)$ consists of a set of vertices(V) and a set of hyperedges(E). A hypergraph is an extension of a graph in the sense that each hyperedge can connect more than two vertices. In our model, the set of vertices V corresponds to the set of data items being clustered, and each hyperedge $e \in E$ corresponds to a set of related items. A key problem in modeling of data items as hypergraph is the determination of related items that can be grouped as hyperedges and determining weights of each such hyperedge. The frequent items computed by an association rule algorithm such as Apriori are excellent candidates to find such related items. Note that the frequent items sets can capture relationship among larger sets of data points. This added modeling power is nicely captured in our hypergraph model.

In our current implementation of the model, each frequent item-set is represented by a hyperedge $e \in E$ whose weight is equal to the average confidence of the association rules, called essential rules, that have all the items of the edge and has a singleton right hand side.

The hypergraph representation can be used to cluster together relatively large groups of related items by partition it into highly connected partitions. One way of achieving this is to use a hypergraph partitioning algorithm that partitions the hypergraph into two parts such that the weight of the hyperedges that are cut by the partitioning is minimized. HMETIS[8] is a multi-level hypergraph partitioning algorithm that has been shown to produce high quality bi-sections on a wide range of problems arising in scientific and VLSI applications. HMETIS minimizes the weighted hyperedge cut, and thus tends to create partitions in which the connectivity among the vertices in each partition is high, resulting in good clusters. By use of HMETIS, we partition the overall hypergraph into K parts which act as signatures of the signature table.

3.2.3 knn Query Algorithm for the Signature Table

We know that each entry in the signature table points to a set of transactions which corresponds to a particular supercoordinate. It is the partitioning created by these supercoordinates which may be used in order to perform the branch and bound method. The branch and bound method[9] is a classical technique in combinatorial optimization of the data in order to avoid searching many of the partitions. Pruning is done by finding good optimistic bounds on the distance of a target point to each set representing a partition of the search space. This bound is an optimistic bound(upper bound) on the value of the similarity function between the target and any transaction in this set. If this optimistic bound is less than the similarity of the target to some solution R which has already been determined, then the corresponding set may be pruned from contention. The process of pruning reduces the size of the accessed space substantially, and thereby leads to improve running times.

```
Procedure   knnQuery(TargetTransaction:T,
SignatureTableEntries:{1,2,…,2^K}, integer:k)
1. for i=1 to k do
        NNTL[i]:= (tid: dummy, sim:0);
2. for each table entry i do
        Opti[i]=FindOptimisticBound(T,i);
3. for each table entry i, in decreasing order of Opt[i] do
4.    if Opt(i)>=NNTL[k].sim then
5.       T[i]=Transactions indexed by entry i;
6.       for each transaction S∈T[i] do
7.          if Hsim(S,T)>=NNTL[k].sim then
8.             NNTL[k].tid=S.tid;
9.             NNTL[k].sim=Hsim(S,T);
10.            sort NNTL in decreasing of sim;
11.         endif
12.      enddo
13.   endif
14.enddo
15.output(NNTL);
```

Fig. 1. k-nearest neighbor Query algorithm

k-nearest neighbor query algorithm is illustrated in Fig. 1. we maintain the k best candidates found so far at each stage of the algorithm. The k best candidates and their similarity to the target are stored in a neighbor list NNTL(Nearest Neighbor Transaction List). In procedure knnQuery, as an initialization, entries of the NNTL are set to $NNTL[i]=[dummy,0]$ $(i=1,...,k)$, i.e. tid's are undefined and sim=0 (step 1). Then we compute the optimistic bounds from the target transaction to each entry in the signature table(step 2) and perform a main memory sort of the entries in the signature table in decreasing order of the optimistic bounds. This sort provides the order in which the supercoordinates of the signature table should be scanned. The purpose of the sorting is to order the partitions created by the supercoordimates in such a way that the partitions which are most likely to contain the nearest transaction to the target are visited.

The supercoordinates in the signature table are scanned one by one. If the optimistic bound from the target transaction to an entry is not less than $NNTL[k].sim$, we compute the similarity between the target transaction and the transactions indexed by that entry. The similarity is computed by our function Hsim(). If the similarity of a transaction S to target is not less than $NNTL[k].sim$, we replace $NNTL[k].tid$ with S.tid and $NNTL[k].sim$ with $Hsim(S,T)$ and NNTL is sorted in decreasing of sim.

For our similarity function Hsim(), How to found the optimistic bounds is the key to the algorithm. According to the formula (1), $Hsim(X,Y) \leq \dfrac{m}{h+m}$. In order to evaluate the optimistic bounds, we introduce theorem 1.

Theorem 1 Let f be a function satisfying:
$$\frac{\partial f(x,y)}{\partial x} \geq 0$$
$$\frac{\partial f(x,y)}{\partial y} \leq 0$$

Let γ be an upper bound on the value of x and θ be a lower bound on the value of y. Then $f(\gamma,\theta)$ is an upper bound on the value of the function $f(x,y)$.

Proof: let (x^0,y^0) be any realization of the value of (x,y). Then, $x^0 \leq \gamma$ and $y^0 \geq \theta$. It follow from the above conditions that:
$$f(x^0,y^0) \leq f(\gamma,y^0) \leq f(\gamma,\theta)$$

The result follows.

Let $f(h,m)=m/(h+m)$, it is easy to prove $\partial f(m,h)/\partial m \geq 0$, $\partial f(m,h)/\partial h \leq 0$. if m_{upper} is the lower bound on value of m and h_{lower} is the upper bound on the value of the h, we know $f(h,m) \leq f(m_{upper},h_{lower})$.

So $Hsim(X,Y) \leq f(h,m) \leq f(m_{upper},h_{lower})$. That is to say, $f(m_{upper},h_{lower})$ is the upper bound on the value of Hsim( ). Once we detemined m_{upper} and h_{lower} for a partitioning of the data, we can consider $f(m_{upper},h_{lower})$ as the optimistic bound of the partitioning. The algorithm of finding optimistic bounds for each entry in signature table is illustrated in fig. 2.

```
Procedure  FindOptimisticBound(TargetTransaction:T,
signatureTableEntry:i)
1. m_upper=FindUpperMatch(T,i);
2. h_lower=FindLowerDist(T,i);
3. Return(m_upper/(m_upper+h_lower));
```

Fig. 2. Evaluating the optimistic bounds on the match and hamming distance

Next we discuss how to determine m_{upper} and h_{lower}. Let $\{S_1,...,S_K\}$ be the sets of signatures. Let r be the activation threshold, and r_j be the number of items common to each of the K signature sets S_j from the target transaction. Let B be an entry in the signature table, and let the K bits representing its supercoordinate be denoted by $\{b_1...b_K\}$. The bit b_i corresponds to the signature S_i. The algorithm of Evaluating the lower bounds on the hamming distance is illustrated in fig. 3. The variable *dist* will contain the lower bounds on the hamming distance between the target transaction and the signature table entry B. In the beginning, *dist* is initialized to 0. For each $j \in \{1,...,K\}$ such that $b_j=0$, we know that every transaction indexed by that entry must have less than r items from S_j in it. On the other hand, if the target transaction has $r_j \geq r$ items in common with that signature, we know that an upper bound on the hamming distance between the target and any transaction indexed by that signature entry must be r_j-r+1. Thus, for each $j \in \{1,...,K\}$ such that $b_j=0$, we add $max\{0, r_j-r+1\}$ to *dist*. For each $j \in \{1,...,K\}$ such that $b_j=1$, we know that every transaction indexed by that entry must have less than r items from S_j in it. On the other hand, if the target transaction has $r_j<r$ items in common with that signature, we know that an upper bound on the hamming distance between the target and any transaction indexed by that signature entry must be $r - r_j$. Thus, for each $j \in \{1,...,K\}$ such that $b_j=1$, we add $max\{0, r -r_j\}$ to *dist*.

The algorithm of evaluating the upper bounds on the match is illustrated in fig. 4. The variable match denotes the upper bound on the number of match between the target transaction and any transaction indexed by supercoordinate B. For each $j \in \{1,...,K\}$ such that $b_j=0$, we add $min\{r-1, r_j\}$ to *match*. For each $j \in \{1,...,K\}$ such that $b_j=1$, we add r_j to *match*.

```
Procedure  FindLowerDist(TargetTransaction:T,
SignatureTableEntry:i)
1. dist=0;
2. for each j∈{1,…,K}  do
3.    r_j = number of items which are in both S_j and T;
4.    if  b_j=0  then
         dist=dist+max(0,r_j-r+1);
5.    else
         dist=dist+max(0,r-r_j);
6.    endif
7. enddo
8. return(dist);
```

Fig. 3. Evaluating the lower bounds on the hamming distance

```
Procedure  FindUpperMatch(TargetTransaction:T,
SignatureTableEntry:i)
1. match=0;
2. for each j∈{1,…,K}  do
3.    r_j = = number of items which are in both S_j and T;
4.    if  b_j=0  then
          match=match+min(0,r_j-r+1);
5.    else
          match=match+r_j;
6.    endif
7. enddo
8. return(match);
```

Fig. 4. Evaluating the upper bounds on the match

3.3 Generation of Recommendation

Once the proximity neighborhoods are determined, two types of recommendations can be produced.

1. Prediction of how much a customer C will like a product P. In our algorithm, prediction on product P for customer C is computed by computing a weighted sum of corated items between C and all his neighbors and then by adding C's average rating to that. This can be expressed by the following formula:

$$C_P = \overline{C} + \frac{\sum_J (J_P - \overline{J})W_{CJ}}{\sum_J W_{CJ}}$$

Here, W_{CJ} denotes the similarity weight between user C and neighbor J. J_P is J's ratings on product P. $\overline{J}$ and $\overline{C}$ are J and C's average ratings. Here W_{CJ} is defined by:

$$W_{CJ} = Hsim(C, J)$$

2. Recommendation of a list of products for a customer C. This is commonly known as top-N recommendation. Once a neighborhood is formed, the recommender system algorithm focuses on the products rated by neighbors and selects a list of N Products that will be liked by the customer.

4 Experimental Evaluation

4.1 Data Sets

We used two different data sets to evaluate the algorithm we presented. The details of the data sets are the following:

E-commerce data. This dataset contains ratings of 14156 customers on 3096 catalog products. The dataset contains 50000 records. The sparse level is 1-50000/(14156*3096)=0.9989.

Movie data. The data set used contained 100,000 ratings from 943 users and 1650 movies, with each user rating at least 20 items. The data was divided into 80% training set and 20% test set. The sparse level of the training set is 1-80000/(943*1650)=0.9486.

4.2 Evaluation Metrics

We use PE(Pruning Efficiency) as a metric to evaluation the scalability of our algorithm. PE was defined as percentage of the data which was pruned by the branch and bound technique when the algorithm was run to completion.

To evaluate an individual item prediction, we used MAE(Mean Absolute Error) as our choice of evaluation metric to report prediction experiments because it is most commonly used and easiest to interpret directly. MAE is the mean absolute error between the predicted ratings and the actual ratings of users within the test data.

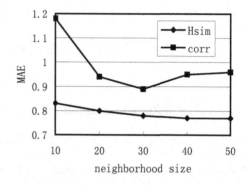

Fig. 5. The quality of the recommendations

4.3 Experimental Results

We are currently performing experiments on movie rating data to evaluate an individual item prediction. Because the size of the neighborhood has significant impact on the recommendation quality. We performed an experiment where we varied the neighborhood size to determine the effectiveness of the recommendations by computing MAE. Results from the different experiments are shown in fig. 5.

As we can see from fig. 5, the size of the neighborhood does affect the quality of prediction. In general, the quality increases as we increase the number of neighbors. However, after a certain point, the MAE converges to a constant, say 0.77. we also calculate the MAE on the same dataset using Pearson correlation. When the size of the neighborhood

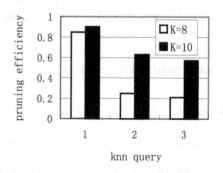

Fig. 6. Scaling of pruning performance

is 30, the minimum of MAE is 0.89. So our similarity functions provide better quality of prediction than Pearson correlation.

We evaluation the scalability of our algorithm on the e-commerce data. Since the pruning efficiency is related to target transaction. We design three kinds of query which represent good, better and worst case. As is apparent from fig. 6, the algorithm pruned 21% to 85% percent of the transactions when the value of the signature cardinality K was 8. But when the value of the signature cardinality was 10, the algorithm pruned 57% to 90% percent of the transactions. the reason for this is that higher values of K create a more fine grained partitioning.

5   Conclusions and Future Work

In this paper, according to the feature of the ratings data, we present a new similarity function Hsim(), and a signature table-based algorithm for performing collaborative filtering. This method partitions the original data into sets of signature, then establishes a signature table to avoid a sequential scan. Our preliminary experiments based on a number of real data sets show that the new method can both improve the scalability and quality of collaborative filtering. Because the new method applies data clustering algorithms to ratings data, predictions can be computed independently within one or a few partitions. Ideally, partition will improve the quality of collaborative filtering predictions. We'll continue to study how to further improve the quality of predictions in the future research.

References

1. Karypis, G.: Evaluation of Item-based Top-N Recommendation Algorithms. In: Proceedings of the Tenth International Conference on Information and Knowledge Management (CIKM), Atlanta (2001)
2. Konstan, J., Miller, B., Maltz, D., Herlocker, J., Gordon, L., Riedl, J.: GroupLens: Applying Collaborative Filtering to Usenet News. Communications of the ACM, 40(3) (1997) 77–87
3. Resnick, P., Iacovou, N., Suchak, M., Bergstrom, P., Riedl, J.: GroupLens: An Open Architecture for Collaborative Filtering of Netnews. In: Proceedings of CSCW'94, Chapel Hill, NC (1994)
4. Sarwar, B., Karypis, G., Kinstan, J., Riedl, J.: Analysis of Recommendation Algorithms for E-commerce. In: Proceedings of ACM E-commerce (2000)
5. Aggarwal, C.C., Wolf, J.L., Yu, P.S.: A New Method for Similarity Indexing of Market Basket Data. In: Proceedings Of the ACM SIGMOD Conference (1999) 407–418
6. Agrawal, R., Imielinski, T., Swami, A.: Mining Association Rules Between Sets of Items in Large Databases. In: Proc. Of the ACM-SIGMOD Int. of Conf. on Management of Data. Washington D.C. (1993) 207–216
7. Agrawal, R., Srikant, R.: Fast Algorithms for Mining Association Rules. In: Proc. of the 20th VLDB Conference. Santiago Chile (1994) 487–499
8. Karypis, G., Aggarwal R., Kumar, V., Shekhar, S.: Multilevel Hypergraph Partitioning: Application in VLSI Domain. In: Proc. ACM/IEEE Design Automation Conference (1997)

9. Roussopoulos, N., Kelley, S., Vincen, F.: Nearest Neighbor Queries. In: Proc. Of the ACM SIGMOD Conference Procceedings. San Jose CA (1995) 71–79
10. ACM.: Special Issue on Information Filtering. Communciations of the ACM, 35(12) (1992)
11. Breese, J.S., Heckerman, D., Kadie, C.: Empirical Analysis of Predictive Algorithms for Collaborative Filtering. In: Proceedings of the 14th Conference on Uncertainty in Artificial Intelligence(UAI-98), San Francisco (1998) 43–52
12. Goldberg, D., Nichols, D., Oki, B.M., Terry, D.: Using Collaborative Filtering to Weave an Information Tapestry. Communications of the ACM, 35(12) (1992) 61–70
13. Billsus, D., Pazzani M.J.: Learning Collaborative Information Filters. In: Proceedings of ICML (1998) 46–53
14. Kitts, B., Freed, D., Vrieze, M.: Cross-sell: A Fast Promotion-tunable Customer-item Recommendation Method Based in Conditional Independent Probabilities. In: Proceedings of ACM SIGKDD International Conference (2000) 437–446
15. Wolf, J., Aggarwal, C., Wu, K., Yu, P.: Horting Hatches and Egg: A New Graph-theoretic Approach to Collaborative Filtering. In: Proceeding of ACM SIGKDD International Conference on Knowledge Discovery &Data Mining (1999)
16. Good, N., Schafer, B., Konstan, J., Borchers, A., Sarwar, B., Herlocker, J., Riedl, J.: Combining Collaborative Filtering with Personal Agents For Better Recommendations. In Proceedings of the AAAI-'99 conference (1999) 439–446
17. Sarwar, B.M., Konstan, J.A., Borchers, A., Herlocker, J., Miller, B., Riedl, J.: Using Filtering Agents to Improve Prediction Quality in the GroupLens Research Collaborative Filtering System. In: Proceedings of CACW'98, Seattle, WA (1998)
18. Sarwar, B.M., Karypis, G., Konstan, J.A. Riedl, J.: Application of Dimensionality Reduction in Recommender System-A Case Study. In ACM WebKDD 2000 workshop (2000)
19. Beyer, K., Goldstein, J., Ramakrishnan, R., Shaft, U.: When is Nearest Neighbors Meaningful? In: ICDT Conference. Jerusalem Israel (1999) 217–235
20. Yang, F.Z., Zhu, Y.Y., Shi, B.L.: An Efficient Method for Similarity Search on Quantitative Transaction Data. Technique Report. Department of Computing and Information Technology, Fudan University (2002).

Architecture for a Component-Based, Plug-In Micro-payment System

Xiaoling Dai[1] and John Grundy[1,2]

[1] Department of Computer Science
[2] Department of Electrical and Electronic Engineering
University of Auckland, Private Bag 92019, Auckland, New Zealand
{xdai001, john-g}@cs.auckland.ac.nz

Abstract. Micro-payment systems have the potential to provide non-intrusive, high-volume and low-cost pay-as-you-use services for a wide variety of web-based applications. However, adding micro-payment support to web-sites is usually time-consuming and intrusive, both to the web sites soft ware architecture and its user interface implementation. We describe a plug-in, component model for adding micro-payment support to web applications. We use J2EE software components to encapsulate micro-payment E-coin debiting and re-demption and discrete user interface enhancement. A CORBA infrastructure is used to inter-connect J2EE and non-J2EE vendors and micro-payment brokers. We demonstrate the feasibility of our approach with an on-line, pay-as-you-use journal portal example and outline an approach to using web services to further generalize our architecture.

1 Introduction

Many current e-commerce systems adopt a macro-payment model and architecture [16], [17], [18]. A customer makes a small number of purchases which have a reasonably high cost per purchase. In order to pay for purchases, a "heavy weight" interaction between the vendor of the product or service and an authorisation agent (bank, credit-card company etc) system is carried out. This typically involves the customer supplying credit card details or "digital money" certificates, which are communicated to the authorisation system using complex encryption algorithms. Business processing logic and database updates are performed by the authoriser before the purchase is approved. The vendor system waits for approval before providing the customer with goods or services. This approach works well for relatively small numbers of transactions and relatively high purchase price (to offset the cost of authorisation) [3]. In some e-commerce scenarios this approach has a number of fundamental flaws. It requires the authorisation system to always be on-line. High numbers of transactions or low-price purchase items are infeasible, due to bottle- necking or prohibitive cost per-transaction. In addition, with some approaches the customer's identity can not generally be hidden from the vendor and customers are charged for products, services or information even if they don't use them [3].

X. Zhou, Y. Zhang, and M.E. Orlowska (Eds.): APWeb 2003, LNCS 2642, pp. 251–262, 2003.

We describe the NetPay micro-payment model and a component-based software architecture that we have been developing for NetPay. NetPay provides an off-line micro-payment model using light-weight hashing-based encryption. A customer buys a collection of "E-coins" using a macro-payment from a broker. These coins are cached in an "E-wallet" on the customer's machine. The customer, when buying many small-cost items from a vendor, pays for these transparently by the passing of E-coin information to the vendor. Periodically the vendor redeems the E-coins with the broker for "real" money. E-coins can be transparently exchanged between vendors when the customer moves to another site. In previous work we have described the hard-coding of NetPay support into web-based applications, an approach used by most macro- and micro-payment solutions [4]. Major disadvantages of such an approach is the difficulty and time to add micro-payment support to existing applications, the mis-match of implementation technologies and application services if trying to reuse code, and potential design and software architecture mis-matches.

We describe a new component-based approach for encapsulating micro-payment support for web-based applications - "vendors" of products, services or information to be purchased by micro-payment. We use an example web-based application, an E-journal portal system, that we have developed independently for a teaching project and then have enhanced by adding NetPay components via J2EE Enterprise JavaBean components and Java Server Page proxies. These reusable NetPay components are plugged into the existing journal site to enhance it with micro-payment support with minimal or no code changes. We describe our approach's architecture and design and we illustrate the E-journal interface after plugging in these components. We discuss related work, the advantages and disadvantages of our approach and outline possibilities for further research.

2 Example Application Domain

On-line journals have become popular and are usually paid for on a macro-payment, subscription basis. Using subscription-based payment, a customer first has to subscribe to the journal by supplying payment details (credit card etc) and the journal system would make an electronic debit to pay for their subscription by communicating with an authorisation server. The customer would then normally go to the journal's site where they login with an assigned customer name and password. The journal looks up their details and provides them access to editions of various journals if their subscription is still current. The E-journal site may provide a range of journals for a specific publisher or act as a portal for multiple publishers, paying each on a per-subscription or per-usage basis. If the customer's subscription to a particular journal has run out, they must renew this by authorising a payment from their credit card.

Fig. 1 (a) outlines some of the key interaction use cases for this scenario. Problems with this approach are that there is no anonymity for the customer (the journal system knows exactly who they are and when and what they read), they can not move to other sites without first subscribing to them too, and they must pay for the whole journal (often very expensive), even if they want just one or two sections or articles. These issues apply to many other information sources on the internet where vendors want to charge for a variety of information content [1], [7].

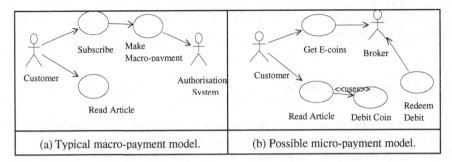

| (a) Typical macro-payment model. | (b) Possible micro-payment model. |

Fig. 1. Two on-line newspaper interaction scenarios

An alternative approach is a micro-payment model. There are several approaches to micro-payment [5], [6], [8], [9], [10]. We outline the basic interactions of our Net-Pay model [2]. Fig. 1 (b) outlines the key interaction use cases for this scenario. The customer first goes to a broker and purchases "E-coins" using a single macro-payment. These are stored in an E-wallet on the customer's machine. The customer can then visit any journal site or newspaper site or music site they wish, their wallet giving the site an E-coin. Each time they view an article (or section or page, depending on the item charged for) or download a song their E-coin is debited. The vendor redeems debits with the broker (for "real" money") periodically e.g. each night/week. The customer can move to another site and unspent money associated with their E-coin is transferred from the first vendor to the second. If E-coins run out, the customer communicates with the broker and authorises another macro-payment debit. The standard macro-payment methods cannot be effectively or efficiently applied for buying inexpensive information goods, like single articles of an on-line journal, because transaction costs are too high. Encryption mechanisms used are slow and each transaction typically "costs" a few cents. Macro-payment suits spending small numbers of large amounts. An Internet micro-payment system allows spending large numbers of small amounts of money at web sites in exchange for various content or services, as in the E-journal scenario above. The design of micro-payment systems is usually quite different from existing macro-payment systems, since micro-payment systems must be very simple, secure, and efficient, with a very low cost per transaction.

The rapid growth of the Internet has led to the appearance of thousands of different web sites, which are created to provide information to millions of people around the world. Producing and maintaining a quality web site takes a great deal of time, dedication and money. To help offset the development costs, web site producers are keen to use their site as a source of income. Therefore, an efficient micro-payment system whose components can be plugged into the existing sites to handle such a trade is needed. Such a micro-payment system would ideally be easily reusable i.e. not require extensive redevelopment to integrate with the web application's architecture; not require any modification to the web application itself; provide effective and efficient debiting of customer "E-coins" and redemption of these coins via a broker for "real" money; and integrate seamlessly with both the architecture and user interfaces of the web application. In our E-journal example, the journal provider would want to charge small amounts on a per-article basis (perhaps varying amounts) and have this micro-payment support integrated seamlessly and with minimum effort with their existing web application architecture.

3   An Overview of NetPay

A new micro-payment protocol called NetPay allows customers (e.g. journal readers) to purchase information from vendors (e.g. on-line E-journal) using "E-coins" on the WWW [2]. A broker provides a source for E-coin purchase and vendor redemption of E-coins for "real" money. NetPay is intended to provide a secure, cheap, widely available, and debit-based protocol for micro-payment applications. NetPay differs from previous micro-payment protocols in the following ways: NetPay uses "touchstones" signed by the broker and E-coin indexes signed by vendors which are passed from vendor to vendor. The signed touchstone is used by a vendor to verify the electronic currency – the "paywords" encoding E-coins, and the signed index is used to prevent double spending by customers and to resolve disputes between vendors. There is no dependency on customer trust required with this approach. Customers have an "E-wallet" that manages their available E-coins: the wallet may reside on the customer's PC or may reside on the broker and vendor machines, being passed from vendor to vendor as the customer accesses information at their web sites. The micro-payments only involve customers and vendors, and the broker is responsible for the registration

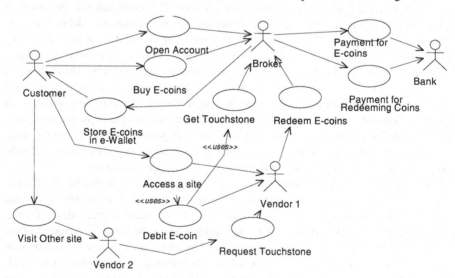

Fig. 2. Basic NetPay component interactions

of customers and for crediting the vendors' account and debiting customers' accounts. Fig. 2 outlines some of the key NetPay system interactions.

Initially a customer accesses the broker's web site to open an account and acquire a number of E-coins from the broker (bought using a single macro-payment). The broker sends an "E-wallet" that includes the E-coin ID and E-coins to the customer and the customer's host caches this information. The customer browses the home page of the journal web site and finds a desired article to read. Each article will have a small cost e.g. 5-10c, and the customer would typically read a number of these. When wishing to read the details of an article, the customer clicks on the article heading and the vendor system debits the customer's E-coins by e.g.. 10c. The vendor verifies that the E-coin provided by the customer's E-wallet is valid by use of a "touchstone" obtained once only from the broker. If the payment is valid (coin is verified and sufficient credit remains), the article is displayed on the screen. The customer may browse other articles, their coins being debited (the index of spent coins incremented) each time an article is read. If E-coins run out, the customer is directed to the broker's site to buy more. When the customer changes to another site, the new vendor site first requests the current E-coin touchstone information from previous vendor's site. The new vendor contacts the previous vendor to get the E-coin touchstone and "spent coin" index and then debits coins for to further news articles. At the end of each day, the vendors all send the E-coins to the broker redeeming them for real money.

4   A Component-Based NetPay Architecture

We initially developed a software architecture for implementing NetPay-based micro-payment systems for thin-client web applications that used hard-coded vendor facilities for micro-payment [4]. We have extended this work to develop component-based NetPay vendor services, supporting much more easily and seamlessly reused vendor server-side NetPay functionality. NetPay micro-payment transactions involve three key parties: the Broker Server, the Vendor Server, and the Customer browser.

This architecture is illustrated in Fig. 3. The Broker server and the Customer browser are same as the previous NetPay architecture [4]. The **Vendor** web sites provide a web server and possibly a separate application server, depending on the web-based system architecture they use. The Vendor web server pages provide content that needs to be paid for and each access to these pages require one or more E-coins from the customers' E-wallets in payment. In our architecture Vendor application server accesses the Broker application server to obtain touchstone information to verify the E-coins being spent and to redeem spent E-coins. They communicate with other vendor application servers to pass on E-coin indexes and touchstones.

Vendors may use quite different architectures and implementation technology. In the example above, Vendor #1 uses a web server with Perl-implemented CGI scripts, C++-implemented application server and relational database. Vendor #2 uses a J2EE-based architecture with J2EE server providing Java Server Pages (web user interface services) and Enterprise Java Beans (application server services), along with a relational database to hold vendor data.

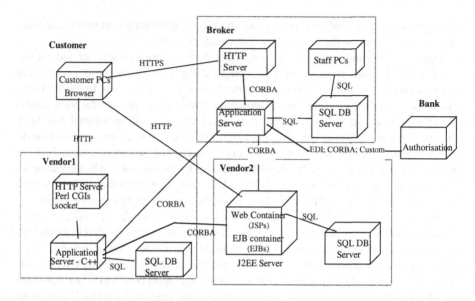

Fig. 3. Basic NetPay software architecture

5 NetPay Component

Our example E-Journal system has a number of customer web browser clients used by customers to access the journal site and read article contents. Another web client is used by staff to manage the redemption of spent E-coins with the NetPay broker server. The vendor J2EE server has a number of web pages e.g. JSPs or servlets and EJBs providing an implementation of the E-journal web system. We add to this a number of NetPay components: EJBs to provide E-wallet management (tracking spending of E-coins by customers; E-coin exchange with the client-side E-wallet application or server-side W-wallet management; touchstone exchange with the NetPay broker or other vendors and E-coin validation). We also provide redemption support for the vendor to communicate with the NetPay broker and redeem customer-spent E-coins for real money.

Fig. 4 shows a high-level view of how these various components interact. The end-user clients access only the session beans. Within the enterprise bean tier, the session beans are clients of the entity beans. On the back end of the system, the entity beans access the database tables that store the entity states. The Session beans access the client-side E-wallet application, broker server and other NetPay-implementing vendor servers via CORBA remote object interfaces.

In our E-journal example system one session bean, `ArticleDBEJB`, represents an interface to the journal article database and is used to select article records. A number of JSPs provide for customer login (if required), journal information and high-level organisation, journal searching and article display.

There are two NetPay session beans that have been added to this E-journal system, `EwalletControllerEJB` and `RedeemControllerEJB`. These session beans provide a client's view of the application's business logic such as MakePayment, ValidateECoins, EwalletReqest and RedeemPayment. Hidden from the clients are the server-side routines that implement the business logic, access databases, manage relationships, and perform error checking.

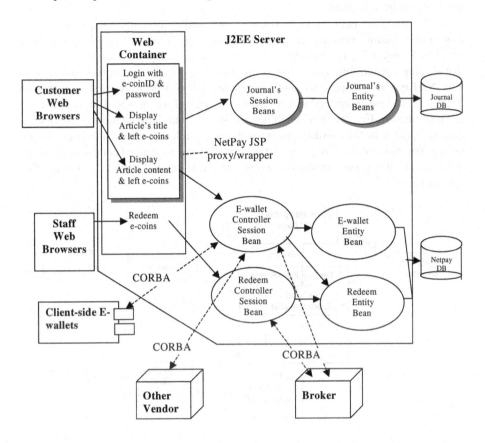

Fig. 4. E-Journal system with NetPay components

For each NetPay business entity the system has a matching entity bean, in this case an EwalletEJB and RedeeemEJB. These beans provide a component-based interface to various database tables: `EWallet` and `RedeemCoin`. For each column in a table, the corresponding entity bean has an instance variable. The NetPay database tables that are used by our entity beans may be added to the existing E-journal database if this is possible, or may be stored in a separate database of their own if required. In order to add our NetPay micro-payment facility to the E-journal, or to other 3rd party J2EE-based applications, we need to be able to add our EJBs to their J2EE server and to detect when pages are being accessed by customers that need to be paid for. We also need to ensure that if the customer attempting access does not have enough E-coins they are directed to the NetPay broker site to buy some more. If the customer wants a server-side E-wallet managed by the vendor vs running a client-side E-wallet application, we need to have the vendor obtain the customer NetPay user-name/password and obtain the E-wallet from the NetPay broker or the previously-visited NetPay-enabled vendor. In addition the customer usually wants an idea about the cost of an article or other information/service before purchase, and access to their available credit in E-coins.

There are three main ways to integrate the NetPay user interface facilities: (1) modify the existing system web pages to incorporate NetPay information (we have developed some JSP page includes so this can be done easily); (2) generate web pages that display the existing system pages in frames and make appropriate interactions with NetPay EJB components; and (3) generate proxy web pages that interact with NetPay session beans and redirect access to the original web pages. These approaches are illustrated in Fig. 5 below. Each has advantages and disadvantages – the first re-quiring updates to the existing system web page implementations, the later two re-quiring renaming of these pages so the generated pages are passed control at appropri-ate times. In this paper we show examples of the E-journal extended using the first approach.

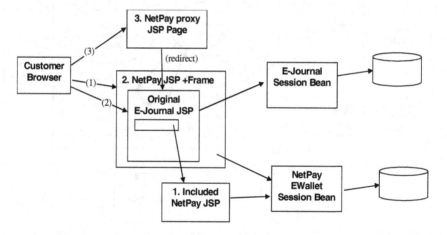

Fig. 5. Ways of integrating NetPay micro-payment functionality with E-journal web pages

A sequence diagram is used in Fig. 6 to show how interactions occur between various components in our NetPay-enabled E-Journal application. For example, when buying an article the customer selects the article for reading e.g. clicking on the URL in a returned article search page or in a journal content page. The web browser requests the article content from the appropriate JSP, and this JSP or its generated proxy requests payment for the content of the article from the NetPay E-wallet session bean. The E-wallet session bean communicates with either the client-side E-wallet or the server-side E-wallet (managed by the E-wallet entity bean) to debit the customer's E-coins to pay for the article. If insufficient coins are available, the customer is directed to the broker site to buy more. Otherwise, the journal article content is displayed to the customer.

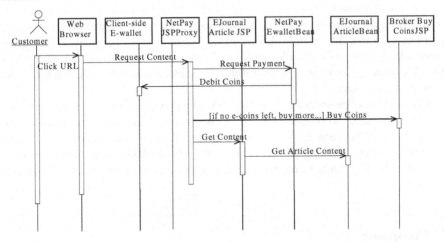

Fig. 6. Click-buy Article and Redeem E-coins Sequence Diagram

6 Implementation

In previous work we implemented a CORBA-based vendor architecture [3]. However, these NetPay components are not optimally reusable and substantial modifications may need to be made to an existing web-based application to incorporate them.

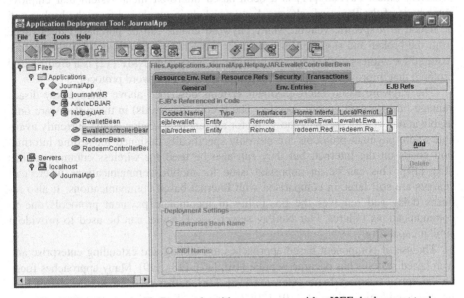

Fig. 7. Plugging in the NetPay vendor-side components with a J2EE deployment tool

We implemented these new NetPay J2EE EJBs and JSP includes to allow for much easier plug-in of NetPay micro-payment facilities into existing J2EE applications. The Ewallet and Redeem EJB components are plugged into the existing E-journal system by deploying them into the E-journal system's J2EE server. The Ewallet component is used to obtain E-wallet from broker or another vendor, make payments by using the client-side or server-side Ewallet managed E-coins, and to generate redeem request data. The Redeem component is responsible for selecting payments and sending these to the NetPay broker.

EJB deploytool provides interface to define relationships between enterprise beans. That makes it easier to plug-and-play components. Fig. 7 illustrates the interface and the relationship between Ewallet component and Redeem component. There is no relationship among existing journal component (ArticleDBJAR) and NetPay components. The NetPay components are plugged in the existing system very straightforwardly.

7 Discussion

The area of micro-payment on the Internet has attracted much recent research attention. Besides NetPay, there are several micro-payment systems that are based on a payword-based micro-payment protocol. These systems can be classified as credit-based and debit-based. Payword [10] is an off-line credit-based system where a user's account is not debited until some time after purchases. This provides more opportunity for fraud since a large number of purchases can be made against an account with insufficient funds. PayFair [11] is a debit-based micro-payment system that employs some parts of the Payword scheme. A payword chain purchased from the broker will be bound to a specific vendor. Many payword chains can be purchased in advance from the broker and stored in the customer's machine. There is no digital-signature required for witness of the payment promise in the system. NMP [12] is a credit-based protocol that improves the fairness for customers from Payword protocol.

The Payword-based micro-payment systems described above share a key disadvantage - they are all vendor specific. The E-coin (paywords) in the systems are only usable at one vendor and have no value for any another vendor. Some currently available micro-payment protocols are not only specifically designed for selling information goods on the Internet, but they can also be used for wireless communications [13], [14]. This can be an important issue for mobile communications where call charges are still large in comparison with Internet based communications. It also reduces delay and removes the possibility of incomplete payment protocols due to communications failures. Our NetPay server-side E-wallet can be used to provide a similar capability.

The use of component-based approaches to building and extending enterprise and web-based systems has become popular [16], [17], [18], [19]. Many approaches focus on enterprise business logic extension [16], [18], rather than a combination of user interface and logic extensions [19], [20]. Our approach to adding NetPay to an existing E-journal uses a similar technique to that we developed for adding collaborative work components to an existing travel-planning application [20]. We plugged in EJBs into the E-journal's existing application server and annotated the E-journal's JSPs to make appropriate E-coin balance, article cost, credit checks and coin debits to the NetPay EJBs. This allows for minimal or no code impact (none if using proxy JSP pages) to the existing system's infrastructure. The use of an EJB-based software architecture enables the application developer to work on the business logic aspects of the application without having to be concerned with system-level issues, such as transactions, security, multithreading, and so forth. In addition, the NetPay EJBs are completely separated from the particular domain knowledge of the web application, enabling each enterprise bean to be reused in different EJB-based vendor systems via plug-and-play with the existing vendor components. While our approach to adding NetPay user interface support to existing J2EE-based vendor application JSPs is basic, usability evaluation of this NetPay-enabled application has indicated it provides a good user interface to users.

We are currently designing a portal infrastructure using web services that will allow a NetPay-enabled vendor to act as a purchasing portal to non-NetPay supporting vendors by redirecting page accesses to these vendors and charging the customers E-coins in the process. This approach will allow for dynamic registration of vendors and support cross-vendor product searching. We are investigating approaches to using NetPay for mobile information content micro-payment applications, both with a server-side E-wallet and client-side E-wallet storage by the mobile device. Our other work focuses on the development of tools to allow existing component-based applications to be NetPay-enabled without any manual component programming, deployment and configuration. We will apply these to experimenting with adding NetPay to other 3rd party J2EE web applications.

8 Summary

We have described the design and development of software components to enable NetPay to be seamlessly added to existing J2EE-based web applications. NeyPay functionality is embodied in Enterprise JavaBean software components and JSP includes or proxies, allowing the existing application to be easily micro-payment enabled. Our NetPay EJBs use a CORBA infrastructure to communicate with customers' client-side E-wallet applications, with a broker server, and with other vendor application servers, whether J2EE-based or not. We have successfully added NetPay components to as separately-developed J2EE-implemented E-journal application to demonstrate our approach's feasibility.

References

1. Blankenhorn, D.: Charging for Content, E-commerce Times.
    http://www.ecommercetimes.com/perl/story/306.html.
2. Dai, X. and Lo, B.: NetPay – An Efficient Protocol for Micropayments on the WWW.
    Fifth Australian World Wide Web Conference, Australia (1999)

3. Dai, X., Grundy, J. and Lo, B.: Comparing and contrasting micro-payment models for E-commerce systems, International Conferences of Info-tech and Info-net (ICII), China (2001)

4. Dai, X., Grundy, J.: Architecture of a Micro-Payment System for Thin-Client Web Applications. In Proceedings of the 2002 International Conference on Internet Computing, Las Vegas, CSREA Press, June 24–27, 444–450

5. Furche A. and Wrightson, G.: SubScrip – An efficient protocol for pay-per-view payments on the Internet, The 5th Annual International Conference on Computer Communications and Networks, USA (1996)

6. Herzberg, A. and Yochai, H. : Mini-pay: Charging per Click on the Web, 1996 http://www.ibm.net.il/ibm_il/int-lab/mpay

7. Herzberg, A.: Safeguarding Digital Library Contents - Charging for Online Content. D-Lib Magazine (1998), ISSN 1082-9873

8. Hwang, M-S., Lin, I-C. and Li, L-H.: A simple micro-payment scheme. Journal of Systems & Software, 55(3)(2001) 221–229

9. Manasse, M.: The Millicent Protocols for Electronic Commerce. First USENIX Workshop on Electronic Commerce. New York (1995)

10. Rivest, R. and Shamir, A.: PayWord and MicroMint: Two Simple Micropayment Schemes. Proceedings of 1996 International Workshop on Security Protocols, Lecture Notes in Computer Science, Vol. 1189. Springer (1997) 69–87

11. Yen, S-M.: PayFair: a prepaid internet ensuring customer fairness micropayment scheme. IEE Proceedings-E Computers & Digital Techniques, vol.148, no.6, Nov. 2001, pp.207–13. Publisher: IEE, UK.

12. Ji, D-Y. and Wang, Y-M.: A micropayment protocol based on PayWord. Acta Electronica Sinica, 30(2)(2002) 301–303

13. Sangjin, K., Heekuck, O.: An atomic micropayment system for a mobile computing environment. IEICE Transactions on Information & Systems. E84-D(6) (2001), 709–716

14. DongGook, P., Boyd, C., Dawson, E.: Micropayments for wireless communications. Information Security and Cryptology - ICISC 2000. Third International Conference. Proceedings (Lecture Notes in Computer Science Vol.2015). Springer-Verlag, Berlin, Germany (2001), 192–205

15. McGarvey, R.: Micropayments enable teensy content purchases. Econtent, 24(1) (2001) 18–21

16. Allen, P.: Realising E-Business with Components. Addison-Wesley, October 2000.

17. Bichler, M., Segev, A., Zhao, J.L.: Component-based E-Commerce: Assessment of Current Practices and Future Directions. *SIGMOD Record* 27(4)(1998) 7–14

18. Fingar, P.: Component-Based Frameworks for E-Commerce. Communications of the ACM(2000)

19. Chong, N.S.T., Sakauchi, M.: e-CoBrowse: co-navigating the Web with chat-pointers and add-ins - problems and promises. Parallel and Distributed Computing and Systems 2(2000) 803–808

20. Grundy, J.C., Wang, X., Hosking, J.G.: Building Multi-device, Component-based, Thin-client Groupware: Issues and Experiences. In Proceedings of the 3rd Australasian User Interface Conference, Melbourne, Australia (2002) 28–30

Verifying the Purchase Request in SET Protocol

Qingfeng Chen, Chengqi Zhang, Shichao Zhang, and Chunsheng Li

Faculty of Information Technology
University of Technology, Sydney
P.O. Box 123, Broadway, NSW 2007, Australia
{qchen, chengqi, zhangsc, csli}@it.uts.edu.au

Abstract. The Secure Electronic Transaction (SET) protocol has been jointly developed by Visa and MasterCard toward achieving secure online-transactions. This paper presents formal verification of the Purchase Request phase of SET, by using ENDL (extension of non-monotonic logic). The analysis unveils some potential flaws. To overcome these vulnerabilities, some feasible countermeasures are proposed accordingly during the validation. Also, the modelling of Purchase Request is described to implement the mechanically model checking instead of manual verification.

1 Introduction

The emergence of electronic commerce over the past decade has radically transformed the economic landscape. There is no doubt that electronic commerce is going to have a profound effect on business, government and consumers and on the way people live and work. In the US, business to business e-commerce is now expected to reach 1.3 trillion by 2003. Similarly business to consumer e-commerce is thought to have reached 7 billion in 1998 and to be on track to reach between 40 billion and 80 billion by 2002 [1].

However, E-commerce causes enormous challenges to the safety of online shopping. The communication medium can be manipulated by malicious principals who can interfere with network traffic. Thus, it is of great importance to have protocols that can authenticate principals and messages under these circumstances, but time has proven authentication protocols to be extremely error prone. Flaws are found in the protocols years after they were published [2]. To prevent the use of incorrect protocols, it is imperative to design methods and tools for formal verification of security protocols.

Formal verification of security protocols have received much attention in recent years. There are many remarkable efforts on developing methodologies, theories, logics, and other supporting tools. These efforts are effective to overcome the weakness and reduce the redundancies in the protocol design stage. Below is a brief introduction to these approaches based on the survey of Gritzalis [3].

Existing approaches to validating security protocols can be classified into two categories: constructing possible attacks using algebraic properties of the algorithms in the protocols (called attack-construction approach), and designing

X. Zhou, Y. Zhang, and M.E. Orlowska (Eds.): APWeb 2003, LNCS 2642, pp. 263–274, 2003.

inferences using specialized logics based on a notion of knowledge and 'belief' (called inference-construction approach).

The *Attack-construction approach* is the construction of probable attack sets based on the algebraic properties of a protocol algorithm, involving the work of Dolev-Yao [4] model and the NRL Analyzer [5]. This work figures out how to ensure authentication and security property, which do not depend on the validity of a designated logic.

The *Inference-construction approach* utilizes modal logics similar to those that have been developed for the analysis of the evolution of knowledge and belief in distributed systems. This includes the BAN logic [6] and the GNY logic [7]. The BAN logic abstracts all but the information intended to convey from the sender to the recipient. Thus, it is simple and has been successfully applied to discover flaws in a variety of authentication protocols (e.g., [8]). The GNY logic is a rather complicated approach, which increases the scope of BAN logic.

However, there are two limitations in existing methods. (a) The attack-construction approach has low-efficiency in detecting attacks for its huge state space. (b) The inference-construction approach is still too complicated to be used.

In addition, there have been attempts to model more realistic protocols, such as the Cybercash coin-exchange [9]. Meadows and Syverson [10] have designed a language for describing the SET specifications [11][12][13], but have left the actual analysis to future researchers. However, the methods for verification of e-commerce protocols are not quite as mature as those used for authentication protocols. The new type of threats, such as payment card transaction, caused by new requirements of on-line transaction will be a significant challenge to the analysis of e-commerce protocols. To our knowledge, existing tools cannot cover these problems in many cases. In this paper, a new protocol analysis approach, ENDL [14], is used to validate the SET's Purchase Request. Also, we present how the verification can be implemented by using mechanically model checking.

The rest of this paper is organized as follows. In Section 2, the SET protocol is cursorily described. Section 3 presents the terms and notations. Section 4 gives the verification to the Purchase Request. Section 5 presents the modelling of the Purchase Request. Finally, Section 6 concludes this paper.

2   Overview of SET

Toward achieving secure on-line transaction using payment card products Visa and Mastercard designed the SET protocol. It addresses several major business requirements:

1. Provide confidentiality of payment information and enable confidentiality of order information.
2. Ensure the integrity of all transmitted data.
3. Provide authentication that a cardholder is a legitimate user of a branded payment card account.

4. Provide authentication that a merchant can accept branded payment card transactions.

Although each of the requirements is described as a distinct component all of them must be carried out together. To achieve these objectives, the SET protocol is divided into five main sub-protocols:

- Cardholder Registration describes how the cardholder registers with a Certificate Authority (CA). The cardholder includes some information, such as the account number, expiration date in the request message. At last, a response message containing the cardholder's certificate, *primary account number* (PAN) and other information is transmitted to the cardholder.
- Merchant Registration is similar to the Cardholder Registration. In order to communicate with the cardholder and the payment gateway, the merchant has to register the signature key and encryption key.
- Purchase Request starts after the cardholder has completed browsing, selection, and ordering. The dual signature is applied to ensure the merchant can not see the Cardholder's account details nor can the payment gateway see the order information. The merchant processes the order and forwards the payment authorization to the payment gateway. If the transaction is accepted, the merchant will ship the goods or perform the service indicated in the order.
- Payment Authorization actually happens during the processing of an order from the cardholder. It permits the merchant to verify the PI and the account information with the payment gateway.
- Payment Capture allows the merchant to request an actual payment from the cardholder via a payment card payment system.

We have employed ENDL to verify the Cardholder Registration and Merchant Registration [15][16]. Compared with them, the Purchase Request phase is more complicated since the cardholder and the merchant have to interact with a third party, Payment Gateway, which is responsible for the payment authorization. Also, it includes some sensitive financial information, which should be kept secret. Thus, we have to consider more details during the validation. In addition, the model checking is introduced here instead of the former manual verification.

3   Basic Terms and Notations

This section reviews briefly the formal definitions for the function word, predicate and action of ENDL.

Principal is some participant who carries out the protocol.

Uppercase X, Y, A, B, C, and CA (Certificate Authorities) range over particular principals.

m_1, m_2, ... , and m_n denote specific messages.

T denotes a specific timestamp that can be used to authenticate the validity of message and to assert that the message is created for a current session.

Cert denotes the certificate that needs to be verified; *CertS()* denotes the signature certificate; *CertK()* denotes the key-exchange certificate.

k denotes the encryption, or decryption, keys.

Generate and *Send* denote specific actions (Encryption and digital signature etc. are some mapping operations on messages, but not actions).

Function word: The abstract description of the operations on a message. These operations consist of the encryption, signature, message digest, and associated mapping relation of the key.

    e(m, k): This represents the operation that message *m* is encrypted by the symmetric (communication) key *k*.

    E(m, k): This represents the operation that message *m* is encrypted by the public key *k*, namely *Kpb(X)* and *Spb(X)* listed below.

    S(m, k): This represents the operation that message *m* is encrypted by the private key *k*, namely *Kpv(X)* and *Spv(X)* listed below.

    H(m): This represents the message digest of message *m* encoded by the one-way hashing algorithm *H(x)*. The one-way Hash function has the property that, given the output, it is difficult to determine the input.

    Kpb(X): This represents the public key-exchange key of *X*.

    Kpv(X): This represents the private key-exchange key of *X*.

    Spb(X): This represents the public signature key of *X*.

    Spv(X): This represents the private signature key of *X*.

    $<m_1, \ldots, m_n>$: This represents the combination of messages $m_1, m_2, \ldots,$ and m_n.

Action is applied to describe the communication process in which a principal is the executant of action and tries to execute some appointed tasks. There are two types of actions listed below:

    Generate(X, m): Applied to represent that *X* generates the message *m*.

    Send(X, Y, m): Applied to represent that *X* sends the message *m* to *Y* after *X* has successfully generated the message *m*.

Predicate is applied to express the knowledge state and belief relation of principals. There are three kinds of predicate listed below:

    Know(X, m): This represents that *X* knows message *m*. It is possible that *X* generates the message *m* by itself or receives *m* from *Y*.

    Auth(X, Y, m): This represents that *X* authenticates message *m* sent by *Y* and *m* has not been modified. If *X* can authenticate the message *m* is valid, then the return value is true; otherwise the return value is false.

    Equal(m, m'): This represents that, if message *m* is equal to message *m'*, then it returns true, otherwise it returns false.

4   The Verification of Purchase Request

Currently, there are a variety of works are being developed to analyze security protocols. However the secure transaction protocol is more complicated than the traditional security protocols, so we cannot find much works in this area. On the other hand, the specifications of SET protocol is incomplete and sometimes blurry [10]. Thus, it is not surprising that some potential drawbacks can be detected during the verification of Purchase Request. Also, some feasible methods of resolution are proposed and would like to draw the attention of the protocol designers.

In this stage, some sensitive information, such as order information (OI) and Payment Instruction (PI), are generated. Therefore, it is necessary to formally verify this phrase before SET is applied into the practical circumstance. For the sake of brevity, some hidden materials and complex operation, such as secret value and hashing algorithm are abstracted away here. Actually, the validation of Purchase Request can be separated into five steps.

4.1   Initiate Request

The cardholder should have completed browsing, choice, and ordering before this flow begins. The main objective of this step is to obtain a copy of the Payment Gateway's certificate. The message from the cardholder C to the merchant M indicates the payment card brand *BrandID* which will be used for the transaction. Actually, the initiate request *PInitReq* can be described by next formal expression.

$$C \longrightarrow M: Send(C, M, PInitReq)$$

The cardholder's challenge Chall-C is included in the *PInitReq* to guarantee the freshness of response messages. There is nothing to be validated since the *PInitReq* message does not contain any message need to be kept secret.

4.2   Initiate Reponse

After M processes the *PInitReq*, it will construct the response message and assign a transaction identifier *TransIDs* to the message. The response message *PInitRes* contains the requested data, including the Merchant's and Payment Gateway's certificates. These are provided within the signature of the response message. Also, the merchant replies with the Chall-C copied from the transaction record and adds a challenge Chall-M of its own. Finally, M sends the response messages to C.

$$\alpha = Generate(M, PInitRes) \circ Send(M, C, <CertS(M), CertK(P)>)$$
$$\circ Send(M, C, <PInitRes, S(H(PInitRes), Spv(M))>)$$

In the programmer's guide of SET, it verifies Chall-C against the Chall-C recorded in the previous transaction to ensure the cardholder's freshness. If the

Chall-C has never been disclosed it can vouch for the freshness, but if not we are really concerned with the replay attacks to the response message. In fact, the intruder Z can intercept the communication between the cardholder and the merchant and replay this message later.

(1)$C \to Z(M)$: *PInitReq*
(2)$Z(C) \to M$: *PInitReq'*
(3)$M \to Z(C)$: $<CertS(M), CertK(P), PInitRes', S(H(PInitRes')), Spv(M))>$
(2')$Z(C) \to M$: *PInitReq''*
(3')$M \to Z(C)$: $<CertS(M), CertK(P), PInitRes'', S(H(PInitRes'')),$
$\qquad\qquad Spv(M))>$
(4)$Z(M) \to C$: $<CertS(M), CertK(P), PInitRes', S(H(PInitRes')), Spv(M))>$

The intruder Z can intercept the initiate request *PInitReq* and replace it with a new request message *PInitReq'*. When the merchant receives *PInitReq'*, he constructs the response message (3) and sends it to C. However, Z intercepts the message and impersonates C to send a new request message (2') to the merchant. M answers C with a new response message (3') accordingly, which is intercepted by Z. Finally, Z impersonates C to send an outdated message (4) that is intercepted by Z from message (3). This attack is continuously used until C wants to bring about the authentication between C and M again.

The instance proves that we cannot exclude the possibility that the Chall-C can be disclosed and used for the replay attacks. In our opinion, it is unfeasible, at least dangerous, to guarantee the freshness of response message by just comparing the current Chall-C with a record from *Initiate Request*. This paper gives an optional method, in which a timestamp T is involved in the response message instead of Chall-C.

(3)$M \to C$: $<CertS(M), CertK(P), PInitReq', S(<T, H(PInitReq')>,$
$\qquad\qquad Spv(M))>$

This prevents the above attack from working because the intruder will be unable to replay the message as before [17].

In addition, M may alter the response message for the sake of network block. If M does not let C know what has been changed on *PInitRes*, or just let C know the modification but the content of the message does not keep the same as the original one, C should pause the current processing and verify *PInitRes* again.

4.3   Cardholder Purchase Request

After the validation of initiate response message, the cardholder may now proceed with the purchase request. It consists of two parts: an order information (OI), for the merchant, and a Payment Instruction (PI), tunnelled through M to P. C does not want P to see what is being bought nor does he want M to see his account details. To achieve this objective, SET introduces a *dual signature* by hashing the concatenation of the messages digest of the OI and PI, and signing the result with the Cardholder's private signature key. Also, the Cardholder's PAN is included to authenticate him.

$$\alpha = Generate(C, OI) \circ Generate(C, PI) \circ$$
$$Send(C, M, S(<OI, H(PI), H(<H(OI), H(PI)>)>, Spv(C))) \circ$$
$$Send(C, M, e(S(<PI, H(OI), H(<H(OI), H(PI)>)>, Spv(C)), k_1)) \circ$$
$$Send(C, M, E(<k_1, PAN>, Kpb(P))) \circ Send(C, M, CertS(C))$$

When M receives the order, it verifies the cardholder signature certificate. Then M validates the dual signature on OI by decrypting it with $Spb(C)$ and comparing the result with a newly generated hashing of the $H(OI)$ and the $H(PI)$. If they are not equal, M returns an error message and stops processing *PReq*. Finally, M transfers the signature on PI to the Payment Gateway. The verification of PI will be described in our future work.

As to the application of dual signature, it strengthens the protection of OI and PI from the malicious attacks. Thus, the merchant may believe the response message published by the cardholder has not been tampered.

However, the cardholder may alter the symmetric key k_1 or the contents of OI and PI since C wonders these messages have been masqueraded or the network is blocked. On the other hand, whether the principals have the memory function is also a critical factor. The detailed description is beyond this paper. Therefore we only list three cases below:

(1) C alters OI and PI , but does not modify k_1;
(2) C alters k_1, but does not change OI and PI;
(3) C alters k_1, OI, and PI.

In case (1), the cardholder constructs the new OI and PI. If C does not let M know what have been changed or notices M the modification but the contents is not identical to the original one, M will fail to authenticate the *PReq*; in case (2), C generates a new key k_1. If C does not let M know the alteration about k_1, M will fail to authenticate $<k_1, PAN>$; in case (3), C alters all the three messages. If C does not let M know the modification or lets M know the changes but the content is not identical to the original one, M will fail to authenticate *PReq*. In this time, the merchant should stop the processing of *PReq* and not send *PRes* to C. At last, the participants have to risk the unending dispute with each other. Thus, our works can be a complement of SET. The detailed verification procedures, such as the certificates by PKI tree, have been presented in our previous works [14], so we do not repeat it here.

4.4   Purchase Response

When M completes the processing of OI, it will create the response message by using the merchant private signature key to digitally sign the hashing of the purchase response. Actually, M will not ship the goods or perform the service in the order until the transaction is authorized. Finally, the Merchant transmits the *PRes* to the cardholder. Let *PRes* = $<Chall\text{-}C, TransIDs, XID>$.

$\alpha = Generate(M, Chall\text{-}C) \circ Generate(M, TransIDs) \circ Genrate(M, XID) \circ$
$Send(M, C, <PRes, S(H(PRes), Spv(M))>) \circ Send(M, C, CertS(M))$

The problem in purchase response is analogous to the purchase initiate response. The intruder can use this security leak to do the replay attacks, which will cause a serious damage to the transaction. Next, we will present the verification of the *purchase response*.

(1) *Generate(M, Chall-C)*   [action]
(2) *Generate(M, TransIDs)*   [action]
(3) *Generate(M, XID)*   [action]
(4)   *Know(M, PRes)*   (1)(2)(3)[R-2]
(5)   *Know(M, <PRes, S(H(PRes), Spv(M))>)*   (4)[2-5][4-2]
(6) *Send(M, C, <PRes, S(H(PRes), Spv(M))>)*   (5)[action]
(7)   *Know(C, PRes)*   (6)[R-1]
(8)   *Know(C, S(H(PRes), Spv(M)))*   (6)[R-1]
(9) $\neg$ *Auth(C, M, PRes)*   (7)(8)[5-1][R-5]

On the other hand, the merchant may alter maliciously the contents of *PRes* for the sake of wrong format or input. If *M* does not let *C* know the alteration or notices *C* the change but it is not identical to the original one. The cardholder will fail to authenticate *PRes*.

From the above observation, we give fully the formal verification to the purchase request phrase. The results disclose some subtle flaws in SET. It is mainly because the specifications of SET do not provide the detailed description and sometimes are misleading. Thus, it is inevitable that some potential flaws can be utilized by the intruder. Next, we will present how to established the modelling of purchase request. This can aid us to verify the protocol automatically instead of the manual validation.

5   Modelling Purchase Request

This Section presents the design of an automatic inference framework, which extricates us from the manual verification. The modelling requires the distinct description to all the processes of purchase request. However, the specifications of SET cannot keep consistent at all the times. In this paper, the business description of SET is acted as the primary reference.

5.1   Designing the Inference Engine

The inference engine is the kernel of the whole inference framework. It knows how to actively use the knowledge in the knowledge base. Normally, a user interface is necessary for smooth communication between the user and the system. It is convenient to view the inference engine and interface as one module, in which contains four basic functions:

- Adopt the external file as the infrastructure of the knowledge base;
- Input the facts and new knowledge by the interaction with the user;

- Access the knowledge base;
- Output the results to the database.

The verification flow is depicted in Fig. 1. When the user detects some sus-pectable problem during the transaction, it collects the related proofs and sub-mits the authentication requirement to the authentication server. By the inter-action with the user, some known facts should be input beforehand. The user interface takes charge of the communication between the user and the authentica-tion server. Then the server will try to find the matched rule from the knowledge base. If all the rules have been searched thoroughly, the authentication will be halted. If not, it will go ahead to check whether the conclusions of the rule have been stored in the database. If the conclusion can be found, the system will skip it and go to next rule. If not, we have to match all the conditions of this rule one by one. If and only if the return value is true the server can create the response and store the results into database, otherwise we have to check the next rule.

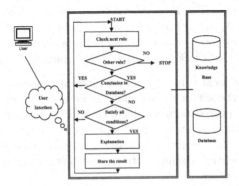

Fig. 1. The algorithm flow of inference engine

5.2   Handling the Knowledge and Facts

Two kinds of methods are applied to handle the knowledge base here. One is inputting the new knowledge and the other is accessing the existing knowledge base. They can be denoted by 'a' and 'b' respectively.

> *process ('a') if acquisition.*
> *process('b') if write ('Name of the knowledge base'),*
> *readln (Name),*
> *consult(Name).*

If the system fails to find the name, it will send an error message to the user. Actually, a rule can be divided into condition and conclusion. Also, a predefined functor *facts_ reading* is used to collect the known facts. Every time, when the user inputs the facts, the system will ask user whether it is a terminal symbol *"yes"*. If so, the processing is halted. If not, the internal functor *assertz* is used to store them into the database.

5.3   Recognition

Next, we want to employ an instance from purchase request to describe how to mechanically verify it by this model. The introduction of the whole verification procedure however is outside this paper so we just focus on the rules handling, which actually is one of the most important components.

The instance comes from the purchase response, in which $Auth(C, M, PRes)$ is the proposition that we want to authenticate. Also, the system may interact with user and collect the facts, such as $Know(C, PRes)$ by functor $facts\_reading$. Some known facts, for instance $Know(M, Spv(M))$, should have been stored in the database previously. The facts collection will continue until the user inputs a terminal symbol "*yes*". Next, we will build up the knowledge base by storing the rules with the serial number by sequence. We cannot include all the rules for the limited space and therefore we just list four rules below.

rule (1, ["*Know(X, m)*"], "*Know(X, H(m))*")
rule (2, ["*Know(X, m)*", "*Know(X, Spv(Y))*"], "*Know(X, S(m, Spv(Y)))*")
rule (3, ["*Know(X, m)*", "*Know(X, Spv(Y))*"], "*Know(X, S(H(m), Spv(Y)))*")
rule (4, ["*Know(X, m)*", "*Know(X, Spb(Y))*", "*Know(X, S(<ID$_Y$, T, H(m)>,
        Spv(Y)))*", "$|Clock\text{-}T| < \triangle t_1 + \triangle t_2$"], "*Auth(X, Y, m)*")

where *Clock* is the local time, $\triangle t_1$ is an interval representing the normal discrepancy between the server's clock and the local clock, and $\triangle t_2$ is an interval representing the expected network delay time [17]. Actually, each rule consists of conditions and conclusion, which are split by the square bracket.

After inputting the facts and establishing the knowledge base, the user can submit an authentication command to the authentication server now:
?- *Auth(C, M, PRes)*.
Following the flow in Fig. 1, the system tries to match the rules in the knowledge base. To match the conditions of a rule, the user may find them from the database or ask user by the user interface. Finally, the system fails to authenticate the *PRes* sent by cardholder, so the system will stop the process and response an error message. Also, the system will retract all the out-date messages, including the rules and facts.

It is convenient for us to verify a more complex instance, we just need to extend the knowledge base and facts. From the observation, our framework is promising in verifying the security protocols.

6   Conclusions

E-commerce has played an important role in global economic growth today. At the same time, its 'evolution', however, has resulted in the increase of both the vulnerability of e-commerce system to security violations and the damages that such violation may cause. Therefore, some secure transaction protocols have been developed, but some proportions of them are subject to attacks. Therefore a variety of formal methods have been produced.

The traditional approaches cannot qualify for the verification of secure transaction protocols because it involves some complicated processes, such as payment card transaction. In this paper, we present how to verify the purchase request of SET by using a new analysis approach. Some potential flaws are detected during the verification. In addition, we propose some available solutions to the protocol designer accordingly.

In particular, a modelling framework is introduced to establish a authentication system with the client/server architecture. To evaluate this modelling, we use an instance from the purchase response to prove its utilities. From the observation, it is cable of detecting the subtle flaws of SET instead of manual validation, which actually eases the people's burden.

References

1. http://www.idc.com
2. Needham R. and Schroeder M., Using Excryption for Authentication in Large Networks of Computers. *Comm. of the ACM*, 21(12), pages 993–999, Dec 1978.
3. Gritizalis S., Security Protocols over Open networks and distributed systems: Formal methods for their Analysis, Design, and Verification, *Computer Communications*, 22(8), pages 695–707, May 1999.
4. Dolev D, Yao A., On the Security of Public Key Protocols. *IEEE Transaction on Information Theory*, 29(2), pages 198–208, 1983
5. Meadows C., The NRL Protocol Analyzer: An overview, *Journal of Logic Programming*, 26(2), pages 113–131, 1996.
6. Burrows M., Abadi M., Needham R., A logic for Authentication. *ACM Transactions on Computer Systems*, 8(1):18–36, February 1990.
7. Gong L, Needham R, and Yahalom R., Reasoning about belief in cryptographic protocols. *Proceeding of the Symposium on Security and Privacy*, pages 234–248, Oakland, CA, May 1990.
8. Meadows C., The NRL Protocol Analyzer: An overview, *Journal of Logic Programming*, 26(2), pages 113–131, 1996.
9. Brackin S., Automatic formal analyses of two large commercial protocols. *Proceedings of the DIMACS Workshop on Design and Formal Verification of Security Protocols*, September 1997.
10. Meadows C, Syverson P., A formal specification of requirements for payment transactions in the SET protocol. *Proceedings of Financial Cryptography* 98, volume 1465 of Lecture Notes in Comp. Sci. Springer-Verlag, pages 122–140, 1998.
11. SET Secure Electronic Transaction Specification, Book 1: Business Description, Version 1.0, May 31, 1997.
12. SET Secure Electronic Transaction Specification, Book 2: Programmer's Guide, Version 1.0, May 31, 1997.
13. SET Secure Electronic Transaction Specification, Book 3: Formal Protocol Definition, 1.0, May 31, 1997.
14. Chen Q.F, Zhang C.Q, Zhang S.C., A Logical Framework ENDL for Verifying Secure Transaction Protocols. *Journal of Knowledge and Information Systems*, Springer, accepted, forthcoming.
15. Chen Q.F, Zhang C.Q, Lu J., The Verification of Merchant Registration in SET Protocol, *Proceedings of The International Conference on Internet omputing*, Las Vegas, pages 1098–1104, 2002.

16. Chen Q.F, Zhang C.Q., Using ENDL to Verify Cardholder Registration in SET Protocol, Proceeding of International Conference on e-Business (ICEB2002), Beijing, pages 616–623, 2002.
17. Denning D., Sacco G., Timestamp in Key Distribution Protocols,Communications of ACM, 24(8), 533–536, August 1981.

Appendix

(1) Axiom

2-5 $Know(X, Spv(X))$

That is X knows its own private signature key. It is computationally unfeasible for anyone to deduce it from the public signature key.

4-2 $Know(X, m) \wedge Know(X, Spv(Y)) \longrightarrow Know(X, S(H(m), Spv(Y)))$

That is, if X knows message m and private signature key $Spv(Y)$ of Y, then X knows the message digest $H(m)$ and $S(H(m), Spv(Y))$ by using $Spv(Y)$ to encrypt $H(m)$.

5-1 $Know(X, m) \wedge Know(X, S(<ID_Y, T, H(m)>, Spv(Y))) \wedge Know(X, Spb(Y))$
$$\xrightarrow{\substack{|Clock - T| < \\ \Delta t_1 + \Delta t_2}} Auth(X, Y, m)$$

This means that, if X knows message m, $S(<ID_Y, T, H(m)>, Spv(Y))$ and $Spb(Y)$, then X can authenticate that Y sent m, and m has not been modified by checking that $|Clock - T| < \Delta t_1 + \Delta t_2$.

(2) Inference Rules

(R-1) Revealation

$$\boldsymbol{Know(X, m)} \vdash_{Send(X, Y, m)} \boldsymbol{Know(Z, m)}$$

states that the secret cannot be protected when plain text is transferred in a practical distributed system and an open network.

(R-2) Generation

$$\vdash_{Generate(X, m)} \boldsymbol{Know(X, m)}$$

states that if message m is generated by X then X itself must know m.

(R-5) Non-monotonic

$$\frac{\nRightarrow P \vdash_\alpha \boldsymbol{Auth(X, Y, m)}}{P \mid \sim_\alpha \neg \boldsymbol{Auth(X, Y, m)}}$$

says that if we cannot conclude that a principal X successfully authenticates m after a sequence of action α, then we non-monotonously assume that X does not believe the validity of m.

Self-organizing Coefficient for Semi-blind Watermarking

Sung-kwan Je[1], Chang-jin Seo[2], Jin-young Lee[2], and Eui-young Cha[1]

[1]Dept. Computer Science,
[2]Dept. Multimedia,
Pusan National University, Korea
jimmy@harmony.cs.pusan.ac.kr

Abstract. In this paper, we present a watermarking scheme based on the DWT (Discrete Wavelet Transform) and the ANN (Artificial Neural Network) to ensure the copyright protection of the digital images. To embed the watermark, the interested regions where the watermark is embed must be decided by the SOFM (Self-Organizing Feature Maps). Among the classified nodes, we select the middle of nodes and establish the average of node as threshold. The established threshold applies the only wavelet coefficients of the selected node, so we can reduce the time cost. Using the SOFM that much safer than other algorithms because unauthorized user can't know the result of training by the SOFM. So even the watermark casting process is in public, the attackers or unauthorized users still cannot remove the watermark from the watermarked image. As the result, the fidelity of the image is excellent than any other algorithm, and the process is good at the strength test-filtering, geometric transform and etc. Furthermore, it is also robust in JPEG compression as well.

1 Introduction

These days, mass copies of data are increasing through the internet and networks because the information data have been digitalized and the multimedia data has been developed rapidly. Several studies protecting the copyright of digital multimedia contents have been proposed [1-5].

The most important character of digital watermarking is imperceptible. If the watermark is embedded, viewers should not see nor notice the mark. Usually the watermark is used proper number by owner, manufacturers, sellers and buyers. If the information of image is being distributed illegally, we can trace the flow of the data using the embedding the watermark in the information of the image. We can find the man who has distributed it. In order to be effective, the watermark should have the characteristics outlined below [4].

- Fidelity; In earlier work. We called it as the term 'imperceptible'. The watermark should not be noticeable by viewers, and the quality of the image embedding the watermark should not be loss. If viewers can notice the watermark, it can be damaged.

Supported in part by the East West Cyber University.

X. Zhou, Y. Zhang, and M.E. Orlowska (Eds.): APWeb 2003, LNCS 2642, pp. 275–286, 2003.

- Robustness; When the watermarked image tests in image processing operations; to improve image quality, attacked by image cropping, image blurring, image sharpening, image enlarge, image reduction and lossy compression, the watermark must be survived.
- Security; Even the watermark verification process is in public, the attackers or unauthorized users still cannot remove watermark from the watermarked image, and neither retrieve the watermark.
- False positive rate; In most applications, it should be distinguished whether the image has been embedded or not. If the watermark is extracted through the image having no watermark, the algorithm should lose the reliability.

Recently, digital watermarking has been classified by two ways; Spatial Domain and Frequency Domain. In the spatial domain, the watermark is embedded directly in the spatial domain. In this process, various researches have been developed as PN-Sequence (Pseudo random Noise Sequence) [6] and statistical method, etc.

The process to embed the watermark in spatial domain is simple and fast but it has disadvantaged that it's weak from the external attack, noise and JPEG compression. Because of the result, the study of the watermarking is mainly researched in the frequency domain in recent. The process of watermarking in the frequency domain is that the watermark is embedded in the repetitive and characteristic coefficient among the generated coefficients that are transformed from FFT, DCT, Wavelet, and etc.

Cox [4-5] proposed the process of watermarking using the DCT. In the process, signal spread of frequency domain is widely distributed to transmit effectively the watermark signal without noise; filtering and compression transform using spread spectrum communication. The energy of the specific signal spread is too small to be noticed, but the signal is extracted by PSNR (Peak Signal to Noise Ratio) using the location and variation of the original image signal. The problem of the process is not clear to select important coefficient, and partly characters can not be effective because of transforming the whole image. It is hard to select important coefficients for embedding watermark using the DCT. Further, the watermark embedded by the robustness of JPEG compression is easily loss because compression used the 8×8 block DCT. Besides, at this scheme, it could be happened the Block phenomenon because it does block transformation, so it brings the loss of image.

Kundur [7] proposed the scheme of watermarking using the wavelet transform and binary watermark. For embedding the watermark, decompose the original image with DWT to 3-levels of MRA (Multi-Resolution analysis) and then each sub-band lines up. In the case of the middle value among coefficients of the sub-band, if watermark is 1, the size of Δ should be added, and if that is -1, the size of Δ should be subtract.

$$\Delta = \frac{f_{k3,l}(m,n) - f_{k1,l}(m,n)}{2Q-1} \tag{1}$$

In the equation (1), l is level of the wavelet transform, and $f_{k,l}(m,n)$ is value of arranging each coefficients of the sub-band. Parameter Q is used to choose trade-off of fidelity and robustness to control the amount of watermark. It is necessary to control suitable amount of watermark.

This paper is organized as follows; we propose the watermarking scheme in section 3 and the experimental result and conclusion at the final section.

2 Wavelet & Artificial Neural Network

2.1 Wavelet Transform

The wavelet transform expresses well the locality characteristic that spatial or time - frequency, as is MRA. So, it used to image analysis and signal processing. The wavelet is a signal on which energy is concentrated on definite time (t); we can create a wavelet function with the scaling and translation of mother wavelet (φ) like equation (2).

$$\varphi^{a,b}(t) = |a|^{-1/2}\,\varphi((t-b)/a) \tag{2}$$

It needs so many calculations to calculate wavelet coefficients about every scale (a) and every location (b) in the wavelet transform, as so, it is proved that if we do the wavelet transform in the moment the scale and location are at 2^n, we could get an effective and correct result. It called the DWT. Mallat [10] suggested the scheme that we could discrete transform with effect using filters. The Wavelet transform for the discrete signal can be accepted by using the FIR (Finite Impulse Response) digital filter from regular orthogonal based function.

2.2 Artificial Neural Network

There are various algorithms in the ANN algorithm. Each algorithm has each application field. In general, when the purpose is to classify the cluster of the data in the characteristic similarity, the applications; ART (Adaptable Resonance Theory) , SOFM and Fuzzy-ART, should be used in large. Many biological neural networks in the brain are found to be essentially two-dimensional layers of processing neurons densely interconnected.

In usual, when the watermark is embedded in a certain image, it is important to decide the location where it is embedded. It is difficult to select the location that has robustness from the attack. The extract of this region is generally expressed to ROI (Region Of Interest).

In this paper, we apply the SOFM algorithm among ANNs for ROI. They are known as the SOFM; of topology preserving maps from the fact the weights (from input node i (wavelet coefficient) to output node j) will be organized such that topologically close nodes are sensitive to inputs that are physically similar. Every input neuron is connected to every output neuron through a variable connecting weight, and these output neurons are extensively interconnected with many local (lateral) connections. The strengths of the lateral connection depend on the distance between the neuron its neighboring neurons. The self-feedback produced by each biological neuron connecting to itself is positive, while the neighboring neurons would produce positive (excitatory) or negative (inhibitory) action depending on the distance from the activation neuron. The essence of Kohonen's SOFM algorithm is that it substitutes a simple geometric computation for the more detailed properties of the Hebb-like rule and lateral interactions. There are three basic steps involved in the application of the algorithm after initialization, namely, sampling, similarity matching, and updating. These three steps are repeated until the map formation is completed, and have the characteristics outlined below [11].

- Approximation of the Input space
  - Represented by the set of synaptic weight vectors provides a good approximation to the input space
- Topological Ordering
  - The SOFM algorithm is topologically ordered in the sense that the spatial location of a neuron in the lattice corresponds to particular domain of feature of input patterns.
- Density Matching
  - Improving the density-matching property of the SOFM algorithm is to add heuristics to the algorithm, which force the distribution computed by the algorithm to match the input distribution more closely.

The SOFM can be applied in binary input pattern and analog input pattern. Furthermore, a variable connecting weight of SOFM gets the average of the whole input pattern, so it responses equally to generate the node. We use generated the character of similar pattern node of SOFM to decide the location of embedding the watermark. The SOFM can select the location of node where users want to embed, so it has a strong point that the embedding location can be controlled by the character of the image.

3 Proposed Algorithm

3.1 Watermark

The signal in the communication channel should not be affected by noise, filtering and compression transmission during the transmission. Spread spectrum communication is introduced for embedding a watermark in image data and unauthorized users should not notice it. When the watermark spreads in various frequency domain of the image, the energy of the special frequency is difficult to notice. For not to changed and noticed the embedding data by unauthorized users, the data should have random characteristic and constitute watermark using the PN-Sequence to extract embedded data by statistical measurement. PN-sequence that shows pseudo-noise signal to random signal has these characters [12].

- Repeat cycle is long enough. Repeat cycle is infinite that is random sequence.
- The coefficient of 0 and 1 is almost same in one cycle.
- Cross-correlation in each sequence is very small in one cycle.
- Small sequence piece cannot regenerate the whole sequence.
- It can be regenerated by suitable regeneration algorithm.

We use the signal of the watermark as the average is 1, and variance is 1: Gaussian normal distribution. N is the length of the signal -amount of the watermark- Gaussian random vector is invisible when it is embedded, and it's also stronger than the binary watermark [4].

3.2 Embedding Watermark

We decompose the original image with the DWT to 3-levels of MRA. In most natural images, the energy is concentrated on the lower frequency domain that relates with human vision. So, if the image data damaged in the lower frequency, people could notice it. Accordingly, for protecting the quality of the image and making the watermarked image, we embed the watermark at the highest frequency domain where a little information of images are in.

Using the DWT, embedding watermark calculated the threshold to embed the watermark with equation (3) that it is to calculate the threshold, which decides to embed each sub-band.

$$T = 2^{\lfloor \log_2 MAX(Wavelet\ Coefficient) \rfloor} \tag{3}$$

It is the one of the image compression algorithm that Shapiro [13] proposed to calculate the threshold, which used zero padding in the EZW (Embedded zerotree wavelet algorithm). EZW method is very efficient to encode important wavelet coefficient and express the energy concentration phenomenon by the wavelet transform. It used the first calculated threshold to embed the watermark. But, It is to embed the watermark which a several bigger wavelet coefficient using the maximum of sub-band. So, it couldn't express the characters of the image nor adjust the length of the watermark. By selecting the location of embedding the watermark by the ANN, we can adjust the quantity of the watermark in the same image, so we can say that it is strong for the image procession like compression or cropping.

In this paper, we choose the SOFM algorithm among these ANNs because it self-organized learning without given correct information of input pattern. We classify wavelet coefficients of the highest sub-band (LH, HL and HH) using the SOFM. In the case of the ART, which is one of other competitive learning proposed by Grossberg and Capenter, it creates the clusters dynamically, so it is not influenced by the size of the image. But, according to the sequence of the input pattern of the ART2, it has disadvantage the result of training occurs differently. The reliability of the ANN cannot be stable because this characteristic takes the influence at the order of the training course about the same image. We use the characteristic of similar pattern cluster of the SOFM to select location to embed the watermark. It has a strong point that users can control freely the location to embed the watermark depends on the characteristic of the image. We classify wavelet coefficients to nodes by self-similarity, and each node has the characteristic of image. Using this characteristic, we select one of nodes in the middle frequency domain and we embed the watermark to classified wavelet coefficients of the node. The embedding the watermark is figure (1) below.

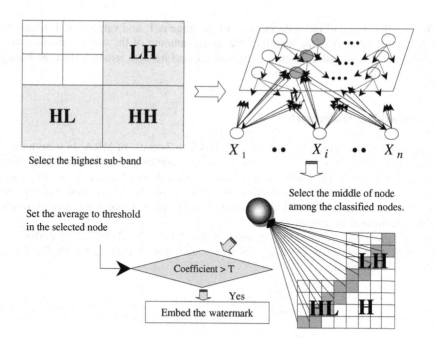

X is a wavelet coefficient, W is a connecting weight

Fig. 1. Embedding watermark

If we decide the location where the watermark is embedded using a threshold for the whole image, it would spend much time. So for resolving this problem, we used the ANN to the highest sub-band, we reduce the time-cost when the threshold is applied to only wavelet coefficients in the selected node, not to apply the whole wavelet coefficients. And we could adjust the number of watermark in the same image and could do that following the specialties of each image.

As we tested, we set the initial weight to 0.5 in the SOFM algorithm, and we select the middle of node among the classified clusters. We set the average to threshold and we embed the watermark to the coefficient what is bigger than that of the average in the middle of nodes. If we do the IDWT (Inverse Discrete Wavelet Transform) the wavelet coefficients in which the watermark is embedding by biorthogonal 4.4 that is mother wavelet, we could synthesis it to the embedded watermark image. Biorthogonal is each vector that it doesn't create a orthogonal set but it has orthogonality each other, it could be FIR filters are possible, symmetric filters are possible and flexible design (use different filters in analysis and synthesis) as the watermark could have a few differences according to the test image.

$$X_i^{'} = X_i + \alpha W_i \qquad (4)$$

$$X_i^{'} = X_i \left(1 + \alpha W_i\right) \qquad (5)$$

$$X_i' = X_i \left(e^{\alpha W_i} \right) \tag{6}$$

X_i' is a watermarked coefficient, X_i is a wavelet coefficient, and W_i is a watermark. When we embed watermark to the image to obtain the watermarked image using equation (4), (5) and (6). Equation (4) is just adding the watermark, so it is not proper when the variation of the value has extreme differences. In equation (5) and (6), the variation of a scaling parameter affects largely the embedding watermark. As a result, we used equation (5), and value is 0.6, 0.8 and 1 according to variance of coefficients.

3.3 Extracting Watermark

We decompose the watermarked image like the processing of embedding watermark to 3-level using the DWT. We calculated the information of the middle of node that classified by using the SOFM in the embedding processing. It use for extracting the watermark without original image. The information has a location and average of embedding the wavelet coefficient.

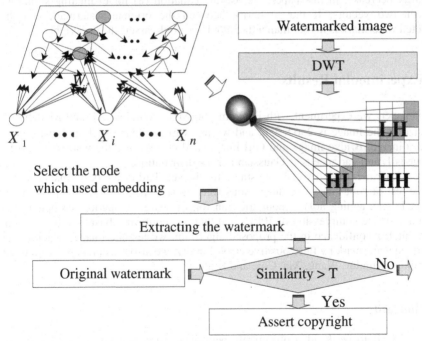

X is a wavelet coefficient, W is a connecting weight

Fig. 2. Extracting watermark

Unauthorized users know about location of embedding the watermark, and the watermark will remove easily. So, in this paper, nobody knows about the location of embedding watermark using the SOFM. Even the watermark is embedded using the SOFM and the watermark verification process is in public, unauthorized users don't know about the information of the trained data. Further, when they execute the SOFM in the same processing, the information of the trained data was different form the result of ours. As a result, the algorithm is safer than others.

For evaluating similarity, there are some schemes. One is the way of calculating Vector Projection, other is the way of calculating correlation, other is the way of calculating Bit Error, and etc [4].

$$Similarity(X, X^*) = \frac{X^* \cdot X}{\sqrt{X^* \cdot X^*}} \tag{7}$$

$$Correlation(X, X^*) = \frac{\sum XX^*}{\sqrt{\sum X^2 \sum X^{*2}}} \tag{8}$$

X is a original watermark, X^* is a extracted watermark. Equation (7), value of similarity is variable according to the size of vector, that is, if the size of vector increases, the value of similarity increase, if the size of vector decreases, the value of similarity decrease. In this paper, we use the equation (8) for evaluating similarity between two vectors. If the similarity between the original watermark and the extracted watermark is higher than a threshold, we could assert the copyright.

4   Experimental Results

In this paper, we experiment with Pentium 700 MHz, Window XP and Matlab 5.2. The size of the image is 256 × 256, and we test various image such as Lena image, Barbara image, Bridge image and Girl image, and etc. We use the watermark as the average is 1, and variance is 1: Gaussian normal distribution.

We experiment fidelity and robustness for the standard of the performance value. For the test of robustness, we did various filtering (Lowpass Filter, Highpass Filter, Wiener Filter), adding noise, geometric transform (enlarge, reduction, cropping) and the attack of the compression of JPEG, and then we confirm robustness. In addition, for the higher confidence in the proposed algorithm, we test the image, which is not embedded watermark by false positive error. Finally, we also are compared with other algorithms (Kundur, Wang, Xia, Cox, and Kutter).

4.1 Similarity

We get PSNR to be decided objectively between the original image and the image embedded watermark, and we calculate fidelity through the equation (8) from the extracted watermark and the original watermark in the table 1, the value of objective PSNR is maintained over 40dB.

(a) Original image   (b) Watermarked image

Fig. 3. Similarity Test

Table 1. Similarity between orignal image and watermarked image

Image	PSNR	Image	PSNR
Lena	48.52	Camera man	47.48
Barbara	47.13	Crowd	47.42
Bridge	47.29	Oleh	46.99
Girl	46.35	Pepper	46.98

4.2 Robustness

We tested the watermarked image in Lowpass filer, Highpass filter, and Wiener filter. We used Highpass filter that the mask of the 3 × 3 size, [0 -1 0; -1 8 -1; 0 -1 0]/4, and Lowpass filter that the 3 × 3 size of the Gaussian filter, average is 0, and standard deviation is 0.5, and Wiener filter is the 3 × 3 size of the Wiener filter. Wiener filter is less similarity than other filters but it is not influenced to extract the watermark. We tested the watermarked imaged about geometric transform (rescaled a twice enlarged the watermarked image, rescaled a twice reduced the watermarked image, and the 156 × 156 size of the center cropping). The result is powerful efficiency in the geometric transform and adding noise of Salt & Pepper and Gaussian.

Table 2. Correlation between the orignal watermark and the extracted watermark.

Image	Lowpass filter	Highpass Filter	Wiener filter	Rescaled enlarge	Center cropping	S&P noise
Lena	0.99	0.97	0.77	0.98	0.89	0.83
Barbara	0.98	0.97	0.76	0.97	0.79	0.88
Bridge	0.99	0.98	0.73	0.99	0.88	0.90
Girl	0.98	0.99	0.77	0.97	0.91	0.79

4.3 Compare with Others

We also compare with other watermarking using PN-Sequence. In the frequency domain, the original image needed Wang [8] and Xia [9] using the wavelet transform,

Kundur [7] without the original image, the original image needed Cox [4] using the DCT, Kutter's [6] algorithm embedded watermark using the spatial domain.

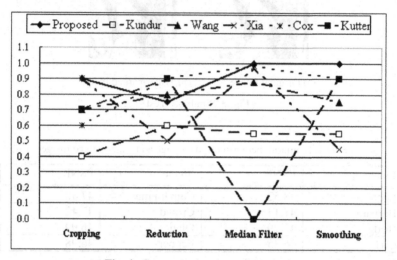

Fig. 4. Compare robustness with others

In the test of robustness such as cropping and filtering, the result is powerful efficient. In the geometrical transformation such as reduction, the process is less similarity than other algorithms; Wang, Cox and Kutter. But, it doesn't matter to decide the watermark exist because the similarity is over than detection value. Compare with Kundur's algorithm, which doesn't need the original image, the process get better result as figure (4).

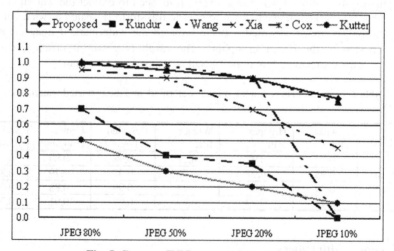

Fig. 5. Compare JPEG compressing with others

Even though the efficiency of the process is weaker than other algorithms, which needed the original image but it is not influence to extract the watermark. In this paper, without the original image, the process is better than other blind watermarking in comparison. Furthermore, compare with Cox in the same DCT situation, it can't be extracted under JPEG 10%, the watermark is extracted in the process even the value is low.

When the image that is not embedded the watermark is experimented in FPE, the watermarking algorithm can't be reliable, if the watermark is extracted in FPE. We test the proposal process at the same situation (simulation) and the watermark isn't extracted from the image.

5 Conclusion

In this paper, we propose the watermarking considering of human vision character and embed the watermark in the highest sub-band that has fewer amounts of image data in visual. The process uses the wavelet transform by using the SOFM. The process considers the character of the image that is adaptive watermarking. Using the clustering data that is used in embedding, the watermark is extracted without the original image. We reduce the time cost when the threshold is applied to only the wavelet coefficients in the selected node, not to apply the whole wavelet coefficients. The algorithm is much stronger than the others because unauthorized users can't know the result of training by the SOFM.

In the result, the value of objective PSNR is maintained over 40dB, and there is not to significant visual difference in subjective observation. As the result, the proposal algorithm is much efficient than any other algorithm.

References

[1] M.D. Swanson, M. Kobayashi, and A. TewFik, "Multimedia Data-Embedding and Watermarking Technologies," *Proc. of IEEE*, vol. 86, no. 6, June 1998.

[2] I. Pitas and T.Kaskalis, "Applying Signatures on Digital Images," *In Proc. 1995 IEEE Nonlear Signal Processing Workshop*, Thessaloniki, Greece, 1995.

[3] C. F. Osborne, R. G. Schyndel and A. Z. Tirkel, "A Digital Watermarking," *Int. Conf. on Image Processing*, Nov. 1994.

[4] I. J. Cox, J. Kilian, T. Leighton and T. Shamoon, "Secure Spread Spectrum Watermarking for Multimedia," *IEEE Trans. on Image Processing*, Vol 6, No.12, pp.1673–1687, 1997.

[5] I. J. Cox, J. Kilian, T. Leighton and T. Shamoon, "Secure Spread Spectrum Watermarking for Images, Audio and Video", *International Conf. on Image Processing*, Vol III, pp.243–246, 1996.

[6] Martin Kutter, Frederic Jordan, and Frank Bossen. "Digital signature of color images using amplitude modulation." *In Ishwar K. Sethi, editor, Proceedings of the SPIE Conference on Storage and Retrieval for Image and Video Databases*, volume 2952, pp. 518–526, San Jose, USA, 1997.

[7] Deepa Kundur and Dimitrios Hatzinakos, "Digital watermarking using multiresolution wavelet decomposition." *In Proceedings of IEEE ICASSP '98*, volume 5, pp. 2969–2972, Seattle, WA, USA, May 1998.

[8] Houng-Jyh Wang, Po-Chyi Su, and C.-C. Jay Kuo. "Wavelet-based digital image watermarking". *Optics Express*, 3 pp. 497, December 1998.

[9]   Xiang-Gen Xia, Charles G. Boncelet, and Gonzalo R. Arce. "Wavelet transform based watermark for digital images." *Optics Express*, 3 pp. 497, December 1998.

[10] S. Mallat, "Multi-Frequency Channel Decomposition of Images Wavelets Models", *IEEE Trans. on Information Theory*, vol. 11, no. 7, July 1992.

[11] Simon Haykin, "Neural Networks: A Comprehensive Foundation", *MacMillan*, 1994.

[12] Tae-sook Ha, "Lecture in CDMA", *KTF*, 1999.

[13] J. M. Shapiro. "Embedded Image coding using zerotrees of wavelet coefficients," *IEEE Trans. on Signal Procsseing*, vol. 41, no. 12, pp. 3445–3462, Dec. 1993.

Applying RBAC Providing Restricted Permission Inheritance to a Corporate Web Environment

YongHoon Yi[1], MyongJae Kim[1], YoungLok Lee[1], HyungHyo Lee[2], and BongNam Noh[1]

[1] Chonnam Nat'l University, Dept. of Computer Science, 500–757, Gwangju, Korea
{yhyi,markkim,yrlee,bongnam}@athena.jnu.ac.kr
[2] Wonkwang University, Div. of Information and EC, 570–749, Iksan, Korea
hlee@wonkwang.ac.kr

Abstract. A successful marriage of Web and RBAC technology can support effective enterprise-wide security in large-scale systems. But RBAC has a role hierarchy concept that senior role inherits all permissions of junior roles. In the corporate environments, senior role need not have all authority of junior roles, and unconditional inheritance in role hierarchy causes undesirable side effects(permission abuse) and violates the principle of least privilege. In this paper[1], we re-explore role and permission inheritance and propose a new model providing restricted permission inheritance. To do this, we divide a single role into sub-roles(Corporate/Department Common role, Restricted Inheritance role, Private Role) based on the degree of inheritance and business characteristics and make role hierarchy with sub-roles. It is very useful to solve unconditional inheritance problem in a corporate environment. And we describe formal description of proposed model. Lastly, we show a system architecture applying RBAC with proposed model within a corporate web environment.

1 Introduction

Role-based access control(RBAC) is known as a proper security model within a corporate intranet. And there are several researches[1,2,3] for Web implementation using RBAC. But we cannot use RBAC providing unconditional inheritance in role hierarchy within a corporate web environment. It is because there are some functions for a job position that are essential but are not inherited to its higher job position(senior role)[4]. For example, *manager* is a senior job position to that of *clerk*, however, *manager* doesn't automatically inherit the 'register purchase' job function of *clerk*[5].

---

[1] This research was supported by University IT Research Center Project

X. Zhou, Y. Zhang, and M.E. Orlowska (Eds.): APWeb 2003, LNCS 2642, pp. 287–292, 2003.

2   Proposed Model

In this section, we propose a model to solve unconditional inheritance problem using sub-role. A single role is divided into sub-roles according to the degree of inheritance and business characteristics. And sub-roles are useful to satisfy restricted inheritance that is needed in a corporate environment.

2.1   Role

A role[6] is a job function within the organization that describes the authority and responsibility conferred on a user assigned to the role. Administrators can create roles according to the job functions performed in the organizations. This is very intuitive and efficient approach except inheritance concern. We discuss a role to apply RBAC providing restricted permission inheritance rather than unconditional inheritance in a corporate environment. Fig.1 shows proposed role concept compared with a single role.

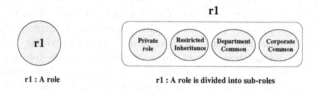

Fig. 1. Proposed role concept for corporate environment

In Fig.1, r1 means a role and this is divided into sub-roles considering corporation which consists of departments and positions. Sub-roles are categorized Corporate Common role, Department Common role, Restricted Inheritance role and Private role. And each sub-role's characteristics of inheritance on role hierarchy are described in [4].

2.2   Role Hierarchy

Like ordinary roles, sub-roles also have role-hierarchy relation among themselves. Corporate and Department Common role unconditionally inherit all permissions to their senior roles. Restricted Inheritance role has the degree of inheritance represented permissible range of permission inheritance.

In Fig.2, the solid line arrow means unconditional inheritance relation among sub-roles and the dotted line arrow shows Restricted Inheritance(RI) relation in accordance with degree of inheritance. Case 1), 2) show unconditional inheritance relation. r_{k3}, r_{j3}, r_{i3} are members of RI relation. In RI relation of r_{k3}, r_{j3} and r_{i3}, permissions are restrictively inherited on sub-role hierarchy. Details of RI relation are described in [4].

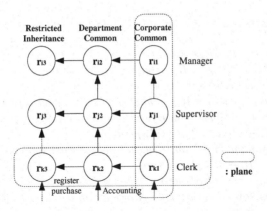

Fig. 2. An example of role hierarchy of proposed model

Case 1) $r_{k1} \rightarrow r_{k2}$ relation

Both r_{k1} and r_{k2} are on same sub-role hierarchy(Horizontal plane). So, r_{k2} inherit all permission of junior sub-role rk1.

Case 2) $r_{k2} \rightarrow r_{j3}$ relation

Both r_{k2} and r_{j2} are on Department Common hierarchy ($r_{k2} \rightarrow r_{j2}$: Vertical plane) and r_{j2} and r_{j3} are on the same sub-role hierarchy ($r_{j2} \rightarrow r_{j3}$: Horizontal plane). So, r_{j3} inherit all permission of junior sub-role r_{k2}.

3   Formal Description of Proposed Model

3.1   Definition

We define a set of components to formally describe the characteristics and behavior of the proposed RBAC model in a corporate environment as follows:

$\mathbf{R}$: *a set of roles*($r_1, r_2, r_3, ..., r_n \in R$)
$\mathbf{R_{CC}}$: *a set of Corporate Common roles*
$\mathbf{R_{DC}}$: *a set of Depratment Common roles*
$\mathbf{R_{RI}}$: *a set of Restricted Inheriance roles*
$\mathbf{R_{PR}}$: *a set of Private roles*
$\mathbf{R_{POS}}$: *sum of roles related to positions*(*i.e vertical plane*)
$\mathbf{R_{JOB}}$: *sum of roles related to jobs*(*i.e horizontal plane*)
$\mathbf{R_{Pi}}$: *a set of sub* − *roles in position i* (R_{Pi}, *where* $1 \leq i \leq n$)
$\mathbf{RH}$: *Role Hierarchy*
       [$RH \subseteq R \times R$, *partially ordered*]
$\mathbf{RH_{CC}}$: *Hierarchy of Corporate Common roles*
       [$RH_{CC} \subseteq R_{CC} \times R_{CC}$, *partially ordered*]

RH$_{DC}$: *Hierarchy of Department Common roles*
$$[RH_{DC} \subseteq R_{DC} \times R_{DC}, \; partially \; ordered]$$
RH$_{RI}$: *Hierarchy of Restricted Inheritance roles*
$$[RH_{RI} \subseteq R_{RI} \times R_{RI}, \; partially \; ordered]$$
RH$_{Pi}$: *Hierarchy of sub − roles*
$$[RH_{Pi} \subseteq R_{Pi} \times R_{Pi}, where \; 1 \leq i \leq n, \; partially \; ordered]$$
role_jobs : *a function to return which job role(r) is related to,*
$$[R \to R_{CC} \cup R_{DC} \cup R_{RI} \cup R_{PR}]$$
role_positions : *a function to return which position role(r) is related to,*
$$[R \to R_{Pi}, 1 \leq i \leq n]$$
ancestor_roles : *a set of senior role on role(r),* $[R \to 2^R]$
mutex_roles_set : *a set of role pair with mutually exclusive relation,*
$$[mutex\_roles\_set \subseteq R \times R]$$
$\geq$: *a partial order on RH (if $r_2 \geq r1$, then r_2 is a senior to r_1)*

3.2   Properties

We examine properties to specify proposed model as follows:

Property 1. $R = R_{job} = R_{pos}$
Property 2. $R_{JOB} = R_{CC} \cup R_{DC} \cup R_{RI} \cup R_{PR}$
Property 3. $R_{POS} = \bigcup_{i=1}^{n} R_{Pi}(1 \leq i \leq n)$
Property 4. $RH_{POS} = RH_{P1} \cup RH_{P2} \cup RH_{P3} \cup ... \cup RH_{Pn}$
Property 5. $RH_{JOB} = RH_{CC} \cup RH_{DC} \cup RH_{RI}$
Property 6. $\forall \, r \in R, role\_positions(r) = \{R_{Pi}|1 \leq i \leq n\}$
$\qquad\qquad\quad role\_jobs(r) = \{R_{JOB}\}$
Property 7.   (a) $(r_i, r_j) \in RH_{POS} : role\_jobs(r_i) \geq role\_jobs(r_j)$
$\qquad\qquad$ (b) $(r_i, r_j) \in RH_{JOB} : role\_positions(r_i) \geq role\_positions(r_j)$

3.3   Principle of Least Privilege

Principle of least privilege means that a user is not given to more permissions than is necessary to perform his/her job functions. The reason of violating this principle is that a role has unnecessarily too many permissions or a role can inherit all permissions of its junior roles. Using restricted inheritance hierarchy, we can easily satisfy this principle. First, a user can only be assigned to role on private role that are at least permission on role hierarchy. Second, Restricted inheritance hierarchy can restrict junior's permission to senior role with degree of inheritance and business characteristics.

3.4   Separation of Duty

Separation of Duty(SoD) means constraints that if a user is authorized as a member of one role, the user is prohibited from being a member of the other role. With SoD, an organization can address potential conflict-of-interest issues at the time a user's membership is authorized for a role. Proposed role hierarchy can satisfy SoD constraints as follows:

$$assigned\_users : (r : ROLES) \rightarrow 2^{USERS}$$

$$\forall(r_i, r_j) \in mutex\_roles\_set \cdot assigned\_users(r_i) \cap assigned\_user(r_j) = \emptyset$$

4 RBAC Architecture

In this section, we suggest RBAC architecture integrating proposed model for a corporate web environment. We use various existing technologies such as Secure cookies, smart certificates applied in previous RBAC implementation[2,7] for Web. Fig. 3 shows RBAC architecture in a corporate web environment. The role server has user-role assignment information for the corporate environment. After a successful user authentication, the user receives his or her private role. Later, when the user requests access to a Web or intranet server with assigned roles, the server allows the user to execute operations in the server based on the user's roles after getting permissions. Administration of role server can be performed in a decentralized manner by administrators.

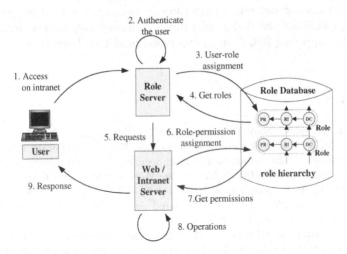

Fig. 3. RBAC Architecture in a corporate web environment

Fig. 4 indicates permission assignment in a corporate web environment and shows a result of Fig. 2 role hierarchy of proposed model. It displays that *manager* and *supervisor* are a senior role than that of *clerk*. *supervisor* inherit the 'register purchase' role of *clerk* and *manager* does not inherit the role of *clerk*.

5 Conclusion

In this paper, we apply RBAC providing restricted permission inheritance to a corporate web environment. Main contribution of this paper is as follows. First,

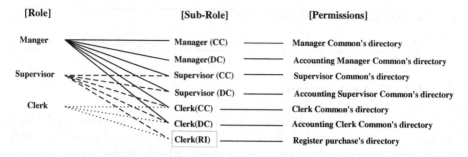

Fig. 4. Permission assignment in a corporate web environment

we categorize a single role into four sub-roles based on the degree of inheritance and business characteristics. And proposed RH_{CC}, RH_{DC}, RH_{RI} and RH_{PR} are well matched with corporate environment. Second, we find an answer to block permission abuse occurred by unconditional inheritance. As a result, Restricted inheritance role hierarchy is very useful to keep the principle of the least privilege. Third, within a corporate web environment, we show a way of applying RBAC providing restricted permission inheritance to a corporate web environment. We believe that applying RBAC in the proposed model for large-scale enterprises is useful.

References

1. David F. Ferraiolo, John F. Barkley, and D. Ricard Kuhn: A Role-Based Access Control Model and Reference Implementation With a Corporate Intranet. ACM Transactions on Information and System Security, Vol2, No.1(1999) 34–64
2. Joon S. Park, Ravi Sandhu: RBAC on the Web by Smart Certificates, Proceedings of the fourth ACM workshop on RBAC(1999) 1–9
3. Zahir Tari, Shun-Wu Chan: A Role-Based Access Control For Internet Security. IEEE Internet Computing(1997) 24–34
4. MyongJae Kim, YongHoon Yi, HyungHyo Lee and BongNam Noh: A Design Methodology of Role Hierarchies providing Restricted Permission Inheritance. Proceeding of Conference on Information Security and Cryptology, Korea institute of Information Security & Cryptology(2002) 326–329
5. Sejong Oh, Seog Park: Task-Role Based Access Control(T-RBAC): An Improved Access Control Model for Enterprise Environment. DEXA2000(2000)
6. Ravi S. Sandhu: Role-Based Access Control Models IEEE Computer, Feb(1996)
7. Joon S. Park, Ravi Sandhu, and SreeLatha Ghanta: RBAC on the Web by secure cookies. In Proceedings of the IFIP WG11.3 Workshop on Database Security(1999)

eSignature Verification on Web Using Statistical Mining Approach

Joseph Fong[1], San Kuen Cheung[2], and Irene Kwan[3]

Department of Computer Science, City University of Hong Kong, Kowloon, Hong Kong
[1] csjfong@cityu.edu.hk   [2] joe.c@student.cityu.edu.hk
Department of Information Systems, Lingnan University, Tuen Mun, N.T., Hong Kong
[3] drikwan@ln.edu.hk

Abstract. This research is related to the field of biometrics. The biometrics research consists of fingerprint scans, retina scans, voiceprint analyses, and so on [1]. Although an electronic signature (eSignature) does not actually come from human, it comes from an indirect tissue (i.e. handwriting) of a human. For instance, a handwritten signature will be collected from a cardholder when filling out the application form of credit card and formularized from a normal signature to an electronic signature. This eSignature will then be transmitted and stored into XML document in a data center. We will extract the eSignature that is a group of numbers from the database. This group of numbers is a factor in preceding the Online Analytical Mining (OLAM) [2]. We use the Internet as a network channel. We will also use the XML-RPC [6] to implement the active rules and apply OLAM to verify incoming eSignatures.

1 Introduction

A report was recently published on the South China Morning Post regarding fake credit cards, about 600 fake credit cards and equipment as the largest single haul of bogus cards in the year between 2001 and 2002. If all items seized in the factory had been turned into counterfeit credit cards, the potential loss suffered by the bank would have been about HKD$14 million [4]. There is certainly an urgent need to stop these frauds. In the current market of pattern recognition system, the electronic signature (eSignature) is a quick method to identify a sender of a document so as to speed up a progress of specific procedures, such as a banking services or credit card payments. For instance, confirmation of a signature from a cheque will be in connection with offices between a headquarters and a subsidiary. In the credit card payment, a shopkeeper may want to confirm a cardholder's signature to protect the shop income. This result of a need motivates us to develop a methodology to quickly verify the human signature by using electronic devices. In this paper, we focus on signature of the credit card payment. In common practice, credit card users will hand their card to shop keeper who will verify the credit card from the card center through a network channel. This procedure only ensures corresponding information contained in the credit card but not to identify the customer or cardholder. With our methodology, we could verify the truth of card owner by confirming the cardholder's signature.

X. Zhou, Y. Zhang, and M.E. Orlowska (Eds.): APWeb 2003, LNCS 2642, pp. 293–300, 2003.

We employ XML-based active rules in our research for creating dynamic features and data interoperability between the data center and clients. In the data center, we will build up a XML document as well as XML-based active rules. The former will be stored for all information regarding credit card, such as cardholder, credit amount, transactions and so on. As for the latter, we will apply event-condition-rule and XML-RPC mechanisms to form active XML-based rules. The advantage of using XML-based model in our research is that the model will more likely become a dominant standard in the Internet. Data could then be exchanged and rules could be triggered through the Internet.

2   Methodology

An initial eSignature will be obtained when a client submits an application form with his/her signature to the card center. The handwritten signature will be converted to a file and transformed to a group of numbers representing the eSignature. The eSignature will then be transmitted over the Internet to the card center. In the card center, OLAP will be deployed to verify an eSignature whether it is a genuine card-owner's signature. Our OLAM will apply the neural network and the XML-based active rules to implement. Figure 1 is the architecture of our proposed OLAM for eSignature confirmation.

2.1 Steps for Transforming "TIFF" Format to eSignature

Steps 1-4 are the procedures for transforming a handwritten signature from a graphical mode into a group of numbers (i.e. eSingnature). Assume that we use an eSignature encoder to scan a customer's signature from the receipt. In our test, we will use the Internet as the network channel. Then, the handwritten signature will be stored in a file in the "TIFF" format. And also, it will go through the following steps.

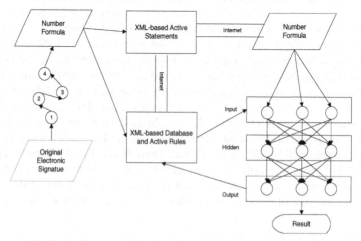

Fig. 1. Architecture of Online Analytical Mining for eSignature

Step 1 - Co-ordinate Points
Building co-ordinate points, we set up four points from left to right and from top to down extracted from the handwritten signature. According to the co-ordinate points, we can build up a rectangle that is the scope of our proposed eSignature.

Step 2 – Pixel Allocation
According to the rectangle from the step one, we can cut the rectangle into many small boxes. Each box may occupy either "0" or "1". The "0" stands for no pixel color inside the box and the "1" stands for a pixel color inside the box.

Step 3 – Weight Correction
According to the standard weight (i.e. each eSignature will be collected and stored in a standard size), we will adjust the handwritten signature by enlarging or shrinking into one size so as to evaluate with the sample record correctly.

Step 4 - Formulation
Adding a formula on top of the derived data collected from the steps 1 and 2, we can protect the data of handwritten signature when it is going to transmit from source location to target destination.

According to the steps 1 to 4, we can obtain an initial eSignature from the application form of credit card. The eSignature will be stored in the XML document. When the system is required to do the analytical mining by this cardholder, the system will extract the initial eSignature to perform analyses. If the result of analyses is positive, the tested eSignature will be stored in our database as a record.

Encoding handwritten signature to eSignature
Begin
        Read a "TIFF" handwritten signature file
        Project the handwritten signature to our scan area of eSignature // Step 1
        Do while - scan the handwritten signature from the area row by row until end of
file
            Do while - scan the row until end of row
                Do while - scan group pixels in 8 pixels per each row // Step 2
                    Match the group pattern to the matching table I
                    Store the temporary numbers in memory
                Enddo
                Match a group of temporary numbers to the matching table II
                Store a row number obtained by matching the temporary numbers
            Enddo
        Enrich the data into a standard weight // Step 3
        Consolidate all the row numbers to form an eSignature // Step 4
        Enddo
End

3   Online Analytical Mining Components

Logically, we apply two components in our methodology to carry out the online analytical mining. The first is the XML-based active rules and the second is the neural network. The neural network can refer to the [6]. The XML-based active rules are for storing static data and dynamic data during the transforming process from "TIFF" format to eSignature and during the evaluation for each transaction information. As for the neural network, we apply this technique from data mining concept to evaluate a tested pattern whether it matches with the initial record or not.

Online analytical mining process (OLAM)

Begin
> If card # from client = card # from server   //Rule 1
> Then call Rule 2
> If cardholder name from client = cardholder name from server   //Rule 2
> Then call Rule 3
> If card expired date from client = card expired date from server   //Rule 3
> Then call Rule 4
> If requested amount <= accumulated amount of limitation   //Rule 4
> Then call Rule 5
> Tested eSignature for evaluation from Internet channel   //Rule 5
> Do while - read eSignature from XML native database until end of eSignature
>> Compare the data between initial record and tested source
>> // enlarge or shrink the tested eSignature
>> Make adjustment to the tested eSignature to fit the compare processes
>> Compare the pixel factor
>> Store the result of the comparison to temporary memory
> Enddo
> Retrieve the result of all the comparison from the temporary memory
> Compute the result using statistics method with initial record // first round test
> If the first round test with the initial eSignature = negative
>> Compute the result with the latest positive record //second round test
> Endif
> Store the final result to the XML native database
> Display the result to the client shop where requests to start the analyses

End

3.1   Active XML-Based Rules

An introduction for the active XML-based rules (shown in the Figure 2) is necessary to comprehensive the details of our research. The active rules consist of some actions triggered by XML-RPC. Its remote procedure callings use HTTP as the transport and XML as the encoding. XML-RPC is designed to be as simple as possible, while allowing complex data structures to be transmitted processed and returned [7]. For instance, each credit card will be temporary restricted to access in the month if the cardholder makes purchases over his/her monthly credit limit. The active rules will examine information stored on corresponding record for matching both information between server and client.

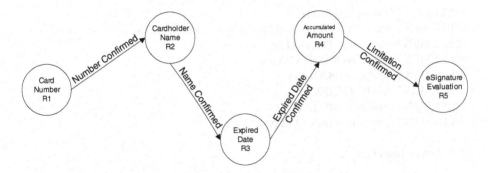

Fig. 2. Active Rule Process for eSignature Evaluation

3.2 XML DTD

```
<!ELEMENT matchRow (row*)>
<!ELEMENT row (uin, columnNo+)>
<!ELEMENT uin (#PCDATA)>
<!ELEMENT columnNo (#PCDATA)>

<!ELEMENT matchPixel (pixel*)>
<!ELEMENT pixel (unit_no, unit_pixel)>
<!ELEMENT unit_no (#PCDATA)>
<!ELEMENT unit_pixel (#PCDATA)>

<!ELEMENT inputEsignature (inEsig*)>
<!ELEMENT inEsig (esig, date_time_in, client_no, card_no, date_time_out, result)>
<!ELEMENT esig (#PCDATA)>
<!ELEMENT date_time_in (#PCDATA)>
<!ELEMENT client_no (#PCDATA)>
<!ELEMENT card_no (#PCDATA)>
<!ELEMENT date_time_out (#PCDATA)>
<!ELEMENT result (#PCDATA)>

<!ELEMENT storeEsignature (stEsig*)>
<!ELEMENT stEsig (esig, date_time_store, holder_name, card_no, band_no,
expire_date)>
<!ELEMENT esig (#PCDATA)>
<!ELEMENT date_time_store (#PCDATA)>
<!ELEMENT holder_name (#PCDATA)>
<!ELEMENT card_no (#PCDATA)>
<!ELEMENT band_no (#PCDATA)>
<!ELEMENT expire_date (#PCDATA)>
```

```
<!ELEMENT transaction (trans*)>
<!ELEMENT trans (date_time, client_no, amount, result, currency, transaction)>
<!ELEMENT date_time (#PCDATA)>
<!ELEMENT client_no (#PCDATA)>
<!ELEMENT amount (#PCDATA)>
<!ELEMENT result (#PCDATA)>
<!ELEMENT currency (#PCDATA)>
<!ELEMENT transaction (#PCDATA)>
```

3.3 Active Interface

```
<html><head><title>activerules</title></head>
<body>
<!--#include virtual="\xmlrpc\code\xmlrpc.asp" -->
<%
sub writeResponse (url, method, myresp)
    response.write("Server: " & url & "<br>")
    response.write("Method: " & method & "<br><br>")
    response.write("We         sent:        <br><pre>"        &
    Replace(functionToXML(method, params), "<", "&lt;",
    1, -1, 1) & "</pre><br>")
    response.write("We       received:      <br><pre>"       &
    Replace(serverResponseText, "<", "&lt;", 1, -1, 1) &
    "</pre>")
    response.write("<p>")
end sub
Dim url, method, params(1), flag
if request.querystring("url")&"" ="" then
    url="http://localhost/interop.asp"
else
    url = Trim(request.querystring("url"))
end if
%>
<form method=get action=activerules.asp>
Rule # 1 <input type=text name=rule1 size=40 > e.g.  4509
5948 2031 9432<br>
Rule # 2 <input type=text name=rule2 size=40 > e.g.
Thomas White<br>
Rule # 3 <input type=text name=rule3 size=40 > e.g.
dd/mm/yyyy<br>
Rule # 4 <input type=text name=rule4 size=40 > e.g.
USD300.00<br>
Rule # 5 <input type=text name=rule5 size=40 > e.g.
/esignature/client23trans11.txt<br>
<input type=submit value="Submit"><input type=reset
value="Reset">
</form>
You can type information to the spaces above for checking
the conditions using XML-RPC.<br><br>
```

```
<%
flag = 0
if request.querystring("rule1")&"" <> "" then
    method="interopEcho.echorule1"
    params(0)=request.querystring("rule1")&""
    myresp = xmlRPC1 (url, method, params)
    call writeResponse(url, method, myresp)
    flag = flag + 1
end if
if request.querystring("rule2")&"" <> "" then
    method="interopEcho.echorule2"
    params(0)=request.querystring("rule2")&""
    myresp = xmlRPC2 (url, method, params)
    call writeResponse(url, method, myresp)
    flag = flag + 1
end if
if request.querystring("rule3")&"" <> "" then
    method="interopEcho.echorule3"
    params(0)=request.querystring("rule3")&""
    myresp = xmlRPC3 (url, method, params)
    call writeResponse(url, method, myresp)
    flag = flag + 1
end if
if request.querystring("rule4")&"" <> "" then
    method="interopEcho.echorule4"
    params(0)=request.querystring("rule4")&""
    myresp = xmlRPC4 (url, method, params)
    call writeResponse(url, method, myresp)
    flag = flag + 1
end if
if flag = 4 then '-- applying rule 5
    method="interopEcho.echorule5"
    params(0)=request.querystring("rule5")&""
    myresp = xmlRPC5 (url, method, params)
    call writeResponse(url, method, myresp)
end if
%>
</body></html>
```

4   Conclusion

In this paper, we have explored another approach of pattern recognition using OLAM and neural network. Our contributions of this paper are: (1) we have successfully transformed from a handwritten signature (i.e. graphical format) to an electronic signature (i.e. numeric format), (2) we have also used a linear representation to evaluate the eSignature, and (3) we have weighted the eSignature by using statistical method. We concluded that our methodology could provide a more formal verification of the card owner is cardholder via computerized matching the handwritten signature with the pre-stored eSignature at the point when a sale transaction is raised at the shop. At present, we use four steps on converting a graph format of handwritten signature to a group of number of electronic signature. These numbers are then transmitted to the other side (i.e. card center) for further processes. In the card center, we apply the XML document and XML-RPC to assist the neural network for completing the online analytical mining. Our methodology of using the online analytical mining on verifying the electronic signature is proved feasible using a case study approach.

References

[1]   E.D. Zwicky, S.Cooper, & D.B. Chapman, "Internet and Web Security - Building Internet Firewalls", O'Reilly 2nd Edition 2000, pp 591–627.
[2]   Joseph Fong, H.K. Wong, & Anthony Fong, "Online Analytical Mining Web-Pages Tick Sequences", Journal of Data Warehousing, Vol. 5, No. 4, Fall 2000, pp 59–68.
[3]   "The GIF Controversy: A Software Developer's Perspective", Last revision February 2, 2002. Web shortcut to this page: lzw.info. Parts are quoted with permission from CompuServe Information Service. Parts are excerpted from the PNG specification.
[4]   South China Morning Post, Hong Kong, March 9 2002, Page 2.
[5]   B. Erickson & F. Romano, "Professional Digital Photography", Prentice Hall PTR, 1999, pp 54–127.
[6]   J. Fong and S.K. Cheung, "Online Analytical Mining for eSignature", Proceedings of the IASTED International Conference – Information Systems and Databases 2002 Tokyo Japan, ACTA Press, ISBN 0-88986-362-8, ISSN 1482-793X, pp 287–292.
[7]   "XML-RPC", UserLand Software, Inc., http://www.xmlrpc.com, 1998–2002.

Deriving Architectures of Web-Based Applications

Weiquan Zhao and David Kearney

School of Computer and Information Science, University of South Australia, Mawson Lakes, SA 5095, Australia
{Weiquan.zhao, David.Kearney}@unisa.edu.au

Abstract. Web-based applications that features intensive date manipulation, user-interaction and complicated business processing have been widely used especially in areas such as e-commerce. They are comparable to traditional GUI client/server applications in terms of functionality, structure and development activities but unique in the fact that they must use the web as an infrastructure for their deployment and execution. In this paper we present a procedure of deriving an architecture specific for web-based applications based on the analysis their features attributed to the uniqueness. We illustrate how this architecture accommodates the features and compare it with other commonly used architectures.

1 Introduction

Modern web-based applications are data intensive, user interactive and business logic centered (also referred to as web-based information systems [1]). Unlike web applications in their primitive form as a repository of inter-linked web pages, a web-based application in this context is software-like, i.e. application logic is significant in defining the behavior of the application rather than navigation paths as represented by hyperlinks in URL. They are comparable to traditional GUI client/server applications that are not based on the web. For example, technically there is no problem to implement a typical web-based on-line billing system in a "traditional" GUI client/server application environment. As a consequence development of web-based application involves increasingly intensive programming apart from activities such as page authoring, art design and data modeling, etc. Therefore software engineering principles and practices should be and have been applied to developing web-based applications, which has been recognized in the research community and contributed to the shaping of the new area – web engineering [2].

Recent researches and practices in the web area have been moving towards investigating structured approaches to developing large and complex web-based applications [9], especially in response to growing challenges on the maintenance of them. This is well supported by technologies in industry including enterprise applications platforms such as J2EE [11] and implementation frameworks such as WAF [6], Barracuda [11], etc. There is a great demand for explicit support of higher-level design abstraction that

X. Zhou, Y. Zhang, and M.E. Orlowska (Eds.): APWeb 2003, LNCS 2642, pp. 301–312, 2003.

can bridge preceding development activities such as business analysis into implementation.

Software architecture fills in as a software engineering technique that helps developers capture major design concerns that have significant impacts on the functionality and quality of the product at a higher-level and at an early stage. An architecture serves as a bridge between the business requirement and the implementation [4]. In particular, domain-specific architectures are useful in promoting reuse of design expertise and in achieving a well-recognized understanding in a specific area, for instance web-based applications.

In this paper we will present a procedure in which we derived a software architecture for web-based applications. We start with an original architecture without considering the specialty of the web and then examine what is the consequence when it is moved in the web environment. The original architecture is then modified to accommodate the characteristics of the web as a mandatory application infrastructure.

The paper is organized as follows. In section 2 we present the initial architecture and then in section 3 we examine what the initial architecture presumes and the impacts once the web is introduced. In section 4 we explain the derivation procedure. Related issues in the supporting implementation framework are discussed in section 5 and typical related works are briefly reviewed in section 6. Finally the paper is concluded in section 7.

2   Architecting without Involvement of the Web

For software like web-based applications, the web can be boiled down to merely another application distribution mechanism like CORBA [15] and DCOM [16] used for partitioning an application into parts and joining them together. A web-based application must be split into two parts by its communication protocol – Hypertext Transmission Protocol (HTTP) and then "glued" together via web browsers and web servers, the protocol implementations at client and server ends respectively. We characterize web-based applications as that they must be partitioned by HTTP and must use a web-browser to render its user interface.

2.1   Dividing an Application into Tiers

We adopt three tiers architecture [10] as the starting point. It is a widely used architectural pattern [8] in distributed complicated GUI application. By tiering an application can be divided based on their functionality, frequency of change, and demanded skill sets, etc. The initial architecture can be depicted as in Fig. 1.

As shown in the diagram, the application is divided into three tiers, which takes care of various application tasks respectively. In implementation, the client tier usually sits on desktops machines and connects via middleware to the application server, which in turn is linked to typically a database server using database access protocols.

In most cases when the web is not involved, this architecture can be mapped in a straightforward way onto an implementation environment. For example, in the J2EE [11] environment, these tiers are referred to as client, EJB and EIS and implemented as standalone Java applications, Enterprise Java Beans and database servers respectively.

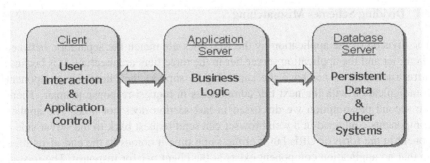

Fig. 1. The three tiers architecture

2.2 The Implicit Presumption

There are some implicit presumptions of the architecture on the support from the implementation environment. They can hold in most cases in a traditional environment thus will not be a problem. The major one is that the execution environment can transparently maintain the integrity of logic of the client tier component(s) of the application. In a traditional execution environment the only access point of such an application to the user is the user interface provided and controlled by the client tier. By no means the end user can affect the application's behavior via a mechanism other than the user interface. The end user's actions are "controlled" by the application's logic and any interaction internal to the application is invisible thus inaccessible to the end user.

Another presumption is that the implementation environment is capable of supporting all the computation and communication undertaken by the application components.

Interacting with end user. The client components need to present the end user with the outputs of the computation and take in inputs from the end user. In a GUI application, this is done via a sufficient set of user interface controls.

Communicating with the application server. The client needs to send requests to the application server for performing business processing and gets responses back to update its own state.

3   How the Web Matters

When applied to web-based applications, the three tiers of architectural components must be mapped onto the implementation environment. The most prominent consequence is that the front end (the one near end users) of the application must be split across the HTTP channel. In [3] we have generally examined the characteristics of web-based applications, in this section we will see how an application of the three-tier architecture will be affected once deployed in the web environment.

3.1 Dividing Schemes Mismatching

The division of the application by the web does not match the separation between the client tier and the application server tier in the three tiers architecture. It is because the infrastructure does not have the capability to support the client tier components to communication with the next tier components in request-response manner. Therefore the second presumption we discussed in last section does not hold. The application components contained in a web browser can send request back to the server side component in the form of URL but it at the same time it comes to the end of its lifecycle so that no application component exists at the client tier for response. The receiver of the HTTP response is the web browser that resides at the lower level than the application.[1]

As a result the HTTP channel divides the application in the middle of the client tier component(s) as depicted in the following diagram Fig. 2.

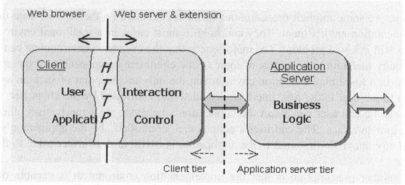

Fig. 2. The impact of HTTP – partition in client tier

3.2 Segmenting of Client Components

Another consequence of the limited capability of the web browser and HTTP is that the client tier architectural components cannot be fully deployed and executed in one piece. At any time only a small portion of the client tier component(s) can be deployed in the form of web page rendered (executed) in the browser. The runtime image of the application can be depicted in the way as shown in Fig. 3., regardless how the client

---

[1] Implementations in which the client components, e.g. a Java applet, creates another channel using protocols other than HTTP is not considered as web based applications in this context. In that case, HTTP is not part of the infrastructure that supports the whole application.

tier component is architect. Note the web does not necessarily affect the application server tier and the database tier, neither of which has to be web-specific. They can still be implemented in a straightforward way using non-web technologies.

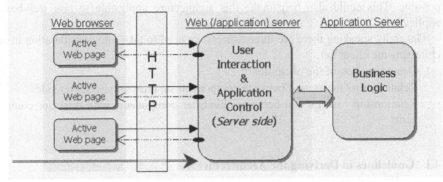

Fig. 3. The impact of HTTP – segmentation of client components

3.3 Internal Communication Exposed to External

The most significant consequence of this division by web is that the communication over HTTP, which is meant to be internal to the application, is exposed to the external because the server side is inherently accessible by end users via URL. The end user can take use of the facilities provided by the web browser such as the navigation buttons, address box and bookmarks to send arbitrary URLs to the server side. It cannot be assumed that the requests received by the server side components are sent from a particular web page. Reaction of the server side components upon such requests without validation could cause unexpected result. Therefore the first presumption on integrity of logic in the client tier of the architecture fails.

3.4 Architecting with Infrastructure

In normal cases, the architecture of a software application should be independent of the implementation environment. But when factors at the implementation level cannot be ignored and the application could be implemented unexpected otherwise, they should to be taken into consideration in architecting, as also recognized and emphasized such as in [5].

4   The Architecture

In this section we will go through several steps to derive the architecture by applying the division introduced by the web to the initial architecture. In the previous section we have shown the uniqueness of web-based applications is attributed to the division by HTTP into the client tier. In the derivation of the architecture we try to restrict the impact of this division so that specialty in development of web-based applications can be kept to the minimum to help reuse existing technologies and expertise as much as possible. This could also help make this architecture applicable to non web-based applications.

Generally speaking there are three aspects we need to take into consideration in architecting the client tier.

−   Decomposition of the client tier
−   Relationship / interaction between components on browser and server sides
−   Relationship / interaction between client tier components with next tier components

4.1   Guidelines in Deriving the Architecture

Generally speaking we aim the architecture to be of high modularity thus possibly of high maintainability. This is especially important to web-based application as they are normally under frequent changes through their lifecycle. In particular we try to solve the problems we have identified in last section that fail the two presumptions.

Synchronizing the user's input with the application
Requests sent from the web browser side, either the target or the accompanying data could be unexpected. Such inputs must be validated and synchronized with the state of the application to ensure the application is not out of track in its execution. Also the application should not be over burdened with unexpected, out-of-order requests.

Decreasing the coupling among client tier components
As requests sent from web browser side is regarded as internal communication between client tier components, the client tier could have heavy coupling if such requests are allowed arbitrary. This will also increase the complexity of the control logic in the client tier components. In the worst case, each client tier component has global control logic, which will result in low modularity and poor maintainability.

Restricting the influence of the web within the client tier
It is preferable to keep the impact of the web as little within the client tier as possible by introducing some isolation tier. This isolation tier is web specific and exposes a web-neural interface to the rest of the application. This is useful because web technologies are volatile thus normally the source of change. Meanwhile expertise in developing non web-based applications can be reused beyond the isolation tier.

Enforcing the application's modularity
Since web-based applications are usually subject to frequent changes, it is important to have a flexible modular structure thus changes can be made easily with limited impact. This can be achieved by separating components of different concerns and of different

frequency of changes. A hierarchical structure is helpful as changes can be localized without rippling effect and the integrity of the global logic can be enforced through the hierarchy.

4.2 H-PCA Architecture for Web-Based Applications

The architecture we have derived is named as Hierarchical Presentation-Control-Abstraction (H-PCA). Its components and structure are shown in Fig. 4.

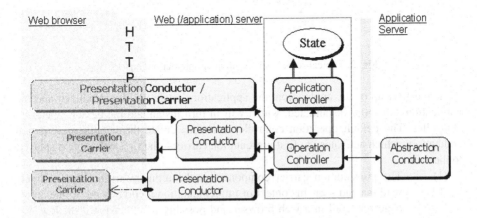

Fig. 4. The H-PCA architecture

H-PCA is similar to the architectural pattern Presentation-Abstraction-Control[2] (PAC) [8] in that the application components are categorized into *Presentation, Abstraction* and *Control*, and presentation and abstraction components are connected to controller components but not to each other. In PAC the whole application is decomposed into a hierarchy of modules each having all these three kinds of components and connected via control components. Differently, in H-PCA the hierarchy is composed of control components organized in two predefined levels and only the lower level control components have access to the other two types of components.

As shown in Fig. 4., the presentation and control components fall in the client tier in the initial architecture and the abstraction components correspond to those in the application server tier. The database server tier is irrelevant in this architecture and omitted for simplicity.

We use a typical interaction scenario (as shown in Fig. 5) between the end user and the application to illustrate the role and responsibility of each kind of component in this H-PCA.

---

[2] Some times PAC is regarded as a variation of MVC.

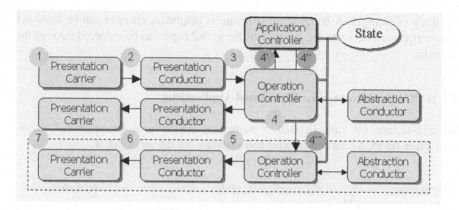

Fig. 5. Typical scenario of component interaction in H-PCA

At the start-up of the application, the applications' state will be initialized and the application controller instantiated, which will in turn instantiate the default operation controller. The default operation controller will then create the default presentation conductors, which activates the first presentation carrier – the first web page displayed to the user.

(1)   The presentation carrier component is the ultimate artifact that interacts with the end user. In context of implementation it corresponds to the active page rendered in a web browser and possibly its extension ("shadow") at the server side. The presentation conductor component is responsible for interacting with controller component through a "web neutral" interface. These presentation conductors consist the "de-webbing" tier that isolates the web from the rest of the application. At run time a presentation carrier component can only be associated with the presentation conductor component that instantiates it and pass the control back to it over HTTP at the end of its lifecycle. The communication in the other direction from the conductor to the carrier is implementation dependent and could be implicit.

(2)   The presentation carrier passes control back to its presentation conductor.

(3)   The presentation conductor validates the request and then passes the control to the controllers. The controllers are organized into a two-level hierarchy. There is an application controller on the top that controls the overall logic of the application. The application controller manages a group of operation controller each of which is responsible for only a portion of application task. All controllers can access and change the state space global to the application. Only operation controllers can access presentation conductors and abstraction conductors for interacting with end users and for performing the business logic respectively. Operation controllers take initiative to activate these conductors and an active conductor only reports back to its initiating operation controller.

(4)   The operation controller, once got control back, may access certain abstraction conductors to perform business processing. The abstraction conductor component may in turn access external systems and other resources, such as database and legacy systems that reside in (or behind) the third tier in the three tiers architecture. As the result of the action of the operation controller, the state of the application may change subsequently. Should the operation controller have finished its task, it will hand over the control to the application controller at the above level, which will either terminate the whole application or activate another operation controller, as shown in steps 4', 4'' and 4'''.

(5)   The operation controller will choose an appropriate presentation conductor to perform the next user interaction.

(6)   The selected presentation conductor receives command from its managing operation controller and then initiates the corresponding presentation carrier and gets it deployed to the end user. In implementation, this is to generate the next active page to be sent back to the browser.

(7)   The new presentation carrier will interact with the end user till it finishes it. Note the page might have its own logic to perform interaction task local to the page.

4.3 Webbing and De-webbing

The key idea of this architecture is to localize therefore to limit the impact of the web on the application and turn the design of web-based applications into being modular and logic-centric as much as what we do with traditional applications. From the point of view of software development, the web introduces a special way of producing user interface and of joining the user interface with the rest of an application. Its implementation technologies are often used in such a way that the controlling logic and even the business logic are mixed together with user interface generation. In addition, the user interface has to be segmented into small pieces connected with the application over a channel exposed to intervention from the environment. However the business logic of the application could be free of this mess and be implemented in traditional technologies.

Based on these facts, we introduced the presentation carrier and the presentation conductor components to deal with web specific features. The presentation conductors form an isolation tier that can hide the web from the rest of the application. We can call this a process of "webbing" and "de-webbing" (or webb-ification and de-webb-ification), which adapts the application to the web environment. The interface between presentation carrier and presentation conductor is not fixed to allow employing various technologies. In particular the core control logic of an application is hidden as well behind the presentation conductors in a hierarchical structure.

In this way the interaction over the web can be well tracked and shielded. The design of the application can be logic-centric instead of user-interface driven. This can help bridge the design with higher-level analysis and maintain the integrity of the application. In addition, the hierarchical organization of components further enforces the modularity of the application, which can help save efforts in understanding, modifying and error locating in development and maintenance.

5   Implementation Framework

To facilitate implementation of the architecture in a specific environment and reuse of code, it is desirable to have an implementation framework that conforms to the architecture while effectively takes use of available implementation technologies. Since the infrastructure has been taken into account in deriving the architecture it should be easy to map architectural components onto implementation ones. We have constructed implementation frameworks for this architecture in PHP [12] and J2EE technologies respectively in a start-from-scratch approach. We have also been conducting experiment to implement this architecture using existing implementation frameworks such as WAF [6]. As those frameworks normally have their own "implied" architecture, so the key to a successful application is to establish a proper mapping between architectural components and those in the implementation framework and to ensure any compromise made in the process is acceptable in terms of application functionality and performance.

In designing the implementation framework one of the key issues that must be addressed is how to simulate the control flow in the hierarchy. According to the architecture the low level components need to return the control back to its upper level managing component once it has finished its own task. However HTTP is a stateless protocol hence any control flow in the "return" direction is treated as "calling" or "initiating" ones. Therefore a mechanism is needed to handle the "return" of control from low level up to the higher level. According to our experience, we recommend a "dispatcher" component that incepts requests over HTTP and then directs them to the right place level by level based on the "call-return" relationship it keeps track of.

6   Related Work

It has been recognized that high-level design is needed for development of web-based applications and it has been well accepted that tiered architecture is applicable to web-based applications as one special case of distributed GUI applications. There are general architectures (pattern) in this arena and special ones specifically proposed for web-based applications. Since the impact of the web upon the application is mostly within the client tier or the alike, it is how to architect this tier that differentiate this our architecture from the others. As summarized in section 4.3 it is mainly restricting the impact of the web from the rest of an application including its control logic that makes this architecture advantageous.

Model-View-Controller (MVC) [8] is a widely used pattern for architecting GUI applications. It is adopted and advocated in the Blueprints program from SUN [6] for demonstrating J2EE technologies. One of its advantages is the flexibility. Components (in categories of model, view and controller) can be linked up together with no centralized control and little limitation on their topology. Normally a triad is used for illustrating this interconnection relationship among the components. However this could cause difficulty in maintenance due to possible chaining impact effect when some components are changed. This is especially serious for web-based applications that are always undergoing changes. Moreover when implemented in the web environment, the view components will be split by HTTP, which can result in even more complex interrelationship among the components to maintain and keep trace of.

This problem is also realized by [7] in which a variation of MVC pattern is proposed. A centralized state chart engine is added to the original MVC pattern to which all the view and controller components are attached. View components correspond to states in the state chart engine and controller components to state transitions. Requests sent over HTTP are mapped to events in the state chart so that they can be validated against what to be expected and synchronized with the state. This is similar to our approach in that view/presentation components correspond to application states. Differently we distributed the state management into controllers organized in a hierarchy instead of having a centralized monolithic state engine. States associated with view components are local to controller and controllers are the first-class components for maintaining the applications' state. Centralized state engine can help maintain the integrity of the application globally but could result in complex state space and fine-grained components that are heavily dependent on it. Furthermore view components can still access model components directly. Above all in our architecture the web is isolated from the control logic

In [9], an architecture called OOHDM-Java2 is proposed that is based on the MVC architecture used in the J2EE environment and also takes use of the implementation framework WAF presented in [6]. It extends the view component in the architecture with support of navigational logic by adding "Navigational Node" in between selection of view component and generation of the deliverable page. In this way the computation part of the application is incorporated with the traditional navigation part of web applications. It did not impose essential changes to the architecture and implementation framework in [6] in the aspect of computing.

7   Conclusion

In this paper we have presented an architecture for software like web-based applications. We illustrated the process how we derived this architecture along with discussion on the specialty introduced by the web. This architecture is specifically aimed at enforcing the modularity of web-based applications and reconciling the uniqueness of web-based applications and the expertise we have in development of traditional applications. We have implemented application on different platforms based on this architecture and are moving on to issues related to supporting more complex applications in terms of concurrency. At the same time we are investigating approaches to integrating this architecture with existing requirement engineering and conceptual design methodologies at the higher level and methodologies on analysis of web-based applications at the architecture level.

References

1. Preuner, G., and Schrefl, M., A Three-Level Schema Architecture for the Conceptual Design of Web-Based Information Systems: From Web-Data Management to Integrated Web-Data and Web-Process Management, World Wide Web Journal, Special Issue on World Wide Web Data Management, Vol. 3, No. 2, Baltzer Science Publishers, pp. 125–138, (2000)
2. Deshpande, Y., Murugesan, S., Ginige, A., Hansen, S., chewabe, D., Gaedke, M., and White, B., A Software Architecture for Structuring Complex Web Applications, Journal of Web Engineering, Vol. 1, No.1 (2002) 003-017
3. Zhao, W., and Kearney, D., Architectures of Web Based Applications, in Proceedings of 4th Australasian Workshop on Software and Systems Architectures (February 2002), http://www.dstc.monash.edu.au/awsa2002/papers/Zhao.pdf
4. Garlan, D. and Shaw M., An Introduction to Software Architecture, Advances in Software Engineering and Knowledge Engineering, Vol. 1, World Scientific Publishing Co., 1993
5. Lockemann, P., Database Systems Architecture: A Study in Factor-Driven Software System Design, in Proceedings of the 13th International Conference on Advanced Information Systems Engineering (CAiSE 2001), Lecture Notes in Computer Science, Vol.2068 (2001), Springer, pp. 13–35
6. Singh, I., Stearns, B., Johnson, M., and Enterprise Team, Designing Enterprise Applications J2EE, ISBN: 0201702770, Addison Wesley, (June 2002) 2nd edition
7. Three-levels Server-side MVC architecture, June 2000, uidesign.net, http://www.uidesign.net/1999/papers/webmvc_part1.html
8. Buschemann, F., Meunier, R., Rohnert, H., Sommerlad, P., and Stal, M., Pattern Oriented Software Architecture: A System of Patterns, John Wiley & Sons, 1996
9. Jacyntho, M., Schewabe, D., and Rossi, G., A Software Architecture for Structuring Complex Web Applications, Journal of Web Engineering, Vol. 1, No.1 (2002) 037–060
10. Sadoski, D., and Comella-Dorda, S., Three Tier Software Architectures, http://www.sei.cmu.edu/str/descriptions/threetier.html
11. JavaTM 2 Platform, Enterprise Edition (J2EE™) web site, Sun Microsystems, Inc. http://java.sun.com/j2ee/
12. PHP web site. http://www.php.net
13. Apache Struts web site. http://jakarta.apache.org/struts/
14. Barracuda web site. http://barracuda.enhydra.org/cvs_source/Barracuda/
15. OMG's CORBA web site, http://www.corba.org
16. DCOM's web site, http://www.microsoft.com/com/tech/DCOM.asp

A New Agent Framework with Behavior Delegation Using SOAP

Ki-Hwa Lee[1], Eui-Hyun Jung[2], Hang-Bong Kang[3], and Yong-Jin Park[1]

[1] Network Computing Lab., Hanyang University, 17,Haengdang-dong,
Sungdong-Ku, Seoul, Korea
{khlee, park}@nclab.hyu.ac.kr
[2] Smart Card Technology Inc., 17, Haengdang-dong,
Sungdong-Ku, Seoul, Korea
ehjung@sct.co.kr
[3] Dept of Computer Eng., The Catholic University, #43-1 Yokkok 2-dong,
Wonmi-Gu, Puchon City, Kyonggi-do, Korea
hbkang@catholic.ac.kr

Abstract. The functional extension of intelligent agents has been a difficult problem because typical software should be edited and recompiled when it needs modifications or replacements in functions after launching. To extend agent's functions dynamically, it is desirable to separate functions from the agent's hard-coded source. In this paper, we propose a new agent framework based on the concept of behavior delegation. We design a new behavior description language, called BDL, for users to assemble agent functions without programming. All behaviors in agent are executed on external server using SOAP. Proposed BDL editor provides users with easy way to assemble agent applications. An example, called Intelligence Price Finder, is implemented to show the use of proposed BDL and the editor.

1 Introduction

Rapid growth of the Internet has given users an easy way of accessing information and services. However, users sometimes have faced the information overload problem [1]. To deal with the information overload problem, it is desirable to use intelligent agents because they have an ability to process the information effectively without human intervention [2].

Typically an intelligent agent should be autonomous and have the properties such as adaptability, reactivity and proactivity [3]. Among these features, adaptability is one of the most important properties because an agent should be able to extend and modify its intelligence and functions dynamically depending on its environment in dealing with information overload problem. Most researches in the agent's adaptability have mainly focused on the enhancement of agent intelligence not on functional extension [4].

In general, the functional extension of an agent is not an easy task because agent functions are hard-coded in the agent's source code [5]. To extend an

X. Zhou, Y. Zhang, and M.E. Orlowska (Eds.): APWeb 2003, LNCS 2642, pp. 313–323, 2003.

agent's function, the agent's code should be edited and recompiled in the source code level. Even though some solutions are proposed using genetic programming [6], they still have complex development process.

In this paper, we propose a new intelligent agent framework in which agents delegate their functions to the external servers using Simple Object Access Protocol (SOAP) and eXtensible Markup Language (XML). Behavior Description Language (BDL) is designed to handle an agent's functions and is used in writing XML documents. In the proposed framework, users can assemble their agent functions at starting time or on runtime using external XML documents. The proposed framework also provides agents with enormous function adaptability without complex development process. Since functions are not hard-coded in agents, they are easily replaced and modified in the proposed system.

The paper is organized as follows. Section 2 discusses existing binary binding mechanisms to describe the method of extending software without code modification. Section 3 addresses our proposed system and Behavior Description Language (BDL) defined for agent's decision. Section 4 presents an example, "Intelligent Price Finder", developed in our proposed agent framework.

2   Functional Extension Methods in Agents

Several methods have been suggested to extend running code's functions in software engineering. In this section, we will briefly discuss these methods.

2.1   Dynamic Linking Library

Dynamic Linking Library (DLL) is a standardized way of extending running code's functions [7]. The DLL can be loaded and connected to calling process whenever it is needed. However, the calling process must contain the functional prototype provided with the DLL to connect it dynamically. This makes software to extend its functions only through predefined functional prototype, so this leads to the restriction of functional extension. Remote Method Invocation (RMI) and Common Object Broker Architecture (CORBA) have also similar mechanism to DLL except using stub. Although they have a dynamic binding mechanism, it is needed to load proper interfaces in the code level.

2.2   SOAP and Invocation Framework

The SOAP provides a way of communication between processes on heterogeneous computing platforms using XML for information exchange [8]. It is somewhat similar to the Internet Inter-ORB Protocol (IIOP) that is a part of the CORBA, and RMI protocol except binding mechanism. The SOAP has been approved as a promising protocol for the Web Services [9]. In the Web Services, text-based binding information, called Web Services Description Language (WSDL) files, describes binding information such as parameter, protocol, host address, and etc.

There are two ways of SOAP invocation: static and dynamic. In static invocation, the generation of stub is an important process and the stub has to be compiled with calling process code. This kind of invocation is similar to the conventional static binding and has the same limitation. As compared with this, dynamic invocation needs no compilation cycle in generating stubs. It just takes parameters described in WSDL files and then calls the SOAP binding using those parameters. To achieve dynamic invocation in the code, Invocation Framework (IF) has been proposed [10,11]. Whenever applications delegate SOAP calling, the IF initiates SOAP-binding after loading given WSDL files and invokes specific operation defined in WSDL files. Using the IF, applications don't need to be recompiled, but just know calling parameters when new WSDL files are added or existing WSDL files are modified.

2.3   Proposed Design

The IF is a desirable method to separate calling codes and called functions in software engineering. However, there are some technical challenges in adopting the IF to the intelligent agent because the IF is just a mechanism to call functions. First of all, agents don't know why and when they call SOAP message. Although binding information is described in the WSDL file, it doesn't help agent's decision for action. So, additional information should be given to agent to make a decision. Secondly, typical agent's task cannot be performed with simply one SOAP call, but may be logically composed of several SOAP calls. The structural information of SOAP calls cannot be described in WSDL files.

To cope with these problems, we propose a new framework in which a number of features are provided. First, the agent framework should separate an agent's functions from an agent using SOAP bindings. In addition, new information schema including WSDL information is designed for an agent's action. The designed schema has a flow control mechanism in which several functions for one task can be expressed.

3   Architecture

In this section, we describe our proposed system architecture. The proposed system consists of agent framework, BDL document, and external behavior server.

3.1   System Component

The components and internal action flows of proposed agent framework are shown in Fig. 1.

Agent Core. Each agent in the agent framework has a form of Agent Core, which loads BDL files and decides when and how to invoke functions according to an agent's environment. Since Agent Core is the base class for all agent applications, it should be customized for each application's need and intelligent activity.

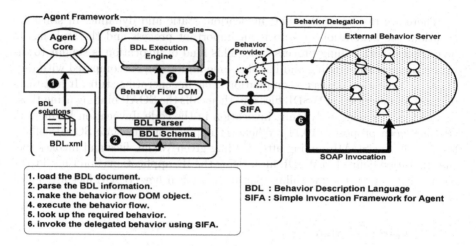

Fig. 1. Agent Framework Architecture

BDL Document. Each function is modeled as "behavior" that describes the information for execution and binding information. These behavior descriptions and flow information are grouped as a "solution". Typically one BDL document for an agent can contain several solutions.

Behavior Execution Engine. Agent Core has its own Behavior Execution Engine (BEE) that parses agent's BDL document and composes behavior flow Document Object Model (DOM), and executes behaviors according to behavior flows described in BDL document.

Behavior Provider. When the BEE needs to invoke real functions, it requests these functions to Behavior Provider (BP) which uses a Simple Invocation Framework for Agent (SIFA) implemented to support dynamic SOAP binding for connecting external Behavior Server (BS). The BS maintains real functions corresponding to behaviors and can service SOAP requests from the BP.

3.2   BDL Schema

BDL is a description language to express the delegated behavior and behavior flow information for the proposed agent framework. Although delegated behaviors are executed on external servers and described in WSDL document, agent system requires information about when the delegated behaviors are called and how the delegated behaviors are composed. This requirement is accomplished by BDL description. There are four types of schemas, which are Port components, Behavior component, I/O components and Flow Control components.

Port components. Port components are attached modules. They present additional I/O information for other BDL component. There are "InPort", "OutPort", "ExInPort", and "ExOutPort" in Port components symbols as shown in Fig. 2. InPort and OutPort define parameter information used for connecting BDL components in BDL description. InPort accepts data and delivers them to its attached BDL component. OutPort publishes data from its attached BDL component to other BDL component's InPort.

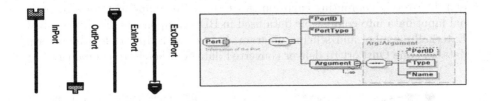

Fig. 2. Port components' symbols and its schema diagram

ExInPort and ExOutPort provide the communication path between the agent framework and external computing actors like I/O devices. Since these ports provide the inter-operability between the agent framework and external I/O, agent developers can make the customized external I/O as long as they satisfy the corresponding interface.

Behavior component. Behavior component is a basic component designed to express one behavioral unit. As shown in Fig. 3, Behavior component has one InPort and OutPort to connect other components in the BDL document. Real function of the Behavior component is delegated to the external servers using SOAP binding. Since delegated services are accomplished by the Web Services, Behavior component has the information about the WSDL location and Web Services operation name for the delegated behavior.

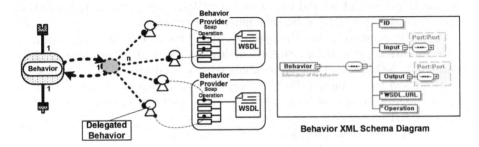

Fig. 3. Behavior component's symbol and its schema diagram

At the Behavior execution time, InPort converts input data to the request message of the Web Services operation and, then the BP invokes the delegated behavior using the SIFA. After completion of behavior execution, OutPort collects the response message from the Web Services operation and delivers them to other components' InPort.

I/O components. I/O components connect external I/O to other BDL components. "ExternalIn" and "ExternalOut" provide channels between an agent and its external computing environment. ExternalIn component converts external input data into compatible data used in BDL components. Fig. 4-(a) shows ExternalIn symbol and schema diagram. It has one ExInPort for the external data and one OutPort to deliver converted data to other BDL components.

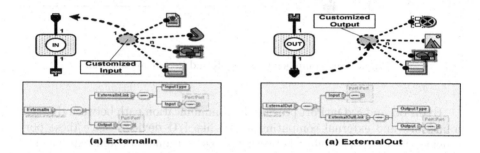

Fig. 4. I/O components's symbols and their schema diagrams

ExternalOut component has the opposite role of ExternalIn. Fig. 4-(b) shows ExternalOut symbol and schema diagram. It also has a mapping mechanism of how the inner data in the agent are mapped onto external data.

Flow Control components. Flow Control components control the flow of behaviors in agents. They are "SourceBar", "SyncBar" and "Branch". SourceBar component launches new execution path. It delivers one input data to several output ports for parallelism. Fig. 5-(a) shows SourceBar symbol and schema diagram. It has one InPort and two or more OutPorts. After executing SourceBar, execution paths are divided into the number of OutPorts.

SyncBar component has the opposite role of SourceBar. It aggregates multiple execution paths using attached multiple InPorts and synchronized these paths. Fig. 5-(b) shows SyncBar symbol and schema diagram. SyncBar has one OutPort and two or more InPorts. Whenever a BDL component needs multiple inputs from different execution paths, SyncBar synchronizes execution until all data are arrived.

Branch component provides behavior flow such as loop or branches using its condition. It seems like switch syntax in programming language. Fig. 5-(c) shows Branch symbol and schema diagram. It has one InPort and at least two or more OutPorts. When InPort accepts data, the Branch component judges the matched condition for input data, and then selects appropriate flow. Branch can only select one OutPort at a time according to internal condition unlike other flow components.

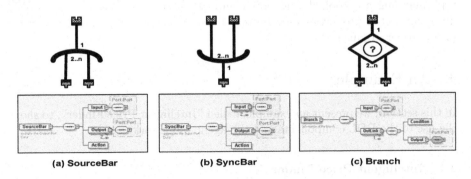

| (a) SourceBar | (b) SyncBar | (c) Branch |

Fig. 5. Flow Control components' symbols and their schema diagrams

3.3   BDL Editor

Since it is not easy for an XML expert to make BDL documents from scratch, we provide a graphical BDL editor. The BDL editor enables users to assemble behaviors expressed in WSDL documents at design time. As shown in Fig. 6, all components and relations between them are generated to proper BDL documents. By using Computer Aided Design (CAD) style BDL editor, whole design process can be simplified.

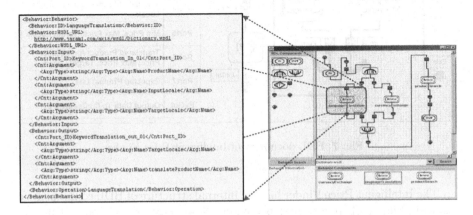

Fig. 6. Relation between BDL diagram and generated document

In the BDL editor, users may select behavior, port and flow control components from behavior palette and drag & drop the components to the editing workspace. In the behavior palette, users can add behaviors dynamically using proper WSDL files' URL. Components on the workspace can be connected with related components using rubber band lines anytime. However, restrictions from type mapping are applied whenever components are connected. In the procedure, connected properties may be set. These properties are used for BEE to make proper arguments.

4   An Example

In this section, we present an example, called "Intelligent Price Finder", to show the use of the BDL components and the agent framework.

4.1   Intelligent Price Finder

A lot of search engines have been developed to find products in the Web. However, the main concern of these search engines is to retrieve exact results without providing additional intelligence such as language translation of the product name or currency exchange of the product price. Proposed Intelligence Price Finder performs multi-locale search only using product name and price given locale.

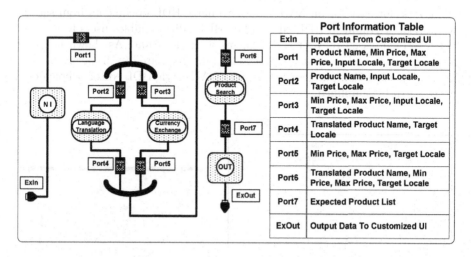

Port Information Table	
ExIn	Input Data From Customized UI
Port1	Product Name, Min Price, Max Price, Input Locale, Target Locale
Port2	Product Name, Input Locale, Target Locale
Port3	Min Price, Max Price, Input Locale, Target Locale
Port4	Translated Product Name, Target Locale
Port5	Min Price, Max Price, Target Locale
Port6	Translated Product Name, Min Price, Max Price, Target Locale
Port7	Expected Product List
ExOut	Output Data To Customized UI

Fig. 7. BDL document of Intelligent Price Finder

The Intelligent Price Finder has the internal structure of BDL components as shown in Fig. 7. There are three behaviors, "Language Translation", "Currency Exchange", and "Product Search" in the given BDL document. After loading these BDL documents, the agent takes user data about the product information through the customized UI. ExternalIn component converts the external input data into internal BDL data and delivers them through Port1.

At source bar, the execution paths are divided into Port2 and Port3. At Port2, data from Port1 flow into Language Translation behavior. Port3 injects the data from Port1 to Currency Exchange behavior. Language Translation behavior translates the product name into target locale name and delivers it to Port4. Currency Exchange behavior also executes currency exchange for target locale currency and delivers it to Port5. SyncBar aggregates data from the Port4 and Port5 and delivers it to Port6. Product Search behavior searches product information using input data which were changed and translated. Finally, ExternalOut translates data from Port7 and delivers it to external customized UI. Fig. 8 shows the usage of our BDL editor in designing of Intelligent Price Finder's BDL document. In the BDL editor, users can load behaviors from the Internet using WSDL location URL. These loaded behaviors are added to the behavior palettes dynamically.

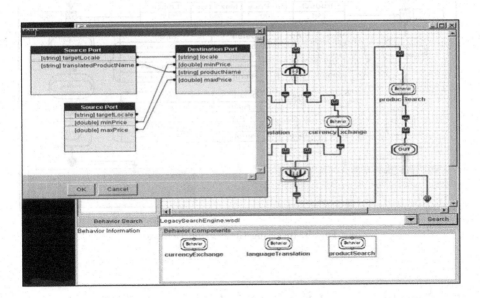

Fig. 8. Design process in BDL editor

4.2 Evaluation

The developing process of agent applications using our proposed framework is quite simple. As shown in our Intelligent Price Finder, new application can be easily assembled with existing functions and simple BDL document. For an Intelligent Price Finder, users write only BDL document for the application using given BDL editor. After completion of the BDL document, the framework loads it and starts to make a new agent instance of Intelligent Price Finder. To test the functional extension that we assume, a new behavior is added to the existing BDL document. Added behavior is "Sorting" that provides sorting function with user's preference. This behavior is inserted into Port7. The modified Intelligent Price Finder is well performed without recompiling and modifying its agent's source after inserting the sorting behavior. Fig. 9 shows the result when the Sorting behavior is inserted into the BDL document. While the previous Intelligent Price Finder has obtained unsorted results, new one shows the sorted result according to the price order.

The proposed framework has provided a new approach of functional extension in software agent system. Besides, the framework can easily integrate various functions made by other developer without knowing of programming languages. It also contributes to increase the reusability of the agent function.

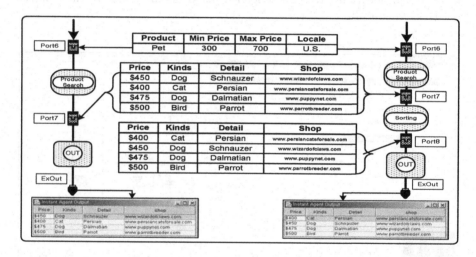

Fig. 9. Inserting the Sorting Behavior

5   Conclusion and Future Work

The functional extension of an Intelligent Agent has been a difficult problem because typical software should be edited and recompiled if it needs modification or replacement of functions after launching. To extend an agent's functions dynamically, the functions should be separated from the agent's hard-coded source. We adopt SOAP dynamic binding mechanism to solve this issue and implemented SIFA to make a SOAP dynamic binding in the agent's code. SIFA makes the delegated function to be loosely coupled with the agent system. In this architecture, agent's functions are delegated and executed on the external server through SOAP.

BDL schema is designed to describe agent's behavior information and flows. It can hold all information related to agent execution. Using BDL schema, agent developers simply make their own agent application without programming. Another advantage of the framework is function reusability in the agent community.

In the future, we will work on Dynamic Function Locating (DFL) using Universal Description, Discovery and Integration (UDDI) [8,11]. The DFL provides agents with finding proper functions automatically.

References

1. Mates, P. : Agents that Reduce Work and Information Overload, CACM, Vol. 37, no. 7, pp.31–40 (1994)
2. Wooldridge, M. : Agent-based software engineering, IEE Proc. on Software Engineering, Vol. 144, no. 1, pp.26–37 (1997)
3. Hermans, B. : Intelligent Software Agents on the Internet: an inventory of currently offered functionality in the information society & prediction of (near-) future developments, Thesis, Tilburg University, Tilburg, The Netherlands (1996)
4. Sloman, A. : What sort of architecture is required for a human-like agent?, Cognitive Modeling Workshop, Aug. (1996)
5. Nicholas, R., Jennings. : A Roadmap of Agent Research and Development, Autonomous Agents and Multi-Agent Systems, pp. 7–38 (1998)
6. Banzhaf, W. : Genetic Programming, Morgan Kaufman Publishers, Inc. (1998).
7. Introducing Dynamic Link Libraries, http://webclub.kcom.ne.jp/ma/colinp/win32/dll/ intro.html
8. Jepsen, T. : SOAP cleans up interoperability problems on the Web", IT professional, Vol.3 no.1, pp.52–55 (2001)
9. Curbera, F., Duftler, M. : Unraveling the Web Services Web : an introduction to SOAP, WSDL, and UDDI. ,IEEE Internet computing, Vol.6 no.2, pp.86–93 (2002)
10. Matthew J.D. , Nirmal, K. Mukhi : Web Services Invocation Framework (WSIF), OOPSLA 2001 workshop on Object-Oriented Web Services
11. Harshal, D. : The need for a dynamic invocation framework, http://www.webservices.org/index.php/article /articleview/469
12. UDDI White Page, http://www.uddi.org/whitepapers.html

Improving the Web Presentation Layer Architecture

Dirk Draheim, Elfriede Fehr, and Gerald Weber

Institute of Computer Science
Free University Berlin
Germany
{draheim,fehr,weber}@inf.fu-berlin.de

Abstract. In this paper we provide a discussion of the Model 2 architecture for web interface programming. We show how the main purpose of Model 2, namely separation of concerns, can be achieved solely by functional decomposition. Enabling technology for this is NSP, a typed, composable server pages technology. The chosen approach is seamlessly integrated with Form-Oriented Analysis.

1 Introduction

Web application frameworks are used for building presentation layers in multi-tiered web-enabled applications. In this paper we review current web application frameworks based on the Model 2 approach. Special attention is paid to the proposed composition mechanisms within the frameworks. Afterwards we show, how certain problems can be overcome by our own approach, NSP.

In section 2 we outline the driving forces for web application frameworks as they have been proposed and explain the Model 2 architecture used in these framework. In section 3 we give our own analysis of the problem domain addressed by the Model 2 architecture and evaluate the current approaches. We will critically reflect on the current practice to use system architecture as a means of implementing processing/presentation separation. In section 4 we give an overview of NSP, an improved server page technology, and outline how it can be used for building well-designed presentation layers. Finally we give in section 5 an outline of Form-Oriented Analysis.

2 Web Application Frameworks

Server pages are HTML pages with embedded script code. In practice the tight coupling of code with layout has become a drawback for server pages. Therefore, separation of business logic processing and presentation generation, called processing/presentation separation in the following for short, has become a goal.

We focus in the following on Java as a scripting language. In the discussion on how to reach processing/presentation separation, Sun has become influential by proposing several server side architectures, especially the "redirecting request" application model, later coined as "Model 2 architecture" [10].

Model 2 web application frameworks target separation of presentation, content and logic. Further objectives of these web application frameworks can be integration with

X. Zhou, Y. Zhang, and M.E. Orlowska (Eds.): APWeb 2003, LNCS 2642, pp. 324–332, 2003.

enterprise application frameworks, rapid development by providing an integrated development environment, support for internationalization, support for security, or support for dynamic form field validation. A prominent commercial Model 2 web application framework is the Sun ONE Application Framework (JATO) [12]. The most widespread application servers according to [11], namely Oracle9iAs, IBM WebSphere, and BEA WebLogic, come along with Model 2 Web application frameworks, too. WebMacro [14] is an early open source project that allows the separation between Java and HTML. Other prominent open source web application frameworks are Struts [9] and Cocoon [2] - both hosted by the Jakarta project. Wafer (Web Application Research Project) [13] is a research project that collects, investigates and compares existing open source web application frameworks.

The Model 2 architecture uses a threepart design in which the request is first directed to a front component, typically a servlet, which triggers the creation of a content object, typically a Java bean (Figure 1). The bean is then passed to a presentation component, typically a scripted server page where the data within the bean is embedded in HTML. Webmacro uses server pages with a special interpreted scripting language different from Java while other approaches rely on Java Server Pages. In Model 2, processing/presentation separation is achieved by using the server pages for presentation purposes only. The Struts framework is widely accepted as the reference implementation of the Model 2 architecture. Struts proposes an interaction between the code components based on a proprietary approach in which business processing units do inform the controller object about the next processing step. Parameter passing between processing units is not established by the Java method parameter passing mechanism, but by emulating a parameter passing mechanism through transferring bean objects.

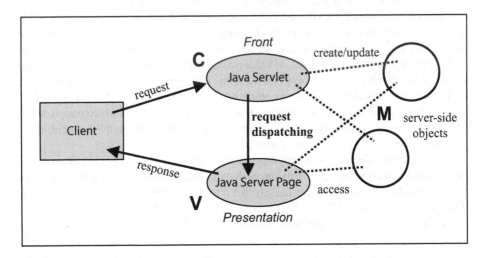

Fig. 1. Model 2 architecture.

3   Request Processing for Web Applications

For the evaluation of Model 2 frameworks we first develop a description of the required behavior of a web application framework. Web applications are used in a submit/response style [15]. The server system is only contacted if the user submits a form or uses a link. The browser of the user then waits for a response page. In the browser of the user this leads to a page change. The complete old page is replaced by the response page, which is completely parsed and rendered. This interaction style is fundamentally different from interaction in GUI's, in fact with respect to presentation HTML interfaces are arguably rather simple. In that regard web presentation layers are similar to presentation layers for traditional transaction processing systems based on mainframe architectures [1]. The processing of a single request (called server action) can be performed in an input/processing/output style. After the user request has been received, the system state may be updated, then information necessary for the page generation has to be gathered from the business logic tiers, then from this information the output page has to be generated. We will later argue that simple functional decomposition as it is achieved with subprograms is fully sufficient for this task. Accordingly, the standard parameter passing mechanisms for programming languages are the appropriate communication mechanism between the components during a server action.

3.1   Misconception of the Model View Controller Paradigm

It is important to clarify a serious misunderstanding in architecture proposals for web site development, namely that web application frameworks following the Model 2 approach do not follow the Model View Controller paradigm. Model View Controller [8] was introduced in Smalltalk for GUI programming and is a completely different concept. It only has superficial similarities in that it has three components from which one is related to the user interface, another to the application. However, the problem solved by the MVC paradigm is totally different. MVC is related to event notification problems within a GUI that provides different views on the same data, which have to be synchronized. MVC is renamed within the pattern community as observer pattern [6]. The misnomer is even more astounding if one considers that the property of GUI's which makes MVC necessary, namely view update, i.e. push technology, is well known to be absent in the pull based approach of HTML interfaces.

The fact that Model 2 web application frameworks rely on a misconception of the MVC paradigm does not necessarily imply that these frameworks have a bad design. But the argument for this architecture, namely that it follows a proven good design, is flawed. Only by recognizing that this argument is invalid the way is free for a new evaluation of the architecture and a recognition of advantages as well as drawbacks.

3.2   Component Interaction in the Model 2 Architecture

The Model 2 architecture defines a fixed decomposition combined with an intended separation of concerns. The incoming request is processed in the front component, then a response page is created in the presentation component. The difficulty with the approach lies not in the proposals for separation of concerns, but in the composition mechanism offered. The question is, which semantics governs the interplay between the components.

The Model 2 architecture offers a complex communication mechanism based on the passing of beans. Beans are attached to a hashtable by the generating unit and retrieved from the hashtable by the target unit. In that way data is transmitted from the servlet to the scripted page. This mechanism is semantically nothing more than a parameter passing mechanism, but without static type safety. The semantics of the composition paradigms of presentation and business logic is only conceivable by direct reference to the runtime architecture, i.e. to the components found in the running system. In contrast, we will later use our NSP approach, where simple method call semantics is sufficient and allows for a sound architecture. Hence in the Model 2 architecture a considerable part of the architecture redefines a parameter passing mechanism which delivers no added value beyond method invocation. It is rather a workaround for the problem, that Server Pages have no typesafe parameter mechanism.

4   Statically Typed Server Pages

The aforementioned problems can be overcome by using the statically typed server page technology NSP (Next Server Pages) [5][4]. NSP offers a procedure call semantics for server pages which views every server page as a strongly typed procedure. Server pages can call each other. The NSP method call mechanism has identical semantics as the Java method call with respect to parameter passing. It is the only composition feature that is needed to build sound and well understood web presentation layers. NSP can be seen as generalization of another approach of the JSP specification, named "including requests" [10]. NSP as a language is realized as a set of XML tags. Therefore NSP documents are well formed XML documents.

4.1   Type System for Server Pages

The NSP approach is derived from the following basic considerations about client/server interaction in web applications. In web interfaces, server requests are triggered by the user following a link or submitting a form. In the case of submitting a form, the contents of the input fields are sent together with the command to the server. Hence submission of a form can be seen as a method call with a parameter list to the server. In web applications links can be used to submit parameters in the same manner. Hence all user interaction with the server, regardless of via links or forms, can be seen as remote method calls by the user. However, the HTTP request is an untyped remote method call. NSP starts with offering a static typing mechanism for client/server communication. The parameters of a server page can be specified in a type system which allows primitive as well as user-defined types. User defined types can be lists, records, and combinations thereof. NSP offers a static type check which is performed on the complete collection of server pages for a web application. Such a collection is called an NSP collection. The static type check compares forms with the server page that is called by the form and checks whether the signature of both do match. The static type check works even for server pages which demand complex types, e.g. a user defined record. In this case, an input field for each primitive typed element of the record must be provided. One of the most advanced features of the NSP type check is that it works even in server pages which use control structures. This is achieved by the so called NSP coding rules.

The parameters provided by the request are presented to the script in the page in the native types of the language. NSP consequently enforces the view that server pages are strongly typed functions in the scripting language. NSP even offers advanced widgets, which perform client side type checks and allow to specify declarative concepts like required form fields.

4.2   Functional Decomposition of Server Pages

The HTML output generated by a server page can be seen as a special return value concept. In a further project formal semantics for this concept will be given. It should be noted that the page output cannot be further processed within most of the server page mechanism. Once textual output is generated, filters and stylesheets are the more adequate solution for further processing. Hence, good practice coincides here with the restrictions of the server page concept. However, there is still need for functional decomposition on the server side. The developer should be able to create separate server pages which provide commonly used elements of several pages and reuse these pages. This desired behavior can be interpreted within the paradigm of special return values: if one server page calls another server page, this automatically implies that the special return value of the callee is textually included into the special return value of the caller and cannot be used in any other way by the caller. In NSP other pages can be called from a page with a special tag. Such calls follow the semantics just described with respect to the output.

The example in Listing 1 shows the implementation of a login dialogue. The dialogue starts with a login page. The customer enters her user identification and her password. If she enters a wrong combination of user identification and password, an error page shows up, which contains an error message and again the login capability. Otherwise the respective user is welcome. The form of the Login page targets the Validate page. The Validate page has two parameters userid and passwd. It is checked at compile time, if the form in its entirety matches the type of the targeted server page. In the Validate page, the WelcomeCustomer page or the Error page is called. Like form input capabilities, an actual parameter of a call explicitly targets a formal parameter by referencing its name.

NSP allows for arbitrary application architectures based on the NSP functional decomposition. NSP frees the developer from considering the implementation details of the parameter passing mechanisms. Hence all special runtime architecture which is needed in NSP to deliver the method call semantics is hidden from the developer. Processing/presentation separation is in the first place a pattern for source code organization. NSP allows to solve the challenges in processing/presentation separation without considering system architecture. Instead in NSP the functional decomposition mechanism allows for the desired separation of concerns.

Listing 1 Example NSP dialogue

```
<nsp name="Login" kind="presentation">
  <html>
    <head><title>Login</title></head>
    <body>
      <form callee="Validate">
          <input type="String" param="userid"></input>
          <input type="String" param="passwd"></input>
          <submit></submit>
      </form>
    </body>
  </html>
</nsp>

<nsp name="Validate" kind="business">
  <param type="String" name="userid"></param>
  <param type="String" name="passwd"></param><java>
  import myBusinessModel.CustomerBase;
  if (! (CustomerBase.validLogin(userid,passwd))){</java>
    <call callee="Error"></call><java>
  } else {
    String cn=CustomerBase.getCustomerName(userid);</java>
    <call callee="WelcomeCustomer">
      <actparam param="customer"> cn </actparam>
    </call><java>
  }</java>
</nsp>

<nsp name="WelcomeCustomer" kind="presentation">
  <param type="String" name="customer"/></param>
  <html>
    <head><title>Welcome</title></head>
    <body>
      Hello Mr. <javaexp>customer</javaexp> !
      ...
    </body>
  </html>
</nsp>

<nsp name="Error" kind="presentation">
  ...
</nsp>
```

In JSP, parameter passing to a JSP differs fundamentally whether the JSP is called across the net or called on the server side. In the first case, parameters come as raw string data, as it is inherited from the CGI model. However, if a server page is called locally, it is established coding practice to pass the parameters by a bean object attached to the request parameter. Hence, a page must be designed either to be callable form the net or to be callable from the server and in both cases the developer has to face a parameter passing mechanism different from any usual parameter passing mechanism. Also the combination of the JSP actions `jsp:include` and `jsp:param` does not provide a usual type-safe parameter passing mechanism, it just provides a convenient notation for the low level Java Servlet include mechanism.

Figure 2 shows a typical control and data flow in a Model 2 architecture system up to details of request dispatching and the improvement of a counterpart system build on NSP technology.

5   Form-Oriented Analysis

NSP can be seamlessly integrated with Form-Oriented Analysis [15][3], an analysis method specifically designed for submit/response style systems. In Form-Oriented Analysis we model such a submit/response style application as a bipartite state machine, which alternates between presenting a page to the user and processing the data submitted by the user. This bipartite state machine is depicted in the key artifact of Form-Oriented Analysis, the form chart. Form-Oriented Analysis describes then, how to annotate this bipartite state machine with constraints, which specify the behavior of the system.

The bipartite state machine describing the system is alternating between two kinds of states. The first kind of states corresponds to the pages of the system as before. These states are called client pages, they are depicted by rounded rectangles. The system remains in such a client page state until the user triggers a page change. In that moment the record with her previous input is sent to the system. The system then switches into one state of the second partition. Such states represent the systems action in response to a submit and are therefore called server actions. These states are left automatically by the system and lead to a new client page.

Form-Oriented Analysis yields a complete and executable system specification. Form-Oriented Analysis leads directly over to system implementation with NSP. The server actions in the form chart will become NSP business components, while the client pages will become presentation components.

6   Conclusion

A research study [7] conducted by the Gartner Group has shown that more than three-quarter of the cost of building an e-commerce site is labor related. Consequently improving the web presentation layer architecture is important.

Our analysis of web application frameworks based on the Model 2 architecture has shown:

- The subsumption of these frameworks under the Model View Controller paradigm is flawed and based on a misunderstanding of Model View Controller.
- Within these frameworks a separation of concerns can be reached and the content parts as well as the presentation parts can be placed in different code units.

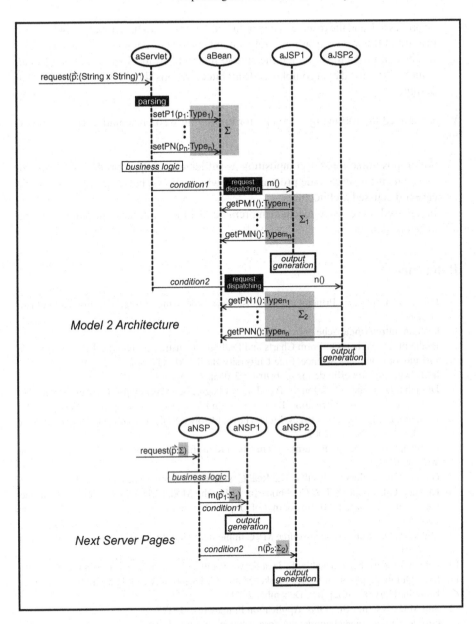

Fig. 2. Model 2 architecture versus NSP technology.

- The composition mechanism used for combining the different code units is proprietary and based on consideration of the runtime object structure of the system. No abstraction layer has been reached.
- The Model 2 approach unfolds complex architecture at a place where architecture is certainly not needed. Page request handling is simple: a request is fully received, can

be processed, and the result can be produced. This allows a functional decomposition in a straightforward way as it is rarely possible in today's complex system landscape. If a design problem for which the simple method call mechanism is the adequate solution is realized by a complex code architecture, this should be considered as bad design.

We recognized the following as crucial for improving web presentation layer architecture:

- We propose functional decomposition as sufficient and appropriate decomposition mechanism for server side programming, which allows, but is not restricted to the earlier discussed architectures.
- In the used server page mechanism, remote and local call have the same style, but different semantics.

References

1. Philip A. Bernstein. Principles of Transaction Processing. Morgan Kaufmann Publishers,1997.
2. Cocoon. http://xml.apache.org/cocoon/
3. Draheim, D., Weber, G.: Form Charts and Dialogue Constraints. Technical Report B-02-08, Institute of Computer Science, Free University Berlin, March 2002
   http://www.inf.fu-berlin.de/inst/pubs/tr-b-02-08.abstract.html
4. Draheim, D., Weber, G.: Strongly Typed Server Pages. In: Proceedings of The Fifth Workshop on Next Generation Information Technologies and Systems, LNCS. Springer-Verlag, 2002.
5. Draheim, D., Typed Server Pages, Ph.D-Thesis, October 2002. Institute of Computer Science, Free University Berlin, 2002.
6. Gamma, E. et al. Design Patterns – Elements of Reusable Object-Oriented Software. Addison-Wesley, 1995.
7. Gartner Group. Survey Results: The Real Cost of E-Commerce Sites. Gartner Group, 1999.
8. Krasner, G.E., Pope, S.T. A Cookbook for Using the Model-View-Controller User Interface Paradigm in Smalltalk-80. In: Journal of Object-Oriented Programming, August/September 1988 26–49
9. Malcolm, D. Struts, an open-source MVC implementation. In: IBM developerWorks, February 2001.
10. Pelegri-Llopart, E.; and Cable, L. Java Server Pages Specification, v.1.1. Sun Press, 1999.
11. Evan Quinn. Application Server Market Share – A Different Angel. Hurwitz Balanced View Bulletin. Hurwitz Group Inc, December 2001.
12. Sun Microsystems. Sun ONE Application Framework (JATO).
    http://developer.iplanet.com/tech/appserver/framework/index.jsp
13. Wafer – Web Application Research Project.
    http://www.waferproject.org/index.html
14. Webmacro. http://www.webmacro.org/, 2002.
15. Gerald Weber. Semantics of Form-Oriented Analysis. Dissertation. Freie Universität Berlin, October 2002.

An Event Based Approach to Web Service Design and Interaction

Wilfried Lemahieu, Monique Snoeck, Cindy Michiels, and Frank Goethals

Katholieke Universiteit Leuven, Department of Applied Economic Sciences,
Naamsestraat 69, B-3000 Leuven, Belgium
{wilfried.lemahieu, monique.snoeck, cindy.michiels,
frank.goethals}@econ.kuleuven.ac.be

Abstract. This paper advocates an approach to web service design and interaction that is based on web services simultaneously participating in shared *business events*. In contrast to one-to-one method invocations, such events are *broadcast in parallel* to all web services that participate in it. Moreover, the transactional business events are distinguished from non-transactional *attribute inspections*. The paper first discusses the role of the business event concept as the cornerstone for a methodical analysis and design phase. Then, it is shown how the event broadcasting paradigm can be implemented by means of SOAP messaging.

1 Introduction

The advent of the web services paradigm brought about a revolution in the way business partners can integrate their information systems and allows for innovative organizational forms that were unthinkable before. The enabling technology for web service interaction is SOAP [1], which can be seen as a lightweight RPC (Remote Procedure Call) mechanism over the Web. In this way, SOAP resembles distributed object architectures such as DCOM, RMI and CORBA, where interaction consists of objects on different hosts remotely invoking one another's methods. However, these can hardly be used over the Internet because they are too heavyweight and don't cope well with firewalls. SOAP, on the other hand, deals well with firewalls because it allows for remote method invocations and their parameters to be represented as *XML messages*, which are transmitted over "native" Web protocols such as HTTP or SMTP. Web services can then be defined as self-contained software components that expose specific business functionality on the Internet and that allow for heterogeneous information systems to be coupled in a very loose way.

Although the web service concept looks very promising, it hasn't fulfilled its full potential yet. One of the primary reasons may be the fact that XML based RPC is essentially a *one-to-one mechanism*: web service A invokes a method on service B, after which B may or may not send a return value to A. Such mechanism is indeed suitable for simple request/response services, e.g. currency converters, stock information services etc. but is inherently difficult to co-ordinate in a complex transactional environment where numerous business partners interact in shared business processes. One-to-one messaging as a mechanism to co-ordinate processes that are shared by

X. Zhou, Y. Zhang, and M.E. Orlowska (Eds.): APWeb 2003, LNCS 2642, pp. 333–340, 2003.

many parties inevitably results in intricate sequences of message exchanges, over which it becomes nearly impossible to co-ordinate transaction management. Also, whereas traditional LAN/WAN information systems based on distributed object/component architectures such as CORBA, DCOM or RMI/EJB typically resulted from a rigid analysis and design phase, this is often not the case with regard to web services. Frequently, individual services providing some functionality are published without a thorough analysis regarding their position within the business processes and the global information system architecture. Again, such approach is only suitable to isolated request/response services [2].

Therefore, this paper advocates an *event based* approach to web service development. Interaction between services is based on the simultaneous participation in (and processing of) *shared business events*. Such transactional business events are distinguished from (non-transactional) *attribute inspections*. Moreover, events are not propagated one-to-one but are *broadcast* in parallel to all services that have an interest in an event of the corresponding type. The remainder of the paper is structured as follows: in section 2, the concept of business events is used as the basis for a methodical analysis and design phase. Section 3 describes an *implementation* approach for event based interaction between web services by means of SOAP messaging. Conclusions are formulated in section 4.

2 Event Based Analysis and Design

The event based interaction mechanism as proposed in this paper directly reflects an underlying object-oriented analysis and design methodology: MERODE [3; 4]. This method represents an information system through the definition of business events, their effect on enterprise objects and the related business rules. Although it follows an object-oriented approach, it does not rely on message passing to model interaction between domain object classes as in classical approaches to object-oriented analysis. Instead, *business events* are identified as independent concepts. An object-event table (OET) allows defining which types of objects are affected by which types of events. When an object type is involved in an event, a method is required to implement the effect of the event on instances of this type. Whenever an event actually occurs, it is broadcast to all enterprise objects involved.

For example, let us assume that the domain model for an order handling system contains the four object types CUSTOMER, ORDER, ORDER LINE and PRODUCT. The corresponding UML Class diagram is given in Fig. 1. It states that a customer can place 0 to many orders, each order being placed by exactly one customer. Orders consist of 0 to many order lines, each order line referring to exactly one order and one product. Products can appear on 0 to many order lines.

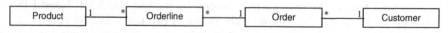

Fig. 1. Domain model for an order handling system

Business event types are e.g. create_customer, modify_customer, create_order, ship_order, etc. The object-event table (see Table 1) shows which object types are affected by which types of events and also indicates the type of involvement: C for creation, M for modification and E for terminating an object's life. For example, create_orderline creates a new occurrence of the class ORDERLINE, modifies an occurrence of the class PRODUCT because it requires adjustment of the stock-level of the ordered product, modifies the state of the ORDER to which it belongs and modifies the state of the CUSTOMER of the order. Full details of how to construct such an object-event table and validate it against the data model and the behavioral model is beyond the scope of this paper but can be found in [3; 4].

The event based data model is combined with a *behavioral model*. Indeed, the enterprise objects are allowed to put *preconditions* on the events in which they participate. Some of these are based on *class invariants*, others on *event sequence constraints* that can be derived from a finite state machine associated with the object type. An example of the finite state machine for an ORDER object is shown in Figure 2. The combined sequence constraints over all object types mimic the general business process(es).

Table 1. Object-event table for the order handling system

	CUSTOMER	ORDER	ORDERLINE	PRODUCT
create_customer	C			
modify_customer	M			
end_customer	E			
create_order	M	C		
modify_order	M	M		
end_order	M	E		
customer_sign	M	M		
ship_order	M	M		
bill	M	M		
create_orderline	M	M	C	M
modify_orderline	M	M	M	M
end_orderline	M	M	E	M
create_product				C
modify_product				M
end_product				E

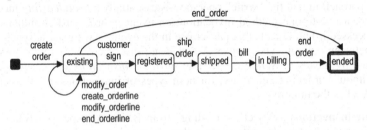

Fig. 2. State machine for an ORDER object

The event concept as described in this section in the first place pertains to the *analysis* and *design* of an information system. The approach allows for the precise identification of an information system's behavior, which is related to real world *business events*. Moreover, the constraints on this behavior can be accurately represented as preconditions imposed by individual enterprise objects. The results from an event-based analysis can be implemented by means of both object-oriented and non-object-oriented technologies. Previously, the main focus was upon implementations where the scope was a standalone system or a LAN based distributed object framework. Even if the applications themselves were distributed, there was always a common *enterprise layer* that contained the "primary copy" of all enterprise objects [5]. The next section discusses how the same approach can also, mutatis mutandis, be applied in a Web environment. It is shown how web services may greatly benefit from an event based approach, at the analysis and design level as well as at the implementation level. In this respect, it is not our goal to come up with a competing mechanism to the current de facto standard web services stack of SOAP, WSDL and UDDI. Instead, the entire approach will be fit into this framework, i.e. event notifications being dispatched as SOAP messages over HTTP.

3 Application of the Event Paradigm to Web Service Interaction

3.1 SOAP as a Mechanism for Event Dispatching

SOAP is a *method based* interaction mechanism: SOAP messages represent remote procedure calls between web objects. Note that initially, we will discuss the interaction between "web objects" in general and use the terms "enterprise objects" and "web services" intermittently. From section 3.2 onwards, we will explicitly distinguish between fine grained *enterprise objects* and coarse grained *web services*. In general, a SOAP-based remote method invocation from object A to object B may have two effects: it may cause a state change in B, i.e. updates to one or more of B's attributes (as part of the *execution* of the method) and it may pass information from B to A (by means of its *return value*). Also, the interaction is essentially one-to-one: between the object that invokes the method and the object on which the method is invoked.

The *event* paradigm differs from the standard RPC approach as applied in SOAP in that the cases of A provoking a state change in B and A retrieving information from B are separated. With an event based approach, a firm distinction can be made between operations (as invoked by A) that "*read from*" attributes in B and that "*write to*" attributes in B. The latter is called the *Command-Query Separation* design principle, which, as discussed in [6], makes software much more transparent and makes classes easier to (re)use. Moreover, the event based paradigm also differs from the standard SOAP approach in that the "write" operation is essentially a *broadcasting* mechanism instead of a one-to-one method invocation: an event is broadcast simultaneously to (and processed in) all objects that participate in the event. Two generic types of interaction between web objects/services A and B are discerned, which will both be implemented by means of SOAP messaging: *attribute inspection* and *event broadcasting*. Without burdening generality, for both types of interactions, we'll assume that object A takes the initiative.

Attribute inspections. Object A "reading" from B, i.e. A inspecting B's attributes, occurs if object A "needs" information that is stored as attribute values in B, e.g. because this information is used by object A to provide output to a human user or to test a precondition. Because the interaction does not cause a state change on either of the two objects, it should not be the subject of transaction contexts. For the same reason, preconditions resulting from class invariants or sequence constraints are not applicable to attribute inspections. SOAP messages that represent attribute inspections are very similar to calling a *getAttribute()* method on an entity Bean in the Enterprise JavaBeans (EJB) framework. Applications or services can call directly upon published *getAttribute()* methods to retrieve data from an entity. Obviously, in a SOAP environment, performance can be boosted if multiple correlated attribute inspections are bundled into a single message exchange. Hence a SOAP message type should be defined for each type of (combined) attribute inspection and for the corresponding return value(s). Figure 3 (left) presents the example of a web service implementing an online retail shop, which, when providing product information to its users, retrieves the detailed product specifications from the respective manufacturers.

Event dispatching. The situation where object A "writes" to B, i.e. causes attribute values in B to be updated, is a bit more complex: because the updates that result from a given business event are to be co-ordinated throughout the entirety of all enterprise objects that participate in the event (the combined updates can be considered as a single transaction), an object should never just *update* individual attributes of another object (in EJB terminology: *setAttribute()* methods should never be published in an entity Bean's public interface). Changes to an object's attributes are only to be induced by generating *business events* that affect the state of all enterprise objects involved in the event. This type of interaction results from an event that occurs in the real world, e.g. a customer issuing a purchase order, a stock dropping below a threshold value, an order being shipped, ... The respective enterprise objects can subscribe to business events that are relevant to them (as denoted in the object event table). This relevancy can exist because their *state* is affected by the event and/or because they entail certain constraints that may decide whether or not the event is allowed to happen at all. These constraints are defined as *preconditions* on the corresponding event type.

An event based interaction paradigm can be implemented by programming languages that incorporate a native "event" construct. However, as applied in our approach, it is also possible to "mimic" event propagation by means of *simultaneous method invocations* on all object instances that participate in a particular event. An object type should have an appropriate method for each event type in which it may be involved. In a SOAP context, the latter is implemented by means of an *event dispatcher* (cf. infra) sending SOAP messages simultaneously to all objects that participate in the event. Such message refers to the method that implements the object's reaction to the event and contains the event's attributes, which are passed as parameters to the invoked method. Hence there will be an XML message type for each event type that may occur and a web object will have a method that implements the object's reaction for each event type in which it may participate. If a relevant event occurs, each participating object receives a SOAP message and executes the corresponding method with the parameters provided in the message. However, in contrast to the "pure" SOAP approach with one-to-one method invocations, these are *simultaneous, coordinated method invocations on several objects*, with each method having the same name, as associated with a particular event type. These methods check constraints pertinent to the corresponding (object type, event type) combination and execute the necessary updates to attributes of that particular object if all constraints are satisfied. If not all constraints are satisfied, an exception is generated.

An example is presented in Figure 3 (right). For instance a *create_orderline* event is broadcast to three web services, each possibly putting constraints on the event and possibly changing its state because of the event. The online *Retail* service checks that the line number is unique and adds the orderline to the appropriate order. The *Manufacturer* service checks whether the ordered product is in stock and adapts its stock level. The *Customer* service checks whether the order's total bill does not exceed a certain amount. The global result of the business event corresponds to the combined method executions in the individual web objects. The transaction is only committed if none of the objects that take part in the event have generated an exception. Otherwise, a rollback is induced[1]. Note that no return values are sent (as is the case with traditional method invocation), other than possibly a status variable for transaction management purposes, i.e. to determine whether the transaction can be committed or should be rolled back.

---

[1] Or, instead of a global rollback, corrective actions are taken. A "hard" commit-or-rollback strategy is often too limiting in a web services context with long-standing transactions.

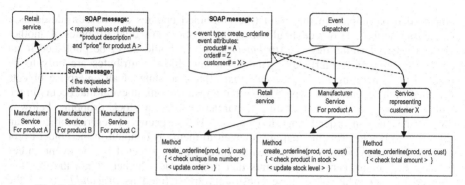

Fig. 3. Examples of attribute inspection and event dispatching between web services

3.2 Staged Event Based Interaction and Explicit Subscription to Remote Events

The interaction mechanism described so far indeed corresponds to event based inter-action over SOAP. This interaction currently takes place between *enterprise objects*, similar to the LAN based distributed object approaches such as DCOM, CORBA and RMI. However, an important difference between a Web based approach and a standalone or LAN based "enterprise layer" is that the enterprise objects and the busi-ness logic of the interacting organizations are to be grouped into coarser grained com-ponents: the actual *web services*. Indeed, it would not be feasible for a company to publish individual interfaces to its respective enterprise objects. Rather, it will pub-lish one or more *web services* that fulfill a certain business function and that are com-posed of (and affect) multiple internal enterprise objects. Moreover, the enterprise layer, i.e. the entirety of enterprise objects that shapes the business process(es), is now itself distributed across different sites/services, with each service control-ling/consisting of a subset of the enterprise objects. Therefore, from a given service's perspective, we can distinguish between *local* objects (the ones that make out the service) and *remote* objects (the ones that are part of other services, possibly on other sites). A single service can be considered as the unified *public interface* of the un-derlying local enterprise objects, which *hides* the complexity of its constituting ob-jects, much like an individual object's implementation is hidden from the other (local or remote) objects it interacts with.

In a LAN based implementation, "real world" events are translated into business events in the information system by means of so-called *input services*. In general, these will encompass user interface components that receive input from human be-ings, e.g. the "sign" button in a sales order form. The business event is then broadcast by the *event dispatcher*. The latter "knows" which event types are relevant to which object types by consulting the object-event table. The same principle can be applied in a web services environment. Now each web service may have its own local input services. Events can be dispatched to the service's local objects, by means of a "lo-cal" object-event table. However, the assumption of a single, central event dispatcher that also automatically knows all *remote* objects to which a certain event may be of interest is unrealistic: in many cases, web services are developed without prior knowl-edge of the other services they are to interact with, and certainly without knowledge about these services' internal enterprise objects. Therefore, as to remote services to which the event may be relevant, the approach should cater for an explicit *subscrip-*

tion mechanism. A given web service's event dispatcher will dispatch its events to all local objects *and* to all remote services that are explicitly subscribed to the corresponding event type. Subscription by a remote service comes down to a local *stub object* being created, which locally "represents" this remote service and contains a reference to its URL. The resulting event based interaction mechanism takes place in four stages, as illustrated in Figure 4. First, the input service associated with a web service detects a real world event (1). This event is broadcast by the service's event dispatcher to all *local* objects, among which some stub objects (2). Each stub *propagates* the event to the remote service it represents (3). Each remote service's event dispatcher in its turn broadcasts the event to its own local objects (4). Figure 3 already depicted how the appropriate (local and remote) objects then each execute a corresponding method, in which preconditions are checked and/or updates are executed.

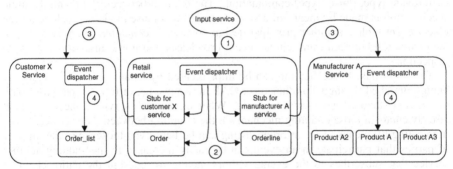

Fig. 4. Example of event notification by means of stub objects

Hence the event based interaction mechanism can be applied on two different levels in the web service architecture: in the first place for interaction *between* web services, where each web service is perceived as an atomic unity by its peer services. The services will interact by responding to communal events. A second interaction mechanism exists at the level of the *intra-service* interaction, i.e. between the respective enterprise objects that make out a single service. This approach can easily be generalized into an n-level system: a service or component receives an event notification and propagates it to its constituting components (and, through the stubs, to the appropriate remote services), which in their turn propagate it to their components etc. In this way, the event is propagated recursively at each level in a hierarchy of complex web services with a complex task, that in their turn are conceived of more simple services with a simpler task until a level of atomic services is reached. On the other hand, at each level, a component that receives an event notification may be a "wrapper" that internally consists of components that interact by means of another mechanism.

The event based interaction mechanism can be applied to web services that belong to long standing business partners with more or less established interaction patterns and to partners that participate in short lived, ad hoc partnerships. In the first case, one could start out from a "unified" analysis and design over the extended enterprise, resulting in a "unified" business model that entails the enterprise objects of all partners involved. In this approach each web service, from the moment it is deployed, has a stub object for each remote service it interacts with. As to ad hoc interaction, stub objects will be created at runtime, as the consequence of certain events occurring.

Such events will represent the explicit *subscription* of one service to another. From then on, two services can start interacting, through mediation of the newly created stub. In a similar way, events that induce the deletion of a stub object terminate the interaction between two services.

4 Conclusions

Regardless of the implementation environment, it is of utter importance when developing an information system to start with a rigorous analysis and design phase. In our approach, the explicit identification of business events has the advantage that constraints, representing the actual business logic, can be identified as preconditions for each (event type, object type) combination. The relation between static and dynamic specification is made by means of a very elegant and concise modeling technique: the object-event table. Another principal design concept is *command-query separation*: the distinction between transactional event broadcasts and non-transactional attribute inspections.

The event based specification can be implemented by means of event dispatching being mimicked through simultaneous SOAP messages, i.e. in full compatibility with the current standard web services stack. Whereas the web service concept in itself already entails a loose coupling mechanism, the coupling between web services communicating by means of event broadcasting can be kept even looser, e.g. the number of parties that participate in an event can be easily increased by just adding another service that subscribes to the event, without having to redesign the entire chain of one-to-one message exchanges.

As already discussed in section 3.2, event propagation can be used both for interaction between peer services and for a complex service to co-ordinate the behavior of its components. The clear distinction between attribute inspections and business events allows for focusing on only the latter with respect to *transaction management*. Also, transaction specification is simplified: a single business event results in multiple simultaneous updates in multiple enterprise objects. The latter is much easier to describe than the myriad of one-to-one message exchanges that could make out a single business transaction in a pure RPC based approach.

References

1. Seely, S., Sharkey, K.: SOAP: Cross Platform Web Services Development Using XML, Prentice Hall PTR, Upper Saddle River, NJ (2001)
2. Frankel, D., Parodi, J.: Using Model-Driven Architecture to Develop Web Services, IONA Technologies white paper (2002)
3. Snoeck, M., Dedene, G.: Existence Dependency: The key to semantic integrity between structural and behavioral aspects of object types, IEEE Trans. Software Engineering, Vol. 24 No. 24, pp.233–251 (1998)
4. Snoeck, M., Dedene, G., Verhelst M., Depuydt A. M.: Object-oriented Enterprise Modeling with MERODE, Leuven University Press, Leuven (1999)
5. Lemahieu, W., Snoeck, M., Michiels C.: An Enterprise Layer Based Approach to Application Service Integration, Business Process Management Journal (forthcoming)
6. Meyer, B.: Object-oriented software construction, 2nd edition, Prentice Hall PTR, Upper Saddle River, NJ (1997)

Active Document Framework ADF: Concept and Method[1]

Hai Zhuge

Knowledge Grid Research Group, Key Laboratory of Intelligent Information Processing,
Institute of Computing Technology, Chinese Academy of Sciences, Beijing, 100080, China
zhuge@ict.ac.cn

Abstract. This paper proposes the concept and method of the active document framework ADF, which is a self-representable, self-explainable and self-executable document mechanism. The content of the document is reflected by granularity hierarchy, template hierarchy, background knowledge, and semantic links between document fragments. An ADF has a set of build-in engines for browsing, retrieving, and reasoning. It can work in the manners that are best suited to the content. The ADF supports not only the browse and retrieval services but also intelligent services like complex question answering and online teaching. The client side service provision mechanism is only responsible for obtaining the required ADF mechanism that provides the particular information services. This improves the current Web information retrieval approaches in efficiency, preciseness and mobility of information services as well as enabling intelligent services.

1 Introduction

Web information services are evolving from low to high level and from simple to complex. The first level services are for information retrieval (IR). The basic premise underlying traditional IR approaches is that related documents will use the same words. Efforts to deal with the synonymy and polysemy issues encountered in the current IR systems have achieved limited success [1, 3]. The second level services are for question answering. Efforts to realize complex question answering have also been made. Previous works focus on the representation, understanding, and processing of fine-granularity documents.

The main obstacle of providing intelligent services is that the common search engines do not know the content of the HTML-based Web documents, and the current web document cannot reflect "machine" understandable content. The Semantic Web is an attempt to solve this issue [2, 4].

A document is a communication media between people. During the content transformation process from the writer to the reader, the content will be distorted more or less during writing and understanding. The content distortion will become serious when the writer and reader do not share knowledge of the same field and at the same level. The current Web-document processing approaches have met with the

---

[1]This work was supported by the National Science Foundation of China.

X. Zhou, Y. Zhang, and M.E. Orlowska (Eds.): APWeb 2003, LNCS 2642, pp. 341–346, 2003.
© Springer-Verlag Berlin Heidelberg 2003

same issue.   Traditional content representation approaches (like the SVM) are based on very fine document fragments like words and phrases.   But small granularity semantics could not directly arrive at large-granularity semantics.   Software tools without any ontology cannot achieve a satisfied efficacy of document understanding. A document incorporating the relevant ontology can be processed or understood more easily and accurately by any software than that without incorporating it. Unfortunately, the capability of current ontology is not strong enough to support a good document understanding.

In the proposed approach, a document content transformation during the writing process and understanding process carries out not only with its ontology but also with its background knowledge, structural knowledge, and semantic knowledge, in which the information content will be kept to the highest extent.   The content of a document is described top-down by four aspects: *granularity hierarchy*, *template hierarchy*, *typed semantic links*, and *background knowledge* (ontology is only a part of it), which can relieve the synonymy and polysemy issues and minimize the search space of IR. We extend the traditional unary semantic similar link to the multi-type semantic link to reflect semantic relationship between different granularity documents, and then investigate document reasoning based on the multi-type semantic links.

2   Content Representation

2.1   Granularity Hierarchy

A document concerns two types of granularities: *document granularity* and *content granularity*. Document granularity is defined according to the size of the document. A large-granularity document usually includes several small-granularity documents. The structure hierarchy of a document is a natural partition of different granularity document fragments.   The document granularity of an ancestor in the hierarchy is larger than that of the successor.

The content granularity can be defined according to the abstraction relationship between document fragments.   In a content granularity hierarchy, a predecessor is more abstract than the successor.   Generally, a large document granularity fragment may not lead to a large content granularity fragment.   But people usually divide a document into fragments according to their understanding of the content so as to enable other people to understand the document easily.   Granularity hierarchy provides a problem-solving approach based on algebra theory and analogy approach [5].

2.2   Template Hierarchy and Background Knowledge

Documents belong to the same category can be described by a certain template. The fragments of a document can also have their templates. A *template hierarchy* can be formed according to the relationship between the document template and its fragments' templates.   The template hierarchy is helpful for understanding a document, and it can also be used to assist the automatic composition of a new document.

B*ackground knowledge* of a document is crucial in entirely understanding content. It relates to a set of theories and a set of related application fields. A *theory* usually consists of a set of conceptual ontologies, a set of axioms, a set of reasoning rules, a set of methods (problem-solution pairs or problem-solving processes), and a set of constraints. A theory can have several sub-theories, each of which can further have several sub-theories. A leaf-node of the theory hierarchy can be represented as a frame. With the background knowledge, the synonymy and polysemy issues can be reduced. Accordingly, documents can be understood more accurately than with the approaches that only consider conceptual ontology.

2.3 Semantic Link Network

A *semantic link* reflects semantic relationship between two semantic nodes. It can be represented as a pointer with a type directed from one node (predecessor) to another (successor). A semantic link can be one of the following types:

- *Cause-effective link*, denoted as *d-ce->d'*, which defines that the predecessor is the cause of its successor, and the successor is the effect of its predecessor. The cause-effective link has the transitive characteristic. Cause-effective reasoning can be formed by chaining cause-effective links according to the transitive characteristic.
- *Implication link*, denoted as *d-imp-> d'*, which defines that the semantics of the predecessor implies that of its successor. The implication link has the transitive characteristic. The implication link can help the reasoning mechanism to find the semantic implication relationship between documents.
- *Subtype link*, denoted as *d-st-> d'*, which defines that the successor is a part of its predecessor. The subtype link has the transitive characteristic.
- *Similar-to link*, which defines that the semantics of the successor is similar to that of its predecessor, denoted as *d-(sim,sd)->d'*, where *sd* is the similar degree between *d* and *d'*. Similar to the partial-inheritance relationship [6], the similar-to link does not have the transitive characteristic.
- *Instance link*, denoted as *d-ins->d'*, which defines that the successor is the instance of the predecessor.
- *Sequential link*, denoted as *d-seq-> d'*, which defines that *d* should be browsed before *d'*, i.e., the content of *d'* is the successor of the content of *d*. The sequential link has the transitive characteristic. The transitive characteristic enables the relevant sequential links to be connected to form a sequential chain.
- *Reference link*, denoted as *d-ref->d'*, which defines that *d'* is the further explanation of *d*. The reference link has the transitive characteristic.

A *semantic link network* (*SLN*) is a directed network where the nodes are document fragments (descriptions or identities) and the edges are the typed semantic links. The *main chain* of the *SLN* is a sequential chain that connects the main fragments of the document from the beginning to the ending node. The content of a document could be wholly browsed if the browser follows the main chain. An *SLN* of a document is connective if all the fragments are linked onto its main chain. A well-defined *SLN* of a large-scale document should be connective at all granularity levels.

The *SLN* can also be used for describing the semantic relationship between a set of related documents. For example, research papers about the same topic can be sequentially connected through the sequential link according to their publication date, and in each paper, the sections can be sequentially connected according to the content dependence relationship between them.

3 Document Reasoning

Document reasoning is for chaining the relevant semantic links and obtaining the reasoning result according to the chaining rules. For example, if we have two links: *d-ce->d'* and *d'-ce->d"*, we can get the reasoning result: *d-ce->d"* according to the transitive characteristic of the cause-effective link. The reasoning process can be represented as a reasoning rule: *d-ce->d', d'-ce->d"=>d-ce->d"*. A reasoning rule can also be simply represented as $\alpha \cdot \beta => \gamma$, where α, β, $\gamma \in \{ce, imp, ins, st, sim, ref, seq\}$, for example, the above reasoning rule can be represented as *ce • ce=>ce*.

A simple case of the reasoning is that all the semantic links have the same type. According to the transitive characteristic of the semantic links, we have the following reasoning rule: $d_1\text{-}\beta\text{->}d_2$, $d_2\text{-}\beta\text{->}d_3$, ..., $d_{n-1}\text{-}\beta\text{->}d_n => d_1\text{-}\beta\text{->}d_n$, where $\beta \in \{ce, imp, st, ref\}$. The heuristic rules for connecting different types of links can be formed. Similar to the definitions and proofs of the inheritance rules in [6], these rules can be formally proved after formally defining the semantic links.

An order relationship exists between these semantic links: $ref \leq ins \leq st \leq imp \leq ce$, where the right one reflects a stronger relationship between two documents than the left one does. In order to obtain a good reasoning result, the reasoning mechanism should find the strongest link between the candidate links. Semantic links can also be in inexact form so as to reflect the possibility of its existence. Different types of inexact semantic links can be also chained for inexact reasoning.

4 Framework Mechanism

An ADF mechanism encapsulates the textual document, content, and operations. It can work like a teacher with a textbook. The reader does not necessarily know too much background knowledge about the document and have reading skills but can learn from the document like a student.

An *ADF* mechanism is a function of the input requirement (denoted as *I*). The output (denoted as *O*) corresponding to the input depends on the content of the document (denoted as *C*) and a set of engines (denoted as *E*). So an ADF mechanism can be described as: *O=ADF(I, C, E)*.

The document content consists of the structural knowledge (*SK*), the background knowledge, and the semantic link network (*SLN*), represented as *C=<SK, BK, SLN>*. *SLN =<FS, LINK>*, where *FS* is a set of different granularity document fragments, and the *LINK* is a set of semantic links between the fragments. The reader working with the network can be regarded as a workflow [7], where the reader can be one or more people, and can be at one place or geographically distributed at different places. The difference is that the flows herein are multiple types of semantic link, so we call the network *text-flow* so as to differentiate it from the workflow. A view of *SLN* is a subgraph that only consists of single type of links or about the same topic. The *SLN* operations can be carried out on views of different topics.

The active document engine consists of the following three components:

- *Execution engine*, which is responsible for the execution of the text-flow according to the order view of its *SLN* like the workflow engine.
- *Search engine*, which is responsible for searching the fragment that matches the input requirement according to the *SLN*. The reasoning rules enable the flexible search result.
- *Reasoning engine*, which is responsible for reasoning according to the *SLN* and the reasoning rules.

Any web user can retrieve the required ADF using a search engine, and can activate it to provide services. The internal engine is responsible for performing the service operations. ADFs can be classified into categories, each of which is a set of documents that share the same background knowledge. To avoid redundancy, an active document can only contain the structural knowledge and the semantic link network. The background knowledge is shared by all the ADFs within the same category. The category can be represented as: $ADFC=<\{ADF_1, ..., ADF_n\}, BK>$, the output of ADF_i is represented as $O_i=ADF_i(I_i, C_i, E_i)$ and $C_i=<SK_i, SLN_i>$.

5 Discussion

The ADF is useful in forming active services for large-scale web documents or a large collection of inter-related web documents. The ADF can be used to realize the complex question answering. If we regard a question as a document, then the question answering process is a reasoning process for finding the matching document. The proposed reasoning rules can provide more candidates for the match-maker of the reasoning mechanism. Many approaches for realizing the matching between two documents have been proposed. These approaches are based on the fact that two documents that are about the same thing will tend to use similar words. Similar to the question-answering application, the ADF can also be used to assist users to solve problems whose solutions exist in or are implied by a document fragment.

The ADF can further be used to provide online learning services, which can help users to learn from large-scale documents like encyclopedias and textbooks. Compared with the existing HTML-based online teaching approaches, the advantages of the ADF-based teaching are that it could actively guide students to read necessary materials and could answer students' questions according to teaching principles and the document content, and that it could provide the background knowledge of the document to the student during the learning process.

6 Conclusion

The advantages of the proposed framework include three major aspects. First, the representation of the document content incorporates not only the ontology and structural knowledge but also the background knowledge and semantic links, so can reflect the document's content more accurately and completely than the traditional document representation approaches do. This can enhance the preciseness of information services and enabling intelligent services. Second, the operations of the document are encapsulated in the document. The document authors or knowledge engineers design the operations according to the document content. This conforms to the fact that only the document author can best know its content and the relevant operations. Third, the client side service provider does not need to search for the information from large-scale web information resources based on a word-level match as the current web search engine, but just needs to subscribe to a relevant indexing mechanism, which suggests the proper active document that could provide the active information services. Users need to only provide their requirements and then get the solution / answer from the service provider. This can raise the efficiency and mobility of Web information services. The proposed semantic link network will form an important part of the knowledge grid [9, 10].

As the generalized form of the ADF, we have proposed the soft-devices model that simulates versatile resources in the future web [8]. Ongoing work includes two aspects: 1) to develop the theoretical model about the active document framework and conduct applications; and 2) investigate the cooperation model for soft-devices.

References

1. Green, S.J. Building Hypertext Links by Computing Semantic Similarity, IEEE Trans. On Knowledge and Data Engineering, 11(1999) 713–730.
2. Hendler, J., Agents and the Semantic Web, IEEE Intelligent Systems, 16(2001)30–37.
3. Henzinger, M.R., Hyperlink Analysis for the Web, IEEE Internet Computing, (2001)45–50.
4. Klein, M., XML, RDF, and Relatives, IEEE Internet Computing, (2001)26–28.
5. Zhuge, H., Abstraction and Analogy in Cognitive Space: A Software Process Model, Information and Software Technology, 39(1997) 463–468.
6. Zhuge, H., Inheritance Rules for Flexible Model Retrieval, Decision Support Systems, 22(1998) 383–394.
7. Zhuge, H., Cheung, T.Y. and Pung, H.K., A Timed Workflow Process Model, Journal of Systems and Software, 55(2000)231–243.
8. Zhuge, H., Clustering Soft-device in the Semantic Grid, IEEE Computing in Science and Engineering, (2002)60–62.
9. Zhuge, H., VEGA-KG: A Way to the Knowledge Web, the 11th international world wide web conference, May, Honolulu, Hawaii, USA, http://www2002.org/CDROM/poster/53.pdf, (2002).
10. Zhuge, H., A Knowledge Grid Model and Platform for Global Knowledge Sharing, Expert Systems with Applications, 22(2002)313–320.

Goal-Oriented Analysis and Agent-Based Design of Agile Supply Chain

Dong Yang and Shen-sheng Zhang

CIT lab, Department of Computer, Shanghai Jiaotong university,
200030, Shanghai, China
dongyangcn@hotmail.com

Abstract. In dynamic enterprise environment, it is a pressing problem to reconfigure supply chain swiftly with the formation and dissolution of virtual enterprises. Multiagent technology provides a promising solution to this problem. In this paper, we present the approach for developing agent-based agile supply chain from goal-oriented analysis to agent-based design. To begin with, a metamodel used for the analysis and design of agile supply chain is given, which defines the abstract entities identified in the analysis and design phase as well as their relationship, such as goal, role, activity, rule and agents. In the analysis phase, the goal of supply chain is represented in AND-OR goal graph and then activities, roles and business rules are identified accordingly. In the design phase, roles are late binded (assigned) to agents and thus the analysis model can be reused. Finally, the architecture of multiagent supply chain based on CORBA platform is described.

1 Introduction

Supply chain is a set of activities across function departments in or outside factories, such as the acquiring of raw materials, the transforming of product, and the delivery of products to customers. The activities involve a number of actors, such as supplier, factories, warehouse, distribution centers and retailers, who are regarded as the participant of supply chain. The aim of supply chain management (SCM) is to manage and coordinate these activities so that products go through the business network in the shortest time and at the lowest costs possible. Agile supply chain differs from average supply chain in the reconfiguration of the system. The agile supply chain can be adjusted or reconfigured with the formation and dissolution of virtual enterprises. Software agents provides a promising solution to the problem with reconfigurable supply chain by adapting behavioral rules of agents without changing function unit of agents [1][2][10]. An agent is an autonomous, goal-oriented software entity that operates asynchronously, communicating and coordinating with other agents as needed. In recent years, a number of researches have applied agent-based technology to supply chain system. Fox firstly proposed to construct supply chain based on multi-agent technology and pointed out that "reconfigurable" is one of characteristics of next generation supply chain management system [10]. Also, D. zheng models different business entities in supply chain as autonomous software agent via internet [12]. Barbuceanu proposed a "structured conversation" model for the coordination of agents and designed a coordination language named COOL for explicitly representing, ap-

X. Zhou, Y. Zhang, and M.E. Orlowska (Eds.): APWeb 2003, LNCS 2642, pp. 347–356, 2003.
© Springer-Verlag Berlin Heidelberg 2003

plying and capturing coordination knowledge [3]. Weiming Shen addressed the implement of supply chain and proposed a general architecture for internet-based multi-agent supply chain systems [11]. The above approaches are mainly concerned about implementation of agent-based supply chain system as well as the coordination between agents. However, they pay a little attention to the analysis of agent-based supply chain and thus lack a uniform framework for constructing supply chain system from the analysis to the design phase.

In this paper, we present the GASCM approach for modeling supply chain (i.e. Goal-oriented analysis and Agent-based design of constructing multiagent Supply Chain Management system).

2 The GASCM Methodology for Modeling Supply Chain

From the definition of supply chain described in section 1, it can be seen that supply chain typically has the following characteristic:

1) Supply chain contains various activities, such as the acquiring of raw material, the approval of order, the distribution of products, etc.

2) Supply chain involves a variety of actors, for example, suppliers, distributors, retailers.

3) Different from hierarchy management in traditional organizations, supply chain focus on the "process" that places emphasis on the coordination among functional department in or outside enterprises.

4) Supply chain has definitive objective (goal), such as the reduction of leadtime and the improvement of customer services quality.

Therefore, we can define supply chain as the process which coordinates the activities involving various participants. The modeling of supply chain can be regarded as "process modeling", i.e. the representation of coordination between participants in supply chain. In the analysis phase of GASCM, we adopt the goal-oriented approach for supply chain modeling. Goal capturing is an important means of requirements analysis [5]. The main advantages of goal-oriented modeling approach include:

1) Goal expresses intentions and captures the reasons of the system to be built.
2) Compared to business process, the goal is much stable. Thus, it is more helpful for analysis and design of information system.
3) Agent is proactive (goal-oriented). Therefore, it is natural transition from the goal-oriented analysis to the agent-base design under unified framework.

In the GASCM approach, the identified abstract entities to be used in the analysis and design phase include goal, role, activity, rule and agent. The entities are explained as follows.

Goal: Goal is the state which system desire to achieve. And it explains why system is built. The goal can be further decomposed into sub-goals. The goal can be realized by satisfying its sub-goals.

Activity: also called task, a basic function unit in business processes.

Role: Role defines the responsibilities of actors as well as a set of activities carrying out the responsibilities. The role is assigned to agent during the design phase.

Rule: Rule specifies the business polices of enterprise and behaviors of business operations.

Agent: Agent is participant or software entity that actually executes the activities.
In the goal-oriented analysis, the following questions need to be answered, i.e.

1) Why: defines the goal of business process.
2) What: defines the activities according to goal of business process.
3) When: defines the control logic between activities.
4) Who: defines the roles in organization and assign activities to roles.

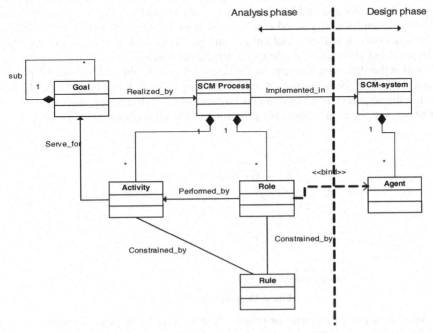

Fig. 1. The meta-model for supply chain modeling

Figure 1 shows the meta-model that we uses for supply chain modeling. The meta-model describes these entities identified in analysis and design phase as well as the relationship between the entities. The left part in the dashed line shows the abstract entities identified the analysis phase while the right part represents the entities in the design (implementation) phase. In the analysis phase, the identified entities contain goal, SCM process, role, activity, rule. The goal is realized by supply chain process and can be further decomposed into sub-goals. The SCM process consists of activities and roles. And the activity is performed by role. Moreover, activity serves for certain goal. The rule places constraint on role and activity. During the design phase, the identified entities include SCM-system and agent. The SCM-system consists of agents. By late binding roles to agents until the design phase, the results of analysis phase can be reused. Another advantage is that the architecture of agent-base supply chain can be free to be chosen in the implementation phase.

3 The Analysis Phase of GASCM Methodology

3.1 The Identification of Goal

Requirement analysis is the first step in the development of software systems. Traditional modeling approaches (such as DFD, IDEF, ER) only describe what system can do or what system is to be, and fail to express the motivation, intention or reason behind the behaviors and entities. In contrast, goal-oriented analysis is the complement of object-oriented analysis and can be used in early stages of requirement analysis [13]. It not only describes social entities and goal entities that o-o analysis often fails to express, but also represents the characteristics of business process in enterprises.

Goal is the state which enterprise desires to achieve. Compared to business process and activity, goal is much more stable. For example, some typical goals include "satisfying the requirement of customer's buying goods", "decreasing approval time for customer's application", "increasing the competitive edges in the markets", etc.

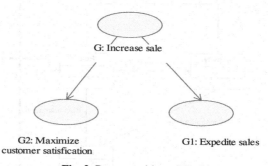

Fig. 2. Decomposition of Goal

After identifying enterprise or supply chain's overall objective, the top-level goal can be determined. The top-level goal is usually abstract and thus abstract goal has to be further decomposed into sub-goals. The procedure of decomposition finishes until the most low-level sub-goal is operational. The decomposition forms a goal graph which is represented in AND-OR diagrams [5]. For example, in figure 2, the overall goal is to increase sales and can be decomposed into sub-goal G1 and G2. The goal G1 is to speed up the progress of sale while the goal G2 is to maximize customer satisfication.

In order to realize the goal G1, the three function departments, i.e. sale department, accounting department and inventory department, need to coordinate their activities. Thus, G1 can decomposed into there sub-goals: (1) goal G1.1, i.e. handling order effectively. (2) goal G1.2, i.e. Keep sufficient goods in stock. (3) goal G1.3, i.e. Manage Accounting effectively. The AND-OR graph of goal G1 is depicted in figure 3. Note that in the figure 3, all the goals belong to AND-decomposition. The further explanation about the part of the goal graph is shown in table 1.

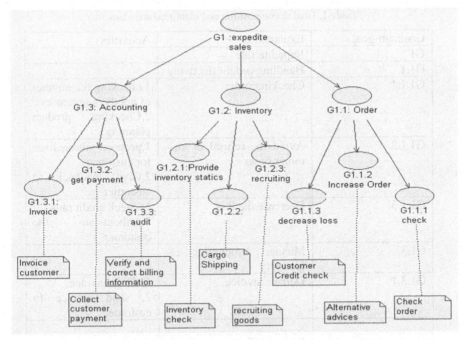

Fig. 3. AND-OR graph of Goal G1

3.2 Activity

By analyzing the AND-OR graph of goal decomposition, the activities can be identified. The activities corresponding to sub-goals are shown in the right column of table 1. For every activity, precondition and post-condition are described, which are later saved in agent's knowledge base. The precondition is a necessary condition for activity to be executed. For example, the precondition for the activity "propose alternatives for customer" is "the order not approved ".

Moreover, the constraints on activities (control dependency) decide when to execute activities and thus can be expressed in behavioral rule. The behavioral rule is described by PSL (Process Specification language)[14], which adopts the syntax of KIF[6] and can express control dependencies between activities, such as concurrency, synchronization, non-determinate choice, etc.

Therefore, the specification of activity can be defined as follows:

```
Activity    activity-name
ID              activity-ID
Precondition   variable expression (e.g. variable>...)
Postcondition variable expression (e.g. variable>...)
Constraint   PSL expression
```

Table 1. Goal decomposition and identified activities

Goal/sub-goal	Explanation	Activities
G1	Expedite sale	
G1.1	Handling order effectively	
G1.1.1	Checking order	1,checking the number of goods in inventory. 2,Checking product planning
G1.1.2	Avoid the refusal of customer order	1,propose alternatives for customer. 2,Give feedback to customer
G1.1.3	Decrease the loss	1, check credit rank. 2,authenticate the customer
G1.3	Manage Accounting effectively	
G1.3.1	Deliver invoice	1, fill in invoice 2. send invoice to customer
......	......	......
G1.2	Keep sufficient goods in stock	
......	......	......

3.3 Role

Role defines the responsibilities of actors as well as a set of activities carrying out the responsibilities. However, role is abstract concept different from actor (i.e. agent) who performs activity actually. The separation of role from actor is of the following advantages: role can be assigned to agents until the design phase, thus the analysis models can be reused.

For example, in our example, the following roles can be identified from the analysis phase:

Sale role: responsible for Goal G1.1.
Accounting role: responsible for Goal G1.3.
Inventory role: responsible for Goal G1.2.
Coordinator role: responsible for Goal G1.
The roles will be assigned to agents in the design phase.

3.4 Business Rules

Business rule defines the policy for business process and constrains dynamic behavior of business process. The rule explicitly states when to start an activity and thus express control logic between activities. In agent-base system, business rule also constrain the interaction between roles (agents). For example, in the agile supply chain system, the following rules are identified:

Rule 1: An order is valid only when the customer is ruled out in the customer blacklist.

Rule 2: For the order placed by average customer, the activity "making payment" should be followed by the activity "delivery to customer".

Rule 3: For the order placed by customer with good record histories, the activity "delivery to customer" may starts before the activity "making payment".

Business rule can be expressed in textual or formal languages. We adopt KIF as the syntax of representing business rules. KIF is based on first-order predicate logic as a knowledge exchange format between different application or programs[6]. KIF language has well-defined formal semantics and provides basic building blocks for expressing simple datatype, constraints, rule, arithmetic expression, etc.

The above three business rules can formally expressed in KIF:

Rule1: (defrelation Rule1_orderValid (?Order) := (and (not (Blacklistedcustomer Of ?Order)) (purchaseOrder ?Order)))

Rule 2 : (defrelation Rule2_processRouting (?Order):= (and (processRouting2 ?Order) (and (averageCustomer(?Order) (purchaseOrder ?Order))))

Rule 3 : (defrelation Rule3_processRouting (?Order) := (and (processRouting3 ?Order) (and (subsidiaryCompanyOf (?Order) (purchaseOrder ?Order))))

In the above rule 2 and rule 3, *processRouting2* and *processRouting3* are behavioral rules which define the processing of order for average customer and the customer with good histories respectively. They can be expressed in PSL as follows:

(defrelation processRouting2 (?Order) := follows (makePayment (?Order), deliver (?Order)))

(defrelation   processRouting3 (?Order) := follows (deliver (?Order), makePayment (?Order)))

Where *follows* is relation defined in PSL to express the ordering between two activities. And *deliver* and *makePayment* are objects of *activity* or *subactivity* in PSL.

4   The Design Phase of GASCM Methodology

In the above analysis phase of GASCM, goal, activity, role and rule are identified. Therefore, the main task in the design phase is to design agents. The agent can be derived from the roles in the analysis phase. Usually, there is one-one mapping from role to agent. However, several roles can be assigned to an agent in order to reduce the cost of communication brought about the interactions between roles.

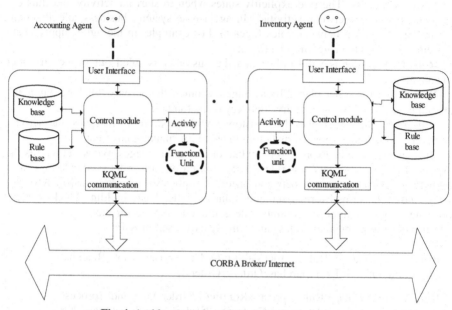

Fig. 4. Architecture of multiagent supply chain system

For instances, the four agents we identified in the analysis phase will be corresponds to inventory agent, accounting agent, order agent and coordination agent respectively by one-by-one mapping in our example. Since supply chain is typical heterogeneous, distributed system, we adopt CORBA-base multiagent architecture as shown in figure 4. The internal architecture of individual agent contains control module, knowledge base, rule base, KQML communication module and activity module. In this figure, the dashed box represents optional part. The knowledge base contains the knowledge that agent believe about itself as well as the environment, the knowledge about domain necessary for agent to cooperate with other agent, and the knowledge about the precondition of activities. The rule base maintains business rule (behavioral rule) in KIF which specify when to start an activity. The KQML communication module is responsible for the delivery of output messages, the receiving of incoming messages as well as the analysis of KQML contents from messages. The components of KQML communication module are designed in the form of CORBA objects. As a result, agents communicate in low level via CORBA object while in high level agents interact with each other in KQML that expresses the knowledge about coordination and the sharing of information. Since CORBA acts as a distributed computing infrastructure for heterogeneous systems, the combination of CORBA and KQML not only enable the exchange of high-level knowledge, but also integrate heterogeneous agents in supply chain. According to KQML contents abstracted from incoming messages, the control module responds differently. For the messages from other agents for the query of knowledge, the control module gets related knowledge from its knowledge base and then replies to the request via KQML communication module. For the messages about business events as well as the request for services, the control module check the business rules in the rule base and evaluate the precondition of activity according to the information in knowledge base. If the rule satisfies, the control module will invoke activity module according to the specification in business rule. In turn, the activity will invoke function unit, which is wrapped into CORBA object if function unit is an external application. The execution of activity may update agent's knowledge base according to post-condition of activity. By modify business rule, function units can be reused and thus supply chain can be reconfigured in a short time.

5 Conclusion

With the formation and dissolution of dynamic alliances, it is of importance to reconfigure supply chain shortly. Agent-base technology provides a promising solution to configurable supply chain. In this paper, we focus on how to develop an agile, reconfigurable supply chain. The approach of goal-oriented analysis and agent-base design of agile supply chain is presented. In the analysis phase, abstract concepts, such as goal, role, rule, are identified and used for modeling supply chain in high-level. By assigning roles to agents in the design phase, agent-base supply chain is constructed. In contrast to the approaches that start with the identification of agents in systems, our approach that separates roles from agents has the following advantage: the models in the analysis phase can be reused. Moreover, supply chain can be configured shortly by adapting business rules without changing function unit of agents. Finally, we present CORBA-based architecture of multiagent supply chain system.

References

1. Wang Liang-zhu, Zhang Shen-Seng, A software-reused-oriented agile supply chain model based on software agents, *Journal of Computer Research and Development*, 2002,2, In Chinese.
2. Duan Yong-Qiang, Gao Guo-jun, The architecture of agile supply chain, *Computer Application Research*, 1999,2, In Chinese.
3. Barbuceanu M. Fox s, Integrating communicative action, conversation and decision theory to corordiante agents, *Proceedings of the First international Conference on Autonomous Agent(Agents'97)*,1997.256–262.
4. Li Qiu-ming, Zhang Shi-lian, Development of the CORBA-based multi-agent supply chain management, *Information and Control*, 2000,12, in Chinese.
5. A. I. Anton, *"Goal-Based Requirements Analysis"*, In *Proceedings of the Second International Conference on Requirements Analysis*, ICRE'96, 1996.
6. Genesereth, M.R., R. E. Fikes: Knowledge Interchange Format, Version 3.0, Reference Manual, Logic Group Report Logic-92-1, Computer Science Department, Stanford University, Stanford, California.
7. Finin, T et al., 1994, "Specification of the KQML agent-communication language," Report of The DARPA Knowledge Sharing Initiative, External Interfaces Working Group.
8. R otte & P Ratrick, Understanding CORBA, prentice Hall, New Jerswy.
9. Fox, M.S., Chionglo, J.F., and Barbuceanu, M., (1993), The Integrated Supply Chain Management System. Internal Report, Dept. of Industrial Engineering, Univ. of Toronto. (Appears to be the fist to propose organizing the supply chain as a network of cooperating, intelligent agents.) aminathan .

10. J.M., Smith, S.F., and Sadeh, N.M. (1996). A Multi-Agent Framework for Supply Chain Dynamics. In *Proc. of NSF Research Planning Workshop on AI & Manufacturing*, Albuquerque, NM.
11. Weiming Shen, Mihaela Ulieru & Douglas Norrie. (1999). "Implementing the Internet Enabled Supply Chain through a Collaborative Agent System", *Agents'99 Workshop on Agent Based Decision-Support for Managing the Internet-Enabled Supply-Chain*, Seattle, WA.
12. K. Sycara and D. Zeng, "Dynamic Supply Chain Structuring for Electronic Commerce Among Agents," Intelligent Information Agents: Cooperative, Rational and Adaptive Information Gathering on the Internet, Matthias Klusch, ed., Springer Verlag, 1999.
13. John Mylopoulos, Lawrence Chung, Eric S.K.Yu. From Object-Orented to Goal-Oriented requirement analysis [J]. *Communication of the ACM*, January 1999,42(1):31~37.
14. Schlenoff, C., Gruninger M., Tissot, F., Valois, J., Lubell, J., Lee, J., The Process Specification Language (PSL): Overview and Version 1.0 Specification, NISTIR 6459, National Institute of Standards and Technology, Gaithersburg, MD (2000).

Methodologies and Mechanism Design in Group Awareness Support for Internet-Based Real-Time Distributed Collaboration

Minh Hong Tran, Gitesh K. Raikundalia, and Yun Yang

Centre for Internet Computing and E-Commerce (CICEC)
Swinburne University of Technology
PO Box 218, Hawthorn, Australia, 3122
{mtran, graikundalia, yyang}@it.swin.edu.au

Abstract. The first purpose of this paper is to provide an overview of the most commonly-used awareness mechanisms, namely, What You See Is What I See, telepointers, multi-user scrollbars, radar views and distortion-oriented views. These mechanisms were derived from researchers' intuition, without prior experimental investigation of what awareness information end-users really need. This research utilised a completely user-centered approach to determine relevant awareness mechanisms. The novelty of this approach is in the use of usability experiments to identify awareness mechanisms. In addition to the illustration of several innovative mechanisms, this research has also successfully differentiated the importance of different awareness information in maintaining group awareness. The significance of different awareness information has been thoroughly compared. These results help designers to know which information must be provided to all team members.

1 Introduction

Real-time, distributed, collaborative writing systems facilitate the task of joint authorship in a distributed environment. Many systems have been produced such as GROVE [6], REDUCE [23], SASSE [1] and ShrEdit [5], but only a small number amongst them are used in the real world. The reason for this lack of usage is that existing systems have not yet matched the diversity and richness of group interaction. Knowing the activities of other collaborators is a basic requirement for group interaction. In face-to-face interaction, people find it naturally easy to maintain a sense of awareness about who is in a workspace, what others' responsibilities are, what others are doing and so on. However, when collaborators are geographically distributed, supporting spontaneous interaction is much more difficult due to various reasons such as limited capabilities of input and output devices, restricted views or weak communication [13].

To support synchronous distributed collaborative writing effectively, systems must provide *group awareness* (GA). GA is defined as *"an understanding of the activities of others, which provides a context for your own activity"* [5]. GA provides information

X. Zhou, Y. Zhang, and M.E. Orlowska (Eds.): APWeb 2003, LNCS 2642, pp. 357–369, 2003.

such as users' identities, their past actions, current activities and future intentions. GA plays an essential and integral role in collaboration by simplifying communication, supporting coordination [6], managing coupling, assisting "anticipation" [13] and supporting "convention" [10]. Various awareness mechanisms have been produced to support GA. Examples of commonly used mechanisms include telepointers [9], radar views [14], multi-user scrollbars [1, 14], and distortion-oriented views [7, 8, 22]. The systems can also incorporate audio and video facilities for supporting communication [2, 4]. Although these mechanisms have enriched GA to some extent, many aspects of GA have not yet been supported. Some awareness mechanisms are implemented in an ad-hoc manner and some may even generate contradictory results. For instance, multi-user scrollbars were reported ineffective in a collaborative page layout task [14]. However, multi-user scrollbars were found useful in collaborative editing as reported in [1].

The remainder of this paper is organised as follows. Section 2 reviews five awareness mechanisms: *What You See Is What I See*, *telepointers*, *multi-users scrollbars*, *radar views* and *distortion-oriented views*. Section 3 introduces the authors' user-centered methodology and the experiment used to identify awareness mechanisms. Section 4 describes several novel mechanisms followed by further discussions in Section 5. The paper is concluded in Section 6 with directions for the authors' future research and development.

2   Overview of Existing Awareness Mechanisms

What You See Is What I See (WYSIWIS)
Conventionally, maintaining GA in face-to-face interaction relies heavily on the short distance between people, i.e., physical proximity [12]. To support GA, early groupware systems provide close view proximity by enforcing strict-WYSIWIS views, where all users see the same set of cursors and the same view of a document. Strict-WYSIWIS applications allow only one user to use mouse or keyboard at a time [17, 18]. Strict-WYSIWIS is relatively easy to implement from a designer's point of view and it helps to maintain GA in the sense that users can identify easily what others are doing as they see the same view.

However, enforcing all users to see the same view makes strict-WYSIWIS an inflexible style of collaboration in which the users are unexpectedly forced to work as a tightly-coupled unit [17]. This design ensures that users can stay aware of others' activities, but it is often too restrictive for many kinds of collaboration where user regularly move back and forth between individual and shared work [16]. Another drawback of strict-WYSIWIS is disruption since all users' movements and actions are entirely visible to all of the users [17].

Due to the inflexibility of strict-WYSIWIS, recent synchronous collaborative editors have relaxed the strict application of WYSIWIS to accommodate natural interactions. As a result, a looser variation of WYSIWIS has been introduced, namely *relaxed-WYSIWIS* view sharing. The idea of relaxed-WYSIWIS view sharing systems is that users are allowed to move and change their viewports independently. However, when users view different parts of the document, they are effectively blinded to the actions happening outside their viewports. To resolve this problem, many awareness mechanisms have been developed specifically for relaxed-WYSIWIS view sharing such as telepointers, multi-user scrollbars, radar views and distortion-oriented views as discussed next.

Telepointers

Telepointers allow a user to see both his/her own mouse cursor and others' mouse cursors. To distinguish telepointers of different users, each telepointer can be assigned a different colour or a different shape and/or even have the user's name and image attached to it [9, 15].

The major advantage of telepointers is providing awareness about users' presence and their activities, foci of attention and degree of interest. By watching telepointers move, a local user knows that the remote user is currently working in the workspace. In addition, telepointers allow users to know that an activity is occurring, and often the kind of actions as well, if names of users' actions are attached to the telepointers.

Although telepointers are able to provide the mouse positions of other users, telepointers can only be used when all participants see the same information on the screen. Telepointers fail to convey awareness information when they are removed from the local user's view. For example, if two users are working on two completely different areas of a document, telepointers become inaccessible. Another problem in implementing telepointers is disruption. Since telepointers show all of the other users' movements, telepointers can easily distract a local user. Another limitation of the telepointer is that it fails to provide users with information about the location at which a remote user is working. In the case of collaborative drawing, telepointers are able to show working locations of other users, because the position of a mouse cursor is a position at which a user is drawing. However, in the case of document editing, the position of a mouse cursor is not a position at which a user is typing. Therefore, the position of a telepointer does not indicate exactly the location at which a remote user is working in a document. In addition to the issues mentioned above, there are other unsolved issues in implementing telepointers such as:

- *Cursor size*: What is the most appropriate cursor size when there are two, four or more users in the workspace? Should cursor size be unchanged or reduced proportionally as group size grows?
- *Cursor lifetime,* especially for inactive cursors: Whilst displaying cursors at all times is useful to indicate who is present and what are they doing, presence of an inactive cursor is intrusive to larger groups [15].
- *Cursor position*: Since users are allowed to scroll and adjust screen size independently, whether cursors should be positioned relatively to the underlying objects in the workspace or absolutely with regard to the window [9].

Multi-user Scrollbars

Multi-user scrollbars show both a local user's position and remote users' positions in a document. The viewport of each user is represented in multi-user scrollbars as a coloured bar locating at the right-hand side of the window [1, 14]. There are two variations of multi-user scrollbars. The major difference between these two variations is that in version 1, each remote scrollbar is located in a different vertical region; however, in version 2, all remote scrollbars are located in the same vertical region. These two variations of multi-user scrollbars offer the same advantages. First, they provide information about other users' locations in the document such as whether users are near the top, the middle or the end of the document. When users have completely different views, telepointers are of no value since they are not visible, but multi-users scrollbars are still capable of conveying information about other users' whereabouts in the workspace. Second, multi-user scrollbars deliver information about relative positions amongst users. Another benefit of the multi-user scrollbar is that this scrollbar makes navigating to another user's location simple by moving the local scrollbar to the same level as the remote user's scrollbar.

The first disadvantage of multi-user scrollbars is that it is difficult to determine the exact position in the document where other users are located, what they can see and what they are doing. This is because all the scrollbar shows is the relative position of the user in the document. The second disadvantage of multi-user scrollbars occurs when a large number of users are working in the workspace. In version 1, the display of a large number of remote users' scrollbars causes space constraints – it forces the area of the document portion viewed to be reduced. In the case of version 2, when views of more than two users intersect, it is difficult to know exactly the location of remote users because many remote scrollbars overlap one another. The third disadvantage is disruption in using multi-user scrollbars. When remote users perform a substantial amount of vertical movement in the document, the remote scrollbars move extensively. Since the scrollbars are placed next to the view of the document, constant movement of remote users' scrollbars become very distracting to a local user.

Radar Views

Radar views render the entire shared workspace within a miniature overview, on which each user's location of activity is superimposed. Radar views present the locations of other users as rectangles. To indicate which rectangle belongs to whom, each rectangle can have a different text label and/or a picture of the user [14]. Telepointers can be added in miniature form to show others' mouse positions and movements. A major advantage of radar views is to provide a high-level view of the shared workspace. A radar view can be seen as an integration that combines advantages offered by telepointers and multi-user scrollbars within a single mechanism. In collaborative writing, radar views provide information about the general structure of the document, locations in the document at which other users are working and their activities upon the document when users work in the same view or different views.

However, radar views have four major problems need to be overcome. First, the major problem with a miniaturisation technique is that it has limited scalability. The low-resolution representation of radar views conceals details of users' actions; a radar view of an extremely large data space contains too little detail to be useful. Second, radar views create a "physical and contextual virtual gap" [7] between local details and global contexts. Third, if users perform a substantial amount of movement, the rectangles in the miniature view change constantly, causing a user's screen to appear very busy. Finally, a problem similar to that of telepointers – radar views fail to distinguish between viewing areas and working areas. Users' viewports drawn in a radar view could be either their viewing or working regions. As a result, if a solely radar view is implemented in an editor, information about other users' working locations provided by radar views could be either insufficient or incorrect.

Distortion-oriented Views

To overcome radar view's limitations, especially to bridge the gap between local details and the global structure of a document, a distortion-oriented display is used. Distortion-oriented views include two categories: *magnifying lenses* (irrelevant to GA) and *fisheye views*. Fisheye views present a single view which displays both local detail and global context on a continuous "surface" [7].

Fisheye views offer two central advantages, which are not provided by any mechanisms described above. First, a fisheye representation bridges the gap between local detail and the global context by providing a seamless and smooth transition between these two views. Second, the usage of multiple focal points – assigning one focal point to each user – allows fisheye views to reveal the location of other users and the details of their actions performed upon the workspace [8]. Extensive technical detail of how fisheye views function is described clearly in [8, 11, 22].

Although fisheye views can provide improved GA of where other users are and what they are doing in a shared workspace, some awareness elements are still poorly supported and some technical issues need to be solved. First, remote users' focal points can be out of a local user's view, when a shared document is too large to fit in the local user's view. The local user apparently loses track of the remote users' whereabouts and what they are doing. Second, since magnified regions representing other users' working areas are adjusted by a local user, these areas do not exactly match with actual viewport size. Third, when more than two enlarged areas overlap they hide one another. This is problematic, as part of document appears to be lost and a local user could be misled when assuming that a hidden remote user has left the workspace.

3   Integrated Approach for Determining Awareness Mechanisms

GA research has exploited a solely "bottom-up" approach in finding awareness mechanisms, i.e., testing mechanisms based on researcher's intuition without prior experimental study of what awareness information end-users really need. Although the solely "bottom-up" approach has exposed some mechanisms, many other possible mechanisms are easily overlooked or require excessive experimentation to be found. To design usable mechanisms, a designer must be directed by the philosophy of user-centered design. This research adopts a completely user-centered approach – a "top-down" approach merged with a "bottom-up" approach [19]. However, this paper only focuses on the work of the "top-down" approach in identifying awareness mechanisms.

• *Top-down approach*

This research started with a "top-down" approach before the "bottom-up" approach. The top-down approach determines user needs and identifies relevant awareness mechanisms by conducting a laboratory-based usability experiment – a top-down experiment. The top-down experiment was conducted with REDUCE – Real-time Distributed Unconstrained Cooperative Editor [23]. REDUCE was selected as the editor for experiments because it has been recommended by the prestigious ACM SIGGROUP (Special Interest Group on Supporting Group Work) as a demonstration editor for trial worldwide. At present, REDUCE provides almost no GA support; hence, conducting the experiment with REDUCE determines valuable awareness information and highly applicable mechanisms. This section describes briefly the setting of the top-down experiment. The full details of the setting were described exhaustively in [19].

• *Bottom-up approach*

The functionality awareness mechanisms derived from the "top-down" approach must be evaluated. After the mechanisms are implemented in REDUCE, the "bottom-up" approach will then determine further awareness support by conducting another series of usability experiments.

Top-Down Experiment

The usability experiment involved *ten pairs* of subjects working on three writing tasks, including *creative writing* (CW) (e.g., writing short essays), *technical document preparation* (TD) (e.g., writing research papers) and *brainstorming* (BS) (e.g., generating ideas). Four pairs worked on CW, three pairs worked on TD and three pairs worked on BS.

Subjects included lecturers and Ph.D. students in Information Technology. They were selected as experimental subjects because their experience in cooperative work and their well-established computer knowledge would give valuable feedback. Identifying relevant awareness mechanisms is the major objective of this research, so choosing technologically-trained experimental subjects is key to the experiment. Each pair participated in a two-and-a-half hour session including:

• *Training* (30 minutes): Each subject was fully trained in using REDUCE.

• *Experiment* (1 hour): Subjects worked on two tasks – one task with verbal communication for thirty minutes and on another task without verbal communication for thirty minutes. Conducting the experiments with and without support of verbal communication allowed identification of problems users had in collaborating and the workarounds users resorted to when silence occurred.

• *Questionnaire and interview* (1 hour): A questionnaire includes twenty five-point scale questions and seventeen open-ended questions. Subjects completed the questionnaire within an interview to discuss awareness information and awareness mechanisms.

4   Awareness Mechanisms from the Top-Down Experiment

Modification Director Mechanism

Assisting users in monitoring who edits their work and which parts of their work are being modified is the inspiration for the emergence of *Modification Director* (MD). The MD maintains awareness by notifying users instantly when their work is modified by other users. Whenever a user's work is modified, a corresponding coloured icon flashes on the local user's screen. The user can easily view the modified area simply by clicking on the flashing icon [21]. MD notifies users immediately whenever their work is modified by others and allows users to find out quickly which part of their work is altered and who makes the modification. Although a pop-up window is used in MD, the window is controlled by users; the window only pops up when a user clicks a flashing icon. Hence, disruption is significantly minimised, because a user is aware of the presence of the pop-up window.

A design issue needs to be addressed when implementing MD; if user A modifies more than two different sections of user B's work at the same time, which section should be shown in the pop-up window? One solution to resolve this problem is to organise the pop-up window in page format, which allows users to go backward and forward amongst the modified areas.

Toggle Multi-user Scrollbar Mechanism

The *Toggle Multi-user Scrollbar* (TMS) is an advanced variation of traditional multi-user scrollbars introduced in [1, 14]. TMS provides all functionality available in traditional multi-user scrollbar plus the ability to hide and show remote scrollbars [20]. Additionally, TMS provides the ability to hide remote user scrollbars. TMS also displays a remote user's name next to their scrollbar, which prevents a user from memorising and mapping many pairs of users and corresponding scrollbars.

One problem in designing TMS occurs when viewports of more than two users intersect, which causes remote scrollbars to overlap. A solution to overcome this problem is to make remote scrollbars transparent; transparency allows all remote scrollbars to be visible when overlapping one another. Another problem with TMS is when the remote scrollbar is set to visible; the screen could be very busy due to a substantial amount of vertical movement. One resolution to this problem is to allow a local user to choose which particular remote scrollbar is visible.

Split Window View Mechanism

In collaborative writing, authors' working areas can be different from their viewing areas [3]. Existing mechanisms such as telepointers, multi-user scrollbars and radar views show users' current viewing areas, but not their working areas. The *Split Window View* (SWV) mechanism enables a user to view both other users' viewing *and* working sections. In SWV, remote insertion cursors are also added to the display. Remote insertion cursors assist a local user in tracking down easily and precisely other users' working areas [21]. These cursors have different functionality to telepointers, thus do not suffer from the disadvantages of telepointers. SWV allows a user to observe more than one users' work at the same time and a user is able to request explicitly whether or not the user wants to retain other users' views. Thus the presentation of awareness information is controlled by users.

Although SWV allows a user to view other collaborators' work simultaneously, this mechanism raises two problems in display and design issues: *space constraints* and *display fidelity*. Since the visible size of a screen is limited, a problem occurs when having multiple views in a single window screen at the same time. The more users that are viewed, the smaller the size of the main editor. This limits the local user's main view of the workspace. Additionally, when both viewing and working areas of a particular user are displayed, SWV might need to implement a low-fidelity presentation of the document in order to fit the entire view in a window of half normal size. Depending on the fidelity, the contents in miniature views can be difficult to read and to understand. Besides that, with low-fidelity views users might have difficulty seeing the remote insertion cursors. If the fidelity is not too low, horizontal scrollbars can be added to each view.

Dynamic Task List Mechanism

The *Dynamic Task List* (DTL) is a task-based awareness mechanism that presents an active and frequently-updated list of all collaborators' tasks [20]. Users' names, their corresponding text colours and their tasks are shown in the list. The display of this list is immediately updated whenever there are changes in collaborators' tasks such as when a new task is assigned, a task is modified or a task is removed from the list. The DTL provides an active awareness information presentation: users can select a particular task to view the corresponding section of the document.

DTL provides high-level awareness information about members' responsibilities, i.e., the tasks for which each member is responsible. DTL also presents a relative comparison and correlation of workloads of all collaborators. For example, when more than one collaborator is responsible for one common task, DTL provides all collaborators with sufficient information about other collaborators with whom they need to cooperate closely. None of the mechanisms covered in Section 2 is capable of supporting this type of awareness information.

Although DTL conveys information about what comments others make on any collaborator's work, the nature of information delivery (a pop-up window) could be intrusive. Especially with those who do not want to know other people's comments while concentrating seriously on their own work. Additionally, though DTL is viewed as possibly a useful and valuable addition to a real-time editor, collaborators need to provide extra effort, apart from writing goals, to build and to maintain the task list. Besides that, the task list might not be useful for a small document, as it is neither convenient nor effective to form the list of tasks for a small-sized document.

5   Further Discussions on Awareness

The preceding sections have reviewed existing awareness mechanisms derived from a solely bottom-up approach and described innovative mechanisms determined by the top-down approach used by the authors. Further issues to be addressed are covered here.

- The top-down approach reveals that many important aspects of group awareness have been mostly ignored by previous research.

Using the top-down approach is better than using a solely bottom-up approach in the sense that the top-down approach ensures that identified mechanisms are definitely based on real data, not imagination, about these users, and what users need. Most previous research has mainly focused on inventing mechanisms to provide information about members' location in the workspace, i.e., information about where in a document other users are currently viewing. However, the results of the top-down approach shows that other important information needs to be provided to end-users such as information about other users' responsibilities, their current working areas and their

Awareness elements	Mean*	Std Dev
• Being able to *comment* on what other users have done	4.53	0.51
• Knowing what *actions* other users are *currently* taking	4.50	0.61
• In the case of nonverbal communication, *having a communication tool* that supports communication between users	4.50	0.61
• Knowing parts of a document on which other users are currently *working*	4.50	0.61
• Knowing tasks for which other users are *responsible*	4.35	0.75
• Knowing if other users know what you have been doing	4.25	0.72
• Knowing *who* is in the workspace	4.15	0.81
• Knowing if other users are *satisfied* with what you have done	4.10	0.64
• Knowing parts of a document at which other users are currently *looking*	3.95	0.83
• Knowing to what extent a portion of a document has been *completed*	3.85	0.88
• Having *voice* communication	3.80	1.11
• Knowing what actions other users are going to take in the *future*	3.75	1.07
• Seeing the position of other users' *cursors*	3.70	0.80
• Knowing to what extent you have completed your work compared to the extent others have completed their work	3.50	0.76
• Being able to view the list of *past* actions carried out by a specific user	3.40	1.14
• Knowing how much time has *elapsed* since other users have used REDUCE	3.40	1.23
• Having *video* communication	3.25	0.97
• Knowing *how long* other users have been in the workspace	2.40	1.19
• Knowing where other users are *geographically located*	1.68	0.95

*Rated on a 5-point scale ranging from 1-"not important" to 5-"very important"

current actions and so on. As shown in the table, "Knowing if other users are satisfied with what you have done" is even more important than knowing other users' viewports, however none of current mechanisms support this type of group awareness. Awareness mechanisms discovered by the top-down approach have demonstrated that designers must consider such information as fundamental requirements when developing awareness mechanisms. For instance, the emergence of Dynamic Task List indicates that supporting group-structural awareness, which has been largely ignored by previous research, is as important as supporting workspace awareness.

- Comparison of different awareness elements

Each question in the five-point scale questionnaire represents one *awareness element*. Thus the importance of an awareness element was determined by the value of the *mean* of a corresponding question. The higher a mean is, the more important that awareness element is. The table shows a sorted list of the means and associated standard deviations of different awareness elements. Overall, standard deviations are small, meaning there is little spread in the scores of each question. The four most important awareness elements rated by the experimental subjects were "Being able to comment on what other users have done" (4.53), "Knowing what actions other users are currently taking" (4.50), "In the case of nonverbal communication, having a communication tool that supports communication between users" (4.50), and "Knowing parts of a document on which other users are currently working" (4.50).

As shown in the table, "Knowing if other users are satisfied with what you have done" was considered as important information by the subjects. It is more or less as important as "Knowing who is in the workspace". However, none of previous research has developed mechanisms to support such information. Interestingly enough, the relative importance of knowing other users' *"past"*, *"current"* and *"future"* actions is also revealed: knowing other users' current actions is the most important, whereas knowing other users' past actions is the least important.

"Knowing where other users are geographically located" was considered the least important by the experimental subjects: the majority of the subjects believed that such information was not all at important. In the interviews, the subjects explained that it was much more important for them to know who other authors are rather than where they are physically located.

- Other suggestions on supporting group awareness

In addition to the discovery of the mechanisms addressed in the previous section, the interview was also used to identify the difficulties, which subjects had to face when writing collaboratively. Several group awareness issues, which are not supported by those mechanisms, have been identified by the interview.

Issue 1: Subjects suggested that a system should allow a user to tell others which part of document that user wants other users to look at.

Issue 2: Several subjects suggested that a system should provide an effective chatting tool, which allows document objects to be embedded into a message before being transferred to the other end. A chat tool should also support private and public chat options.

Issue 3: Almost all subjects suggested that an editor should use *colour* to indicate the status of document objects.

Issue 4: Nearly half of the subjects wanted the system to provide information about "How long other users remain in the shared workspace".

6 Conclusion and Future Work

This paper has thoroughly reviewed the principal awareness mechanisms of What You See Is What I See (WYSIWIS), telepointers, multi-user scrollbars, radar views and distortion-oriented views. *WYSIWIS* is useful in tightly-coupled interaction, but too inflexible to accommodate natural collaboration when users often shift between individual and group work. *Telepointers* provide information about users' presence, but telepointers are inaccessible when users have wholly different viewports. Telepointers could be very intrusive to users in many cases. *Multi-user scrollbars* present relative locations of users, but fail to provide exact users' locations and activities in the workspace. *Radar views* provide a high-level view of the entire workspace, but create a virtual gap between a local view and the global structure of a document. Radar views scale poorly for a large workspace as data presented in radar views becomes too small to be useful. *Distortion-oriented views* display both local details and the global view on one window. However, distortion-oriented views are problematic when remote users' focal points are outside a local user's view or when more than two focal sections overlap.

This research adopts a completely user-centered approach in designing awareness mechanisms; that is, an integrated approach merging a "top-down" approach with a "bottom-up" approach. The "top-down" approach has discovered four innovative mechanisms of *Toggle Multi-user Scrollbar* (TMS), *Split Window View* (SWV), *Modification Director* (MD), and *Dynamic Task List* (DTL). In brief, *TMS* tackles the issue of distraction residing in traditional multi-user scrollbars by giving users the ability to control the visibility of remote scrollbars. *SWV* allows users to gauge easily other users' viewing areas and working areas in the shared document. *MD* notifies a user instantly whenever their work is modified by other users. *DTL* provides high-level information about users' responsibilities, a correlation of workloads of all users. This research provides the successful *differentiation* of the importance of various awareness elements. The results of comparing different awareness elements help designers to have better understanding of which information should be provided to support group awareness. No analysis of the importance of awareness elements has been done by other researchers.

In the future, a "bottom-up" approach will evaluate the effectiveness of these awareness mechanisms by conducting a further set of usability experiments.

Acknowledgement. We sincerely thank Professor Penelope Sanderson for her initial support and valuable insight of this research. We gratefully acknowledge SCHIL for useability experiments support, and Professor Chengzheng Sun for REDUCE support.

References

1. Baecker, R. M., Nastos, D., Posner, I. R., Mawby, K. L.: The User-centred Iterative Design of Collaborative Writing Software, Proc of CHI'93, Amsterdam (1993) 399–405.
2. Beaudouin-Lafon, M., Karsenty, A.: Transparency and Awareness in a Real-Time Groupware System, Proc of UIST'92, CA (1992) 171–180.
3. Benford, S., Bowers, J., Greenhalgh, C., Snowdon, D.: User Embodiment in Collaborative Virtual Environments, Proc of CHI'95, USA, (1995) 242–249.
4. Bly, S. A., Harrisor, S. R., Irwin, S.: Media Spaces: Bringing People Together in a Video, Audio, and Computing Environment, Communications of ACM, vol. 36 (1993) 28–47.
5. Dourish, P., Bellotti, V.: Awareness and Coordination in Shared Workspaces, Proc of CSCW'92, Toronto, Canada (1992) 107–114.
6. Ellis, C. A., Gibbs, S. J., Rein, G.: Groupware: Some Issues and Experiences, *Communications of the ACM,* vol. 34 (1991) 39–58.
7. Greenberg, S., Gutwin, C., Cockburn, A.: Awareness through Fisheye Views in relaxed-WYSIWIS Groupware, Proc of Graphics Interface 1996, Toronto, Canada (1996) 28–38.
8. Greenberg, S., Gutwin, C., Cockburn, A.: Using Distortion-oriented Displays to Support Workspace Awareness, Proc of the HCI'96, Imperial College, London (1996) 229–314.
9. Greenberg, S., Gutwin, C., Roseman, M.: Semantic Telepointers for Groupware, Proc of OzCHI'96, Australia (1996) 54–61.
10. Grudin, J.: Groupware and Social Dynamics: Eight Challenges for Developers, Communications of the ACM, vol. 37 (1994) 92–105.
11. Gutwin, C.: Improving Focus Targeting in Interactive Fisheye Views, Proc of CHI'02, Minneapolis, Minnesota, USA (2002) 267–274.
12. Gutwin, C., Greenberg, S.: The Effects of Workspace Awareness Support on the Usability of Real-time Distributed Groupware, ACM Transactions on Computer-Human Interaction, vol. 6 (1999) 243–281.
13. Gutwin, C., Greenberg, S.: A Descriptive Framework of Workspace Awareness for Real-Time Groupware, Computer Supported Cooperative Work, The Journal of Collaborative Computing, vol. 11 (2002).
14. Gutwin, C., Roseman, M., Greenberg, S.: A Usability Study of Awareness Widgets in a Shared Workspace Groupware System, Proc of CSCW'96, Massachusetts (1996) 258–267.
15. Hayne, S., Pendergast, M., Greenberg, S.: Implementing Gesturing with Cursors in Group Support Systems, Journal of Management Information Systems, vol. 10 (1994) 42–61.
16. Salvador, T., Scholtz, J., Larson, J.: The Denver Model for Groupware Design, ACM SIGCHI Bulletin, vol. 28 (1996) 52–58.
17. Stefik, M., Bobrow, D. G., Foster, G., Lanning, S., Tatar, D.: WYSIWIS Revised: Early Experiences with Multiuser Interfaces, ACM Transactions on Office Information Systems, vol. 5 (1987) 147–167.
18. Suthers, D. D.: Architectures for Computer Supported Collaborative Learning, IEEE International Conference on Advanced Learning Technologies (ICALT'01), Madison, Wisconsin (2001) 25–28.

19. Tran, M. H.: A Group Awareness Framework for Real-time Cooperative Editing based on Experimental Study using REDUCE, Research Report of Master of Information Technology, School of Information Technology, Swinburne University of Technology, Australia (2002).
20. Tran, M. H., Raikundalia, G. K., Yang, Y.: Usability Experiments for Determining Document-Related Awareness in Real-time Cooperative Editing, Proc of the Sixth Australasian Document Computing Symposium ADCS'01, Coffs Harbour (2001) 95–98.
21. Tran, M. H., Raikundalia, G. K., Yang, Y.: Split Window View and Modification Director: Innovative Awareness Mechanisms in Real-time Collaborative Writing, Proc of the Conference on Human Factors HF'2002 (CD ISBN: 0-85590-789-5), Melbourne, Australia (2002).
22. Weir, P., Cockburn, A.: Distortion-oriented Workspace Awareness in DOME, British Computer Society Conference on Human-Computer Interaction, Sheffield Hallam University, Sheffield (1998) 239–252.
23. Yang, Y., Sun, C., Zhang, Y., Jia, X.: Real-time Cooperative Editing on the Internet, IEEE Internet Computing, vol. 4 (2000) 18–25.

Statistics Based Predictive Geo-spatial Data Mining: Forest Fire Hazardous Area Mapping Application

Jong Gyu Han[1], Keun Ho Ryu[2], Kwang Hoon Chi[1], and Yeon Kwang Yeon[1]

[1] Korea Institute of Geosciences & Mineral Resources,
30 Gajung-dong Yusong-ku Daejeon, Republic of Korea
{jghan, khchi, ykyeon}@rock25t.kigam.re.kr
[2] Chungbuk National University,
361-763 Cheongju, Republic of Korea
khryu@dblab.chungbuk.ac.kr

Abstract. In this paper, we propose two statistics based predictive geo-spatial data mining methods and apply them to predict the forest fire hazardous area. The proposed prediction models used in geo-spatial data mining are likelihood ratio and conditional probability methods. In these approaches, the prediction models and estimation procedures depend on the basic quantitative relationships of geo-spatial data sets relevant to the forest fire with respect to the selected areas of previous forest fire ignition. In order to make the prediction map for the forest fire hazardous area prediction map using the two proposed prediction methods and evaluate the performance of prediction power, we applied a FHR (Forest Fire Hazard Rate) and a PRC (Prediction Rate Curve) respectively. When the prediction power of the two proposed prediction models is compared, the likelihood ratio method is more powerful than the conditional probability method. The proposed model for prediction of the forest fire hazardous area would be helpful to increase the efficiency of forest fire management such as prevention of forest fire occurrences and effective placement of forest fire monitoring equipment and manpower.

1 Introduction

The emergence of remote sensing, scientific simulation and survey technologies has dramatically enhanced our capabilities to collect geo-spatial data. However, this explosive growth in data makes the management, analysis and use of data much more difficult. Geo-spatial data mining technique can be used to overcome these difficulties. Geo-spatial data mining is to discover and understand non-trivial, implicit, and previously unknown knowledge in large spatial databases. Widespread use of spatial databases [1, 2] is leading to an increasing interest in mining interesting and useful but implicit patterns [3,4]. The focus of this work can be of importance to the organizations which own large geo-spatial data sets. Recently, knowledge extraction from geo-spatial data has also been highlighted as a key area of research [5]. The organization which makes decisions based on large spatial data sets spreads across numerous domains including ecology and environmental management, public safety, transporta-

X. Zhou, Y. Zhang, and M.E. Orlowska (Eds.): APWeb 2003, LNCS 2642, pp. 370–381, 2003.
© Springer-Verlag Berlin Heidelberg 2003

tion, public health, business, etc. In this study, we has focused on the application domain of forest fire prevention where forestry managers are interested in finding spatio-temporal distribution of forest fires and predicting forest fire hazardous areas from large spatial/non-spatial data sets such as forest maps, topography maps and fire history data. Forest fire provides a good example in examining spatio-temporal representations for GIS applications because of its spatio-temporal variability. A key element in the forest fire hazardous area prediction modeling is a forest fire hazard model, which estimates the fire hazard potential mainly based upon forest attributes, forest utilization, and topography.

In this paper, a statistics based predictive geo-spatial data mining method is developed into predict a forest fire hazardous area in the Youngdong region of Kangwon province, Republic of Korea. We show that, by analyzing historical data on fire ignition point locations, we can gain the necessary predictive capability, making it possible to quantify the ignition probability in space. The analysis is performed using inductive approaches in a raster geographic information system (GIS), and it explores the information contained in the spatial attributes of the phenomenon.

The raster GIS database used in the study contain a layer with the location of ignition events and a set of layers corresponding to potentially explanatory attributes. This spatial data set is analyzed using conditional probability and likelihood ration prediction models.

2 Related Works

The predictive data modeling, while predicting the unknown values of certain attributes of interest based on the values of other attributes in the large amount of database, is a major task in data mining. Predictive data mining has wide applications, including credit evaluation, sales promotion, financial forecasting, and market trend analysis.

Statistical data analysis and inference have studied many parametric and non-parametric methods towards the prediction problems. The statistical linear regression analysis provides a means to obtain the prediction of the continuous attribute by inserting the new values of the explanatory attributes into the fitted regression equation [6]. This method is a purely parametric approach which assumes that the response attribute has a normal distribution, which sometimes could be violated. Statistical pattern recognition, neural nets, and machine learning techniques deal with the prediction of categorical attributes [7].

Bayesian approach is a probabilistic method, which is designed to yield the minimum overall error rate. The problem can be formulated in precise mathematical terms, and an optimal solution can theoretically be found by the probabilistic theory of Bayesian analysis. Unfortunately, however, there are serious obstacles to the direct application of this theory [7]. Nevertheless, there are still some successful applications derived from Bayesian analysis. [8] proposes a finite mixture model by adopting the Bayesian approach for the predictive data mining. A finite mixture model is acquired from instantiated attributes. The conditional predictive distribution of the attribute can be calculated from the model. [8] shows a relatively good performance of this approach by some empirical results.

Neural nets (networks) provide another type of predictive method. Unlike the normal discriminant method described above, most neural network methods are nonparametric: no assumption is made about the underlying population distribution. The back-propagation network (BPN) which is also sometimes referred as a multilayer perceptron, is currently the most general-purpose, and commonly used neural network paradigm [9].

Decision trees are currently the most highly developed techniques for partitioning samples into a set of covering decision rules. A decision tree is a flowchart-like structure consisting of internal nodes, leaf nodes, and branches. Each internal node represents a decision, or test, on a data attribute, and each outgoing branch corresponds to a possible outcome of the test. Each leaf node represents a class. In order to classify an unlabeled data sample, the classifier tests the attribute values of the sample against the decision tree. A path is traced from the root to a leaf node, which holds the class prediction for that sample. ID3 [10, 11] and CART [12] procedures for induction of the decision trees have been well established for a highly effective method.

Other procedures, such as SLIQ [13] and SPRINT [14], have been developed for very large training sets. [15] proposes an efficient algorithm of decision tree induction. The algorithm addresses not only the efficiency and scalability issues, but also the innovative multi-level classification.

3   Proposed Prediction Model for Geo-Spatial Data Mining

In this paper, we proposed and applied two prediction models for spatial data mining based on spatial statistics [16].

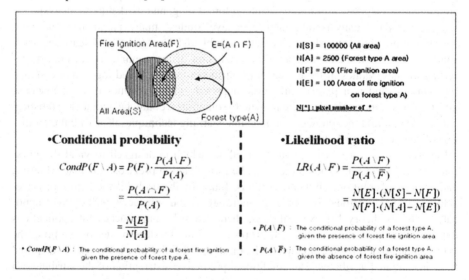

Fig. 1. Schematic diagram and explanation of the proposed prediction models

These are conditional probability and likelihood ratio methods. In these approaches, the prediction models and estimation procedures depend on the basic quantitative relationships of spatial data sets relevant to the forest fire with respect to the selected area of previous forest fire ignition. The two models used in this study are described briefly as follows.

3.1 Conditional Probability Prediction Model

The left side of Figure 1 shows the conceptual description of the conditional probability prediction model. For example, consider the problem of locatiiong a forest fire ignition location area in a region that covers an area of 10,000 pixels and suppose that 500 pixels covered by forest fire ignition are known within the region. The average density of the known fire ignition area in the region is $N[F]/N[S]$, or 500/100,000=0.005, where $N[F]$ is the pixel number of the forest fire ignition area and $N[S]$ is the pixel number of the total region. This is the probability that 1 pixel, chosen at random (with a random generator for example), contains a known forest fire ignition area. Where no other information is available, this ratio can be used as the prior probability of a forest fire ignition area, $P(F)$. Suppose that a binary indicator map such as a forest type map and that 100 out of the 500 pixels of fire ignition area, where the forest type A is on. Clearly the probability of finding a forest fire ignition area is much greater than 0.005, if the forest type A is known to be present; conversely, the probability is less than 0.005 if the forest type A is known to be absent. The favourability for finding a forest fire ignition area, given the presence of the evidence such as the forest type A, can be expressed by the conditional probability:

$$CondP(F \setminus A) = \frac{P(F \cap A)}{P(A)} \qquad (1)$$

where $CondP(F\setminus A)$ is the conditional probability of a forest fire ignition area given the presence of a forest type A. However, $P(A \cap F)$ is equal to the proportion of the total area occupied by F and A together, or $P(A \cap F) = N[A \cap F] / N[S] = N[E]/N[S]$, and similarly $P(A) = N[A]/N[S]$, where $P(A)$ and $N[A]$ are, respectively the probability and area where pattern A is present, respectively. So that the conditional probability of a forest fire occurrence given the presence of the forest type A is 100/2500=0.04, 8 times larger than 0.005, the prior probability of a forest fire ignition area. Effectively, the prediction for new forest fire occurrence of the same type now becomes more focused, because if the forest type A is used as a critical indicator, the search area is reduced from 100,000 pixels to 2,500 pixels.

In order to obtain an expression relating the posterior probability of a forest fire occurrence in terms of the prior probability and a multiplication factor, we note that the conditional probability of being on the forest type map A, given that the presence of a forest fire ignition area is defined as:

$$P(A \setminus F) = \frac{P(A \cap F)}{P(F)} \qquad (2)$$

which for the present case has the value 100/500 = 0.2, Because $P(A \cap F)$ is the same as $P(F \cap A)$, Equations (1) and (2) can be combined to solve for $CondP(F\setminus A)$, satisfying the relationship.

$$CondP(F \setminus A) = P(F) \cdot \frac{P(A \setminus F)}{P(A)} \qquad (3)$$

This states the conditional (posterior) probability of a forest fire occurrence, given that the presence of the forest type A equals the prior probability of the forest fire ignition area $P(F)$ multiplied by the factor $P(A\backslash F)/P(A)$. The numerator of this factor is 0.2 and the denominator is 2500/100000=0.025, so the factor is 0.2/0.025=8. Thus given the presence a forest type A, the posterior probability of a forest fire occurrence is 8 times greater than the prior probability.

3.2 Likelihood Ratio Prediction Model

The likelihood ratio prediction model has been applied to solve the problems of predicting in various disciplines. In particular, it has been applied to quantitative medical diagnoses from clinical symptoms to predict some diseases, e.g.[17, 18, 19]. In [20], a likelihood ratio prediction model is used in ecological GIS application. In geology, the prospector model, which was originally developed in a non-spatial mode [21, 22], uses a likelihood ratio prediction model to search the potential mineral deposit area in an expert system. [23] applies the same approach to the prediction of base-metal deposits in a greenstone belt.

The likelihood ratio prediction model is described here in the context of forest fire hazardous area mapping, where the goal is to locate the forest fire ignition places in advance. The spatial datasets used in this study are formatted in a set of pixel objects. The set of point objects (the past forest fire occurrence area, forest type, digital elevation model (DEM), aspect, slope, road networks, human habitat, and so on) are treated as being binary, either present or absent. In fact, the model requires that each point (pixel) be treated as a small area object, occurring within a small unit cell.

In this study, the likelihood ratio represents the ratio of the two spatial distribution functions, those with the forest fire and those without any occurrences. The right side of Figure 1 shows the conceptual description of the likelihood ratio prediction model. In this model, we assume that the spatial distribution functions of the areas with forest fire happened and those without any occurrences should be distinctly different. For example, LR(A\F), the likelihood ratio of the forest fire occurrences at forest type A in Figure 1 is $P(A\backslash F)/P(A\backslash\overline{F})$ $= N[E]\cdot(N[S]-N[F])/N[F]\cdot(N[A]-N[E])$ and substituting number for the example leads to $P(A\backslash F) = 100 * (100,000 - 500) = 9,950,000$, $P(A\backslash\overline{F}) = 500 * (2,500 - 100) = 1,200,000$, and therefore $P(A\backslash F)/P(A\backslash\overline{F})$ $=$ 9,950,000/1,200,000 = 8.2916. If the value of LR is greater than 1, then the presence of the binary pattern, forest type A, is an important positive evidence for forest fire ignition. However, if the pattern is negatively correlated with the forest fire, LR would be in the range (0, 1). If the pattern is uncorrelated with the forest fire, then LR=1. Thus, for each thematic layer, two spatial distribution features for the areas with forest fire and those without any occurrences are initially computed, firstly. Then the likelihood ratio function for the layer is computed. Using the Bayesian combination rule, the likelihood ratio functions for all data layers are combined. Afterwards, the forest fire hazard prediction map is generated from these joint likelihood ratio functions.

This prediction model is not restricted to this case, however, and can be applied to the prediction of the other environment changes and natural hazard.

4 Forest Fire Hazardous Area Prediction Procedure

The procedure for making a forest fire hazardous area prediction map is as follows (Figure 2);

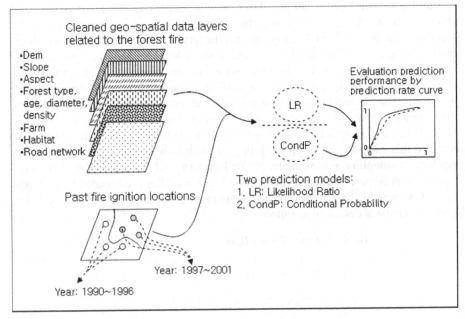

Fig. 2. Procedure for locating forest fire hazardous area

First of all, we established the spatial dataset related to the past forest fire ignition area. And we have constructed thematic maps like forestry maps (forest type, diameter, density, ages), topography maps (DEM, slope, aspect), human activities maps (road networks, farm and building boundaries) and fire history data (ignition location, year, month date, time, climate conditions, cause, burned area). These thematic maps are pre-processed for spatial data mining of forest fire hazardous area prediction. In the pre-processing step, the gridding as well as multi-buffering data processing techniques are used for spatial computation. To extract general forest fire ignition patterns such as spatial distribution features, it may be better to use elevation, slope, road netwoks and farm boundary thematic maps.

Secondly, we performed the relevance analysis to select suitable thematic maps related to forest fire occurrences. Usually, there may be a large number of thematic maps associated with forest fire. However, it is neither desirable nor feasible to use all the thematic maps to do prediction. In most cases, only a few of them are highly relevant to the response attribute and are valuable for prediction.

Thus, it is necessary to perform an effective relevance analysis to filter out those attributes which are weakly relevant to the response attribute. However, the decision on whether an attribute or the combination of attributes is weak or not given its relevance measure is still subjective to the individual's or expert's opinions. So the purpose of our relevance analysis is to provide the users with an index of attribute relevance of each predictor. The choice of the predictors to be used in prediction depends on the user's judgment.

Thirdly, we employed a multiple layer integration method that predicts the probability of forest fire occurrences using the two proposed predictive spatial data mining methods regarding topography, forestry, fire history data and the distance to human built infrastructures. This method integrates the relevance analysis and prediction modeling at single level and enables the user to perform prediction at an optimal level abstraction interactively. For flexible and efficient multiple level prediction, we have used to the sharing method, which shares some intermediate analysis results with the neighborhood levels of abstraction rather than performing the prediction analysis. FHR (Forest fire Hazard Rate) is used to integrate multiple layers in this study. It is required that each layer used in the proposed prediction models is conditional independence assumption. For example, if two layers (V_1 and V_2) are conditionally independent with respect to a set of fire ignition locations, FHR is computed by multiplying the predicted values at the attribute value at the point thematic map 1 and 2. The general formula is described as follows

---

•FHR: Forest fire Hazard Rate

$$FHR(p)_{CondP} = CondP(V_1'(p)) \times \cdots \times CondP(V_m'(p)), i = 1, \cdots, m$$

$$FHR(p)_{LR} = LR(V_1'(p)) \times \cdots \times LR(V_m'(p)), i = 1, \cdots, m$$

$V_i'(p)$: *Attribute value at the point thematic map (i)*

LR *Likelihood ratio*

$CondP$ *Conditional probability*

Lastly, we have carried out the efficiency and effectiveness of the proposed prediction modeling for forest fire hazardous area. For this step, we have used the strategy of cross validation for the prediction power using different fire history information of two forest fire occurrence periods. Moreover, in order to validate of prediction accuracy, the prediction rate curve method has been applied.

5 Experiments and Results

The study area for predicting forest fire hazardous area is Youngdong area of Korea which is composed of Samchuk, Donghae, Gangneung, Yangyang, Kosung and Sokcho city. The largest forest fire in modern history of Korea occurred in April, 2000 in Youngdong area. Youngdong area is located in the east of the Taeback Mountains, which divide Kangwon province into Youngdong region and Youngseo region, the eastern part and the western part of that, respectively. The locations of ignition points are marked on 1:25,000 scale topographic maps, and each point is associated with a field form where other information such as the time of ignition, area burned, and land use are recorded. These point location data are digitized to a point layer. The geographic database sets for fire ignition prediction analysis are described in section 4. At first, an analysis of the relationship of each individual independent attribute with the response attribute was performed to get an idea of the relative importance of each attribute in explaining fire ignition. The results of the analysis of relevance of each independent attribute for the data sets corresponding to fire ignition is that forest type, elevation, slope, road networks, farm and building boundaries thematic maps have significant attributes in the data set corresponding to fire ignition. However, tree diameter, density, ages and aspect maps have the less significant attributes in the data set.

In the spatial database, it was assumed that the time of the study was the year 1996 and that all the spatial data available in 1996 were compiled, including the distribution of the forest fire ignition locations, which had occurred prior to that year. The occurrences play a pivotal role in constructing prediction models by establishing probabilistic relationships between the pre-1996 forest fires and the remainder of the input data set. The predictions based on those relationships were then evaluated by comparing the estimated hazard classes with the distribution of the forest fire ignition locations that had occurred after 1996, i.e., during the period 1997 to 2001.

To make the forest fire hazardous area map using the two proposed methods and evaluate the performance of its prediction power, we applied a FHR (Forest Fire Hazard Rate) and a PRC (Prediction Rate Curve) respectively. The FHR for each prediction model was calculated by the formula described in section 4. For validation purpose, the past fire ignition location data sets were partitioned into two independent data sets (one is the forest fire ignition data set of pre-1996 and the other one is that of during the period between 1997 to 2001) for model training and validation, respectively.

Figure 3 shows the prediction rates of the two proposed models with respect to the 1997 to 2001 forest fire occurrences. In Figure 3, the prediction rates with respect to the "future" 1997 to 2001 occurrences of "likelihood ratio" are more powerful than "conditional probability".

For the visualization of a prediction pattern, the relative ranks of the models were applied to the pattern. To obtain the relative ranks for the prediction pattern, the estimated probabilities of all pixels in the study area were sorted in descending order. Then the ordered pixel values were divided into 11 classes (colored red to blue) as follows. The pixels with the highest 5 percent estimated probability values were classified as the "100"class, shown in "red" in Figure 4, occupying 5 percent of the study area. The pixels with the next highest 5 percent values were presented in "orange", occupying additional 5 percent of the study area, and were classified as the "95" class. We repeated the classification process eight more times, for classes 5 percent apart, and the resulting ten classes are shown in the ten different colors. Finally, the "blue" color was assigned to the remaining 50 percent of the area.

Figure 4 represents the forest fire hazardous area map predicted by the likelihood ratio prediction model. From the result of the prediction map (Figure 4), hazardous or non-hazardous areas can be identified. The pixels with the red, orange or yellow colors in the predicted map can be interpreted as having higher likelihood of future fire occurrence. On the other hand, less hazardous areas are covered by the blue pixels in the predicted map. The circles with the red color are the past forest fire ignition locations.

The forest fire hazardous area prediction model described in this paper provides an effective method for estimation of the degree of forest fire hazard. It is based upon the forestry, topography, human activity attributes, which contribute to fire hazard and risk. Those we have found out in the multiple thematic maps emerged as affective to forest fire occurrences are elevation, slope, forest type, road network, farm and habitat zone condition. The effectiveness of the models estimated, tested, and showed acceptable degree of goodness. The proposed model developed would be helpful to increase the efficiency of forest fire management such as detection of forest fire occurrences and effective disposition of forest fire prevention resources.

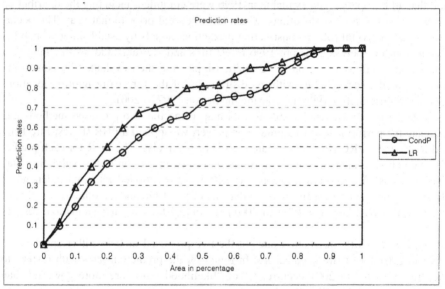

Fig. 3. Prediction rate curve of each models; the curve shows that the likelihood ratio method is more powerful than conditional probability method.

6 Conclusion

Spatial data mining is one of the most efficient tools in discovering interesting, potentially useful and high utility patterns from large spatial data sets. In this study, we proposed and applied two prediction models for spatial data mining based on spatial statistics. These are conditional probability and likelihood ratio methods. In these approaches, the prediction models and estimation procedures depend on the basic quantitative relationships of spatial data sets relevant to forest fire with respect to the

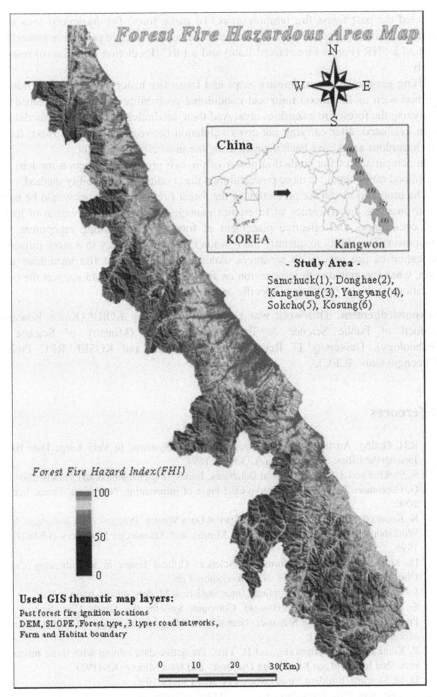

Fig. 4. Forest fire hazardous area map produced by predictive geo-spatial data mining using likelihood ratio prediction model.

selected the past forest fire ignition areas. To make forest fire hazardous area map using the two proposed methods and evaluate the performance of prediction power, we applied a FHR (Forest Fire Hazard Rate) and a PRC (Prediction Rate Curve) respectively.

Using geographic maps, forestry maps and forest fire history, a spatial data mining method such as likelihood ratio and conditional probability has been developed for analyzing the forest fire hazardous area. And then, predictive power of each model has been evaluated, after carrying out cross validation between the models. Next, forest fire hazardous areas have been mapped using the most effective model.

In comparison of the prediction power of the two proposed prediction models, the likelihood ratio method is more powerful than the conditional probability method.

The proposed model for prediction of the forest fire hazardous area would be helpful to increase the efficiency of forest fire management such as prevention of forest fire occurrences and effective placement of forest fire monitoring equipment and manpower. The ability to quantify the ignition risk can be the key to a more informed allocation of fire prevention resources. Additionally, the forest fire hazardous area map, when integrated with information on fire propagation risk, can support the optimization of silvical practices in specific areas.

Acknowledgement. This work was supported in part by KORP (Korea Research Council of Public Science & Technology), MOST (Ministry of Science & Technology), University IT Research Center Project and KOSEF RRC Project (Cheongju Univ. ICRC).

References

1.   R.H. Guting. An Introduction to Spatial Database Systems. In Very Large Data Bases Jorunal(Publisher: SpringerVerlag), October 1994.
2.   S. Shekhar and S. Chawla. Spatial Databases: Issues, Implementation and Trends. 2001.
3.   G. Greenman. Turning a map into a cake layer of information. New York Times, Feb 12 2000.
4.   K. Koperski, J. Adhikary, and J. Han. Spatial Data Mining: Progress and Challenges. In In Workshop on Research Issues on Data Mining and Knowledge Discovery (DMKD'96), 1996.
5.   D. Mark. Geographical Information Science: Critical Issues in an Emerging Cross-Disciplinary Research Domain. NSF Workshop, Feb.
6.   J. Neter and L. Wasseman. Applied Linear Statistical Models, 4th ed. Irwin,
7.   S. M. Weiss and C. A. Kulikowski. Computer Systems that Learn: Classification and Prediction Methods from Statistics, Neural Nets, Machine Learning, and Expert Systems. Morgan Kaufman, 1991.
8.   P. Kontkanen, P. Myllym.aki, and H. Tirri. Predictive data mining with finite mixtures. Proc. 2nd Int. Conf. on Knowledge Discovery and Data Mining (KDD'96)
9.   D. M. Skapura. Building Neural Networks. ACM Press, 1996.
10.   J. R. Quinlan. Induction of decision trees. Machine Learning.
11.   J. R. Quinlan. C4.5: Programs for Machine Learning. Morgan Kaufmann, 1993.

12. L. Breiman, J. Friedman, R. Olshen, and C. Stone. Classification and Regression Trees. Wadsworth International Group, 1984.
13. M. Mehta, R. Agrawal, and J. Rissanen. SLIQ: A fast scalable classifier for data mining. In Proc. 1996 Int. Conference on Extending Database Technology (EDBT'96), Avignon, France, March 1996.
14. J. Shafer, R. Agrawal, and M. Mehta. SPRINT: A scalable parallel classifier for data mining. In Proc. 1996 Int. Conf. Very Large Data Bases.
15. M. Kamber, L. Winstone, W. Gong, S. Cheng, and J. Han. Generalization and decision tree induction: Efficient classification in data mining. In Proc. of 1997. Int. Workshop on Research Issues on Data Engineering (RIDE'97)
16. Jong Gyu Han, Yeon Kwang Yeon, Kwang Hoon Chi and Keun Ho Ryu, Prediction of Forest Fire Hazardous Area Using Predictive Spatial Data Mining, Proc. of Int. Conf. on Information and Knowledge Engineering. P348–358, 2002
17. Lusted, L.B., Introduction to Medical Decision Making: Charles Thomas, Springfield, 271p.
18. Aspinall, P. J. and Hill, A.R., Clinical inferences and decisions-I. Diagnosis and Bayes' theorem: Opthalmic and Physiological Optics, v.3, p.295–304, 1983.
19. Spiegelhalter, D.J. and Knill-Jones, R.P., Statistical and knowledge-based approaches to clinical decision-support systems, with an application in gastroenterology: Journal of the royal Statistical Society, A, Part 1, p. 35–77, 1984,
20. Aspinall, R.J., An inductive modeling procedure based on Bayes' theorem for analysis of pattern in spatial data: Internationl Journal of Geographical Information System, v.6(2), p.105–121, 1992.
21. Reboh, R. andReiter, J., A knowledge-based system for regional mineral resource assessment: Final report, SRI project 4119, p 267, 1983.
22. McCammon, R.B., Prospector II –The redesign of Prospector: AI system in Government, March 27–31, 1989, Washington, D.C., p.88–92, 1989.
23. Reddy, R.K., Bonham-Carter, G.F. and Galley, A.G., Developing a geographic expert system for regional mapping of Volcanogenic Massive Sulphide (VMS) deposit potential: Nonrenewable Resources, v. 1(2), p.112–124, 1992.

Knowledge Representation, Ontologies, and the Semantic Web*

Evimaria Terzi[1], Athena Vakali[1], and Mohand-Saïd Hacid[2]

[1] Informatics Dpt., Aristotle University,
54006 Thessaloniki, Greece
`evimaria,avakali@csd.auth.gr`
[2] Université Claude Bernard Lyon 1,
Laboratoire d'Ingénierie des Systèmes d'Information,
69622 Villeurbanne, France
`mshacid@.bat710.univ-lyon1.fr`

Abstract. A unified representation for web data and web resources, is absolutely necessary in nowdays large scale Internet data management systems. This representation will allow for the machines to meaningfully process the available information and provide semantically correct answers to imposed queries. Ontologies are expected to play an important role towards this direction of web technology which defines the so called, Semantic Web. The goal of this paper is to provide an overview of the Knowledge Representation (KR) techniques and languages that can be used as standards in the Semantic Web .

1 Introduction

The development of standards that guarantee interoperability at various levels, has been one of the major factors contributing in the successful establishment of the World Wide Web (*WWW*). As pointed out in [5], the current Web can be classified as the second generation Web. The first generation started with the "handwritten" HTML web pages. The second generation, made a step forward introducing machine - generated web pages or even active HTML pages. The common characteristic between the first two web generations is that they are both human - oriented. The third generation of the Web is what is widely known as the "Semantic Web" and its main difference from the previous two generations is that it aims to machine - readable information ([1]).

1.1 Applications of the Semantic Web

The Semantic Web will enable intelligent services (such as information brokers, search agents and information filters) to process information automatically and it

* This work is supported by the bilateral research collaboration programme Platon between Greece and France, 2002–2004 financed by the French and Greek Secretariat of Research and Technology, Ministry of Development.

X. Zhou, Y. Zhang, and M.E. Orlowska (Eds.): APWeb 2003, LNCS 2642, pp. 382–387, 2003.

is expected that the existing e-services (of limited functionality) will be replaced. A more detailed description of the applications and the areas of impact of the Semantic Web, that include search engines, intelligent agents and push systems, is given in [9].

The remainder of the paper is organized as follows: The next section identifies the role of Ontologies in the Semantic Web. Section 3 describes the core of support of semantics on the web, with reference on the XML and RDF standards, while in Section 4 the most popular Ontologies languages are outlined. Conclusions are given in Section 5.

2   Ontologies in the Semantic Web

For web-based systems in specific, the poor communication and lack of a common understanding (due to the different languages, the overlapping and/or mismatched concepts, the differences in structures and methods) may entail to poor knowledge and software interoperability. This problem of poor communication can be solved by the introduction of ontologies. Ontologies are expected to have a major impact in the development of the Semantic Web, and mainly in the information exchange process.

The definition of the ontology given in [11] can be adopted: "An ontology is a logical theory accounting for the intended meaning of a formal vocabulary, i.e., its ontological commitment to a particular conceptualization of the world. The intended models of a logical language using such a vocabulary are constraint by its ontological commitment (and the underlying conceptualization) by approximating these intended models." This definition captures the two most important and necessary features of an ontology which are the vocabulary and the corresponding definitions. The vocabulary includes the terms for classes and relations, while the definitions of these terms may be informal text, or may be specified using a formal language like predicate logic. The advantage of formal definitions is that these definitions allow a machine to perform much deeper reasoning, while the disadvantage is that these definitions are much more difficult to construct. Typically, a layered approach is adopted, in order to represent the knowledge on the web and in order to define the ontologies. At the lowest level, there is a need for a generic mechanism that will allow for expression of machine-readable semantics of data. The Schema layer lies on top of this layer whereas a formal *KR* language will be used as the third logical layer.

Ontology models and languages need to be established so that the potential of ontologies to be fully exploited. In order for this to be done, these languages and models should be based on existing mechanisms and schemata like RDF and XML. In this paper We mainly focus on the third layer and we present an overview of the already proposed languages which provide Web-based *KR* and knowledge sharing, mainly via ontologies. These languages are mostly based either on XML or RDF and their goal is satisfy the following three requirements [5]:

- *Global Expressive and Modeling Power:* which is ecessary to the existing high degree of heterogeneity.
- *Syntactic Interoperability:* High syntactic interoperability is achieved when the data expressed in a specific format can be easily read by many applications that use even already existing parsers. If such parsers do not exist and there is extra effort for the data to be read, then the interoperability is low.
- *Semantic Interoperability and Reasoning Support:* Semantic interoperability refers to the mapping between the unknown terms and known terms in the data.

3   XML/RDF to Support Semantics on the Web

3.1   The XML Standard

XML [2] is intended as a markup language for arbitrary document structure,as opposed to HTML, which is a markup-language for a specific kind of hypertext documents. Regarding XML syntax it looks very familiar to this of HTML. An XML document consists of a properly nested set of open and closed tags, where each tag can have a number of attribute-value pairs. The important thing about XML is that the vocabulary of the tags as well as the way these tags can be combined is not predefined and it determined by the application and gives additional information about the text itself.

Although XML is characterized by high flexibility, there may be some problems that will occur when it comes to the machine processing issues of XML documents. In order for these problems to be solved, there is a need to define grammars for XML tags. This information is contained in a Document Type Definition (DTD) that specifies the valid elements, the contents of these elements and which attributes may modify an element. An XML document that is associated with a DTD and conforms to the rules that are defined by it is said to be valid. Notice though, that the DTD just provides the syntax of the XML document and gives no information about the semantics. The semantics of the DTDs and the XML Documents are just implicit and can only be perceived by humans that read the document's source code.

Recently, W3C has released an alternative to DTDs called XML Schema. XML Schemas provide greater flexibility in the definition of an XML application, even allowing the definition of complex data types, while they also use the same syntactic style as other XML Documents. However, XML Schema provides just an advanced XML grammar specification and data typing, and it still suffers from the semantic drawbacks of DTDs.

3.2   The RDF Schema

The real value and the basic conception of RDF [13] is its data model. More specifically, it defines a very simple data model of triples (subject, value, object). Every object O has an attribute A with value V. Such a triple corresponds to the relation that is commonly written as A(O,V). With this simple model objects and their properties may be presented. Coming back to the graph representation the RDF triples can also be represented by a labeled edge between two nodes: [O]-A→[V]. This notation allows the first and third elements of the triple to be combined in many ways.

Once we have the data model, there is a need to describe the characteristics of the objects being modeled. Just as XML Schema provides a vocabulary definition facility for XML, RDF Schema provides a similar facility for RDF. The main difference between RDF and XML Schemas is that in RDF case the schemas do not define a permissible syntax but instead classes, properties, and their interrelation: they operate directly at the data model level, rather than the syntax level. Scaled up to the Web RDF schemas are a key technology, as they will allow machines to make inferences about the data collected from the web.

3.3   XML – RDF and the Semantic Web Language Requirements

The Table 1 below shows whether XML and RDF described in the previous subsections can satisfy the basic three requirements imposed by the semantic web:

Table 1. XML/RDF and the Semantic Web Requirements

	Universal Expressive Power	Syntactic Inter- operability	Semantic Inter -operability
XML	Yes	Yes	Several Disadvantages
RDF	Yes	Yes	Several Advantages

4   Ontology Languages

There are two main approaches that have been followed towards the development of languages for ontologies representation. The first class of languages is based on First Order Logic (*FOL*), whereas the second class is based on ontology-representation. *FOL*-based languages have been adopted by organizations and cooperating partners whose main concern is not to make their knowledge publicly available over the Web. A relatively detailed description of the above ontology languages and their relationship with the previously analyzed web standards will follows.

4.1   SHOE – Simple HTML Ontology Extensions

SHOE is a *KR* language that allows ontologies to be designed and used directly to the World Wide Web (WWW). Based on the description provided in [8], SHOE's basic structure consists of ontologies, entities which define rules guiding what kind of assertions may be made and what kind of inferences may be drawn on ground assertions, and instances that make assertions to these rules. Regarding the *syntax* of SHOE, it has been primarily selected to fit seamlessly with that of HTML. Using similar syntax with HTML makes it easy for those that know HTML to learn SHOE as well. A slight variant of SHOE syntax also exists for compatibility with XML [14], which is a requirement for compatibility with today's applications since XML is an emerging standard for transmitting web documents. Two applications of SHOE developed in Univeristy of Maryland for research reasons are summarized in [8].

4.2   XOL – XML-Based Ontology Exchange Language

XOL is a language for ontology exchange. It is "designed to provide a format for exchanging ontology definitions among a set of interested parties. The ontology definitions that XOL is designed to encode include both schema information (meta-data), such as class definitions from object databases, as well as non-schema information (ground facts), such as object definitions from object databases. The syntax of XOL is based on XML that is a widely adopted web standard with high expressive power and syntactic interoperability, which are the basic requirements for the syntax of a language that can be used in the context of the Semantic Web. The semantics of XOL are based on OKBC-Lite, which is a simplified form of the knowledge model for the OKBC (Open Knowledge Base Connectivity.) [3], that is an API (application program interface) for accessing frame knowledge representation systems. The XOL was designed in response to a study of ontology languages performed by the Bio-Ontology Core Group. The study had found that no existing ontology-exchange language satisfied the requirements of the bio-informatics community.

4.3   OIL – Ontology Interchange Language

OIL [4,6,7] proposes a "joint standard for integrating ontologies with existing and arising web standards". OIL is a Web-based representation and inference layer for ontologies, which combines the widely used modeling primitives from frame-based languages with the formal semantics and reasoning services provided by description logics. OIL's *syntax* is layered on RDF. One of the design goals of OIL was to maximize integration with RDF applications. Thus most RDF Schemas are valid OIL ontologies and most of OIL ontologies can be partially understood by RDF processors. However, unlike RDF, OIL has very well defined *semantics.*

There are mainly multiple layers of OIL, where each subsequent layer adds functionality to the previous one. Core OIL is basically RDFS without reification. Standard OIL adds a number of description logic primitives to the Core OIL, and is the base of most of the work done with OIL today. Instance OIL adds the capability to model instances essentially using their description in RDF. Finally, Heavy OIL is an undefined layer that will include future extensions to the language. This layered approach allows applications to use pre-defined subsets of the language to manage complexity.

Nowadays, DARPA Agent Markup Language + Ontology Interchange Language (DAML+OIL) [10], [12] is a new language created with the best features of SHOE, DAML, OIL and several other markup approaches. It is considered to be the most advanced web ontology language, and it is expected to provide the basis for future web standards for ontologies.

5   Conclusions

Ontologies are expected to play an important role in the context of Semantic Web. This paper identifies on the major role of the Ontologies in the Semantic web, identifies the currently used standards and describes languages that have been proposed in order to define and describe ontologies on the web.

References

1. T. Berners – Lee: "Weaving the Web". Harper, San Francisco 1999.
2. T. Bray, J. Paoli and C. Sperberg-McQueen: " Extensible Markup Language (XML)". W3C (World Wide Web Consortium), February 1998. Available at http://www.w3.org/TR/1998/REC-xml-19980210.html.
3. V.K. Chaudhri, A. Farquhar, R. Fikes, P.D. Karp, J.P. Rice: "Open Knowldege Base Connectivity 2.0.2".http://WWW-KSL-SVC.stanford.edu:5915/doc/release/okbc/okbc-spec/okbc-2-0-2.pdf, 1998.
4. S. Decker, D. Fensel, F. Harmelen, I. Horrocks, S. Melnik, M. Klein and J. Broekstra: " Knowledge Representation on the Web". In Proceedings of the 2000 International Workshop on Description Logics (DL2000). Aachen, Germany, August 2000.
5. S. Decker et al: " The Semantic Web – on the respective Roles of XML and RDF.
6. D. Fensel et al.: "OIL in a nutshell". In Knowledge Acquisition, Modeling, and Management, Proceedings of the European Knowledge Acquisition Conference (EKAW-2000), R. Dieng et al. (eds.), Lecture Notes in Artificial Intelligence, LNAI, Springer-Verlag, October 2000.
7. D. Fensel et al.: "OIL: An ontology infrastructure for the Semantic Web.". In IEEE Intelligent Systems, 16(2):38–45, 2001.
8. J. Heflin, J. Hendler and S. Luke: "SHOE: A Knowledge Representation Language for Internet Applications". Technical Report CS-TR-4078 (UMIACS TR-99-71). 1999.
9. J. Heflin: " Towards the Semantic Web: Knowledge Representation in a Dynamic, Distributed Environment". PhD Thesis, University of Maryland, Computer Sciences Dept. 2001.
10. J. Hendler and D. McGuinness: " The DARPA agent markup language". IEEE Intelligent Systems, 15(6):72–73, November/December 2000.
11. N. Guarino: "Formal Ontology and Information Systems". In Proceedings of Formal Ontology and Information Systems, Trento, Italy, June 1998. IOS Press.
12. Joint US/EU Ad Hoc Agent Markup Language Committee. DAML+OIL, 2001.
13. "Resource Description Framework (RDF) Schema Specification 1.0", W3C Recommendation, March 2001. Available at http://www.w3.org/RDF/
14. eXtensible MArkup Language (XML) 1.0, Available at: http://www.w3.org/XML/

Web Wrapper Validation

Eng-huan Pek[1], Xue Li[1], and Yaozong Liu[2]

[1]School of Information Technology and Electrical Engineering
The University of Queensland
Brisbane, Queensland 4072, Australia
xueli@itee.uq.edu.au
[2] National University of Defence Technology
Changsha, Hunan, China

Abstract. Web wrapper extracts data from HTML document. The accuracy and quality of the information extracted by web wrapper relies on the structure of the HTML document. If an HTML document is changed, the web wrapper may or may not function correctly. This paper presents an Adjacency-Weight method to be used in the web wrapper extraction process or in a wrapper self-maintenance mechanism to validate web wrappers. The algorithm and data structures are illustrated by some intuitive examples.

1 Introduction

A wrapper (also referred to as web wrapper) is an information extraction software program. Its goal is to transform data items, extracted from a semi-structured document (for example, an HTML document), into a self-described representation (for example, a XML document) that then can be used by a variety of database-oriented applications.

The wrapper validation can be compared with the web wrapper verification. Web wrapper verification [1] uses a machine learning technique to determine whether a wrapper is operating correctly against the content of the web document. For example, it calculates the similarity between web pages with respect to a set of predefined fields which are described by a collection of global numeric features, such as word count, average word length, the number of punctuation and upper-case characters in the strings etc. It then estimates the probability based on the measured values to yield an overall probability that identifies whether the page was correctly wrapped. In other words, this is a content-based approach to verify wrappers. However, in the real world the information extraction is mostly based on the information presentation structures. The usage of this property of the information extraction is feasible and must not be ignored. Hence, in this paper we present an Adjacency-Weight method to record the information extraction path for validating web wrappers. Our approach is structure-oriented and will exploit the relevance between the information content and information presentation logic.

A wrapper extraction path will follow the HTML structure in a top-down fashion. Our approach makes use of the complete extraction path starting from the root of data node of an HTML file. The concept of Adjacency-Weight is defined as the number of children nodes per parent node, and the number of possible data nodes that are

X. Zhou, Y. Zhang, and M.E. Orlowska (Eds.): APWeb 2003, LNCS 2642, pp. 388–393, 2003.
© Springer-Verlag Berlin Heidelberg 2003

extractable using this extraction path. The information of Adjacency-Weight recorded at time T_1, will then be used for wrapper validation at time T_2. Our wrapper validation algorithm is then developed for the validation of any wrapper used in the WWW environment.

Section 2 briefly introduces the wrapper validation problem. It will show some rationale behind our ideas. Section 3 describes our proposed web wrapper validation algorithm. The conclusions are given in section 4.

2 Wrapper Validation Problem

A wrapper consists of a set of extraction rules and is specific to one source only. The extraction rules are based on the document-object model (DOM) [2]. This model uses the hierarchical structure of a web document to identify and extract relevant information. A wrapper can be constructed manually, or by using semi-automatic or automatic wrapper generation toolkits. Wrapper development and maintenance by hand is both labor intensive and error-prone because web sources are seldom static. Therefore, information extraction from web source has led to researches into semi-automatic construction of wrappers [3, 4, 5, 6, 7, 8] and automatic construction of wrappers [1, 9, 10] using machine learning techniques [11, 12, 13], which are based on inductive learning that can perform some wrapper verification and maintenance tasks. However, for a large number of manually or semi-automatically constructed wrappers, the maintenance of wrappers requires a mechanism that can make those wrappers self-maintainable. So that the changes in the underlying document structures will be detectable. In other

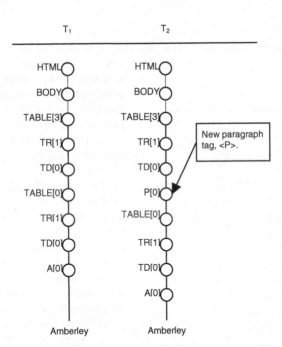

Fig. 1. Behaviour of two extraction processes on the same data item. Extraction rule relies on HTML hierarchy structure and its extraction rule. The horizontal axis is time.

words, we need to build in the wrappers with the capacity of self-maintainable extraction rules.

Web developers may constantly adjust their sites to make web pages more user-friendly, or attractive that would often compromise the accuracy of the wrappers. Using a wrapper to extract information from HTML document is unlike a database where data items are identified by attributes. The wrapper's weakness is that it cannot interpret the types of changes occurred in HTML structures. This means that wrapper does not understand semantic representations of HTML document. The implementation of extraction rule strictly depends on the HTML structure, this is known as the "Scaling Problem" in literatures. We use the following examples to show that wrappers may extract information incorrectly. In this paper's discussion, we use the *dot notation* convention to represent the extraction path. More details on the extraction languages can be found in [4].

Example 1. Consider a fragment of an HTML tree structure in Fig.1. Suppose we have constructed a wrapper using single-dot notation expression to describe an extraction rule for extracting the data item "Amberley" at time T_1. The extraction path (EP) is defined as follows:

```
EP(T1) =
HTML.BODY.TABLE[3].TR[1].TD[0].TABLE[0].TR[1].TD[0].A[0].txt.
```

Later at time T_2, suppose the information contents remain unchanged when the web document is restructured by adding a paragraph tag P to the tree structure. So that the P tag becomes the parent node of the table tag *TABLE[0]* and the *TABLE[0]* tag becomes the children node of the P tag. Though the information contents remains consistent, the wrapper stops extracting information because of a broken extraction path. This extraction rule is too strict and in most cases the wrapper will fail to work.

However, the wrapper using double-dot notation expression to extract the same data item may continue to extract information correctly as long as there is a descendent path similar to *TABLE[0].TR[1].TD[0].A [0].txt* anywhere in the

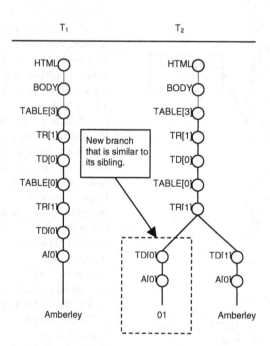

Fig. 2. It is impossible for wrapper to distinguish each operation that its extraction path is invalid. The horizontal axis is time.

document relative to the ancestor path. The extraction rules using double-dot notation expression will depend on the ancestor definition. For instance, in the case of ancestor path defined as:

```
HTML.BODY.TABLE[3].TR[1].TD[0].TABLE[0]
```

and its descendent path as:

```
TD[0].A[0].txt
```

That is,

```
EP(T₁) = HTML.BODY.TABLE[3].TR[1].TD[0].TABLE[0]..TD[0].A[0].txt
```

This double-dot notation expression extraction rule is broken because of the strict extraction rule defined in the ancestor path.

Example 2. In Fig.2, a new branch of nodes similar to the sibling nodes is added at one level higher in the hierarchy tree structure at time T_2. Both extraction rules defined in example 1, which use single- and double-dot notation expressions, are syntactically correct. But, the extracted data item is semantically incorrect.

In example 1 we have identified that the wrapper extraction rules are dependent on HTML structure. In example 2 we have identified that the wrapper does not understand semantic changes. In general, it is impossible for a wrapper to distinguish each operation in which its extraction path is valid. In these examples, the structures of the page are syntactically different but semantically consistent. This consistency is essentially an agreement between wrapper and data source, and is the ultimate goal we want to achieve. It is basically saying that if a wrapper agrees to obey certain rules, the data source would promise to work correctly.

3 Adjacency-Weight Method

Assuming a web document is represented in an HTML hierarchical tree structure, the Adjacency-Weight algorithm is designed to compare: the extraction path; the value of a node which represents the number of adjacent children nodes; and the number of leaf-nodes which are also extractable by the specific extraction path at time T_1 with that information obtained by the same wrapper at time T_2.

Particularly, an Adjacency-Weight of an HTML structure is a representation of the number of children nodes. For example, in Fig.3 (Region R0) the TABLE[0] node has

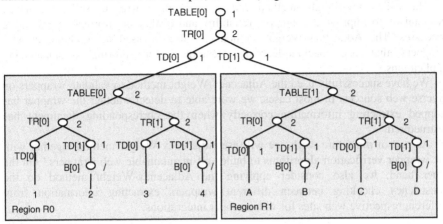

Fig. 3. A region consists of data items and HTML tags. Two similar regions have different data items.

an Adjacency-Weight of 2, and the TD[1] node of TR[1] node of TABLE[0] has an Adjacency-Weight of 1. If a child node is a leaf node, its Adjacency-Weight is marked by a forward slash "/" to indicate the end of extraction path.

The Adjacency-Weight method needs to keep three kinds of data describing extraction paths of an HTML structure at time T_1. They are:

1. A set of complete **extraction paths** for all data items starting from the root node to leaf nodes of an HTML tree structure. That means, we record all the tag names of every node and its node index written inside the square brackets. We denote an extraction path by $EP(T_1)$.

2. The **Adjacency-Weight** of extraction path. It is always written in front of the node tag name. A Node that contains a leaf node is indicated by a forward slash "/".

3. The sum of leaf nodes derivable from extraction path. This sum is called a **reflection** of an extraction path and is denoted by $\theta(T_1)$.

The Adjacency-Weight Method compares Adjacency-Weight value of each node recorded at time T_1 with that of HTML structure obtained at time T_2. If Adjacency-Weight value of a node is different from that of time T_2, its children and descendent nodes at each hierarchical level are compared with the extraction path $EP(T_1)$. If all nodes of new branches are similar to $EP(T_1)$ the reflection at time $\theta(T_2)$ is to be incremented by 1. Whenever $\theta(T_2)$ is greater than $\theta(T_1)$, wrapper $W(T_2)$ is considered invalid. Otherwise wrapper $W(T_2)$ is considered valid if $\theta(T_2)$ is less than or equal to $\theta(T_1)$.

4 Conclusions

In this paper, we have presented the Adjacency-Weight method for web wrapper validation. We have also identified some types of changes that would cause wrappers to extract information incorrectly. The proposed algorithm should be complementary to web wrapper verification [1].

The Adjacency-Weight method can be used in a wrapper self-maintenance mechanism, to improve the wrapper reliability and quality in information extraction processes. The Adjacency-Weight method can also be used in combination with wrappers that use machine-learning techniques for information-management applications.

We have successfully used the Adjacency-Weight method to validate wrappers on diverse web sources. In most cases, we were able to detect whether the wrapper has stopped extracting information correctly when the corresponding document has restructured.

As part of the future work, we will use Adjacency-Weight method together with the wrapper verification algorithms to build self-maintainable web wrappers. On the other hand, we also consider applying the Adjacency-Weight method on the consistency checking between different wrappers extracting information from different respective web sites for web wrapper integrations.

Acknowledgement. The authors would like to acknowledge Dr. Xiaofang Zhou for his initial ideas and many constructive discussions.

References

1. N. Kushmerick. (2000). "Wrapper Verification". *World Wide Web Journal.* 3(2): 79–94; Jan 2000.
2. J. Robie. (1998). "What is the Document Object Model?" *W3C Recommendation (Document Object Model (DOM) Level 1 Specification version 1.0).*
3. A. Sahuguet, F. Azavant. (1999). "Building light-weight wrappers for legacy Web data-sources using W4F". *In Proc. of the Intl. Conf. on Very Large Data Bases (VLDB).*
4. A. Sahuguet, F. Azavant. (1999). "Looking at the Web through XML glasses". *In Proceedings of the 4th Intl. Conf. on Cooperative Info. Systems.*
5. Sahuguet, F. Azavant. (2000). "Building Intelligent Web Applications Using Lightweight Wrappers". *Proceedings of Data and Knowledge Engineering.*
6. A. Sahuguet, F. Azavant. (1999). "WysiWyg Web Wrapper Factory (W4F)". *http://db.cis.upenn.edu/DL/WWW8/.*
7. L. Liu, W. Han, D. Buttler, C. Pu, W. Tang. (1999). "An XML-based Wrapper Generator for Web Information Extraction". *Proceedings of the ACM SIGMOD International Conference,* June 1–4, Philadelphia.
8. L. Liu, W. Han, C. Pu. "An XML-enabled Wrapper Construction System for Web Information Sources". *Proceedings of the 16th International Conference on Data Engineering (ICDE'2000),* San Diego CA (February 28 - March 3, 2000).
9. N. Kushmerick. (1999). "Regression testing for wrapper maintenance". *AAAI/IAAI.*
10. N. Kushmerick, D.S.Weld, R. Doorenbos. (1997). Wrapper induction for information extraction. *In International Joint Conference on Artificial Intelligence (IJCAI).*
11. C. Sammut. (1993). "The Origins of Inductive Logic Programming: A Prehistoric Tale". *Proceedings of the 3rd International Workshop on Inductive Logic Programming.*
12. T. Lau, D. S. Weld. (1999). "Programming by Demonstration: An Inductive Learning Formulation". *Intelligent User Interfaces.*
13. B. Chidlovskii. (2000). "Wrapper Generation by K-reversible Grammar Induction", Proceedings, Machine Learning: ECML 2000, 11th European Conference on Machine Learning, Barcelona, Catalonia, Spain, May, 2000.

Web-Based Image Retrieval with a Case Study

Ying Liu[1] and Danqing Zhang[2]

[1] School of InfomationTechnology and Electrical Engineering
University of Queensland, Brisbane QLD 4072 Australia
liuying@itee.uq.edu.au
[2] Creative Industries Faculty
Queensland University of Technology, Brisbane QLD 4001 Australia
d.zhang@qut.edu.au

Abstract. Advances in content-based image retrieval(CBIR)lead to numerous efficient techniques for retrieving images based on their content features, such as colours, textures and shapes. However, CBIR to date has been mainly focused on a centralised environment, ignoring the rapidly increasing image collection in the world, the images on the Web. In this paper, we study the problem of distributed CBIR in the environment of the Web where image collections are represented as normal and typically autonomous websites. After an analysis of challenging issues in applying current CBIR techniques to this new environment, we explore architectural possibilities and discuss their advantages and disadvantages. Finally we present a case study of distributed CBIR based exclusively on texture features. A new method to derive texture-based global similarity ranking suggests that, with a deep understanding of feature extraction algorithms, it is possible to have a better and more predictable way to merge local rankings from heterogeneous sources than using the commonly used method of assigning different weights.

1   Introduction

Digital image capturing devices, such scanners, digital cameras and digital video cameras, become part of our daily life. Huge collections of images are now stored in computers. Efficient management and search of image data becomes a very important issue. Typically, image retrieval can be done in three different ways: by keyword-based search using text annotations attached to image data, by browsing, or by content-based image retrieval (CBIR). Text-based image search, which takes advantages of mature data technologies for text retrieval, is highly efficient and accurate, but suffers from the problem that all images must be annotated and the type of search must be anticipated at the time the text is edited. On the other side, browsing, even thumbnail-based browsing, is only useful when the number of images is small (say, less than a few thousand). Therefore, CBIR remains to be the most promising way to handle the problem of image retrieval for very large and diversified image collections. CBIR retrieves images using content features, such as colours, shapes or textures. Typically, a query retrieves from a data collection all the images which "look" similar to a

X. Zhou, Y. Zhang, and M.E. Orlowska (Eds.): APWeb 2003, LNCS 2642, pp. 394–405, 2003.

given image or drawing by comparing their content features. More sophisticated image search engines can take some user feedback into consideration in order to improve accuracy [1].

In this paper we investigate the problem of CBIR meta-search. Assume that there are a number of independently developed CBIR systems (*local systems*). A new system, the *global system*, will be developed such that the user issues a single query to the global system, which will select relevant local systems, direct the query to them (possibly with necessary modifications), merge the results from the local systems and return the combined results to the user. Further, we assume that each local system is presented as a normal website (that is, the queries are accepted as an HTML form and how a local system retrieves data is unknown to the global system except any parameters that can be selected from the query interface). In other words, each local system is autonomous and will be presented to the user as a single system.

The contributions of this paper are twofold. First, we present a systematic analysis of the meta CBIR problem in the Web environment. Second, we investigate the problem of combining rankings from local systems which may use different feature extraction algorithms and similarity measures, and present a case study for texture features. This case study indicates the possibility of using new strategies for global ranking other than some previous known simple strategies such as assigning different weights to different local sites [2].

The rest of this paper is organised as follows. We review related work in CBIR and meta-search for Web search engines in Section 2. Architectures for Web-based image retrieval are discussed in Section 3. A case study of combining search results from three sites where different texture features are used to find globally most similar images based on textures is presented in Section 4. We conclude this paper in Section 5.

2   Related Work

In this section, we give a brief review of the related work in the areas of CBIR and text-based meta-search currently used by Web search engines. We also identify key differences and challenges for Web-based CBIR in comparison to traditional CBIR and text informational retrieval.

CBIR was introduced in the early 90's. It searches images using visual features, such as colours, textures and shapes. Typically, a query retrieves from a data collection all the images that "look" similar to a given image or drawing.

Basic visual features: Colour is an important feature in CBIR. The most commonly used colour feature representation is colour histogram [3], where the colour spectrum is divided into a number of bins and the value of each feature represents the number of pixels of an image in that colour range.

Texture is the visual patterns that have properties of homogeneity that do not result from the presence of only a single colour or intensity [4]. Texture contains important information for image retrieval and has been one of the most active research areas since the 70's. In early 90's, Wavelet transform was introduced

[5]and it is proven as proper for texture description because of its non-uniform frequency decomposition, similar to the human perception system.Discrete Cosine Transformation [6] and Steerable Pyramid [7]are other popular feature extraction methods.

Shape feature is required by many applications and can be classified as boundary-based and region-based representations in general. Boundary-based shape representation uses the outer boundary of the shape. Region-based shape representation uses the entire shape region. The most successful representatives for shape representations are Fourier Descriptor and Moment Invariant [8].

Layout and segmentation: Global feature often provides false positive information especially when an application database set is large.Feature layout is a better approach because it contains both features and spatial relations among them. Several colour layout representations were proposed by different studies[9].

Reliable image segmentation lead to a high accuracy in image retrieval using feature layout. In general, segmentation techniques can be categorised into three classes: automatic, semi-automatic, and manual. Automatic segmentation techniques can be based on techniques such as morphological operation [10],fuzzy entropy[11],etc. Normally, an automatic segmentation can only segment regions but not objects. Manual segmentation can obtain high-level objects,however,it is not practical because the amount of human work need is too much for large image data set. As a trade off, semi-automatic segmentation algorithms are widely adopted. The main idea is to combine manual inputs from the user with the image edge generated by the computer. One positive semi-automatic segmentation algorithm based on clustering and grouping in spatial-colour-texture space was developed in [8].

Web-Based CBIR: From above literature review, it is clear that what features should be used often depends on applications. Therefore, it is unavoidable to cope with different feature extraction algorithms when performing meta CBIR search.

Identification of multimedia elements such as images and video in large collections such as the Web usually require the integration of textual and visual information [12]. A system called Diagenes [13]classifies facial images from the Web using different methods of Evidence Combination[14]. WebSeer is a prototype for Web-based CBIR [15]. It classifies images into different category such as cartoons, photographs to improve search accuracy. WebSEEK emphasizes colour information of images and allows for visual query by example[16].

Web Search and Meta-search: A Web search engine is essentially a text retrieval system for Web pages plus a Web interface. A robot is used to collect Web pages following hyperlinks on the pages already processed. Web pages are indexed,using information derived from links, tags and collective user behaviours [17].

Web metasearch addresses the problem of using multiple search engines, which may be specialised in different topics, user communities, or geographical regions, such that the user issues a single query, which will be decomposed into sub-queries dispatched automatically by the metasearch engine and the query results from multiple search engines are merged into a single sorted list [2]. The main issues in metasearch include data source selection (only sources likely to provide high quality answers are visited), document selection (not every locally most similar documents are returned but those that are likely to be globally relevant), and result merger (return a globally sensible ranking with respect to autonomy and heterogeneity of local systems).

3   Web-Based CBIR

The problem of Web-based CBIR is defined as follows. There are n web sites $S_1, S_2, ..., S_n$ (these are called *local sites*). Each local site S_i has a data set D_i. It accepts a query q_i according to its own Web-based query interface, and returns top k_i results $\{r_{ij} \mid 1 \leq j \leq k_i\}$ that match the query condition from D_i. The user issues a query Q to these n web sites via a meta-search site (the *global site*), and a set of k results are returned to the user by the mediator such that these k results are the top k matches to Q from $\cup_{i=1}^{n} D_i$. For simplicity, we assume that all sites have the same search capability to the global system. In other words, query Q can be processed by all web sites.

Web-based CBIR can be implemented using the following architectures.

1. *Centralised system architecture:* The mediator sends a robot to all Web sites and collect images from these sites, then builds a centralised image databases using its own image processing and database software. This approach is efficient to answer queries once the centralised database is built, and has the advantage of requiring no CBIR functionality of local web sites. However, the large size in image data makes it difficult for the robot to collect images due to website local robot access policies and network traffic.

2. *Distributed system architecture:* The distributed system architecture requires highest level of local support. It has the benefit of minimising data transfer from local sites to the global site. However, it requires local sites to accept agents which may consume a significant amount of resources to process local data (feature extraction and query processing). When local sites allow permanent data to be stored there, this approach eventually builds a distributed database system, in the sense that the data is distributed but the software and metadata are centrally designed and fully cooperational with the global site. The distributed system may be built as a peer-to-peer (P2P) to avoid having a central coordinator [18].

3. *Interoperable system architecture:* The distributed approach requires the local sites to scarify too much local autonomy, and it is very difficult to have independently developed local sites to answer a global query without any special consideration for the local sites to work together with the global site or other sites. The interoperable system architecture provides a trade-off. A local site is interoperable if it is standard-based, for both its local query interfaces and the format of their query results. We also assume that the results are returned as a collection of image thumbnails with a hyperlink by clicking which the full image will be returned, and each image thumbnail has

a overall similarity score in relation to the query as determined by the local site.

4. *Mediator-wrapper architecture:* The wrapper-mediator architecture has been extensively used in integrating web sites (for text-based retrieval). Each local site is fully *autonomous*. The wrapper developed for each local site has a uniform upper interface to the mediator so the query from the mediator can be understood and the results returned from the wrapper is standard. The mediator typically has a registry of all local sites (about what data there and how to invoke them). It performs query execution planning by selecting proper local sites, decomposing the global query into local queries, activating and monitoring local executions and merging local results. This architecture can now be implemented using the support provided by the Web Services technology.

Our discussion hereafter focuses on the third and fourth architectures, which are more practical for today's Web. A query Q to find top k best results can be modified to q_i, $1 \leq i \leq n$, and each q_i is sent to S_i which returns the k best local results. Thus, a total of n queries will be executed and $k * n$ results will be returned. The global site needs to merge the results from all local sites and return the globally best k results. This merger process is non-trivial. It is too expensive to get $k * n$ full images and re-process them at the global site to select the globally top k results, in particular when n or image sizes are large. Thus, it is necessary to merge local similarity scores for the global site to fetch the final k images in full sizes. Local scores can be combined in three different ways:

1. *Direct sorting with normalisation:* Local scores are first normalised to the range(0..1). Then, these normalised numbers are sorted to generate global ranking, and the top k results are selected as the query results.

2. *Weighted sorting:* for site s_i, a weight w_i is chosen (experimentally for example) such that the top k are selected by sorting $s_i \times w_i$. It is difficult to chose these weights properly, in particular in the dynamic environment of the Web. It is often necessary to have the user's feedback in order to assign weights.

3. *Directed sorting with parameter tuning:* This is similar to direct sorting with normalisation, however, the local scores are guaranteed to be compatible by selecting proper input parameters if the local sites support parameter selection. Comparing to the weighted sorting approach, this approach is not based on experiments or user feedback, but on the understanding of CBIR theory and local algorithms.

Obviously, directed sorting is the most easy method. But it risks of combining non-compatible scores thus may not lead to desired accuracy. The weighted sorting approach sometimes is the only applicable approach, but it is difficult to assign weights without too many iterations of user involvement to provide feedback. The final approach can be very attractive and might be feasible to design some sample queries to understand local algorithms for input parameter tuning.

4   Rank Merger for Texture Features

As discussed before, merging local rankings from heterogeneous sources is an important topic in web-based image retrieval. In this section, we provide a case study using texture features. Firstly, we give an introduction to three frequently used texture feature extraction methods. Then we study the problem of making them compatible by selecting different parameters. Finally we compare the performance of global ranking by input parameter tuning with two other global ranking methods.

We denote the width and height of an image as w and h, so an image is represented as $\{f(i,j) \mid 0 \le i \le h - 1, 0 \le j \le w - 1\}$, where $f(i,j)$ is the intensity of the pixle at row i and column j.

4.1   Three Common Feature Extraction Methods

Wavelet is the most popularly used texture description method. Tree-structured wavelet is well developed, and fast algorithms are available [19]. We simply denote it as Discrete Wavelet Transform (DWT).

A block diagram of a 2-level 1-D DWT is shown in Figure 1. H_0 and H_1 are the highpass filters used in level 1 and 2, L_0 and L_1 are lowpass filters used. Apply 1-D DWT in both horizontal and vertical directions, we get 2-D DWT of an image. A L-level 2-D DWT produces $3 * L + 1$ subbands. Figure 1 shows the 16 subabnds of a 5-level DWT. Statistical features such as mean and variance can be extracted from each subband to describe textures.

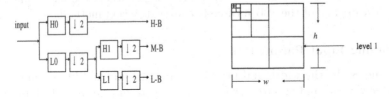

Fig. 1. 1-D DWT Diagram and 16 Subbands in a 5-level 2-D DWT

Another technique often used for texture featuring is Discrete Cosine Transform (DCT). DCT separates the image into spectral subbands of different importance with respect to the image's visual quality. In [20], the author classified the coefficients into 4*4 subbands, as shown in Figure 2, and features of these subbands were extracted. For image $f(i,j)$, the DCT coefficients C_f are

$$C_f(k_1, k_2) = 4 \cdot \sum_{i=1}^{h-1} \sum_{j=0}^{w-1} f(i,j) \cdot cos(\frac{\pi k_1(2i+1)}{2h}) cos(\frac{\pi k_2(2j+1)}{2w})$$

where $C_f(k_1, k_2)$ is the DCT coefficient in row k_1 and column k_2 of the DCT matrix.

Both DWT and DCT suffer from lack of translation and rotation invariance properties[7].The result is that texture patterns with similar spatial properties but different directional properties may not be recognised. To overcome this problem, steerable pyramid(SP)[7] is introduced. Basis functions of SP are directional derivative operators that come in different sizes and orientations. The system diagram of SP is shown in Figure 2. Image analysis is implemented by 1) decomposing the image into lowpass and highpass subbands using steerable filters L_0 and H_0; 2) decomposing the lowpass subband into a set of bandpass subbands B_0, ...,B_n and a lower lowpass subband L_1, where $n = N - 1$ with N being the number of orientations;3) Sub-sampling L_1 by a factor of 2 and repeating step 2). L-level SP decomposition will produce $L \times N$ bandpass subbands, 1 highpass subband and 1 lowpass subband.

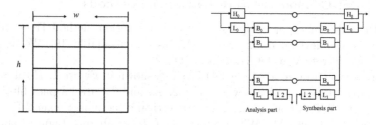

Fig. 2. DCT Subbands and SP Diagram

In the rest of this section, we conduct a case study where there are three web sites each using one of the above three texture extraction methods.

4.2   Tuning Input Parameters

Let S_w and S_h be the width and height of a certain subband in decomposition domain, mean (m) and variance (var) of the coefficients can be calculated as

$$m = \frac{\sum_{i=1}^{S_h-1} \sum_{j=0}^{S_w-1} C_f(i,j)}{S_w \times S_h} \qquad var = \sqrt{\sum_{i=1}^{S_h-1} \sum_{j=0}^{S_w-1} (C_f(i,j) - m)^2}$$

where $C_f(i,j)$ is the transform coefficient.

[20] included a DWT-based texture descriptor, where a 5-level DWT results in 16 subbands as shown in Figure 1. The DCT-based texture descriptor included has 4*4 subbands as shown in Figure 2.Then m and var of each subband were calculated and formed texture descriptor of 32 terms. We denote these two descriptors as DWT($m + var$) and DCT($m + var$) hereafter. As for SP, we use a 4-orientation 3-level SP which results in 14 subbands.

Next we use the SP domain as an example to discuss the significance of the parameters m and var in discriminating images. These discussions apply to DWT and DCT as well.

In SP decomposition, except the lowpass subband, m of all subbands is close to zero [21]. Hence, we expect that m would not provide good retrieval performance. var is proved to be much more efficient for texture retrieval than m does. However, we found that using var as descriptor, textures with similar pattern but different luminance property can not be distinguished, for example, d101 and d102 in the Brodatz album [22] will be classified into same group. Hence we consider combing a parameter describing the luminance property of the whole texture, with var to describe the texture. Luminance property of a texture can be described by its average intensity as

$$mA = \frac{\sum_{i=0}^{h-1} \sum_{j=0}^{w-1} f(i,j)}{w \times h}$$

So, mA combined with var form a new descriptor $var + mA$.

Hence, we have four descriptors:1) m of 14 terms; 2) var of 14 terms; 3) the mean and the variance together form a descriptor $m + var$ of 28 terms; and 4) $var + mA$ of 15 terms, denoted as $(v_1, v_2, \cdots v_{14}, mA)$, where v_1 is the variance value of the lowpass subband, v_{14} is of the highpass subband, v_2 to v_{13} are of the 12 bandpass subbands. A smaller weight should be assigned to v_1 and mA, as their magnitudes are usually much larger than other terms.

4.3   Experimental Results

Brodatz textures are widely recognized as a standard test set. In our experiment, each of the 112 Brodatz textures (of size 512*512) is segmented into 4 tiles of size 256*256, thus form a database of 448 textures. L2 distance between texture features is used to measure texture similarity.

We use *recall* and *precision* to measure the performance of image retrieval methods. Recall indicates the proportion of relevant images retrieved from the database when answering a query, and precision is the proportion of the retrieved images that are relevant to the query. Taking one of the four tiles from the same texture as query image, for homogeneous textures (most textures in Brodatz Album are homogeneous), the other three tiles are the most similar ones to be found; for inhomogeneous textures, we consider the similar tiles from the whole database. We conduct 112 queries using each of the 112 Brodatz textures as the query image.

For query image Q_i, among the top k similar tiles retrieved, the number of relevant images found is C_i and the number of relevant images in the database is T_i. For all 112 queries, the total number of relevant images found is $T_c = \sum_{i=1}^{112} C_i$, the total number of relevant images in the database is $T_t = \sum_{i=1}^{112} T_i$, and the number of texture retrieved is $T_n = k * 112$. Then, we have

$$Recall = T_c/T_t \quad Precision = T_c/T_n$$

We now compare the retrieval performance of the three different feature extraction algorithms by using different parameters. As expected, retrieval performance of m is very poor compared with var as shown in Figure 3. Figure 4 compares the performance of features using parameters var, $m + var$, and $var + mA$

based on SP. It shows that the proposed feature set $var + mA$ provides good retrieval performance. Note that weights 0.1 and 0.5 were assigned to v_1 and mA, respectively.

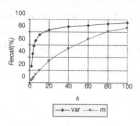 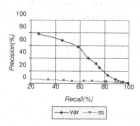

Fig. 3. var and m (SP)

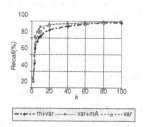 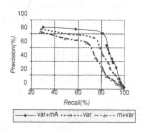

Fig. 4. var, $m + var$ and $var + mA$ (SP)

Applying $var + mA$ to DWT and DCT, we obtain two new descriptors DWT($var + mA$) and DCT($var + mA$),or denoted as New-DWT, New-DCT. The weights to v_1 and mA are 0.1 and 0.2 for DWT($var + mA$), 0.25 and 0.5 for DCT($var + mA$).

To merge local rankings from heterogeneous sources efficiently, we hope the performance of systems from which local ranking results are obtained be comparable. Figure 5 compares the performance of SP($m + var$), DWT($m + var$), and DCT($m + var$). Figure 6 displays the results of SP($var + mA$), DWT($var + mA$) and DCT($var + mA$) together. We observe that with parameter $m + var$, retrieval performance of SP, DWT and DCT are different, while using $var + mA$, their performances become comparable. We expect that this will make global ranking easier and more efficient.

Normalising the distance values between textures into range $[0, 1]$, we compare the retrieval performance of three algorithms:

1. *Direct sorting with normalisation*: Select k most similar textures using SP($m + var$), DWT($m + var$), DCT($m + var$) respectively, and sort the

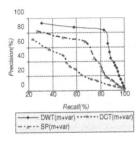
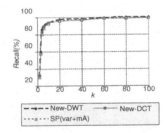

Fig. 5. Performance of $SP(m + var)$, $DWT(m + var)$ and $DCT(m + var)$

$3 * k$ distance values of these textures between the query texture image, the k smallest distances correspond to the k final selected textures.

2. *Weighted sorting*: Considering the performance of each individual feature sets (Figure 5), experimentally, we assign different weights 1.0, 1.2 and 1.5 to the distances of the k locally selected candidates by $DCT(m+var)$, $SP(m+var)$ and $DWT(m + var)$ respectively. Then sort the $3 * k$ distance values and choose the final k.

3. *Directed sorting with parameter tuning*: Since performance of $SP(var +mA)$, $DWT(var + mA)$, $DCT(var + mA)$ are comparable, we directly choose the k most similar tiles with smallest distances from the $3 * k$ candidates.

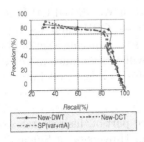
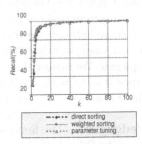

Fig. 6. Performance of $SP(var + mA)$, $DWT(var + mA)$ and $DCT(var + mA)$

In Figure 7, we compare the retrieval performance of the three ranking algorithms. It shows that recall values of all three algorithms are very close; however, precision of the third algorithm is much better. This proves that with a deep understanding of feature extraction algorithms, parameter tuning could be an efficient way for global ranking.

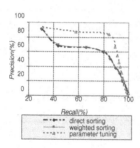
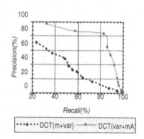

Fig. 7. Performance of the three global ranking methods

5 Conclusions

Web-based image retrieval raises many new research issues to traditional CBIR in a centralized environment. A particularly difficult problem is to combine local rankings returned by local systems which may use different and sometimes unknown local similarity ranking algorithms to generate a sensible global ranking. In this paper, we have analyzed the problem of Web-based CBIR. A case study of combining local rankings using three popular texture feature extraction algorithms has illustrated that, with a good understanding of general texture feature extraction methods and under the assumption that a Web-based CBIR system allow some input parameter selection, the local rankings from these systems can be made compatible. This input parameter tuning method performs better than assigning different weights to different sources, where the process is empirically based and not really predictable.

This paper presents some preliminary results of Web-based CBIR research. Currently we are building a prototype for Web-based CBIR, and also investigating methods of understanding local CBIR systems by imposing a set of purposely designed queries. We expect that this new area will attract much more attention in the future due to both the importance of this problem and immaturity of research in this area.

Acknowledgement. The first author conducted part of this research when she was attached to School of Computing, National University of Singapore. The second author would like to thank Professor Binh Pham and Dr Xuefeng Li of QUT for many helpful discussions on the topic of texture-based CBIR.

References

1. Smith, J.R., Chang, S.F.: Automated image retrieval using color and texture (1995) Technical report CU/CTR 408-95-14, CTR, Columbia University.
2. Meng, W., Yu, C., Liu, K.: Building efficient and effective metasearch engines. ACM Computing Surveys **34** (2002) 48–89
3. Swain, M., Ballard, D.: Color indexing. International Journal of Computer Vision **7** (1991) 11–32

4. Smith, J.R., Chang, S.F.: Automated binary texture feature sets for image retrieval. In: IEEE International Conference on Acoustic, Speech, Signal Processing. (1996)
5. Chang, T., Kuo, J.C.C.: Texture analysis and classification with tree-structured wavelet transform. IEEE Transaction on Image Processing **2** (1993) 429–441
6. Jain, A.K.: Fundamentals of digital image processing. Prentice Hall (1986)
7. Freeman, W.T., Adelson, E.H.: The design and use of steerable filters. IEEE Trans. Pattern Analysis and Machine Intelligence **13** (1991) 891–906
8. Rui, Y., Alfred, C., et al: Modifies fourier descriptors for shape representation – a practical approach. In: Proc. of First International Workshop on Image Databases and Multimedia Search. (1996)
9. Huang, J., Kumar, S., et al: Image indexing using color correlogram. In: Proc. IEEE Conference on Computer Vision and Pattern Recognition. (1997)
10. Lybanon, M., Lea, S., et al: Segmentation of diverse image types using opening and closing. In: Proc. IEEE International Conference on Image Processing. (1994) 3013–3016
11. Li, B., Ma, S.D.: On the relation between region and contour representation. In: Proceedings of IEEE International Conference on Image Processing. (1994)
12. Aslandogam, Y.A., T.Yu, C.: Automatic feedback for content based image retrieval on the web. In: Proc. of International Conference on Multimedia and Expo (ICME). (2002)
13. Aslandogam, Y.A., T.Yu, C.: Multiple evidence combination in image retrieval: Diogenes searches for people on the web. In: Proc. of ACM SIGIR. (2000) 88–95
14. Shafer, G.: A Mathematical Theory of Evidence. Princeton University Press (1996)
15. Swain, M.J., Frankel, C., Athitsos, V.: Webseer: An image search engine for the world wide web (1996) Technical report TR-96-14, University of Chicago, Department of Computer Science.
16. Smith, J.R., Chang, S.F.: Visually searching the web for content. IEEE Multimedia (1997) 12–20
17. Kleinberg: Authoritative sources in a hyperlinked environment. In: Proc. of ACM-SIAM Discrete Algorithms. (1998)
18. Ng, W.S., Ooi, B.C., Tan, K.L., Zhou, A.: PeerDB: A P2P-based system for distributed data sharing. In: ICDE. (2003)
19. Mallat, S.G.: A theory for multiresolution signal decomposition: The wavelet representation. IEEE Trans. Pattern Analysis and Machine Intelligence **11** (1989) 674–693
20. Smith, J.R., Chang, S.F.: Transform features for texture classification and discrimination in large image databases. In: IEEE International Conference on Image Processing. (1994) 407–411
21. Areepongsa, S., Park, D., Rao, K.R.: Invariant features for texture image retrieval using steerable pyramid. In: WPMC 2000, Bangkok. (2000)
22. Brodatz, P.: Textures: a Photographic Album for Artists and Designers. Dover, New York (1966)

Extracting Content Structure for Web Pages Based on Visual Representation

Deng Cai[1][*], Shipeng Yu [2][*], Ji-Rong Wen[*] and Wei-Ying Ma[*]

[*] Microsoft Research Asia
{jrwen, wyma}@microsoft.com
[1] Tsinghua University, Beijing, P.R.China
caideng00@mails.tsinghua.edu.cn
[2] Peking University, Beijing, P.R.China
ysp@is.pku.edu.cn

Abstract. A new web content structure based on visual representation is proposed in this paper. Many web applications such as information retrieval, information extraction and automatic page adaptation can benefit from this structure. This paper presents an automatic top-down, tag-tree independent approach to detect web content structure. It simulates how a user understands web layout structure based on his visual perception. Comparing to other existing techniques, our approach is independent to underlying documentation representation such as HTML and works well even when the HTML structure is far different from layout structure. Experiments show satisfactory results.

1 Introduction

Today the Web has become the largest information source for people. Most information retrieval systems on the Web consider web pages as the smallest and undividable units, but a web page as a whole may not be appropriate to represent a single semantic. A web page usually contains various contents such as navigation, decoration, interaction and contact information, which are not related to the topic of the web page. Furthermore, a web page often contains multiple topics that are not necessarily relevant to each other. Therefore, detecting the content structure of a web page could potentially improve the performance of web information retrieval.

Many web applications can utilize the content structures of web pages. For example, some researchers have been trying to use database techniques and build wrappers for web documents [3]. If a web page can be divided into semantic related parts, wrappers can be more easily matched and data can be more likely extracted. Link structure analysis can also make good use of the content structures of web pages. Links at different parts of a page usually act as different functions and contribute to the PageRank [2] or HITS [11] differently. Recent works on topic distillation [4] and focused crawling [5] show the usefulness of page segmentation on information analysis. Furthermore, adaptive content delivery on small handheld devices also requires the detection of underlying content structure of a web page to facilitate the browsing of a large page by partitioning it into smaller units [10].

X. Zhou, Y. Zhang, and M.E. Orlowska (Eds.): APWeb 2003, LNCS 2642, pp. 406–417, 2003.

People view a web page through a web browser and get a 2-D presentation which has many visual cues to help distinguish different parts of the page. Generally, a web page designer would organize the content of a web page to make it easy for reading. Thus, semantically related content is usually grouped together and the entire page is divided into regions for different contents using explicit or implicit visual separators such as lines, blank areas, images, font sizes, colors, etc [16]. This motivates our work to segment a web page into semantically related content blocks from its visual presentation. If we can reconstruct the structure of a page corresponding to human visual perception, it will better reflect the semantic structure. In this paper, we propose VIPS (**VI**sion-based **P**age **S**egmentation) algorithm to extract the content structure for a web page. The algorithm makes full use of page layout features and tries to partition the page at the semantic level. Each node in the extracted content structure will correspond to a block of coherent content in the original page.

The paper is organized as follows. Section 2 presents the related works. Section 3 defines the web page content structure based on vision. The details of the VIPS algorithm are introduced in Section 4. The experimental results are reported in Section 5. Section 6 summarizes our contributions and concludes the paper.

2 Related Works

The applications mentioned in the introduction indicate the need of techniques for extracting the content structure of a web page. Tag tree or Document Object Model (http://www.w3.org/DOM/) provides each web page a fine-grained structure, illustrating not only the content but also the presentation of the page. Many researchers [10, 12, 15] have considered using the tag information and dividing the page based on the type of the tags. Useful tags include <P> (for paragraph), <TABLE> (for table), <UL> (for list), <H1>~<H6> (for heading), etc.

Some other algorithms also consider the content or link information besides the tag tree. Embley [8] use some heuristic rules to discover record boundaries within a page, which assist data extraction from the web page. Chakrabarti [4] addresses the fine-grained topic distillation and dis-aggregates hubs into regions by analyzing link structure as well as intra-page text distribution.

A Function-based Object Model (FOM) of a web page is proposed by Chen [6] for content understanding and adaptation. Every undividable element in the tag tree is called a basic object and can be grouped into a composite object. A function type can be defined to each object and helps to build a hierarchical structure for the page. However, the grouping rules and the functions are hard to define accurately, and thus make the whole tree-constructing process very inflexible.

In [16] and [6], some visual cues are used in DOM analysis. They try to identify the logic relationships within the web content based on visual layout information, but these approaches still rely too much on the DOM structure. Gu [9] tries to construct a web content structure by breaking out the DOM tree and comparing similarity among all the basic DOM nodes. Since a normal web page may have hundreds of basic elements, the algorithm is time-consuming and inflexible, not capable to deal with a large amount of web pages.

3   Vision-Based Content Structure for Web Pages

Similar to [6], we define the *basic object* as the leaf node in the DOM tree that cannot be decomposed any more. Although a DOM structure provides a hierarchy for the basic objects in a web page, it is more for representation rather than content organization. In this paper, we propose the *vision-based content structure*, where every node, called a *layout block*, is a basic object or a group of basic objects. The nodes in the content structure do not necessarily have a mapping to the nodes in the DOM tree.

Similar to the description of document representation in [14], the basic model of vision-based content structure for web pages is described as follows.

A web page Ω is specified by a triple $\Omega = (O, \Phi, \delta)$. $O = \{\Omega^1, \Omega^2, ..., \Omega^N\}$ is a finite set of objects or sub-web-pages. All these objects are not overlapped. Each object can be recursively viewed as a sub-web-page and has a subsidiary content structure. $\Phi = \{\varphi^1, \varphi^2, ..., \varphi^T\}$ is a finite set of visual separators, including horizontal separators and vertical separators. Every separator has a weight indicating its visibility, and all the separators in the same Φ have same weight. δ is the relationship of every two blocks in O and can be expressed as: $\delta = O \times O \rightarrow \Phi \cup \{NULL\}$. Suppose Ω_i and Ω_j are two objects in O, $\delta(\Omega_i, \Omega_j) \neq NULL$ indicates that Ω_i and Ω_j are exactly separated by the separator $\delta(\Omega_i, \Omega_j)$ or we can say the two objects are adjacent to each other, otherwise there are other objects between the two blocks Ω_i and Ω_j.

Since each Ω_i is a sub-web-page of the original page, it has similar content structure as Ω. Recursively, we have $\Omega'_s = (O'_s, \Phi'_s, \delta'_s)$, $O'_s = \{\Omega^1_{st}, \Omega^2_{st}, ..., \Omega^{N_s}_{st}\}$, $\Phi'_s = \{\varphi^1_{st}, \varphi^2_{st}, ..., \varphi^{T_s}_{st}\}$ and $\delta'_s = O'_s \times O'_s \rightarrow \Phi'_s \cup \{NULL\}$ where Ω'_s is the tth object in the sub-web-page level s, N_{st} and T_{st} are the number of objects in O'_s and number of separators in Φ'_s.

Fig. 1 shows an example of visual-based content structure for Yahoo! Auctions page. It illustrates the layout structure and the vision-based content structure of the page. In the first level, the original web page has four objects or visual blocks VB1~VB4 and three separators $\varphi^1 \sim \varphi^3$, as specified in Fig. 1(d). Then we can further construct sub content structure for each sub web page. For example, VB2 has three offspring objects and two separators. It can be further analyzed like Fig. 1(e).

For each visual block, the *Degree of Coherence* (DoC) is defined to measure how coherent it is. DoC has the following properties:

- Ranges from 0 to 1;
- The greater the DoC value, the more consistent the content within the block;
- In the hierarchy tree, the DoC of the child is not smaller than its parent's.

We can pre-define the *Permitted Degree of Coherence* (PDoC) to achieve different granularities of content structure for different applications. The smaller the PDoC is, the coarser the content structure would be. For example in Fig. 1(a), the visual block VB2_1 may not be further partitioned with an appropriate PDoC.

The vision-based content structure is more likely to provide a semantic partitioning of the page. Every node, especially the leaf node, is more likely to convey a semantic meaning for building a higher semantic via the hierarchy. For instance, in Fig. 1(a) we can say that VB2_1_1 denotes the category links of Yahoo! Shopping auctions, and that VB2_2_1 and VB2_2_2 show details for two different comics.

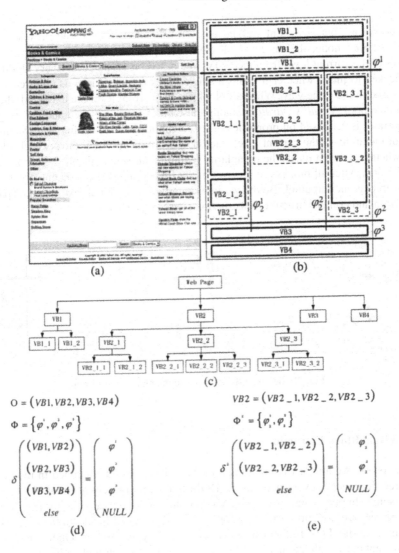

Fig. 1. The layout structure and vision-based content structure of an example page. (d) and (e) show the corresponding specification of vision-based content structure.

4 The VIPS Algorithm

In the VIPS algorithm, the vision-based content structure of a page is deduced by combining the DOM structure and the visual cues. The segmentation process is illustrated in Fig. 2. First, DOM structure and visual information, such as position, background color, font size, font weight, etc., are obtained from a web browser. Then, from the root node, the visual block extraction process is started to extract visual blocks of the current level from the DOM tree based on visual cues. Every DOM node is checked to judge whether it forms a single block or not. If not, its children will be processed in the same way. When all blocks of the current level are extracted, they are put into a pool. *Visual separators* among these blocks are identified and the weight of a separator is set based on properties of its neighboring blocks. After constructing the layout hierarchy of the current level, each newly produced visual blocks is checked to see whether or not it meets the granularity requirement. If no, this block will be further partitioned. After all blocks are processed, the final vision-based content structure for the web page is outputted. Below we introduce the visual block extraction, separator detection and content structure construction phases respectively.

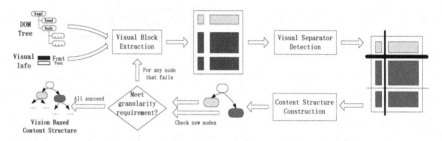

Fig. 2. The vision-based page segmentation algorithm

4.1 Visual Block Extraction

In this phase, we aim at finding all appropriate visual blocks contained in the current sub-tree. In general, every node in the DOM tree can represent a visual block. However, some "huge" nodes such as <TABLE> and <P> are used only for organization purpose and are not appropriate to represent a single visual block. In these cases, the current node should be further divided and replaced by its children. On the other hand, we may not extract all leaf nodes in the DOM tree due to their high volume.

At the end of this step, for each node that represents a visual block, its DoC value is set according to its intra visual difference. This process is iterated until all appropriate nodes are found to represent the visual blocks in the web page.

The visual block extraction algorithm DivideDomtree is illustrated in Fig. 3. Some important cues are used to produce heuristic rules in the algorithm are:

- Tag cue: Tags such as <HR> are often used to separate different topics from visual perspective. Therefore we prefer to divide a DOM node if it contains these tags.
- Color cue: We divide a DOM node if its background color is different from one of its children's.
- Text cue: If most of the children of a DOM node are Text nodes (i.e., no tags surround them), we do not divide it.

```
Algorithm DivideDomtree(pRoot, nLevel)
{
    IF (Dividable(pRoot, nLevel) == TRUE){
    FOR EACH child OF pRoot {
        DivideDomtree(child, nLevel);
    }
    } ELSE {
    Put the sub-tree (pRoot) into the
        pool as a block;
    }
}
```

```
Algorithm Dividable(pRoot, nLevel)
{
    IF (pRoot is the Top Block){
    RETURN TRUE;
    } ELSE {
        Special routines for TABLE, TR,
            TBODY, TD, P, UL, FORM;
        Heuristic rules for general tags;
    }
}
```

(a)   (b)

Fig. 3. The visual block extraction algorithm

- Size cue: We prefer to divide a DOM node if the standard deviation of size of its children is larger than a threshold.

The Tag cue and Color cue are relatively straightforward to produce corresponding heuristic rules. Below we give the details of how to use text and size cues to generate heuristic rules for block extraction. First, several definitions are given:

1. *Valid Node*: a node that can be seen through the browser. The node's width and height are not equal to zero.
2. *Block Node*: the node with tag not <A>, <B>, <FONT>, <HR>, <I>, <P>, <STRONG>, <TEXT>.
3. *Text Node*: the DOM node that only contains free text.
4. *Virtual Text Node*: The node that is not a block node and only have text node as children.

According to the above definitions, we use the following text cue and size cue based heuristic rules to further enhance the block extraction process:

- A node will be dropped if it has no valid child.
- If a node only has one valid child and this child is not Text node, then trace into the child.
- If all the children of a node are Text nodes or Virtual Text nodes, then set the DoC 1.
- If the node's size is 3 times greater than all his children's total size, divide it.
- If the node has Text node child or Virtual Text node child and the node's width or height is smaller than a threshold, set the DoC 0.8.
- Split the node which has more than two successive <BR> children. (It means there are many space in the middle, may be two different topics)

In addition, some tags, such as <TABLE>, <TBODY>, <TR>, <TD>, <P>, <UL> and <LI>, are very important and common in web page and are more likely to form a content coherent sub-tree. So we define some special routines in our algorithm to handle these tags and set higher thresholds for these tags in the above rules.

Take Fig. 1 as an example. VB1, VB2_1, VB2_2, VB2_3, VB3 and VB4 will be extracted at the first round. The detailed process is as follows. In Fig. 4, a DOM tree structure of VB2 is shown. In the block extraction process, when the <TABLE> node is met, it has only one valid child <TR>. We trace into the <TR> node according to the heuristic rules. The <TR> node has five <TD> children and only three of them are valid. The first child's background color is different from its parent's background color, so the <TR> node is split and the first <TD> node is not divided further in this round and is put into the pool as a block. The second and fourth child of <TR> node is not valid and will be dropped. When the third and fifth children of <TR> are considered, we use another rule to improve the efficiency – because the first <TD> is not divided, so there will be no horizontal separators in this round projection. It is unnecessary to divide the third and fifth <TD> and they should be taken as a block in this level.

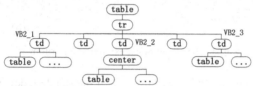

Fig. 4. DOM tree structure of VB2 in the sample page

4.2 Visual Separator Detection

After all blocks are extracted, they are put into a pool for visual separator detection. Separators are horizontal or vertical lines in a web page that visually cross with no blocks in the pool. From a visual perspective, separators are good indicators for discriminating different semantics within the page. A visual separator is represented by a 2-tuple: (P_s, P_e), where P_s is the start pixel and P_e is the end pixel. The width of the separator is calculated by the difference between these two values.

Separator Detection. The visual separator detection algorithm is described as follows:

1. Initialize the separator list. The list starts with only one separator (P_{be}, P_{ee}) whose start pixel and end pixel are corresponding to the borders of the pool.
2. For every block in the pool, the relation of the block with each separator is evaluated
   - If the block is contained in the separator, split the separator;
   - If the block crosses with the separator, update the separator's parameters;
   - If the block covers the separator, remove the separator.
3. Remove the four separators that stand at the border of the pool.

Take Fig. 5(a) as an example in which the black blocks represent the visual blocks in the page. For simplicity we only show the process to detect the horizontal separators. At first we have only one separator that is the whole pool. As shown in Fig. 5(b), when we put the first block into the pool, it splits the separator into S1 and S2. It is same with the second and third block. When the fourth block is put into the pool, it crosses the separator S2 and covers the separator S3, the parameter of S2 is updated and S3 is removed. At the end of this process, the two separators S1 and S3 that stand at the border of the pool are removed.

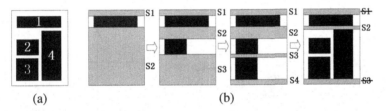

(a)   (b)

Fig. 5. A sample page and the separator detection process

Setting Weights for Separators. The separators are used to distinguish blocks with different semantics, so the weight of a separator can be assigned based on the information difference between its neighboring blocks. The following rules are used to set a weight to each separator:

- The more the distance between blocks on different side of the separator, the higher the weight.
- If a visual separator is at the same position as some tags such as <HR>, its weight is made higher.
- If the differences of font properties such as font size and font weight are more clearly on two sides of the separator, the weight will be increased. More over, the weight will be increased if font size before the separator is smaller than that after the separator.
- If background colors are different on two sides of the separator, the weight will be increased.
- When the structures of the blocks beside the separator are very similar (e.g. both are text), the weight of the separator will be decreased.

Take the third <TD> node in Fig. 4 as an example. The sub-page corresponding to this node is shown in Fig. 6(b) and the DOM tree structure is shown in Fig. 6(a). We can see that many nodes in the DOM tree are invalid in our definition and cannot be seen on the page. They are ignored in the block extraction process. After the block extraction phase, six blocks are put in a pool and five horizontal separators are detected. Then the weights of these separators are set based on the rules we described. In this example, the separator between Block 2 and Block 3 will get higher weight than the separator between Block 1 and Block 2 because of the different font weights. For the same reason, the separator between Block 4 and Block 5 will also get a high weight. The final separators and weights are shown in Fig. 6(c), in which a thicker line means a higher weight.

4.3 Content Structure Construction

When separators are detected and separators' weights are set, the content structure can be constructed accordingly. The construction process starts from the separators with the lowest weight and the blocks beside these separators are merged to form new virtual blocks. This process iterates till separators with maximum weights are met. The DoC of each new block is also set via similar methods described in Section 4.1.

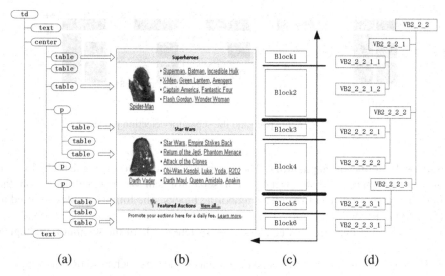

(a)   (b)   (c)   (d)

Fig. 6. Separators and weights among blocks

After that, each leaf node is checked whether it meets the granularity requirement. For every node that fails, we go to the Visual Block Extraction phase again to further construct the sub content structure within that node. If all the nodes meet the requirement, the iterative process is then stopped and the vision-based content structure for the whole page is obtained. The common requirement for DoC is that DoC > PDoC, if PDoC is pre-defined.

Take Fig. 6 as an example. In the first iteration, the first, third and fifth separators are chosen and Block 1 and 2 are merged to form the new block VB2_2_2_1. Similar merging is conducted for Block 3 and 4 (resulting a new block VB2_2_2_2) and Block 5 and 6 (resulting a new block VB2_2_2_3). The new blocks VB2_2_2_1, VB2_2_2_2 and VB2_2_2_3 are the children of VB2_2_2 and can also be viewed as a partition of VB2_2_2. Every leaf node, such as VB2_2_2_1_1, VB2_2_2_1_2 and VB2_2_2_2_1, will be checked to see whether it meets the granularity requirement. After several iterations, the final vision-based content structure of the page is constructed.

In summary, the proposed VIPS algorithm takes advantage of visual cues to obtain the vision-based content structure of a web page and thus successfully bridges the gap between the DOM structure and the semantic structure. The page is partitioned based on visual separators and structured as a hierarchy closely related to how a user would browse the page. Content related parts could be grouped together even if they are in different branches of the DOM tree.

VIPS is also very efficient. Since we trace down the DOM structure for visual block extraction and do not analyze every basic DOM node, the algorithm is totally top-down. Furthermore, the PDoC can be pre-defined, which brings significant flexibility to segmentation and greatly improve the performance.

5 Experiments

We provide some performance evaluation of our proposed VIPS algorithm based on a large collection of web pages from Yahoo. We also conduct experiments to evaluate how the algorithm can be used to enhance information retrieval on the Web.

5.1 Performance of VIPS Algorithm

We selected 140 web pages from popular sites listed in 14 main category of Yahoo directory (http://www.yahoo.com). The web content structure detection algorithm is run against these pages and the results are assessed by human judgments. Table 1 shows the result.

Table 1. Evaluation of the quality of page analysis

Human judgment	Number of pages
Perfect	86
Satisfactory	50
Failed	4

As can be seen, 86+50=136 (97%) pages have their content structures correctly detected. For those "failed" cases, one major reason is that the browser (i.e. Internet Explorer in our experiments) provides wrong position information so that our algorithm cannot get the correct content structure. Another reason lies in that several pages use images (e.g., a very thin image that represents a line) to divide different content blocks. Our algorithm currently does not handle this situation.

5.2 Experiments on Web Information Retrieval

Query expansion is an efficient way to improve the performance of information retrieval [7]. The quality of expansion terms is heavily affected by the top-ranked documents. Noise and multi-topics are two major negative factors for expansion term selection in the web context. Since our VIPS algorithm can group semantically related content into a segment, the term correlations within a segment will be much higher than those in other parts of a web page. With improved term correlations, high-quality expansion terms can be extracted from segments and used to improve information retrieval performance.

We choose Okapi [13] as the retrieval system and WT10g [1] in TREC-9 and TREC 2001 Web Tracks as the data set. WT10g contains 1.69 million pages and amounts to about 10G. We use the 50 queries from TREC 2001 Web Track as the query set and only the TOPIC field for retrieval, and use Okapi's BM2500 as the weight function and set $k_1 = 1.2$, $k_3 = 1000$, $b = 0.75$, and $avdl = 61200$.

An initial list of ranked web pages is obtained by using any traditional information retrieval methods. Then we apply our page analysis algorithm with a PDoC 0.6 to the top 80 pages and get the set of candidate segments. The most relevant (e.g. top 20) segments from this candidate set are used to select expansion terms. These selected terms are used to construct a new expanded query to retrieve the final results.

We compared our method with the traditional pseudo-relevance feedback algorithm. Note that our method selects expansion terms from blocks while traditional methods select expansion terms from entire web pages. The experimental result is shown in Fig. 7.

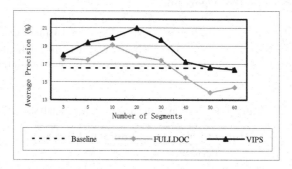

Fig. 7. Performance comparison of pseudo-relevance feedback based on two different ways of selecting query expansion terms. VIPS is our method which selects query expansion terms from blocks while FULLDOC represents traditional approaches where the entire pages are used for expansion term selection.

From Fig. 7, we can see that pseudo-relevance feedback based on web page content structure significantly outperforms traditional methods and achieves about 27% performance improvement on the Web Track dataset (refer to [17] for more details). The experiments clearly show that web page content structure is very helpful to detect and filter out noisy and irrelevant information. Thus better expansion terms can be selected to improve retrieval performance.

6   Conclusion

In this paper a new approach of extracting web content structure based on visual representation was proposed. The produced web content structure is very helpful for applications such as web adaptation, information retrieval and information extraction. By identifying the logic relationship of web content based on visual layout information, web content structure can effectively represent the semantic structure of the web page. An automatic top-down, tag-tree independent and scalable algorithm to detect web content structure was presented. It simulates how a user understands the layout structure of a web page based on its visual representation. Compared with traditional DOM based segmentation method, our scheme utilizes useful visual cues to obtain a better partition of a page at the semantic level. It also is independent of physical realization and works well even when the physical structure is far different from visual presentation. The experimental result has shown that our proposed scheme achieves very satisfactory performance. We plan to apply the scheme for adaptive content delivery to facilitate better web browsing on mobile devices for our future works.

References

1. Bailey, P., Craswell, N., and Hawking, D., Engineering a multi-purpose test collection for Web retrieval experiments, Information Processing and Management, 2001.
2. Brin, S. and Page, L., The Anatomy of a Large-Scale Hypertextual Web Search Engine, In the Seventh International World Wide Web Conference, Brisbane,Australia, 1998.
3. Buneman, P., Davidson, S., Fernandez, M., and Suciu, D., Adding Structure to Unstructured Data, In Proceedings of the 6th International Conference on Database Theory (ICDT'97), 1997, pp. 336-350.
4. Chakrabarti, S., Integrating the Document Object Model with hyperlinks for enhanced topic distillation and information extraction, In the 10th International World Wide Web Conference, 2001.
5. Chakrabarti, S., Punera, K., and Subramanyam, M., Accelerated focused crawling through online relevance feedback, In Proceedings of the eleventh international conference on World Wide Web (WWW2002), 2002, pp. 148-159.
6. Chen, J., Zhou, B., Shi, J., Zhang, H., and Wu, Q., Function-Based Object Model Towards Website Adaptation, In the 10th International World Wide Web Conference, 2001.
7. Efthimiadis, N. E., Query Expansion, In Annual Review of Information Systems and Technology, Vol. 31, 1996, pp. 121-187.
8. Embley, D. W., Jiang, Y., and Ng, Y.-K., Record-boundary discovery in Web documents, In Proceedings of the 1999 ACM SIGMOD international conference on Management of data, Philadelphia PA, 1999, pp. 467-478.
9. Gu, X., Chen, J., Ma, W.-Y., and Chen, G., Visual Based Content Understanding towards Web Adaptation, In Second International Conference on Adaptive Hypermedia and Adaptive Web-based Systems (AH2002), Spain, 2002, pp. 29-31.
10. Kaasinen, E., Aaltonen, M., Kolari, J., Melakoski, S., and Laakko, T., Two Approaches to Bringing Internet Services to WAP Devices, In Proceedings of 9th International World-Wide Web Conference, 2000, pp. 231-246.
11. Kleinberg, J., Authoritative sources in a hyperlinked environment, In Proceedings of the 9th ACM-SIAM Symposium on Discrete Algorithms, 1998, pp. 668-677.
12. Lin, S.-H. and Ho, J.-M., Discovering Informative Content Blocks from Web Documents, In Proceedings of ACM SIGKDD'02, 2002.
13. Robertson, S. E., Overview of the okapi projects, Journal of Documentation, Vol. 53, No. 1, 1997, pp. 3-7.
14. Tang, Y. Y., Cheriet, M., Liu, J., Said, J. N., and Suen, C. Y., Document Analysis and Recognition by Computers, Handbook of Pattern Recognition and Computer Vision, edited by C. H. Chen, L. F. Pau, and P. S. P. Wang World Scientific Publishing Company, 1999.
15. Wong, W. and Fu, A. W., Finding Structure and Characteristics of Web Documents for Classification, In ACM SIGMOD Workshop on Research Issues in Data Mining and Knowledge Discovery (DMKD), Dallas, TX., USA, 2000.
16. Yang, Y. and Zhang, H., HTML Page Analysis Based on Visual Cues, In 6th International Conference on Document Analysis and Recognition, Seattle, Washington, USA, 2001.
17. Yu, S., Cai, D., Wen, J.-R., and Ma, W.-Y., Improving Pseudo-Relevance Feedback in Web Information Retrieval Using Web Page Segmentation, To appear in the Twelfth International World Wide Web Conference (WWW2003), 2003.

XML Data Integration and Distribution in a Web-Based Object Video Server System

Shermann Sze-Man Chan[1] and Qing Li[2]

[1] Department of Computer Science,
[2] Department of Computer Engineering and Information Technology,
City University of Hong Kong,
83 Tat Chee Avenue, Kowloon, Hong Kong SAR, China
{shermann@cs., itqli@} cityu.edu.hk

Abstract. Data integration and distribution, albeit "old" topics, are necessary for developing a distributed video server system which can support multiple key functions such as video retrieval, video production and editing capabilities. In a distributed object video server (DOVS) system, objects from (homogeneous and heterogeneous) servers usually need to be integrated for efficient operations such as query processing and video editing. On the other hand, due to practical factors and concerns (such as resource cost and/or intellectual property concerns), raw/source video files often need to be well protected. XML is becoming the standard for multimedia data description (e.g. MPEG-7), and is very suitable for Web-based data presentation owing to its expressiveness and flexibility. In this paper, we describe our approach to process XML descriptions for data integration and distribution in a Web-based DOVS system.

1 Introduction

Web-enabled multimedia search and management systems become important in multimedia information management. Video is a rich and colorful media widely used in many of our daily life applications like education, entertainment, news spreading etc. Digital videos have diverse sources of origin such as tape recorder and Internet. Expressiveness of video documents decides their dominant position in the next-generation multimedia information systems. Unlike traditional types of data, digital video can provide more effective dissemination of information for its rich content.

Collectively, a digital video can have several information descriptors: (i) media data - actual video frame stream, including its encoding scheme and frame rate; (ii) metadata - information about the characteristics of video content, such as structural information and spatio-temporal features; (iii) semantic data - text annotation relevant to the content of video, obtaining by manual or automatic understanding. Metadata is created independently from how its contents are described and how its database structure is organized later. It is thus natural to define "video" and other meaningful constructs such as "scene", "frame" as objects corresponding to their respective inher-

X. Zhou, Y. Zhang, and M.E. Orlowska (Eds.): APWeb 2003, LNCS 2642, pp. 418–429, 2003.
© Springer-Verlag Berlin Heidelberg 2003

ent semantic and visual contents. Meaningful video scenes are identified and associated with their description data incrementally. Depending on user's viewpoint, same video/scene may be given different descriptions. On the other hand, XML is becoming the standard for multimedia data description (e.g. MPEG-7), and it is very suitable for Web-based data presentation owing to its expressiveness and flexibility. More specifically, video data can be separated into XML data description and raw videos. Using XML data description and a newly proposed Bi-Temporal Object-oriented XML Processing and Storage model, data integration and distribution can be easily achieved over the Web while the server keeps its own raw videos.

1.1 Background of Research

Over the last few years, we have been working on developing a generic video management and application processing (VideoMAP) framework [4], [5], [13]. A central component of VideoMAP is a query-based video retrieval mechanism called CAROL/ST, which supports spatio-temporal queries. While the original CAROL/ST has contributed on working with video semantic data based on an extended object oriented approach, little support has been provided to support video retrieval using visual features. To come up with a more effective video retrieval system, we have made extensions to the VideoMAP framework, and particularly the CAROL/ST mechanism to furnish a hybrid approach [6]. Meanwhile, we have worked out a preliminary version of our Web-based prototype called VideoMAP* [2], [3].

1.2 Paper Contribution and Organization

In this paper, we introduce a generic data conversion mechanism between Temporal Object-oriented Database and Temporal Object-oriented XML Data. The mechanism converts binary object data into XML packets for transmission. We also propose a Bi-Temporal Object-oriented XML Processing and Storage model as the central integration mechanism. The central mechanism can process and store infinite incoming XML packets (streams) from group of servers for data integration and distribution. The rest of the paper is organized as follows. We review some related work on Web-based video data model and issues of data streams in sect. 2. Sect. 3 is a preliminary introduction of our Web-based VideoMAP* framework. In sect. 4, we describe the architecture and mechanisms for data integration and distribution in detail. Finally, we conclude the paper and offer further research directions in sect. 5.

2 Related Work

2.1 Web-Based Video Data Management

The DiVAN project [8] built a distributed audio-visual digital library system providing TV broadcasters and video archives owners with: (i) facilities to effectively compress, annotate, organize and store raw material; (ii) coherent content-based access facilities via user-friendly interface paradigms. It can demonstrate and assess the applicability and acceptability of the system through experiments based on the archives of major European broadcasters and audio-visual Institutions. The A4SM project [11] integrated an IT framework into video production process: (i) pre-production (e.g., script development, story boarding); (ii) production (e.g. collection of media-data by using an MPEG-2/7 camera); (iii) post-production (support of non-linear editing). In collaboration with TV-reporters, cameramen and editors, a MPEG-7 camera is designed in combination with a mobile annotation device for reporter, and a mobile editing suite suitable for generation of news-clips.

2.2 Data Stream Modeling

Data streams become useful for online analysis of continuous data e.g., sales transaction, stock market. Compared with the large volume of incoming data streams, most systems for stream processing have relatively limited amount of memory and space. Whatever the size of data streams, data streams will be removed once they are processed. Important information extracted from the data streams is stored in a data summary (intermediate results) repository for further processing. For example, sales transactions need to be stored in customers' profiles. Therefore, some ACID (atomic, consistent, isolation, and durability) characteristics of a relational database are necessary to maintain and some data models should be derived in order to handle data streams over the Web. Dionisio et al. [7] proposed a unified data model that represented multimedia, timeline, and simulation data utilizing a single set of related data modeling constructs. They developed a knowledge-based multimedia medical distributed database, which can handle time-based multimedia streams with structural information. Another research effort advocates a Data Stream Management System (DSMS) for network traffic management [1]. DSMS supports collecting and processing data streams using four data stores (Stream, Store, Scratch, and Throw). In addition, another complete DSMS called STREAM (Stanford stREam datA Manager) [9] is to be built to manage continuous and rapid data streams, which will have functionality and performance similar to a traditional DBMS.

2.3 XML Data Stream

For the purposes of data integration and distribution, XML (text-based) format is suitable due to its expressiveness and presentation power over the Web. Ives et al. [10] provided an overview of their Tukwila data integration system, which is based on a query engine designed for processing network-bound XML data sources. Tufte et al. [16] proposed merge operation and template for aggregation and accumulation of XML data. XML document can be created by integrating several XML documents, which are collected from the Internet. Their approach is simply to merge the documents semantically together, but without updating. Besides the research work on XML data integration, recent research on punctuated XML streams focuses on the format of XML streams, which aim is to handle fast processing of sequence of streams [14].

Suppose some blocking operators (such as sort) from data streams may block and delay stream processing, data streams should be embedded with some priori knowledge, which can be expressed in the form of punctuations.

3 Overview of the Web-Based Object Video Management System

3.1 VideoMAP* Architecture

The architecture of our Web-based object video management system (VideoMAP*) is shown in Fig. 1. There are two types of components: server- and client- components. The client-components are grouped inside the gray boxes; the server-components are shown below the network backbone. The main server-components providing services to the clients include Video Production Database (VPDB) Processing, Profile Processing, and Global Query Processing. Four kinds of users can utilize and work with the system: Video Administrator (VA), Video Producer (VP), Video Editor (VE), and Video Query Client (VQ). Each type of users is assigned with a priority level for the VPDB Processing component to handle the processing requests from a queue. The user priority levels of our system, in descending order, are from VA, VP, VE, to VQ. Detailed discussions of the main components are described in [2].

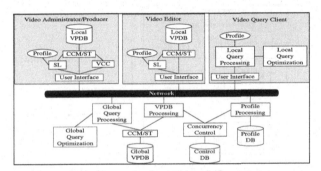

Fig. 1. Architecture of VideoMAP*: a Web-based Object Video Management System

3.2 Global and Local Video Production Databases

In the Web-based environment, cost of data communication is an important issue worth great attention. In order to reduce this overhead, databases can be fragmented and distributed into different sites. There are many research efforts on data fragmentation of relational databases. On the contrary, there is only limited recent work on data (object) fragmentation in object databases [12], [15]. In VideoMAP*, different types of users can retrieve the Global Video Production Database (Global VPDB) into their Local VPDBs for processing, and their work may affect, and be propagated to, the Global VPDB. In particular, each type of users may work on a set of video segments and create dynamic objects out of the video segments. Therefore, a generic mechanism for object data integration and distribution is necessary to address the problem of inconsistency among databases.

4 Object Data Integration and Distribution

4.1 Architecture and Process Flow

In Fig. 2, there are two servers: Video Server (VS) and Central Integration Server (CIS). In VS, there are four data stores: (i) Video Production Database (the VPDB described in sect. 3); (ii) temporary Transaction-timestamped Object-oriented XML Database (Txn-OO-XMLed Data and Operation); (iii) Bi-Temporal Object-oriented XML Database (BiT-OO-XML Storage); (iv) Video Server Domain Database (Video Domain/Timestamps). Besides, processes and mechanisms in between those data stores include (i) filtering process of inconsistent transaction-timestamped objects (Filtering out Inconsistent Txn-Objects); (ii) conversion processes between transaction-timestamped objects and XML (Txn-Object to XML Conversion, and XML to Txn-Object Conversion); (iii) transaction-timestamped object-oriented XML stream processing (Txn-OO-XML in-Stream/out-Stream Processing). In CIS, there are three data stores: (i) BiT-OO-XML Storage; (ii) Filtered Txn-OO-XMLed Data and Operation; (iii) XML Vocabulary for VideoMAP. The processes in CIS include Txn-OO-XML in-Stream/out-Stream Processing, and Domain Filtering.

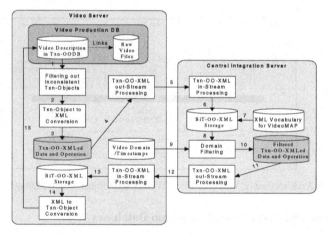

Fig. 2. Add-on Components for Object Data Integration and Distribution

The numberings shown in Fig. 2 depict the process flow of data integration and distribution between VS and CIS. Starting from process 1 of VS, some inconsistent objects (cf. Fig. 3) from the Transaction-timestamped Object-oriented Database (Txn-OODB) are first filtered out by the algorithm (i.e., *FilterInconsistentObject*) described in Appendix. Then, follow process 2 to 3, inconsistent objects are converted to XML format with proper transaction timestamps (Txn-OO-XMLed). The outputs of the filtering and conversion processes are shown in Fig. 4, Fig. 5, and Fig. 6 respectively. The description of each component and process is provided in the subsequent sections. The Txn-OO-XMLed Data and Operation component in VS is a temporary data store, in which XML data will then be trimmed into small pieces for sending out to CIS. XML data received by CIS are processed by the structural information of VideoMAP (XML vocabulary for VideoMAP), and the output is stored in the Bi-Temporal Object-oriented XML (BiT-OO-XML) Storage finally. Data from various VSs are integrated into CIS. According to the domain of each VS, data is then filtered and distributed to VS (from process 9 to 13). Once groups of XML packets are collected in the BiT-OO-XML Storage in VS, the data will be converted instantly to Txn-OODB (from process 14 to 15) for VPDB processing.

4.2 Component Description

Video Production Database. Video Production Database (VPDB) is a temporal (transaction-timestamped) object-oriented database designed for object data integration and distribution. With the introduction of transaction timestamps, inconsistent objects can be easily filtered out. Meanwhile, with the introduction of duplicate (backup) data, object can be rollback if the process of integration and distribution in CIS failed. It is also necessary to identify equivalent and/or identical objects in CIS, in which the objects are logically the same but exist separately among various VSs. Txn-OODB includes some base classes: *TxnObject*, *ObjectId*, *ObjectRef*, and *TxnTimestamp*. All classes of VideoMAP can be derived from *TxnObject*, which is embedded with three main features of object orientation: object identifier, object inheritance, and object composition. ObjectId contains a global identifier (*global_id*), a local identifier (*local_id*), and a *version*. With a *global_id*, object can be identified among different sites. *local_id* is for local processing in local site. *version* is useful for object versioning. *TxnObject* only stores the object identifiers of other objects for inheritance relationships and composite relationships. Therefore, conversion and extraction of binary objects (*TxnObject*) are relatively easy to perform, and dynamic construction of video programs can be performed. The structure of *ObjectRef* consists of an update frequency and a timestamp, type of operation, and a reference counter. All these data items are valid in the current local site only. The timestamps are obtained from a centralized controller once the user logons to the system. This information may be useful for integration.

Inconsistent Object Filtering. Inconsistent objects in Txn-OODB can be filtered out using the algorithm (i.e., *FilterInconsistentObject*) in Appendix. The timestamp *TS* of the last updated VPDB by CIS is used to compare with the transaction timestamps stored in each object. If one of the timestamps in an object is greater than *TS*, it means that this object is in an inconsistent state, and the object should be filtered out. An example of two inconsistent objects is shown in Fig. 3. The object shown in the left-side box was previously inserted with a timestamp of "20010102.223411". The format of the timestamp is "yyyymmdd.hhmmss". Then, data integration and distribution was performed at the timestamp of "20010102.223411", therefore *TS* was set to "20010102.223411". At the timestamp of "20020907.0000", the "name" attribute of the left-object was updated. At this moment, a second object (shown in the right-side box of Fig. 3) is being inserted into the database with the timestamp of "20020908.105502". As the second object is a child object of the first one, the inheritance relationship between these two objects is being updated at this time, with the timestamp of "20020908.105502". Therefore, by comparing *TS* with the timestamps of objects, these two objects are marked as inconsistent.

```
object Scene : TxnObject
  attributes
    id.global_id.SITE="192.168.1.100"
    id.global_id.SEQ=1
    id.local_id.SITE="192.168.1.100"
    id.local_id.SEQ=1
    id.version=1

    freq_info.update_freq=2
    freq_info.update_freq_ts.last_update="20020908.105502"
    freq_info.operation_type="update"
    freq_info.reference_count=1

    // static data
    name="MyFirstScene"
    name_bak="MyScene"
    name_ts.last_update="20020907.000000"

    // dynamic inheritance
    parent_id_list=0
    parent_id_list_bak=0
    parent_id_list_ts.last_update="20010102.223411"
    child_id_list[0].global_id.SITE="192.168.1.100"
    child_id_list[0].global_id.SEQ=2
    child_id_list[0].local_id.SITE="192.168.1.100"
    child_id_list[0].local_id.SEQ=2
    child_id_list[0].version=1
    child_id_list_bak=0
    child_id_list_ts.last_update="20020908.105502"

    // dynamic composite
    component_id_list=0
    component_id_list_bak=0
    component_id_list_ts.last_update="20010102.223411"
    container_id_list=0
    container_id_list_bak=0
    container_id_list_ts.last_update="20010102.223411"
```

```
object Scene : TxnObject
  attributes
    id.global_id.SITE="192.168.1.100"
    id.global_id.SEQ=2
    id.local_id.SITE="192.168.1.100"
    id.local_id.SEQ=2
    id.version=1

    freq_info.update_freq=1
    freq_info.update_freq_ts.last_update="20020908.105502"
    freq_info.operation_type="insert"
    freq_info.reference_count=1

    // static data
    name="MySecondScene"
    name_bak=""
    name_ts.last_update="20020908.105502"

    // dynamic inheritance
    parent_id_list[0].global_id.SITE="192.168.1.100"
    parent_id_list[0].global_id.SEQ=1
    parent_id_list[0].local_id.SITE="192.168.1.100"
    parent_id_list[0].local_id.SEQ=1
    parent_id_list[0].version=1
    parent_id_list_bak=0
    parent_id_list_ts.last_update="20020908.105502"
    child_id_list=0
    child_id_list_bak=0
    child_id_list_ts.last_update="20020908.105502"

    // dynamic composite
    component_id_list=0
    component_id_list_bak=0
    component_id_list_ts.last_update="20020908.105502"
    container_id_list=0
    container_id_list_bak=0
    container_id_list_ts.last_update="20020908.105502"
```

Fig. 3. Example of Inconsistent Objects

```
<Operation type="update">
  <Object type="Scene">
  <ObjectId>
    <id.global_id.site value="192.168.1.100" />
    <id.global_id.seq value="1" />
    <id.local_id.site value="192.168.1.100" />
    <id.local_id.seq value="1" />
    <id.version value="1" />
  </ObjectId>
  <StaticData>
    <name value="MyFirstScene" />
    <name_bak value="MyScene" />
    <name_ts.last_update value="20020907.000000" />
  </StaticData>
  <Inheritance>
    <child_id_list.0.global_id.site value="192.168.1.100" />
    <child_id_list.0.global_id.seq value="2" />
    <child_id_list.0.local_id.site value="192.168.1.100" />
    <child_id_list.0.local_id.seq value="2" />
    <child_id_list.0.version value="1" />
    <child_id_list_bak value="0" />
    <child_id_list_ts.last_update value="20020908.105502" />
  </Inheritance>
  </Object>
</Operation>
```

```
<Operation type="insert">
  <Object type="Scene">
  <ObjectId>
    <id.global_id.site value="192.168.1.100" />
    <id.global_id.seq value="2" />
    <id.local_id.site value="192.168.1.100" />
    <id.local_id.seq value="2" />
    <id.version value="1" />
  </ObjectId>
  <StaticData>
    <name value="MySecondScene" />
    <name_bak value="" />
    <name_ts.last_update value="20020908.105502" />
  </StaticData>
  <Inheritance>
    <parent_id_list.0.global_id.site value="192.168.1.100" />
    <parent_id_list.0.global_id.seq value="1" />
    <parent_id_list.0.local_id.site value="192.168.1.100" />
    <parent_id_list.0.local_id.seq value="1" />
    <parent_id_list.0.version value="1" />
    <parent_id_list_bak value="0" />
    <parent_id_list_ts.last_update value="20020908.105502" />
  </Inheritance>
  </Object>
</Operation>
```

Fig. 4. Example of Inconsistent Object to XML Conversion

XML Data Conversion from Inconsistent Object. After filtering out the inconsistent objects, they are converted into plain-text XML format. The XML format would restore the object-oriented features and contain transaction timestamps. It also includes operation information. Such information is important and useful for other databases to do further processing. Then each attribute (such as name) of Scene is compared with its backup value (i.e., name_bak). If the timestamp of the attribute is greater than TS (cf. *FilterInconsistentObject* in Appendix) and the value is different from its backup value, this attribute will be copied to the format as shown in Fig. 4. The format of the result is named Transaction-timestamped Object-oriented XML Data (Txn-OO-XMLed Data and Operation).

```
<Stream>
  <Head>
    <Stream.Total value="1" />
  </Head>
  <Stream.TxnId value="192.168.1.100.1.1.345" />
  <Stream.Id value="1"/>
  <Stream.Operation value="update" />
  <Body>
    <Object type="Scene">
    <ObjectId>
      <id.global_id.site value="192.168.1.100" />
      <id.global_id.seq value="1" />
      <id.local_id.site value="192.168.1.100" />
      <id.local_id.seq value="1" />
      <id.version value="1" />
    </ObjectId>
    <StaticData>
      <name value="MyFirstScene" />
      <name_ts.last_update value="20020907.000000" />
    </StaticData>
  </Body>
</Stream>
```

```
<Stream>
  <Head>
    <Stream.Total value="1" />
  </Head>
  <Stream.TxnId value="192.168.1.100.2.1.456" />
  <Stream.Id value="1" />
  <Stream.Operation value="insert" />
  <Body>
    <Object type="Scene">
    <ObjectId>
      <id.global_id.site value="192.168.1.100" />
      <id.global_id.seq value="2" />
      <id.local_id.site value="192.168.1.100" />
      <id.local_id.seq value="2" />
      <id.version value="1" />
    </ObjectId>
    <StaticData>
      <name value="MySecondScene" />
      <name_ts.last_update value="20020908.105502" />
    </StaticData>
  </Body>
</Stream>
```

Fig. 5. Example of Independent XML Packets

XML Processing. In order to allow immediate (stream) processing in CIS (due to limited size of space and memory of buffers), two groups of XML data as shown in Fig. 4 are further trimmed into four smaller pieces (i.e., XML packets shown in Fig. 5 and Fig. 6) in VS. If the object data is a simple attribute type (static data), the inconsistent value (e.g. name) will be copied to the packet. However, if the data is a list (e.g. parent_id_list), then the list is needed to compare with its backup value in order to further trim the elements of the list into more pieces (cf. *ObjectList2Packets* in Appendix). Two out of the four packets (cf. Fig. 7) can be processed independently (immediately), but some cannot.[1] Therefore, dependent packets are grouped together for transmission. The first packet of each group contains the head of packet ("/Stream/Head"). Inside the Head, it stores the total number of data packages ("/Stream/Head/Stream.Total") in each group. If this value is one, it means the packet is an independent packet. Each group of packets has a unique transaction identifier ("/Stream/Stream.TxnId"). Each packet has a packet transmission order ("/Stream/Stream.Id") and the type of operation ("/Stream/Stream.Operation"). There are three types of operations: update, insert, and delete. More specifically, operations are: (i) insert a new object; (ii) delete an object; (iii) insert object id to the object id list; (iv) delete object id from the object id list; (v) update static attribute data. Fig. 5 shows two independent packets, each belonging to its own group; Fig. 6 shows two dependent packets from an identical group.

---

[1] Therefore, data processing in CIS is semi-streaming.

```
<Stream>
  <Head>
    <Stream.Total value="2" />
  </Head>
  <Stream.Txnld value="192.168.1.100.2.1.457" />
  <Stream.Id value="1" />
  <Stream.Operation value="insert" />
  <Body>
    <Object type="Scene">
    <ObjectId>
      <id.global_id.site value="192.168.1.100" />
      <id.global_id.seq value="2" />
      <id.local_id.site value="192.168.1.100" />
      <id.local_id.seq value="2" />
      <id.version value="1" />
    </ObjectId>
    <Inheritance>
      <parent_id_list.global_id.site value="192.168.1.100" />
      <parent_id_list.global_id.seq value="1" />
      <parent_id_list.local_id.site value="192.168.1.100" />
      <parent_id_list.local_id.seq value="1" />
      <parent_id_list.version value="1" />
      <parent_id_list_ts.last_update value="20020908.105502" />
    </Inheritance>
  </Body>
</Stream>
```

```
<Stream>
  <Stream.Txnld value="192.168.1.100.2.1.457" />
  <Stream.Id value="2" />
  <Stream.Operation value="insert" />
  <Body>
    <Object type="Scene">
    <ObjectId>
      <id.global_id.site value="192.168.1.100" />
      <id.global_id.seq value="1" />
      <id.local_id.site value="192.168.1.100" />
      <id.local_id.seq value="1" />
      <id.version value="1" />
    </ObjectId>
    <Inheritance>
      <child_id_list.global_id.site value="192.168.1.100" />
      <child_id_list.global_id.seq value="2" />
      <child_id_list.local_id.site value="192.168.1.100" />
      <child_id_list.local_id.seq value="2" />
      <child_id_list.version value="1" />
      <child_id_list_ts.last_update value="20020908.105502" />
    </Inheritance>
  </Body>
</Stream>
```

Parent and Child are related

Fig. 6. Example of Dependent XML Packets

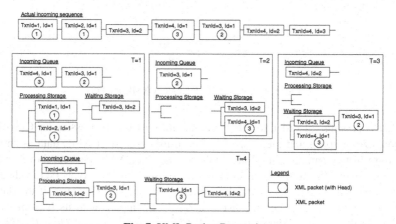

Fig. 7. XML Packet Processing

A scenario of XML packet transmission is shown in Fig. 7. XML packets are sent from VS to CIS during the process of Txn-OO-XML out-Stream Processing. The first two packets (i.e., with TxnId=1 and TxnId=2) are independent packets of Fig. 5. The dependent packets of Fig. 6 are illustrated by the packets with TxnId=3. The Actual Incoming Sequence shows the packets received by CIS. CIS receives the packets and stores them in the Incoming Queue. In addition, two temporary storages are used to process the incoming packets. As memory may be limited, the window processing size for the Processing Storage can be set to an optimal value according to the configuration of CIS. Besides window processing size, there are some other parameters and checking needed (e.g., time period for processing, checking of whether the size of next packet is over the size of window, and checking of the size of packet, etc.). For simplicity of the scenario, the value of the window processing size is infinite here, and all packets in the Processing Storage can be processed in one unit time of timestamp. Fig. 7 shows four snapshots of the process from timestamp T=1 to T=4. At T=1, the first two independent packets are received and stored into the Processing Storage for instant processing. As the third packet is a dependent packet, it is received and stored into the Waiting Storage. At T=2, the packet of TxnId=4 is stored into the Waiting Storage as it should wait for its dependent packets. Then at T=3, all packets in the group of TxnId=3 are completely received, therefore at T=4, this group of packets is sent to the Processing Storage.

The Bi-Temporal Object-oriented XML Model. Packets from the Processing Storage of Fig. 7 are stored into a Bi-Temporal Object-oriented XML (BiT-OO-XML) model. The model is bi-temporal because it contains transaction timestamps of the incoming XML packets and valid timestamps. By the assumption of limited space of CIS and large amount of video descriptions from VPDBs, data stored in the model will be removed periodically and/or when it is demanded, according to the valid timestamps. Therefore, the temporal structure of the model is designed for easy removal of data (cf. Fig. 8). According to the amount of resources, the structure grouped in the darker grey box is created and defined dynamically by the server with valid time. The root node named as "3d" means the model stores data for three days only. (It can be five days or even longer). The nodes in the second level (or further levels) further divide and group the packets according to the valid time.

Objects inside XML packets are to be stored in the structure below the grey box (cf. Fig. 8). Objects from the same transaction are first grouped together. Then the objects are clustered by their object types (e.g. scene, video), and are stored in a Data Pack with indices and a new valid timestamp. Once a Data Pack is formed, a scheduler would trigger the distribution process from CIS to all VSs. When the valid timestamp is expired, the Data Pack will be removed. Otherwise, if an object inside the Data Pack needed to be updated (by *global_id*, *local_id*, *version*, and *txn_timestamp*), the updated object will be migrated to a new Data Pack with a new valid timestamp and the distribution process will be triggered. We assume that objects are evolved from the same source, i.e. they are of their unique global ids. Different users can get an object, modify it, and then store it with a new *local_id*. However, *global_id* will never change. Other logical index structures can be formed (e.g., domain and any important attribute), with links to the physical structure. As domain information can be collected from VS, objects created from VSs with similar domains can be grouped together in the index structure. In order to facilitate the retrieval of XML data, indexes are created according to the XML Vocabulary for VideoMAP.

Domain Filtering. Domain filtering is to extract necessary data from Bi-Temporal Object-oriented XML Storage of CIS by the requirement specified by the VS. An indexing structure shown in Fig. 8 has grouped objects together from different VSs, which have similar domains information. Moreover, data can also be extracted based on the timestamps. Therefore, packets from different VSs with similar domain can be integrated and sent back to VSs in order to complete the cycle of data integration and distribution. VPDB can then be updated to a consistent state or started the process of rollback.

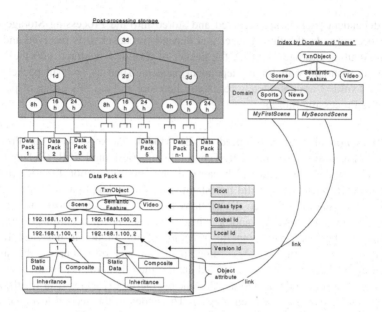

Fig. 8. Bi-Temporal Object-oriented XML Packet Storage

5 Conclusion and Future Research

In this paper, we gave an overview of our Web-based object video management system (i.e., VideoMAP*), from which the problem of data (object) inconsistency arose. In order to fix the problem, we introduced a generic data conversion mechanism between Temporal Object-oriented Database and Temporal Object-oriented XML Data. Both temporal data include transaction-based timestamps. In addition, we proposed a Bi-Temporal Object-oriented XML Processing and Storage model as the central integration mechanism. There are a number of issues for us to further work on. Among others, we plan to develop an *object XML* query language with a sufficient expressive power to accommodate VideoMAP* user queries adequately. Performance evaluation of processing such object XML queries is another important issue and will be conducted upon the VideoMAP* prototype system.

References

1. Babu, S., Subramanian, L., Widom, J.: A Data Stream Management System for Network Traffic Management. Proc. Workshop on Network-Related Data Management (2001)
2. Chan, S.S.M., Li, Q.: Architecture and Mechanisms of a Web-based Video Data Management System. Proc. IEEE ICME, New York City (2000)
3. Chan, S.S.M., Li, Q.: Architecture and Mechanisms of a Multi-paradigm Video Querying System over the Web. Proc. Int. Workshop on Cooperative Internet Computing, Hong Kong (2002) 17–23

4. Chan, S.S.M., Li, Q.: Facilitating Spatio-Temporal Operations in a Versatile Video Database System. Proc. Int. Workshop on Multimedia Information Systems (1999) 56–63

5. Chan, S.S.M., Li, Q.: Developing an Object-Oriented Video Database System with Spatio-Temporal Reasoning Capabilities. Proc. Int. Conf. on Conceptual Modeling (1999) 47–61

6. Chan, S.S.M., Wu, Y., Li, Q., Zhuang, Y.: A Hybrid Approach to Video Retrieval in a Generic Video Management and Application Processing Framework. Proc. IEEE ICME, Japan (2001)

7. Dionisio, J.D.N., Cárdenas, A.F.: A Unified Data Model for Representing Multimedia, Timeline, and Simulation Data. IEEE TKDE, Vol. 10, No. 5 (1998) 746–767

8. The DiVAN project. http://divan.intranet.gr

9. The DSMS project. http://www-db.stanford.edu/stream

10. Ives, Z.G., Halevy, A.Y., Weld, D.S.: Integrating Network-Bound XML Data. Bulletin of IEEE Computer Society TCDE, Vol. 24, No. 2 (2001) 20–26

11. The A4SM project. GMD IPSI – Integrated Publication and Information Systems Institute, Darmstadt. http://www.darmstadt.gmd.de/IPSI/movie.html

12. Karlapalem, K., Li, Q.: A Framework for Class Partitioning in Object Oriented Databases. Distributed and Parallel Databases, Kluwer Academic Publishers (2000) 317–350

13. Lau, R.W.H., Li, Q., Si, A.: VideoMAP: a Generic Framework for Video Management and Application Processing. Proc. Int. Conf. on System Sciences: Minitrack on New Trends in Multimedia Systems, IEEE Computer Society Press (2000)

14. The Punctuated Stream project. http://www.cse.ogi.edu/~ptucker/PStream

15. Ozsu, M.T., Valduriez, P.: Principles of Distributed Database System, Prentice Hall, Upper Saddle River, New Jersey (1999)

16. Tufte, K., Maier, D.: Aggregation and Accumulation of XML Data. Bulletin of IEEE Computer Society TCDE, Vol. 24, No. 2 (2001) 34–39

Appendix: Algorithms

```
FilterInconsistentObject
  input :
    objects of Video Production DB, IN-OBJ
    timestamp of consistent Video Production DB, TS
  output :
    inconsistent objects, OUT-OBJ
  begin
    /* Compare Transaction Timestamps */
    for each object A in IN-OBJ do
      if A.freq_info.update_freq_ts.last_update > TS, then
        Mark object A as OUT-OBJ
      else if there is any timestamp in object A > TS, then
        Mark object A as OUT-OBJ
      end-if
    end-for
  end. {FilterInconsistentObject}
```

```
ObjectList2Packets
  input :
    ordered object list, NEW-LIST
    ordered object list backup, OLD-LIST
  output :
    packets
  begin
    for each element A in NEW-LIST do
      compare A and with all elements in OLD-LIST
      if A is in OLD-LIST then
        Mark the element of OLD-LIST
      else if A is not in OLD-LIST then
        create an "insert" packet for element A
      end-if
    end-for

    for all unmarked elements in OLD-LIST do
      create a "delete" packet for each unmarked element
    end-for
  end. {ObjectList2Packets}
```

Genetic Algorithm-Based QoS Multicast Routing for Uncertainty in Network Parameters

Layuan Li and Chunlin Li

Department of Computer Science. Wuhan University of Technology, Wuhan 430063.P. R. China
jwtu@public.wh.hb.cn

Abstract. This paper discusses the multicast routing problem with multiple QoS constraints in networks with uncertain parameters, and describes a network model that is suitable to research such QoS multicast routing problem. The paper mainly presents GAQMR, a multicast routing policy for Internet, mobile network or other high-performance networks, that is based on the genetic algorithm, and can provide QoS-sensitive paths in a scalable and flexible way, in the networks environment with uncertain parameters. The GAQMR can also optimize the network resources such as bandwidth and delay, and can converge to the optimal or near-optimal solution within few iterations, even for the networks environment with uncertain parameters. The incremental rate of computational cost can close to polynomial and is less than exponential rate. The performance measures of the GAQMR are evaluated using simulations. The results shows that GAQMR provides an available approach to QoS Multicast routing for uncertainty in network parameters.

Keywords: QoS; multicast routing; genetic algorithm; uncertainty; network parameters

1 Introduction

Broadband integrated services networks are expected to support multiple and diverse applications, with various quality of service (QoS) requirements. Accordingly, a key issue in the design of broadband architectures is how to provide the resources in order to meet the requirements of each connection. The establishment of efficient QoS routing schemes is, undoubtedly, one of the major building blocks in such architectures. Indeed, QoS routing has been the subject of several studies and proposals[1~6], and references therein. It has been recognized that the establishment of an efficient QoS routing scheme poses several complex challenges. One of the major challenges results from the inherent uncertainty of the information available to the QoS routing process.

QoS multicast routing relies on state parameters specifying resource availability at network nodes or links, and uses them to find paths with enough free resources. In turn, the successful routing of new flows together with the termination of existing ones, induce constant changes in the amount of resources available. These must then be communicated back to QoS multicast routing. Unfortunately, communicating such

X. Zhou, Y. Zhang, and M.E. Orlowska (Eds.): APWeb 2003, LNCS 2642, pp. 430–441, 2003.
© Springer-Verlag Berlin Heidelberg 2003

changes in a timely fashion is expensive and, at times, not even feasible [2,4]. As a result, changes in resources availability are usually communicated either infrequently or uncertainly. There are two main components to the cost of timely distribution of changes in network state: the number of entities generating such updates and the frequency at which each entity generates updates.

In network operation, parameters about the state of nodes or links may be lost. This loss of certainty in state information can have a substantial impact on the multicast routing. For route selection, the main consequence of this loss of accuracy in network state information is that it now needs to consider not only the amount of resources that are available, but also the level of certainty with which these resources are indeed available. The second contributor to the cost of maintaining certain parameters information is the frequency of state changes, and therefore updates. Specifically, each advertisement of a state change consumes both network bandwidth on all the links over which it is sent, and processing cycles at all nodes where it is received. Keeping this overhead to a minimum is, therefore, desirable, if not mandatory. There are many different methods that can be used to achieve such a goal (see [2], [3] for in-depth investigations of this issue and its impact on QoS routing), but they typically involve waiting for either a large enough change or until a minimum amount of time has passed.

The providing a comprehensive set of solutions for computing good paths in the presence of uncertainty is a daunting task that goes well beyond the scope of a single paper. The goal of this paper is to present a QoS multicast routing policy based on genetic algorithm (GA) which can be suitable to the networks with uncertain parameters.

The rest of the paper is organized as follows. Section 2 describes the related work. Section 3 introduces a network model. Section 4 presents the GAQMR. Some simulation results are provided in Section 5. The paper concludes with Section 6.

2 The Related Work

The traditional multicast routing protocols, e.g., CBT and PIM [3-6], were designed for best-effort data traffic. They construct multicast trees primarily based on connectivity. Such trees may be unsatisfactory when QoS is considered due to the lack of resources. Several QoS multicast routing algorithms have been proposed recently. Some algorithms [3] provide heuristic solutions to the NP-complete constrained Steiner tree problem, which is to find the delay-constrained least-cost multicast trees. These algorithms however are not practical in the Internet environment because they have excessive computation overhead, require knowledge about the global network state, and do not handle dynamic group membership. Jia's distributed algorithm [7] does not compute any path or assume the unicast routing table can provide it. However, this algorithm requires excessive message processing overhead. The spanning join protocol by Carlberg and Crowcroft [1-3] handles dynamic membership and does not require any global network state. However, it has excessive communication and messsage processing overhead because it relies on flooding to find a feasible tree branch to connect a new member. QoSMIC [3], proposed by Faloutsos et al., alleviates but does not eliminate the flooding behavior. In addition, an extra control element, called Manager router, is introduced to handle the join requests of new members. Multicast routing and its QoS-driven extension are indispensable components in a QoS-centric network architecture [8-19]. Its main objective is to construct a multicast tree that optimizes a certain objective function (e.g., making effective use of network resources) with respect to performancerelated constraints (e.g., end-to-end delay bound, interreceiver delay jitter bound, minimum bandwidth available, and maximum packet loss probability).

To provide input to the multicast routing algorithm used, each node in the network has to keep either local or partial network state. Several state update policies have been proposed to determine when a state update should be triggered. As summarized in [1-3], the most commonly used policies are: (1) Relative change or threshold-based triggers (i.e., a state update is triggered when the amount of change in the state variable exceeds a threshold). (2) Absolute change or class-based triggers (i.e., a state update is triggered when the state changes from one class to another). (3) Timer-based triggers (i.e., a state update is periodically triggered).

To control the protocol overhead and to limit it to a tolerable level, large clamp-down timers are used to limit the rate of updates. The accuracy of network state is also affected by, for example, the scope of an update message, and the types of value advertised (exact state values or quantized values).There is a fundamental trade-off between the certainty of state information and the protocol message overhead. Moreover, in large and dynamic networks, the growth in the state information makes it practically impossible to maintain accurate knowledge about all nodes and links. Instead, the state information is usually aggregated in a certain hierarchical manner, and the aggregation process inherently decreases the information accuracy and introduces imprecision. The uncertain state information kept at each node imposes difficulty in QoS provisioning. Guerin and Orda investigated the problem of QoS routing when the state information is uncertain or inaccurate and expressed in some probabilistic manner [2,12]. Their objective was to identify a path that is mostly likely to satisfy the delay requirement, which they achieved by decomposing the end-to-end requirement into local delay constraints and deriving tractable, near-optimal solutions for a certain class of probability distributions. Lorenz and Orda also considered the same problem, but in the context of networks with rate-based schedulers (i.e., networks that employs fair queuing scheduling disciplines for link sharing) [12]. Chen et al. considered a simplified probability model for link parameters (i.e., link parameters are allowed to distribute uniformly over an interval) [18]. They then proposed a distributed ticket-based probing routing algorithm.

Most of the work in QoS routing in the presence of uncertain state information is still in the theoretical development stage.

3 Network Model

A network is usually represented as a weighted digraph $G = (V, E)$, where V denotes the set of nodes and E denotes the set of communication links connecting the nodes. $|V|$ and $|E|$ denote the number of nodes and links in the network, respectively, Without loss of generality, only digraphs are considered in which there exists at most one link between a pair of ordered nodes[13].

Let $s \in V$ be source node of a multicast tree, and $M \subseteq \{V - \{s\}\}$ be a set of end nodes of the multicast tree. Let R be the positive weight and R^+ be the nonnegative weight. For any link $e \in E$, we can define the some QoS metrics: delay function *delay* (e): $E \to R$, cost function *cost* (e): $E \to R$, bandwidth function *bandwidth* (e); $E \to R$, and delay jitter function *delay-jitter* (e): $E \to R^+$. Similarly, for any node $n \in V$, one can also define some metrics: delay function *delay* (n): $V \to R$, cost function *cost* (n): $V \to R$, delay jitter function *delay-jitter* (n): $V \to R^+$ and packet loss function *packet-loss* (n): $V \to R^+$. We also use T (s,M) to denote a multicast tree, which has the following relations:

1) $delay\ (p\ (s,t)) = \sum_{e \in P(s,t)} delay\ (e) + \sum_{e \in P(s,t)} delay\ (n)$.

2) $cost\ (T(s,M)) = \sum_{e \in T(s,M)} cost\ (e) + \sum_{e \in T(s,M)} cost\ (n)$.

3) $bandwidth\ (p(s,t)) = \min\{bandwidth\ (e),\ e \in P(s,t)\}$.

4) $delay\text{-}jitter\ (p\ (s,t)) = \sum_{n \in P(s,t)} delay - jitter\ (e)$

$$+ \sum_{n \in P(s,t)} delay - jitter\ (n)\ .$$

5) $packet\text{-}loss\ (p\ (s,t)) = 1 - \prod_{n \in P(s,t)} (1 - packet\text{-}loss(n))$

where $p\ (s,t)$ denotes the path from source s to end node t of T (s, M). With QoS requirements, the problem can be represented as finding a path P^*, such that (1) $\Pi_{l \in P*} pl\ (W) \geq \Pi_{l \in P} pl\ (W)$, where $l \in E$ are the links in the path and $p_l\ (W)$ is the probability that the link l can accommodate a flow which requires w units of bandwidth, and (2) $\Pi_{l \in P*} pl\ (\delta) \geq \Pi_{l \in P} pl\ (\delta)$, where $p_l\ (\delta)$ is the probability that delay for link l is less than δ. QoS multicast routing problem for uncertain parameters is a NP-complete hard problem, which is also a challenging problem for high-performance networks.

4 GAQMR

Genetic algorithms are based on the mechanics of natural evolution. Throughout their artificial evolution, successive generations each consisting of a population of possible solutions, called individuals (or chromosomes, or vectors of genes), search for beneficial adaptations to solve the given problem. This search is carried out by applying the Darwinian principles of "reproduction and survival of the fittest" and the genetic operators of crossover and mutation which derive the new offspring population from the current population. Reproduction involves selecting, in proportion to its fitness level, an individual from the current population and allowing it to survive by copying it to the new population of individuals. The individual's fitness level is usually based on the cost function given by the problem (e.g., QoS multicast routing) under consideration. Then, crossover and mutation are carried on two randomly chosen individuals of the current population creating two new offspring individuals. Crossover involves swapping two randomly located sub-chromosomes (within the same boundaries) of the two mating chromosomes. Mutation is applied to randomly selected genes, where the values associated with such a gene is randomly changed to another value within an allowed range. The offspring population replaces the parent population, and the process is repeated for many generations. Typically, the best individual that appeared in any generation of the run (i.e. best-so-far individual) is designated as the result produced by the genetic algorithm.

4.1 Coding

The coding is one of important problems to solve the QoS multicast routing problem using genetic algorithm. In our coding scheme, all possible paths between the source and a destination will be stored a buffer. The paths which satisfy the bandwidth constraint can be selected, and the paths which do not satisfy the bandwidth constraint should be excluded. Still the number of possible paths could be large, especially for large networks. These buffers of feasible paths between the sender and multiple receiver are provided. We then take on solution randomly from each buffer to provide a multicast solution. The multicast solution string can be at-most of length $c*n$, where c is the number of destinations and n is the number of network nodes. These solution strings can be called chromosomes.

4.2 Selection of Initial Population

Suppose the source of multicast group is the root of the multicast tree $(T(s,M))$, and the destinations are the leaves of the multicast tree. The multicast tree is constructed by the search method of random depth first. Note that multicast tree which is based on the above method may satisfy the QoS constraints, or may not satisfy the QoS constraints.

4.3 Fitness Function

Fitness function should describe the performance of the selected individuals. The individual with good performance has high fitness level, and the individual with bad performance has low fitness level. Let links be service queues where packets to be transmitted get serviced. For most cases this service can be assumed to follow Poisson distribution. The service time should follow an exponential distribution. Let the delay for link l be denoted by the variable d_l, which is a random variable following exponential distribution with parameter equal to λ. So the delay over a path consisting of k links would be the sum of k independent random variables all having the same exponential distribution and so would follow an Erlang-K distribution. From the definition of Erlang-K distribution we get that the probability that the delay over a path P of length k is less than g is given by the following equation:

$$up(g) \frac{\lambda^k g^{k-1} e^{-\lambda g}}{(k-1)!}.$$

Let the maximum delay allowed in a multicast service be D. The measure that the selected multicast route would meet the delay constraint can be obtained by taking the product of $up(D)$ over individual paths in the multicast tree. Thus the probability, $p(D)$, of the selected multicast $M \subseteq E$ meeting the delay requirements would be given by the following equation:

$$p(D) = \Pi_{p \in M} up(D)$$

To find an optimal path, our objective is to maximize this probability of satisfying delay requirements. The measure of the bandwidth guarantee can be obtained by assuming a similar model for the network links. If the service rate or the transmission rate, which is basically a measure of link bandwidth, is assumed to follow a poisson distribution, the probability that a link $l \in E$ can provide bandwidth of w is given by

$$w_l(w) = \Pi_{p \in M} wp(W)$$

So the probability with which the bandwidth guarantee of W is satisfied for an entire path P is given as $wp(W) = \Pi_{l \in E} w_l(W)$. Therefore for all the paths belonging to a multicast T (s,M), the probability of satisfying bandwidth guarantee of W units is $w(W) = \Pi_{p \in M} wp(W)$.

The normal conjecture is that the path which is capable of providing with greatest residual bandwidth is the best choice. The total residual bandwidth in the network after allocating bandwidth for a multicast $T (s,M)$, is given by $\Sigma_{l \in E}(c_l - w_l)$, where c_l is the capacity of a link $l \in E$ and w_l is the bandwidth allocated for all the paths in the multicast $T(s,M)$, along the link l. Obviously, w_l is 0 if $l \notin p$ where $p \in P$. The fraction of total bandwidth available as residual bandwidth is given as

$$rw = \frac{\Sigma_{l \in M}(c_l - w_l)}{\Sigma_{l \in M} c_l}$$

The fitness function of GAQMR can be defined as follows.

$$f(T) = f_c (Af_d + Bf_w + Cf_{rw} + Rf_j + Sf_l), \text{ where}$$

$$f_c = \frac{\alpha}{cost[T(s,M)]},$$

$$f_d = \Pi_{p \in M} up(D) \cdot \Phi_d$$

$$f_w = \Pi_{p \in M} wp(W) \cdot \Phi_w$$

$$f_{rw} = \Sigma_{l \in M} (c_l - w_l) / \Sigma_{l \in M} c_l \cdot \Phi_{rw}$$

$$f_j = \prod_{l \in M} \Phi_j [delay - jitter(p_T(s,t)) - J],$$

$$f_l = \prod_{l \in M} \Phi_l [packet - loss(p_T(s,t)) - L],$$

$$\Phi_d(Z) = \begin{cases} 1, & Z \le 0 \\ h_d, & Z > 0 \end{cases}, \quad \Phi_w(Z) = \begin{cases} 1, & Z \le 0 \\ h_w, & Z > 0 \end{cases},$$

$$\Phi_{rw}(Z) = \begin{cases} 1, & Z \le 0 \\ h_{rw}, & Z > 0 \end{cases}, \quad \Phi_j(Z) = \begin{cases} 1, & Z \le 0 \\ h_j, & Z > 0 \end{cases},$$

$$\Phi_l(Z) = \begin{cases} 1, & Z \le 0 \\ h_l, & Z > 0 \end{cases}.$$

where A, B, C, R and S are the positive weight of f_d, f_w, f_{rw}, f_j and f_l, respectively, which denote the probability of the selected route meeting the delay constraint, the probability of satisfying bandwidth constraint, the bandwidth utilization, the rates for delay-jitter and packetloss of the fitness function. The $\Phi_d(Z)$, $\Phi_w(Z)$, $\Phi_{rw}(Z)$, $\Phi_j(Z)$ and $\Phi_l(Z)$ are the penalty functions. The $\Phi_d(Z)$ is the penalty function of delay metric. If individual can satisfy delay constraint (D) then the value of $\Phi_d(Z)$ is 1 else the value is h_d $(0<h_d<1)$. The $\phi_j(Z)$ is the penalty function of delay jitter metric. If individual can satisfy delay jitter constraint (J) then the value of $\phi_{dj}(Z)$ is 1 else the value will be h_j $(0<h_j<1)$. Similarly, $\phi_l(Z)$ is the penalty function of packet loss metric. If individual can satisfy packet loss constraint (L), (packet loss $(P_T(s,t)) \le L_t$) then the value of $\phi_l(Z)$ is 1 else the value will be h_l $(0<h_l<1)$. The value of h_d, h_w, h_{rw}, h_j and h_l can be dynamically set in terms of practical cases.

4.4 Crossover

Two individuals can randomly be selected from current population by crossover operation. The crossover rules can be described as follows.

(1) The selection features of GA shows that individual with higher fitness level can be selected with larger probability. The parent individual which can satisfy QoS constraints is selected with larger probability, which is advantageous to improve convergence performance of the genetic algorithm. The networks topology that is consists of these good links may be constructed by some subtrees, which may not have connectivity.

(2) If all selected parent individuals can not satisfy QoS constraints, these subtrees are connected by using probability A/ (A+B+C+R+S), B/ (A+B+C+R+S), C/ (A+B+C+R+S), R/(A+B+C+R+S), and S/(A+B+C+R+S), respectively. If one of the selected parent individuals can satisfy QoS constraints, the subtrees are connected using shortest path cost. The connected subtrees will continuously join the successive connection operation. This process will be repeated until a multicast tree $(T(s,M))$ is constructed.

4.5 Reproduction

Reproduction is mainly the operation to increase the number of good solutions in the population in every iteration of the algorithm. The solutions are assigned a probability of being selected in the next generation which is proportional to its fitness function. Thus a solution with a greater value for its fitness function is more probable of being selected in the next generation than another one with lower value for the fitness function. In this way better solutions replaces the inferior ones in the next generation. The selection of the next generation solutions are done by the roulette wheel scheme once the probabilities of selection are given.

4.6 Mutation

Some intermediate nodes of the new children individuals are randomly selected according to the mutation probability. Breaking the multicast tree into some separate sub-trees by removing all the links that are incident to the selected nodes. Meanwhile, it re-connects those separate sub-trees into a new multicast tree by randomly selecting the least-delay or the least-cost paths between them. These sub-trees are connected in similar way to crossover operation. This operation also has the similar role in optimization procedure like that of the crossover operation. This mutation operation can improve the performance of the genetic algorithm, which should be advantageous to break through of local optimal solution of the algorithm and to close in on the global optimal (or near optimal) solution of the algorithm (QoS constraints are satisfied and cost is lower).

5 Simulations

We conduct simulations to evaluate GAQMR, GAQMR is implemented by using the Network Simulator (NS) and its performance is compared with some existing protocols or algorithms[3-7]. Network topologies used in the simulations are deliberately manipulated to simulate wide area sparse networks. A large network is likely to be loosely interconnected [9]. An n-node graph is considered to be sparse when less than 5% of the possible edges are present in the graph. The network graphs used in the simulations are constructed by the Waxman's random graph model [20,21].

In this random graph, the edge's probability can be

$$P_e(u, v) = \beta exp(-\frac{d(u, v)}{aY})$$

where $d(u,v)$ is geometric distance from node u to node v, Y is maximum distance between two nodes, parameter a can be used to control short edge and long edge of the random graph, and parameter β can be used to control the value of average degree of the random graph.

We first compare the quality of routing trees by network cost of GAQMR, CSPT, BSMA and QoSMIC. The network cost is measured by the mean value of the total number of simulation runs. At each simulation point, the simulation runs 100 times. Each time the nodes in the group G are randomly picked out from the network graph. The network cost is simulated against two parameters: delay bound D and group size. In order to simulate the real situations, group size are always made less than 20% of the total nodes, because multicast applications running in a wide area network usually involve only a small number of nodes in the network, such as video conference systems, distance learning, co-operative editing systems, etc.

Fig.1 shows the network cost versus group size. In this round of simulations, the network size is set to 500 and D is $d_{max}+3/8d_{max}$. From Fig.1, we can see when group size grows, the network cost produced by GAQMR, QoSMIC and BSMA increases at a rate much lower than CSPT. QoSMIC, BSMA and the proposed GAQMR can produce trees of comparable costs.

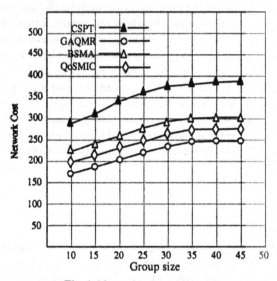

Fig. 1. Network cost vs. group size

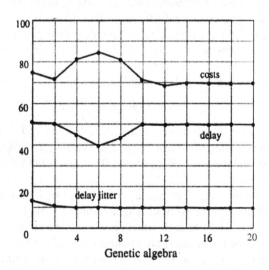

Fig. 2. Network costs, delay and delay jitter vs. Genetic algebra

We then examine the convergence of GAQMR. In simulation experiment, the network size is set to 50, delay constraint D is 60, packet loss constraint $L=0.002$ and

$W=80$. The probability for crossover operation is set to 0.2, and the probability for mutation is set to 0.02. For simplicity, we assume that QoS constraints of all leaves nodes (end nodes) are same. Fig.2 shows the varied curves of cost, delay, and delay jitter of the multicast tree with the increasing genetic algebra. From Fig.2, we can see that GAQMR can quickly break away from local optimal solution, and achieve global optimal solution using the above instructional mutation operations.

In the following simulation experiment, we assume $h_d=h_w=h_{rw}=h_j=h_l=0.5$, $A=B=C=R=S=1$, the network size is 50, $D=60$, $L=0.002$, $W=80$, $\lambda=90$, the probability for crossover operation is 0.2 and the probability for mutation is 0.02. The results of simulation experiments are shown in Fig.3. To find the probabilities of delay guarantees, we have used Erlang K distribution with parameters (k,l) is used, where k denotes the number of links in the selected path. Results for exhaustive methods (EXHM) are derived by searching exhaustively for the optimal solution in terms of the QoS requirements, from the entire population. The figure shows that GAQMR is able to catch up with the optimal solution within a few iterations.

Fig.4 shows the numbers of iterations versus the numbers of nodes, from Fig.4, it can be seen that the computation cost does not go up at least in a non-polynomial fashion and varies roughly in a linear fashion with the growth of the numbers of nodes. From these results it is evident that for large networks it is possible to get optimal solutions within feasible time, even with uncertain network state information. Many simulation experiments show that quadratic fitness function does not help much

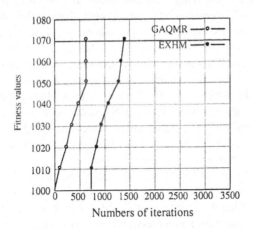

Fig. 3. Fitness value vs. numbers of iterations

compared to linear fitness function, which is desirable in the sense that it is possible to do with only linear fitness function and add to the saving of computation cost. The study has also shown that the rate of computational cost of GAQMR is less than exponential and close to polynomial rate. Also from the absolute values for the path computation cost by the above method it is evident that for large networks it is possible to get optimal solutions within feasible time, even with uncertain network parameters.

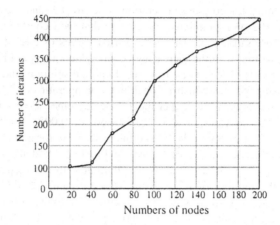

Fig. 4. Numbers of iterations vs. numbers of nodes

6 Conclusions

Multicast applications involving real-time audio and/or video transmissions require strict QoS constraints (end-to-end delay bound. bandwidth availability and loss probability) to be met by the network. To guarantee real-time delivery of multimedia packets, a multicast channel needs to be established in advance using a path selection policy that takes into account the QoS constraints. Among numerous advances in high-performance networking technology, the multicast routing with QoS constraints has continued to be a very important research area. This paper has discussed the multicast routing problem with multiple QoS constraints in the networks environment with uncertain parameters. The paper has presented the GAQMR, a multicast routing policy for Internet, mobile network or other high-performance networks, that is based on the genetic algorithm, and can provide QoS-sensitive paths in a scalable and flexible way in the networks environment with uncertain parameters. The GAQMR can also optimize the network resources such as bandwidth and delay, and can converge to the optimal on near-optimal solution within few iterations, even for the networks environment with uncertain parameters. The incremental rate of computational cost can close to polynomial and is less than exponential rate. The availability and efficiency of QGMRP have been verified by simulation. Our study shows that GAQMR can provide an available approach to QoS multicast routing in networks environment with uncertain parameters.

Acknowledgment. The work is supported by National Natural Science Foundation of China and NSF of Hubei Province.

References

[1]   Bin Wang and Jennifer C. Hou, "Multicast routing and its QoS extension: Problems, algorithms, and protocols," *IEEE Network*, Jan/Feb, 2000. pp. 22–36.

[2]   Roch A. Guerin and Ariel Orda. "QoS routing in networks with inaccurate information: Theory and algorithms," *IEEE/ACM. Trans. On Networking*, No.3, Vol.7. June. 1999. pp. 350–363.

[3]   Li Layuan and Li Chunlin, Computer Networking, National Defense Industry Press, Beijing, 2001.

[4]   Moses Charikar, Joseph Naor and Baruch Schieber, Resource optimization in QoS multicast routing of real-time multimedia, *Proc of IEEE INFOCOM*. 2000. pp. 1518–1527.

[5]   Li Layuan and Li Chunlin, "The QoS routing algorithm for ATM networks", *Computer Communications*, NO.3–4, Vol.24, 2001, pp. 416–421.

[6]   Li Layuan. "A formal specification technique for communication protocol". *Proc of IEEE INFOCOM*, April. 1989, pp. 74–81.

[7]   X. Jia. "A distributed algorithm of delay-bounded multicast routing for multimedia applications in wide area networks", *IEEE/ACM Transactions on Networking*, No.6, Vol.6, Dec. 1998, pp. 828–837.

[8]   Li Layuan and Li Chunlin, "The QoS-based routing algorithms for high- speed networks" *Proc of WCC*, Aug. 2000, pp. 623–1628.

[9]   Li Layuan and Li Chunlin, "A multicast routing protocol with multiple QoS constraints." *Proc of WCC*, Aug. 2002.

[10] Zhang Q, Lenug Y W, "An orthogonal genetic algorithm for multimedia multicast routing." *IEEE Trans Evolutionary Computation*, 1999, 3(1): 53–62.

[11] F. Xiang, L. Junzhou. W. Jieyi and G. Guanqun. "QoS routing based on genetic algorithm", *Computer Communications*, 22(1999), pp. 1392–1399.

[12] Dean H. Lorenz and Ariel Orda. "QoS routing in networks with uncertain parameters" *IEEE/ACM Transactions on Networking*. Vol.6, No.6, DEC.1998, pp. 768–778.

[13] Li Layuan and Li Chunlin, "A routing protocol for dynamic and large computer networks with clustering topology," *Computer Communication*, No.2, Vol.23, 2000, pp. 171–176.

[14] D. G. Thaler and C. V. Ravishankar, "Distributed center-location algorithms," *IEEE JSAC*, Vol.15, April 1997, pp. 291–303.

[15] I. Cidon, R. Rom, and Y. Shavitt, "Multi-path routing combined with resource resetvation," *Proc of IEEE INFOCOM*, April 1997, pp. 92–100.

[16] J. Mog. "Multicast routing exeensions to OSPF." RFC 1584. March.1994.

[17] Y. Xiong and L.G. Mason, "Restoration strategies and spare capacity requirements in self-healing ATM networks,' *IEEE Trans on Networks*, Vol. 7, No. 1, Feb, 1999, pp. 98–110.

[18] S. Chen and K. Nahrstedt, "Distributed QoS routing in ad-hoc networks," *IEEE JSAC*, special issue on ad-hoc networks, Aug. 1999.

[19] Li Layuan. "The routing protocol for dynamic and large computer networks". Journal of computers, No.2, Vol.11, 1998, PP. 137–144.

[20] B. M. Waxman. "Routing of multipoint connections." *IEEE Journal of Selected Area in Communications*, Dec. 1998, pp. 1617–1622.

[21] R.G. Busacker and T. L. Saaty, Finite Graphs and Networks: An introduction with applications, McGraw-Hill, 1965.

Tagged Fragment Marking Scheme with Distance-Weighted Sampling for a Fast IP Traceback

Ki Chang Kim[1], Jin Soo Hwang[2], Byung Yong Kim [1], and Soo-Duk Kim [1]

[1] School of Information and Communication Engineering, Inha Univ.,Korea
[2]Department of Statistics, Inha Univ., Korea

Abstract. IP traceback technique allows a victim to trace the routing path that an attacker has followed to reach his system. It has an effect of deterring future attackers as well as capturing the current one. FMS (Fragment Marking Scheme) is an efficient implementation of IP traceback. Every router partici-pating in FMS leaves its IP information on the passing-through packets, par-tially and with some probability. The victim, then, can collect the packets and analyze them to reconstruct the attacking path. FMS and similar schemes, how-ever, suffer a long convergence time to build the path when the attack path is lengthy. Also they suffer a combinatorial explosion problem when there are multiple attack paths. This paper suggests techniques to restrain the convergence time and the combinatorial explosion. The convergence time is reduced consid-erably by insuring all routers have close-to-equal chance of sending their IP fragments through a distance-weighted sampling technique. The combinatorial explosion is avoided by tagging each IP fragment with the corresponding router's hashed identifier.

1 Introduction

DOS (Denial Of Service) attack typically is performed by sending a large number of packets to the victim system[4,10]. To hide the attacker's location, it often uses a spoofed IP address[3,11]. There are several IP traceback techniques that can trace the attack path in spite of IP spoofing[1,2,9,14]. Most of them, however, requires a heavy traffic or log analysis in the intermediate routers and are impractical without the man-agement support at the routers.

Recently, efficient IP traceback techniques based on IP marking have been sug-gested[16,19]. In these schemes, the routes in the packet-traveling path mark their IP on the passing-through packets. If all routers write their IP's on all packets, the packet length will be increased out of control. To avoid that, the routers mark their IP's only probabilistically; that is, they mark only if a randomly generated number (between 0 and 1) is less than a certain sampling probability. Since a full IP address is still too large, they split it into a number of fragments (e.g. 8 fragments) and write only one of them. To let the victim know which fragment it is, they include the offset of that par-ticular fragment in the packet. Also, since there could be several routers on the attack

X. Zhou, Y. Zhang, and M.E. Orlowska (Eds.): APWeb 2003, LNCS 2642, pp. 442–452, 2003.

path, the routers need to convey information about the distance or hop counts from the victim. For this purpose, a distance field is included in the packet, too. Finally, to facilitate error-checking process, a hashed value of the original IP is included (in fragmented form).

These solutions are based on an observation that a DOS attack typically involves a large number of packets, and even though the intermediate routers mark their IP's occasionally, the victim can construct the full attack path by collecting all the IP-marked packets. Since the attack path can be constructed automatically without further helps from routers, these solutions are superior to previous IP traceback techniques. However, they still have a number of drawbacks. First the constant sampling probability chosen by FMS, one of the prominent IP marking techniques, tends to penalize distant routers from the victim. The further is the router from the victim, the harder for it to deliver its IP fragments to the victim. Because of this, the time to collect all necessary IP fragments to reconstruct the full attack path (the convergence time, in short) becomes unnecessarily longer. Secondly, they are weak to multiple attack paths[5,7,8]. With multiple attack paths, the victim receives multiple IP fragments with the same offset and distance. Since there are multiple routers at the same distance, the victim has no way of knowing which IP fragment belongs to which router. In FMS, the victim has to try all possible combinations of IP fragments to recover the original IP's. [19] suggests a technique to avoid this, but it requires the victim to maintain a map of upstream routers.

In this paper, we suggest techniques to solve above two problems. The convergence time can be minimized by insuring all routers have equal chance of sending their IP fragments. Since all routers have an equal chance, there are no particular routers that are unduly penalized, and the victim wouldn't have to wait for the slowest router sitting idle. Giving a fair chance is possible through a distance-weighted sampling technique. Each router samples packets based on the values of the distance the packet has traveled so far. Our algorithm encourages the routers to choose short-traveled IP fragments over long-traveled ones for IP marking. This strategy tends to equalize the arrival rates of IP fragments from different routers. We analyze what would be the optimal sampling function that would make all routers have the same chance of IP marking.

The combinatorial explosion is avoided by tagging each IP fragment with the corresponding router's hashed identifier. Since IP fragments are tagged with a particular router's identifier, the victim can easily extract IP fragments belonging to the same router. However, this hashed identifier could collide, and we give an explanation about how often this collision could happen and what can be done when that happens. The rest of the paper is structured as follows. Section 2 surveys related researches. Section 3 explains the distance-weighted sampling technique. Section 4 explains the Tagged Fragment Marking Scheme. Section 5 gives the experimental results. And finally, Section 6 draws a conclusion.

2 Related Researches

Reconstructing an attack path during or after an attack is not an easy problem[6,14]. There are several techniques that are varied in cost and performance. Input Debugging technique[18] utilizes the input debugging feature provided in most routers. Using this feature, a router operator can associate a packet's egress port to the corresponding ingress port. Starting from the closest router, the victim can construct an attack path by identifying the upstream link at each router. This technique, however, requires the router operator's manual searching of the right upstream link.

Controlled Flooding technique[2] is proposed as a solution for the above problem. The victim somehow coerces the upstream routers to flood each of their egress ports. By monitoring the change in attack packet volume, the victim can tell which upstream link the attack packet is coming from. This technique does not require help from the operators, but it assumes the victim knows the upstream router map and is weak for multiple attack paths. Logging technique[15] suggests a way of keeping efficient logs at key routers. Only the minimum information is logged to avoid data explosion, however it still calls for massive accumulation of data.

ICMP technique[1] takes a different approach. Rather than relying on the victim's blind search for the attack path, it requires the routers to sample their packets with a very low probability, copy them into special ICMP packets with information on adjacent routers, and forward them. The victim, then, can construct an attack path based on this information. However, since the sampling probability is very low (e.g. 1/20000), the victim needs a huge number of packets to complete the attack path.

FMS (Fragment Marking Scheme)[16] is based on a similar idea as ICMP technique: the router sends information about its location to the victim. However, in this case the router writes its partial IP address directly in the passing packets. Since it does not need to generate additional ICMP packets, it can write the IP address more frequently without worrying about traffic increase. In order to write the router's IP address without increasing the original packet size, it uses the 16-bit IP "identification" field that is rarely used these days (less than 0.25% in typical packets[1][12,17]). Since multiple routers compete for this field, and 16-bit is not enough for even a single IP address, FMS requires each router to run some probability function and write its partial IP (e.g. one eighth of it) only when the result is below some threshold value. The offset of the chosen IP fragment and the distance of the router from the victim along the attack path are also written in the "identification" field as shown in Fig.1.

FMS is efficient and allows an automatic attack path discovery. However it still has a number of problems such as a weakness against multiple attach paths or a long convergence time for computing attack path. Advanced Marking Scheme[19] provides a solution that is robust under multiple attack paths. However, it requires each victim has a map for upstream routers beforehand, which is not a trivial problem.

---

[1] [16] gives out a technique to handle the case when the "identification" field is actually used for its original purpose.

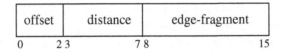

offset	distance	edge-fragment

0   2 3   7 8   15

Fig. 1. The structure of an IP fragment in FMS.

3 Distance-Weighted Sampling

In this section, we deal with the long convergence time. In Section 4, we address the problem of combinatorial explosion. A convergence time is the time to construct the attack path. In FMS, each router sends its IP by fragments, and the victim should wait until the last router sends its last IP fragment. Therefore, the convergence time is determined by the slowest router. For a constant sampling probability, as adopted by FMS, the furthest router from the victim is the slowest because its IP fragments are most of time overwritten by other routs in the downstream path. In [16], sampling probability $p = \frac{1}{n}$, n being the number of hops in the attack path, is suggested as one that can optimize the convergence time. However, the routers in the middle of the attack path do not know what would be the total number of hops of the attack path, and as explained later a constant sampling probability penalizes the furthest router and fails to optimize the convergence time.

We propose a distance-weighted sampling technique in which the sampling probability depends on the distance the target packet has traveled so far such that the probability is inversely proportional to it.

$$p = \frac{1}{f(d)} \text{ (where } d \text{ is the distance)}$$

Since the convergence time will be minimized when the IP fragments of different routers arrive at the victim with equal rates, our question is what $f(d)$ will make the arrival rate equal. To find the right $f(d)$, we need to look at the sampling process more closely as shown in Fig. 2.

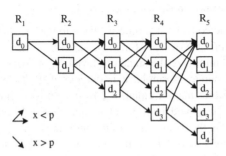

Fig. 2. Sampling process at each router.

Fig. 2 shows how an attack packet gets a new IP fragment and a distance value at each router. All packets leaving R1 has an IP fragment of R1 and distance d=0. These packets are denoted by d0 box in R1. Upon receiving these packets, R2 samples them with $p = \frac{1}{f(0)}$ since all packets have distance zero. For those sampled, it overwrites the existing IP fragment with its own and set d = 0 again. For those not sampled, R2 XORs its corresponding IP fragment and increases the distance by 1. The d0 and d1 box in R2 denotes these two kinds of packets. The arrow in the figure shows a possible transition from one state to another.

Now R3 receives two kinds of packets: packets with d = 0 that are marked by R2 and packets with d = 1 that represent the edge between R1 and R2. For packets with d = 0, R3 uses sampling probability $p = \frac{1}{f(0)}$ to transform them into two different kinds of packets as shown by the arrows in the figure. For packets with d = 1, R3 uses $p = \frac{1}{f(1)}$ to produce again two kinds of packets. As shown in the figure, d0 box collects packets from all kinds of packets in the previous router while other boxes receives packets from only one kind (the one-level lower box in the previous router). This regularity can be exploited to construct a recursive formula on arrival rates of various kinds of packets at various routers as follows.

First, let's define X(n,i) as the number of IP fragments with distance i arrived at router n. Then, the recursion below holds.

$$X(n+1, 0) = X(n,0)*\frac{1}{f(0)} + X(n,1)*\frac{1}{f(1)} + \ldots\ldots + X(n,n)*\frac{1}{f(n)}$$
$$X(n+1, d) = X(n,d-1)*\left(1 - \frac{1}{f(d-1)}\right) \text{ for } d = 1, \ldots , n+1$$

That is, packets with d=0 at router R(n+1) has been collected from all kinds of packets at router Rn. The contribution factor of each box in Rn is $\frac{1}{f(d)}$, where d is the distance value, meaning that packets belonging to a particular box in Rn moves to d0 box in R(n+1) with the probability of $\frac{1}{f(d)}$. Other boxes in R(n+1) collects members from the one-level lower box in Rn with factor of $\left(1 - \frac{1}{f(d-1)}\right)$.

In order to minimize the convergence time we have to choose f(0), f(1), .., f(n) in such a way that the minimum of X(n+1, i) for i =0, ..., n+1 would be maximized. It turns out to be equivalent to minimize the standard deviation of X(n+1, i) for i =0, ..., n+1. Based on the above recursion formula, it is obvious that f(0) would be 2. The next value f(1) would be greater than or equal to 2 to sustain the minimum value 1/4. The theoretical optimal value would be 1/3 but in our case 1/4 would be the maximal minimum value. But in the sense of minimizing standard deviation and maximal minimal value in the next step, f(1) would be 4. Continuing our argument about selecting f(d) values, we can reach the general formula by a mathematical induction. The optimal value of f(d) would be 2(d+1). This choice of f(d) value guarantees that we will have the minimum standard deviation. At each router the distribution of packets of different distances is symmetric, that is, we have the smallest or two smallest packets (depending on whether we have an even or odd number of different distance packets) of the middle distance. The shape of packet distribution is a symmetric V shape in optimal case. We can find two largest packets of the nearest and the farthest distance.

4 Tagged Fragment Marking Scheme

In FMS, each router makes a decision for each input packet whether it is going to mark its IP or not. If marking is decided, it computes a 32-bit hash out of its own IP, interleaves them with its IP, and splits the 64-bit result into k fragments. One of these fragments will be written on the packet. As explained in previous sections, an offset and a distance value are also included to facilitate the path reconstruction process. If the router decides not to mark, the distance field will be merely increased. The victim then can differentiate IP fragments by the distance field. Fragments with the same distance would have come from the same router at that distance, and the victim can recover its IP address. The problem with this scheme is when there are multiple attack paths. If there are m routers at distance d participating in the attack, the victim will receive m IP fragments for each offset value. To calculate the original m IP addresses, the victim needs to try all possible combinations of these IP fragments. With $k=8$ and $m=10$, the number of possible combination is 10^8.

To cope with the combinatorial explosion, we propose to tag each IP fragment with a 4-bit hash value of the original full IP. Since we don't have additional space in the IP identification field, we reuse the 4-bit hash field as in FMS[2]. Instead of sending 1/8 hash fragment, we tag each IP fragment with the same 4-bit hash value as in Fig. 3.

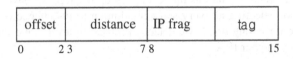

Fig. 3. Tagged Fragment Marking Scheme.

The victim can collect IP fragments with the same tag and recover the original IP. The problem with this scheme is collision. Since 32-bit IP address space is hashed into 4-bit space, there can be collisions between routers. Collisions between routers at different distances do not cause a problem because the victim can differentiate them. Collisions between routers at the same distance, however, do cause a problem. In this case, the victim should try all possible combinations to recover the original IP's as in FMS. However, the number of collided routers at the same distance should be much less than the total number of routers.

The more serious problem is when the recovered IP's all hashed into the same tag value we are looking for, but not the right IP's. This could happen because we validate

---

[2] The hash fragment is 4-bit when k = 8. We assume k=8 in the following arguments.

the correctness of the selected combination of IP fragments by hashing them and comparing the value with the attached hash value. A wrong combination still could produce a correct hash value through collision. This kind of nested collision should occur to all selected combinations; otherwise we wouldn't have accepted them as the recovered IP's. We first argue that this nested collision happens quite rarely, and that even though it happens, we still can recover the true IP's through backtracking.

Suppose there were m routers that collided, and the hash value is H. The probability of m routers to collide is $\left(\frac{1}{16}\right)^{m-1}$. Furthermore, assume the victim has selected wrong IP combinations, and all of these wrong combinations still produce the same hash value, H. The probability that this would happen is $\left(\frac{1}{16}\right)^{m} m^{7}$ (assuming $k=8$). Therefore the probability that m routers at the same distance collide, and the victim computes wrong IP's without knowing the incorrectness is $\frac{m^{7}}{16^{2m-1}}$.

For m=2,3,4,…, the probability decreases rapidly as 1/32, 1/479, 1/16384, … Even though the probability becomes very small especially as m increases, we still need a systematic way of dealing with this collision. The basic observation is that since the IP fragments except ones with distance=0 come in edge-id forms, to recover the original IP we need to XOR the candidate edge-ids with a known IP address. This XORing should be applied to all combinations of IP fragments. If our selection of IP's at distance 0 was wrong, the extracted IP's through XORing with them at the next distance level in most cases have a rare chance of being correct. They could again produce the right hash value even though they are not the correct IP's, but the probability of this is quite low. The probability would be the multiple of wrong selection probability at distance 0 and the probability of producing the same hash value. And even though we pass the second level, the probability of not detecting faulty IP's at the next higher levels becomes extremely small as the level goes up because we have to multiply the probability of not detecting at every stage in addition to the chance of producing the same hash value for wrong IPs. If we detect a problem at level x, we should backtrack to level x-1 to try another IP's.

5   Experiment

5.1   Effectiveness of Distance-Weighted Sampling

In Section 3, the sampling function was given by

$$p = \frac{1}{ai+b}$$

where i is the distance field value of the target packet, and a and b are some constants. The optimal one was found when $a=b=2$. We vary a and b to see how the function performs. Assuming a 31-hop attack path, we have measured the arrival rate of IP fragments of the routers under various a and b, and computed the standard deviation of the arrival rates. The result is in Fig. 4.

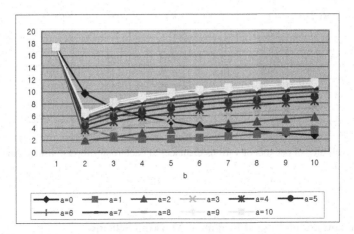

Fig. 4. Standard deviation produced by various *a* and *b* in p=1/(ai+b). X axis is *b*, and Y is standard deviation.

With a constant *p* (when *a=0*), the standard deviation decreases as predicted[16]. However, even with *b=31*, it still doesn't reach the optimal value. For *a=1*, the minimum standard deviation occurs at *b=5* which is still greater than the optimal one. For *a=b=2*, it reaches the optimum, 1.975759. For greater *a*'s, the minimum standard deviation become larger.

Fig. 5 shows the case when *a=b=2* in more detail. The distribution of packets at each router in terms of distance shows an interesting property. It is symmetric along the distance axis. The smallest arrival rate is due to the middle distance packets, and the largest due to the other two extremes – distance zero and maximum packets. Furthermore the smallest arrival rate is about half of the largest one always. This figure is in contrast with that in Fig. 6. Fig. 6 shows another distribution of packets under a constant *p*, especially when *a=0* and *b=2*. The smallest arrival rate is always due to the packets that have come from the furthest router. The closest router arrives fastest, and it covers exactly half of the total arriving packets. The arrival rate declines monotonically as the router's location becomes more distant. With larger *b*, the steepness of this declining will be reduced, and the standard deviation will be decreased. But as proved in Section 3, this monotonic declining cannot achieve optimal standard deviation. The V-shaped distribution in Fig. 5 is the one that achieves it.

	R1	R2	R3	R4	R5	R6	......
d=0	50	37.5	31.25	27.3437	24.6093	22.5585	......
d=1	50	25	18.75	15.625	13.6718	12.3046	......
d=2		37.5	18.75	14.0625	11.7187	10.2539	......
d=3			31.25	15.625	11.7187	09.7656	......
d=4				27.3437	13.6718	10.2539	......
d=5					24.6093	12.3046	......
d=6						22.5585	......
......							......

Fig. 5. Arrival rates of packets of various distances at each router for Distance-Weighted Sampling with *a=b=2*.

	R1	R2	R3	R4	R5	R6	......
d=0	50	50	50	50	50	50	......
d=1	50	25	25	25	25	25	......
d=2		25	12.5	12.5	12.5	12.5	......
d=3			12.5	6.25	6.25	6.25	......
d=4				6.25	3.125	3.125	......
d=5					3.125	1.5625	......
d=6						1.5625	......
....							......

Fig. 6. Arrival rates of packets of various distances at each router for a constant sampling probability 1/2.

5.2 Performance of Tagged Fragment Marking Scheme

Tagged FMS allows the victim to differentiate packets that has come from the same routers by looking at the tag. However, since the tag value is obtained through hashing, there could be a number of routers at the same distance from the victim that produce the same tag value. When a collision happens, the Tagged FMS should try possible combinations of IP fragments among the collided ones, as in FMS. We have measured the total number of combinations needed to compute the original IP's given m routers at the same distance, m begin a number between 1 and 10. The result is in Fig. 7. In the figure, "m" is the number of routers at the same distance. The needed combinations are computed for various m's repeatedly, and the average is shown. The number of tried combinations for Tagged FMS includes those trials due to backtracking. When a set of wrong IP's are selected due to secondary collision as explained in Section 4, the Tagged FMS uses this IP set to compute the next level routers, and if the incorrectness of it is detected during the process, the Tagged FMS backtracks to the current level, re-computes another set of IP's, and retry the next level. The number inside a parenthesis in the figure shows the number of backtracks tried to find the correct IP's.

	M=1	M=2	m=3	m=4	m=5	m=6	m=7	m=8	m=9	m=10
FM S	1	129	3282	$3.1*$ 10^4	$1.8*$ 10^5	$8.3*$ 10^5	$2.8*$ 10^6	$8.1*$ 10^6	$2.0*$ 10^7	$4.9*$ 10^7
TF MS	1 (0)	2 (0)	4 (0.2)	6 (0.2)	5.7 (0.1)	7.9 (0.1)	31.3 (0.3)	12.4 (0.6)	17.9 (1.1)	28.9 (0.6)

Fig. 7. Number of combinations tried to find correct IP's in FMS and Tagged FMS.

6   Conclusion

IP tracing is an important technique to defend a computing system from attackers. FMS (Fragment Marking Scheme) is one of the promising IP tracing techniques that is simple and efficient. However, FMS has a number of drawbacks: the convergence time to reconstruct the attack path gets considerably long when the path is lengthy, and there is a combinatorial explosion problem under multiple attack paths. In this paper, we have proposed Distance-Weighted Sampling technique to reduce the convergence time and Tagged FMS to avoid the combinatorial explosion. We have proved that the Distance-Weighted Sampling technique gives the optimal convergence time and showed that the Tagged FMS technique reduces the number of combinations considerably.

Acknowledgements. The work reported in this paper has been supported by the Korea Science and Engineering Foundation under the Grant R05-2002-000-01048-0.

References

1. S. M. Bellovin, "The ICMP Traceback Messages," Internet Draft: draft-bellovin-itrace-00.txt, *http://www.research.att.com/~smb*, Mar. 2000.
2. Hal Burch and Bill Cheswick, "Tracing anonymous packets to their approximate source," Unpublished paper, December 1999.
3. Computer Emergency Response Team (CERT), "CERT Advisory CA-1995-01 IP Spoofing Attacks and Hijacked Terminal Connections," *http://www.cert.org/ advisories/CA-1995-01.html*, Jan. 1995.
4. Computer Emergency Response Team (CERT), "CERT Advisory CA-2000-01 Denial-of-service developments," *http://www.cert.org/advisories/CA-2000-01.html*, Jan. 2000.
5. David A. Curry, "UNIX System Security," Addison Wesley, pp.36–80, 1992.
6. Drew Dean, Matt Franklin, and Adam Stubblefield, "An algebraic approach to ip traceback," in Network and Distributed System Security Symposium, NDSS '01, February 2001.
7. Dave Dittrich, "Distributed Denial of Service (DDoS) attacks/tools resource page," http://staff.washington.edu/dittrich/misc/ddos/, 2000.
8. Sven Diettrich, Neil Long, and David Dittrich, "Analyzing distributed denial of service attack tools: The shaft case," in 14th systems Administration Conference, LISA 2000, 2000.
9. P. Ferguson and D. Senie, "Network Ingress Filtering: Defeating Denial of Service Attacks Which Employ IP Source Address Spoofing," RFC 2267, Jan. 1998.
10. J.D. Howard, "An analysis of security incidents on the internet," Phd thesis, Carnegie Mellon University, Aug. 1998.
11. L.T. Heberlein and M. Bishop, "Attack Class: Address Spoofing," In 1996 National Information Systems Security Conference," pages 371–378, Baltimore, MD, Oct. 1996.
12. S. Kent and J. Mogul, "Fragmentation Considered Harmful," In Proceedings of the 1987 ACM SIGCOMM Conference, Pages 390–401, Stowe, VT, Aug. 1987
13. Jon Postel, "Internet Protocol-Darpa Internet Program-Protocol Specification," RFC 791, *http://www.faqs.org/rfcs/rfc791.html*, Sept. 1981.
14. "Project IDS – Intrusion Detection System," *http://www.cs.columbia.edu/ids/index. html*, 2002.
15. G. Sager. Security Fun with Ocxmon and Cflowd. Presentation at the Internet 2 Working Group, Nov. 1998.
16. Stefan Savage, David Wetherall, Anna Karlin, and Tom Anderson, "Practical network support for IP traceback," in *Proc. of ACM SIGCOMM*, pp. 295–306, Aug. 2000.

17. Ion Stoica and Hui Zhang, "Providing guaranteed services without per flow management," in *SIGCOMM' 99*, pp. 81–94, 1999.
18. R. Stone, "CenterTrack: An IP Overlay Network for Tracking DoS Floods," In to appear in *Proceedings of thje 2000 USENIX Security Symposium*, Denver, CO, July. 2000.
19. Dawn Xiaodong Song and Adrian Perrig, "Advanced and Authenticated Marking Schemes for IP Traceback," in *Proc. IEEE INFOCOM*, April. 2001.

An Ant Algorithm Based Dynamic Routing Strategy for Mobile Agents [1]

Dan Wang, Ge Yu, Mingsong Lv, Baoyan Song, Derong Shen, and Guoren Wang

School of Information Science and Engineering
Northeastern University, Shenyang, China 110004
{wangdan,yuge }mail.neu.edu.cn

Abstract. Routing strategy is one of the most important aspects in a mobile agent system, which is a complex combinatorial problem. Most of current mobile agent systems adopt static routing strategies, which don't consider dynamic network status and host status. This is a hinder to the performance and autonomy of mobile agents. Ant Algorithm is good at solving such kind of problems. After analyzing existing routing strategies of typical mobile agent systems, this paper summarizes factors that may affect routing strategy of mobile agents, proposes an Ant Algorithm based dynamic routing strategy by using both experience and network environment such as resource information, network traffic, host workload, presents an acquiring and storing method of routing parameters and decision rules according to the major characteristics of mobile agent migration. The simulation experiment is implemented and the results show our dynamic routing strategy can effectively improve the performance and autonomy of mobile agents.

1 Introduction

The mobile agent is a software entity with certain intelligence, which has the ability to migrate independently in the network environments and can carry out tasks on behalf of their users [1]. Since the mobile agent can migrate dynamically to the host where resources are available to achieve asynchronous computing, a number of network connections as before become unnecessary so that the distributed computing efficiency is greatly improved. A mobile agent can migrate in a range of hosts on a network, using the resources and services provided by the hosts to execute the tasks given by its user. The migration of a mobile agent is directed by a routing strategy. The routing strategy is based on a routing table, called an *itinerary* [2], which contains the hosts to be visited and the visiting sequence. How to make an efficient itinerary involves many factors such as the network's traffic, the host workload and the available resources. The goal of a routing strategy is to execute user's tasks successfully with minimal time and overhead.

[1] This work is supported by the National Natural Science Foundation of China (60173051), the Cross Century Excellent Young Teacher Foundation of the Ministry of Education, and the National 863 High-tech Program (2001AA415210)

X. Zhou, Y. Zhang, and M.E. Orlowska (Eds.): APWeb 2003, LNCS 2642, pp. 453–464, 2003.

Generally, a mobile agent's routing strategy can be categorized as static approach and dynamic approach [3]. The static approach is adopted in most mobile agent systems, by which the itinerary is predefined by the task designer before an agent migrates and can not be changed. The major difference among the systems that adopt static approach is that some systems such as Aglet[4] implicate their itineraries within program codes, while other systems such as Concordia[5] explicitly keep their itineraries outside of program codes to reduce the burden of the mobile agent's migration.

Internet is such a highly dynamic environment that the load of the networks and hosts on it is uncertain, thus mobile agents should have the ability to adjust dynamically the sequence of hosts to be visited according to network situation and tasks to reduce time or the amount of data transmission. With dynamic routing strategies, the itinerary can be adjusted according to agents' tasks and network status during the process of migration. An initial itinerary is defined by users, and can be frequently revised by migrating agent to adapt to the changing environment. So it supports well agent's characteristics such as reactivity, adaptability and autonomy [3].

This paper analyzes existing routing strategies, summarizes factors that affect the migration of mobile agents and proposes an Ant Algorithm based dynamic routing strategies, for which, the storing and acquiring method of parameters and routing decision rules is designed according to the major characteristics of mobile agent migration. Moreover, a simulation experiment is implemented and the system performance is evaluated

The reminder of this paper is organized as follows. Section 2 discusses the related work. Section 3 analyzes the factors of routing strategies for mobile agents, and the problems of applying Ant Algorithm into mobile agent routing strategies. In Section 4, an Ant Algorithm based dynamic routing strategy is proposed and the implementation techniques are presented. In Section 5, the performance evaluation is explained. Finally, Section 6 concludes the paper and gives the future work.

2 Related Work

There are many research works have been done on the routing strategies of mobile agents. In paper [6], the routing strategy is defined as a problem of finding the minimal visiting sequence to complete the tasks in the minimal time with the assumption that network status and directory service are available. Three parameters including the latency of two adjacent hosts, the execution time on every host and the probability of completing the tasks on every host are presented. In paper [7], a heuristic algorithm is presented to realize the minimal execution time and the minimal number of agents that accomplish the tasks together. The authors think more than one agent can accomplish a specific task, and the number of agents to accomplish a task and the total execution time are two main performance factors. Paper [8] analyzes the behavior of agents in a network, i.e., whether the agents merely migrate or make the RPC communication with adjacent hosts, or even the combination of the two. The algorithm presented only focused on the amount of data that is transmitted across hosts. An optimization algorithm is presented in reference [9]. The spending of time and data transmitted in migration and RPC communication is available in advance. A process of alternative migrations and RPC communications characterizes the behavior of an agent. The concept of itinerary is presented in paper [2].

However, the following problems still are not solved well by the existing works:

- **The combination of migration and RPC communication or merely migration as the working mode for mobile agents.** Some algorithms claim that rather than merely migration or RPC communication, the combination of the two is the most efficient way. Agents should decide whether to migrate or to communicate according to the cost of each mechanism.
- **Static approach or dynamic approach.** The algorithms above are mostly static strategies, so agents are less sensitive or adaptive to the environment. Since Internet is a large-scale network and agents may carry numerous kinds of tasks, it's impractical to maintain the network status and the host status in advance.
- **Critical Factors.** Some algorithms considered only the amount of data that are transmitted across network; others comprehensively considered network load, host load and the probability of resources existing on hosts. Few algorithms took agents' migration experience into account. Such neglect shouldn't occur in agent systems with high intelligence.
- **Different optimization targets.** Some are focused on minimizing data transmitted, and others try to minimize total migration time.

3 Routing Strategies for Mobile Agents and Ant Algorithm

This section first analyzes the characteristics and related factors in mobile agent routing strategies, then introduces Ant algorithm, and discuss how to apply Ant algorithm into the dynamic routing strategy.

3.1 Routing Strategy

The characteristics and critical factors in mobile agent routing strategies include:

- **Adopting dynamic approach to have high sensitivity and adaptability**

  Static approach requires collecting knowledge about network and hosts, but it's impractical to accomplish such a collecting process on the Internet that has so many hosts and complex topological structures. At the same time, hosts also change frequently in load status due to a large amount of information they have to process. Thus routing strategies should be highly sensitive to network status and host status and can make accordingly adjustment to the changing environment. Therefore, we choose the dynamic approach.

- **Testing and collecting of network information in distributed style**

  The complexity of Internet topological structure and the huge number of hosts in it make it unfeasible to introduce a unified or centralized monitoring mode, so it is indispensable to make the distributed collecting of network information and resource information. The information acquired is stored in corresponding hosts instead of a small set of hosts in charge of preserving information. It's also impossible for a host to maintain comprehensive information about the network and all the hosts.

- **Both resource information and network information should be emphasized**

Resources drive the migration of agents; hence the nodes in the network monitor not only status of network and hosts but also information about resources, and the selected routes for an agent should imply resource guidance.

- **Both the execution time and the amount of data transmitted should be taken into account as major aspects of the optimization target**

The drawback of network and resource monitoring is excess data transmission, which exacerbates network burden in some degree. An optimization strategy should keep a balance between the economized time and the excess data transmission.

- **Previous Experiences should be considered.**

Directing the next migration by use of previous experiences can improve mobile agent's execution efficiency.

3.2 Overview of Ant Algorithm

Ant Algorithms, which was inspired by the observation of real ant colonies, were first proposed in 1991 by Dorigo as an approach to solve difficult combinatorial optimization problems, such as the traveling salesman problem (TSP) and the Job Shop Scheduling problem (JSP) [10]. Research results revealed that ants have the ability to find the shortest path between their nests and the food source. The path is acquired by rather the whole ant colony than a single ant. While walking from food sources to the nest and vice versa, ants deposit on the ground a substance called pheromone, forming in this way a pheromone trail. Ants can perceive pheromone and tend to choose paths with strong pheromone concentrations. Higher density of pheromone is deposited on shorter paths, and the tendency makes it possible for a colony of ants to find the shortest path [11-13].

Take TSP problem for example, the topological graph of a network is defined as G = (N, E), and there are arcs between any two nodes. The problem solving process by Ant Algorithm is as follows. At the beginning of the algorithm, m ants are generated at time point t and are distributed randomly on the nodes in the graph. A tabu list $Tabu_k$, which records the nodes that ant k has visited up till now, is introduced to ensure that any node cannot be visited more than once by the same ant in a cycle. The probability of ant k migrating from node i to node j at time point t is decided by the formula (1):

$$P_{ij}^k = \frac{(\tau_{ij}(t))^\alpha (\eta_{ij})^\beta}{\sum_{l \in N^i} (\tau_{ij}(t))^\alpha (\eta_{ij})^\beta}, \quad \forall j \in N^i \wedge j \in N_k - Tabu_k(i) \tag{1}$$

$\tau_{ij}(t)$ represents the density of pheromone on the arc$_{ij}$ at time t. At the beginning, every arc with be given a rather small pheromone value, and this value is frequently updated in the consecutive steps. $\eta_{ij}=1/d_{ij}$ is the local heuristic information which represents the expectation of migrating from node i to node j. d_{ij} is the Euclid distance between node i and node j. α,β are two parameters that control the proportion of pheromone and local information when calculating probability P_{ij}. N^i is the adjacent node set of the node i. After |N|-1 steps, each of the ants has finished a journey covering every nodes and m feasible solutions emerges, this process is called an iteration or a cycle. Then pheromone on arcs is updated according to the quality of acquired paths.

Ant Algorithm is categorized into three classes, **Ant-Cycle, Ant-Density** and **Ant-Quantity**. They are different in the updating moment and the mechanism. The pheromone increments of Ant-Cycle, Ant-Density and Ant-Quantity are given in the formula (2),(3),(4), respectively:

$$\Delta\tau_{ij}^{k}(t) = \begin{cases} 1/L_k(t) & \forall(i,j) \in T_k(t) \quad \text{$L_k(t)$ is the length of path that ant k find} \\ 0 & \text{otherwise} \end{cases} \tag{2}$$

$$\Delta\tau_{ij}^{k} = \begin{cases} Q_1 & \text{ant k moves from i to j during } (t, t+1) \\ 0 & \text{otherwise} \end{cases} \tag{3}$$

$$\Delta\tau_{ij}^{k} = \begin{cases} Q_2/d_{ij} & \text{ant k moves from i to j during } (t, t+1) \\ 0 & \text{otherwise} \end{cases} \tag{4}$$

The total increment of pheromone on arc $_{ij}$ is calculated by formula (5):

$$\Delta\tau_{ij}(t) = \sum_{k=1}^{m} \Delta\tau_{ij}^{k}(t) \tag{5}$$

A pheromone evaporation mechanism, which reduced the amount of pheromone on every arc, is introduced to reduce old pheromone information. Let the evaporation proportion is ρ, and then pheromone on arc$_{ij}$ is finally updated according to the formula (6):

$$\tau_{ij}^{new}(t) = (1-\rho)\tau_{ij}^{old} + \Delta\tau_{ij}(t) \tag{6}$$

In Ant-Cycle algorithm, pheromone is updated at the end of period *(t0, t+(n-1))*, this is called *delayed updating*; In Ant-Density and Ant-Quantity algorithm, pheromone is updated at the end of every step, and this is called *online updating*. Due to slow convergence of the basic Ant Algorithm, many improved algorithms emerge by revising the pheromone updating mechanism. A universal algorithm framework called Ant Colony Optimization is given in [10].

On one hand, Ant Algorithm has a comprehensive consideration of both historical experience information that is represented by pheromone and local heuristic information, different values of weighting parameters control the extent of effect of the two factors; on the other hand, the optimal solution is worked out by a group of ants and the existence of pheromone provides a special channel for ants' asynchronous communication. Learning mechanism of ants and utilization of the ant colony's knowledge are also implied since ants need pheromone when deciding the next migration host.

There are also some shortcomings inherited in the algorithm: (1) the searching process is much too long; (2) an inappropriate choosing of parameters α and β might cause stasis or convergence to local optimization; and (3) the updating mechanism will affect the proportion of pheromone and experience information when deciding the paths. So we claim that, when the Ant Algorithm is chosen to solve some problems, the following factors must be emphasized:

- **Appropriate selection of parameters α and β.** the values of them are directly related with the stasis and convergence to the local optimization.
- **Updating mechanism of the pheromone.** This includes the amount of increment, updating occasion and frequency, which affect the sensitivity of the algorithm.
- **Adoption of the randomizing scheme.** A good randomizing scheme can enable ants to extend searching space.

3.3 Applying Ant Algorithm for Dynamic Routing Strategies

We consider it feasible to use Ant Algorithm to solve the mobile agent routing problems on the Internet, based on the major reasons as follows:

- **There are essential similarities between problems that Ant Algorithm can solve and that emerging in mobile agent routing on the Internet**

  We think the routing problem is a complex combinatorial problem on a weighted graph, whose weights on arcs change with time and there are numerous hosts on the Internet, on the moment, Ant Algorithm is good at solving this kind of problems.

- **Mobile agent execution environment (MAE) provides carrier for Ant Algorithm**

  Pheromone can be stored and collected. On MAE. On the moment, mobile agents, with certain memory and learning ability are perfect substitutes of artificial ants;

- **The mobile agent routing problem itself is a process that agents and MAE learn from circumstance and accumulate experience**

  When first sent to a network, the mobile agent system has little knowledge about the network and resources information, hence it's indispensable for the mobile agent system to learn from circumstance and store corresponding information on it. The pheromone storage mechanism is very suitable for mobile agent systems.

- **The variety of network load and host load requires flexibility and adaptability of a routing strategy**

  This requirement is satisfied by local heuristic information and flexible pheromone storage mechanism of Ant Algorithm.

  On the other hand, although it is effective and efficient for Ant Algorithm to solve the TSP problem, the new problems may occur when using it to solve mobile agent routing problems as follows:

- **Control Mechanism**

  The termination of a mobile agent is decided by whether it has accumulated enough resources or whether the specific tasks are fulfilled, i.e., for information search, thus a mobile agent has no definite target host or definite migrating steps. These factors don't exist in the process of solving TSP problem by Ant Algorithm. So a control mechanism of migrating steps or time is needed.

- **Skip the non-resource host**

  Resource driven migration may cause that two hosts with certain resource is separated by a host without such resource. The algorithm should ensure the agent skip the non-resource host.

- **Obtaining of major parameters**

  The approach of obtaining network latency, host load and existence of resources is different. In TSP problem, weights on arcs are explicit before algorithm starts; while in mobile agent routing problem, major parameters are obtained by distributed monitoring.

- **Pheromone updating mechanisms are different**

  Some work reveal that too many ants in Ant Algorithm may cause descend in performance by changing the pheromone. In this situation, special pheromone updating mechanisms are necessary to avoid such decline in performance.

So, we want design an Ant Algorithm based dynamic routing strategy for mobile agents. By this strategy, when related factors in mobile agent routing strategies described above is input, a probability value is given as output after calculation, which will direct mobile agent to choose proper hosts to migrate to.

4   Dynamic Routing Strategy Based on Ant Algorithm

The entire mobile agent routing problem is a complex one, so it's hard to meet all the requirements. To simplify, the following restrictions is made, as shown in Table 1. Besides achieve dynamic routing strategy, we assume that RPC is not taken into consideration, and the whole process is made of many migrating steps. At the same time, one specific task is carried by only one mobile agent.

Table 1. Considered Parameters

Number of agents to complete a task	Considering resource?	Dynamic / Static?	Combining RPC mechanism?	Existing multiple related tasks?
Single agent	Yes	Dynamic	No	No

4.1 Routing Parameters

The parameters are defined as follows in our algorithm: (1) d_{ij}: Network latency between two adjacent hosts i and j; and we assume $d_{ij} \neq d_{ji}$. (2) $l_i(j)$: Record stored on host i about load information on host j; it's an estimation of average waiting time calculated from length of waiting queue. (3) *ResItem*: Resource content, a string describing the resources that an agent needs. It can be either a specific content or a summarization of similar contents. (4) $p_i(j)$: Existing probability of resource j on host i, $p \in [0,1] \lor p = -1$. $p = -1$ means that there is no record about the existence of resource j on host i. (5) τ^R_{ij}, τ^L_{ij} : The former is the value of resource pheromone and the latter is the value of load pheromone. Similar to Ant Algorithm, both resource pheromone and load pheromone are recorded.

MAE is responsible for storage of parameters. There are two tables on every MAE. Take host i for example, one of the tables is to maintain local resource information and resource pheromone on adjacent hosts; the other table is to maintain local load information between host i and adjacent hosts and load pheromone. The acquiring approach of parameters is shown as Table 2.

Table 2. Acquiring Approach of Routing Parameters

Parameters	Executed by Mobile Agent	Executed by MAE
d_{ij}	Acquire before migrate to the next host by means of communication	Periodically send Ping command to acquire latency
$l_i(j)$	Taken along with agents while migrating to the next host	Periodically send load information to adjacent hosts for updating
ResItem, $p_i(j)$	Taken along with agents	
τ^L_{ij}	Updated when agents finished its task	
τ^R_{ij}	Updated by returning agents	

Since time synchronization is hard on the Internet, it is impossible for agents to calculate latency between two hosts. Thus MAE maintains d_{ij}. MAE will periodically send host load information to adjacent hosts and hosts receive and store coming information. Another way of transmitting the host load information and latency is when an agent has finished executing on a host, it will communicate with adjacent hosts for this information. This approach may be accurate, but the acquiring process may be more frequent. The storage of resource information depends on the tasks that agents carry. Only information about frequently used resources will be stored while others rarely used is seldom stored to economize storage consumption.

4.2 Pheromone Updating Mechanism

The updating of load pheromone is similar to that of Ant-Quantity algorithm and the updating of resource pheromone is similar to that of Ant-Cycle algorithm. When migration is terminated, a returning agent is generated and backtracks to update resource pheromone on visited hosts. The difference between them is the result of the different changing features of the two major factors. Network latency and host load change frequently, while resource information seldom change with such a high frequency. Thus the updating of load pheromone should be more frequent to reveal accurate changes of local load information. We also introduced a cyclic evaporating process that does not exist in traditional Ant Algorithms. In some period, the number of agents on some part of the network may be small, since the pheromone updating is triggered by agents, the pheromone on such hosts may change much too slow and originally stored pheromone may represent out-of-date information. The cyclic evaporation is introduced to replace old information in good time.

[Algorithm 1] Execution and updating pheromone

    Step1 Initialization: Set initial value such as maximum migrating steps, maximum migration time, etc.;

    Step2 Updating corresponding *ResItem* and $P_i(j)$ on this host according to information taken along with the agent;

    Step3 Turning the agent into sleep mode, add the agent into waiting queue;

    Step4 Taking out from the waiting queue, and waken up to execute the task;

    Step5 Calculating P_{ij}(refer to the formula13 in section 4.3), decide the next hosts;

    Step6 Updating load pheromone on this host: τ^L_{ij}

    Step7 Sending resource information on this host to the latest visited host;

    Step8 If (maximum migrating steps or maximum migration time is reached)

    Then   Send a returning agent; Update resource pheromone τ^R_{ij} on visited hosts;

            Terminate migration; Go to Step 9;

    Else   Migrate to the next host, go to Step 2;

    Step9 End

The updating Formulas (7)- (12) are relative to the pheromone updating process:

Load Pheromone Updating: $\tau^L_{ij} = (1 - \rho_L) \cdot \tau^L_{ij} + \Delta\tau , \quad 0<\rho_L<1$ (7)

Resource Pheromone Updating: $\tau^R_{ij} = (1 - \rho_R) \cdot \tau^R_{ij} + \rho_R \cdot \Delta\tau , 0<\rho_R<1$ (8)

Load Pheromone Cyclic Evaporation: $\tau^L_{ij} = e_L \cdot \tau^L_{ij}$ (9)

e_L is load pheromone cyclic evaporation ratio, and $0<e_L<1$.

Resource Pheromone Cyclic Evaporation: $\tau_{ij}^R = e_R \cdot \tau_{ij}^R$ (10)

e_R is resource pheromone cyclic evaporation ratio, and $0 < e_R < 1$

Load Pheromone Increment: $\Delta \tau_{ij}^L = Q_L$ (11)

Resource Pheromone Increment $\Delta \tau_{i,i+1}^R = \Delta \tau_{i+1,i}^R = Q_R \cdot \sum_{i=1}^{n-1} p_i(i+1)$ (12)

Q_L is adjustment constant and Q_R is the adjustment constant.

Resource pheromone updating is designed similar to that of Ant-Cycle algorithm in order to reflex the resource-distributing situation on a relative long path. The updating of resource pheromone is symmetric, $\Delta \tau_{ij}^R = \Delta \tau_{ji}^R$.

4.3 Routing Decision Rules

Routing Decision Rules is to calculate a probability value using the value of pheromone and the local heuristic information according to a specific ratio, which directly affect the choosing of the next host to migrate to. The load status of network always changes very fast, so the algorithm needs to converge in a high speed. We adopt the decision rules in ACS Algorithm [10]:

- A tunable parameter q_0 is predefined with range $0 < q_0 < 1$;
- When making decision, a random parameter q, which is evenly distributed within [0, 1], is generated. Decision is made according to the formula (13):

$$\begin{cases} if \ q \le q_0 & then \ P_{ij} = \begin{cases} 1 & j = \text{argmax} A_i(l) & l \in N^i - tabu(i) \\ 0 & otherwise \end{cases} \\ if \ q > q_0 & then \ \text{make decision according to value of probability } A_i(j) \end{cases}$$

$$A_i(j) = \frac{(\tau_{ij}^L)^\alpha \cdot (\tau_{ij}^R)^\beta \cdot (1/(d_{ij} + l_i(j))^\gamma \cdot (p_i(j))^\eta}{\sum_{l \in N^i - tabu_i} [(\tau_{ij}^L)^\alpha \cdot (\tau_{ij}^R)^\beta \cdot (1/(d_{ij} + l_i(j)))^\gamma \cdot (p_i(j))^\eta]}$$ (13)

[Example 1] Assume that an agent is on host i now, the candidates of the next host are l, m, n, we also assume that $A_i(l)=0.5$, $A_i(m)=0.3$, $A_i(n)=0.2$.

- If $q \le q0$, the host with the largest value of $A_i(j)$ will be chosen, i.e., $P_{il}=1$, $P_{im}=0$, $P_{in}=0$, so the next host to migrate to is l.
- If $q > q0$, then $P_{il} = A_i(l)$, $P_{im} = A_i(m)$, $P_{in} = A_i(n)$. The next host to be visited is not definite, and is decided according to the probabilities above. This mechanism allows searching in broader space, and the probability of stasis is reduced.

5 Performance Evaluation Experiment and Results

The experiment model is shown as Fig.1, which maintains five modules: **Simulator**: The entrance of the program, initialize global data structure, start monitors; **IMap**: The map on which the agents migrate; **AgentGenerator**: Generate agents in succession, and send the agents to the simulating network; **ResMonitor**: Record the resource information into documents for latter analysis; **Host Set**: Manage all the

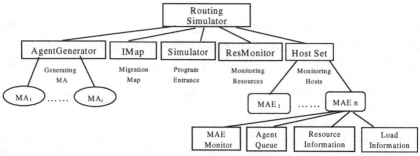

Fig. 1. Experiment Model

hosts in the simulating network. Each of the hosts has an agent queue, a load monitor, a resource information table and a load information table.

Major data structures are initialized and monitors are started when program starts. Simulating hosts collect resource and load information cyclically and update corresponding tables. Agents are generated and sent to the simulating network. If the task is completed, an agent will terminate by itself. Resource information is written to documents cyclically for latter analysis. We simulated a network with 20 hosts. To simplify the simulation, we only tested the performance under static environments, i.e., parameters about all the hosts didn't change while simulating. Hence cyclic evaporation is canceled. The whole simulation went on for 2 hours, which simulated a 20-hour situation in the network.

In Fig.2 and Fig.3, only the performance about the agents that started at host 1 and host 11 is illustrated since agents that started from other hosts have similar performance.

The execution time of agents from the same host are stable, and there is an increase trend in the resource that an agent gets after approximately 300 agents have started from each host. The result implies that with the procession of the algorithm, agents are directed to the route on which there is more targeted resource, and can get a larger amount of resource within the same time.

Experiments show that different sets of parameters can lead to different results, even in networks with the same scale. At the same time, networks with different scales require adjusting parameters. Some sets of parameters cannot even give any performance improvement. We think It's apparent that the determinative factor in selecting routes is the value of P_{ij}. In calculation, the four values in it may counteract with each other. For example, a high value of resource pheromone and a relatively low value of the load local information don't guarantee a high calculative value of P_{ij}. it's quite difficult to design a set of parameters that possesses both high adaptability and high resource directivity. In practical applications, parameters should be set carefully by adjusting the four weighting parameters in formula (13) to achieve only some of the targets but not all.

The disseminating speed of resource information is directly related to the scale of the network, and the larger networks require the longer period.

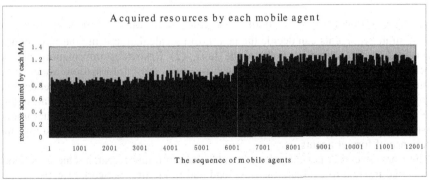

Fig. 2. Acquired resources

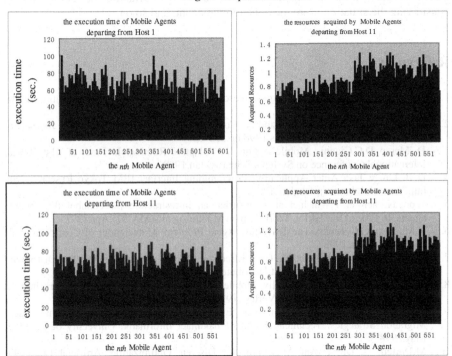

Fig. 3. The acquired resources and average execution time departing from Host 1 and Host 11

6 Conclusions and Future Work

This paper analyzed the feasibility and new problems of using Ant Algorithm to solve mobile agent routing problem and developed corresponding algorithm, which can direct agents to select routes sensibly considering network status, host status and resource information. Experiments reveal that this routing strategy for mobile agents has many advantages, some aspects of the algorithm have satisfied the requirement for designing mobile agents' routing strategies, such as: (1) Adopting dynamic routing strategy. Agents can decide the next host by calculation using the information about load and resources stored on the host. (2) Resources information can be disseminated quickly between adjacent hosts and only information about used resources instead of that about all the resources on hosts is spread; thus reduce the storage consumption on hosts. (3) Distributed acquiring of resource information and load information is achieved by cyclical collecting mechanism.(4) Pheromone constructs a special communication channel and enables agents to study the experience of former agents.

There are several issues that are to be addressed in future research. One is to adopt an accurate method to evaluate the host load and to monitor network effectively; the others includes implementing an effective resource information directory service, considering the situation more than one mobile agent, and so on.

References

1. DB.Lange, M. Oshima, Seven good reasons for mobile Agents. Communication of the ACM, 1999,Vol.42(3): pp.88-89.
2. M.Strasser, K.Rothermel. Reliability Concepts for Mobile Agents. Int. Journal of Cooperative Information Systems.1998.pp.355-82
3. D, Marco.,D.C.Gianni,. Mobile Agents for Adaptive Routing. In Proc. of 31st Hawaii International Conference on Systems Sciences, Jan.1998.
4. D B. Lange Java Aglet Application Programming Interface.IBM Tokyo Research Lab. http://www.trl.ibm.co.jp/ Aglets.1997.
5. Wong,N.Paciorek,T.Walsh,et al. Concordia: an infrastructure for collaborating mobile agents. In Proc.of the 1st Int. Workshop on Mobile Agents(MA'97),Apr.1997.
6. K.Moizumi,G.Cybenko. The Travelling Agent Problem. Mathematics of Control, Signals and Systems,Jan.1998.
7. J.Baek, J. Yeo, G..Kim et al, Cost Effective Mobile Agent Planning for Distributed Information Retrieval. In Proc. of Distributed Computing Systems, Apr. 2001.
8. T.Chia, S.Kannapan. Strategically Mobile Agents. In First International Workshop on Mobile Agents MA97, Springer Verlag, 1997.
9. M. Ashraf, J.Baumann, M. Strasser. Efficient Algorithms to Find Optimal Agent Migration Strategies. Technical Report of Fakultaet Informatik, University of Stuttgart, May 1998.
10. M.Dorigo, G. DiCaro.Ant Algorithms for Discrete Optimization. Artificial Life,1999. Vol.5(3). pp.137-172.
11. Colorni, M.Dorigo,V.Maniezzo. Distributed Optimization by Ant Colonies. In Proc. of ECAL91 - European Conference on Artificial Life, Paris, France, ELSEVIER Publishing, pp.134-142.
12. C.Alberto, M.Dorigo, V. Maniezzo. An Investigation of Some Properties of an Ant Algorithm. In Proc. of the Parallel Problem Solving from Nature Conference (PPSN92), Brussels, Belgium, 1992.pp.509-520.
13. Dorigo, V. Maniezzo, A. Colorni, The Ant System: Optimization by a colony of cooperating agents. IEEE Transactions on Systems,1996.26, pp.29–41.

Integration of Mobile IP and NHRP over ATM Networks

Tae-Young Byun and Moo-Ho Cho

School of Computer and Electronic Engineering, Gyeongju University,
Hyohyun-dong, Gyeongju, Kyungpuk, KOREA
{tybyun, mhcho}@gyeongju.ac.kr

Abstract. In this paper, we propose a scheme to integrate the Mobile IP and NHRP over NBMA networks including ATM network. This paper also defines the signaling and control mechanisms required to integrate NHRP and Mobile IP. The integration decreases the end-to-end path delay between a MN and CN by using the features of ATM which are fast switching and high scalability. We mathematically analyze the end-to-end path delay between end hosts in integrated Mobile IP networks, also shows the improvement of delay by simulation.

1 Introduction

NHRP(Next Hop Resolution Protocol)[1] is an excellent technology for creating shortcut paths across an ATM campus network interconnecting routers. Because of its scope, the rollout of this service into next-generation networks may flow from the campus networks, next possibly to include a few ISP networks, and finally allowing cut-through of international networks. Since NHRP and NBMA(Non-broadcast Multiple Access) networks such as ATM network are very closely related, it would be desirable to incorporate NHRP into these core networks too. NHRP adds cut-through routing as an ATM service and hosts in LAN communicate with NHRP clients through a router. This routing function allows NHRP clients that are members of different LIS(Logical Internet Subnetwork) to establish a shortcut path through the ATM cloud. NHRP is a kind of address resolution service, which maps IP address of destination host into ATM address of the host, and provides shortcut routing between ATM hosts.

Mobile IP is designed to support mobile computing over the Internet and could potentially provide host mobility solution in these future networks. A Mobile IP scheme has been adopted by the IETF for standardization in IPv4[2,3]. A Mobile Node(MN) is identified by the IP address it has when it is in its home network, called its home address. When a MN moves away from its home network to a foreign network, it obtains a temporary Care-of-Address(COA) from the Foreign Agent(FA) in the foreign network. The MN registers with a Home Agent(HA), which is typically a router, in its home network, informing the latter of its COA. Any Correspondent Node(CN) wishing to communicate with the MN need not be aware that the MN has moved. It

X. Zhou, Y. Zhang, and M.E. Orlowska (Eds.): APWeb 2003, LNCS 2642, pp. 465–470, 2003.

simply sends IP packets addressed to the MN's home address. These packets are routed via normal IP routing to the MN's home network, where they are intercepted by the HA. The HA encapsulates each such packet in another IP packet which contains the MN's COA as destination address. Thus these packets are delivered to the MN's new location by a tunneling process.

Currently there are several proposals to incorporate IP-based technologies into the core networks of future wireless cellular systems such as Universal Mobile Telecommunications System(UMTS)[4], Cellular IP[5]. In this paper, we propose a scheme to integrate the Mobile IP and NHRP over ATM network. The integration improves the end-to-end path delay between hosts. Our work here provides a solution for incorporation of both the Mobile IP and NHRP into these future IP-based core networks, and also provides mobility support for NHRP.

The organization of the rest of the article is as follows. In Section 2, we present our scheme to integrate NHRP into the Mobile IP in details, and also explain how our scheme reduces end-to-end path delay between MN and CN compared with conventional IP forwarding. Evaluation results by simulation are presented in Section 3. Finally, our conclusion is presented in Section 4.

2   Integration of NHRP and Mobile IP

Generally, routers are responsible for delivering IP packets to destination. These routers exist on boundaries between two different networks, thus networks can be either LAN-based IP network or ATM-based IP network. Especially, considering that every packet forwarded by the routers which are over ATM-based IP networks has to undergo comparably long processing delay due to IP forwarding mechanism based on 'store-and-forward' in each router. But, we will improve the end-to-end path delay by utilizing cut-through forwarding function that is an important capability of ATM switch. With conforming the basic operation of Mobile IP, AER(ATM Edge Router) or HA in ATM networks can set a shortcut VC to FA. The shortcut VC has a role of tunnel partially or fully. Here, NHRP has a crucial role of setting a shortcut VC.

We enumerate four integration scenarios as follows, also assume that CN, HA, FA and MN are distributed across LAN-based IP networks and ATM-based IP networks.

□ **Scenario 1: Shortcut VC between AER(ATM Edge Router) and FA.** A typical network conforming to scenario 1 is illustrated in Fig. 1. Each entity consisting of Mobile IP network is distributed across LAN or ATM. CN and HA are located in LAN-based IP network, FA and MN are located in a LIS over ATM network.

□ **Scenario 2: Shortcut VC between HA and FA.** An example network of scenario 2 is illustrated in Fig. 2. Differently to previous scenario 1, HA is located in ATM. In this, we can fully establish a shortcut VC over tunnel between HA and FA. This indicates that our scheme can be superior to tunneling using existing IP routing in view of tunnel path length. This possibility is due to more shortened shortcut tunnel in comparison with existing tunnel using IP routing based on store-and-forward. Additionally, cut-through switching of ATM switch reduces tunneling path delay. Once a shortcut VC has been established, all packets along with shortcut VC do not experience store-and-forward delay that is   occurred in each router. Instead, packets directly are delivered along with VC shortcut to FA not via router.

□ **Scenario 3: Shortcut VC between AER and FA.** An example network of scenario 3 is illustrated in Fig. 3. Scenario 3 is similar to scenario 1 in that HA is located in LAN-based IP network, but FA or MN is in ATM-based IP network. So, we can establish a shortcut VC that covers partial tunneling paths between AER and FA. This indicates that the partial tunnel path using shortcut VC gives less path delay than tunnel path using existing IP routing based on store-and forward mechanism.

□ **Scenario 4: Shortcut VC between HA and FA.** An example network of scenario 4 is illustrated in Fig. 4. Scenario 4 is similar to scenario 2 in that both of the HA and FA exist in ATM-based IP network. So, we can establish a shortcut VC that fully covers tunneling paths between HA and FA. This indicates that the full path of tunnel along shortcut VC gives less path delay than existing tunnel path along IP.

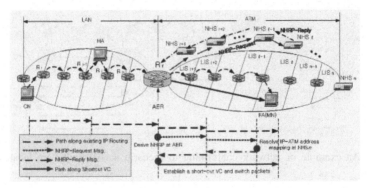

Fig. 1. An example of network conforming to scenario 1: CN and HA are located in LAN-based IP network, FA and MN are located in a LIS over ATM network.

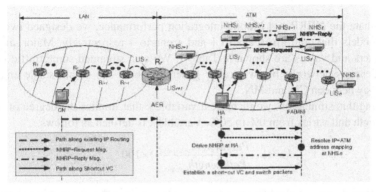

Fig. 2. An example of network conforming to scenario 2: CN is located in LAN-based IP network and HA, FA and MN are located in ATM network.

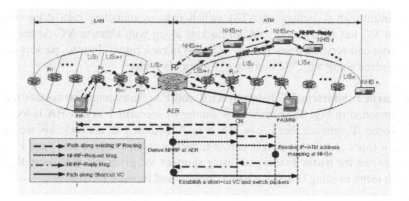

Fig. 3. An example of network conforming to scenario 3: HA is located in LAN-based IP network and CN, FA and MN are located in ATM network.

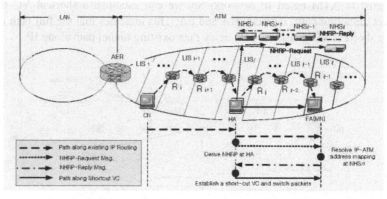

Fig. 4. An example of network conforming to scenario 4: All entity are located in ATM network.

3 Performance Evaluation

To evaluate the NHRP and Mobile integration performance, we designed two IP network models that conform scenario 1 and scenario 4 respectively. Major simulation parameters and values are shown in Table 1. We also streamed some traffic into two heterogeneous networks by two traffic generation nodes to obtain stable end-to-end path delay between CN and MN.

During this simulation, we increase a variable k that implies the degree of reduced path length and varies from 0% to 50%. Variable k is defined as follows.

$$k = (1 - \frac{PathLength_{shortcutVC}}{PathLength_{ipRouting}}) \times 100 \qquad (1)$$

$PathLength_{shortcut}$ means the path length of shortcut VC that is established after successful NHRP operation, exists between AER(or HA) and FA. But on the other hand,

PathLength$_{ipRouting}$ means the length of path that is established by normal routers. Generally, *PathLength$_{shortcut}$* is smaller than *PathLength$_{ipRouting}$*. So, if we assume $k=10(\%)$, this indicates that path length of shortcut VC is equivalent to 90 percent of the path length by IP routing, that shortcut VC was decreased compared with path length by IP routing about 10 percent.

Table 1. Simulation parameters

Parameter		Value
LAN-based IP network	The number of LANs	8
	Bandwidth (Mbps)	100
ATM-based IP network	The number of LISs	3
	The number of ATM switches in a LIS	19
	The number of NHSs	3
	Bandwidth (Mbps)	155
NHRP Control Messages	Message Length (byte)	1024
	Occurrence Frequency (sec)	Poisson(5.0)
Traffic Load (Tr)	Two nodes flow traffic in networks as a mount of Tr (10MBytes or 5MBytes) per a second respectively	

To verify the enhancement of our scheme compared with existing IP routing, we measured end-to-end path delays in three cases, which each case is described below.

□ **Case 1**: End-to-end path delay from CN to MN by existing IP routing based on store-and-forward method. In this case, we do not use any shortcut VC over ATM network.

□ **Case 2**: Differently to Case 1, we use a shortcut VC between AER(or HA) to FA in this case. Additionally, the end-to-end path delay includes total address resolution delay by NHRP for the first packet flowed in ATM networks.

□ **Case 3**: This case is similar to Case 2 in using a shortcut VC between AER(or HA) to FA, but differently to Case 2, this does not include address resolution operations using NHRP. Because address resolution has already completed for the first packet flowed in ATM network, the following packets do not need to resolve ATM address of FA, are switched along shortcut VC which was established in Case 2.

The measurements are plotted in Fig. 5 and Fig. 6. We can find that delay of Case 2 is slightly greater than that of Case 1 due to additional address resolution overhead. But, as shown in case 3 on graphs, after either HA or AER has completed address resolution using NHRP, following packets are faster than packets in Case 1. The most important reason of that result is that the store-and forward processing delay on routers over ATM networks are removed in Case 3.

Also, we note that as k grows, delays in Case 2 and Case 3 decrease. That results from the reduced path length of shortcut VC.

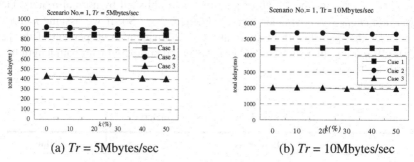

(a) Tr = 5Mbytes/sec   (b) Tr = 10Mbytes/sec

Fig. 5. Averaged end-to-end path delay from CN to MN in scenario 1

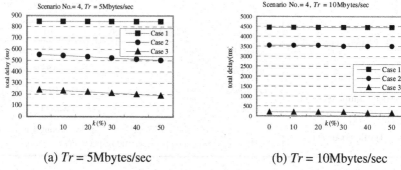

(a) Tr = 5Mbytes/sec   (b) Tr = 10Mbytes/sec

Fig. 6. Averaged end-to-end path delay from CN to MN in scenario 4

5 Conclusions

In this paper, we provided detailed mechanisms to integrate Mobile IP and NHRP. We use NHRP and establish a shortcut VC to switch the packet between CN and MN. Switching is much faster than conventional IP forwarding, the transmission delay and packet-processing overhead is reduced. By simulation, we showed that integration of NHRP and Mobile IP superior to existing Mobile IP operation based on IP routers in view of end-to-end path delay. This work can easily be extended for optimized path routing in Mobile IPv6 and proposed scheme also can be applied to another NBMA networks in addition to ATM network.

References

1. J. Luciani, D. Katz etc., "NBMA Next Hop Resolution Protocol(NHRP)", RFC 2332, Apr. 1998
2. C. Perkins, ed.,"IPv4 Mobility Support", RFC 2002, Oct. 1996
3. C. Perkins, "Mobile IP", IEEE Communication Magazine", Vol. 35, No. 5, pp. 84–99, 1997
4. Andrew T. Campbell, Javier Gomez, Andras G. Valko, "An Overview of Cellular IP", IEEE Wireless Communications and Networking Conference (WCNC'99), New Orleans, Sept. 1999
5. D. O'Mahoney, "UMTS: the fusion of mixed and mobile networking", IEEE Internet Computing. Volume:2, pp.49–56, 1998

e_SWDL : An XML Based Workflow Definition Language for Complicated Applications in Web Environments[1]

Wei Ge, Baoyan Song, Derong Shen, and Ge Yu

Department of Computer Science and Engineering
Northeastern University, Shenyang, China 110004
babysmile_gloria@sina.com

Abstract. e_SWDL is the workflow definition language of a prototype WfMS –e_ScopeWork, which is designed to support complex cross-enterprises workflow applications among heterogeneous sites by using XML approach. On this basis, e_SWDL follows WfMC's XML-based process definition language standard (XPDL), and makes necessary extensions for semantics-rich modeling ability in three major aspects: (1) the complicated transitions between tasks for workflow process modeling; (2) the workflow relevant data and workflow environment data for data modeling; and (3) the role, participant and participant group for organization modeling. Furthermore, Compensation entities (CDSet) are provided for failure handling of distributed workflow scheduling, and Concurrency entities (ConSet) are provided for correctness of concurrent workflow concurrency execution. e_SWDL provides strong modeling ability for complicated workflow logic and suits distributed and heterogeneous Web environments.

1 Introduction

Workflow is a collection of tasks (or activities) to implement the automation of business processes of intra-enterprises and/or inter-enterprises, and these tasks are coordinated to fulfill business needs. A workflow system typically consists of two parts: the specification module (workflow model) and the execution module (workflow engine) [1]. As a result of more complication for business processes on Internet such as e-Business and CIMS, the workflow model must be sophisticated enough to capture more semantics of these complicated applications and to be able to evolve dynamically when necessary. Hence, a workflow model should have good comprehensibility, i.e. ability of users to understand, modify and construct business process models. To do this, a workflow definition language that can describe workflow logic with rich semantics must be provided.

e_SWDL is the workflow definition language of a prototype WfMS for complicated applications – e_ScopeWork being developed by us. It adopts XML

[1] This work is supported by the National 863 High-tech Program (2001AA415210), the Foundation for University Key Teacher and the Teaching and Research Award Program for Outstanding Young Teachers in Higher Education Institutions of the Ministry of Education

X. Zhou, Y. Zhang, and M.E. Orlowska (Eds.): APWeb 2003, LNCS 2642, pp. 471–482, 2003.

standard to define workflow process model, data model and organization model, with the goal to describe business process clearly and provide the flexibility and portability effectively.

The rest of the paper is organized as follows. The related work of some typical workflow definition languages is discussed in Section 2, and then the workflow model of e_ScopeWork is introduced in Section 3. The design of e_SWDL is presented in detail in Section 4. A case study using e_SWDL is given in Section 5. Finally, the summary and future work is given in Section 6.

2 Related Work

Till now, many workflow products, mainly for office automation, have been developed [2], besides them, many WfMS prototypes oriented to complicated applications are also developed and corresponding workflow definition language are provided, typically, MFDL designed by Middle East Technical University [3,4], and WFSL/TSL & WIL [5] designed by Georgia University. MFDL is for a WfMS based on CORBA by fully using the characteristics of CORBA, and extends the CORBA-IDL language properly with obvious advantage of the CORBA infrastructure. They can describe certain complicated business processes, however, they cannot describe the complicated execution and control semantics such as loop, and concurrency control.

With the emerging of Web service technology, several new workflow languages are proposed. Web Services Flow Language (WSFL) [6] and BPEL4WS (Business Process Execution Language for Web Service) [7] are new proposed standard from IBM that addresses workflow. WSFL defines a public interface that allows business processes to advertise themselves as web services. It tries to describe simple process in low cost and short time. The essential in WSFL is recursive composition, which provides a method of integrating services from various providers into a single solution. BPEL4WS devotes to more sophisticated process descriptions. It defines an interoperable integration model that should facilitate the expansion of automated process integration in both the intra-corporate and the business-to-business spaces.

XPDL (XML Process Definition Language) [8] is a new standard proposed by WfMC to standardize interface one of its meta-model. It provides a common method to access and describe workflow definitions, and supports process definition import and export for the interoperability among different workflow products. Comparing with WSFL, XPDL focuses on advanced workflow applications other than simple process definition. Its interoperability, together with the extensibility, gives e_SWDL design basis and extensible space.

In e_SWDL, we inherit these two features and extend some entities and attributes to get sophisticated description and fit into complicated workflow environment. It handles the intricacy of process, furthermore, provides the powerful definition of various data structure and describes the changeful organization structure of world-wide enterprises clearly.

3   Workflow Model of e_ScopeWork

Workflow model can be divided into three sub-models logically: workflow process model, workflow data model and workflow organization model to describe workflow process semantic precisely. Each sub-model is depicted independently by its entities so as to provide the flexibility, and on the other hand, they coordinate to describe business processes, where workflow process model is in dominant position, and the other two can be connected with it by reference (illustrated in Fig.1).

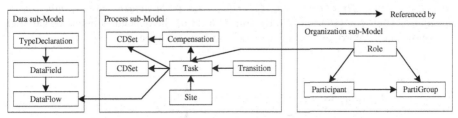

Fig. 1. Workflow reference model of e_ScopeWork

Workflow process model is composed of tasks and transitions (control flows) between tasks. Each task represents a work item, which is a logical and self-contained unit. Transition joins the tasks together to control the process running from one task to another, so it consists of from-task, to-task and condition of this transition as the transition may be conditional or unconditional. In addition, site description is necessary in distributed environment.

Workflow data model is described by the definition of *TypeDeclaration*, *DataField* and *DataFlow*, so that workflow environment data, as well as workflow relevant data such as the data available to tasks or applications during the workflow execution, and the data may be used to pass persistent information or intermediate results between tasks and for evaluations in condition expressions can be defined semantically.

Workflow organization model contains the definition of *Participant* and some extended entities: *Role* and *PartiGroup*. *Role* entity defines all roles in a specific workflow organization, and *Participant* entity provides descriptions of resources that can act as the performer of the various tasks in the process definition. The particular resource, which can be assigned to perform tasks, may have one or more roles, and inversely, one role probably contains one or more participants. The workflow participant declaration does not necessarily refer to a human or a single person, but may also identify person with appropriate skill or responsibility, or machine resource. In addition, we can bind several participants, who are grouped suitably for a specific responsibility, as a *PartiGroup*. For example, we can bind all the appropriate participants as a *PartiGroup* whose ages less than 35 and have excellent professional skill. The role defined in organization model can fulfill some specific tasks, and during scheduling, the optimal participant (or participant group) of all suitable ones for this role will be chosen as the performer of this task. This is relevant to the scheduling of workflow [9], and the algorithm is discussed in [10].

In e_ScopeWork, task can be clarified as *Transactional Task* or *Nontransactional Task*, or particularly as *User Task*, a kind of *Nontransactional Task*, according to the action features of it (i.e. whether supporting the ACID properties or not, and the supporting degree). A certain task may also be *Task* or *Compound Task* according to the complicated degree of task. *Task* cannot be divided any more, and *Compound Task* can be divided into *Task(s)* and other *Compound Task(s)*. This classification ensures the workflow modularity, which enforces locality of modifications; only the parts of the scripts are directly affected by a change. Modularity provides a flexible way of workflow schema definition. Compound Task perhaps has transactional properties, so there are *Compound Transactional Task*, *Compound Nontransactional Task* and particularly, *Compound User Task*.

In e_ScopeWork, 6 kinds of transition structures are provided for complicated application environment (illustrated in Fig.2): *Serial Structure*, *Contingency Structure*, *Split Structure*, *Join Structure*, *Loop Structure* and *Compensation Structure*. Their combination is sufficient to describe the dependencies in all varieties of complicated environments between tasks in our prototype.

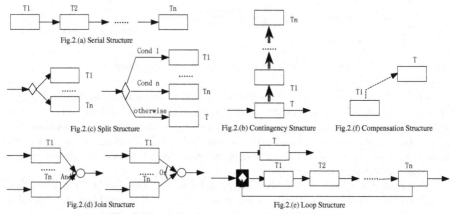

Fig. 2. Transition Structure of e_ScopeWork

The complex structures are explained here. Figure 2(b) illustrates *Contingency Structure*. It shows that T_2 start when T_1 abort or fail, until T_n analogically. Once there is one among T_i completes, the whole structure completes.

Figure 2(e) illustrates *Loop Structure*. It shows the *While Loop Structure*, but there is the other structure, i.e. *Repeat-Until Loop Structure*. Just as the figure illustrate, if the condition is true, T_1 start. When T_1 complete T_2 start, until T_n analogically. The structure implement until the condition change to false or either of T_i abort or fail.

Figure 2(f) illustrates *Compensation Structure*. T' represent the compensation task of T.

4 Definition of e_SWDL

The flexibility and portability is the most important characteristics of e_SWDL. The extensibility of XPDL provides flexible definition of workflow schema to handle the frequent change of workflow running environment, and portability is the coherent purpose of WfMC to support interoperation among a variety of workflow products and prototypes.

To get flexibility, *ExtendedAttributes* entity was inherited from XPDL that can be used in all entities, where necessary, allows users to extend the functionality of this specification to meet individual product needs. They can express any additional entity characteristics that need to be exchanged between workflow systems. Any run-time semantics associated with the use of the extended attributes during process enactment are separately specified and require bilateral agreement. In addition, the separation of three sub-models description can perform flexibility in some extent.

As mentioned above, the portability of e_SWDL supports the interoperation of workflow process definitions between separate products, and hides the difference of our graphical definition tool from WfMC's standard with an import/export function to map to/from the standard at the product boundary. In all cases the process definition must be expressed in a consistent form, which is derived from the common set of entities and attributes expressing its underlying concepts [11]. It also agrees with our ideas on e_ScopeWork, which is implemented on Microsoft .NET infrastructure to equip the prototype with the portability by web service.

It is noticed that *Description* entity that is short textual description can also be used in all entities. *Documentation* entity can specify path and filename of help file and/or description file. Now we will introduce entities in e_SWDL respectively below. They are expressed with XML DTD for the conformance and extension to XPDL.

4.1 Container Entities Definition

Package act as a container for grouping together a number of individual process definitions and associated entity data, which is applicable to all the contained process definitions (and hence requires definition only once). *Package* contains *WorkflowProcess*, *Participant*, *Site*, *CDSet*, *ConSet*, etc.

WorkflowProcess defines the elements that make up a workflow. It is a container for the process itself and provides information associated with administration (creation date, author, etc.) or to be used during process execution (execution priority, time limits to be checked, etc.). *WorkflowProcess* contains definitions, respectively, for *Task*, and, optionally, for *Transition*, *Participant*, *Site*, etc.

There are some entities that can be defined in both *Package* and *WorkflowProcess*. Those entities are: *Role*, *Participant*, *PartiGroup*, *Site*, *TypeDeclaration*, *DataField*, *CDSet*, *Compensation* and *ConSet*. The scope of definitions within a package is global and these entities can be referenced from all workflow process definitions contained within the package. Definitions within *WorkflowProcess*, however, can only be referenced from the entities in this workflow process.

The grammar of *Package* and *WorkflowProcess* definitions is listed below:

```
<!ELEMENT Package
(PackageHeader?,ExternalPackages?,Roles?,Participants?,PartiG
roups?,Sites?,TypeDeclarations?,DataFields?,WorkflowProcesses
,Compensations?,CDSets?,ConSets?)>
<!ATTLIST Package Name ID #IMPLIED
xmlns:xpdl CDATA #FIXED
http://www.wfmc.org/standards/docs/xpdl>

<!ELEMENT WorkflowProcesses (WorkflowProcess*)>
<!ELEMENT WorkflowProcess
```

```
(ProcessHeader?,Roles?,Participants?,PartiGroups?,Sites?,Type
Declarations?,DataFields?,Applications?,Tasks,Transitions,Dat
aflows?,Compensations?,CDSets?,ConSets?,ExtendedAttributes?)>
<!ATTLIST WorkflowProcess Name ID #IMPLIED>
```

4.2 Workflow Process Model Definition

Task Definition. A workflow process consists of one or more tasks, each comprising a logical, self-contained unit of work within the process. In *Task* definition, the information related with task will be defined such as name, implementation and runtime relevant information (e.g. priority, etc.) specifically. In addition, as workflow is a specific field of information application, the task of it can be limited by starting time, duration and ending time, so the *limited* entity is defined. In addition, a task will be processed by a combination of resource, so we need to specify task performer in task definition. Data used, site of task and organization element are only references and the specification is defined in respective entity.

There are difference between the definition of *Transactional Task* and *Nontransactional Task*, for *Transactional Task* is atomic at least. It's necessary, therefore, to specify "*Execute*", "*Commit*" and "*Abort*" in "*TImplementation*" entity, but "*Execute*", "*Done*" and "*Fail*" in "*NTImplementation*" entity for *Nontransactional Task* correspondingly.

The grammar of *Transactional Task* definition is listed below:

```
<!ENTITY % TransactionT
"Limit?,TImplementation,TaskSite,Performer,Priority?,Document
ation?">
<!ELEMENT TTask (%TransactionT;)>
<!ATTLIST TTask Name ID #IMPLIED>
```

Modularity is ensured through the compound task structure, which provides a flexible way of composing an application out of other applications. In compound task definition, we should define its name, begin and end task as references, and other optional features such as limit, priority, etc. Its grammar is omitted here.

Route Definition. There are some *Route* tasks in e_SWDL. *Route* task is "functional" task, that is, it only helps to construct complicated transition structure or workflow process, so there is no implementation definition, performer or site reference in it. There are 6 kinds of Route tasks: *Begin Route* (i.e. the first task in workflow process), *End Route* (i.e. the last task in workflow process), *Split Route, Join Route, DoWhile Route* and *RepeatUntil Route*. The logic of Split, Join, DoWhile and RepeatUntil will be mentioned in transition definition.

The grammar of *Route* definition is listed below:

```
<!ELEMENT Route EMPTY>
<!ATTLIST Route
Name ID #IMPLIED
Type (BR | ER | SR | JR | DWR | RUR) #IMPLIED>
```

Transition Definition. Workflow process consists of one or more tasks, and transition link tasks according to workflow logic. 6 kinds of transition structures defined in e_SWDL (illustrated in Fig.2).

The grammar of *Transition* definition is listed below:

```
<!ELEMENT Transitions (Transition*)>
<!ELEMENT Transition (Branch*)>
<!ATTLIST Transition
Name ID #IMPLIED
Type (SERIAL | SPLIT | JOIN| LOOP | COMPENSATION |
CONTINGENCY )
Logic (AND | OR | DOWHILE | REPEATUNTIL)>
<!ELEMENT Branch (Condition)>
<!ATTLIST Branch
From IDREF #REQUIRED
To IDREF #REQUIRED>
```

Compensate Dependent Set (CDSet) and Compensation Definition. The failure handling and recovery are critical in workflow systems, and it is implemented in hierarchical manner: task and schema failure, task manager failure and WfMS failure. The latter two should be captured and handled by scheduler or take other mechanisms, and they are beyond the scope of this paper. Schema is verified when it is defined in our prototype, we provide some modeling criterion to support the verification [12].

In e_SWDL definition, we define *CDSet* and *Compensation* to provide failure handling. *Compensation* defines the actions of a specific task to handle the task failure. How to recover failure system back to normal state is a worthy issue to penetrate, and we can fulfill it by completely compensation and re-execution, but more practically, by partially compensation and incrementally re-execution if the previous result is useful in workflow running environment. To implement partially compensation and incrementally re-execution we define *CDSet* that specifies several tasks that have compensation dependency. The tasks in a certain *CDSet* will be compensated in the reverse execution order, and the failure handling mechanism can perform the recovery that will be discussed in other paper.

The grammar of *CDSet* and *Compensation* definition is listed below:

```
<!ELEMENT CDSet (RelativeTask, RelativeTask+)>
<!ELEMENT RelativeTask EMPTY>
<!ATTLIST RelativeTask
Wfref IDREF #REQUIRED
Taskref IDREF #REQUIRED)>

<!ELEMENT Compensation
 (ReExecution | IncreReExe | PartiallyComp)>
<!ATTLIST Compensation Taskref IDREF #REQUIRED)>
<!ENTITY %CI "Condition, Implementation">
<!ELEMENT ReExecution (%CI;)>
<!ELEMENT IncreReExe(%CI;)>
<!ELEMENT PartiallyComp(%CI;)>
```

ConSet Definition. How to coordinate the exclusive requirements so as to ensure the execution of workflow instances not to be influenced by another in a multi-workflow execution environment is the important problem to be resolved, i.e. workflow concurrency control. In e_SWDL definition, we can define relative tasks that conflict one another. The concurrency control of workflow depends on some algorithms described in [13,14].

The grammar of *ConSet* definition is listed below:

```
<!ELEMENT ConSets (ConSet*)>
<!ELEMENT ConSet
(RelativeTask,RelativeTask+,Condition,Implementation)>
```

4.3 Data Model Definition

Workflow environment data and workflow relevant data describe workflow data model together. Workflow environment data is maintained by WfMS or local system environment, but may be accessed by tasks or used by the WfMS in the evaluation of conditional expressions in the same way as workflow relevant data. Workflow relevant data represent the variables of a workflow process. They are typically used to maintain decision data (used in conditions) or reference data values, which are passed among tasks.

TypeDeclaration and DataField Definition. *TypeDeclaration* explicitly specifies all data types needed for a schema to define appropriate data objects, and *DataField* specifies data object whose type is a reference of *TypeDeclaration*.

The grammar of *TypeDeclaration* and *DataField* definitions is listed below:

```
<!ELEMENT TypeDeclarations (TypeDeclaration*)>
<!ELEMENT TypeDeclaration
((%Type;),Description?,ExtendedAttributes?)>
<!ATTLIST TypeDeclaration Name ID #REQUIRED>


<!ENTITY %Type "%ComplexType;| BasicType">
<!ELEMENT BasicType EMPTY>
<!ATTLIST BasicType Type (STRING | FLOAT | INTEGER | BOOLEAN
| DATETIME) #REQUIRED>
<!ENTITY %ComplexType "RecordType | UnionType |
EnumerationType | ArrayType| ListType">


<!ELEMENT DataFields (DataField*)>
<!ELEMENT DataField
(DataType, InitialValue?, Length?, Description?,
ExtendedAttributes?)>
<!ATTLIST DataField Name ID #REQUIRED>
```

Dataflow Definition. In WfMS, besides control flow (transition) there is data flow between tasks. We can take two points of view to define dataflow in WfMS. One is task-centered, that is, data object is defined as In, Out or InOut object of task, and in this way the data consistency should be verified. The other is data-centered, that is, source task and target task is defined for a specific data object. We adopt the latter in e_SWDL. The data object is defined in *DataField* definition, and here is just a reference to it.

The grammar of *Dataflow* definition is listed below:

```
<!ELEMENT Dataflows (Dataflow*)>
<!ELEMENT Dataflow (Data*)>
<!ATTLIST Dataflow
Name ID #IMPLIED
Source IDREF #IMPLIED
Target IDREF #IMPLIED>
<!ELEMENT Data EMPTY>
<!ATTLIST Data Dataref IDREF #REQUIRED>
```

4.4 Organization Model Definition

This definition contains *Role*, *Participant* and *Partigroup*, which have been mentioned in Section 4. They provide descriptions of resources that can act as the performer of the various tasks in the process definition.

The grammar of Organization model definition is listed below:

```
<!ELEMENT Roles (Role*)>
<!ELEMENT Role (Description?, ExtendedAttributes?)>
<!ATTLIST Role Name ID #IMPLIED>

<!ELEMENT PartiGroups (PartiGroup*)>
<!ELEMENT PartiGroup (Participants, Description?,
ExtendedAttributes?)>
<!ATTLIST PartiGroup
Name ID #IMPLIED
Role IDREF #IMPLIED>

<!ELEMENT Participants (Participant*)>
<!ELEMENT Participant
(PartiSpty*, Description?, ExtendedAttributes?)>
```

4.5 Implementation of e_SWDL

e_SWDL has been implemented in our WfMS prototype e_ScopeWork. It accepts process definition as input, verifies it from lexical, grammatical and semantic points by step, then abstract the semantic of process and stores into WfDD (Workflow Data Dictionary), the repository of our prototype.

The meta-data in WfDD is modeled according to workflow model logic, so the definition information of process can be captured completely and stored precisely into

WfDD. Information stored in WfDD provides the basis for workflow scheduling, concurrency control and recovery. When a process is activated, one workflow instance is created and proceeds forward automatically according to the logic defined by user, which is enacted and monitored by workflow scheduler [9].

In our prototype, a graphical definition tool is also provided for convenience and easy operation. Graphical definition can be translated into language description in text, and inversely also. Some rules is enforced to verify model in both graphical and text description.

5   Case Study

In this section, we describe e-Commerce scenario (illustrated in Fig.3) as a workflow application. It is obvious that the implementation of workflow definitions can be conducted in very short time and thus with very low cost. In this example, we focus on data, split and join structure description and omit others due to limited space.

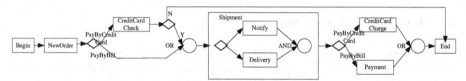

Fig. 3. E-commerce workflow example

```xml
<?xml version="1.0" encoding="utf-8"?>
<Package Name="eCommerce">
  <WorkflowProcesses>
    <WorkflowProcess Name="eCommerceWf">
      <Roles>
        <Role Name="provider" /><--other are omitted-->
      </Roles>
      <Participants><-- omitted--></Participants>
      <Sites>
        <Site Name="China" /><-- other are omitted-->
      </Sites>
      <TypeDeclarations>
        <TypeDeclaration Name="Result">
          <BasicType Type="BOOLEAN"/>
        </TypeDeclaration>
      </TypeDeclarations>
      <DataFields>
        <DataField Name="PayCheck">
          <DataType DataTyperef="Check" />
        </DataField>
        <DataField Name="CheckResult">
          <DataType DataTyperef="Result" />
        </DataField>
        <-- other datafields are omitted-->
      </DataFields>
      <Tasks>
```

```
        <Route Name="begin" Type="BR"/>
        <UTask Name="CreditCardCheck">
    <NTImplementation><--omitted--></NTImplementation>
            <Performer Roleref =" provider " />
            <TaskSite Siteref="China" />
        </UTask>
        <Route Name="SR2" Type="SR"/>
        <CompoundTTask Name="Shipment">
            <BeginTask Taskref="SR3" />
            <EndTask Taskref="JR2" />
        </CompoundTTask>
        <-- other tasks are omitted -->
        </Tasks>
        <Transitions>
            <Transition Name="begin" Type="SERIAL">
                <Branch From="begin" To="NewOrder" />
            </Transition>
            <Transition Name="begin" Type="SERIAL">
                <Branch From="NewOrder" To="R1" />
            </Transition>
            <Transition Name="Pay" Type="Split" Logic="OR">
                <Branch From="R1" To="CreditCardCheck" >
                    <Condition>:CheckCard="Credit":</Condition>
                </Branch>
                <Branch From="R1" To="J1" >
                    <Condition>:CheckCard="Bill":</Condition>
                </Branch>
            </Transition>
            <-- other transitions are omited-->
        </Transitions>
        <Dataflows>
            <Dataflow Name="CheckResult" Source="R2">
                <Data Dataref="CheckResult"/>
            </Dataflow>
            <-- other dataflows are omitted here-->
        </Dataflows>
    </WorkflowProcess>
  </WorkflowProcesses>
</Package>
```

One dataflow "CheckResult" is defined with Source attribute but no Target for it's a unilateral dataflow produced from "CreditCardCheck". More practically, the business process with complicated data and organization structure can be described precisely in e_SWDL. It is obviously found out every entity is defined separately in this language, so the interaction of entities is reduced in a great extent to provide the flexible definition in changeful environment.

6 Conclusion

This paper describes an XML-based workflow definition language e_SWDL that provides the definitions of multiple entities and attributes to describe workflow schema semantically. The combination of those entities and attributes can describe the advanced and complicated workflow logic and the actions in workflow's executing, failure handling and concurrency control precisely, and furthermore, equip this language with the flexibility and portability for distributed and complicated environment.

Future work of our prototype includes the formal verification of workflow model that has been started. Furthermore, we plan to provide dynamic reconfiguration and integration in changeful environment, so more sophisticated language should be implemented.

References

1. Clarence E, Karim K. ML-DEWS: Modeling Language to Support Dynamic Evolution within Workflow Systems. University of Colorado, CTRG Labs, Dept of Computer Science.
2. Rob Allen, et al. Workflow: An Introduction. www.wfmc.org 2001.
3. Gokkoca E, Altinel M, Dogac A. Design and Implementation of a Distributed Workflow Enactment Service. Tech. Report of SRDC, Middle-East Technical University, 1997.
4. Tatbul. N, Arpinar. S, Karagox. P, Gokkoca E. et al. A Workflow Specification Language and Its Scheduler. Tech. Report of SRDC, Middle-East Technical University, 1997.
5. Krishnakumar. N, et al. Specification of Workflows with Heterogeneous Tasks in METEOR, Tech. Report of University of Georgia, 1997.
6. James Shell. IBM DeveloperWorks: Web service, Part 4: Introducing the Web Services Flow Language, Part7: WSFL and recursive composition. IBM:developerWorks 2002.
7. Francisco Curbera, et al. IBM DeveloperWorks: Web service, Business Process Execution Language for Web Services, Version 1.0. 31 July 2002
8. Workflow Management Coalition Workflow Standard. Workflow Process Definition Interface–XML Process Definition Language. www.wfmc.org 2001.
9. Tang Weiping, Ge Wei, Song Baoyan, Yu Ge. The Task Scheduling of .NET-Based WfMS e_ScopeWork. Computer Science 2002,Vol.29: 325–327.
10. SONG Baoyan, YU Ge, HE Qiang, WANG Guoren. Handling Mechanism of User Task in ScopeWork. Journal of Northeastern University (Natural Science) 2000.6,Vol.21 No.6.
11. Workflow Management Coalition. Workflow and Internet: Catalysts for Radical Change A WfMC White Paper. www.wfmc.org June 1998.
12. Zeng Chun, SONG Baoyan, et al. A Workflow Model Supporting Complicated Applications. Journal of Northeastern University (Natural Science), 1999, 20(5): 464~467.
13. GE Wei, SONG Baoyan, YU Ge. The Concurrency Control Mechanism of ScopeWork. Mini-Micro Systems. 2002.8,Vol.23: 5–8
14. Song Baoyan, YU Ge, GE Wei, WANG Guoren. The Concurrency Control Mechanism for Complicated Applications of Workflow. Journal of Northeastern University (Natural Science) 2002.1,Vol.23 No.1: 12–15

An Efficient User Task Handling Mechanism Based on Dynamic Load-Balance for Workflow Systems[1]

Baoyan Song, Ge Yu, Dan Wang, Derong Shen, and Guoren Wang

Department of Computer Science and Engineering,
Northeastern University, Shenyang, China 110004
{bysong,yuge,wangdan,shendr,wanggr}@mail.neu.edu.cn

Abstract. User task is one of the major task types of complicated workflow applications. The way how to handle user tasks impacts the performance of a workflow system significantly, which involves many issues such as description of the duty of each participant, calculation of the workload of each participant, and policy to dispatch work items among participants. After analyzing the characteristics of user tasks, this paper proposes an efficient user task handling mechanism based on dynamic load-balance approach. To do this, the organization model and the workload model are defined, the load-balance policies and the workload dispatching algorithms are designed, and the implementing techniques in a prototype WfMS – e_ScopeWork are presented. The performance experiments are made and show that the new mechanism can improve the workflow system performance effectively.

1 Introduction

A workflow can be simply defined as a set of tasks (also called activities) together with the specification of the control and data-dependency between these tasks, which coordinate execution for a business goal. A task is defined as a work unit that can be executed independently and is either the operations of an auto-executing software system or an activity involving persons or organizations [1]. A workflow that describes a complicated application involves various types of tasks is also very complicated. The complicacy not only refers to the handling logic of task itself but also the complex dependencies among tasks and the large scale of tasks. Therefore, it is necessary to design different scheduling schemes in terms of different task types so as to schedule the workflows more efficiently and effectively.

User task is one of the major task types to be handled for complicated applications in WfMSs. A user task is done by a person or a group in an enterprise. The handling mechanism of user tasks is different from that of other types of tasks, since it depends on the organization structure and involves in many issues including how to describe the duty of participants, calculate the workload of each participant, track the work history of each participant, dispatch work items of a user task among the participants,

---

[1] This work is supported by the National 863 High-tech Program (2001AA415210), the Cross Century Excellent Young Teacher Foundation of the Ministry of Education, and the National Natural Science Foundation of China (60173051)

X. Zhou, Y. Zhang, and M.E. Orlowska (Eds.): APWeb 2003, LNCS 2642, pp. 483–494, 2003.

and so on. This paper will focus on the development of an efficient handling mechanism of user tasks. To begin with, the basic concepts are defined at first.

Definition 1 (User task) A special task that is done by a person or an organization, but not by an automated software system, noted as T.

Definition 2 (Participant) The related persons or organizations that serves as the executors or handling units of a user task T, noted as P.

Definition 3 (Work item) The instance of a user task T at run-time, noted as Q. Usually, work items are managed with a work list.

After analyzing the characteristics of user tasks, this paper proposes a handling user task mechanism based on dynamic load-balance approach. The mechanism includes an organization model for describing the organization structure and organization rules, the algorithm for calculating participant's workload, the dispatching work items policy for dynamic load-balance. This paper also presents the implementing techniques of the mechanism in a prototype WfMS – e_ScopeWork and gives the performance evaluation results by experiments.

The major contributions of this paper are: 1) A novel scheduling algorithm of user tasks for dynamic load-balance in terms of the characteristics of user tasks; 2) A dynamic load-balance dispatching policy for multi-goal optimization, which considers multiple goals including task types, importance levels of work items, organization structures, handling capabilities, current workload of participants, and so on; and 3) the implementing techniques in a prototype workflow management system.

2   Related Work

In recent years, many famous prototypes [2-7] of WfMSs have been developed to deeply research workflow techniques for complicated application fields, including tasks handling [2], distributed workflow scheduling based on inter-task dependencies [3-6], and the concurrency control of workflows [7]. But to the best of our knowledge, so far almost all researches on distributed scheduling architectures consider only the tasks that are automatically executed by software systems, and few deal with user task handling.

WfMC [1] has proposed handling scheme for user tasks, but didn't tell how to define organization structure and dispatch work items. Papers [8,9] indicate that when modeling a workflow, it should be allowed for modeling organization structure at the same time. Thereby, definition of organization structure should be considered at first when handling user tasks in this paper. In order to share the organization structure among different workflow process in an enterprise, we allow the definition of organization structure and the workflow process in two different stages.

The technique of dynamic load-balance is discussed in a distributed workflow system [10], which proposes two load-scheduling policies: Round-robin and Load-aware. Round-robin policy that schedule the handling units in turn is very effective in the condition that the handling units have equal capabilities and that tasks executed have equal workloads. Otherwise, unbalanced workload will arise among distributed handling units. To deal with this problem, Load-aware policy supports load-balance among handling units according to the workload of each handling unit. But, paper[10] only consider the case when the handing units are computers. In the case that handling units are persons, the load-balance factors are different and much more complex. The flexible work-list management based on status chart and activity chart is discussed in [11]. It discusses the factors that would be considered in handling user tasks for load-balance, but don't give its algorithm.

3   User Task Model and User Task Handling

A workflow schema is defined at workflow build-time. While at run-time, it is possible that more than one workflow instance of the same schema and execute forward with different speed. Fig.1 shows the example of the execution status of a multi-instance workflow, where T_2 is a user task (e.g. preparing documents) for which two secretaries are competent, and there can be four instances of T_2. The problem occurs with how to dispatch the four work items to the two secretaries, considering different work items might involve different workload, e.g. preparing a simple notice is quite different from working out a developing plan of an enterprise.

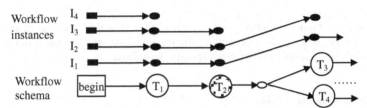

Fig. 1. Execution status of a multi-instances workflow

Generally, there are two different approaches for handling user tasks:

- **Fetching work items by participant:** At workflow build-time, the members of an organization who are competent for the user task are appointed to the participant of a user task in advance. While at run-time, the member self-consciously (i.e. actively) fetches work items from a centralized location where the work items are kept.
- **Appointed work items by system:** For each user task, the work items are not appointed to the participant at workflow build-time. Instead, they are appointed dynamically by the system at run-time, and then the appointed members do the corresponding work items.

The advantages of approach 1 are simple and easy to implement. But, the system performance greatly depends on the consciousness of the involved members. If the appointed members are very active and self-conscious to get the next work item to do after finishing the current one, the system performance might be good. Otherwise, some are busy while others are idle such that uncertain delay will arise in processing. On the other hand, even that all members are active, if a member with poor capability fetches a heavy work item, the total work still cannot finish although all others have done the work and become idle. In this way, load-balance among members becomes impossible. The approach 2 can avoid the load-unbalance problems resulted in fetching work items by members. It can dynamically determines the optimal ones from members who have the abilities to complete the task in time by the scheduling system on the basis of the current status of resource utility in a workflow environment. However, how to get the current status of resource utility is a key problem to be studied.

To effectively deal with user tasks, we adopt the approach 2 and propose a handling mechanism to support dynamic load-balance. The basic steps to efficiently handle user tasks are as follows:

- Define the proper organization structure which can represents the real situation of complicated workflow applications correctly, including the description of the members of the organizations and the roles of the organization.
- Select the participant for each user task at workflow build-time. The participant is identified by a specific role of the organization.
- Schedule the user tasks at workflow run-time according to the exiting definitions and running workload status to keep load-balance and achieve minimum finish time.

4 Organization Model

An organization model consists of the organization structure and the organization rules. The former defines the elements of the organization, and the latter defines how to organize those elements to perform a specific workflow.

4.1 Organization Structure

Executing a user task depends on the responsibility of personnel in an enterprise. So the organization structure must be defined before defining a workflow process. We allow that organization structures and workflow processes are defined separately, such that the definition of organization structure can be shared by different workflow processes.

Definition 4 (Role) A role is an abstract representation that describes the characteristics of task participants, note as R.

The set of all roles in an organization is represented as *RoleSet*. Each role distinguishes itself from others by some characteristic attributes such as name, business duty and so on. The characteristic attributes for a role are dependent on concrete applications. Role R can be described as n-tuple:

$R = <$ *name, businessDuty, ... $>$

Definition 5 (Actor) An actor is a member in an organization, noted as A.

The set of all actors in an organization is represented as *ActorSet*. Each actor distinguishes himself from others by some characteristic attributes such as name, gender, age, title of technical position, technical rank and specialties, etc. An actor can act as one or more than one roles. Actor A can be described as n-tuple:

$A = <$ *name, gender, age, title, rank, specialties,...... $>$

Some time, it is necessary that several actors work together for a specific task.

Definition 6 (Group) A group consists of several actors who work together for a user task, noted as G.

The set of all groups in an organization is represented as GroupSet. Each group distinguishes itself from others by some characteristic attributes such as group name, the number of actors in the group, the description of the function, and so on. The characteristic attributes of a group are also dependent on specific applications. A group can act as one or more than one roles. Group G can be described as n-tuple:

$G = < name, numberOfActors, functionDesc,......>$

In summary, in an organization structure, an actor is the most basic element, a group is the composite element that consists of several actors, and a role is the element used to organize actors and groups. In the following, the discussions for actors are also true to the groups.

4.2 Organization Rule

Since the personnel migration in an organization such as the changes of the roles that the actors or the groups act as, the organization rules on organization structure should support the dynamic changes, so as to enable actors act as a given role dynamically.

Definition 7 (Dynamic relationship) The dynamic relationship among organization elements be described by $\{ t \mid \phi(t)\}$. Here, t is a tuple, and $\phi(t)$ is a predication expression, in which in addition to Boolean operators, two new role operators ∇ and $\angle$ are defined as follows.

Definition 8 (Role operation) Sub-expression $P \nabla R$ checks if participant P (actor or group) can act as role R. and sub-expression $A \angle G$ checks if actor A belongs to group G.

Two organization rules are defined as followed:
1) **Basic rule:** It is used to perform simple functions, for example, to find appropriate actors according to the role who can act as, to find appropriate actors according to the limited conditions of the role and so on.

Example 1 Choose the actors who are competent for the role *Secretary*.
Secretary_actor_set={ a | a∈ActorSet ∧ r∈RoleSet ∧ r[name] = 'secretary' ∧ a ∇r };

Example 2 Choose the actors who can type.
Typing_actor_set = { a | a∈ActorSet ∧ Typing∈a[specialities]};

Example 3 Choose all young managers (i.e. age<=35).
Young_Managers_actor_set = {a | a∈ActorSet ∧ a[age]<=35 ∧ r∈RoleSet ∧ r[name]='manager' ∧ a ∇r}

2) **Compound rule:** It is defined by combining the basic rules by set operators (∪, ∩,−) to perform complex functions.

Example 4 Choose Secretary who can type.
Typing_Secretary_actors_set = Secretary_actor_set ∩ Typing_actor_set

5   User Task Scheduling Algorithm

At build-time of a workflow, we should first define tasks, and then the inter-task control dependencies and data dependencies. When defining user tasks, the participants must be appointed. Here, they are identified by pre-defined roles with their limited conditions but not to correspond to a given actor or group.

At workflow run-time, the scheduling system finds all actors or groups who can act as the roles defined in user tasks, then selects a competent one from them to execute work item according to some policies, such as types, importance levels of work items, organization structure, handling capabilities (including professional rank and work achievement) and current workload of actors. The policies will be introduced in following section in detail.

The purpose of keeping load-balance among actors by dynamic dispatching work items is to make use of the resources adequately and get optimized execution efficiency.

5.1   Work Item Dispatching

Now let's describe the dynamic dispatching procedure of work items with the following example.

Example 5 Find all young managers (i.e. age<=35) and then dispatch development task of project 1 to the one with the lightest workload.

The scheduling system first finds all young managers, Young_Managers_actor_set, according to the definition information of user task at build-time (i.e. role: manager; limited condition: age<=35). If only one actor is found, we have no choice but to dispatch the task to him (her). While if more than one actor is found, we should select an appropriate actor from them according to the dynamic load-balance dispatching policy that will be explained in next section in detail. Thereby, the following algorithm of dispatching work items is designed.

Algorithm 1 (Algorithm of dispatching work items Q)

Step 1 The system finds all actors who can act as the role with the conditions and puts them into the set *AvailableActorSet*, according to the definitions (i.e. the role and condition) defined at build-time;

Step 2 If Cardinality(*AvailableActorSet*) = =1 then goto Step 4;

Step 3 The system chooses the optimal actor a in AvailableActorSet according to Algorithm 2 and 3;

Step 4 Dispatching Q to a;

Step 5 End.

5.2   Dynamic Load-Balance Policy

In this section, we describe the implementing policy in Step 3 of Algorithm 1 in detail. Choosing an appropriate policy to ensure that workloads could be dispatched among actors as evenly as possible and the work items can be executed as soon as possible is the aim of the enterprise management. At first, the workload concept used in this paper is defined as follows.

Definition 9 (Workload) The execution time required by a work item is defined as workload.

All work items belonging the same task are classified into different types and different importance level. The work item Q with the type k and the importance level h is noted as $Q^{k,h}$. The workload of $Q^{k,h}$ is noted as wl^k, where wl^k is assessed by business contents and experiences. If $Q^{k,h}$ is to be done by actor Ai for the first time and the technical rank of Ai is higher than $Rank^h$, then the workload of $Q^{k,h}$ for Ai is wl^k_i and $wl^k_i = wl^k$, where $Rank^h$ is the lowest technical rank that a participant must have to do $Q^{k,h}$ (otherwise, Ai cannot do $Q^{k,h}$). If Ai has done the work items whose type is the same as $Q^{k,h}$, the wl^k_i is the average value of all his/her successful execution time for those work items.

To design a dynamic load-balance policy, the following factors are considered:
- Different actors might spend different execution time for even the same work item, because the working ability of each actor might be different.
- The workload of each type of work items might be different from others, for example, drafting out a notice and working out an enterprise plan are different workload.

Therefore, the dynamic load-balance policy is as follows:
- Classify work items of a user task, according to their business contents and the management experiences, and determine the important levels and the types.
- Evaluate workload of each actor for the work item $Q^{k,h}$ that will be dispatched.
- Evaluate the business ability for each actor. Here the business ability is defined by the success rate who has done the work item $Q^{k,h}$. In order to calculate business ability, the working log for an actor is kept by the scheduling system. The log includes the successful flag, the executing time, and the type of work items.
- Choose an actor whose business ability is suitable for work item $Q^{k,h}$ according to that his/her workload is the lightest. Moreover, in order to ensure that the important work item is done by the outstanding actor, a given value $rate^h$ is defined for $Q^{k,h}$, which requires that the success rate of $Q^{k,h}$'s actor must be greater than $rate^h$. The value of $rate^h$ can be set from 0 to 1. When the $rate^h$ is 0, it means the least important work item.

5.3 Calculation of wl^k_i

The calculation of wl^k_i is as follow:

Algorithm 2 (Calculate wl^k_i of actor A_i on work item $Q^{k,h}$)

Step 1 Calculate the total execution times tc which actor A_i has done work item $Q^{k,h}$;
Step 2 If $tc == 0$ then goto step5;
Step 3 Calculate the total times sc which A_i has done $Q^{k,h}$ successfully, and then the value of sc/tc;

Step 4 If $sc/tc \geq rate^h$, then $\lambda=1$, and then calculate workload wl_i^k.

$$wl_i^k = (\sum_1^{sc} wl_{i,j}^k)/sc, \text{ where, } wl_{i,j}^k \text{ is the workload of the jth success execution}$$

of Ai for $Q^{k,h}$. Then goto step 6;

Step 5 if $A_i[\text{rank}] \geq rank^h$ then $\lambda=1$, $wl_i^k = wl^k$ else $\lambda=0$, $wl_i^k=0$;

Step 6 End.

5.4 Finding the Actor with the Lightest Workload

Suppose that there are n actors who are competent for the work item Q of task T in a workflow. In run-time, since different instances of the workflow will advance with different speed, some actors are dispatched with work items while some are not. Let m be the number of work items that actor A_i ($1 \leq i \leq n$) is undertaking, and $wl_{i,j}$ represent the *jth* workload of A_i, then the total workload of A_i is $\sum_{j=1}^{m} wl_{i,j}$.

Therefore, when a work item $Q^{k,h}$ is to be dispatched, then the workload wl_i^k ($1 \leq i \leq n$) should be calculated respectively by Algorithm 2. Our policy is to find the actor A_i who can satisfy the following expression and dispatch the work item to him (her):

$$\min\left\{ wl_i \mid wl_i = \lambda(wl_i^k + \sum_{j=1}^{m} wl_{i,j}) \wedge wl_i \rangle 0, i = 1,2,..., n \right\}$$

Algorithm 3 (Find actor A_l who is excellent and has the lightest workload)
Step1 Set i=1;

Step2 Calculate wl_i^k and λ according to Algorithm 2;

Step3 Repeat Step4, Step5 and Step6 until i == n;

Step4 If $\lambda==0$ then loadSum=0 else loadSum=$\sum_{j=1}^{m} wl_{i,j}$;

Step5 $wl_i = \lambda(wl_i^k + \text{loadSum})\}$;

Step6 i=i+1,

Step7Select A_i such that $wl_i = \min\{wl_i, i=1,2,..,n, \text{ and } wl_i > 0\}$

Step8 End

In this algorithm, in the case of more than one actor having equal workload at the same time, some policies can be used to ensure dispatching work averagely. For example, for each actor, we can log the time when the task was dispatched to him (her) last time. Then we can dispatch the work item to him (her) who has not got task to execute for the longest time among all actors with equal workload. In this way,. a novice will have chances to execute more important work items if he/she has sufficient high technical rank. This could ensure to find the actors with the lightest workload from outstanding actors.

In some application environments, the above viewpoint can be simplified as: considering that all corresponding actors of a role appointed in a task have equal working abilities, that is, they spend equal time in handling a work items, and the workload is equal for all work items of the same user task. In this case, the dispatching policy becomes as Round-robin algorithm.

6   Implementation Issues in e_ScopeWork

e_ScopeWork [12-14] is a prototype system of WfMS to support large scale and complicated applications. It is built on Microsoft .NET and all components are implemented as web services. Each task (except user task) also can be implemented by a Web service that is distributed on Intranet or Internet.

6.1 Distributed Task Scheduling

e_ScopeWork implements fully-distributed scheduling. Either simple or compound task is associated with a task manager (i.e. TM) that is generated automatically based on workflow schema at building scheduling system. According to the type of tasks, task managers are divided into three types: transactional TM, non-transactional TM and user TM. All the scheduling information is distributed into these TMs. TMs are responsible for scheduling a workflow as well as the execution and supervision of tasks. TMs determine whether associated tasks can start and when they start, according to inter-task dependencies. Once the current task has been completed, the corresponding TM activates its directly successive TM according to the dependencies. Existed applications (i.e. legacy tasks) in original system are wrapped as Web services, and then are scheduled. A user task is activated by the actor who gets work item from work list by work list handler. The work items in work list are managed by user task managers.

6.2 Scheduling of User Tasks

In nature, user TMs, responsible for user tasks, are almost the same as non-transactional managers except its interactive objects. The interactive objects of user TMs are dispatcher, no longer general tasks. The dispatcher for different user task is different, which is also generated automatically at building scheduling system. The algorithm for dispatchers might be Algorithm 1 or Algorithm Round-robin in the paper. Work list is an ordered-set of work items to be executed by an actor, and the work items in it are filled in by dispatcher. In e_ScopeWork, work list services are Web services that are distributed to different nodes over the whole network. All actors retrieve their work list to get necessary information, and then complete the work items according to the requirements. After completing, actors notify their TMs the completion information by work list handler. The TMs are responsible for logging part of completion information to history information tables and activate directly successive TMs. The handled process of user tasks in e_ScopeWork is shown in Fig.2.

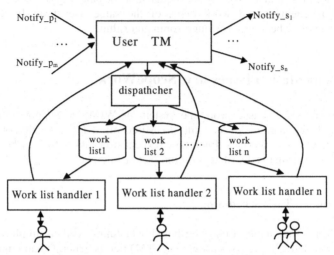

Fig. 2. Handling approach of user tasks

C# is core language of Microsoft .NET for Web service of next generation and the interface of work list service is described by C# as follow:

```
Interface WorkList {... ...
long AddItem ();      //add work items
long GetItem ();      //get work items
long DeleteItem ();   //delete work items
}
```

The interface of work list handler is described by C# as fellow:

```
Interface WorkListHandler {... ...
long Retrieve ();   //retrieve work items from work list
long Reply ();      //inform TM of handling results
}
```

7   Performance Evaluation

To evaluate the performance of Algorithm 1, the experiments are made in the environment of the prototype system of WfMSs for Algorithm 1 and Algorithm Round-Robin.

Suppose T_2 is a user task in a workflow schema as shown in Fig.1. All work items of T_2 can be divided into three types. The estimated workload for each type of work items is 7, 12, and 22 minutes respectively. There are different important levels in each type of work items. Let the important level is be 1, 2 or 3, and the $rate^h$ is 0, 0.8 or 0.9 (here h=1, 2 or 3). The actors who can be competent for T_2 are a1 and a2. The business ability of a1 is higher than a2. The successful executing rate of a1 for more important work items is higher than a2. The executing time of a1 for the same work item is shorter than a2. The same 200 instances of T_2 are used in follow experiments.

The workloads status of a1 and a2 for Algorithm round-robin is shown in Fig.3. 100 work items will be finished by a1 and a2 respectively. The unbalance of workloads is serious with the growth of instances. The total successful executing rate is 84% because more important work items are executed by a2.

The workloads of a1 and a2 for Algorithm 1 are shown in Fig.4. The numbers of work items that will be finished by a1 and a2 respectively are not same. The balance of workloads is kept with the growth of instances approximately. The total successful executing rate is 99% because more important work items are executed by a1. If the workload is always unbalancing in an application environment under Algorithm 1, it should be considered to add the new actors with appropriate technical rank.

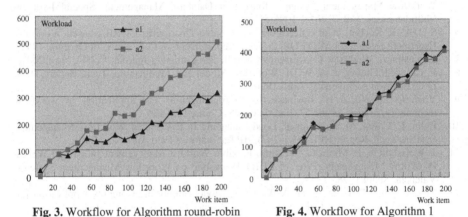

Fig. 3. Workflow for Algorithm round-robin   **Fig. 4.** Workflow for Algorithm 1

8 Conclusion

To make use of the resources adequately and get optimized executing efficiency, a user task handling approach supporting dynamic load-balance is proposed in this paper. The handling ability of each actor is considered to be different from another one because the factors such as technical rank, experience and so on. The workload of each work item for a user task in it is considered to be different from another one because the type, the important level of work items and so on. Thereby, the scheduling performance of the approach is much better. From the performance evaluation experiments, it can be seen that the workloads are balancing, the successful rate is higher and the response time is shorter. The approach can ensure to find the actor who has the lightest workload in higher technical rank or excellent actors and make him (her) execute more important work items. It also ensures to find the actor who has the lightest workload to execute general work items. The method can be exploited to improve the performance of complicated and distributed workflow applications.

There are still some works we need to do in the future, e.g. we will consider the priorities of work items in user task handling mechanism, so as to improve the scheduling performance of WFMS.

References

1. D. Hollingsworth, The workflow Reference Model, Workflow Management Coalition, TC00-1003,Nov.1994.
2. P. Karagoz, S. Arpinar, P. Koksal, et al., Task Handling in Workflow Management Systems, in Proceedings of International Workshop on Issues and Applications of Database Technology, IADT'98, Berlin, Jun. 1998.
3. P. Attie, M. Singh, E. Emerson, et al., Scheduling Workflows by Enforcing Intertask Dependencies Distributed Systems Engineering Journal, Vol. 3, 1996.
4. E. Gokkoca, M. Altinel, I. Cingil, et al., Design and Implementation of a Distributed Workflow Enactment Service, in Proc. of Intl. Conf on Cooperative Information Systems, Charleston, USA, June 1997.
5. J. Miller, A. Sheth, K. Kochut et al., CORBA-Based Run-Time Architectures for Workflow Management Systems, Journal of Database Management, Special Issue on Multidatabases, Vol. 7, No. 1 1996.
6. S. Das, K Kochut, et al ,ORBWork: A Reliable Distributed CORBA-based Workflow Enactment System for METEOR_2, Tech. Report, Dept. of C. S. ,Univ. of Georgia, 1997.
7. J. Puustjarvi. Workflow Concurrency Control, The Computer Journal, Vol.44, No.1 2001.
8. F. Castal, P.Grefen, et al, WIDE Workflow Model and Architecture, Tech. Report, Dept. of C. E, Twente University, April 1996.
9. Yuan Q L, Wu Z H, Business flow reorganization: The application of workflow technology, in Proc. of the 5th Conf on CIMS, China, 122~126.
10. L Jin, F. Casati, M. Sayal, et al, Load Balancing In Distributed Workflow Management System, Tech. Report(HPL-2001-287), HP Laboratories Palo Alto, Nov. 2001.
11. J. Weissenfels, P. Muth, G. Weikum, Flexible Worklist Management in a Light-Weight Workflow Management, Proc. of EDBT Workshop on Workflow Management Systems, Valencia, Spain 1998.
12. Zeng C, Song B Y, and et al. A Workflow Model Supporting Complex Application [J]. Journal of Northeastern University (Natural Science Edition), 20(5): 464~467, 1999.
13. Song B Y, Yu G, and et al. Architecture for a CORBA-Based Workflow Management System, MINI-MICRO SYSTEMS, 21(12): 1320~1323 2000.
14. Song B Y, Yu G, and et al. Workflow Concurrency Control Mechanism for complicated Application. Journal of Northeastern University (Natural Science Edition), 23(1): 12~15 2002.

Exception Specification and Handling in Workflow Systems

Yoonki Song and Dongsoo Han

Information and Communications University,
58-4 Hwaam-Dong, Yuseong-Gu, Daejeon, 305-732, Korea
{ysong, dshan}@icu.ac.kr

Abstract. Various unexpected events frequently happen in workflow system supporting web-based business processes. Thus workflow system should be equipped with handlers to cope with the unexpected events. But in practical terms, we cannot expect for a workflow system to prepare all the handlers for events that might potentially occur. It is more reasonable to let process designers specify exceptional situations and define corresponding exception handlers at process build time. At that time, when exceptional events occur, the workflow system detects the exceptions and invokes corresponding exception handlers. To support this mechanism, a workflow system should provide a means of specifying exceptions and facilities to detect exceptions and invoke corresponding exception handlers. In this paper, we devise an exception specification method using an event-transition approach and its handling mechanism using a design pattern. Detecting exceptions and mechanism for invoking exception-handling routines are developed and incorporated into our research workflow system (ICU/COWS).

1 Introduction

Workflow Management System (WfMS) is a software system that creates and manages business processes by integrating existing software. Defining a business process implies the specification of various components of the model in a particular business environment. In that situation, we frequently come across failures and exceptions during workflow enactment service and they may cause serious problems especially in mission-critical applications on web environment. As a result the need of exception handling is generally recognized. In general, the role of exception handling is to mainly enhance reliability and robustness of a system.

Exception in a workflow is defined as events or conditions that hinder the execution of an activity from being normally completed. Many WfMSs have their own methods for handling them in a disciplined way. These methods can be divided into event-transition approach and rule-based approach. The event-transition approach [1][9] allows the process designer to specify exceptional situations in process activities and when an exception occurs while executing the activity, the control-flow makes a transit into the attached exception handler. But the event-transition approach is not so good at coping with the situation

X. Zhou, Y. Zhang, and M.E. Orlowska (Eds.): APWeb 2003, LNCS 2642, pp. 495–506, 2003.

when multiple exceptions need to be attached to the definition of an activity (or activities). The direct specification of multiple exceptions to an activity makes the process model to be very complex. WAMO [2][3] identifies the importance of incorporating the exception handling mechanism into WfMSs. It uses *Sagas* and flexible transactions to deal with workflow exceptions. It also offers a preliminary classification of exceptions. OPERA [4][5] integrates programming language primitives for exception handling to workflow management systems. On the other hand the rule-based approach generally provides a rule-based language for the exception specification. The event part defines the symptoms of an exception and the condition is a boolean expression that describes that the symptoms really coincide with an exception to be handled. The action part is an operation in the exception occurrence. However, the rule language is intrinsically complex. WIDE [6] provides a process definition language which includes a rule language for defining expected exceptions, called *Chimera-Exc*. WIDE devises a pattern-based environment that supports the design and reuse of exception in workflows. However, reuse and management of exception handlers are presented with only some implementation details in the research prototype. ADOME-WfMS [7] also takes rule-based approach with meta-model features. METEOR$_2$ [8] uses the 'justified' ECA rules to capture more contexts in workflow modeling. Justification (J) provides a reasoning context for the evaluations of ECA rules to support context dependent reasoning processes in dealing with uncertainties. XPDL (XML Process Definition Language) is a language for describing workflows. It provides the meta-model that is used to define the objects and attributes contained within a process definition. However, it does not contain facility for exception specification.

In this paper we develop an exception specification and handling mechanism using event-transition approach. We adopted XPDL to integrate our exception specification, because XPDL is accepted as *de facto* standard in workflow society. Moreover, we have found that, in accommodating the nature of workflow in exception specification, XPDL is the most suitable language to work with. We keep the strong points concerning the event-transition approach and try to complement its drawback by providing a handy graphical user interface, which helps the process designer easily model and understand the process. The objectives and contribution of this paper include: (1) developing an exception specification scheme considering the nature of workflow and extending XPDL, (2) constructing an exception handling workflow system class structure using design pattern.

We have organized this paper as follows. Section 2 and 3 describe our scheme for exception specification and an exception handling mechanism is devised in the workflow system. The graphical user interface is presented in section 4 and we draw our conclusion in section 5.

2   Exception Specification

Our exception mechanism is composed of two parts. One part is for exception specification at process build time and the other part is for exception handling at runtime. In this section, we describe each part respectively with the introduction of general exception properties.

2.1   Properties of Workflow Exceptions

Exceptions in a workflow are events or conditions that hinder the execution of an activity from being normally completed. If an exception occurs in a process, it cannot be completed in a normal fashion. Thus a workflow system must be equipped with exception handlers to cope with the exceptions. But in fact, we cannot expect a workflow system to have all the potential exception handlers. If one can anticipate the possible exceptions beforehand, the corresponding exception handlers could be prepared for the exceptions. In our exception mechanism, we let the process designer define an exception handling activity and if an exception occurs the corresponding exception handling activity is invoked.

If an exception occurs in an activity and its exception handling activity is successfully completed, the activity is considered to have been successfully completed. But as an exception handling activity might cause another exception, we keep hierarchy among exception handlers and propagate the exceptions that are not handled on the spot to upper exception handlers in the hierarchy.

Meanwhile we can classify exceptions into several categories according to the nature of exceptions. Characteristics such as data, state, properties of entity (process or activity), source of failure (application or infra structure) are typically used for the classification. More details regarding classification of exceptions are given in [10]. Moreover for the proper exception handling of workflows, we consider the following features of workflows.

1. **Long-lived Activities**: A workflow process usually has a long lifetime and integrates diverse applications of enterprises. The long-running processes have a much higher possibility of being abnormally stopped by unexpected events during their execution.
2. **Separating Normal Activities from Exceptional Activities**: By separating normal activities from exceptional activities, we can improve several aspects of a system in terms of quality, such as readability, maintainability, and reusability.
3. **Hierarchy of Exception Handlers**: Process designers should organize their business processes by attaching handler to different areas of specialization such as process and activity. Handlers associated with a process are in a upper stratum than the handlers associated with activities.
4. **Exception Propagation**: By keeping hierarchy among exception handlers and propagating unresolved exceptions to the upper level exception handlers in the hierarchy, process designers specify exception handling activities in more organized way. Several exception handlers can be summarized in one exception handling activity and it can be given at some proper place in the process definition.
5. **Guarded Block**: Guarded block is a range of processes where exceptions can be raised and a guarded block can be nested into another guarded block. Each guarded block has its exception handling activity and when an exceptional event is encountered during the execution of a guarded block, an exception is raised and control is passed on to an appropriate handler for the block. If the corresponding handler is not found in the handler the exception is propagated to the outer guarded block. This propagation continues all the way up to the process level until it finds one.

6. **Sequential or Concurrent Execution**: Exception can occur either in sequential or concurrent execution mode. While exception specification in sequential execution mode is resolved by previous considerations, exception specification in concurrent execution mode requires some more constraints. That is, a guarded block cannot be set across concurrent activities and the end of exception handler must never flow into other concurrent activities. This constraint can be easily enforced by our graphical user interface.

2.2   Exception Specification

Exception specification includes our considerations discussed in the previous subsection. Contents to specify exceptions include the following attributes.

- **ID**: Identifier of an exception.
- **Name**: Symbolic name of an exception.
- **Description**: Short textual description of an exception.
- **Exception Handling Models**: There are 5 types of handling models. Our research supports 5 types of exception handling and process designer can specify one of models he/she has selected. Fig. 1 shows 5 types of our exception handling models.

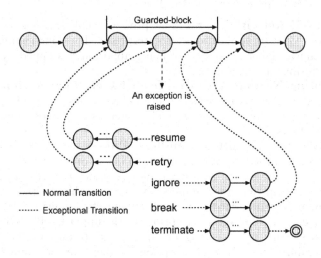

Fig. 1. Handling Models

- **Handling Mode**: It defines the degree of automation when triggering and terminating exception handling. Automatic mode denotes the fact that exception is fully controlled by the workflow system and manual mode denotes that an exception is handled through user interaction.
- **Exception Handler**: An exception handler is defined as a set of activities to be executed when some exceptions are detected while executing a group of activities in a guarded block.

- **Pre-condition**: It needs to check the violation of certain assertions on relevant data or the status of an invoked activity. A pre-condition is specified to represent the condition to be satisfied before a process goes into a guarded block. (e.g. 'contract' = $20,000)
- **Post-condition**: A post-condition expression is given to represent the condition to be satisfied after the process of finishing the execution of a guarded block. If the condition is evaluated to be valid, the activities in the guarded block are regarded as having been successfully terminated.

To accommodate above specifications in XPDL of WFMC, we extend the XPDL DTD according to XPDL convention:

```
<!ELEMENT Package (PackageHeader, ..., Exceptions?, ExtendedAttributes?)>
<!ELEMENT WorkflowProcess (ProcessHeader, ...,
    Exceptions?, GuardedBlocks?, ExtendedAttributes?)>
<!ELEMENT Activity (Description?, ..., PreCondition,
    PostCondition, ExtendedAttributes?)>
<!ELEMENT PreCondition (#PCDATA | Xpression)*>
<!ELEMENT PostCondition (#PCDATA | Xpression)*>
<!ELEMENT Transitions (Transition*, ExceptionalTransition*)>
<!ELEMENT ExceptionalTransition (Condition?, Description?,
    ExtendedAttributes?)>
<!ATTLIST ExceptionalTransition Id NMTOKEN #REQUIRED
    From NMTOKEN #REQUIRED To NMTOKEN #REQUIRED
    Loop (NOLOOP | FROMLOOP | TOLOOP) #IMPLIED Name CDATA #IMPLIED>
<!ELEMENT Exceptions (Exception*)>
<!ELEMENT Exception (Description?)>
<!ATTLIST Exception Id NMTOKEN #REQUIRED Name CDATA #IMPLIED>
<!ELEMENT GuardedBlocks (GuardedBlock*)>
<!ATTLIST GuardedBlock Id NMTOKEN #REQUIRED From NMTOKEN #REQUIRED
    To NMTOKEN #REQUIRED Name CDATA #IMPLIED>
<!ELEMENT OnExceptions (OnException*)>
<!ELEMENT OnException ANY>
<!ATTLIST OnException Id NMTOKEN #REQUIRED Name CDATA #IMPLIED
    ExceptionID CDATA #IMPLIED HandlingModel (IGNORE | RESUME | RETRY |
    BREAK | TERMINATE) "RESUME" RetryCount #IMPLIED>
```

The previous code shows some extracted part of an extended XPDL DTD and extended elements for the specification are given below.

1. `Activity`: `PreCondition` and `PostCondition` elements are newly added. Thus one can specify exceptions that might occur in an activity.
2. `Transition`: `Transitions` element is divided into (normal) `Transition` and `ExceptionalTransition` elements. An `ExceptionalTransition` element is for exceptional control flow and it does not affect transition restriction such as join/split. That is, when an exception occurs, `ExceptionalTransition` only can be considered and the control flow follows along the path specified by it. Explicit separation between normal and exceptional transition provides readability and maintainability.

3. **Exception:** A process designer can define exceptions using the `Exception` element. It comprises the information stated in the previous paragraph. Handling model can be specified graphically and compensating activities are linked by `ExceptionalTransition` element.

4. **GuardedBlock:** `GuardedBlock` contains `OnExceptions` and attributes such as `Id`, `Name`, `From` and `To`. `GuardedBlocks` element is specified within the `WorkflowProcess` element. `OnExceptions` element can contain zero or more `OnException` elements. `OnException` element contains attributes such as `Id` and `Name`, and `RetryCount` element.

Now consider the following scenario. `timeout_ex` is attached to guarded block. `timeout_ex` occurs during the execution of `a3`, the control follows along the path `ex_t1` designate which means `a5` is invoked as an exception handler. Here, the circle denotes the activity and the triangle denotes exception.

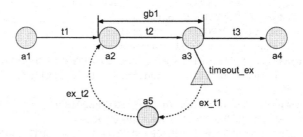

Fig. 2. An Example Scenario

The XPDL excerpt in the following script shows the specification of the example scenario:

```
<Package Id="1" Name="Sample Model">
  <WorkflowProcesses>
    <WorkflowProcess Id="1" Name="Sample Process1">
      ...
      <Activities>
        <Activity Id="1" Name="a1">...</Activity>
        <Activity Id="2" Name="a2">...</Activity>
        <Activity Id="3" Name="a3">...</Activity>
        <Activity Id="4" Name="a4">...</Activity>
        <Activity Id="5" Name="a5">...</Activity>
      </Activities>
      <Transitions>
        <Transition Id="1" From="1" To="2" Name="t1">...</Transition>
        <Transition Id="2" From="2" To="3" Name="t2">...</Transition>
        <Transition Id="3" From="3" To="4" Name="t3">...</Transition>
        <ExceptionalTransition Id="4" From="3" To="5" Name="ex_t1">...
        </ExceptionalTransition>
        <ExceptionalTransition Id="5" From="5" To="2" Name="ex_t2">...
```

```
          </ExceptionalTransition>
        </Transitions>
        <Exceptions>
          <Exception Id="1" Name="timeout_ex">
            <Description>Timeout occurred</Description>
          </Exception>
        </Exceptions>
        <GuardedBlocks>
          <GuardedBlock Id="1" From="2" To="3" Name="gb1">
            <OnExceptions>
              <OnException Id="1" ExceptionId="1" HandlingModel="RETRY"
                RetryCount=2>
            </OnExceptions>
          </GuardedBlock>
        </GuardedBlocks>
      </WorkflowProcess>
      ...
    </WorkflowProcesses>
    ...
</Package>
```

3 Exception Handling

Once a process designer specifies the exception to handle the specified exception completely, the enactment service should provide the exception handling mechanism at execution time. As suggested in section 3.1, we show how to apply the consideration using design pattern. For the mechanism, we extend *ManageDistributed-Workflows* pattern from our previous research [11]. The extended structure for exception handling is shown in Fig. 3. We add *Observer* pattern [13] which is one of the behavioral patterns to *ManageDistributed-Workflows* pattern for exception listening and notification at runtime. Fig. 4 shows the structure of ExceptionObject, GuardedBlock, TMI and GTMI in detail.

ExceptionObject and GuardedBlock are newly added while ExceptionObject, GuardedBlock, TMI and GTMI are the main classes in the structure.

1. ExceptionObject: It plays a role of being a runtime object of user-defined exception that contains the context. ExceptionObject is extended from EventObject and implements WfException. The purpose of ExceptionObject is to assume the role of a messenger between the point where the exception has ccurred and has been identified, and the place where the exception should be handled. ExceptionObject may contain attributes, carrying information from the point causing exception to the exception handler.

2. TMI(Task Manager Instance): It is responsible for managing a task within a workflow process. It may contain zero or more ExceptionObject(s) that can be created while executing an activity. It is responsible for the detection of exception.

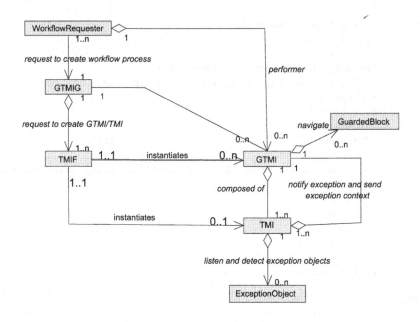

Fig. 3. Extended Structure

3. GTMI(Global Task Manager Instance): It is responsible for managing multiple TMIs that are associated with tasks within a workflow process. It contains TMIs extended from NotificationListener. That is, when an exception is detected by TMI, GTMI obtains the notification from TMIs.
4. GuardedBlock: It contains information such as Id, Name, From and To. It is used for GTMI to decide on an appropriate exception handler.

The following is the typical procedure of our exception handling mechanism, when an exception is detected while the workflow system is running.

1. **Raising Exception**: When an exceptional situation is encountered an exception is raised and an ExceptionObject is created.
2. **Exception Detection**: When an exception is raised, it is detected by TMI and the created ExceptionObject is passed to GTMI.
3. **Catching Exception**: When an exception is detected by TMI, the exception is delivered to GTMI and it looks at guarded blocks for a handler matched with the raised exception. If no handler matching the exception is found, the exception propagates to the outer block. This propagation continues all the way up to the process level until the handler is found. If this fails, the workflow system cannot handle the exception and the process is abnormally aborted. To prevent workflow from falling into such a situation, an uncaught exception of a workflow definition should be analyzed. The details of the technique can be referred to in our previous work [12].
4. **Invoking Handler**: Once corresponding handler is found, it is automatically invoked by the workflow system. A handler is typically used for two

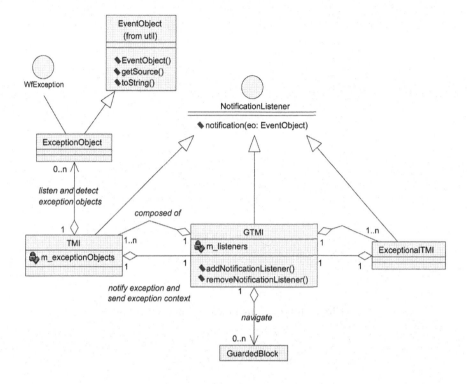

Fig. 4. Detailed Structure

main purposes. First, ideally, a handler will perform some operation that allows the process to recover from the exception and continue the execution. For example, in response to a "time out" exception in a process, a handler might compensate for the event. Second, if recovery is not possible, a handler can at least notify users through a helpful error message before the process is terminated.

An exception is raised if some abnormal state is detected. Signaling an exception by TMI is the communication of an exception occurrence to its invoker. The recipient of the notification is GTMI, which controls the overall process flow. GTMI determines whether internal recovery should be executed and which exceptional TMI should be executed. Then, GTMI invokes appropriate exceptional TMI. Fig. 5 shows the interactions among the classes.

4   Process Builder and Design Process

We have implemented a process builder in which process designers can graphically design business processes. Exceptional conditions and handlers are specified or registered using the process builder. The defined processes are generated, imported, and exported in the form of XPDL. Once an XPDL business process is

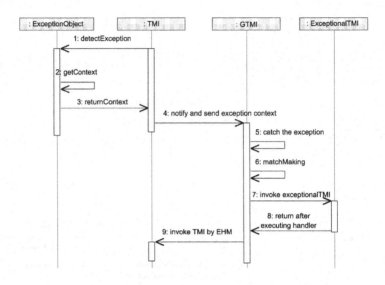

Fig. 5. Interactions in exception occurrence

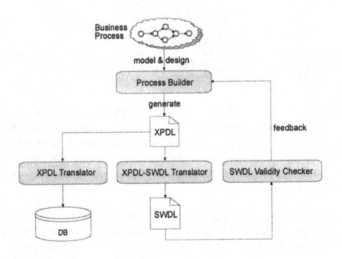

Fig. 6. Processing Steps

created, it is translated into SWDL(Simple Workflow Definition Language) [12] and incorrect exception specifications like uncaught exception specifications are detected through an SWDL validity checker.

The detected errors are reported to the process designer and the check process is repeated until no more errors are detected. When no error is found in the definition, the process is stored in database to be used by workflow system. Fig. 6 depicts the aforementioned processing steps. Fig. 7 shows the image of

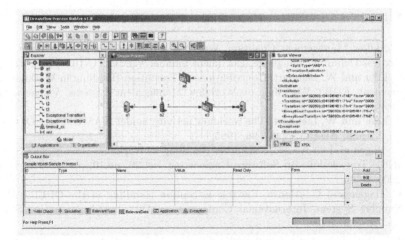

Fig. 7. Process Builder

our process builder. The process builder comprises 4 windows. The upper-left window hierarchically shows entities in a workflow model (or package) including exception specification. The upper-center window is a canvas in which process designers graphically design their processes. The upper-right window is a script viewer. When a process is drawn in the upper-center window, the process is translated into XPDL or WPDL dynamically and viewed in the script viewer. The bottom window has the information of entities such as relevant data, relevant data types, and applications to be used. The designers may refer to the information to specify exceptional conditions.

5   Conclusion

In this paper, we have developed an exception specification method for a workflow definition and an exception handling mechanism of workflow system. To implement our exception specification method, we have extended XPDL of WFMC. The central idea of our exception specification is to isolate exception handling activities (or handler) from normal activities and clarify the control flow of a process. In spite of some difficulties due to the complexity of the event-transition approach, we believe this goal has been achieved in a way because exceptions can be specified in structured way in our scheme and they can be specified using GUI. Another contribution of this paper is that principal workflow characteristics have been considered and reflected in the proposed mechanism. Furthermore, the scheme utilizes well-designed patterns. In the future, we plan to apply our exception specification and handling mechanism for a real-world process especially for inter-organizational workflows.

References

1. Workflow Management Coalition, Workflow Process Definition Interface – XML Process Definition Language, Document number WfMC TC-1024, May 22, 2001.
2. J. Eder and W. Liebhart, Contributions to Exception Handling in Workflow Management, EDBT Workshop on Workflow Management Systems, Valencia, Spain, 1998.
3. J. Eder and W. Liebhart, The workflow activity model WAMO, Proc. Of CoopIS-95, Vienna, Austria, pp.87–98, 1995.
4. C. Hagen and G. Alonso, Exception Handling in Workflow Management Systems, IEEE Transactions on Software Engineering, vol.26, no.10, pp.943–958, October 2000.
5. C. Hagen and G. Alonso, Flexible Exception Handling in the OPERA Process Support System, International Conference on Distributed Computing Systems, pp.526–533, 1998.
6. F. Casati, Specification and Implementation of Exceptions in Workflow Management Systems, ACM Transactions on Database Systems, vol.24, no.3, pp.405–451, 1999.
7. D. K. W. Chiu, Q. Li and K. Karlapalem, ADOME-WFMS: Towards Cooperative Handling of Workflow Exceptions, ECOOP Workshop 2000: Advances in Exception Handling Techniques, Lecture Notes in Computer Science, vol.2022, pp.271–288, 2001.
8. Z. Luo, A. Sheth, K. Kochut, and J. Miller, Exception Handling in Workflow Systems, Applied Intelligence: the International Journal of AI, Neural Networks, and Complex Problem-Solving Technologies, vol.13, no.2, pp.125–147, 2000.
9. D. S. Han, J. Y. Shim and C. S. Yu, ICU/COWS: A Distributed Transactional Workflow System Supporting Multiple Workflow Types, IEICE Transactions on Information Systems, vol.E83-D, no.7, July 2000.
10. J. Y. Shim, D. S. Han and M. K. Lee, Exception Analysis of Structured Workflow Definition, Proc. of the 20th IASTED International Conference on Applied Informatics, Innsbruck, Austria, 2002.
11. S. I. Lee, D. S. Han and D. Lee, A Pattern for Managing Distributed Workflows, Proc. of Pattern Languages of Programs(PLoP) 2000 Conference, Monticello, IL, 2000.
12. M. K. Lee, D. S. Han and J. Y. Shim, Set-Based Access Conflicts Analysis of Concurrent Workflow Definition, Information Processing Letters, vol.80, no.4, Nov. 2001.
13. E. Gamma, R. Helm, R. Johnson and J. Vlissides, Design Patterns: Element of Reusable Object Oriented Software, Addison-Wesley, 1995.

Key Issues and Experiences in Development of Distributed Workflow Management Systems

Hongchen Li[1], Yun Yang[1], and Meilin Shi[2]

[1] School of Information Technology, Swinburne University of Technology
PO Box 218, Hawthorn, VIC 3122 Australia
{hli, yyang}@it.swin.edu.au
[2] Department of Computer Science & Technology
Tsinghua University, Beijing, P.R. China, 100084
shi@csnet4.cs.tsinghua.edu.cn

Abstract. Research on workflow technology has been promoting the development of workflow management systems (WfMSs). Compared to centralised WfMSs, the development of distributed WfMSs are much more complex. Therefore, it needs to analyse their development from the software engineering perspective. This paper first presents the development lifecycle of distributed WfMSs, and then discusses issues of enterprise-wide workflow modeling and implementation of distributed WfMSs. Furthermore, we report on a case study and discuss issues related to the implementation of some components.

1 Introduction

To develop a workflow application, selected business processes are abstracted from the real world and specified using a language, called *workflow specification language*. The result of abstraction is called *workflow specification*. The workflow specification is used by WfMSs to create and control the execution of workflow instances, i.e., representations of real-world processes.

Despite the effort having been made by the workflow community during the past years, it is recognised that WfMSs are still not very successful. There are a lot of open issues and limitations in the existing workflow technology. These issues can be broadly divided into *workflow modeling* issues and *WfMS implementation* issues [2]. The *workflow modeling* issues mainly concern about representation, analysis, evaluation and optimisation of business processes, while the *WfMS implementation* issues highlight development, testing and evaluation of WfMSs.

As far as the development of distributed WfMSs is concerned, to the best of our knowledge, no analysis has been done on this issue from the software engineering lifecycle perspective. In this paper, we first present a development lifecycle of distributed WfMSs, and then open our discussion along this development lifecycle. We, however, mainly discuss key issues related to the development of distributed WfMSs based on our work on workflow management.

X. Zhou, Y. Zhang, and M.E. Orlowska (Eds.): APWeb 2003, LNCS 2642, pp. 507–512, 2003.

2 Development Lifecycle of Distributed WfMSs

Since a distributed WfMS is a kind of software, its development should follow the rationale of software engineering, having the lifecycle including requirement analysis, workflow modeling, architecture definition, component implementation, system testing, running & maintenance, as shown in Figure 1. A distributed WfMS has the similar development lifecycle with other software systems. However, the phrases have their own connotations for the development of distributed WfMSs.

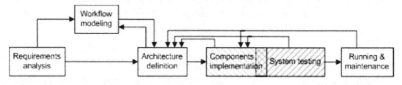

Figure 1: Development lifecycle of distributed WfMS

Given the space limit, we only address requirements analysis, workflow modeling, architecture definition, and components implementation in the development lifecycle, without system testing and running & maintenance.

3 Requirements Analysis

Requirements for Workflow Modeling: Workflow modeling denotes the creation and storage of workflow specifications [10]. Underlying the specification language is a *workflow metamodel*, which is a domain-oriented abstraction, primarily including a set of modeling concepts. The workflow metamodel is the basis for the construction of workflow specification languages. In order to support distributed and dynamic workflow applications, a workflow metamodel should have such properties as *expressiveness, usability, enactability, formal semantics, and flexibility*.

Requirements for System Implementation: Requirements for system implementation depend on the application domain. Some requirements are mapped onto the functionality of distributed WfMSs. Others are the properties owned by the WfMSs. Currently, in order to support enterprise-wide workflow management, some properties are identified for distributed WfMSs, e.g., *scalability, reliability, availability, dynamic reconfiguration, integrability, and interoperability*.

4 Enterprise-Wide Workflow Modeling

Up to now, many workflow metamodels have been proposed by workflow researchers, such as Petri Nets [1], Event-Condition-Action (ECA) [4], Hypermedia Structure [8], State-Activity Chart [16], Concurrent Transaction logic (*CTR*) [5], Script Language [6], State-Entity-Activity-Model (SEAM) [2], Workflow Loop [13], and Three-dimensional Workflow Model [11].

Despite the effort having been taken by the Workflow Management Coalition (WfMC) and Object Management Group (OMG), no standard metamodel has been proposed so far. How to model and specify workflows correctly, we believe, is one of the most important issues in the field of workflow research. Current research on the workflow modeling issues usually involves using formal or semiformal methods to model business processes at a high level. This kind of conceptual models is useful for the purpose of workflow analysis and verification, but does not suit for implementation of workflow management. On the other hand, research on the workflow implementation issues uses informal methods at a concrete level to specify different aspects of workflows. The result has good properties for workflow management, but cannot ensure the correctness of workflows.

5 Implementation of Distributed WfMSs

The system implementation primarily consists of the architecture definition and the components implementation in the development lifecycle of distributed WfMSs (see Figure 1). In this section, we focus on discussing the architecture definition of distributed WfMSs. The components implementation will be addressed with a case study in Section 6.

5.1 Conceptual Architecture

Logically, a distributed WfMS consists of a number of components, each of which encapsulates a specific part of workflow management functionality. From the viewpoint of service supply, the conceptual architecture of a distributed WfMS can be defined in a three-layer model, i.e. *Repository Layer, Infrastructure Layer,* and *User Layer* from the bottom up (see Figure 2). Each layer consists of a few components. The *Repository Layer* provides a persistent storage that is used by the high-level components. The *Infrastructure Layer* contains the primary functionality of workflow management, e.g. workflow engine, transaction manager, exception handler. The *User Layer* provides some tools for workflow users.

5.2 Implementation Architecture

An implementation architecture provides a framework for the integration of components. The distributed architecture has a better performance than the centralised one in support of enterprise-wide workflow management. Along the distribution dimension, J. Miller et al. define five kinds of run-time architectures for workflow management, from highly centralised to fully distributed [14]. Based on the conceptual taxonomy, K. Kim differentiates four types of architectures, from passive architecture to dual-active architecture [9]. In [15], three architecture variations are distinguished from the existing distributed WfMSs *as replicated servers, localised servers*, and *full distribution*.

At present, distributed object-based or lightweight agent-based architectures provide a better infrastructure for dynamic workflow applications and for making the workflow management more integrated. A lot of distributed WfMSs are realised based on middleware products, e.g. WIDE [3]. Recently, a lightweight approach is proposed to meet the needs of highly dynamic business environment. In this approach, the workflow enactment is achieved by a collection of agents, e.g. Serendipity-II [7].

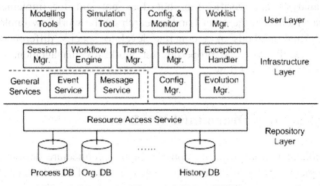

Figure 2: Conceptual architecture of distributed WfMSs

6   Case Study for Components Implementation

In this section, we illustrate our approach to the development of distributed WfMSs using a case study from our project, in which we have developed a web-based distributed WfMS, namely ECCS (E-Commerce-oriented Cooperative System) originated from [11].

6.1   System Overview

To meet the requirements for enterprise-wide workflow modeling discussed in the previous section, we define a workflow metamodel named *three-dimensional workflow model*, which is composed of three sub-models: *process model*, *information model*, and *organisation model* [11].

The architecture of ECCS is composed of multiple domains, each of which is composed of a local server, namely CEServer, and multiple clients, as shown in Figure 3. CEServer runs on WINNT/Windows operating system, and interacts with clients or other domain servers through HTTP and TCP/IP respectively.

6.2   Components Implementation

The remainder of this section discusses the implementation of some components which relate closely to workflow management.

Resource Manager: Most existing WfMSs are directly based on a database system and extend some functions for resource management. But this extension is not enough for the resource management in distributed WfMSs. For this situation, component *Resource manager* (see Figure 3) is realised as a middleware providing some services for workflow execution.

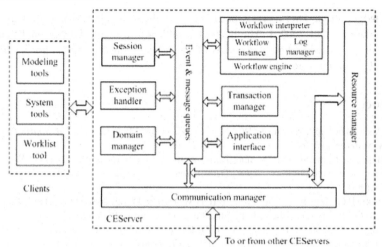

Figure 3: The ECCS architecture

Workflow Engine: The background about workflow execution has been presented in [17]. In ECCS, component *workflow engine*, consisting of *workflow interpreter*, *workflow instance*, and *log manager*, is created dynamically in response to an event of workflow initiation. The *workflow instance* contains information related to workflow execution.

Exception Handler: Like other distributed WfMSs, rule-based approach is adopted in ECCS for exception handling. The exception handling logic is expressed as extended ECA rules, which are stored in a rule repository. An event will be triggered by the exception source when an exception occurs. The event is captured by component *exception handler* (see Figure 3).

Transaction Manager: Transaction management in distributed WfMSs is far more complex than that of database systems. Component *Transaction manager* is introduced to maintain dependences between concurrent transactions and to coordinate their execution. The transaction model in ECCS has a hierarchical structure and a relaxed isolation property to support long-running activities [12]. Resources occupied by a transaction are released during its execution. A compensation-based recovery protocol is used to achieve atomicity and durability of transactions.

7 Conclusions and Future Work

This paper has discussed some key issues in development of distributed WfMSs from the software development perspective. These issues may be interrelated and interdependent. Sometimes, if a best solution for all these issues is impossible, tradeoff is necessary for acquiring a better overall performance.

Our research group is aiming at developing a lightweight, web-based, and dynamic distributed WfMS. Issues and experiences addressed in this paper will be paid more attention in the future workflow research.

Acknowledgements. This work is partly supported by Swinburne VC Strategic Research Initiative Fund 2002-4. The authors would like to thank the National Science Foundation in China for the past support of the research during first author's study at Tsinghua University, P.R. China.

References

1. M. Aalst: The Application of Petri Nets to Workflow Management. *The Journal of Circuits, Systems and Computers*, 8(1): (1998) 21–66
2. A. Bajaj, S. Ram: SEAM: A State-Entity-Activity-Model for a Well-Defined Workflow Development Methodology. *IEEE Transactions on Knowledge and Data Engineering*, 14(2): (2002) 415–431
3. F.Casati, P.Grefen, B. Pernici et al: WIDE Workflow Model and Architecture. Technical Report, Politecnico di Milano, Italy, http://dis.sema.es/projects/WIDE, (1996)
4. G. Cugola, E. Nitto, A. Fuggetta. The JEDI Event-Based Infrastructure and Its Application to the Development of the OPSS WFMS. *IEEE Transactions on Software Engineering*, 27(9): (2001) 827–850
5. H. Davulcu, M. Kifer et al: Logic Based Modeling and Analysis of Workflows. In *Proc. of the ACM Symposium in PODS'98*, Seattle USA, (1998) 25–33
6. N. Glance, D.S.Pagani, R.Pareschi: Generalized Process Structure Grammars (GPSG) for Flexible Representations of Work. In *Proc. of ACM CSCW'96*, Cambridge, MA USA, (1996) 180–189
7. J. Grundy, M. Apperley, J. Hosking et al: A Decentralized Architecture for Software Process Modeling and Enactment. *IEEE Internet Computing*, Sept.-Oct.: (1998) 53–62
8. J. Haake, W.Wang: Flexible Support for Business Processes: Extending Cooperative Hypermedia with Process Support. In *Proceedings of ACM Group'97*: (1997) 341–350
9. K. Kim: A Framework and Taxonomy for Distributed Workflow Architectures. *Telecommunications Review*, SK Telecom, (10): (2001) 781–792
10. M. Kradolfer: A Workflow Metamodel Supporting Dynamic, Reuse-Based Model Evolution. *PhD Thesis*, Dept. of Information Technology, University of Zurich, (2000)
11. H. Li: On Workflow-based CSCW Platforms. *PhD Thesis*, Dept. of Computer Science & Technology, Tsinghua University, China, (2001)
12. H. Li, M. Shi, X. Chen: Concurrency Control Algorithm for Transactional Workflows. *Journal of Software*, Supplement: (2001) 1–8
13. R.Medina-Mora, T.Winograd et al: The Action Workflow Approach to Workflow Management Technology. In *Proc. of ACM CSCW'92*: (1992) 281–288
14. J. Miller, A. Sheth, K. Kochut, X. Wang: CORBA-Based Run-Time Architectures for Workflow Management Systems. *Journal of Database Management*, Special Issue on Multidatabases, 7(1): (1996) 16–27
15. D. Tombros: An Event- and Repository-Based Component Framework for Workflow System Architecture. *PhD Thesis*, Dept. of Info. Tech., Univ. of Zurich. (1999)
16. D. Wodtke, J. Weissenfels et al: The Mentor Project: Steps Towards Enterprise-Wide Workflow Management. In *Prof. of the 12th IEEE Intl. Conf. on Data Engineering*, New Orleans, LA, Mar. (1996)
17. WFMC: Workflow Management Coalition: The Workflow Reference Model. TC00-1003, (1995)

Intelligent Search for Distributed Information Sources Using Heterogeneous Neural Networks

Hui Yang and Minjie Zhang

School of Information Technology and Computer Science
University of Wollongong
Wollongong, 2500, Australia
{hy92, minjie}@uow.edu.au

Abstact. As the number and diversity of distributed information sources on the Internet exponentially increase, various search services are developed to help the users to locate relevant information. But they still exist some drawbacks such as the difficulty of mathematically modeling retrieval process, the lack of adaptivity and the indiscrimination of search. This paper shows how heterogeneous neural networks can be used in the design of an intelligent distributed information retrieval (DIR) system. In particular, three typical neural network models - Kohoren's SOFM Network, Hopfield Network, and Feed Forward Network with Back Propagation algorithm are introduced to overcome the above drawbacks in current research of DIR by using their unique properties. This preliminary investigation suggests that Neural Networks are useful tools for intelligent search for distributed information sources.

1 Introduction

Due to the exponential growth of the Internet as well as advances in telecommunication technologies, online information sources and users have grown at an unprecedented rate during the past twenty years. However, overwhelming information online and heterogeneously distributed over the Internet makes the users difficult to locate the most relevant information at a very low cost with minimal effort.

In order to overcome this difficulty in retrieving information from the Internet, various search services such as AltaVista, Excite, Lycos attempt to maintain full-text indexes of the Internet. However, relying on a single standard search engine has limitations such as incompleteness of retrieval documents and inconsistence of ranking algorithms. The limitations of the search services have led to introduction of meta-search engines, e.g, MetaCrawler and SavvySearch. The primary advantages of current meta-search engines are the ability to combine the results of multiple search engines, and the ability to provide a consistent user interface for searching these engines, but they still exist the following main weaknesses:

- Mathematically modeling retrieval process:
  The retrievals are based on the matching of terms between documents and the user queries, which are often suffering from either inexact and ambiguous descriptions of the user queries; or missing relevant documents which are not indexed by the key

X. Zhou, Y. Zhang, and M.E. Orlowska (Eds.): APWeb 2003, LNCS 2642, pp. 513–524, 2003.

words used in a query, but by concepts with similar meaning to those in the query. All these make retrieval process hard to model mathematically.

- Lacking adaptivity:

The semantic vagueness of keywords in both documents and queries makes the meta-search services low precision and recall rate. Obviously, learning ability is needed for offering the potential of the meta-search services that automatically modify their indices to improve the probability of relevant retrieval.

- Indiscriminate search

Most of the meta-search services usually indiscriminately broadcast the user query to all underlying information sources and merger the results submitted by those information sources. It is inefficient and impractical to search such a huge information space in current research.

Neural networks (NN) as methods of information processing have the ability to deal with partially correct or incomplete input data. Neural networks are considered as good mechanisms to learn the mapping relationship or rules even without knowing the detail of mathematical model between input data and output data. Also, it has already been demonstrated that neural networks can provide good performance as classifiers in areas such as speech and image recognition [10].

In this paper, we propose a framework of a distributed information retrieval system based on heterogeneous neural networks in which three different neural network models are used as major components. This proposed approach attempts to overcome the above limitations in current research in the field by using the main capabilities of artificial neural network, which are intelligence, adaptivity, and classification. Due to different characteristics of different stages during distributed information retrieval, a single neural network technique looks to be inappropriately applied to the whole procedure of distributed information retrieval. So we make use of the unique characteristics of three different types of neural network models - Kohonen's SOFM Network, Hopfield Network and Feed Forword Network with Back Propagation to separately deal with 3 major tasks, namely, information source selection, information extraction and fusion, and relevance feedback during distributed information retrieval.

The remainder of this paper is organized as follows. In Section 2, we first present an overview of neural network techniques for information retrieval. In Section 3, we begin with a description of the basic features of our proposed distributed information retrieval system's construction and operation. Section 4 highlights the structure and operation of three different types of neural networks to address intelligent search for distributed information sources. Finally, conclusions and future work are provided in Section 5.

2   Neural Network and Information Retrieval (IR)

As one of the important techniques in Artificial Intelligence (AI), neural networks have been studied with respect to their learning processes and structures in the hope of mimic human-like behavior. Spread activation search, adaptivity and learning ability, as the significant characteristics of neural networks, seem to be well suited for information retrieval tasks.

Therefore, neural network techniques have drawn attention from researchers in computer science and information science in recent years and been proved to provide great opportunities to enhance the information processing and retrieval capabilities of current information storage and retrieval systems.

Mozer [9] used a two-level neural network with document and term nodes. He used inhibitory links between every pair of documents which were used in "winner take all" network to pick a single alternative in the PDP model.

In the **AIR** system [1], Belew proposed a connectionist approach to build a representation for author, index term and document nodes to overcome the imprecise and vagarious keyword description. A powerful learning algorithm had been developed to automatically modify the weights on existing links by user relevant feedback.

In Kwok's work [8], he also developed a simple 3-layer neural network together with a modified Hebbian correlational algorithm that was used to reformulate probabilistic information retrieval so as to achieve optimal ranking.

Chen and his colleagues [2] developed a single-layer, interconnected, weighted/labeled network for concept-based information retrieval.

We believe that neural networks and their functions are promising for applications in IR and may provide a viable solution to search problem for distributed information sources on the Internet.

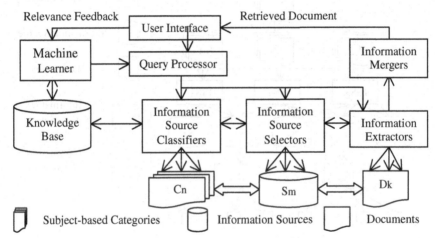

Fig. 1. A Framework of an Information Retrieval System Based On Heterogeneous Neural Networks

3   A Distributed Information Retrieval System Based on Heterogeneous Neural Networks

In this section, we will describe a framework of a distributed information retrieval system based on heterogeneous neural networks called (**HNNDIR**) and the operations for intelligently searching distributed information sources.

3.1   A Framework of HNNDIR System

First, we present the overall framework of **HNNDIR** system. **HNNDIR** system is comprised of several sophisticated components, three of which are built based on neural network techniques. Figure 1 shows the main components and the control flows among them. The function of each component is defined as follows:

User Interface (**UI**). It interacts with the user by receiving user queries and presenting relevant information, including searching results and explanations. In addition, it also observes the user's behavior and provides the *Machine Learner* with the information about the user's relevant feedback to searching results.

Query Processor (**QP**). It is responsible for formulating an initial set of query terms and for revising the query terms as new search terms which are learned in the *Machine Learner*. It firstly uses a stop-list to delete non-useful terms and Porter's stemming algorithm to normalize the query, and then it transforms the query into a set of index terms. Besides, it accepts a set of reformulated search terms that have been refined by the *Machine Learner*.

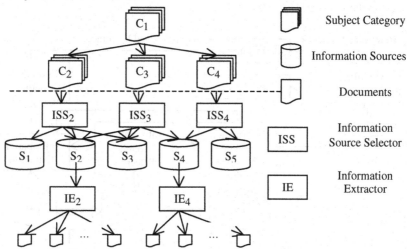

Fig. 2. Hierarchical Organization of Information Sources in HHNNIRSystem

Information Source Classifiers (**ISCs**). To more effectively search information sources available on the Internet and to decrease the probability of analyzing unrelated information, a subject directory with a hierarchical architecture is constructed shown as Figure 2. The tree hierarchy contains nodes at different level indicating the subjects of interests to the users. The leaf nodes point to specific and unambiguous subjects. The nodes of the higher level deal with more extensive and broader topics than those of the subordinate level. The leaf nodes only treat available information sources. The **ISC** uses a multilayered neural network clustering algorithm employing the Kohonen Self-Organization Feature Map (SOFM) to partition the Internet information sources into distinct subject categories according to their content. SOFM will be described in detail in the next section.

Once query index terms are created, the **ISC** browses the subject directory to locate the appropriate partition to launch the keyword search. A series of filtering steps are executed through imposing progressively processed demands and quality standards. During each filtering stage, a test is performed, which will prevent a set of non-relevant information sources from searching at the next stage if it fails.

Information Source Selectors (**ISSs**). The **ISS** contains numerous weight matrices identifying information sources belonging to a particular category. The pertinent characteristics of each information source are stored within each matrix, which consist of such things as its retrieval time and cost, and relevant keywords used for retrieval. The matrices are used by a simple 3-layer Feed Forward network with Back Propagation (BP) learning algorithm which will be discussed in detail in the next section. Once the subject category, whose region is what the user is looking for, is determined, the corresponding **ISS** is activated. A ranked set of information sources is finally produced. The ranking reflects the evaluated relevance of the information sources to the query.

Information Extractors (**IEs**). To reduce the volume of original documents in each information source and to simply represent these documents, the pretreatment is required to extract predefined elements such as a set of representative index terms from these documents text. The **IE** uses co-occurrence function on these extracted elements and transforms them into 2-dimensional binary vectors. Finally, it stores the vectors in the form of matrices.

Information Fusioner (**IF**). The **IF** mergers retrieval documents from different information sources, removes the contradiction, complements the incompleteness, and submits an integrated ranked list of documents to the user.

Machine Learner (**ML**). After the users return the retrieved documents which have been marked as being relevance to their query, a relevance feedback learning process in the **ML** is invoked. During this learning process, the relevance information is analyzed together with the term-association matrixes stored in the **ML**, and some word terms are identified and ranked for their potential usefulness as search terms. Application domain knowledge from the *Knowledge Base* (**KB**) is acquired for providing subject-specific information that suggests alternative terms for searching and for helping articulate the user's needs. The whole process is monitored by a 3-layer NN model with the Hopfield Net learning algorithm [5].

Knowledge Base (**KB**). The **KB** contains various sub-symbolic representations of subject categories. Each is obtained by analyzing the co-occurrence probabilities of keywords in documents in a specific subject category. Such a sub-symbolic representation would suggest the important terms and their weighted relationships with the subject category, which should be used by the **ML** to reformulate precise search terms in light of particular characteristics of a specific subject domain.

All of these components are integrated in **HNNDIR** system. The construction, adaptation and integration of these components were a nontrivial process. In the following subsection, we describe its operations for intelligently searching distributed information sources using the above components.

3.2 The Operation of HNNDIR System

To better illustrate the mechanisms used either within or between **HNNDIR**'s components, we describe a simple information retrieval process that consists of the following 4 stages: query processing, information source selection, information extraction and fusion, and relevance feedback learning, to be executed consecutively.

3.2.1   Query Processing

Query processing is initiated when the user submits his/her information need. The **QP** analyzes the user's query and converts it into a initial set of index terms by eliminating non-content words and stemming, which may be represented by the vector $Q=\{q_1,\ q_2,\ \cdots,\ q_n\}$.

3.2.2   Information Source Selection

The **ISC** starts the process of analyzing the query terms using the knowledge of the **KB** component on subject categories and its own top-down approach to find the most likely subject categories from the subject directory. The **ISC** consults the **KB**, activates related categories in the hierarchical architecture, and then lists the categories that match the query terms.

For each large region, a recursive process of analyzing subject categories in the subject directory would be undertaken. Guided by heuristics, the **LSC** begins to browse the subject directory from the highest layer, and progressively refine the search region by choosing the subject category with maximal likeliness with respect to the user query in the same layer until to the lowest layer (the leaf layer).

Once the preferred subject category is determined, the corresponding **LSS** for this particular category c_i starts to choose the most likely information sources from the subject category (see Figure 2).

3.2.3   Information Extraction and Fusion

When the information on the information sources associated with the relevance documents in response to the query is transferred to the **IE**, the **IE** is activated and the index term matching process is initiated. In the **IE**, representative index terms from documents in a particular information source s are represented by a 2-dimension binary vector, which is $D=\langle d,\ r\ \rangle$, where $d=\{d_1,\ d_2,\ \cdots;\ d_t\}$, t is the number of documents in the information source, and $r=\{r_1 y_1,\ r_2 y_2,\ \cdots;\ r_n y_n\}$ in the vector space V^n, r is the index term and y is the term weight. So the size of the term-by-document weight matrix D is $t \times n$. The document ranking function could be

$$f(d_i)=d_i \cdot Q = \sum_{j,k} r_{ij} y_{ij} w_k q_k = \sum_{j=1}^{n}\sum_{k=1}^{n} r_{ij} c_{jk} q_k = d_i C Q^T \tag{1}$$

Finally, a ranked document list for the information source s is produced as the actual response of the Feed Forward network for a given query Q. The m top-ranked documents will be chosen as the final retrieval result of the information source s that will be given to the **IF**.

The **IF** integrates the retrieved documents from different information sources into a single integrated ranked document list which is submitted to the **UI** to display.

3.2.4   Relevance Feedback Learning

The user gives a relevance rating for the retrieval documents displayed on the **UI** after the user scans the search results. The documents that have been marked relevant by the user are analyzed by the **ML**. When this set of documents as the input nodes are inputted into the Hopfield Neural Network in the **ML**, by using the responding term-association matrix stored in the **ML** and the learning ability of the Hopfield network, some appropriate search terms are triggered and used to refine or reformulate the user's information need which is prepared for the next search.

4   Research Issues in HNNDIR System's Design

The specific system design and research methods adopted by **HNNDIR** system are discussed in this section.

4.1   Relevance Feedback Learning Based on Hopfield Net

Our relevance feedback learning component is based on a variant of the Hopfield Network [5], which incorporates the basic Hopfield net iteration and convergence ideas. The Hopfield network was introduced as the best known of the autoassociation memories with feedback where when an input pattern is presented to the network, the network will yield a response associated with the exemplar pattern to which the input pattern is sufficiently similar.

Here we use a three-layer neural network to implement the relevance feedback learning. Figure 3 shows the configuration of such a network. Document vector $D^I = \{d_1^I, d_2^I, \cdots, d_p^I\}$ is the input to the network. Each node in the input layer D represents a document d_i^I, $d_i^I \in D^I$. Hopfield layer (hidden layer) T is a layer of fully connected nodes which can function as an associative memory. Each node in Hopfield layer T represents a term t_j, $t_j \in T$. The output layer consists of only one node, which pools the input of all the nodes in Hopfield layer T. The weight of the connection between the node d_i^I and the node t_j is denoted by β_{ij}, which represents the degree of their association. There is a bidirectional connection between the node t_j and the node t_k, and the connectional weight is denoted with α_{jk}. The weight γ_j is the output of the node t_j.

Each connection β_{ij} is associated with a constant weight representing the approximate implication strength of the node t_j and the node d_i^I:

$$\beta_{ij} = \frac{tf_{ji} \cdot idf_j}{max\_tf_i \cdot \log n} \tag{2}$$

Where tf_{ji} is the frequency that a term t_j appears in a document d_i^I; idf_j is the inverse of document frequency corresponding to t_j and maximum tf value of the index terms in the document d_i^I [12]; n is the total number of documents D.

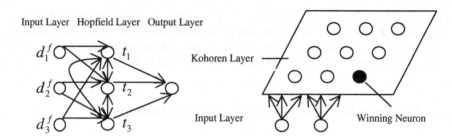

Fig. 3. A vaiant 3-layer Hopfield Network   **Fig. 4.** A Two-Dimention Kohoren SOFM Model

The weight α_{jk} between the node t_j and the node t_k is the similarities computed based on co-occurrence analysis which reveals the explicit semantic relationship between index terms in a particular subject category.

Having the initial input and the weighted links in Hopfield layer, the activated node t_j updates in the Hopfield model over time. At each time step, nodes in Hopfield layer are activated in parallel by performing an associated energy function.

The above process repeats until node outputs remains unchanged. The final output will be the set of concepts which best describe the original search terms.

4.2   An SOFM Based Approach for Categorizing Distributed Information Sources

There are large numbers of information sources maintained by different organizations which deal with specific domains of knowledge on the Internet. Although some Internet services such as search engines are useful to help users explore and find what they want in such a vast information space, they do not provide any effective method for organizing the information sources. It is desirable to provide an effective way to organize and manage information sources.

Categorization or classification is a useful method for managing distributed information sources. Although traditional classifiers and clustering algorithms have produced encouraging result [6], they remain some shortcomings such that the training stage maybe very complex and require large number of storage and computation. Neural net classifier can compute matching score in parallel, and continuously modify the connection weight during training or matching phase for improving performance.

One of the significant characteristics of the Kohoren model is unsupervised clustering technique which can be used to reduce the amount of supervised training data required.

The Kohoren net architecture consists of two layers, an input layer and a Kohorn layer (a output layer). These two layers are fully connected. Each input layer neuron is connected to each output layer neuron via a variable connection weight. The Kohoren layer is one or two dimension grids (lattices) where each node represents a cluster center as shown in Figure 4. A unique property of the SOFM is that cluster centers aggregate geometrically within the network output layer.

The goal of a SOFM is to create effectively a meaningful topographically organization map of the different feature of exemplar patters. Determination of the winning output layer neuron is the neuron whose weight vector has a minimum of the Euclidean norm distance from the input vector. The reason for the use of Euclidean distance to select a winning neuron is that it does not require weights or input vectors to be normalized. The output of the SOFM model is to select a winning neighbor surrounding the winning neuron instead of a single winner.

In order to better organize and manage a great amount of distributed information sources on the Internet, we propose a multiple layered graphical SOFM approach.

The input vector, S, is denoted as following:

$$S = \{d_1, \quad d_2, \quad \cdots, \quad d_p\} \tag{3}$$

Where S represents an information source, p is the number of documents that the information source contains.

In the Kohoren layer, we establish a set of clusters (with associated cluster center) such that the distance between an input vector and the closest cluster center serves to classify the input vector. The set of clusters is expressed as $C = \{c_1, \quad c_2, \quad \cdots, \quad c_k\}$, where k is the number of clusters. The vector, M, represents the cluster center for each of the k cluster. So the vector M is expressed as $M = \{m_1, \quad m_2, \quad \cdots, \quad m_k\}$.

The weight from input neuron d_i ($1 \leq i \leq p$) to output neuron $m_j (1 \leq j \leq k)$ is represented with w_{ij}. To compute w_{ij}, we firstly extract some meaningful words from the document d_i by using a stop-list to delete nonuseful terms and porter's stemming algorithm to normalize the index terms such as "mouse" and "mice". Secondly, use the top (most frequently occurring) n terms to construct the input characteristic vector space, namely, $d_i = (t_1, \quad t_2, \quad \cdots, \quad t_n)$. The connect weight w_{ij} is defined as

$$w_{ij} = \begin{cases} \dfrac{tf_{ij} \cdot idf_j}{max\_tf \cdot \log p} & if \quad t_i \in M \left(1 \leq i \leq n\right) \\ 0 & otherwise \end{cases} \tag{4}$$

Giving the input vector, S, compute distances I_j between the input and each output node m_j by using Euclidean distance function and select the winning neuron m_{k^*}. with a minimum of the Euclidean norm distance.

A neighbor function can be utilized to update the connection weight of the winning neuron and those connection weights of the appropriate neighborhood nodes so that the clusters response may be refined. Finally, the system exits when no noticeable change to the Feature Map has occurs. Apply the above steps recursively to classify information source S to a subject-specific category.

As we known, information sources are constructed in a hierarchical architecture. So our M-SOFM network is organized in the same way. The information source S is firstly classified to a particular category in the top-layer map with Kohoren's SOFM algorithm, and then is sequentially classified to the category on the subordinate layer until the lowest layer (the leaf layer).

As we know, the documents that an information source contains maybe involve in different subjects from the relative domain. For example, if an information source storages a large amount of documents concerning to Neural Network and Information Retrieval, the information source will be reasonably classified into two subjects, separately, "Neural Network" and "Information Retrieval". So we improve the SOFM algorithm on the leaf layer during the processing of the leaf layer. Instead of only selecting the winning neuron m_{k^*}, the choose of the winning neurons will be a set of output layer neurons that have small Euclidean norm distance I_j.

4.3   Feed Forward Network with Back Propagation Algorithm

In the **ISC**, **ISS** and **IE** three components in **HNNDIR** system, we all use the Feed Forward networks to seperately choose the appropriate subject category, the most likely information sources containing relevance documents and the most relevant documents with respect to a given query. These three Feed Forward networks have similar structures and operations, so here we only introduce a simple 3-layer Feed Forward network in the **IE** component to explain the exact operation of such neural network.

This network is also semantic network and works in a spreading activation model. Due to the property of its inference association, spreading activation is theoretically believed to have the potential to outperform some traditional IR techniques, but the experimental results done by Salto & Buckley [11] indicate that simple spreading activation model may not be sufficiently powerful to gain satisfactory retrieval results without a good learning algorithm. So our 3-layer Feed Forward network adopts Back Propagation (BP) algorithm which makes the network to be trained in a supervised manner.

The reason that choosing BP algorithm as the learning algorithm is that BP algorithm provides a way to calculate the gradient of the error function efficiently using the chain rule of differentiation and it adjusts the connection weights of the network in accordance with an error-correct rule in order to minimize the total error over the course of many learning iterations [4].

The structure of such a 3-layer Feed Forward network with BP algorithm is shown in Figure 5. In the input layer Q, Q is represented by the vector $Q = \{q_1, \ q_2, \ \cdots, \ q_n\}$, q_i is a query term. There is a connection link between each node q_i and the corresponding term-by-document node t_j in the hidden layer T if it exists. The weight of this connection is denoted w_{ij}. There is a bi-directional and asymmetric connection between a document node d_k in the output layer and each of the term-by-document nodes corresponding to terms in the document. The weight of the connection from the node t_j and the node d_k is denoted a_{jk}.

Basically, BP learning consists of 2 phrases through the different layers of the network: a training phase and a retrieval phase. Before using it for retrieval purposes, the network must be trained. The weight of the query nodes is fixed at 1.0. The connection weight w_{ij} between the node q_i and the node t_j is computed by

$$w_{ij} = \frac{q_i}{\left(\sum\limits_{i=1}^{n} q_i^{\,2}\right)^{1/2}} \tag{5}$$

The connection weight a_{jk} is determined by using traditional IR techniques such as the vector space model based on TF×IDF.

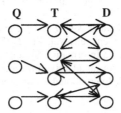

Fig. 5. A 3-Layer Feed Forward Network With BP

Run the network and obtain output layer values by spreading inputs through the network layer by layer using the sigmoid function, and then adapt weight using BP difference equation. Finally, If the total error falls below a preestablished tolerance error threshold or remains unchanged, the network is said to be converged, otherwise start for new training cycle.

When the training phase is halted, the term-association weight matrices are produced, which are stored for further use in the retrieval phase.

During the retrieval phase, when the **QP** creates a new query vector Q, the NN is activated. The activation spreads through the related nodes layer by layer using the weight matrices produced during the training phase. The weight matrices remain unchanged during the retrieval phase. Finally, a ranked list of documents is produced as the actual response of the network, which reflects the evaluated relevance of the documents to the query.

5   Conclusion and Future Works

We have shown that a heterogeneous neural network structure together with the necessary learning algorithms can be used for distributed information retrieval in a flexible fashion. The framework of a distributed information retrieval system with heterogeneous neural network is given where three major components separately make use of different types of neural networks to solve the different tasks during the process of distributed information retrieval. We wish that this preliminary investigation suggests that neural networks provide a sound basis for designing an intelligent information retrieval system.

This is of course only the first step. Our work is currently at a prototypical stage. We still need to explore more appropriate and effective NN techniques for this system. We will report with more details on the complete architecture and on the evaluation of the prototype in further work.

Acknowledgement. This research was supported by a large grant from the Australian Research Council under contract DP0211282.

References

1. Belew, Y. K.: Adaptive Information Retrieval. Proceedings of the 12th International Conference on Research and Development in Information Retrieval. Cambridge, Massachusetts (1989) 11–20
2. Chen, H., Lynch, K. J., Basu, K. and Ng, D. T.: Generating, integrating, and activating thesauri for concept-based document retrieval, Int. J. IEEE EXPERT, Special Series on Artificial Intelligence in Text-based Information Systems, Vol. 8(2). (1993) 25–34
3. Crestani, F.: Learning strategies for an adaptive information retrieval system using neural networks. Proceedings of IEEE International Conference on Neural Networks, Vol. 1. (1993) 244 –249
4. Haykin, S.: Neural Networks: a comprehensive foundation. 2th edn. Upper Saddle Rever, New Jersey, Prentice Hall (1999)
5. Hopfield, J. J.: Neural Network and physical systems with collective computational abilities. Proceedings of the National Academy of Sciences, Vol. 79(4). USA (1982) 2554–2558
6. Huang, W. and Lippman, R.: Network Net and Conventional Classifier. Proceedings of IEEE Conference on Neural Information Processing System-Natural and Synthetic, Boulder, CO(1987)
7. Kohonen, T.: Self-Organization and Associative Memory. 2nd, edn. Springer-Verlag, Berlin (1988)
8. Kwok, K. L.: A Neural Network for Probabilistic Information Retrieval. Proceedings of the 12th International Conference on Research and Development in Information Retrieval. Cambridge, Massachusetts (1989) 21–30
9. Mozer, M. C.: Inductive Information Retrieval using Parallel Distributed Computatio. Technical Report. ICS, UCSD, La Jolla, California (1984)
10. Muneesawang, P. and Guan, L.: A Neural Network Approach for learning Image Similarity in Adaptive CBIR. Proceedings of the IEEE Fourth Workshop on Multimedia Signal. (2001) 257 –262
11. Salton, G. and Buckley, C.: On the use of spreading activation methods in automatic information retrieval. Proceedings of the 11th International Conference on Research & Development in Information Retrieval. New York (1988) 147–160
12. Turtle, H. and Croft, W. B.: Evaluation of an Inference Network-Based Retrieval Model. Int. J. ACM Transaction on Information System, Vol. 9(3). (1991) 187–222

A Localness-Filter for Searched Web Pages[*]

Qiang Ma[1], Chiyako Matsumoto[2], and Katsumi Tanaka[1]

[1] Graduate School of Informatics, Kyoto University.
Yoshida Honmachi, Sakyo, Kyoto, 606-8501, Japan
{qiang,tanaka}@dl.kuis.kyoto-u.ac.jp
http://www.dl.kuis.kyoto-u.ac.jp
[2] Graduate School of Science and Technology, Kobe University.
Rokkodai, Nada, Kobe, 657-8501, Japan
{chiyako}@db.cs.scitec.kobe-u.ac.jp
http://www.db.cs.scitec.kobe-u.ac.jp

Abstract. With the spreading of the Internet, information about our daily life and our residential region is becoming to be more and more active on the WWW (World Wide Web). That's to say, there are a lot of Web pages, whose content is 'local' and may only interest residents of a narrow region. The conventional information retrieval systems and search engines, such as Google[1], Yahoo[2], etc., are very useful to help users finding interesting information. However, it's not yet easy to find or exclude 'local' information about our daily life and residential region. In this paper, we propose a localness-filter for searched Web pages, which can discover and exclude information about our daily life and residential region from the searched Web pages. We compute the localness degree of a Web page by 1) estimating its region dependence: the frequency of geographical words and the content coverage of this Web page, and 2) estimating the ubiquitousness of its topic: in other words, we estimate if it is usual information that appears everyday and everywhere in our daily life.

1 Introduction

Everyone, both novice and expert, can access the vast amount of information that is available on the WWW and find what they are looking for. Conventionally, users input keywords or keyword-based user profiles to search for interesting information. Unfortunately, it's not always easy to specify the keywords for interesting information. That's to say, some kinds of information are not easy to be found via the conventional information retrieval systems. For example, time-series documents, such as news articles, can not be retrieved effectively because that they are incoming information and it is impossible to clearly specify the search keywords. Some new retrieval mechanisms are necessary for such kinds of information. Ma[3,4] and Miyazaki[5] focused on the time-series feature

---

[*] This research is partly supported by the Japanese Ministry of Education, Culture, Sports, Science and Technology under Grant-in-Aid for Scientific Research on "New Web Retrieval Services Based on Discovery of Web Semantic Structures", No. 14019048, and "Multimodal Information Retrieval, Presentation, and Generation of Broadcast Contents for Mobile Environments", No. 14208036.

X. Zhou, Y. Zhang, and M.E. Orlowska (Eds.): APWeb 2003, LNCS 2642, pp. 525–536, 2003.

of information and proposed some meaningful measures, called freshness and popularity, to fetch new valuable information from time-series documents. On the other hand, according to the rapidly progressing and spreading of the World Wide Web (WWW), the information about our daily life and residential region is becoming to be more and more active. However, via conventional methods, it is not yet easy to discover local information from the Web, too. Some portal Web sites[6,7] provide directory type search services for regional information. In such portal Web sites, the regional information is managed manually. The resource may be limited and some valuable local information may be missed. It's also necessary to define some new retrieval criterions for discovering local information.

In our early work[8], we proposed a notion called localness degree for discovering local information from the Web. With the localness notion, we can estimate the dependence of a Web page on a special region. In this paper, we refine our localness estimation methods and propose a localness filter for searched Web page. The localness filter will compute the localness degree of each Web page of search results and select more (or less) local information as the filtering results according to users' intentions. For example, if a user wants to get more local information, the localness filter will return the Web pages that have high localness degree. On the other hand, if a user wants to exclude local information, the Web pages that have lower localness will be returned. In contrast to conventional system, the localness filter is useful to:

– acquire local information, which is not easy to clearly specify in keywords,
– exclude the local information, and
– discover local information over multi-regions.

We say a Web page is local when it only interests the residents (users) of some special regions or organizations. From this perspective, we compute the localness degree of a Web page from two ways: a) estimating its region dependence: the frequency of geographical words and the area of its content coverage, and b) estimating the ubiquitousness of its topic: in other words, we estimate if its information is usual that appeals everywhere and everyday in our daily life.

(a) Region Dependence. If a page has high region dependence, it may describe something about a special region and may interest the residents. Therefore, its probability of being local information may be high.

At first, to estimate the region dependence, we compute the frequency of geographical words within a Web page. We assume that geographical words are words of region name and organization name. The administration level of each geographical word is considered as a weight value when compute its frequency. If geographical words appear frequently, the localness degree is high.

Secondly, we compute the content coverage of a Web page. We plot its geographical words on a map and compute the area of its content coverage based on MBR(Minimum Bounding Rectangle)[9,10]. If this area is small and there are many geographical words, the localness degree of that Web page is considered to be high. In other words, we compute the density of geographical words over the content coverage to estimate the localness degree. If the density is high, localness degree of that page should be high.

Moreover, we compute the document frequency of each geographical word to avoid the effects of usual geographical words on localness degree.

(b)Ubiquitousness of Topic. Some events occur everywhere and some events occur only in some special regions. Information about the latter is a kind of scoop and may interest all users (of all regions). In other words, it may be global information more than local information. Therefore, if a page describes scoop event (the latter), it may not be local information. On the other hand, if a page describes ubiquitous event (the former type. High similarity between these events excluding the locations and times), it may only interest users of some special region because that it's usual information. For instance, summer festivals are held everywhere in Japan. These events (summer festivals) are similar although their locations and times may be different. People may be only interested in the summer festival of their living town (or some special places to them, such as his/her hometown). In other words, the summer festival of a special region may interest the residents only and its localness degree could be high.

To estimate the ubiquitousness of a Web page, at first, we compute its usual words' (which are used often in our daily life) frequency by referring a pre-specified usual words dictionary. Secondly, we compare it with other Web pages to compute their similarities without geographical words and proper nouns. If its usual words' frequency and the number of its similar (excluding geographical words and proper nouns) pages are high, this Web page may represent usual information, such as ubiquitous topic or event. Therefore, its localness degree should be high.

The remainder of this paper is organized as follows: in section 2, we give an overview of related works. In section 3, we describe the mathematical definitions of localness of a Web page and introduce the localness filter for local information retrieval. In section 4, we show some preliminary evaluation results. Finally, we conclude this paper with some discussions and a summary in section 5.

2   Related Work

Mobile Info Search (MIS)[11] is a project that proposes a mobile-computing methodology and services for utilizing local information from the Internet. Their system[12] exchanges the information bi-directionally between the Web and the real world based on the location information. Our research differs in that we define a new concept, the localness degree of a Web page, for discovering 'local' information from the Web automatically.

Buyukkokten et al[13] discussed how to map a Web site to a geographical location, and studied the use of several geographical keys for the purpose of assigning site-level geographical context. By analyzing "whois" records, they built a database that correlates IP addresses and hostnames to approximate physical locations. By combining this information with the hyperlink structure of the Web, they were able to make inferences about the geography of the Web at the granularity of a site.

Geographic Search[14] adds the ability to search for Web pages within a particular geographic locale to traditional keyword searching. To accomplish this, Daniel converted street addresses found within a large corpus of documents to latitude-longitude-based coordinates using the freely available TIGER and FIPS data sources, and built a two-dimensional index of these coordinates. Daniel's system provides an interface that allows the user to augment a keyword search with the ability to restrict matches to within a certain radius of a specified address. In consideration of how much a page has stuck to the area, this point differs from our research. Moreover, our work focuses on how to discover local information from Web contextually: content and correlation with others.

In contrast to these systems and services, the main contribution of our work is that our system can estimate not only which region a Web page relates to, but also how 'local' (or how 'ubiquitous') a Web page is.

3   A Localness-Filter Based on Regional Dependence and Topic Ubiquitousness

In this section, we describe the notion of localness and the localness filter.

3.1   Computing Localness Degree

As we mentioned above, a Web page is local means that its information only interests users of some special regions or organizations. We compute the localness of a Web page from two ways : 1) region dependence and 2) ubiquitousness of its topic. In other words, if its content bears closely to a special region, the localness of that Web page is considered to be high. We also say that a Web page is local if its information (topic) is usual that appears everywhere and everyday in our daily life.

3.1.1 Region Dependence

We noticed that a Web page with a high dependence on a region includes much geographical information, such as the names of the country, state (prefecture), city, and so on. Therefore, we compute the frequency of these geographical words of a Web page to estimate its region dependence.

The content coverage is another factor to estimate a Web page's region dependence. If a Web page describes information about a narrow region, its region dependence may be high. In other words, if the content coverage of a Web page is very narrow, we say that it is local.

(a) **Frequency of Geographical Words.** A Web page has many detailed geographical words, it may deeply depend on some regions. Here, 'detailed geographical word' means that geographical word identifies a detailed location. Usually, we can use the administrative level of each geographical word (region name) as its detailedness[1]. For example, "Xi'an" is more detailed than "China". When compute the frequency, we assign weight values to geographical words according to their detailedness. The simplest rule is to set

---

[1] In our current work, we just consider the detailedness of geographical words based on administrative levels. We also observe that the population density is also important. We will discuss this issue in our future work.

up weight values in the following order: country name < organization name < state (prefecture) < city < town < street(road).

We also compute the document frequency of each geographical word within a Web pages' corpus (i.e., Web pages in the same Web site as the estimating one.) to estimate region dependence of a Web page. That's to say, if the document frequency of a geographical word contained in the estimating Web page is high, such geographical word is a common one and less affects the localness of that page.

In short, if a Web page includes many detailed geographical words that have lower document frequencies, it is local. The formula for computing localness degree based on detailedness, frequency and document frequency of geographical word is defined as follows.

$$local_g(p) = \frac{\sum_{i=1}^{k} weight(geoword_i) \cdot tf(geoword_i)/df(geoword_i)}{words(p)} \quad (1)$$

where, $weight(geoword_i)$ is the detailedness of geographical word $geoword_i$, $words(p)$ is the total words number of page p (excluding stop words). k is the number of distinctive geographical words of p. $tf(geoword_i)$ is the frequency of $geoword_i$ and $df(geoword_i)$ is the document frequency of $geoword_i$.

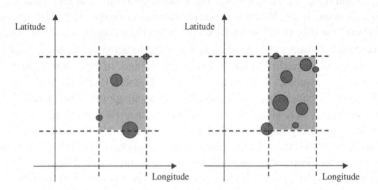

Fig. 1. Example for Effects of Number and Sizes of Geographical Words on Localness

(b) Content Coverage. We convert the region names and organization names to pairs of location data such as $(latitude, longitude)$ and estimate the content coverage of the Web page based on the MBR (Minimum Bounding Rectangle)[9,10].

Each geographical word is converted to a two-dimensional point (latitude, longitude)[2]. We plot all of these points on a map, on which the y-axis and x-axis are latitude and longitude, respectively. The content coverage of a Web page could be approximately computed by the MBR (Minimum Bounding Rectangle), which contains these points.

---

[2] In our current working phase, we use a Japanese location information database[15], which includes latitudinal and longitudinal data for the 3,252 cities, towns, and villages in Japan.

The number and sizes of points plotted on the MBR are also used for estimating the localness. Point size represents the detailedness of a geographical word. A motivation example is illustrated in Fig. 1. Four points are plotted on the left MBR, and eight points are plotted on the right MBR. Even if the areas of the two MBRs are equal, their localness degrees should be different because that the right one may describe more detailed information about that region.

In short, if the content coverage is narrow and there are many detailed geographical words on it, that Web page is local. As mentioned before, the document frequency of each geographical word is also important to avoid the effects of common geographical words on localness degree. The formula is defined as follows.

$$local_{de}(p) = \frac{\sum_{i=1}^{k} weight(geoword_i) \cdot tf(geoword_i)/df(geoword_i)}{MBR(p)} \tag{2}$$

$$MBR(p) = (lat_{max} - lat_{min})(long_{max} - long_{min}) \tag{3}$$

where $local_{de}(p)$ is the localness degree. $weight(geoword_i)$ is the function that we use to estimate the detailedness of geographical words. $tf(geoword_i)$ is the frequency of $geoword_i$ within p. $df(geoword_i)$ is the document frequency of $geoword_i$ within a page corpus. MBR_p is the content coverage of page p. The maximum latitude and longitude are lat_{max} and $long_{max}$, respectively. The minimum latitude and longitude are lat_{min} and $long_{min}$, respectively. When only one point exists in a page and $MBR(p)$ computed by Function (3) will be 0. When such exception has been caught, we set $MBR(p)$ to 1.

Some detailed place names have no match in the location information database[15]. In this case, we downgrade the detailedness of such place name to find an approximate location data. For example, if the location data of "C street, B city, A state" is not found, we could use the location data of "B city, A state" as an approximate match.

Different places may share the same name. To avoid a mismatch, we analyze the page's context to clearly specify its location data. For example, to match up "Futyu city" to its correct location data, we can examine the page content. If "Hiroshima prefecture" appears around the "Futyu city", we could use the location data of "Futyu city, Hiroshima prefecture" to find the location data of "Futyu city" in this page. On the other hand, if "Tokyo metropolitan" appears, we should use "Futyu city, Tokyo metropolitan" to get the proper location data.

3.1.2 Ubiquitousness of Topic

Some events occur everywhere and some events occur only in some special regions. Information about the latter is a scoop and may interest all users (of all regions). Oppositely, a ubiquitous occurrence may have a high localness degree. For example, a summer festival, an athletic meet, and weekend sale are ubiquitous events that appear usually. A ubiquitous occurrence may be a normal part of our daily life. Therefore, if a page describes scoop event, it may not be local information. On the other hand, if a page describes ubiquitous event, it may be local information.

We estimate the topic ubiquitousness of a Web page with two factors: the similarity between pages and the locations where events hold. If the pages are similar in content but different in location or time, their topics are usual. Here, the similarity between page

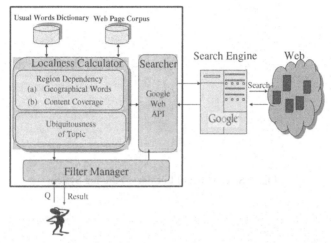

Localness Filter

Fig. 2. Architecture of Localness Filter

A and B is calculated as follows:

$$sim(A, B) = \frac{v(A)v(B)}{|v(A)||v(B)|} \qquad (4)$$

where, $v(A)$ and $v(B)$ are keyword (excluding geographical words and proper nouns) vectors of page A and B, respectively.

We also compute the frequency of daily words within a Web page to estimate its ubiquitousness by referring a pre-specified usual(daily) words dictionary. If the frequency is high, we say that Web page describes usual information and its ubiquitousness is high. The usual words dictionary is constructed from a corpus of user-selected Web pages that describe usual information.

In short, the localness degree $local_u$ based on the ubiquitousness of topic of Web page p is computed as following:

$$local_u(p) = (dailywords(p)/words(p)) * (m/n) \qquad (5)$$

where, $dailywords(p)$ means the frequency of daily words in page p. $words(p)$ means the total number of words in p. m is the number of pages, whose similarities (with page p, excluding geographical words and proper nouns) are greater than threshold Δ. n is the number of pages, which are used for similarity comparison.

3.2 Localness Filter

Although more and more information about our daily life and residential region becomes to be active on the Internet, it's not yet easy to acquire and exclude such kind of information by conventional information retrieval systems and services.

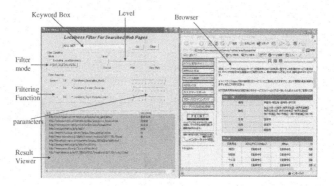

Fig. 3. Screen Shot of Localness Filtering System

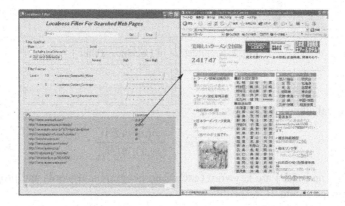

Fig. 4. Running Example: Web Page with High Localness

In this section, we introduce a localness-filter for searched Web pages based on the localness notion. The goal of our localness-filter is to help users to find or exclude local information from the search results.

In our localness filter, the localness of page p is computed as follows:

$$local(p) = \alpha \cdot local_g(p) + \beta \cdot local_{de}(p) + \gamma \cdot local_u(p) \qquad (6)$$

where, $0 \le \alpha \le 1, 0 \le \beta \le 1, 0 \le \gamma \le 1$ are weight values, which can be specified by a user himself/herself. For example, a user can let $\alpha = 1, \beta = 0, \gamma = 0$ to select the geographical words based localness $local_g(p)$ as his/her filtering function.

Localness filter has two modes: exclusion mode and inclusion mode. In exclusion mode, the Web pages whose localness degrees (computed by function (6)) are greater than threshold θ will be excluded from the searched Web pages. On the other hand, in the inclusion mode, only the local Web pages whose localness degrees are greater than threshold will be the survivors.

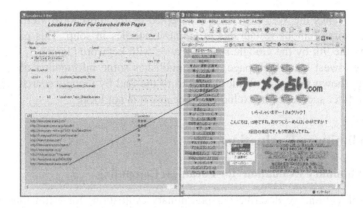

Fig. 5. Running Example: Web Page with Low Localness

A Web page may be local for a wide region while it's considered to be global for a very narrow region. That's to say, localness is a relative concept. According to this feature of localness, the level of localness is defined as a three-grades value ranging from 1 to 3^3, where 1 means normal level (e.g., according to the level of prefecture.), 2 means high local level (e.g., according to the level of city.) and 3 means very high level (e.g., according to the level of county, ward, village.).

Fig. 2 illustrates the architecture of localness-filter. The *filter manager* will accept the request from a user and return the results to the user. The *searcher* receives search request from the *filter manager* and accesses the Google Web service[1] to get search results from the Web via the Google Web API[16]. The searched Web pages will be passed to *localness calculator* to estimate their localness degrees. The parameters for localness estimation are set up by *filter manager* based on user's specification. *filter manager* also generates the filtering results according to the filter mode and level that are specified by a user. *Usual Words Dictionary* is used to compute the frequency of usual(daily) words within a Web page. *Web Page Corpus* includes some collections of Web pages to compute the document frequencies of geographical words and the topic ubiquitousness of each page.

We are developing the localness filter on .net platform[17]. We use Chasen[18] for Japanese morphological analysis to extract geographical words from a Web page. Fig. 3 is a running snapshot of our current system. A user can input his/her query into the keywords box and customize the localness filter: filter mode (by ratio buttons), parameters of filtering function and localness level (by slider bars). In the result viewer, the results are sorted in descending order of localness at this time according to the inclusion mode. The results also can be sorted in ascending order according to the exclusion mode of localness filter. The number of ⋆ signals the degree of localness: high degree of localness will bring more ⋆. By clicking the URL in the result viewer, a Web browser will automatically start up to view the Web page.

---

[3] In our current work, we can adjust the detailedness of geographical words or can adjust the threshold θ for the level feature of localness.

Fig. 4 shows the Web page that is accepted as the most local Web page, which describes some famous restaurants of Chinese noodles in soup. This page has been ranked to the 9th by the Google search service with keyword "lamen"[4]. On the other hand, the lowest local Web page, which publishes some information about fortune-telling, is shown in Fig. 5. While it ranked to the 2nd by Google search service, the localness filter succeeded in excluding it because it is not local.

4   Preliminary Evaluations

4.1   Preliminary Evaluations for Localness Computing

In this subsection, we describe our preliminary evaluations for estimating the localness notion. We used 500 Web pages (written in Japanese) from the ASAHI.COM (http://www.asahi.com/), which is a well-known, news Web site in Japan. Initially, we excluded all of the structural information (e.g., HTML tags) and the advertisement content from the HTML sources of these Web pages.

In the preliminary evaluations, we compute three kinds of localness degrees ($local_g(p)$, $local_{de}(p)$ and $local_u(p)$) from the aspects of region dependence (geographical words and content coverage) and topic ubiquitousness, respectively. One of the limitations of our preliminary evaluation is that we only compare the similarity of a page with different region's pages to compute its topic ubiquitousness. That's to say, we let the portion $dailywords(p)/words(p)$ of Formula (5) to be 1 when we compute the localness of each page from the topic ubiquitousness aspect.

By the localness estimation from the region dependence aspect (frequency of geographical word), there are 327 pages that have been selected as local pages. The number of local pages that have been selected by a user is 362. The recall ratio and precision ration are 0.619 and 0.685, respectively. On the other hand, 283 pages have been selected as local pages by localness estimation from the region dependence aspect(content coverage), and 362 pages were considered to be local pages by a user. The recall ratio and precision ratios are 0.555 and 0.710, respectively.

Moreover, there are 80 pages are selected as local pages by localness estimation from the topic ubiquitousness aspect. The number of Web pages selected as local by a user is 324. This time, the recall ratio and precision ratios are 0.200 and 0.813, respectively. We noticed that recall ratio is very poor. One of the considerable reasons is: we used the news articles as our evaluation targets for the preliminary experiments. Because news articles are more formal and unique than other Web pages, we might fail in estimating the topic ubiquitousness. We are planning to evaluate other kinds of Web pages in the future. The limitations of number and time intervals of evaluation pages are other considerable reasons. Further research to obtain better results need to be carried out.

4.2   Preliminary Evaluation for Localness Filter

We compare the filtering results of localness filter and search results of Google to estimate the localness filter. In the comparison evaluation, we set the parameters of filtering

---

[4] "lamen" is a Japanese word means Chinese noodles in soup.

function (6) as follows: $\alpha = 1.0, \beta = 0, \gamma = 0$. The level of localness is set to normal level. The filter mode is set to inclusion mode. In the comparison evaluation, the evaluation targets are limited to the top 50 pages (ranked by Google) of search results.

The first query for the comparison evaluation is "lamen"[5]. By localness filter, there are 23 pages are accepted as local ones from the top 50 searched pages. The accepted pages are also selected as local pages by a user. On the other hand, there are 27 pages are excluded form the searched Web pages while 15 of them are selected to be local by a user. The recall ratio and precision ratio are 0.605 and 1.0, respectively. The top 10 searched pages' original ranking order by Google and localness based ranking order are $(p_1, p_2, p_3, p_4, p_5, p_6, p_7, p_8, p_9, p_{10})$ and $(p_4, p_9, p_{10}, p_5, p_2, p_6, p_1, p_7, p_8, p_3)$, respectively. This shows that localness filter can help users to find local information quickly.

Another query for the comparison evaluation is "Chocolate Kobe". On the normal level of localness, 33 pages are accepted as local pages by the localness filter while 11 of them are not local by estimation of a user. On the other hand, there are 17 pages are excluded while 3 of them are selected to be local by a user. The recall ratio and precision ratio are 0.880 and 0.667, respectively. On the high level of localness, 14 pages are accepted including 5 incorrect (estimated by a user) pages. On the very high level of localness, 7 pages are accepted including 1 incorrect (estimated by a user) page. The ranking order of top 10 searched pages by localness filter is $(p_8, p_6, p_5, p_7, p_4, p_3, p_{10}, p_9, p_1, p_2)$.

Since our evaluations are limited, there are more improving works needed to be done. Nevertheless, these results can confirm the notion, localness, is useful for discovering local information from massive amount of Web pages. Form the comparison evaluation, at least, we could assume that localness is more useful to filter search results. We also could assume that the level feature of localness is helpful for filtering search results from the query with geographical words. These will be tested in our future evaluations.

5   Conclusion

There are many Web pages, which provide information about our daily life and residential region. These pages are very important for residents and may only interest them. In this paper, We proposed a filter for searched Web pages based on the notion of *localness*. With this filter, users can acquire or exclude more local information from the Web according to their intentions.

In this paper, we estimate a Web page's localness from two aspects: region dependence and topic ubiquitousness. We also noticed that users' location information is useful to estimate the localness of a Web page. If a Web page is often accessed by users from the same region, and there is little access from other regions, we could say that such page only interests users of that special region and its localness is high. On the other hand, if some information is published only from the residents of a same region, and there are few users which report the same information in other regions, we could say that such information is local because that it only interests users of a special region. We will discuss these issues in our future work.

---

[5] "lamen" is a Japanese word means Chinese noodles in soup. In our comparison evaluation, the keywords of query are all in Japanese.

Further experiments to estimate the localness notion and the localness filter need to be carried out, such as comparison evaluations with dictionary-type search in portal region Web sites (Yahoo! Region[6], MACHIGoo[7], etc.) and keywords search in agent-type search services (Google, etc.). Further refinements on the the localness notion and localness filter are also planned to do as our future work, such as, considering well the hierarchical relationships among geographical words to estimate the region dependence, etc.

References

[1] Google. http://www.google.com/, 2002.

[2] Yahoo! Japan. http://www.yahoo.co.jp/, 2002.

[3] Qiang Ma, Kazutoshi Sumiya, and Katsumi Tanaka.   Information filtering based on time-series features for data dissemination systems (in Japanese). *IPSJ TOD7*, 41(SIG6(TOD7)):46–57, 2000.

[4] Qiang Ma, Shinya Miyazaki, and Katsumi Tanaka. Webscan: Discovering and notifying important changes of web sites. *proc. of DEXA2001, LNCS 2113*, pages 587–598, 2001.

[5] Shinya Miyazaki, Qiang Ma, and Katsumi Tanaka.   Webscan: Content-based change discovery and broadcast-notification of web sites (in Japanese).   *IPSJ TOD10*, 42(SIG8(TOD10)):96–107, 2001.

[6] Yahoo!regional. http://local.yahoo.co.jp/, 2002.

[7] MACHIgoo. http://machi.goo.ne.jp/, 2002.

[8] Chiyako Matsumoto, Ma Qiang, and Katsumi Tanaka. Web information retrieval based on the localness degree. *proc. of DEXA 2002, LNCS 2453*, pages 172–181, 2002.

[9] Antonin Guttman. R-trees: A dynamic index structure for spatial searching. *Proc. ACM SIGMOD Conference on Management of Data*, 14(2):47–57, 1984.

[10] Carlo Zaniolo, Stefano Ceri, Christos Faloutsos, Richard T. Snodgrass, V. S. Subrahmanian, and Roberto Zicari. *Advanced Database Systems*. The Morgan Kaufmann, 1997.

[11] Nobuyuki Miura, Katsumi Takahashi, Seiji Yokoji, and Kenichi Shima. Location oriented information integration - mobile info search 2 experiment - (in Japanese). *The 57th National Convention of IPSJ*, 3:637–638, 1998.

[12] KOKONONET. http://www.kokono.net/, 2002.

[13] Orkut Buyukkokten, Junghoo Cho, Hector Garcia-Molina, Luis Gravano, and Narayanan Shivakumar. Exploiting geographical location information of web pages. *proc. of WebDB (Informal Proceedings)*, pages 91–96, 1999.

[14] Daniel Egnor. Google programing contest, 2002.

[15] T. Takeda. The latitude / longitude position database of all-prefectures cities, towns and villages in japan, 2000.

[16] Google Web API. http://www.google.com/apis/, 2002.

[17] Microsoft .net. http://www.microsoft.com/net/, 2002.

[18] Chasen. http://chasen.aist-nara.ac.jp/chasen/whatis.html.en, 2002.

DEBIZ: A Decentralized Lookup Service for E-commerce[1]

Zeng-De Wu, Wei-Xiong Rao, and Fan-Yuan Ma

Department of Computer Science & Engineering,
Shanghai Jiaotong University, Shanghai 200030, China
{Wu-zd, Rao-wx, Ma-fy}@cs.sjtu.edu.cn

Abstract. Existing e-commerce specifications such as ebXML and UDDI manage resource by logical centralized approach, which lead to single point failure and performance bottleneck. As a new computing model, peer-to-peer addresses existing e-commerce resource management problems in a natural way. This paper presents DEBIZ, a decentralized service for resource management in e-commerce. In DEBIZ, resource is managed in peer-to-peer approach, and metadata of the resource and query message is presented in XML document. Experimental results show that DEBIZ has lower space overhead, well-balanced load, and good robustness.

1 Introduction

E-commerce is a huge infrastructure, which is consisted of a great number of business resources. These resources are written with different computer languages, compiled in different platforms, run on different hardware, have different data structures, types and formats, use different transport mechanisms, and support a wide range of different technologies. Management of these resources is of great importance to e-commerce. The emergence and popularity of XML and XML-based e-commerce specification provides good foundation for e-commerce resource management [1].

However, existing e-commerce specifications such as ebXML [2] and UDDI [3] manage resource by centralized approach, which is hard for distributed e-commerce with data distributed over Internet. Centralized data sources require replication of documents and force to manage resources created by others. This is relatively costly and inefficient. Creating a centralized index reduces the richness of the data, and leads to single point failure and performance bottleneck. Thus, a more robust and seamless e-commerce infrastructure is demanded. Especially if it is considered that critical business information is usually stored in various formats and on disparate servers.

Peer-to-peer [4, 5, 6, 7, 8] is an information system model without any centralized control or hierarchical organization, where the software running at each node is equivalent in functionality. The feature of peer-to-peer is self-organizing, scalability,

---

[1] This paper was supported by the Grid Research Program of Shanghai (025115032) and the High Technology Research and Development Program of China (2001AA414140)

X. Zhou, Y. Zhang, and M.E. Orlowska (Eds.): APWeb 2003, LNCS 2642, pp. 537–547, 2003.

and autonomous. Since resource is managed locally, peer-to-peer removed centralized resource management problem. Since resource index is distributed uniformly over all peers, peer-to-peer removed single point failure and performance bottleneck that exists in centralized approach. The core of peer-to-peer systems is peer-to-peer routing algorithm. There are two kinds of peer-to-peer routing algorithms, structured routing algorithm and unstructured routing algorithm. In unstructured routing algorithms such as Gnutella [9], each peer connects to several other peers. The topology is ad hoc and the placement of data is completely unrelated to the overlay topology. Unstructured routing algorithms locate resource by broadcast, and control the broadcast by TTL. There are high possibilities that unstructured routing algorithms may fail to locate resource. Chord [6], Tapestry [7], Pastry [8], CAN [5] are structured routing algorithms, which provide a mapping between the file identifier and location, so that queries can be efficiently routed to the node with the desired file. Since existing peer-to-peer routing algorithms are designed for sharing file, metadata of which is simple and could not apply to e-commerce directly.

This paper presents DEBIZ, a decentralized lookup service to resource manage in e-commerce. Resource in DEBIZ is managed in peer-to-peer approach and the peer-to-peer overlay is organized with Chord [6] protocol. Since Chord cannot apply to e-commerce directly, we extend Chord routing algorithm by append a router repository to each routing table. Query request and router repository items in DEBIZ are presented in XML document.

The rest of this paper is organized as follows. Section 2 presents the decentralized lookup service to manage e-commerce resource. Section 3 presents peer-to-peer resource lookup algorithm. Section 4 presents the evaluation and experimental results. Section 5 gives the conclusions.

2 Decentralized Lookup Service to Manage E-commerce Resource

The key to DEBIZ lies in resource distribution and resource lookup. Fig. 1.a shows the process of resource distribution, and Fig. 1.b shows the process of resource lookup. Before distributing e-commerce resource $\Re$, business partner generate metadata $\Re d$ of e-commerce resource $\Re$. $\Re d$ is used to distribute $\Re$ and presented in form of XML document. Then DEBIZ hash the key of $\Re d$, and get a hash identifier (HID). After that, DEBIZ lookup the distribution peer node N by means of peer-to-peer routing algorithm. Later on, business partner present the XML document $\Re d$ to the peer node N, which save the distribution information to router repository and complete the distribution process.

The process of resource lookup is roughly same as that of resource distribution. The key step in resource distribution and lookup process is to lookup a peer node according to HID, which was achieved by the extended routing algorithm.

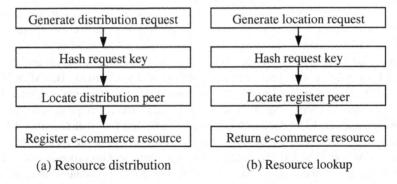

(a) Resource distribution   (b) Resource lookup

Fig. 1. Resource distribution and lookup process

In DEBIZ, e-commerce system of a partner is called e-commerce Unit (EU). To see how DEBIZ works, we need to examine briefly the EU architecture. A EU is a federation of logical machines. Each logical machine consists of three active components called the XML integrator, the core component and the router, and a passive component called the repository. Several logical machines can share one piece of hardware, each can have a dedicated machine, or a single logical machine can use several physical machines, however it is configured, the programs will run the same way.

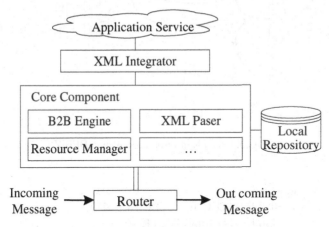

Fig. 2. Key component of e-commerce unit

Fig. 2 shows the key components of EU. XML integrator integrates e-commerce applications (such as ERP, CRM and SRM, etc) and exposes it as business services. Core component consists of B2B engine, XML parser and resource manager, etc. B2B engine executes B2B presented in XML document. XML parser parses the XML document, and resource manager manages the business resource kept in the local repository. Local repository keeps the application service interface, B2B workflow document and business metadata, etc. Router route query request and return routing result.

Fig. 3 shows an example of resource lookup. Suppose EU 1 is an automobile manufacturer, who wants to search information of bearing manufactory in China. EU 1 generates a routing request in form of XML document, which consists of an envelope containing information used by core, and a payload containing the application related data. EU 1 hashes the key 'bearing' and gets an identifier B28AD5C3E516 F6D63AC5. The query condition of the routing request is 'Country = China, BusinessType = manufactory'. Fig. 3 shows the payload of routing request. After generating routing request, EU 1 lookup local routing table and find that identifier EU 2 is closest to B28AD5C3E516F6D63AC5 among all identifiers in the local tables. Then the request is routed to EU 2, which operate the same lookup process as EU 1 and routes the query to the next e-commerce unit. The process continues until the node (EU K for example) with identifier closest to B28AD5C3E516F6D63AC5 is found. EU K searches in local router repository for metadata that satisfies the query condition and return the result to EU 1. Fig. 5 shows the payload of replay to the request. In order to get more detailed business information, EU 1 further communicate with business partner through service interface (such as "61.146.46.46:6666" in fig. 5).

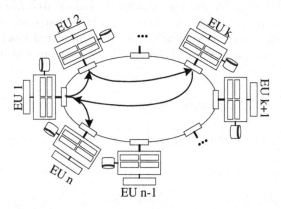

Fig. 3. Example of resource lookup in DEBIZ

```
<Request>
    <HID>B28AD5C3E516F6D63AC5</HID>
    <MainKey>bearing</MainKey>
    <QueryCondition >
        <Country>China</Country>
        <BusinessType>manufactory</BusinessType>
    </ QueryCondition >
</Request>
```

Fig. 4. Payload of routing request

```
<Result>
  <Section>
    <Name>ChangZhou Precision Bearing Co.,Ltd<Name>
    <Interface>61.146.46.46:6666</Interface>
    <Description>...<Description>
  </Section>
  <Section>
    <Name>Harbin Bearing Group co.<Name>
    <Interface>61.146.46.46:6666</Interface>
    <Description>...<Description>
  </Section>
  ...
</Result>
```

Fig. 5. Payload of replay to the request

3 Resource Lookup Algorithm in DEBIZ

Resource lookup algorithm specifies how to find the location of e-commerce resource. Lookup is achieved by peer-to-peer routing algorithm. Existing structured routing algorithms only support exact-match resource lookup, that is: given a key, it maps the key to peer nodes. For application such as e-commerce, conditional resource lookup is of great importance. Because Chord [6] have the features of simplicity, provable correctness, and provable performance compared with other lookup protocols, we use Chord protocol to organize routing table. We extended Chord protocol so that not only can it support exact-match lookup but also conditional lookup.

3.1 DEBIZ Router Component

Fig. 6 shows the structure of DEBIZ Router, which is consisted of routing table and repository map. Structure of DEBIZ routing table is the same as that of Chord, which maintains no more than 160 items. Each is consisted of 160-bit ID and 32-bit IP address. Router repository maintains maps between hashing ID and the corresponding business information lists. For each ID in router repository, there may be more than one business resource item.

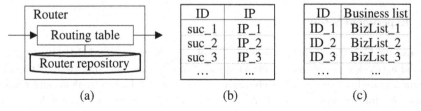

(a)   (b)   (c)

Fig. 6. (a) Structure of DEBIZ router. (b) Items of routing table. (c) Repository map of router repository

3.2 DEBIZ Lookup Algorithm

Before presenting DEBIZ lookup algorithm, we first introduce a definition:

Definition 1. Let Ξ be identifier set, and Ω be the EU set. Then the definition of node and node^{-1} are given as follows:

node: $\Xi \rightarrow \Omega$, Ξ is HID set, and Ω is the EU set. node maps HID to corresponding node. This mapping is achieved by Chord algorithm.

node^{-1}: $\Omega \rightarrow \Xi$, node^{-1} maps node to the HID of the node. This mapping is achieved by consistent hashing.

If EU 1 decides to lookup business information with key biz_key, the DEBIZ works as follows:

1. EU 1 hashes biz_key to get HID id, then generates Msg_query, the structure of which is showed in fig. 4.
2. EU 1 lookups id' which is closest to HID id from local routing table. If id and id' satisfy the following conditions, then jumps to step (5).
   - id<=id'
   - $\forall$ id''$\in \Xi$, id<=id'' $\wedge$ id''<=id' $\rightarrow$ id'=id''
3. Routes Msg_query to node(id').
4. node(id') receives Msg_query, and extracts id from Msg_query. DEBIZ jumps to (2) to continue lookup.
5. Extracts query condition from Msg_query. Finds query results from router repository, and generates Msg_result.
6. Route Msg_result to EU 1.

EU 1 may further communicate with business entities listed in Msg_result for more detailed business information.

4   Evaluation and Experimental Results

In this section, we evaluate DEBIZ by simulation. In order to compare with centralized resource management approach such as UDDI, we also evaluated UDDI approach (UDDI for simplicity). We compared latency, space overhead, load, and robustness of DEBIZ with UDDI.

4.1 Experiment Setup

We use the Georgia Tech Internetwork Topological Models (GT-ITM) [10] to generate the network topologies used in our simulations. We use the "transit-stub" model to obtain topologies that more closely resemble the Internet hierarchy than pure random graph. An Internetwork with 600 routers and 28800 business partners (node for simplicity) are used in our experiment. The latency of physical hops between nodes in the same stub domain, nodes in stub domain and transit domain, nodes in same transit domain, and nodes in different transit domains are 1, 3, 5 and 7, respectively.

The routing process obeys three rules:

1. The path connecting two nodes in the same domain stays entirely within that domain.
2. The path connecting node u in stub domain U to node v in another stub domain V goes form U through one or more transit domains to V, and does not pass through any other stub domains.
3. In case two stub domains are connected directly via a stub-stub edge, the path between two nodes on the two domains may go along that edge and avoid any transit domains.

4.2 Latency Evaluation

Fig. 7 shows the effect of number of nodes on latency. We increase GT-ITM scale by increasing the number of nodes connected to each stub router. Results show that the latency and the number of nodes N_H are in logarithmic relation. This is because the logical hops of Chord $Hop_{Chord} = \log(N_H)$ [6]. Since the routing table of DEBIZ is same as that of Chord, the logical hops of DEBIZ $Hop_{DEBIZ} = \log(N_H)$. If the average latency of single logical hop is κ, thus, latency of DEBIZ $Latency_{DEBIZ} = \kappa \times \log(N_H)$.

Experimental results further show that the latency of UDDI is roughly 47. This is because the logical hops of UDDI is 2, and does not increase with N_H. Although latency of DEBIZ is higher than that of UDDI, DEBIZ has lower space overhead, lower load, and good robustness (refer to 4.3, 4.4, 4.5).

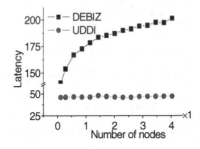

Fig. 7. Effect of number of nodes on latency

4.3 Space Overhead

The space overhead is consisted of two parts: routing table overhead and router repository overhead. In order for analyzing conveniently, we first give a definition and two assumptions:

Definition 2. The memory size of routing ID and corresponding IP is called memory unit, size of which is σ.

Assumption 1. Node ID and file business information ID is distributed uniformly in ID space, and there are n business partners in e-commerce system, each partner distributes m business information in average.

Assumption 2. The average overhead of each business information item is $k \times \sigma$.

Since there are $\log(n)$ items in DEBIZ routing table, and overhead of every item is σ, which is 192 bits, thus, the overhead of routing table is $\log(n) \times \sigma$. Follow the definition and assumptions given above, each router repository have m items, overhead of router repository is $m \times k \times \sigma$. Overhead of DEBIZ is:

$$Space_{DEBIZ} = \log(n) \times \sigma + m \times k \times \sigma \tag{1}$$

Since UDDI maintains all information in central repository, overhead of UDDI is:

$$Space_{UDDI} = n \times m \times k \times \sigma \tag{2}$$

For $m = 80$ and $k = 2$ in Formula 1 and 2, fig. 8 shows the effect of number of nodes N_H on space overhead. Experimental results in fig. 8 shows that the space overhead of DEBIZ is between $171 \times \sigma$ and $175 \times \sigma$, but overhead of UDDI repository between $10^6 \times \sigma$ and $6 \times 10^6 \times \sigma$. When there are 20000 EU in GT-ITM, space overhead of DEBIZ is 18285 times lower than that of UDDI. Thus, space overhead of DEBIZ is much better than that of UDDI.

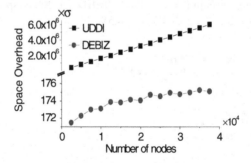

Fig. 8. Effect of number of nodes on Space overhead

4.4 Load Evaluation

Load is one important metric to evaluate e-commerce resource manage approach. This paper uses the number of messages in and out of node as evaluation metric to load. Fig. 9 shows the comparisons in loads between DEBIZ and UDDI. The load of UDDI increases with number of nodes linearly, but the load of DEBIZ and number of nodes is in logarithmic relation. The reason for this is, for each resource lookup request, there is an in message and an out message. Thus, if each business partner sends one request, the load of UDDI registry is $2 \times N$. While in DEBIZ, each resource lookup needs $\log(N)/2$ logical hops in average, thus, total logical hops of N resource lookup request are $N \times \log(N)/2$. Since node ID and file business information ID is distributed uniformly in ID space, then load of each node is well balanced. Thus, each node routes $\log(N)/2$ messages. For each message routing, there are an in message and an out message. Thus, the load of each node is $\log(N)$.

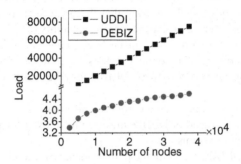

Fig. 9. Load of BEBIZ and UDDI

4.5 Robustness Evaluation

In this experiment, we evaluated the ability of DEBIZ to regain consistency after a large percentage of node fail simultaneously. We consider 28800 nodes with each node distribute 10 piece of business information, and randomly select a fraction of the nodes that fail. After the failures occur, we wait for the network to stabilizing, and then measure the fraction of keys that could not be looked up correctly.

Fig. 10 plots the effect of node failure on resource lookup. The lookup failure rate is almost equal to node fail rate. Since this is just the fraction of keys expected to be lost due to the failure of the responsible nodes. That is to say, there is no significant lookup failure in DEBIZ resource lookup. We conclude that DEBIZ is robust in face of node failure.

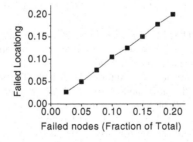

Fig. 10. The effect of node failure on resource lookup

5   Conclusions

Resource lookup and distribution is of great significance to e-commerce. This paper presents DEBIZ, a decentralized lookup service for e-commerce. Experimental results show that, compared with centralized resource management in existing e-commerce specifications, peer-to-peer approach has the following advantages:

1. Better Robustness. DEBIZ is fully distributed and will automatically adjust its routing table when nodes failed, ensuring that the node responsible for a key can always be found. This improves robustness and availability of e-commerce system.
2. Lower load. There is a routing table in each e-commerce unit, and resource is looked up by cooperation of all e-commerce units. Since loads of resource lookup is distributed evenly on all nodes, load of DEBIZ may be much lower than that of UDDI.
3. Better space overhead. Since resource routing information is distributed evenly over all nodes, space overhead of DEBIZ may be much lower than that of UDDI in large-scale e-commerce systems.
4. Easy to manage. In DEBIZ, e-commerce partner manages resource locally. There is no need to setup e-commerce register center, such as UDDI register and ebXML register, which makes resource management easier.

We conclude that peer-to-peer lookup service for e-commerce is practical and promising.

References

1.   WU Zeng-De, Liu Yan, MA Fan-Yuan. Research on service-based e-business application integration framework. Journal of Shanghai Jiaotong University, 2002.09.1341–1345.
2.   Cole J, Milosevic Z. Extending support for contracts in ebXML. Proceedings 2001 Information Technology for Virtual Enterprises. Queensland, AUSTRALIA: ITVE, 2001. 119 –127.
3.   http://www.uddi.org/, UDDI Version 3.0, Published Specification.
4.   WU Zeng-De, RAO Wei-Xiong, MA Fan-Yuan. Efficient Topology-aware Routing in peer-to-peer Network. International workshop on grid and cooperative computing, 2002. Chinese academy of sciences,China computer federation. Hainan, China.
5.   Sylvia Ratnasamy, Paul Francis, Mark Handley, Richard Karp, Scott Shenker. A scalable content-addressable network. Proceedings of ACM SIGCOMM`01, San Diego, September 2001.
6.   Ion Stoica, Robert Morris, David Karger, M. Frans Kaashoek, and Hari Balakrishnan. Chord: a scalable peer-to-peer lookup service for Internet applications. Proceedings of ACM SIGCOMM`01, San Diego, September 2001.
7.   Ben Y. Zhao, John D. Kubiatowicz, and Anthony D. Joseph. Tapestry: an infrastructure for fault-tolerant wide-area location and routing. U. C. Berkeley Technical Report UCB//CSD-01-1141, April 2000. http://oceanstore.cs.berkeley.edu/publications/.
8.   Antony Rowstron, Peter Druschel Lecture Notes in Computer Science. Pastry: scalable, decentralized oject location and routing for large-scale peer-to-peer systems. In Proceedings of the 18th IFIP/ACM International Conference on Distributed Systems Platforms (Middleware 2001). Heidelberg, Germany, November 2001.

9. Qin Lv, Sylvia Ratnasamy, Scott Shenker. Can heterogeneity make gnutella scalable?. Electronic Proceedings for the 1st International Workshop on peer-to-peer Systems (IPTPS '02), 7–8 March 2002 – Cambridge, MA, USA.
10. Zegura, E. w., Calvert. k., and Bhattacharjee, S. How to model an Internetwork. In Proceed-ings of IEEE INFOCOM (1996).

Design of B+Tree-Based Predicate Index for Efficient Event Matching

Botao Wang, Wang Zhang, and Masaru Kitsuregawa

Institute of Industrial Science, The University of Tokyo
Komaba 4–6–1, Meguro Ku, Tokyo, 135–8505 Japan
{botaow, zhangw,kitsure}@tkl.iis.u-tokyo.ac.jp

Abstract. Efficient event matching algorithms are the core of publish/subscribe systems. Such algorithms are typically designed based on memory structure for performance reasons. Given the explosive growth of information, it is *not* always practically feasible to keep the index for event filtering memory-resident, thereby necessitating the need for a secondary storage structure. Incidentally, even though search algorithms designed for active databases and spatio-temporal databases are applicable to publish/subscribe systems, these algorithms are *not* specifically designed for publish/subscribe systems which require both fast search as well as efficient support for dynamic insertions and deletions. To address this problem, we propose a predicate index for secondary storage structures with space complexity $O(n)$ and search time complexity $O(\log n)$. Analytical comparison of our proposed algorithms with existing work indicates that our secondary storage predicate index is efficient for event matching.

1 Introduction

The rapid growth of technology has considerably changed the manner and scale of information management. Users can find and provide information easily through brokers like the Web; at the same time, in various applications, such as stock tickers, traffic control, network monitoring, Web logs and clickstreams, and Sensor networks, input data arrive as continuous ordered data streams[17]. There is a growing necessity for systems to be able to capture the dynamic aspect of Web information. Publish/subscribe systems provide subscribers with the ability to express their interest in an event in order to be notified afterwards of any event fired by a publisher, matching their registered interest. In other words, producers publish information on publish/subscribe systems and consumers subscribe to their desired information[7]. The precursor of publish/subscribe systems was subject-based. In such systems, information consumers subscribe to one or more subjects and the system notifies them whenever an event classified as belonging to one of their relevant subjects is published. A representative example of such a system is a mailing list. Thousands of mailing lists exist, encompassing a wide variety of topics. The user subscribes to lists of his/her interests and receives messages via mail. However, it offers only limited expressiveness.

X. Zhou, Y. Zhang, and M.E. Orlowska (Eds.): APWeb 2003, LNCS 2642, pp. 548–559, 2003.

As an attractive alternative to subject-based publish/subscribe systems, content-based publish/subscribe systems typically introduce subscription schemes based on the properties of the given notifications. Notably, events are not classified according to some pre-defined subject names, but according to properties of the event themselves. For example, a content-based system for a stock market may define a subscription schema as a tuple containing three attributes: *CompanyName*, *Price* and *ChangeRatio* with string, float and float types respectively. The user can choose stock information by the values of attributes not by subject *Stock* only.

The cost of the gain in expressiveness of content-based system is an increase in the complexity of the matching process. The efficiency of matching highly depends on matching algorithms. Input data arrive as data stream and the subscriptions are inserted and deleted dynamically.

As far as we know, many matching algorithms in the context of publish/subscribe are generally proposed based on memory structure [1][3][8][9][13][16][18]. As pointed in [17], input data arrive in form of data stream, it's very difficult to keep all the index data in the memory practically. At the same time, for the similarity of operations(range or interval query), some searching algorithms designed for active database[11], spatio-temporal database [2][5][6][10] can be applied to publish/subscribe system, those algorithms are not designed originally for publish/subscription system and lack of flexibility of insertion and deletion, don't support relational operator "!=" directly.

In this paper, we will propose a secondary storage predicate index structure based on B+tree for efficient event matching. The rest of this paper is organized as follows. Section 2 formally defines the event matching problem. Section 3 introduces the related work. Section 4 describes our predicate index structure: PB+tree and event matching algorithm in this context. In Section 5, analytical comparisons between our proposed algorithm and existing techniques are made. Finally, conclusion is given in Section 6.

2   Event Matching Model

The event matching problem can be expressed as follows. Given an event e and a set of subscriptions S, determine all subscriptions in S that are matched by e. A subscription is a conjunction of predicates. A predicate is a triple consisting of an attribute, a constant, and a relational operator ($<, <=, =, !=, >=, >$). A subscription schema defines the properties of the information to be supported by publish/subscribe system. Attributes are defined in subscription schema. For example, three attributes: *CompanyName*, *Price* and *ChangeRatio* with string, float and float types respectively, can be defined for stock market. Following is a subscription example, ($CompanyName = Yahoo$) AND ($Price>1000$) AND ($ChangeRatio<0.05$). An event is an array of (Attribute, Constant) tuples. The size of array depends on the number of attributes defined in subscription schema. Following is an event example of stock schema, ($CompanyName, Intel$), ($Price, 5000$), ($ChangeRatio, 0.03$). An event e matches a subscription S if all predicates in S are satisfied by some (Attribute, Value) tuples in e. For example, the event ($CompanyName, Yahoo$), ($price, 500$), ($ChangeRatio, 0.1$) matches the following subscription which is expressed as a conjunction of two predicates: (*CompanyName* = *Yahoo*) AND (*Price* < 1000). Event matching algorithms in content-based publish/subscribe systems can be classified into two categories:

- Algorithms based predicate index. The solutions based on predicate indexing consist of two phases:
  - The first phase determines all predicates that are satisfied by event.
  - The second phase finds all the subscriptions matched by the event according to the results of the first phase.

  Algorithms based on predicate indexing techniques use a set of one-dimensional index structures to build indexes for predicates defined in subscriptions. They differ from each other in the way of selecting predicates from subscriptions to index structures[3] [8][9][11][13] [16][18].

  Basically, predicates are grouped by attributes. A predicate family consists of predicates with same attribute. For each attribute, one predicate index is built. For example, for stock schema introduced previously, three predicate indexes will be built on attributes *CompanyName*, *Price*, *ChangeRatio*.
- Algorithms based on subscription index[1][14]. The techniques based on subscription index insert subscriptions into a decision tree. Events enter the tree from root node and are filtered through by intermediate nodes. An event that passes all intermediate testing nodes reaches a leaf node where reference(s) of matched subscriptions are stored.

Our index data structure is designed for predicate index. Although, there are many proposals for predicates selection [8][9][11][18], the predicate index is essential while getting all satisfied predicates according to the event at the first phase. In the following introductions, we will concentrate on the predicate index of one attribute without considering about the second phase. For details of different selection methods of predicates, please refer to [8][9][11][18].

3   Related Work

A lot of algorithms related to event matching have been proposed. Some are proposed for publish/subscribe systems[1] [8] [9][15] [14][18] and continuous queries[3] [4][17]; Some are proposed for active database [11] [12][13], spatio-temporal database [2] [6] [10]. In [8][9][18], predicate indexs are built. The algorithm consist of two phases: the first step gets satisfied predicates, the second step collects matching subscriptions according to the results of the first step. In [8], three predicate indexes are built for operators (=, >, <). For = operator, hash table or binary search can be used. For > and < operator, binary search trees are used. In [8], hash table is used to build index for predicates with = operator. [18] is a information Dissemination System(IDS) for document filtering. There, predicate index is a inverted list which is built based on the vocabularies used in predicates.

Different from predicate index, [1] and [14] built subscription tree based on subscription schema. In [1], each non-leaf node contains a test, and edges from the node represent results of that test. The test and result corresponds to predicate.

A leaf node contains a subscription. The matching is to walk the matching tree by performing the test prescribed by each node and following the edge according to the result of test. if number of matched subscription is greater then one, multiple paths will be walked. In [14], Profile(subscription) tree is built, the height of tree is number of attributes defined in subscription schema. Each non-leaf level corresponds to one attribute of event schema. Each attribute domain is divided non-overlapping subrange by the value of predicate. One leaf node contains multiple subscriptions whose predicates are satisfied by the values of attributes in the subranges. There is only a single path to follow in order to find the matched subscriptions.

In [11][12][13], algorithms related to rule management were proposed. The key component of the algorithm in [11] is the interval binary search tree(IBS-tree). The IBS-tree is designed for efficient retrieval of all intervals that overlap a point, while allowing dynamic insertion and deletion of intervals. In [12], the same idea of IBS-tree is implemented by skip lists. "Expression Signature" is designed to group subscriptions and share computation in [13].

Event filtering is critical step of continuous queries. In [4], Expression Signature is used to group queries for computation sharing. In [16], four data structures: a greater-than balanced binary tree, a less-than balanced binary tree, an equality hash-table, and an inequality hash-table were built(we call them data structure Group Filter in Section 5). The structures are similar to that of [8], but inequality operator(!=) is supported. In [3], predicate index is built based on Red-Black tree. Each node contains five arrays that store queryIDs of the corresponding predicates. Five relational operators ($<, <=, =, >=, >$) are supported directly.

Because the range query of spatio-temporal database uses operators ($<, <=, >=, >$) in the similar way of predicate index, the related data structures can be used to built predicate index. In[6], an index structure for time interval is built. A set of linearly ordered indexing points is maintained by a B+tree, and for each point, a bucket of pointers refers to the associated set of intervals. In [2], Interval B+tree is built and the lower bounds of the intervals are used as primary keys. Multi-dimensional Rtree[10] and its variants may not behave well for one-dimensional interval for the reason of overlap of interval.

4   PB+Tree: Predicate Index Based on B+Tree

4.1   Motivation

B+tree is an efficient secondary storage index structure and all its data are kept in leaf nodes which are linked in an order list. Our idea is that to build a predicate index on secondary storage based on B+tree and make use of the order of leaf node list to share computation. All the predicates of one attribute are kept in one extended B+tree which supports relational operators ($<, <=, =, >=, >, !=$) directly.

4.2 Structure of Predicate Index

The basic structure of the predicate index is shown in Fig.1. The constant defined
in predicate is used as the key of B+tree. As shown in Fig. 1, three lists are added
below the leaf node list of B+tree, where data structure of B+tree leaf node is
extended.

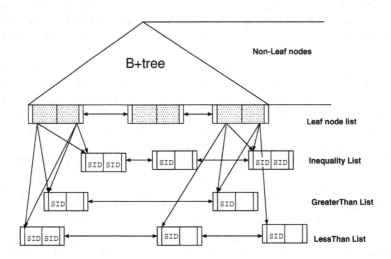

Fig. 1. Basic Structure of PB+tree

Inequality List. Inequality list is used to deal with predicates with operator
(!=). The data structure of its node is shown in Fig.2. Mainly, it consists
of two pointers and an array of items. An item consists of key and SidSet.
The key is the same as the key used in B+tree. It corresponds to predicate
Attribute! = Key. SidSet is ID set of subscriptions which contain predicate *Attribute! = Key*. Because *Attribute! = Key* means a special range
(*Attribute > key* AND *Attribute < Key*) double links are defined in inequality list. Inside one node, the items are arranged in descending order of
key. PreviousPointer points to previous node of inequality list in ascending
order of key. NextPointer points to next node of inequality list in descending
order of key. Logically, Inequality list is an order list of items, where the logically adjacent two items maybe be kept in two different adjacent Inequality
list nodes.

GreaterThan List and LessThan List. GreaterThan list is used to deal
with predicates with operators (>, >=). The data structure of GreaterThan
list node is shown in Fig.3 It is similar to that of Inequality list. The difference is that it has only previousPointer, no nextPointer. For each item,
SidSet is ID set of subscriptions which contain predicate *Attribute > Key*
or *Attribute >= Key*. For two predicates with different keys, the range represented by one predicate will totally cover another on GreaterThan list. It

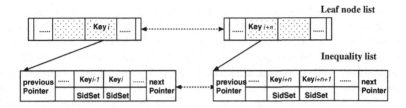

Fig. 2. Data Structure of Inequality List Node

is determined by the value of key. For example, *Attribute* > 10 is true means *Attribute* > 5 is true too. We make use of this property to share computation to collect results on GreaterThan list via previousPointer from the item corresponding to the largest range designated by input.

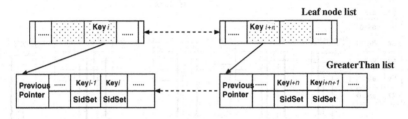

Fig. 3. Data Structure of GreaterThan List Node

LessThan List has similar data structure to GreaterThan List. The difference is that the pointer of node is nextPointer, not previousPointer.

Extended Leaf Node of B+tree. As shown in Fig.1, three lists are added below leaf node list of B+tree. The nodes on these lists are designated by the pointers defined in the items of leaf nodes. The data structure of B+tree leaf node is extended as shown in Fig.4

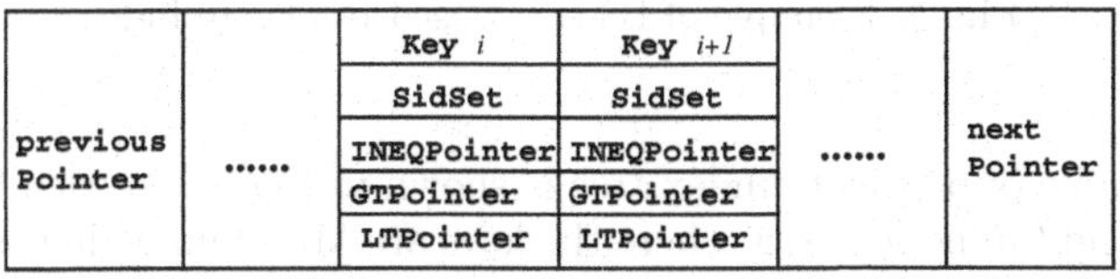

		Key *i*	Key *i+1*		
		SidSet	SidSet		
previous Pointer	......	INEQPointer	INEQPointer	......	next Pointer
		GTPointer	GTPointer		
		LTPointer	LTPointer		

Fig. 4. Data Structure of Leaf Node

It consists of an array of items, previousPointer and nextPointer. The definitions of previousPointer, key and nextPointer are same as those in B+tree respectively. For each item, besides the key, the SidSet is ID set of subscriptions which contain predicates in the forms of *Attribute = Key*, *Attribute <= Key* or *Attribute >= Key*. INEQPointer, GTPointer, LT-Pointer are the pointers of Inequality list node, GreaterThan list node and LessThan list node respectively. GTPointer points to the GreaterThan list node where exits the item with the biggest key less than or equal to the key kept in the item of the leaf node. For example, GTPointers of key 5 and 6 in Fig. 5. LTPointer points to the LessThan list node where exists the item with the smallest key greater than or equal to the key kept in the item of the leaf node. Because Inequality predicate represent two special ranges and has double links, INEQPointer can be set by the same way as that of GTPointer or LTPointer to keep order. In Fig.5, the setting of INEQPointer is the same as that of GTPointer.

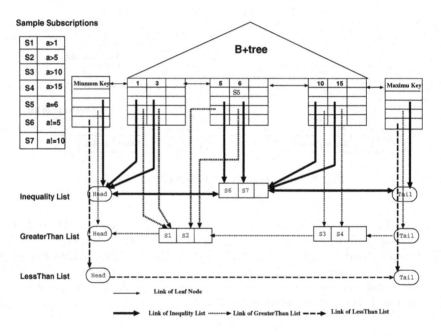

Fig. 5. Example of B+tree-Based Predicate Index

An example of predicate index tree is shown in Fig.5. On each list, there are both head and tail nodes exist where the keys are Minimum value and Maximum value in head and tail node respectively.

4.3   Insert Algorithm

Insert Algorithm has two main steps, 1)the first is insertion of leaf node list of B+tree, where INEQPointer, GTPointer or LTPointer of the new item should be set. 2)the second is insertion of one of the three lists according to the operator

```
Insert(Sid, Predicate, Root)
1   //Sid:Identifier of Subscription. Predicate:input predicate.
2   //Root: root of B+tree
3   Insert Predicate.constant into B+tree
4   Assign  the leaf node holding Predicate.constant to CurrrentLeafNode
5   IF (Predicate.constant didn't exist before insertion)
6      // initialize pointers of new inserted item on the leaf node
7      Assign the item with key Predicate.constant
8                                      to CurrentItem
9      Assign the item with biggest key less than
10                          Predicate.constant to PreviousItem
11     Assign the item with smallest key  greater than
12                          Predicate.constant to NextItem
13     //Set pointers according to nearby item.
14     Assign GTPointer of PreviousItem to GTPointer of CurrentItem
15     Assign LTPointer of NextItem to LTPointer of CurrentItem
16     Assign INEQPointer of PreviousItem to INEQPointer of CurrentItem
17  ENDIF
18  InsertToList(SID, Predicate, CurrentLeafNode)
```

Fig. 6. Algorithm of Inserting Leaf Node List

of predicate. Besides inserting *Sid* of new subscription to SidSet. INEQPointers, GTPointers or LTPointers of related items on leaf nodes should be adjusted as shown in Fig.7(Line 7) according to input.

The first step is shown in Fig. 6. Line 3 inserts *Predicate.constant* into leaf node list. This step is same as that of original B+tree. Line 5 judges whether the key of the added item is new or not. If the key is new, its related pointers must be set. Line6-12 get pointers of new added item, and its previous item and next item. Line 13-16 set pointers of new added item. Line 18 starts the function of the second step **InsertToList()**.

The second step of insertion is executed by function **InsertToList()**. The function first chooses which list should be inserted according to the operator contained in the predicate. Because three lists share the similar idea of ordering predicates according to their constants, here we introduce algorithm of inserting GreaterThan list only. The function name is **InsertToGreaterThanList()** and the algorithm is shown in Fig.7.

For line 3-4, the greaterThan node holding the item with biggest key less than or equal to Predicate.constant, so the operation here guarantee the right order of GreaterThan list. If the greaterThan node splits after insertion at line 5, line 6 inserts the new node into the list in order of key. line 7 adjusts GTPointers kept in the items of related leaf nodes by checking leaf node list according to the minimum key and maximum key kept in the items of two split GreaterThan list nodes. Line 9 adds sid into SidSet if the key of the item exited before insertion.

```
InsertToGreaterThanList(Sid, Predicate, LeafNode)
1  //Sid: Identifier of Subscription, Predicate: predicate with (>, >=)
2  //LeafNode: LeafNode holding the item with key  Predicate.constant
3  Insert GreaterThan list node pointed by GTPointer of the item
4         with key value Predicate.constant in the LeafNode
5  IF (GreaterThan node is split after insertion)
6     Create new node and insert it into GreaterThan list in order of key
7     Adjust GTPointers of items on leaf nodes related two nodes
8  ELSE IF (item with Predicate.constant existed before insertion)
9          Add Sid into SidSet corresponding to the item
10      ENDIF
11 ENDIF
```

Fig. 7. Algorithm of Function InsertToGreaterThanList()

4.4   Search Algorithm

According to the above insertion algorithm, the searching results on GreaterThan list is the part of GreaterThan list from the item with biggest key less than input key to the Head of GreaterThan list.

```
Search(InputKey, Root, Result)
1  //InputKey: input data from event, Root: root of B+tree
2  //Result: Set of Sid and initial value is null
3  Search Inputkey from Root of B+tree
4  IF (found)
5     Assign found LeafNode to CurrentLeafNode
6     Assign found item to CurrentItem
7     Add  SideSet of CurrentItem to Result
8  ELSE //not found
9     Assign leafNode where search(line 3) stopped to CurrentLeafNode
10 ENDIF
11 CollectPreviousINEQ(InputKey, CurrentLeafNode, Result)
12 CollectNextINEQ(InputKey, CurrentLeafNode, Result)
13 CollectGT(InputKey, CurrentLeafNode, Result)
14 CollectLT(InputKey, CurrentLeafNode, Result)
```

Fig. 8. Main Search Algorithm

The main search algorithm is shown in Fig.8. Line5-7 show the case when the *InputKey* is found. In this case, the content of SidSet kept in the found item in the leaf node should be added to the result(Line 7). Line8-10 show the case when the key is not found. In that case, the starting leaf node to get results from each list is set at Line 9. The algorithms of four **CollectPreviousINEQ()**, **CollectNextINEQ()**, **CollectGT()** and **CollectLT()** functions are similar.

In the following, only function collecting GreaterThan list(**CollectGT()**) is introduced. It is shown in Fig.9. Line 4-5 get starting node to collect results on GreaterThan list. Line 6-7 get first result item on GreaterThan list Line 8-12 collect results by scanning GreaterThan list from the first item.

```
CollectGT(InputKey, LeafNode,  Result)
1  //InputKey: input data from event
2  //LeafNode: LeafNode where B+tree search stopped.
3  //Result: Set of Sid
4  Get GTPointer of the item with the biggest key
5                       less than InputKey in LeafNode
6  Get the item which has biggest key value less than Inputkey
7     on the GreaterThan list node pointed the GTPointer(line4-5)
8  Assign the item to CurrentItem.
9  DO
10   Add SidSet of the CurrentItem into Result
11   Assign previous item of the CurrentItem to the CurrentItem
12 WHILE (Head of GreaterThan list is not met)
```

Fig. 9. Algorithm of Function CollectGT()

4.5   Delete Algorithm

The delete algorithm is a reverse procedure of insertion. Here the details are skipped for reason of space.

5   Analytical Comparison

Assume the number of unique predicate is n and the total number of predicates satisfied by event is L, the search time complexity is $O(\log n + L)$. Because pointers of the items on leaf node list need to be adjusted while do insertion as introduced in Fig.7(Line7), the number of leaf nodes accessed for adjustment of pointers is called $Number_{update}$. The minimum time complexity is $O(\log n)$ if all the pointers to be adjusted are kept in one same leaf node. Generally, the time complexity of insert operation is $O(n)$ for the reason of adjustment. Delete operation has same time complexity for the same reason. Our algorithm is built based on B+tree, only the leaf nodes are extended to point to three lists, so the space complexity is $O(n)$. In table 1, the comparisons of complexities are listed.

Considering Complexities of space and search time, we compare with Grouped Filter[16] only for its best complexities. In publish/subscribe systems, the ratio of data arriving is much higher than that of subscriptions updating. It means that performance of search (event matching) has a decisive influence on performance of publish/subscribe system. From the view of event matching, both Grouped Filter and PB+tree have same time complexity $O(\log n + L)$. But

Table 1. Comparisons of Space and Time Complexities

Algorithm	Space	Search	Insert	Delete
PB+tree	$O(n)$	$O(\log n + L)$	MIN:$O(\log n)$ MAX:$O(n)$	MIN:$O(\log n)$ MAX:$O(n)$
Grouped Filter	$O(n)$	$O(log n + L)$	$O(\log n)$	$O(\log n)$
Red-Black tree based	$O(n)$	$O(n)$	$O(\log n)$	$O(\log n)$
IBS-Tree	$O(n \log n)$	$O(\log n + L)$	$O(log^2 n)$	$O(log^2 n)$
Time Index	$O(n^2)$	$O(\log n + L)$	MIN:$O(\log n)$ MAX:$O(n)$	MIN:$O(log n)$ MAX:$O(n)$
Interval B+tree	$O(n)$	$O(n)$	$O(\log n)$	$O(\log n)$

as introduced in Section3, Grouped Filter uses four data structures and PB+tree use only one B+tree structure. Grouped Filter is a main memory predicate index and PB+tree is designed for secondary storage predicate index, which as far as we know, it is a novel predicate index.

Generally, the insertion and deletion complexity of PB+tree are $O(\log n + number_{update})$. In practice, it is reasonable to predicate that the $Number_{update} << n$ in the case that distribution of predicates with different operators and constants is uniform. That means the performance of insert and delete is very near to minimum complexity $O(\log n)$ and far from maximum complexity $O(n)$.

Besides differences in space and time complexities, the data structure designed for spatio-temporal database is used to find all intervals that intersect a input point, which means they mainly support predicates with format (Constant$_{start}$ < Attribute < Constant$_{End}$). In the case that the Constant$_{start}$ or Constant$_{End}$ is infinite, overlap will rise greatly for IBS-tree[11] and Time Index[6], search efficiency will decline greatly for IB+tree[2]. They don't support predicate with single operator directly.

By the comparisons in table1 and above analysises, we can conclude that efficient event matching can be reached by building secondary storage predicate index on PB+tree.

6   Conclusion

In this paper, we introduced a secondary storage predicate index structure based on B+tree. The index structure supports predicates with relational operators($<$,$<=,=,! =,>=,>$). The space complexity is $O(n)$. The time complexity of search operation is $O(\log n + L)$, and both insertion and deletion have Minimum $O(\log n)$ and Maximum $O(n)$ time complexity. Analytical comparison of our proposed algorithms with existing work indicates that our secondary storage predicate index is efficient for event matching.

References

1. Marcos K.Aguilera, Robert E.Strom, Daniel C. Sturman, Mark Astley, Tushar D.Chandra. Matching Events in a Content-based Subscription System. Eighteenth ACM Symposium on Principles of Distributed Computing(PODC), 1999
2. Tolga Bozkaya, Meral Ozsoyoglu. Indexing transaction time database. Information Sciences 112(1998)
3. Sirish Chandrasekaran, Michael J. Franklin. Streaming Queries over Streaming Data. Proceedings of the 28th VLDB Conference, Hong Kong, 2002
4. Jiangjun Chen, David J. DeWitt, Feng Tian, Yuan Wang. NiagaraCQ: A Scalable Continuous Query System for Internet Databases. ACM SIGMOD 2000
5. Y.-J. Chiang and R.Tamassai, "Dynamic Algorithms in Computational Geometry". Technial Report CS-91-24, Dept. of Computer Science, Brown Univ., 1991
6. Ramez Elmasri, Gene T.J. Wuu, Yeong-Joon Kim. THE TIME INDEX: AN ACCESS STRUCTURE FOR TEMPORAL DATA. VLDB 1990
7. P. Th. Eugster, P. Felber, R. Guerraoui and A.-M. Kermarrec. The Many Faces of Publish/Subscribe. Technical Report 200104, Swiss Federal Institute of Technology
8. Francoise Fabret, Francois Llirbat, Joao Pereira, Dennis Shasha. Efficient matching for Content-based Publish/Subscribe Systems. Technical report, INRIA, 2000.
9. Francoise Fabret, H.Arno Jacobsen, Francois Llirbat, Joao Pereira, Kenneth A.Ross, Dennis Shasha. Filtering Algorithms and Implementation for Very Fast Publish/Subscribe Systems. ACM SIGMOD 2001
10. Antonin Guttman. R-Trees: A Dynamic Index Structure for Spatial Searching. ACM SIGMOD 1984
11. Eric N. Hanson, Moez Chaaboun, Chang-Ho, Yu-Wang Wang. A Predicate Matching Algorithm for Database Rule Systems. ACM SIGMOD 1990
12. Eric N. Hanson, Theodore Hohnson. Selection Predicate Indexing for Active Database Using Interval Skip List. TR94-017. CIS department, Univeristy of Florida, 1994
13. Eric N. Hanson, Chris Carnes, Lan Huang, Mohan Konyala, Lloyd Noronha. Scalable Trigger Processing. ACM SIGMOD 1999
14. Annika Hinze, Sven Bittner. Efficient Distribution-Based Event Filtering. International Workshop on Distributed Event Based Systems. Austrai July 2002
15. H.Arno Jacobsen, Francoise Fabret. Publish and Subscribe Systems. Tutorial. ICDE 2001
16. Samuel Madden, Mehul Shah, Joseph Hellerstein, Vijayshankar Raman. Continuously Adaptive Continuous Queries(CACA) over Streams. ACM SIGMOD 2002
17. Rajeev Motwani. Models and Issues in Data Stream Systems. Invited Talk. PODS 2002
18. Tak W.Yan, Hector Garcia-Molina. The SIFT Information Dissemination System. In ACM TODS 2000

Data Replication at Web Proxies in Content Distribution Network

Xuanping Zhang [1], Weidong Wang [2], Xiaopeng Tan [1], and Yonghu Zhu [1]

[1] Department of Computer Science, Xi'an Jiaotong University, Xi'an, P.R.C
{zxp, xptan, yhhu}@mail.xjtu.edu.cn
[2] The High Speed Wire Rod Mill, MaAnShan IRON & STEEL Co. LTD, P.R.C
wdwang@sina.com

Abstract. This paper investigates the problem of optimally replicating objects at the candidate proxies in content distribution network. In our model, each proxy in the set of candidates has a finite storage capacity for replicating objects and charges fee for use. The optimization problem is to find a set of proxies from candidates set for replicating objects at them such that the total access cost is minimized, subject to the constraints that the objects placed at a proxy should not exceed the storage capacity of the proxy and the total fees charged by the proxies should not exceed a pre-specified budget. We formulate this problem as a combinational optimization problem and show that this optimization problem is NP complete. We propose two heuristics and evaluate them by simulation. The simulation results show that these two heuristics could significantly reduce the access cost.

1 Introduction

The proliferation of the Internet has resulted in a rapid increase in the number of Internet users and applications. This growth has led to congested network links, overload Web servers and frustrated users. Content Distribution Network (CDN) has emerged as an effective approach to alleviate the origin server, reduce the network traffic and improve the client response time. A CDN consists of a set of distributed proxy servers that act as intermediaries between the origin servers and end user for efficient delivery of Web content. The proxy servers replicate data objects from origin server and serve requests for these objects from the proxy closest to the Web clients.

CDNs can be classified by the degree of content objects duplication among the proxy servers. One type of CDN duplicates all data objects at every proxy servers. This would waste large amount of storage for replicating data objects that are not frequently requested by clients. In addition, full duplication may generate heavy traffic in the network to upload or update the data objects. The other type of CDN duplicates only subset of data objects at each proxy servers. Duplication of frequently requested objects can balance the workload of the proxy servers and improve the storage utilization. In the latter type of CDN, the two key factors in determining the effectiveness of CDN are the placement of proxy servers and replication of data objects. The proper placement of proxy servers can effectively reduce web access delay, network congestion, and server load. Previous work has shown that a carefully designed placement scheme (i.e., the number and placement of proxies) can improve

X. Zhou, Y. Zhang, and M.E. Orlowska (Eds.): APWeb 2003, LNCS 2642, pp. 560–569, 2003.

system performance significantly [1-6]. Some research work also has been done on the optimally replicating data objects at Web servers [7-9].

The placement of proxy servers and the replication of data objects are two interdependent problems. e.g., the optimally replicating objects at proxies depends on the placement of proxies. Some research work has been done on these problems. But they consider only one of these problems independently. In this paper, we study the problem of optimally replicating objects combining with the proxy placement. Supposed that CDN proxies can be chosen from a number of candidate servers distributed in network. Each candidate server has a finite storage capacity for replicating objects and charge fixed fee if it is used as a proxy. The problem is to find a set of proxies from candidates set for replicating objects at them such that the total access cost is minimized, subject to the constraints of each proxy storage capacity and the pre-specified budget. We formulate this problem as a combinational optimization problem and show that this optimization problem is NP complete. We develop some heuristics and evaluate them by simulation.

The rest of this paper is organized as follow. In section 2 we discuss some of the previous work. In section 3 we formulate the problem and show it is NP complete. Section 4 presents the heuristics we developed. Section 5 contains the performance evaluation results. Conclusions are in section 6.

2   Previous Work

A number of papers have addressed the problem of the placement of Web proxies or the replication of data objects at Web proxies. Li et al.[1] presented the problem of optimal proxy placement in a tree so that the overall latency of accessing the Web sever is minimized. The problem is formulated by using dynamic programming method and the optimal solution is obtained. Jia et al. [2] extended this work to an environment where web servers are replicated. In [4], A more general model for proxy placement in tree that considers both read and write operation to the Web objects was proposed and efficient algorithms were developed. The problem of proxy placement in general network topology is discussed in [3,14]. Cronin et al. [14] studied the problem of proxy placement on a restricted set of hosts with the objective of minimizing the maximum distance between any client to a mirror, and presented three graph theoretic algorithms (Min k-Center, l-Greedy, and Cost-Adjustable Set Cover) and two heuristics. Qiu et al. [3] formulated the problem of Web server replicas placement into the p-median problem, and proposed several heuristics. The problem of proxy placement in above work is assumed that a proxy (or mirrored server) duplicates all data object in the original sever.

Some work has been done on the problem of partially replicating data objects at proxies. Jia et al. [7] studied the problem of data replication in en-route proxies with finite storage capacities and proposed a greedy and a knapsack-based heuristic. Xu et al. [9] discussed the issue of data replication with considering both read and update costs to data objects. An efficient algorithm was developed for tree networks and several heuristics were proposed for arbitrary networks. Kangasharju et al. [8] discussed the problem to replicate data in CND servers with finite capacity for storing objects. They formulated this problem as a combinational optimization problem with objective of the average number of clients traversed is minimized when clients fetch objects from the nearest server containing the requested object. Four natural heuristics were developed and compared numerically using real Internet topology data.

3 The Problem and Model

In this section, we consider the problem to distribute the content of a Web site in the Internet. The Internet is modeled by a connected graph $G(V, E)$, where V represents a set of nodes and E a set of links of the network. For a link $(u, v) \in E$, $d(u, v)$ is the distance of the link. Suppose that a Web server S contains a set of m data objects denoted by $O = \{o_1, o_2, \ldots, o_m\}$. The data objects can be images, video clips, audio files, or large data files, etc. Each data object o_i has a size (i.e., number of bytes), denoted by z_{oi}, and an updated frequency (or up-load frequency) w_{oi}. Each client node $v \in V$ has a read frequency to each data object o_i, denoted by $r(v, o_i)$, $1 \leq i \leq m$. In order to improve the performance for access to these data objects, the Web site owner (called content owner) needs to contract to some ISPs (web servers) to host the contents at their web servers that are close to the end user. We assume that there are t candidates of edge servers (proxies), denoted by $C = \{p_1, p_2, \ldots, p_t\}$. Each proxy, p_j, $1 \leq j \leq t$, has a storage capacity available for S, denoted by Z_{pj}, and will charge S for fees, denoted by F_{pj}, if it is chosen by S for content distribution. Our problem is to find a subset of proxies $P(P \subseteq C)$ and determine a subset of objects that should be replicated at each proxy $p \in P$, such that the overall access cost is minimized, subject to the constraints that the objects placed at a proxy should not exceed the available storage capacity of the proxy and the total fees charged by the proxies should not exceed a pre-specified budget.

We define the data access cost as the data size times the distance that the data is transmitted in the network. This cost reflects the bandwidth consumption for data retrieval and is usually used as the basis for calculation of fees charged by Telecom companies. Let $d(v, o_i)$ denote the distance from v to object o_i. It is usually the distance from v to the closest proxy that holds o_i. $d(v, o_i)$ can be the distance from v to the server S if v is closer to S or o_i is not replicated at any proxy. When a client v requests an object o_i, the request will be forwarded to a proxy (usually the closest one) that holds the object. The weighted cost for v to read object o_i is

$$r(v, o_i) \times z_{o_i} \times d(v, o_i).$$

The total cost for all clients to read object o_i is

$$\sum_{v \in V} r(v, o_i) \times z_{o_i} \times d(v, o_i)$$

There is also a cost for uploading the object to the proxies or updating the object at the proxies. Let $P(o_i)$ denote the set of proxies that hold object o_i, where $P(o_i) \subseteq P$. We assume the multicast model is used to upload (or update) data objects to the proxies. The multicast mechanism uses the shortest path tree to transmit object o_i to the set of proxies $P(o_i)$. Let $SPT(S, P(o_i))$ denote the shortest path tree rooted from S and linking all the proxies in $P(o_i)$. The overall cost to upload (or update) the object o_i is

$$w_{o_i} \times z_{o_i} \sum_{(x,y) \in SPT(S, P(o_i))} d(x, y)$$

The access cost to data object o_i can be represented as:

$$AccessCost\ (o_i) = \sum_{v \in V} r(v, o_i) \times z_{o_i} \times d(v, o_i) + w_{o_i} \times z_{o_i} \sum_{(x,y) \in SPT(S, P(o_i))} d(x, y) \tag{1}$$

The overall access cost to all m data objects can be represented as:

$$AccessCost\ = \sum_{i=1}^{m} AccessCost\ (o_i) \cdot \tag{2}$$

We define the following variables:

$$x_{ij} = \begin{cases} 1 & \text{if object } o_i \text{ is replicated at proxy } p_j \\ 0 & \text{otherwise} \end{cases}$$

The storage constraint on the number of objects that can be replicated at proxy p_j is represented as:

$$\forall p_j \in P: \quad \sum_{i=1}^{m} x_{ij} z_{oi} \leq Z_{pj} \tag{3}$$

The content owner may have a constraint on the total budget, denoted by B, that can be spent for content distribution. The number of proxies selected for content distribution must be subject to this constraint:

$$\sum_{p_j \in P} F_{p_j} \leq B \tag{4}$$

The problem to replicate objects at candidate proxies can be described as follow:

Find P and data replication at proxies in P, such that $AccessCost$ defined in (2) is minimized, subject to constraints (3) and (4) are met.

The problem described above is a constrained optimization problem. If we suppose each candidate proxy has enough storage capacity to hold all objects and pre-specified budget is infinite, this problem will be reduced to the same problem as described in[10] and is proved to be NP-Complete problem.

4 Heuristic Algorithms

Because the problem described above is NP-complete, finding the optimal solution is not feasible. In this section, we will solve this problem by using a greedy heuristic algorithm, which can find a near-optimal solution in polynomial complexity.

Suppose P is a set of proxies selected from candidate servers C. At each proxy $p_j \in P$, some data objects have been replicated. If we replicate an object o_i at the proxy p_j, the cost for clients to read object o_i will be decreased and the cost to update object o_i will be increased. For a client v, if p_j is closer to v than other proxies that hold object o_i, The reduced cost for v to read object o_i is

$$r(v, o_i) z_{oi} [d(v, o_i) - d(v, p_j)]$$

The overall reduced cost for clients to read object o_i can be represent as:

$$\sum_{v \in V \wedge [d(v, o_i) - d(v, p_j)] > 0} r(v, o_i) z_{oi} [d(v, o_i) - d(v, p_j)]$$

To replicate object o_i at proxy p_j, the object o_i must be transmitted along the shortest path from S to p_j. Let $NL(p_j, P(o_i))$ denote the set of links that are included in the shortest path from origin sever S to proxy p_j but not in the shortest path tree $SPT(S, P(o_i))$. The cost increased for updating object o_i is represented as:

$$w_{o_i} \times z_{o_i} \sum_{(x,y)\in NL(p_j,P(o_i))} d(x,y)$$

We define the gain of replicating the object o_i at the proxy p_j, denoted by g_{ij}, which is the reduced cost for read minus the increased cost for update and is represented as:

$$g_{ij} = \sum_{v\in V \wedge [d(v,o_i)-d(v,p_j)]>0} r(v,o_i)z_{oi}[d(v,o_i) - d(v,p_j)] - w_{o_i}z_{o_i} \sum_{(x,y)\in NL(p_j,P(o_i))} d(x,y) \qquad (5)$$

We also define the *Object-Proxy Benefit* from replicating the object o_i at the proxy p_j, denoted by e_{ij}, as follows:

$$e_{ij} = \frac{g_{ij}}{z_{o_i}} = \sum_{v\in V \wedge [d(v,o_i)-d(v,p_j)]>0} r(v,o_i)[d(v,o_i) - d(v,p_j)] - w_{o_i} \sum_{(x,y)\in NL(p_j,P(o_i))} d(x,y) \qquad (6)$$

If we choose the p_j as a replicated proxy, the total gain (denoted by G_j) of replicating some objects at the proxy p_j is:

$$G_j = \sum_{i=1}^{m} x_{ij} g_{ij} \qquad (7)$$

Let G_j^* be the maximum gain for choosing p_j as a replicated proxy, *that is,* the G_j^* is the maximum G_j defined in (7) subject to $\sum_{i=1}^{m} x_{ij}z_i \le Z_{pj}$. We define E_j, the *Max-Proxy Benefit* from selecting the p_j as a replicated proxy, as follow:

$$E_j = \frac{G_j^*}{F_{pj}} \qquad (8)$$

Based on the *Object-Proxy Benefit* defined in (6) and *Max-Proxy Benefit* defined in (8), we propose two data replication heuristics, which are called *OPB(Object-Proxy Benefit)* and *MPB(Max-Proxy Benefit)*.

Heuristic OPB. The value of *Object-Proxy Benefit* e_{ij} in (6) represents the expected benefit if we replicated o_i at p_j. The heuristic *OPB* selects the maximum *Object-Proxy Benefit* to replicate an object at a proxy each time.

```
Algorithm OPB {
  P={S};
  Calculate each e_ij under the condition of no data
      replication, let Ω={ e_ij |i=1,2,...m, j=1,2,..t};
  While Ω≠φ {
    Select a maximum e_ij and eliminate it from Ω;
    If  z_oi ≤ z_pj and e_ij ≥0{
      If  p_j ∉ P and B≥F_pj {
        B=B-F_pj;
        P=P∪{p_j};
      }     /* select p_j as a proxy */
      If  p_j ∈ P {
        Replicate o_i at p_j;
        z_pj =z_pj -z_oi;
        Recalculate e_ik under the condition of current
            data replication for k=1,2...t;
      }
    }    /* end if */
  }   /* end while */
  return;
}  /* end OPB */
```

Heuristic MPB. The value of *Max-Proxy Benefit* E_j in (8) represents the expected maximum benefit if we choose p_j as a replicated proxy. The heuristic *MPB* each time selects a candidate proxy which has maximum *Max-Proxy Benefit* as a replicated proxy and replicate objects to make the total gain maximized.

To approximately compute the maximum gain G_j^*, we choose object one by one in decreasing order by e_{ij}. An object can be replicated at the proxy p_j only if the remaining storage capacity of the proxy p_j is greater than its size and the benefit e_{ij} is positive.

```
Algorithm MPB {
  P={S};
  Calculate each Eⱼ under the condition of no data
      replication, let Ψ={Eⱼ | j=1,2,..t};
  While Ψ≠φ {
    Select a maximum Eⱼ and eliminate it from Ψ;
    If  B≥Fₚⱼ  and Eⱼ ≥0{
      B=B-Fₚⱼ;
      P=P∪{pⱼ};
      Replicate objects at pⱼ to gain Eⱼ;
      Recalculate each Eₖ in Ψ for k=1,2,...t;
    }/* select pⱼ as a proxy and replicate objects at it*/
  }  /* end while */
  return;
}  /* end MPB */
```

The time complexities of the OBP and MPB algorithms are $O(mnt^2+m^2t^2)$, where m is the number of the objects, n is the number of the clients and t is the number of the candidate proxies.

5 Simulation

In this section, we present experimental results of our heuristic algorithms. Network topologies used in the simulations are generated using the BRITE topology generator, downloaded from http://cs-pub.bu.edu/brite/index.htm. The size of the networks used in the simulations is of 300 nodes. We use the Waxman's probability model for interconnecting the nodes of the topology. In the simulation, a server node and 30 candidate proxy nodes are randomly picked up from the graph.

The total number of data objects stored at the web server is 1000. Each object's size, updated frequency, and read frequency by each node are generated randomly. The size of each object is in the range from 1 to 100. The updated frequency and the read frequency by each node are in the range from 1 to 10.

In our simulations, we define the relative access cost as the evaluation metric, which is the access cost as a percentage of the base cost. The base cost means the access cost under the condition of no data replication, that is, all clients access objects from Web server. The metric of relative access cost is independent of network topology.

$$Relative cost = access cost / base cost \times 100\%$$

To evaluate the performance of OPB and MPB heuristics, we compare our algorithms with the random method which randomly picks up one candidate proxy and stores objects as many as possible. We run the random method 10 times and the average relative access cost is used as it's result.

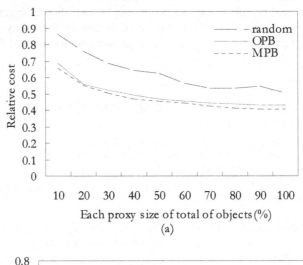

(a)

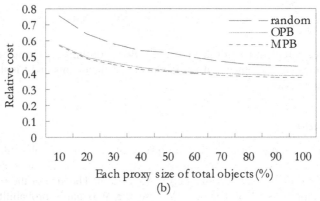

(b)

Fig. 1. Relative cost versus proxy size. (a) Budget=20% of total proxy fees,(b) Budget=40% of total proxy fees.

In the simulation of Figure 1, we assume each proxy has the same size. We give a fixed pre-specified budget and vary the proxy size from 10% of the total object sizes to 100%. In Figure 1a and Figure 1b, the budget is respectively fixed to 20% and 40% of total candidate proxy fees. We find that the OPB and MPB algorithms perform better than random algorithm, and the relative cost will be reduced as the each proxy size is increased.

Figure 2 and Figure 3 illustrated the relative cost versus pre-specified budget varied from 10% of the total candidate proxy fees to 100%, respectively. In Figure 2 we assume each proxy has same size. Figure 2a fixes each proxy size to 60% of total object sizes and Figure 2b fixes each proxy size to 80%. In Figure 3, each proxy size is randomly generated in the range from 10% of total object sizes to 100%. These simulation results show that the OPB and MPB algorithms also perform better than random algorithm, and the relative cost will be reduced as the pre-specified budget is increased.

From Figure 1-3, the following can be observed:

1) The OPB and MPB Algorithm perform significantly better than the random algorithm. When each proxy storage capacities or the budget is tight, the OPB and MPB algorithms produce much better results than random algorithm. As the proxy storage capacities or budget become less constrained, the relative cost of the random algorithm is getting closer to the OPB and MPB algorithms.

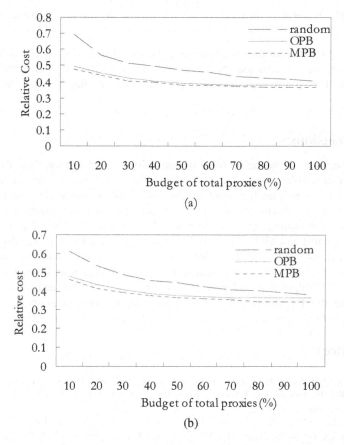

Fig. 2. Relative cost versus budget with each proxy having same size (a) proxy size=60% of total object (b) proxy size=80% of total object

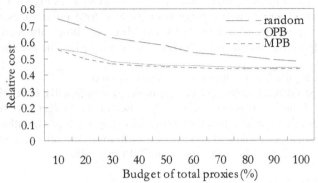

Fig. 3. Relative cost versus budget with each proxy size generated randomly

2) The OPB algorithm is almost as good as MPB algorithm. But through detail observation, we can find the MPB algorithm performs slightly better than the OPB algorithm. This is because that the MPB take the fee charged by each proxy into account.

6 Conclusions

In this paper, we study the problem of optimally replicating objects at the candidate proxies. This problem is to select a set of proxies from candidate servers and replicate objects at them so that the total access cost is minimized under the total budget constraint. We formulate this problem as a combinational optimization problem and show that this optimization problem is NP complete. We develop two heuristic algorithms, OPB and MPB. The simulations are performed and the results reported in this paper show that the OPB and MPB algorithms perform much better than random algorithm when the proxy storage capacities and total budget are limited. On the other hand, the MPB algorithm performs slightly better than the OPB algorithm because the MPB take the fee charged by each proxy into account. In general, the methods proposed in this paper can be used to develop effective content distribution network.

References

[1]   B. Li, M. J. Golin, G.F. Italiano, X. deng and K. Sohraby: "On The Optimal Placememnt of Web Proxies in The Internet", Proc. IEEE INFOCOM 1999, vol. 3, March 1999,pp. 1282–1290.
[2]   X.H. Jia, D.Y. Li, X.D. Hu, D.Z. Du: "Optimal Placement of Web Proxies for Replicated Web Servers in then Internet", The Computer Journal, Vol.44, No.5, Oct. 2001, pp.329–339.
[3]   Q. Lili, V. N. Padmanabhan, and G. M. Voelker: "On the placement of Web server replicas" Proc. IEEE INFOCOM 2001, vol. 3, 2001, pp. 1587–1596.
[4]   X.H. Jia, D.Y. Li, X.D. Hu, D.Z. Du: "Placement of read-write Web proxies on the Internet", Proc. of IEEE 21st International Conference on Distributed Computing Systems, 2001. pp. 687–690.

[5] O. Wolfson, and A. Milo: "The Multicast Policy and Its Relationship to Replicated Data Placement", ACM Transaction on Database Systems, Vol.16, No.1, 1991, pp.181–205.

[6] K. Kalpakis, K. Dasgupta, O. Wolfson: "Optimal placement of replicas in trees with read, write, and storage costs", IEEE Transactions on Parallel and Distributed Systems, Vol. 12, No. 6, June 2001, pp. 628 –637.

[7] X.H. Jia, D.Y. Li, D.Z. Du: "Data Replication in En-Route Web Proxies", submitted to IEEE Intern. Conf. On Distributed Computing Systems, USA, May, 2003.

[8] J. Kangasharju, J. Roberts, and K.W. Ross: "Object Replication Strategies in Content Distribution Networks", Computer Communications, Vol. 25, 2002, pp.376–383.

[9] J.L. Xu; B. Li; D.L. Lee: "Placement problems for transparent data replication proxy services", IEEE Journal on Selected Areas in Communications, Vol. 20, No.7, Sept. 2002, pp. 1383 –1398.

[10] T. Loukopoulos, I. Ahmad: "Static and adaptive data replication algorithms for fast information access in large distributed systems", Proc. of 20th International Conference on Distributed Computing Systems, 2000, pp. 385 –392.

[11] T. Loukopoulos, I. Ahmad, D. Papadias: "An overview of data replication on the Internet", Proc. of International Symposium on Parallel Architectures, Algorithms and Networks, 2002, pp.31–36.

[12] H. Stockinger, A. Samar, B. Allcock, I. Foster, K. Holtman, and B. Tierney: "File and object replication in data grids", Proc. of 10th IEEE International Symposium on High Performance Distributed Computing, 2001. pp. 76 –86.

[13] I. Cidon, S. Kutten, R. Soffer: " Optimal Allocation of Electronic Content", Proc. IEEE INFOCOM 2001, vol. 3, 2001, pp. 1773 –1780.

[14] E. Cronin, S. Jamin, C. Jin. A.R. Kurc, D. Raz, and Y. Shavitt: "Constrained Mirror Placement on the Internet", IEEE Journal on Selected Areas in Communications, Vol.20, No.7, Sept. 2002.

A Hash-Based Collaborative Transcoding Proxy System

Xiu Wu and Kian-Lee Tan

Department of Computer Science,
National University of Singapore, Singapore 119260
{wux, tankl}@comp.nus.edu.sg

Abstract. This paper proposes a hash-based collaborative transcoding proxy system for heterogeneous client environment. The system aims to improve the system performance in two aspects, caching efficiency and workload balancing. This system employs a hash-based object caching strategy, which optimizes the cache storage utilization by removing redundant objects scattering in different locations of the system cache. In addition, cache replacement algorithm deployed at the transcoding proxy is examined. Conclusion is drawn that object access rate should be considered when making eviction decision. On the other hand, a hash-based workload distribution strategy is proposed to share the expensive transcoding load among proxies. This strategy performs well with balanced hash function. With unbalanced hash function, satisfactory load sharing is achieved by an optimized strategy, which allows the overloaded proxy to outsource some transcoding tasks to less overloaded neighbors.

1 Introduction

As the Internet becomes part and parcel of our daily life, many of today's devices (for example, laptops, PDAs and mobile phones) have incorporated Internet access features. These devices have very different capabilities, such as network bandwidth, processing power, storage capacity and screen display size. For the same web content to be accessible by the diversified client devices, it must be adapted to suit the specific device requirements. In other words, there exist several variants for the same object. Here we refer to these variants as different versions of the same object. Different versions of the same object differ in modality and fidelity.

Transcoding is the process of transforming a web object from an existing version to another version with lower resolution, or to a different format. Generally, the version after transcoding has smaller size, and is referred to as a less detailed version. The original version can be transcoded to any less detailed version. While some transcoded versions can be transcoded to some less detailed versions, this is not always possible because of the loss of information during the previous transcoding process. Transcodable versions of an object are also known as its useful versions. As discussed in [1], there are three main approaches to content transcoding in the Internet [1]. In the *server-based approach* [8], transcoding is performed by the content server offline, and various versions of the same object are stored in the server's disk. However, with

X. Zhou, Y. Zhang, and M.E. Orlowska (Eds.): APWeb 2003, LNCS 2642, pp. 570–582, 2003.

today's ever increasing variety of client devices, maintaining multiple versions for the same object at the content server is not cost effective. The second approach is *client-based transcoding* that relies on clients to carry out the resource intensive transcoding operation. This approach is impractical in view of the limited processing power and network bandwidth for weakly connected devices. For these reasons, many studies have been conducted to explore the advantages of proxy-based approach, which transcodes the object at the proxy on-the-fly according to client's requirements [6][7][10]. Proxy in the proxy-based transcoding is referred to as transcoding proxy. Besides transcoding, another important feature of transcoding proxy is caching where objects (original or transcoded) are retained at the proxy so as to reduce network latency as well as avoid repeating some recently performed transcoding operations.

If all the transcoding operations are assigned to the *last hop* proxy that directly connects to the clients, the last hop proxy will be overwhelmed by the costly transcoding operations. In [1], a collaborative transcoding proxy system was presented. The proxies are hierarchically organized and clients are assigned to edge proxies that located at the lowest level in the hierarchy. The basic operation of the system is summarized as follows. Clients send HTTP requests to their respective assigned edge proxies. The request flows up the hierarchy until an exact version or useful version of the requested object is located by one of proxies along the path. These two cache events are referred to as *cache exact hit* and *cache useful hit* respectively. If neither *cache exact hit* nor *useful hit* occurs along the way (*cache miss* event), the request is forwarded to the content server by the root proxy. The content server will reply with the original version object. In proxy-based transcoding, content server would not perform transcoding. The found object (either from a cache or a content server) travels down the proxy hierarchy to the client. When a *useful version* object is sent towards the client, according to the workload distribution strategy, transcoding will be carried out by one of the proxies along the object return path. All objects travels down the cache hierarchy leave a copy at each proxy's cache along the return path. Three workload distribution strategies are suggested for the system, NOINFO, THR (threshold) and LL (Least-loaded). In NOINFO, a proxy performs transcoding whenever it receives an object that requires transcoding, In THR a proxy relies on a preconfigured load threshold and its own load to determine whether to perform the transcoding operation locally or delegate it to lower level proxies. The last approach is LL. A proxy compares its own load with that of lower level proxies along the object return path to make decision. Both THR and LL are shown to outperform THR tremendously. Caching is another issue addressed in [1]. The main focus in is to study which version is more valuable to be cached, the version before transcoding (coverage-based) or the transcoded version (demand-based). With replacement policy sticks to LRU, it is revealed that demand-based caching performs better. This system has certain limitations. Firstly, the workload distribution is limited in balancing the load for proxies along the return path instead of the whole system. Secondly cache storage is not fully utilized due to the presence of duplicate objects. Thirdly, due to a lack of global information about the availability of the various versions for an object in the whole system, the system fails to exploit cached objects effectively to achieve minimum transcoding cost. Lastly, LRU replacement policy overlooks reference rate. We believe a better cache performance may be achieved by other replacement policies.

In this paper, we proposed a hash-based collaborative transcoding proxy system. In the devised system, proxies are organized in a hierarchy and according to a common hash function, web objects are hashed to one of the proxies. This proxy is referred to as the *hashed proxy* for the object. It is responsible for caching as well as transcoding for the set of objects that hashed to it. Our experiment shows that the proposed hash-based collaborative transcoding proxy system not only utilizes the cache well, but also achieves a more balanced workload distribution. As a result, the system outperforms existing method in terms of throughput and response time.

The rest of this paper is organized as follows. Section 2 defines the system environment. After that, we present the proposed hash-based systems in section 3. Simulation setup and results are reported in section 4. Section 5 concludes the paper

2 System Environment

In this section, we define the system environment so as to facilitate our discussion in subsequent sections. In a heterogeneous client environment, transcoding proxies are organized in a hierarchy. Proxy-based approach is employed in the system.

2.1 Collaborative Proxy System and Client Devices

The homogeneous proxies are organized as a hierarchy. Edge proxies are located at the lowest level and are connected to clients directly. The top-most level is the root proxy, which is responsible for communication with content servers. It is assumed that each proxy in the system is capable of performing any transcoding tasks needed. In the system studied, message flow is only between different levels of proxies. The proposed collaborative proxy systems extends the proxy system presented in [1], cooperation is not confined to proxies along the same request path but all proxies. More comprehensive discussion will be provided in section 3.

Clients' capabilities vary drastically in many aspects. Each client is assigned to one of the edge proxies, which will handle all its HTTP requests. Upon connected to the assigned edge proxy, a client needs to register and meanwhile conveys its capability information to the proxy. This information will be used by the proxy system to judge which version best suits the specific client's requirements.

2.2 Hashing

In the hash-based system, a hash function is defined and known by all proxies in the system. As suggested in [9], the hash function can take into account the entire URL, in which objects within the same page will likely be hashed over different proxy caches. This scattering can help to spread the load of popular pages over different proxy caches. Alternatively, we can also hash only the hostname portion of the URL, in which all the objects in the same site have the same hashed proxy [9]. A proxy can always determine the hashed proxy for an object by computing its hash value. Alternatively, upon receiving a request directly from the client, the edge proxy can decide the hashed proxy based on the hash function, and include the hashed proxy identity in the HTTP request as meta–information. This saves other proxies the effort of evaluating the hash function in order to determine the hashed proxy of requested object.

3 Hash-Based Collaborative Proxy Systems

In this section, we propose a basic hash-based proxy system, called *hash-default system*. We then present three optimizations to improve the performance of the basic system. We shall refer to the systems with these optimizations as *hash-dup system, hash-outsrc system* and *hash-dup-outsrc system* respectively.

3.1 Hash-Default System

The proposed *hash-default system* is a hash-based proxy system that employs a hash-based object caching strategy, a replacement algorithm and a hash-based workload balancing strategy. We will also present the message flow of the system.

Hash-Based Object Caching. Constraint by the cache storage, it is not possible to keep all versions of all objects in the proxy caches. Therefore it is crucial to manage the overall cache storage effectively so as to improve cache performance. This can be done by keeping as many objects as possible in the proxy cache, and providing proxies with the knowledge about the availability of various versions of a requested object in the whole system. The former can be achieved by eliminating duplicate objects from proxy caches globally. Meanwhile, by caching various versions of the same objects in the same cache, availability of various versions of a requested object can be retrieved from one of the proxies

In the *hash-default system*, the cache location for each object is determined by the hash function. Only the hashed proxy is responsible for caching the set of objects hashed to it. This prevents the system from caching the same object redundantly in different proxy caches. On the other hand, as all versions for the same object have the same URL, they will be hashed to the same proxy. Therefore, hashed proxy contains the availability information of various versions for the requested object when serving requests. This enables the system to exploit cached objects effectively to achieve minimum transcoding cost imposed.

Cache Replacement Policy. Cache replacement policy is deployed at the proxy cache to ensure more valuable objects get more chances to be cached. To yield optimal cache performance, it is important to identify the set of popular objects. While LRU cache replacement policy considers the access recency when making eviction decision [2][14], the LFU algorithm favors objects with higher reference rate [3][13]. In this paper, the LFU algorithm is extended for deployment at the transcoding proxies as follows: the reference rates of difference versions of an object is considered separately, as among the various versions of an object, some versions may be more popular than other versions due to client devices distribution or different access pattern for different client device. For subsequent sections, if the LRU algorithm is employed, the suffix "LRU" is added to the system name. Similarly, when the LFU algorithm is used, the suffix "LFU" is appended.

For replacement, the time complexity for LFU is O(logN) [3][13], which is more expensive that that of the case for LRU, which is O(1). In this paper, we present a *PartialLFU* cache replacement policy, which is a compromise between LRU and LFU. It is depicted as follows. Generally, entries are organized based on recency, this is the same as LRU. In addition, the reference rate for each entry is kept. Periodically, a proportion of the cache, to be more specific, those most recently accessed entries, will be sorted according to reference rate. The time complexity for *PartialLFU* is O(1) for replacement generally. Sorting for the recently access entries may also be carried out when the proxy is idle. The suffix "*PartialLFU*" is used to indicate the adoption of *PartialLFU* cache replacement policy.

Hash-Based Workload Distribution. In this section, we discuss how to distribute the transcoding workload across the various proxies in the *hash-default system*. When no exact version but a useful version of the requested object is available, the useful version must be transcoded before being delivered to the client. This raises a question: who should perform the transcoding operation? As transcoding operation is resource intensive, an efficient strategy that can distribute the workload evenly across proxies in the system is called for.

A simple hash-based workload distribution policy is proposed for the *hash-default system*, in which the hashed proxy is responsible for all transcoding tasks associated with objects hashed to it. Thus, besides caching the set of objects cached to it, hashed proxy has to handle the transcoding tasks pertaining to the same set of objects. Given a good hash function, this will balance out the transcoding workload across all the proxies in the proxy system. It is robust even in the circumstance where some edge proxies are assigned with more clients, as more clients assigned to the edge proxy does not necessarily lead to more transcoding burden to that particular request path.

This workload distribution strategy also benefits the hashed-based caching strategy proposed. Having both caching and transcoding for an object carried out in the same proxy, it provides the hashed proxy the convenience of caching a new transcoded version immediately after it performs the particular transcoding task, without extra transmission cost incurred.

Message Flow. With the hashed-based strategy and hash-based workload distribution strategy defined, in this session, we outline the network message flow of the *hash-default system*. When a HTTP request arrives at the proxy system, the edge proxy determines its hashed proxy according to the hash function, and forwards it towards the hashed proxy. The HTTP request is forwarded hop by hop until it reaches the hashed proxy. Once the hashed proxy gets the message, it looks for the requested version of the object in its local cache. If an *exact hit* occurs, a copy of the object is returned to the client along the return path. If the hashed proxy does not have the exact version of the object, but a useful version is located in cache, the hashed proxy transcodes the useful version to the requested version, caches the transcoded version and sends it to the client. Lastly, if neither an exact version nor a *useful version* is owned by the hashed proxy, the request is forwarded to the content server, which returns the original version of the object to the root proxy of the system. This original version object is sent to the hashed proxy, where it is transcoded if necessary, cached and returned to the client. Fig 1 and Fig 2 illustrate the message flow. For clarification, the message flow in Fig. 2 is numbered to indicate the order.

As all requests for the same object will be sent to the same hashed proxy, the hashed proxy can precisely keep track of the reference rate for objects hashed to it, which is required when enforcing the LFU cache replacement policy.

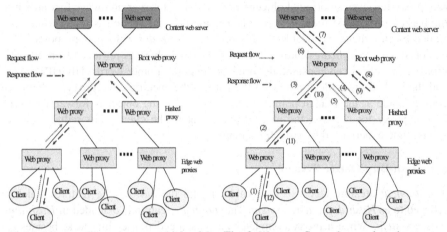

Fig. 1. Message flow when exact hit/useful hit occurs in hashed proxy

Fig. 2. Message flow when cache miss occurs in hashed proxy

3.2 Hash-Outsrc System

In terms of workload distribution, the *Hash-default system* is limited in certain circumstances, to be more specific, when the hash function fails to scatter the objects evenly among the proxies. In this case, some proxies may have more objects hashed to them as compared with others. This imposes more transcoding tasks on these proxies and may cause them to be overloaded. To circumvent this problem, *Hash-outsrc system* is proposed. It is equipped with *outsourcing* feature, which enables the overloaded proxy to outsource some of its transcoding tasks to a less loaded neighbor, which can be its parent or child proxies. When a proxy encounters a transcoding task, if its own load index does not exceed a predefined threshold value, it will proceed with the transcoding. Otherwise, the hashed proxy outsources the transcoding task to its least loaded neighbor proxy. When the outsourced proxy completes the transcoding task, it returns the transcoded version to the hashed proxy, which then caches the transcoded version object and delivers it to the client. Load information exchange among the neighbors can be conveniently done by the following means. When a proxy sends out a HTTP request or response, it piggybacks its load information in the HTTP header. Similarly, when a proxy receives a HTTP request or response, it extracts from the HTTP header the loading information of its *neighbor proxies.*

3.3 Hash-Dup System

Hash-dup system is an optimization of the *hash-default system*. It aims to reduce the user perceived delay for clients with capability to consume original version objects. Apparently, to reduce the user perceived delay effectively, an object should be delivered to the client as soon as it is ready to be consumed by the client. However, in *hash-default system*, the user perceived delay is not optimized. For instance, when the root proxy retrieves an original object from the content server, it always forwards it to the hashed proxy first regardless of whether the original version is ready to be consumed by the client. To deal with this problem, *hash-dup system* is proposed. It is equipped with a *duplicate* feature. In case an original object is retrieved from the root proxy, if the client can consume the original version, in other words, HIGHPC client, and the hashed proxy does not sit in the path to the specific edge proxy, a duplicate copy is made at the branch point. While one copy of the object is forwarded to the hashed proxy for caching, the other copy is sent to the client. This reduces the response time experienced by HIGHPC clients.

3.4 Hash-Dup-Outsrc System

The *duplicate* feature can also be combined with the *outsourcing* feature, which is referred to as *Hash-dup-outsrc system*. The *duplicate* feature is extended in *Hash-dup-outsrc system*. When a proxy completes an outsourced transcoding task, besides returning the transcoded object to the hashed proxy for caching, it makes a duplicate copy of the transcoded object if the hashed proxy does not sit in the path to the client. While one copy travels to the hashed proxy, the other copy is forwarded to the client.

4   Performance Evaluation

4.1 Experiment Setup

To evaluate the hash-based proxy system performance, a simulation model is built. It consists of client model, workload model, proxy system model and network model.

Firstly, as defined in [1], clients are categorized into five classes according to their capabilities, namely HIGHPC, MIDPC, HPC, PDA and SMARTPHONE. Therefore, web objects can be transcoded to five versions to suit the specific client class requirement. In this paper, we only consider HTML and image objects as they constitute 85% of the web objects in the Internet [4]. It is assumed that a *more detailed* version can always be transcoded to a *less detailed* version. The object sizes for the five versions are assumed to be 100%, 75%, 50%, 25% and 5% of the original object size respectively. The client device distribution is defined as [0.15, 0.1, 0.35, 0.25, 0.15].

Secondly, the workload model is defined based on the recent research works on Internet workload pattern [3][4][5][11][12]. Table 1 summarizes the parameter settings in the workload model.

Thirdly, we define the proxy system model. As in [1], the homogeneous proxies are organized hierarchically. Cache size for the proxy is defined in terms of the ratio of

the total original objects sizes. For strategies that require workload information, proxies update their own load information every 8 seconds. New client sessions are generated with exponential interarrival time. In addition to that, a Zipf-like distribution with
α set to 0.35 is used to model how clients are partitioned among the edge proxies.

Table 1. Parameters for workload model

Category	Distribution	Parameters
Number of Pages per session	Inverse Gaussian	μ=3.86, λ = 9.46
User think time	Pareto	α=1.4, k=10
Objects per page	Pareto	α=1.245, k=2
HTML object size	Lognormal	μ=7.630, σ=1.001
In-line object size	Lognormal	μ=8.215, σ=1.46
Object popularity	Zipf	α=0.75

Finally, we summarize the network model. Proxies are inter-connected via a network with bandwidth of 45 Mbps [1]. The delay incurred for the root proxy to retrieve
an original version object from the content server is modeled by an exponential distribution [12] with parameter β set to 1 second. Bandwidth for client to edge proxy is
given as 10Mbps, 56 Kbps, 28.8 Kbps, 19.2 Kbps and 9.6 Kbps for the five client
classes respectively. Table 2 summarizes the parameter settings used.

Table 2. Parameters for client/proxy/network model

Category	Parameter	Value(default)
Web proxy	Number of proxies(Np)	13
	Levels of caches(K)	3
	Nodal out-degree (O)	3
	HTTP processing time	0.001
	Disk transfer rate	10 MB/sec
	Transcoding rate	20 KB/sec
	Bandwidth	45 Mbps
	Cache size	1% of total original object size
	Content server delay	Exp (β=1 sec.)
Client	Interarrival time	Exp (β=1 sec.)
	Edge Proxy	Zipf (α=0.35)
	Bandwidth (bps)	[10M, 56 K, 28.8 K, 19.2 K 9.6 K]
	Device distribution	[0.15, 0.1, 0.35, 0.25, 0.15]

To study the effectiveness of the proposed systems, we use the following three
proxy systems as references. (1) *Simple System*. This is the system proposed in [1]
with LL workload distribution and *demand-based* caching. LRU is the cache replacement policy. (2) *Ideal System*. Each proxy in the system has unlimited cache storage to
hold all the versions for all the objects, therefore, 100% *cache exact hit* ratio is
achieved. (3) *Perfect-Know System*. In this system, proxy cache size is limited. Each
proxy possesses perfect knowledge about the object popularity as well as the cache
contents of all the proxies. Thus, system can always make correct decision in caching
popular objects without redundancy and handling HTTP requests. For load sharing,
LL workload distribution strategy is applied to proxies along the object return path.

We use the *mean user perceived delay* as the primary performance metric. It is the elapsed time between request submission and arrival of the requested object at the client. Another performance metric used is the cache hit ratio that reflects the effectiveness of the proxy cache. The fairness of the workload distribution strategies is explored by measurement of the *mean proxy utilization* for the proxies.

4.2 Experiment Results

Based on the simulation model defined, a simulator was implemented using the CSIM package. Simulations were run on several Linux machines.

***Hash-Default System* Vs Reference Systems.** In this set of experiments, we compare the *hash-default system* and the reference systems with respect to the proxy cache size. The cache size varies from 0.5% - 10% of the total original object size. A balance hash function is assumed in which objects are evenly scattered to the proxies.

The *mean user perceived delay* and the cache performance for the various systems are given in Fig. 3 and Fig. 4 respectively. Fig. 5 shows the *Mean proxy utilization,* and Fig. 6 shows the *mean accumulated queuing delay*, which corresponds to the total queuing delay experienced by a message when passing through the proxy system. It is concluded that *ideal system* always yields the lowest *mean user perceived delay* since it assumes infinite cache storage, which results in 100% *exact hit* ratio. Both *hash-default-LFU system* and the *perfect-know system* outperform the *simple system*. This can be explained by the tremendous enhancement in cache hit ratio in these two systems over the *simple system*, as illustrated in Fig. 4. In *simple system*, the suboptimal cache utilization accounts for the poor cache performance.

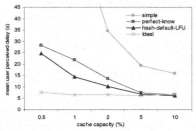

Fig. 3. Mean user perceived delay vs. cache capacity

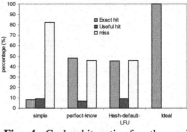

Fig. 4. Cache hit ratio for the various proxy systems (cache capacity = 1%)

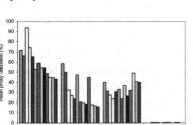

Fig. 5. Mean user perceived delay vs. cache capacity (cache capacity = 1%)

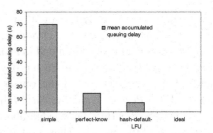

Fig. 6. Mean accumulated Queuing Delay (cache capacity = 1%)

Comparing *perfect-know system* with *hash-default-LFU system*, we observe that although the former contributes to slightly higher cache *exact hit ratio* (see Fig. 4), the *hash-default-LFU system* that does not posses perfect knowledge exhibits lower *mean user perceived delay* (see Fig. 3). This can be explained from the viewpoint of work-load distribution. *Perfect-know system* assigns transcoding task to the Least-Loaded proxy along the object return path. Thus, for transcoding task that arises from a cache-missed request, it is always accomplished by one of the proxies along the path from root proxy to the edge proxy. With clients assigned to edge proxies unevenly, for instance, zipf-like distribution with $\alpha = 0.35$ in our experiments, proxies along a busier path perform more transcoding, and contributes to longer queuing delay. On the other hand, this problem is circumvented by *hash-default-LFU system* that employs a hash function for load distribution. As illustrated in Fig. 5, *hash-default-LFU system* contributes to a fairer workload distribution as compared with *perfect-know system*. This accounts for the lower *accumulated queuing delay* as shown in Fig. 6. Lastly, we notice that even though the employed hash function scatters objects to proxies evenly, however, 100% balanced workload distribution is not achieved by *hash-default-LFU system* due to different access popularity and object sizes exhibited by web objects.

Performance Evaluation for the Various Hash-Based Systems. We evaluated the performance for the various hash-based systems. To provide more insight of the performance evaluation, two scenarios are considered. One is with balanced hash function, the other is with unbalanced hash function.

Scenario 1: Balanced Hash Function. In this scenario, the employed hash function hashes objects to proxies evenly. Fig. 7 and Fig. 8 show the *mean user perceived delay* and the mean proxy utilization respectively. We note that all the hash-based proxy systems outperform the perfect-know system.

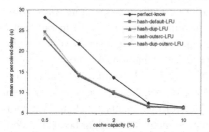

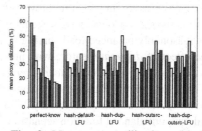

Fig. 7. Mean user perceived delay vs. cache capacity with balanced hash function

Fig. 8. Mean proxy utilization with balanced hash function (cache capacity = 1%)

First, we evaluate the effect of *outsourcing* feature. As shown in Fig. 8, both the *hash-outsrc system* and the *hash-dup-outsrc system*, which allow an overloaded proxy (in this case 50 pending requests in proxy queue) to outsource some transcoding tasks to *neighbor proxies*, outperform other proxy systems in load balancing. However, in terms of *mean user perceived delay*, no obvious enhancement is observed. This can be explained as follows. With a balanced hash function, the hash-based workload distribution strategy performs well in sharing the workload among the proxies. Therefore, *outsourcing* feature is not crucial. Next we discuss the effect of *duplicate* feature.

Duplicate feature helps to reduce the *mean user perceived delay* for clients that consume original version objects, in other words, HIGHPC clients. As shown in Fig. 7, in terms of *mean user perceived delay* for all clients, systems with *duplicate* feature performs slightly better than systems without this feature. However the improvement is not very significant as the *duplicate* feature mainly benefits HIGHPC clients only.

Scenario 2: Unbalanced Hash Function. Fig. 9 and Fig. 10 show the performance of the various hash-based proxy systems with unbalanced hash function, in which one proxy is hashed with two times more objects than that of others. Apparently, the *perfect-know system* is unaffected, as it does not rely on the hash function to make decision. The *hash-dup-outsrc-LFU system* performs best among the various systems.

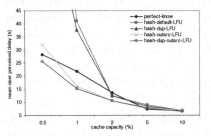
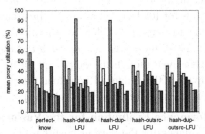

Fig. 9. Mean user perceived delay vs. cache capacity with unbalanced hash function

Fig. 10. Mean proxy utilization with unbalanced hash function (cache capacity = 1%)

It is obvious that with unbalanced hash function, systems without *outsourcing* feature exhibit significant performance degradation with small cache capacity. This is expected as their workload distribution is solely relied on the hash function. An unbalanced hashing will lead to an unbalanced transcoding workload distribution, and in turn, causes longer queuing delay in heavy loaded proxies. Situation is worse with small cache capacity, in which the low *cache exact hit ratio* imposes more transcoding tasks to the system. Conversely, systems with outsourcing feature perform satisfactorily as reasonably balanced load sharing is still ensured (see Fig. 10). Next, we evaluate the effect of *duplicate* feature with unbalanced hash function. As shown in Fig. 9, *duplicate* feature gives lower *mean user perceived delay*. The improvement is more significant than that of the case for balanced hash function. This is due to the fact that *duplicate* feature avoids unnecessary hops in delivering objects to client, which is crucial with unbalanced function scenario in which some proxies might be overloaded.

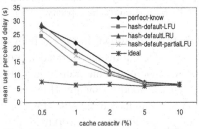
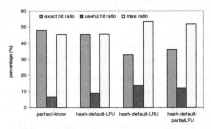

Fig. 11. Mean user perceived delay vs. cache capacity

Fig. 12. Cache hit ratio for the various cache replacement policies (cache capacity = 1%)

Performance Evaluation for Various Cache Replacement Policies. Simulations are carried out to investigate the impact of cache replacement policy to the hash-based system. The experiment results are given in Fig. 11 and Fig. 12. The *partialLFU* algorithm in the simulation is defined as every 10 seconds, 30% of the cache entries that are recently accessed are sorted according to their access rate. It is shown that LFU replacement policy is superior to LRU replacement policy in the hash-based system. On the other hand, the *partialLFU* replacement policy gives the intermediary performance. This is intuitive given the fact that it is a compromise of LFU and LRU.

5 Conclusions

In this paper, a hash-based hierarchical collaborative proxy system is proposed. It is responsible for performing transcoding operations as well as caching various versions for web objects in a heterogeneous client environment. Our study shows that the devised hash-based caching strategy, which eliminates redundant objects in the system cache, improves cache performance. In view of workload distribution, the hash-based workload distribution strategy that scatters the expensive transcoding tasks to the proxies according to hash function, works well with balanced hash function. In case of unbalanced hash function, by applying the *outsourcing* feature, the system presents satisfactory performance. Lastly several cache replacement policies are studies. It is concluded that access rate should be considered when making eviction decision.

References

1. V.Cardellini, P. S. Yu, and Y. W. Huang. Collaborative Proxy System for Distributed Web Content Transcoding. In Proc. ACM CIKM, pages 520–527, 2000.
2. Aggarwal,J. L. Wolf, and P. S.Yu. Caching on the World Wide Web. *IEEE Trans. on Software Engineering*, 11(1): 95–107, Jan. 1999
3. L. Breslau, P.Cao, L. Fan, G. Phillips, and S. Shenker. Web caching and Zipf-like distributions: Evidence and implications. In Proc. IEEE Infocom 1999, Mar. 1999
4. M. Arlitt, R. Friedrich, and T. Jin. Workload characterization of a Web proxy in a cable modem environment. ACM Performance Evaluation Rev. 27(2):25–36, Aug. 1999.
5. P. Barford and M. E. Crovella. A performance evaluation of Hyper Text Transfer Protocols. In Proc. ACM Sigmetrics 1999, pages 188–197, Atlanta, May 1999.
6. S.Chandra C.Ellis, and A.Vahdat. Application-Level Differentiated Multimedia Web Services Using Quality Aware Transcoding. *IEEE Journal on Selected Areas in Communications*, 2000.
7. S. Chandra and C. S. Ellis. JPEG Compression Metric as a Quality-Aware Image Transcoding. In *Proc. USENIX 2nd Symp. On Internet Techonlogy and Systems*, pages 81–92, 1999.
8. R.Mohan, J. R. Smith, and C.-S. Li. Adapting multimedia internet content for universal access. *IEEE trans. On Multimedia*, 1(1):104–114, Mar. 1999
9. K.W. Ross, Hash Routing for Collections of Shared Web Caches, IEEE Network, 11, pp. 37–44, 1997.

10. R. Floyd and B. Housel. Mobile Web Access Using eNetwork Web Express. *IEEE Personal Communications*, 5(5):47–52, 1998.
11. J. E. Pitkow. Summary of WWW characterizations. World Wide Web, 2(1–2):3–13, 1999.
12. W. Willinger and V. Paxson. Where Mathematics meets the Internet. Notices of the American Mathematical Society, 45(8):961–970, Aug. 1998
13. D.N. Serpanos and W.H. Wolf, "Caching Web objects using Zipf's law," in SPIE – The International Society for Optical Engineering. 1998, vol. 3527, pp. 320–6.
14 J. Shim, P. Scheuermann, and R. Vingralek. Proxy Cache Algorithms: Design, Implementation, and Performance. IEEE Trans. on Knowledge and Data Engineering, 11(4):549–561, 1999

Dynamic Materialized View Management Based on Predicates

Chi-Hon Choi[1], Jeffrey Xu Yu[1], and Hongjun Lu[2]

[1] The Chinese University of Hong Kong, Hong Kong, China
{chchoi, yu}@se.cuhk.edu.hk
[2] The Hong Kong University of Science and Technology, Hong Kong, China
luhj@cs.ust.hk

Abstract. For the purpose of satisfying different users' profiles and accelerating the subsequence OLAP (Online Analytical Processing) queries in a large data warehouse, dynamic materialized OLAP view management is highly desirable. Previous work caches data as either chunks or multidimensional range fragments. In this paper, we focus on ROLAP (Relational OLAP) in an existing relational database system. We propose a dynamic predicate-based partitioning approach, which can support a wide range of OLAP queries. We conducted extensive performance studies using TPC_H benchmark data on IBM DB2 and encouraging results are obtained which indicate that our approach is highly feasible.

Keywords: Dynamic materialized view management, data warehousing.

1 Introduction

OLAP systems have been widely used for business data analysis. Precomputing OLAP queries (known as view materialization) becomes a key to achieve high performance in data warehouses. Usually, according to the query statistics on a daily basis, the frequently accessed OLAP queries are selected as views, and are materialized in a time window during night, in order to effectively utilize the computation and storage resources. The materialized views are used to accelerate the OLAP queries in the following day. This type of materialized views is called static materialized views [1,6,7,8,9,13,16]. However, as different users may have different preferences, they may be interested in similar but different portions of data from time to time. Therefore, their query patterns are difficult to predict. Furthermore, ad-hoc queries, which are not known in advance, make the static materialized views quickly become outdated. Hence, static materialized views cannot fully support the dynamic nature of the decision support analysis. In order to fully satisfy users' ad-hoc queries, dynamic materialized views management is highly desirable.

The work related to dynamic view management is summarized in brief below. [11] shows some typical characteristics of OLAP queries which are suitable for caching. In order to speed up the query response time for OLAP queries, different

X. Zhou, Y. Zhang, and M.E. Orlowska (Eds.): APWeb 2003, LNCS 2642, pp. 583–594, 2003.

caching mechanisms have been proposed [2,3,4,10,12,15]. They can effectively reuse the previous query results and speed up the query processing time of the subsequence queries. Ezeife in [5] presents horizontal fragmentation ideas and schema for selecting and materializing views to reduce query response time and maintenance cost. However, Ezeife only considers the static view selection problem.

As most of the existing popular database applications are built on top of relational database systems, like IBM DB2, in this paper, we focus on ROLAP (Relational OLAP) and aim at building a dynamic view management system on top of relational data warehouse. The main advantage of our approach is that it is able to fully utilize the power of relational database systems. We attempt to release the restrictions imposed on the multidimensional fragments [12], and intend to answer more general OLAP queries. Different from [4,12], we partition views/tables based on user predicates dynamically. For the dynamic materialized view management, we further study three issues: (1) predicate selection for partition, (2) repartitioning and (3) view replacement policies.

The rest of the paper is organized as follows: Section 2 gives background of our study. Section 3 outlines two static prepartitioning-based view management approaches. In Section 4, we discuss our new dynamic predicate-based partitioning approach. We present our performance results in Section 5 and conclude the paper in Section 6.

2   Preliminaries and Problem Definition

An M-Multidimensional Database (MDDB) is a collection of relations, $D_1, \cdots, D_M$, F, where D_i is a dimension table and F is a fact table as described in [1,11] (also known as star-schema). Each dimension table has a key attribute. The fact table keeps the foreign keys of the M dimension tables, with additional measures. Figure 1 shows a simple 3-dimensional MDDB with a fact table, Sales, and three dimension tables, Product, Store and Date. In the Sales table, pid, sid and did are the foreign keys of the corresponding dimension tables. The measure in the Sales table is dollarSales. Given an M-dimensional MDDB, a *dependent lattice* can be defined as $(L, \preceq)$ [9], with a set of OLAP queries (group-by queries) L, and a dependence relation $\preceq$ (derived-from, be-computed-from). Given two queries q_i and q_j. We say q_i is dependent on q_j, $(q_i \preceq q_j)$, if q_i can be answered using the results of q_j. A dependent lattice can be represented as a directed acyclic graph, $G = (V, E)$. Here V represents the set of OLAP queries, as vertices. We use $V(G)$ and $E(G)$ for the set of vertices and the set of edges of a graph G. An edge, $v_i \to v_j$, exists in E, if and only if $v_j \preceq v_i$ and $\nexists v_k (v_j \preceq v_k \wedge v_k \preceq v_i)$, for $v_i \neq v_k \neq v_j$. A *datacube* is a dependent lattice with 2^M vertices, for an M-dimensional MDDB, where each vertex represents a group-by. Consider a query (Query 1) that requests to report the detailed measure dollarSales for every combination of product category (pcategory), store (sid) and date (did) below.

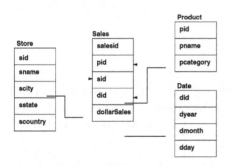

Fig. 1. A Star-Schema

Table 1. Assumed Query 1 result

pcategory	sid	did	dollarSales
biscuit	store1	3	2093
beer	store2	4	2011
bread	store2	5	2010
biscuit	store1	12	1359
milk	store1	1	2356
milk	store1	2	3526
bread	store1	15	2121
biscuit	store1	11	2101
bread	store1	5	1021
beer	store2	16	3216

Query 1 *Find* `dollarSales` *for every combination of* `pcategory`, `sid` *and* `did`.
   select *pcategory, sid, did, dollarSales*
   from *Sales s, Product p*
   where *s.pid = p.pid*

Assume Table 1 shows the result of Query 1 which forms a temporal 3-dimensional MDDB with `dollarSales` as measure. Here, the three dimensions are `pcategory`, `sid` and `did`.

Three OLAP queries (Query 2, Query 3 and Query 4) are shown below. Like Query 1, the subsequence three OLAP queries need to join the fact table **Sales** and the dimension table **Product**. However, they can be computed using Table 1. The derived-from relationships for the four queries are listed below: Query 2 $\preceq$ Query 1, Query 3 $\preceq$ Query 1, Query 4 $\preceq$ Query 1, and Query 3 $\preceq$ Query 2.

Query 2 *Find the total* `dollarSales` *for every* `pcategory`, `sid` *and* `did` *where* `pcategory` *is* `biscuit` *and* `did` *is less than 10.*
   select *pcategory, sid, did, sum(dollarSales)*
   from *Sales s, Product p*
   where *s.pid = p.pid and pcategory = 'biscuit' and did < 10*
   group by *pcategory, sid, did*

Query 3 *Find the total* `dollarSales` *for every* `pcategory` *and* `did` *where* `pcategory` *is* `biscuit` *and* `did` *is less than 8.*
   select *pcategory, did, sum(dollarSales)*
   from *Sales s, Product p*
   where *s.pid = p.pid and pcategory = 'biscuit' and did < 8*
   group by *pcategory, did*

Query 4 *Find the total* `dollarSales` *for every* `pcategory` *and* `did` *where* `pcategory` *is* `biscuit` *and* `did` *is greater than or equal to 10.*

> **select** *pcategory, did, sum(dollarSales)*
> **from** *Sales s, Product p*
> **where** *s.pid = p.pid and pcategory = 'biscuit' and did ≥ 10*
> **group by** *pcategory, did*

The *dynamic materialized view management* is defined as how to maintain some results of OLAP queries (known as materialized views) in a limited space, in order to maximize the possibility to answer other OLAP queries in runtime.

3 Related Work: Static Prepartitioning-Based Materialized View Management

In this section, we outline two static prepartitioning-based materialized view management approaches [4,12]. Both approaches cache the granularity of data as either chunks or fragments to support OLAP queries.

In [4], `chunked-file` is proposed to support OLAP queries. The `chunked-file` uses multi-dimensional arrays to store chunks, where a chunk, ranging at any level in the hierarchy, is proportional to the number of distinct values in the corresponding dimension at that level. For example, assume the result of Query 1 is shown in Table 1. Here, `pcategory` has 4 possible categorical values, `sid` has two categorical values (store1/store2), and `did` has 9 distinctive numerical values in the domain [1, 16]. Accordingly, a chunked file is created with 128 ($= 4 \times 2 \times 16$) chunks. For instance, the chunk [0][0][0] stores a measure for `pcategory` = 'biscuit', `sid` = 'store1' and `did` = 1. The `chunked-file` approach can support all the four queries, Query 1-4.

In [12], a system, called `DynaMat`, is proposed that dynamically materializes information at multiple levels of granularity in the form of fragments. However, `DynaMat` puts some restrictions on the query patterns. `DynaMat` can only efficiently support the following three types of multidimensional range queries: (i) select a full range[1] of a dimension, for instance, for all `did` between 1 and 16; (ii) a single value, like `pcategory` = 'biscuit'; and (iii) an empty range[2]. `DynaMat` cannot support those queries that do not satisfy any of the three types efficiently.

4 A New Dynamic Predicate-Based Partition Materialized View Management Approach

In this paper, we propose a ROLAP-based materialized view management approach, which can be easily developed on top of relational database management systems. Unlike `chunked-file` that uses arrays to store data, we use relations to support materialized views. The space consumption of relations are much

---

[1] A full range means the value is between the minimum value and maximum value of this dimension.

[2] An empty range means the dimension is not in the present in the query

Table 2. A materialized view by partition Table 1 using the two predicates p_1
and p_2

Partition	pcategory	sid	did	dollarSales
R_1	biscuit	store1	3	2093
R_2	beer	store2	4	2011
	bread	store1	5	1021
	bread	store2	5	2010
	milk	store1	1	2356
	milk	store1	2	3526
R_3	biscuit	store1	12	1359
	biscuit	store1	11	2101
R_4	bread	store2	15	2121
	beer	store2	16	3216

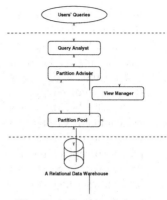

Fig. 2. A System Overview

smaller than that of multidimensional arrays. Unlike DynaMat that selects a dimension to partition data, we use *predicates* used in OLAP queries to partition.
Our approach can support a wide range of OLAP queries, which are attempt to
minimize the space consumption in a relational database system.

The dynamic predicate-based partitioning approach is illustrated with an
example here. Suppose Query 1 is processed and its result is shown in Table 1.
By using two selected predicates from Query 2: pcategory = 'biscuit' (denoted
p_1) and did < 10 (denoted p_2), Table 1 can be horizontally partitioned into four
materialized views: $p_1 \wedge p_2$, $\neg p_1 \wedge p_2$, $p_1 \wedge \neg p_2$, and $\neg p_1 \wedge \neg p_2$. They are shown
in Table 2. Note that each partition will be stored in a table in a commercial
multidimensional database.

Obviously, there is no overlapping between any pair of partitions in Table 2.
Suppose a user issues Query 4. Since Query 4 can be directly answered by the
third partition in Table 2, the query processing cost is to scan 2 tuples. On the
other hand, chunked-file needs to scan 14 chunks. DynaMat cannot efficiently
process Query 4 because Query 4 does not satisfy any of the three query types:
(i), (ii) or (iii) stated in Section 3.

4.1   System Overview

The system overview is depicted in Figure 2. It is built on a relational database
system (IBM DB2), which consists of four main components: Query Analyst,
Partition Advisor, View Manager and Partition Pool. These components
are described as follows.

- Query Analyst: It parses an incoming query and convert the necessary infor-
  mation into internal data structures that will be used in other components.
- Partition Advisor: It first determines which partition candidates in the
  Partition Pool can efficiently answer the query based on the derived-from

relationship. Second, it chooses the best partition(s) among the set of partition candidates to answer the query. If there are no qualified partitions, the query will be answered using the base tables.

- **View Manager**: It monitors the incoming queries and performs two main tasks. First, it decides which predicates are the most beneficial to partition the materialized views. This decision is based on a cost model which estimates the benefit of each predicate. If the predicates used in partitioning are changed, **View Manager** will repartition the materialized views. Second, when the disk space reaches the limit, **View Manager** uses a replacement policy to replace partitions in **Partition Pool**.

- **Partition Pool**: It is the information repository that stores the materialized views which are horizontally partitioned based on the incoming query predicates.

In the following, we will discuss **Partition Advisor** and **View Manager** in detail as they are more complicated.

4.2   Partition Advisor

A typically OLAP query involves selections which are based on some dimension values and/or joining the fact table with one or more dimension tables followed by a group-by operation. Predicate-based partitioning is to horizontally partition a view into a set of disjoint sub-views such that there is no overlapping between any sub-views. The predicates for horizontal partition are those predicates appearing in the where clause. A simple predicate is of the form, $A\theta v$, where A is an attribute, θ is one of the six operations ($=, <, >, \neq, \leq, \geq$), and v is a constant in the domain of A. For example, in Query 2 here are two simple predicates : `pcategory` $=$ 'biscuit' (denoted p_1) and `did` < 10 (denoted p_2). The conjunction of simple predicates is called *minterm predicate* [14]. Each simple predicate can occur in a minterm predicate either in its natural form or its negated form. Recall that it is always possible to transform a Boolean expression into conjunction normal form. For Query 2, there are four minterm predicates, M_1, M_2, M_3 and M_4, as follows:

$$M_1 = p_1 \wedge p_2 \Longleftrightarrow \texttt{pcategory} =' \texttt{biscuit}' \wedge \texttt{did} < 10$$
$$M_2 = \neg p_1 \wedge p_2 \Longleftrightarrow \texttt{pcategory} \neq' \texttt{biscuit}' \wedge \texttt{did} < 10$$
$$M_3 = p_1 \wedge \neg p_2 \Longleftrightarrow \texttt{pcategory} =' \texttt{biscuit}' \wedge \texttt{did} \geq 10$$
$$M_4 = \neg p_1 \wedge \neg p_2 \Longleftrightarrow \texttt{pcategory} \neq' \texttt{biscuit}' \wedge \texttt{did} \geq 10$$

In our system, a materialized view, V_i, is associated with an OLAP query, q_{V_i}. For example, the whole Table 2 is a materialized view represented by Query 1. This materialized view has four partitions: R_1, R_2, R_3 and R_4, for the corresponding four minterms: M_1, M_2, M_3 and M_4 mentioned above. Accordingly, each partition R_i can be represented using a query q_{R_i}.

For an incoming query q, **Partition Advisor** will first determine the set of materialized views that can answer q by checking if $q \preceq q_{V_i}$. In other words, all attributes in q must also be in q_{V_i}, the selection condition used in q implies

---

Algorithm 1 Partition Selection

Input: q: an incoming user query;
Output: a partition to answer the user query.

 1: **begin**
 2: Let bestPartition be the base table(s) that can answer q;
 3: **for** each materialized view V_i in **Partition Pool do**
 4:    Let q_{V_i} be the corresponding query that represents V_i;
 5:    **if** $q \preceq q_{V_i}$ **then**
 6:      **if** $|bestPartition| > |V_i|$ **then**
 7:        bestPartition $\leftarrow V_i$;
 8:      **end if**
 9:      **for** each partition R_j of V_i **do**
10:        **if** $q \preceq q_{R_j}$ **and** $|bestPartition| > |R_j|$ **then**
11:          bestPartition $\leftarrow R_j$;
12:        **end if**
13:      **end for**
14:    **end if**
15: **end for**
16: **return** bestPartition;

---

that it is a subset of q_{V_i}, and the aggregate functions used in the two queries are the same. Second, **Partition Advisor** needs to determine a partition R_j in a materialized view V_i to answer the query q. The partition selection algorithm is shown in Algorithm 1. In order to eliminate the overhead, **Partition Advisor** attempts to select one partition, R_i, to answer a given query. It is because, in general, the cost of selecting partitions is exponential in terms of the number of partitions available. When there is no single partition that can answer the query, there are two ways to solve it as shown in Algorithm 1: (1) use a whole materialized view to answer the query; (2) use the base tables to answer the query. As discussed later, when there is a materialized view available for answering the query, we will consider whether we need to repartition the materialized view after processing the query.

4.3 View Manager

View Manager maintains the top m predicates that give the highest predicate benefits for a materialized view, where m is predefined by a data warehouse administrator. Note that the number of predicates influences how a materialized view is partitioned. In general, m predicates can create a maximum of 2^m minterm fragments during the horizontal partitioning process. To reduce the cost of such huge overhead, we select the most frequent predicates for horizontal partitioning when the number of predicates is large. The process of selecting a predicate, p_i, depends on two factors: its relative access frequency, f_i, and its corresponding partition size, $|R_i|$. The predicate benefit of a predicate, p_i, denoted $PB(p_i)$, is estimated as follows:

Algorithm 2 Selecting top m predicates for a materialized view V

Input: a query q with k simple predicates $\{p_1, p_2, \cdots, p_k\}$, a materialized view V with n simple predicates $\{p_1, p_2, \cdots, p_n\}$.

Output: m highest predicate benefit $(PB(p_i))$ predicates.

```
1: begin
2: for i = 1 to k do
3:     for j = 1 to n do
4:         if the predicate p_i in the query q matches a predicate p_j maintained with the
           view V then
5:             PB(p_j) ← f_i × |R_i| + PB(p_j);
6:         else
7:             create a new predicate benefit PB(p_i);
8:             PB(p_i) ← f_i × |R_i|;
9:         end if
10:    end for
11: end for
12: return the m highest predicates;
```

Algorithm 3 Repartitioning

Input: a query (q_V) and its corresponding materialized view (V);

```
1: begin
2: Let L hold the m highest predicates for V;
3: Let L' the m highest predicates used in V, (selected by Algorithm 2);
4: if L ≠ L' then
5:     remove all existing partitions for V;
6:     generate new minterm predicates;
7:     delete infeasible minterms;
8:     repartition V using the new minterm predicates.
9: end if
```

$$PB(p_i) = |R_i| \times f_i \qquad (1)$$

We select the top m highest benefit predicates using Algorithm 2. Here, suppose the relative query frequency of an incoming query q is f_q. The access frequency of p_i used in q is $f_i = f_q$.

When a user query is issued, and it cannot be answered using a partition but a materialized view, V, `View Manager` will calculate the predicate benefits to see whether there is any change in the m top predicates associated with V, by taking both of the predicates used in q and V into account. If there is any change in the m top predicates, `View Manager` will repartition V using the new m predicates. Otherwise, `View Manager` will not repartition V. The repartitioning algorithm is shown in Algorithm 3.

The query results are stored in `Partition Pool` as materialized views, when there is free space. When `Partition Pool` is full, a replacement policy is adopted to store the beneficial partitions.

5   A Performance Study

All of the experiments are conducted on a Sun Blade/1000 workstation with a 750MHz UltraSPARC-III CPU running Solaris 2.8. The workstation has a total physical memory of 512M. We employ the TPC_H[1] benchmark dataset, and conduct our testing using IBM DB2[2] version 7.1.

5.1   Performance Metrics

In order to evaluate the performance of the predicate-based partitioning approach, we use two performance metrics: average query processing time and cost saving ratio.

- average query processing time: it is the average query processing costs over n randomly selected queries.
- Cost Saving Ratio (CSR) [4]: it measures the results as follows.

$$CSR = \sum_{i=0}^{n} \frac{wcost(q_i) - cost(q_i)}{wcost(q_i)} \times \frac{1}{n}$$

where $cost(q_i)$ is the query processing cost using partitions and $wcost(q_i)$ is the query processing cost using non-partitions, that is using the base tables in the data warehouse.

5.2   Feasibility

In this experiment, we investigate the feasibility of our predicate-based partitioning approach. We design seven different queries templates[3] with respect to each vertex in the datacube. For each query template, at least 10 queries are randomly generated using the TPC_H qgen program. As a result, we totally issue 70 different OLAP queries with randomly generated predicates as well as randomly query frequency. The sequence of these 70 queries are randomly determined.

We compare our predicate-based partitioning approach with an implementation of chunked-file [4] in the relational database system, IBM DB2. We assume that Partition Pool is large enough to store the root vertex (the largest materialized view) in the datacube. In fact, it is about 21% of the base table. When testing the 70 queries one by one, two highest beneficial predicates are selected to generate minterms ($m = 2$). The materialized view will be dynamically divided into 4 partitions based on the two predicates. We will repartition the materialized view dynamically, if necessary.

The chunked-file approach uses a predetermined chunk size statically. In this testing, we pre-partition the materialized view into k even partitions to simulate the chunk-based [4] in ROLAP environments. Three k values are tested:

---

[1] http://www.tpc.org
[2] http://www-3.ibm.com/software/data/iminer/fordata/
[3] No queries access the empty group-by clause vertex in the datacube.

4-chunk, 9-chunk and 25-chunk. We do not compare with DynaMat, because most OLAP queries cannot be efficiently answered by DynaMat due to the restrictions on the query types.

In a relational database, we found that our dynamic predicate-based partitioning approach (PP) outperforms the static pre-partitioning significantly in terms of average query processing time in second as follows: PP: 1.99, 4-chunk: 2.74 9-chunk: 2.70 and 25-chunk: 2.86. It is totally not surprised. The reason is that the dynamic partitioning learns from predicates and attempts to repartition the materialized views in an eager manner. The incoming queries are most likely to be answered by a predicate-based partition. Consequently, the query processing cost must be reduced.

5.3 Query Locality

To study the query locality, we conduct two sets of experiments based on *data access locality* and *hierarchical access locality*:

- **Data Access Locality**: Most users have their own preferences which may last for a while. That is, they may be interested in one part of the data. For instance, a Hong Kong stock analyst is most likely and often to query the Hong Kong stocks rather than all stocks in the world. To simulate the data access locality, a certain percentage of the database is designed as a hot region such that the queries are most likely to access the designated part of the database. H60, H70, H80 and H90 means 60%, 70%, 80% and 90% of the queries access 20% of the datacube, respectively. The rest of queries are uniformly distributed over the database.
- **Hierarchical Access Locality**: Proximity queries are used to model hierarchical access locality. For instance, users may be primarily interested in the Hang Seng Index in early morning. Afterwards, they may be interested in its trend in this week, this month, or this year, based on the time hierarchy. In this experiment, the degree of hierarchical access locality can be tuned by varying the mix of random queries and proximity queries. Q60, Q70, Q80 and Q90 means 60%, 70%, 80% and 90% queries are proximity queries and 40%, 30%, 20% and 10% are random generated, respectively.

Assume that the space available is to hold 10% of the base tables. For each of the query patterns above, we issue 100 queries, calculate the average query processing time and CSR. In the following figures, PP and DW represents the dynamic predicate-based partitioning approach and the non-partitioning approach, respectively. Figure 3 and 4 show that the dynamic predicate-based partitioning approach exploit the locality very good. Figure 3 (a) shows the performance for query pattern with a designated hot region. Note that CSR increases with a larger hot region of the database. Figure 3 (b) shows the comparison of average query processing time between predicate-based partitioning and non-partitioning approach. The dynamic predicate-based partitioning approach can dramatically reduce the average query processing time compared with DW. Figure 4 shows the performance for proximity query pattern. In Figure 4 (a), CSR increases sharply as the proximity percentage increases. This is because more incoming

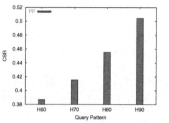
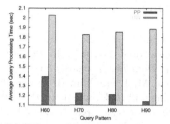

(a) Effect of varying the hot region on CSR

(b) Effect of varying the hot region on query response time

Fig. 3. Testing Different Data Access Locality Patterns

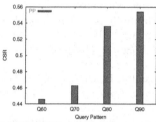
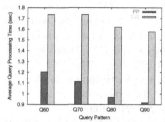

(a) Effect of varying the proximity on CSR

(b) Effect of varying the proximity on query response time

Fig. 4. Testing Different Hierarchical Access Locality Patterns

queries can be derived from the partitions. Note that Q90 reaches the highest CSR, which denotes that the predicate-based partitioning is favorable for roll-up queries. In Figure 4 (b), compared with DW, dynamic predicate-based partitioning diminishes the average query processing time.

6 Conclusions

In this paper, we propose a new dynamic predicate-based partition materialized view management approach for caching OLAP queries in a relational multidimensional database. We focus on ROLAP. We use user predicates to partition views, rather than using a predetermined threshold to pre-partition views. Based on the user predicates, the materialized views are partitioned into horizontal fragments, which allows fine granularity caching as well as coarse caching. Our approach can dynamically materialize the incoming query results and exploit them for future reuse. The experimental results show that predicate-based partition exhibit high query locality, and outperform the pre-partitioning approach in terms of ROLAP.

Acknowledgment. The work described in this paper was fully supported by a grant from the Research Grants Council of the Hong Kong Special Administrative Region. (Project no. CUHK4198/00E).

References

1. E. Baralis, S. Paraboschi, and E. Teniente. Materialized views selection in a multidimensional database. In *Proceedings of 23rd International Conference on Very Large Data Bases*, pages 156–165, 1997.
2. S. Dar, M. J. Franklin, B. T. Jónsson, D. Srivastava, and M. Tan. Semantic data caching and replacement. In *Proceedings of 22nd International Conference on Very Large Data Bases*, pages 330–341, 1996.
3. P. Deshpande and J. F. Naughton. Aggregate aware caching for multi-dimensional queries. In *Processings of 7th International Conference on Extending Database Technology*, volume 1777, pages 167–182, 2000.
4. P. Deshpande, K. Ramasamy, A. Shukla, and J. F. Naughton. Caching multidimensional queries using chunks. In *Proceedings of ACM SIGMOD International Conference on Management of Data*, pages 259–270, 1998.
5. C. I. Ezeife. Selecting and materializing horizontally partitioned warehouse views. *Data and Knowledge Engineering*, 36(2), January 2001.
6. A. Gupta and I. S. Mumick. *Materialized Views: Techniques, Implementations, and Applications*. The MIT Press, 1999.
7. H. Gupta, V. Harinarayan, A. Rajaraman, and J. D. Ullman. Index selection for OLAP. In *Proceedings of the 13th International Conference on Data Engineering*, pages 208–219, 1997.
8. H. Gupta and I. S. Mumick. Selection of views to materialize under a maintenance cost constraint. In *Proceedings of the 7th International Conference on Database Theory*, pages 453–470, 1999.
9. V. Harinarayan, A. Rajaraman, and J. D. Ullman. Implementing data cubes efficiently. In *Proceedings of ACM SIGMOD International Conference on Management of Data*, pages 205–216, 1996.
10. P. Kalnis and D. Papadias. Proxy-server architectures for OLAP. *SIGMOD Record (ACM Special Interest Group on Management of Data)*, 30(2):367–378, 2001.
11. R. Kimball. *The Data Warehouse Toolkit*. John Wiley & Sons, 1996.
12. Y. Kotidis and N. Roussopoulos. Dynamat: A dynamic view management system for data warehouses. In *Proceedings of ACM SIGMOD International Conference on Management of Data*, pages 371–382, 1999.
13. W. Liang, H. Wang, and M. E. Orlowska. Materialized view selection under the maintenance time constraint. *Data and Knowledge Engineering*, 37(2), May 2001.
14. M. T. Ozsu and P. Valduriez. *Principles of Distributed Database Systems, Second Edition*. Prentice Hall, 1999.
15. P. Scheuermann, J. Shim, and R. Vingralek. Watchman : A data warehouse intelligent cache manager. In *Proceedings of 22nd International Conference on Very Large Data Bases*, pages 51–62, 1996.
16. A. Shukla, P. Deshpande, and J. F. Naughton. Materialized view selection for multidimensional datasets. In *Proceedings of 24th International Conference on Very Large Data Bases*, pages 488–499, 1998.

DPR: A Dynamic Partial Replication Protocol Based on Group Communication for a Web-Enable Database Cluster[*]

Chung-Ho Lee[1], Jae-Dong Lee[2], and Hae-Young Bae[1]

[1]Dept. of Computer Science and Engineering, INHA University
Yonghyun-dong, Nam-ku, Inchon, 402-751, Korea
{chlee, hybae}@dblab.inha.ac.kr
[2]Dept. of Information and Computer Science, DANKOOK University
Seoul, 140-714, Korea
letsdoit@dku.edu

Abstract. This paper proposes a dynamic partial replication protocol based upon group communication system for use with a web-enable database cluster. It dynamically combines the advantages of both a partial and a full replication model according to a query pattern. Most eager-update replication protocols that have been suggested as the best replication for a database cluster are based on the full replication. However, an actual database cluster system needs partial replication rather than full replication to achieve high throughputs and scalability. The proposed Dynamic partial Replication (DPR) protocol guarantees consistency among replicas and reduces the overhead due to remote access inherent in the previous partial replication protocols. The proposed protocol consists of three parts: partial replica control, scale-out factor estimation and dynamic replica allocation. Partial replica control part is the framework for the DPR protocol. Scale-out factor estimation part determines the optimal number of replicas according to the current query pattern and access frequency to maximize throughput and efficiency. Dynamic replica allocation part creates or removes the temporary replica in a local site. The simulated evaluation shows that the proposed protocol outperforms the existing eager-update protocols, achieving improvements of approximately 16% in response time and 20% in scalability.

1 Introduction

With the rapid growth of the Internet, significant numbers of web-based information systems have come to rely on database cluster technology to serve large user communities and to deal with peak loads. A database cluster is where multiple database servers each have their own instance of a single database. If one database server fails, another can service queries and write transactions so that applications depending on the database don't fail [1, 11]. The goal of a database cluster is high throughput, high scalability and high availability. In a database cluster, data replication is used as a key

---

[*]This research was supported by University IT Research Center Project of Korea

X. Zhou, Y. Zhang, and M.E. Orlowska (Eds.): APWeb 2003, LNCS 2642, pp. 595–606, 2003.

component for both fault-tolerance and efficiency, in order to guarantee high performance and high availability.

Most eager-update replication protocols that have been suggested as the best replication for a database cluster are based on full replication [8, 9, 10, 13], but in practice an actual database cluster system needs partial replication rather than full replication in order to achieve high throughputs and scalability. Replication protocols based on full replication have excessive writing overhead, i.e., all replica must be kept consistent and must reflect the latest updates. The more nodes a cluster system has, the greater the writing overhead. Therefore, the partial replication is necessary to adapt to changing transaction patterns and to handle large databases. Some previous works have dictated the use of partial replication because partial replication is more useful in actual systems [3, 5, 10]. These previous works, however, have focused on partially replicated data in a distributed computing environment, i.e., an unreliable network. Kemme of [10] have initially presented several issues of partial replication and proposed general solutions. But, he has missed performance study to analyze trade-offs between full and partial replication. To date, no studies have focused on partial replication in a scalable database cluster based on a reliable network. An efficient data propagation scheme for improving scalability has recently been proposed [7], which is realized by lowering the cost of remote write operations compared to the cost of executing its local write operations in the scale-out factor. In spite of this advantage, this scheme still can't expect to achieve high scalability in a large database cluster that must support an unpredictable number of clients and transaction patterns.

This paper proposes a DPR protocol that guarantees consistency and reduces the remote access overhead inherent in the partial replication. Our protocol consists of three parts: partial replica control, scale-out factor estimation and dynamic replica allocation. Partial replica control part is the framework for the DPR protocol. Scale-out factor estimation determines the optimal number of replicas according to the current query pattern and access frequency to maximize the throughput and efficiency. Dynamic replica allocation part creates or removes the temporary replica in a local site.

This paper is organized as follows. Section 2 presents the dynamic partial replication model upon which the proposed DPR protocol is based. Section 3 gives the details of the proposed DPR protocol. Section 4 presents the results that were obtained by running a simulation of proposed protocol. Section 5 summarizes our conclusions.

2   The Dynamic Partial Replication Model

This section presents a dynamic partial replication model upon which the replication approach suggested in this paper is based. Both full and partial replication are considered.

As shown in Fig. 1, the dynamic partial replication model based on a scalable database cluster system, i.e., a database cluster is composed of a scalable set of nodes: a finite set of active nodes ($N_1, N_2, N_3, \dots N_n$) and spare nodes ($N_{n+1}, N_{n+2}, \dots$) for online scaling[1]. A database server resides on each node and its clients are an unknown num-

---

[1] This means that scaling must be done online and must be non-blocking

ber of the general public. Each database is partially or fully replicated. In full replication, each data item resides in every site and has n replicas. On the other hand, in partial replication, data item has one or more sites that have a copy of that data item. In the partial replication model, the set of servers is structured into some groups, g_x, g_y ... g_z. The database consists of a set of data items, $D=\{D_1, D_2, .D_n\}$, for example, X, Y, Z. The unit of each data item is a table or a partition of a table. Each group maintains replicas of a certain data item among all of the data items. For example, group g_x that consists of four nodes maintains replicas of data item X.

The communication among nodes is based on a multicast primitive of group communication systems. Group communication systems manage the message exchanging between groups of nodes. The most important property of multicast is message ordering service which ensures that all messages are delivered in the same serial order at all nodes [2,9,12]. Our scalable database cluster model uses a read-one/write-all-available (ROWAA) approach in which each read operation is translated to a physical read from the replica. A write operation is translated to physical writes on all available replicas [12,13].

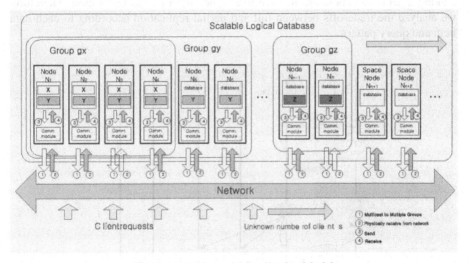

Fig. 1. Dynamic partial Replication Model

3 The Dynamic Partial Replication Protocol

This section presents DPR protocol based on the previous model in section 2. And it consists of three parts: partial replica control, scale-out factor estimation and dynamic replica allocation.

3.1 Motivation

DPR is based on eager-update protocols such as SER, SI, CS, Hybrid, SER-SH, SI-SH and CS-SH [8,9,10]. Firstly, fig. 2 explains the overhead of an existing partial replication protocol presented in Kemme [10]. We call it extended SER protocol.

We assume there are three data items: X, Y and Z in a scalable logical database and three groups: $g_x=\{N_1\}$, $g_y=\{N_1, N_2, N_3\}$ and $g_z=\{N_2, N_3, N_4\}$. Transaction T_i starts at site N_2. It wants to read data items X and Y. Y is stored at N_2. X is only stored at N_1. It sends a read request to N_1 where the transaction is registered as a sub-transaction, the lock is acquired, the read is performed and the response is returned to N_2. Then, N_1 and N_2 build the set of nodes R_i that have registered T_i. In the send phase, N_2 multicasts the write set to all sites. The multicast starts the 2-phase commit among all sites in R_i. When write set WS_i is delivered at N_2, no decision can be made yet since N_2 must either wait for a pre-commit message from all of the sites in R_i or for at least one abort message. In this example, at site N_1 a write set WS_j is delivered before WS_i conflicting with T_i's read operation. As a result T_i must be aborted everywhere and N_2 multicast the corresponding abort message. If there had been no abort at N_1, N_1 would also have sent a pre-commit to N_2 and would have multicast a commit [10].

In the extended SER protocol, if local site doesn't have copies of a data item, a remote access to read it is inevitable. Additionally, T_i's initial node must wait for either a pre-commit message from all sites in R_i or for at least one abort message before making a decision. These are the overhead inherent in partial replication. Therefore, we analyze the trade-offs between full and partial replication according to each data item and query pattern.

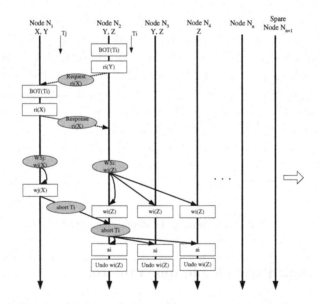

Fig. 2. An example of extended SER protocol for partial replication

3.2 Dynamic Partial Replication

The proposed DPR protocol guarantee complete consistency among replicas and decrease the remote access used in partial replication by creating a temporary replica in a local site. It also periodically makes a decision about duration of the local replica based upon the transaction access pattern and the access frequency. These temporary replicas do not need to be logged for recovery. Therefore, these temporary replicas increase the access efficiency for a transaction that must access remote data.

[Algorithm 1: partial replica control]
INPUT:
  T_i, T_j,...: i^{th} and j^{th} running transactions
  N_i, N_j,...: Nodes on which T_i and T_j initiate
  flags: information whether the temporary replica will be made
       or not
OUTPUT:
  result: result of T_i, {a_i or c_i}
Partial_Replica_Control(*T, N, flags, result*)
`// I. read phase`
```
01: for (every read operation rᵢ(X)∈ Tᵢ)
02:    if (Nᵢ has a replica of data item X in a cache or on a disk)
03:        rᵢ(X) acquires local read lock and is executed locally
04:    else
05:        Send a point-to-point msg to Nⱼ which has a replica of X
06:        Perform a sub-transaction in Nⱼ and receive the result
07:        if (flags of temporary replicas equals 1)
08:            Make a temporary replica of X in the cache
09:            if (the result of the response is not complete)
10:                call the dynamic replica allocation procedure
11:        Build the set of nodes Rᵢ that have registered Tᵢ
12:    end if
13: end for
14: if (there are read only operations in Tᵢ, WSᵢ = ∅)
15:    result = cᵢ
```
`// II. send phase`
```
16: Bundle all write operations in WSᵢ and multicast it
```
`// III. lock phase`
```
17: if (there was remote access to different nodes, Rᵢ ≠ ∅)
18:    Nᵢ either waits for pre-commit msg from all nodes in Rᵢ or
       for at least one abort msg whenever remote access con-
       flicts with a write operation of a remote node
19:    Nᵢ multicast aᵢ or cᵢ to all nodes
20: if (delivery of WSᵢ)
21:    for (every wᵢ(X) ∈ WSᵢ)
22:        if (there is no lock on X)
23:            Grant the lock of Wᵢ(X)
24:        if (there is a write lock on X or all read locks on X
            are from transactions that have already processed
            their lock phase)
25:            Insert the lock request to queue
26:        if (there is a granted read lock rⱼ(X) and the write
            set WSⱼ of Tⱼ has not yet been delivered)
27:            Abort Tⱼ and grant lock of Wᵢ(X)
28:        if (there is a granted read lock rⱼ(X) and WSⱼ has al-
            ready been sent)
            Multicasts abort msg aⱼ
29:    end for
```

```
30:     if (Tᵢ is a local transaction)
31:        Multicast a commit msg cᵢ
32: end if
// IV. write phase
33: if (a write lock is granted)
34:     Perform the corresponding operations
// V. termination phase
35: if (delivery of a commit msg cᵢ and all operations have been
        executed)
36:        Commit, result = cᵢ
37:        Release all locks
38: end if
39: if (delivery of an abort msg aᵢ)
40:     Undo all operations already executed and result = aᵢ
41:     Release all locks
42: end if

End of Algorithm 1
```

The difference between DPR and extended SER are in the read and lock phase. In the read phase (line numbers 01~ 15), if there is a temporary replica for data item X in the cache, there is no need to access a remote site as this is similar to having the data on disk. On the other hand, we need additional overhead to manage the cache area. In the lock phase (line numbers 17~32), we combine the original SER and the extended SER. If there was a remote read, we follow the extended SER. If there was no remote read, we follow the original SER because the temporary replica is the same as the persistent replica. The success of the DPR protocol depends on the following scale-out factor estimation process.

3.3 Scale-out Factor Estimation

In order to improve the scalability and throughput, we will focus on the role of a temporary replica that removes remote accesses. We will describe the scale-out factor and it's estimation process to decide when we create or remove temporary replica. This process runs independently as a back-end processor and uses the properties shown in Table 1 as decision factors.

Table 1. Database parameters

Property	Meaning
	Proportion of write operations (w)
Query Pattern	Proportion of remote read operations (rr)
	Proportion of remote write operations (rw)
Access Frequency	Access frequency of each data item (f)

We will determine equations for the scale-out factor estimation process in the partial replication model. These equations are based on the equations for a full replication model [7]. In the partial replication model, a replicated database consists of a group of nodes (sites). Each site doesn't necessarily have a copy of the database. There are k replicas. Equation (1), t is execution transaction per seconds of a certain item. t is composed of transactions within the group and transactions outside the group. Transactions within the group are composed of x local transactions and a number of remote update transactions. Transactions outside the group are composed of a number of remote read transactions and a number of remote write transactions:

$t = local\ operations + write\ operations\ within\ the\ group + remote\ operations\ outside\ the\ group$

$$t = x + w \times wo \times x \times (k-1) + \sum_{i=1}^{n-k}(\frac{x_i \times rr_i}{k} + x_i \times rw_i \times wo) \tag{1}$$

In Equation (1) above, x is local operations, rr is the proportion of remote read transactions and rw is the proportion of remote write transactions outside the group. In Equation (2), the relative throughput of one node within the group for a data item, or scale-out (so_i), is the proportion it performs on local transactions, x, divided by its nominal capacity, t. Equation (3) is the sum of each node within the group. As Equation (3) indicates, the number of replicas has a significant effect on the scalability. The purpose of a scale-out factor estimation process is to find the optimal number of replicas that reflect the changing query pattern while also considering the frequency in order to improve scalability and performance. Then, we can simply decide whether a temporary replica should be created or removed. If we want to obtain the scale-out factor for all of the data items, we add the scale-out factor of each data item considering access frequency as shown in Equation (4).

$$so_i = \frac{x}{t} = \frac{x}{x + w \times wo \times x \times (k-1) + \sum_{i=1}^{n-k}(\frac{x_i \times rr_i}{k} + x_i \times rw_i \times wo)} \tag{2}$$

$$so_{group-gx} = \sum_{j=1}^{k}(\frac{x}{x + w \times wo \times x \times (k-1) + \sum_{i=1}^{n-k}(\frac{x_i \times rr_i}{k} + x_i \times rw_i \times wo)}) \tag{3}$$

$$so_{group-all} = so_x \times f_x + so_y \times f_y + ... + so_z \times f_z = \sum_{i=data-item} so_i \times f_i \tag{4}$$

However, it is time consuming to obtain the scale out factors of every data item. Therefore, in our algorithm, we obtain the scale out factor of data items that have a high frequency compared to the frequency of other data items.

[Algorithm 2: scale-out factor estimation]

INPUT:
```
evt_interval: predefined time to check scale-out factor es-
              timation periodically (milliseconds)
rep_info: meta-information about replication
stat_info: statistical information of query pattern and ac-
           cess frequency
```

OUTPUT:
   flags: information whether the temporary replica will be
          made

Scaleout_Factor_Estimation (*evt_interval*, *rep_info*,
                            stat_info, flags)

```
01: while (evt_interval equals 1)
02:    Refer to rep_info and stat_info
03:    Select the data items that have high access frequency
04:    for (every selected data item)
05:        Compute the scale-out factor of the data item by
           using equations (3), (4)
06:        Decide the number of replicas to be made or removed
07:        Make new version of flags of the data item
08:    end for
09:    Multicast the new version of flags
10:    evt_interval ← 0
11: end while
```

End of Algorithm 2

As Algorithm 2 indicates, the scale-out factor estimation process consists of three phases. The compute phase (line numbers 02~05) computes the scale-out factor of selected data items by referencing the statistical and replication information. The decision phase (line number 06) decides how many replicas will be made or removed. The send phase (line numbers 09~10) multicasts the changed information to all nodes.

3.4 Dynamic Replica Allocation

As unknown number of clients and a changing query pattern requires a flexible partial replication scheme in which sites can dynamically create replica or remove replicas whenever they are no longer needed. Replica allocation has to be initiated internally. We need two operations on data item X. *Allocate (X, N_s, N_t)* creates a temporary replica at target node N_t with existing data item X at the source node N_s. *Free (X, N)* removes the temporary replica of data item X at the node N. These two operations should be done without interrupting ongoing transactions. If there is a concurrent transaction T_i updating data item X, T_i's update is also reflected in new allocated replica. For this, *Allocate (X, N_s, N_t)* operation is processed by two steps, log shipping and data transfer. The target node N_t multicasts a *Allocate (X, N_s, N_t)* request to the group that has a replica of data item X using total order service. The delivery of this request is recorded in the shipping log of N_s. A shipment is logged starting at the oldest log that is currently active. Once the shipment has been logged, the reader starts the data copy. The reader of N_s puts tuples into a data block for transfer. This enforces the existence of log records at node N_s that are old enough for redo purposes. The copying is done online and is non-blocking and it allows parallel updates and inserts to occur. A data block includes important two fields. *RedoLSN* is the lowest non-executed log sequence number for this data item. This number is registered when starting to fill the data block. *Highkey* is the highest key read when sending the block (Fig. 3). If the algorithms above determine that a temporary replica of data item X should be made, the next step is to allocate new temporary replica.

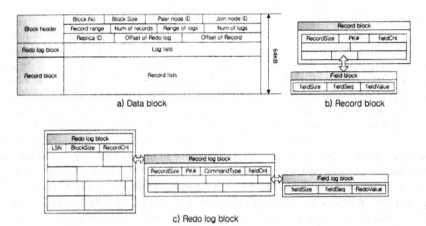

a) Data block

b) Record block

c) Redo log block

Fig. 3. Structures of data block

[Algorithm 3: Dynamic Replica Allocation]

INPUT:

evt_alloc: event for replica allocation request
evt_data: event for informing the end of the data transfer
N_t: target nodes that create temporary replica of X
N_s: source nodes that already have the replica of X
DB: data block to be sent from source nodes to target nodes

Log_Shipping(*evt_alloc*, *evt_data*, N_t, N_s, DB)
```
01: if (delivery of evt_alloc)
02:    Start making the logical redo log in Np
03:    while (there is no evt_data)
04:        Read a log record from log buffer
05:        if (log record's LSN > DB.redoLSN &&
               log record's key <= DB.highkey)
06:            Transfer redo log to Nj
07:    end while
08: end if
End of Log_Shipping
```

Data_Transfer(*evt_alloc*, N_t, N_s, DB)
```
09: if (delivery of evt_alloc && starting of Log_Shipping)
10:    for (every record)
11:        Assigns initial DB.redoLSN and DB.highkey
12:        while (DP.size < 64KB)
13:            Read tuples into data block in Np.
14:            Reassigns DS.highkey with the highest key
15:        end while
16:        Send data block to Nt.
17:    end for
18:    Make evt_data
19: end if
End of Data_Transfer
```

End of Algorithm 3

Algorithm 3 is composed of two sub-algorithms, one is for logging the data shipment and the other is for transferring the data. Once logging has started, the data transfer may start. This enforces the existence of log records at the targets that are old enough for redo purposes. The data block is read sequentially in primary key order (line number 13). Only low-level latches are needed during copy of the tuples within a block. Thus, updates can happen while data are read. The update transactions that are related to tuples that have already been sent are logged in the logical redo log by the log shipping thread. Additionally, there are several points that must be addressed in order for the dynamic replica allocation to be practical. To minimize the overhead of allocation and enhance the availability during the allocation operation, we can use parallel data transfer from several source nodes that have a replica within a group to a target node. For this, the data to be transferred have to be divided by using primary key. In fig. 4, *Fmin* indicates the minimum value of data and *Fmax* indicates the maximum value. Total data area is divided by *N*, the number of replicas (or number of source nodes). This approach is also good for the rearrangement of data transmission area of each node. Fig. 5 shows the rearrangement process when data transmission of node 2 is finished earlier than that of node 1.

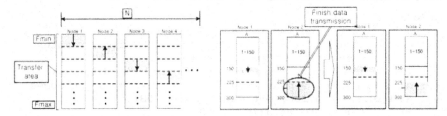

Fig. 4. Data division for parallel transfer   **Fig. 5.** Rearrangement of transmission area

4 Performance Evaluation

In order to evaluate the performance of the proposed protocol, we simulated two experiments. The architecture of the simulation captured the most important components of a partially replicated system. Table 2 summarizes the parameters used for the simulation. The database was modeled as a partially replicated database.

Table 2. Simulation parameters

Parameters	Value
Number of data item in the database	50
Size of total database	100Mbyte
Percentage of partially replicated data	100, 80, 30, 20, 10 (%)
Distribution of partially replicated data	Uniform distribution
Access frequency of data item	50, 20, 15, 10, 5 (%)
Number of nodes in the system	10
Network bandwidth	1Gbps
Number of operations within a transaction	30
Query Pattern (Percentage of write operation)	40, 30, 20, 10, 0 (%)
Distribution of workload	Uniform distribution

Experiment 1 (Impact of changing query pattern and frequency): In practice, there can be a change in the query pattern and access frequency in dynamic environments like the Internet or a mobile computing environment. This experiment analyzed the behavior of three protocols that varies the query pattern and access frequency compared to their initial values. The initial value of query pattern was from 40 % to 0%. The new value of query pattern was from 100 % to 0% (100, 60, 40, 20, 0). This made the disparity between query patterns larger for each data item. All of the other parameters were not changed. The new values were applied when the system reached its mid-load point of 90 transactions per second.

Experiment 2 (Scalability): The ability to scale up the system depends on the number of update operations and the size of the database to be transferred without interrupting ongoing transactions in the system. To analyze the scalability, we conducted an experiment using a transaction with update rates of 30, 20, 10, 0% (each is a uniform distribution). In this experiment, we measured how the system reacted to a changing number of servers.

Analysis: Fig. 6 shows the result of the experiment with a changing query pattern and frequency. We compared the response times of three protocols. We can see that the performance degraded rapidly when the load was around 90 transactions per second. We can also see that our proposed DPR protocol outperformed other protocols, as its response time was about 16% lower than that of any other protocol. The response time of DPR remained significantly lower even when the query pattern was changed, since the DPR protocol can deal with the changing query pattern and frequency by using the scale-out factor estimation process.

Fig. 7 depicts the response time as the number of nodes increases from 10 to 36. The response time for all protocols increased with the number of nodes due to the increased system load and data transfer from one node to scaling node. For 12 nodes and higher, we can observe that the DPR protocol behaved better than the other protocols. While SER had to transfer the total database to a scaling node, DPR transferred only some of the data item, in order to improve the system performance. E-SER also transferred some of data item to a joining node. The choice of which data are to be transferred is random, but since some data are transferred, it can also improve system performance. In this experiment the main factor to consider was the size of the database. As the size of the database increased, our proposed DPR had better performance.

5   Conclusion

This paper was motivated by the development of a scalable database cluster system, which needs high throughputs and linear scalability. Recently, the eager-update replication protocols based on group communication have appeared to be a good mechanism to achieve these goals. Current solutions, however, assume full replication, or can't completely support partial replication. Furthermore, an actual database cluster system needs partial replication rather than full replication to achieve high throughputs and scalability. This paper proposed an eager-update replication protocol, the DPR protocol, to support not only full replication, but also partial replication. The proposed partial replication protocol decreases the amount of remote access inherent in other partial replication protocols by creating temporary replica in local site. It then periodically makes a decision regarding the validation of the local replica, by using scale-out factor estimation that depends on the query pattern and the access frequency.

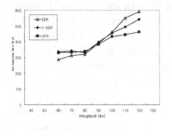

Fig. 6. Experiment 1   **Fig. 7.** Experiment 2

References

1. R. Buyya: High Performance Cluster Computing. Prentice Hall PTR, Vol.1 (1999)
2. P. Felber, R. Guerraoui, A. Schiper: The implementation of a CORBA group communication service. *Theory and Practice of Object Systems*, (1998) 4(2). 93–105
3. U. Fritzke, P. Ingels: Transactions on partially replicated data based on reliable and atomic multicasts. The 21st International Conference on Distributed Computing Systems (ICDCS), Mesa, AZ. (2001) 284–291
4. J. Gray, P. Helland, P. E. O'Neil, D Shasha: The dangers of replication and a solution. In *Proc. of the ACM SIGMOD Int. Conf. on Management of Data*, (1996) 284–291
5. J. Holliday, D. Agrawal, A. El Abbadi: Partial database replication using epidemic communication. In *Proc. of the Int. Conf. on Distributed Computing Systems* (2002)
6. J. Holliday, R. Steinke, D. Agrawal, A. El Abbadi: Epidemic quorums for managing replicated data. In *Proc. of the IEEE Int. Performance, Computing and Communications Conf. (IPCCC)*, Phoenix Arizona (2000) 93–100
7. R.Jimenez-Peris, M.Patino-Martinez, B. Kemme, G. Alonso: Improving the scalability of fault-tolerant database clusters. *The 22nd International Conference on Distributed Computing Systems (ICDCS)*, Vienna, Austria, July (2002)
8. B. Kemme, G. Alonso: Don't be lazy, be consistent: Postgres-R, a new way to implement database replication. In *Proc. of the Int. Conf. on Very Large Data Bases (VLDB)*, Cairo Egypt September (2000)
9. B. Kemme, G. Alonso: A new approach to developing and implementing eager database replication protocols. *ACM Transactions on Database Systems*, September (2000)
10. B. Kemme: Database Replication for Clusters of Workstations. PhD thesis, Department of Computer Science, ETH Zurich Switzerland (2000)
11. Philip Russom: Get answers to your questions about a relatively new form of clustering-the database cluster. Intelligent Enterprise Magazine December 12 (2001)
12. R. van Renesse, K. P. Birman, S. Maffeis. Horus: A flexible group communication system. *Communications of the ACM*, 39(4). (1996) 76–83
13. M. Wiesmann: Group Communication and Database Replication: Techniques, Issues and Performance, PhD thesis, ETH Zurich Switzerland (2002)

Author Index